Encyclopedia of
Reincarnation and Karma

Encyclopedia of Reincarnation and Karma

Norman C. McClelland

McFarland & Company, Inc., Publishers
Jefferson, North Carolina, and London

LIBRARY OF CONGRESS CATALOGUING-IN-PUBLICATION DATA

McClelland, Norman C., 1944–
Encyclopedia of reincarnation and karma / Norman C. McClelland.
p. cm.
Includes bibliographical references and index.

ISBN 978-0-7864-4851-7
softcover : 50# alkaline paper ∞

1. Reincarnation — Encyclopedias. 2. Karma — Encyclopedias.
I. Title.
BL515.M38   2010   202'.3703 — dc22   2009051790

British Library cataloguing data are available

©2010 Norman C. McClelland. All rights reserved

*No part of this book may be reproduced or transmitted in any form
or by any means, electronic or mechanical, including photocopying
or recording, or by any information storage and retrieval system,
without permission in writing from the publisher.*

Front cover image ©2010 punchstock

Manufactured in the United States of America

*McFarland & Company, Inc., Publishers
Box 611, Jefferson, North Carolina 28640
www.mcfarlandpub.com*

CONTENTS

Preface
1

Introduction
3

The Encyclopedia
9

Sources Consulted
283

Index
299

PREFACE

This encyclopedia of reincarnation and karma originally began as a three-page glossary of basic terms dealing with the traditional Buddhist views of rebirth and karma that I wrote for a class on those subjects. However, that very limited glossary almost immediately needed to be expanded as my students asked such basic questions as "What exactly is the difference between Buddhist rebirth and Hindu reincarnation?"; "Didn't the ancient Egyptians and Greeks believe in rebirth or reincarnation?"; "Don't some passages in the Bible, at least, imply rebirth and karma?"; and "Can someone remember a past life through hypnosis?" Some of these, and similar questions, I could answer in a very generalized or sketchy way, but others I had no clue as to the appropriate response.

In seeking answers, I began what turned into eight years of extensive reading on the subject of reincarnation and karma that spanned a spectrum of individuals, beliefs, theories, and practices from the very naïve, sometimes absurd and quite subjective to the very scholarly and objective, as represented in the "Sources Consulted" at the end of this volume. As the work progressed I came to depend more and more on my life partner Lynn Sipe, without whose help in copy editing and critical commentary this work would never have been finished. He has my deepest appreciation.

INTRODUCTION

It is more than likely that a reasonably literate person in Seattle, Paris, Buenos Aires, or Melbourne, upon being asked a question about reincarnation or karma, would make an immediate mental association with what they knew about Hinduism or perhaps something about the Dalai Lama. While they would not be wrong in making this immediate connection they certainly would be focusing on a very narrow aspect of a far-reaching set of issues and ideas, defined differently across a variety of human cultures and times. Apart from the earliest notions of reincarnation and karma in the cultures of South, Central and East Asia, variations on these themes have played a key role in the thought of the ancient Greeks, the Celts, the medieval Cathars, Jewish Kabbalists, certain Sub-Saharan tribes, Australian aboriginal peoples, and various Amerindian tribes. From the late 19th century onward there has been renewed popular interest in the notions of reincarnation and karma in many western countries, particularly in Britain, France, Brazil, and the United States. This has led to a significant outpouring of first- or second-hand accounts of persons claiming past lives along with increased scholarly attention to those claims.

If one is to go to any major bookstore there is a good chance of finding material on reincarnation and karma. This includes autobiographies and biographies of past lives, as well as books on past life therapy, how to improve one's karma in the next life, and, most recently, supposed reincarnational teachings of channeled extraterrestrial beings.

As long as one does not read more than a handful of such books chances are one might encounter only minor conflicting information on the subject. But if one reads many examples of these texts one is assured of finding very little agreement among them as to exactly what constitutes reincarnation, beyond the all too general and simplistic idea of having lived a past life and the prospect of a future one.

It is the purpose of this encyclopedia to demonstrate just how complex the subjects of reincarnation and karma are and how little real agreement there is on them across a very broad range of writings. The most immediate proof of that complexity can be found by investigating the various English terms that have been used in reference to the process of existing across many life times. The four most commonly used of these terms, in order of popularity, are rebirth or reincarnation, transmigration, metempsychosis, and palingenesis. Each of these terms is used, in general, to describe a process in which a single soul or its equivalent survives the death of one body just to enter another body at or soon after the biological conception of that new body. In addition, any one of these terms may, but need not, be accompanied by the phenomenon commonly known as karma.

At the outset we need to understand

that the diversity of names for this re-embodiment process results from the fact that each term can refer to a closely related, but not necessarily identical phenomenon. Another way of saying this is that each term refers to a slightly different re-embodiment process. This results in considerable overlap in meaning between the various terms. The term "rebirth" has the most generalized meaning, and more often than not can be used as a synonym for all the other terms. This is particularly the case in a Hindu or Jain context, where all four of the above terms are fully interchangeable. Such, however, is not the case in a Buddhist context or in some Western contexts.

In Buddhism the only acceptable one of the four English terms is rebirth. This is because Buddhism understands the three terms other than rebirth to describe the process of a very real or concrete entity (soul: *atman*) passing from one body to another, which, at least officially, Buddhist doctrine rejects. For this reason, in this encyclopedia the term rebirth is used only in a specifically Buddhist context, and in those instances it is "not" regarded as being synonymous with reincarnation. In all other non–Buddhist contexts the two terms will be treated as interchangeable.

At the same time, since Buddhism does accept "rebirth" from human to animal and vice versa, transmigration could be used so long as no concrete soul is thought to be included in the process. However, as not to confuse matters, even in this case only the term rebirth is used. Also, in referring to a believer in multiple or serial lives one has a choice between phrases like "a believer in rebirth" or "a reincarnationist." As implied above, I will use these interchangeably except in specific Buddhist contexts.

In the case of western (ancient Greek to modern Euro-American) views of the re-embodiment process the terms rebirth and reincarnation, while usually accepted as synonymous, are often contrasted with the term transmigration. This is because the latter term is usually considered to mean cross-special re-embodiment. In other words, it suggests that former human souls can be reborn into animal bodies (regressive transmigration) and that former animal souls can be reborn into human bodies (progressive transmigration). For a minority of Western reincarnationists this cross-special movement is not a problem, but for the majority no such special boundary crossing is possible; in short, the only possibility is lateral transmigration, that is, human to human.

An important "Western vs. Eastern" difference revolves around the term "mind." As will be discovered in the entry for "mind" many modern Western metaphysicians believe it is better to speak of mind, rather than soul, as undergoing reincarnation because that supposedly places it in a more psychological, hence scientific, context rather than in any sectarian religious context. While I question how valid this attempt at de-emphasizing religion is, this is not the main reason that I have resisted replacing soul as the factor surviving death with mind. The main reason is that in many ancient and modern belief systems a distinction has often been made between a soul, as that which survived bodily death, and mind as that which dies with the body.

As noted above, Buddhism creates some special terminological problems. This is true not only in its rejection of a soul, but even in trying to substitute mind for that which passes from death to rebirth. The standard Buddhist term for mind is *manas*, but this is never used to describe the death-surviving factor. When a psychological term for survival is used it is always *vijnana* (consciousness); however, even this term has often been rejected by many Buddhists as too soul-like. To deal with this wording difficulty and to avoid inconsistency, I have used the more neutral term "rebirth factor" in a variety of

Buddhist, and, as appropriate, some non-Buddhist contexts.

The fourth term to describe the re-embodiment process, metempsychosis, while popular in pre-nineteenth century literature, is rarely used today. When this term is used here it is as a synonym for transmigration, especially in the context of interspecies (regressive and progressive) transmigration of the soul. Even rarer today is the term palingenesis.

Because the term rebirth is both the most generic and is also shorter than reincarnation, most entries titles are listed using the term rebirth, especially if the entry is on a sufficiently general aspect of the subject. However, when pairing the rebirth/reincarnation issue with Western religious views, from ancient Greek to modern times, reincarnation is primarily the term used.

Over-arching conceptual foundations are presented in the various "Argument" entries: the arguments pro and con on an afterlife in general; the arguments specifically against rebirth; the list of sixty-two arguments supportive of rebirth; the detailed examination for each of these entries to which the reader is directed; and the arguments that challenge rebirth on a logical basis. Likewise, the extended themes are continued in the two dozen or so entries on karma in all of their complexities and those entries that deal with pros and cons of reincarnation in the Old and New Testaments.

Similar to the complexity of the rebirth issue is that of karma. As defined in various dictionaries karma is the moral and/or ethical behavior that influences the quality of a person's past, present, and future lives. While this concept was found in a very rudimentary form among some classical Greco-Romans religious groups and later Gnostic cults and is also indigenous in an equally rudimentary form among some present-day West African peoples, the concept of karma never developed to the same worldwide extent that the belief in rebirth did. It was only in India that a full scale karmic concept evolved and it was only from here that it spread to other parts of Asian via Hindu and Buddhist missionary activities; as a result of this activity for over two millennia karma has been a determinative factor in the lives, happiness and suffering of hundreds of millions of inhabitants of south and east Asia.

While covered extensively in the various entries on karma, among the complex issues surrounding the concept of karma is how Buddhism has been able to account for the working of karma without a soul; why did the Greco-Roman rudimentary karmic concept never fully evolve; what were the early Christian fathers' criticism of it; how does karma support and/or conflict with monotheistic religion; how has the very widespread practice of ancestor worship complicated the karma concept and vice versa; and does the issue of blaming the victim negate the very morality that the concept of karma is presumed to uphold?

In most of the West, the concept of rebirth and karma is frequently just a passing thought as in such statements as, "Well, he must have bad karma," referring to some negative thing that has happened to someone in this life, but resulting from something which transpired in a past life. In fact, that speaker may have only the vaguest notion of what karma means beyond this simplistic notion. However, according to a 2000 Harris Poll in the United States, 27 percent of the general population has a deep belief in reincarnation and some form of karma. Furthermore, among those in the population that are 20 to 30 years old this percentage rises to 40 percent, while among those over 65 years old it drops to only 14 percent. Similar percentages have been found in Europe.

A number of reasons have been suggested for this growing interest in rebirth and karma. One major reason is that many Westerners have lost the belief in the concept of a future miraculous bodily Resurrection. However, rather than abandon all hope for a life after death they have adopted the far less miraculous-seeming belief in rebirth. Another major reason is that many people can not harmonize the idea of a just and loving God with the resurrection-related idea of an eternal hell.

What public opinion surveys rarely reflect, however, is that many Americans and Europeans actually adopt reincarnation and karma concepts, not to replace, but to augment their more traditional Christian and Jewish beliefs, as noted in entries such as Christianity, Esoteric; Christianity, Lost Chord of; Kabbalah; New Testament and Reincarnation; Rebirth in the Modern West; Resurrection or Reincarnation; and Rosicrucians.

In addition to the series of broad thematic articles the majority of the encyclopedia's approximately 1,200 entries focus on a highly specific aspect of reincarnation and karma. These entries cover a very diverse range, though they can be conceptually grouped as focusing on: key individuals, both historic and modern, as either advocates or opponents of reincarnation or karma; religious groups, sects, associations, societies and organizations supportive of the notions of reincarnation and karma; and specific beliefs, concepts, and practices across time and cultures.

A Note on Spelling Conventions and Abbreviations

As might be expected, there are many words in the entries that are not found in an average English dictionary because of their foreign or esoteric origin. Many of these words would normally have various types of diacritical marks above, below or between letters. Since the inclusion or exclusion of diacritics rarely influences their pronunciation by an English speaker, I have, for the sake of simplicity, omitted all such marks. Similarly, I have modified the traditional spelling of some words to make their pronunciation clearer to the average English reader. For example, the Sanskrit ś has been spelled as sh, as in Shiva (the deity); the Pali cc- has been changed to ch-, as in *paticha-samuppada*. In some Sanskrit words, such as *jñana* (knowledge), the ñ- immediately after the j- means a nasalizing of the j- which is nearly impossible for the average English speaker, but to try to change this spelling would make it unrecognizable so I have left it alone, though minus the tilde. For the same reason I have also left alone the aspirated "h" as *abhijna* (supernatural power), *bhakti* (devotion), *bhava* (birth), *dharma* (teachings), *duhkha* (dissatisfaction), *lobha* (greed), and *samadhi* (concentration), etc.

It will also be noted that in certain specifically Buddhist focused entries two variant spellings, Sanskrit and Pali, are often given. The first is used by Mahayana Buddhism, while the second is used by Theravada Buddhism. Since many publications on Buddhism will use only one or the other of these I have tried to give both so that a reader, seeking more information on that topic elsewhere will have no difficulty finding it. To be consistent, the first spelling will always be the Sanskrit followed by the Pali, as in ***Abhijna/Abhinna*** (S/P) or (S/P: *akushala/akusala*); however, after the initial double entry (S/P: Karma/*Kamma*) any further use of the term will employ only the Sanskrit as in karma, unless otherwise indicated. If there is only one word as in *bhava* (S/P) or (S/P: *cetana*) it means the word is spelled the same in both languages; however, if there is a set of such words in an entry the S/P will not be constantly repeated, in which case it should be understood that the word is the same in both languages as in body (S/P: *rupa*), desire (*raga*), feelings (*vedana*). If I have given only one of the two spellings it will appear as either (S) or (P) or as in *Bhavanga* (P) or (S: *tiryak*).

There is also an orthographic issue when it comes to the Buddhist doctrine of no-soul or no self (*An-atman/An-atta* or more commonly *Anatman/Anatta*). In early Buddhist India there was no real distinction between the concept of soul and self; in short, the concepts were synonymous. To emphasize this synonymous nature whenever there is mention of the soul or self in a Buddhist context the two words will appear as soul (self) or as no-soul (self) or as *anatman*.

While there is a specific Jain canonical dialect called Ardha-Magadhi the most common Jain terms also have a Sanskrit form such as *Abhavya* which will be treated as noted above.

There are words from other languages in which there is disagreement as to the best way to romanize the spellings; for two or more spellings of these the spellings are separated by an "or" and/or parenthesis, as for example with the Egyptian terms heart (*ab* or *ib*); the *akh* (*akhu, khu,* or *ikhu*); the goddess Ammut (Ammit or Amemait) and the shadow (*khaibit, haibit,* or *sheut*).

Traditional Tibetan spelling involves a number of silent letters as well as some combinations of consonants which are pronounced in a way surprising to most English speakers. For this reason most Tibetan words translated into English tend to be simplified. For example, in the phrase *Chikhai* [Tibetan: *Hchi-khai*] *Bar-do* (Transitional State of the Moment of Death), the *Chikhai* is about as close to the English pronunciation one can get of the Tibetan word which more correctly is romanized as *Hchi-khai*.

This simplification has lead to some problems since there is no one standardizing authority for such simplification. The simplified and the original spellings given here are for the most part those that have been adopted by the Tibetan scholar David L. Snellgrove in his *A Cultural History of Tibet* (1980). Snellgrove, in his "Pronunciation Rules," says that "there are eight prefixed letters, *g, d, b, m, r, s, l* and the apostrophe which represents a distinct letter in the Tibetan alphabet." According to him, all these eight prefixes may be ignored for the purpose of an approximate pronunciation. Thus *blama* will be lama (teacher). I have tried to give both the simplified and the unsimplified versions of such words, but in some cases only one was available to me. If the reader can easily say it then it is most likely the simplified, otherwise it is the unsimplified.

The Chinese terms covered here often have two transliterations. One is the modern *Pin-yin*, transliteration, and the other is the older Wade-Giles transliteration. When both were available to me I have provided each, with the Pin-yin first separated by a diagonal stroke from the Wade-Giles, for example, Dao/Tao. If I have provided only one version and it is the Wade Giles it will appear as either (*ch'i*, WG) or Yaoshi fo (WG); otherwise the entry is in *Pin-yin* (Py).

Use of Abbreviations and Other Editorial Conventions

Words appearing in boldface type within an entry indicate that there is a separate entry for that term within the normal alphabetical sequence of entries. "See also" references to Hinduism, Jainism, and other religions are in boldface, but not Buddhism. The reason is that so many of the entries are Buddhist-related that the entry for Buddhism would be followed by several pages of "see also" references.

In regard to Buddhist, Hindu, Jain, and similar terminology those terms that have become common enough to appear in a major English dictionary, such as karma and nirvana are not italicized, while most of the less familiar terms are italicized. Also, the proper names of deities have been left un-italicized, as have the names of religions or religious sects.

Special mention must be made concerning abbreviations for the various citations from the Pali Canon, the *Tripitaka,* as published by the Pali Text Society, London. The *Tripitaka* is the fundamental corpus of writings of Theravada Buddhism. This very extensive collection is divided into a number of sets of books (*Suttapitaka*), each with several volumes in the English translations. The volumes cited in this encyclopedia are *The Book of the Gradual Sayings or More Numbered Suttas* (*Anguttaranikaya,* hence the abbreviation AN I & II); *The Dialogues of the Buddha* (*Dighanikaya*), DN III; *The Collection of the Middle Length Sayings* (*Majjhimanikaya*), MLD I & III; and *The Book of the Kindred Sayings or Grouped Suttas* (*Sanyuttanikaya*), SN I–V. These are more completely described in the "Sources Consulted."

Finally, the reader will notice the spelling of re-death. The concept of reincarnation includes not just a series of rebirths but of re-deaths; however, while the term rebirth is a long accepted spelling the logical opposite redeath is not; therefore, when referring to repeated death I have hyphenated the word as re-death.

THE ENCYCLOPEDIA

Abhavya (S). In **Jainism** this is a term for a class of souls that can attain a heavenly state (***devaloka***), but no further than that. This means that such souls are never able to gain ***moksha*** (liberation from the round of birth and death). *Abhavya* are in some ways the equivalent of the ***ichantika*** in Buddhism.

See also **Eighth sphere**.

Abhijna/Abhinna (S/P). These terms refer to the psychic or supernatural powers the **Buddha**, Gautama, is said to have gained at the time of his enlightenment. One of these powers was "remembrance of former births" (***purvanivasanusmrti***). This is said to include the ability to recall his five hundred or so past lives in detail, as well as to recall the past lives of others. It is claimed that many monks and nuns who attain full enlightenment (*arhat*) also acquire this ability.

See also *Bhavanga*; **Buddhist stages of liberation**; *Jataka Tales*; **Memories, reasons for loss of past life; Rebirth in Buddhism**.

Abraham of Posquieres, Isaac ben. This 12th–13th century French Kabbalist, besides possibly being the author of the ***Bahir***, was the first known person in Judaism to openly teach the doctrine of reincarnation. Isaac is also known as Isaac the Blind and Isaac the Pious.

See also **Kabbalah**.

Accidentalism (S: *ahetu-apachaya-vada*). The doctrine that there are no really logically discernable causes to actions or results from them. This means that there are really no bases for morality. This is considered a heretical teaching in Buddhism. The opposite of it, and equally heretical, is the doctrine of **determinism** or fatalism, or at least of strong determinism. Buddhism teaches that the truth is the **middle way** between accidentalism and determinism. Buddhism teaches that anyone holding either of these views will be unable to escape the round of rebirth and re-death.

See also **Annihilationism, Buddhist view**.

Acts of the Apostles 2:39. This is one of the biblical passages that have been cited as "possibly" implying that reincarnation was secretly taught by the earliest Christian authors. It reads, "For the promise [of salvation] is to you, and your children, and to all who are far away, everyone whom the Lord our God may call." The argument is that the words "and to all who are far away" could imply that those who lived in the past (far away time) will be given another life in the post-resurrection era in order to receive the promise. Like most of the biblical passages that have been cited to try to prove a reincarnation theme this too has been read out of context.

See also **Cayce, Edgar; Harrowing of hell; Luke, Gospel of; Old Testament and the soul; Possession; Psalms; Resurrection of Jesus; Xenoglossy**.

Acupuncture. This Chinese medical system involves the insertion of needles into specific points on the skin called acupuncture points. The insertion of the needles is thought to stimulate the life-force (*ch'i*, WG). It is believed by some reincarnationists that certain acupuncture processes, as they unblock the *ch'i*, can stimulate past life memories, otherwise blocked.

See also **Chinese religion and reincarnation; Rebirth and cyclical time**.

Adam. According to both the Old and New Testaments this was the first human being. There seems to be some discrepancy in **Genesis** as to whether Adam was at first a collective term for both genders, or from the start exclusively a male being. The first view seems likely from Genesis 1. The second view is almost assured from Genesis 2. However, some esoteric interpretations of Genesis 2 suggest that God split a hermaphroditic being into separate sexes. This interpretation is then easy to harmonize with the popular concept of **soul mates**.

Despite the mythical nature of Adam various reincarnationists incorporate him into the reincarnation issue as if he had once been a real person. This is usually done in relationship to the figures **Melchizedek**, King **David**; and **Jesus**. For example, **Edgar Cayce** was convinced that Adam was not only the collective name for a primordial group of souls undergoing physical embodiment for the first time, but also the personal name of the leader of that group of souls. While the primordial Eve is also assigned later reincarnation by some major reincarnationist teachers, such as Cayce, considering the patriarchal nature of most religious thinkers it ought to be of no surprise that she is mentioned much less than is Adam.

Under the influence of the *Zohar*, some Kabbalic teachers have believed that Adam reincarnated as the biblical patriarch Jacob (Israel).

See also **Christian atonement theories; Corinthians, 1st and 2nd; Creationism, soul; Fall of the souls; Jesus; Kabbalah; Original sin versus karma;** *Pneumatikoi*; **Predestination; Romans; Soul; Soul's existence prior to embodiment.**

Adhi-daivika duhkha. In one of the classifications of ***duhkha*** (dissatisfaction) this is the form caused by past evil karma. The other two forms of *duhkha* are *adhi-bhautika duhkha*, which is caused by external things or beings, and *adhyatmika duhkha*, which is caused by one's present actions.

Adrenocorticotrophin (ACTH) *see* **Memories, reasons for loss of past life.**

Adrishta. This is an invisible, impersonal, cosmic moral force that is another designation for karmic results.

Advaita Vedanta *see* **Brahman; Dualism; Individuality and rebirth;** *Jiva*; *Prakriti*; **Monism; Pantheism and panentheism.**

Aeneas of Gaza (died about 518 CE). This Christian philosopher was a strong supporter of Platonist and Neoplatonist doctrines; nevertheless, he rejected the idea of a **soul's existence prior to embodiment**, not to mention **metempsychosis**, in favor of the orthodox Christian belief in the resurrection of the body after a single life time.

See also **Christian fathers critical of reincarnation; Christianity and reincarnation; Church Council of 553; New Testament and reincarnation.**

Aetherius Society. One of the new religions that combine a belief in reincarnation, karma, and **UFOism**, it was founded in 1954 by George King (1919–1997) shortly after contact with what he believed to be extra-terrestrial beings. Among these beings was the Master Aetherius, hence the name of the Society. According to the teachings revealed to King such teachers as the **Buddha**, Krishna, Lao Tzu, and **Jesus** were, and still are, cosmic masters or members of the (interplanetary) **Great White Brotherhood**. In fact, both Jesus and Aetherius were born on **Venus**, while other masters originated from **Mars**. All of these masters periodically meet at the Interplanetary Parliament on **Saturn**.

The Society teaches that hundreds of thousands of years ago there was a planet called Maldek, which was located between Mars and Jupiter. Destroyed by the misuse of nuclear weapons, nothing remains of it except an asteroid belt; however, refugee souls from Maldek reincarnated into human bodies on Earth. This reincarnation first took place on the **lost continent** of Lemuria (**Mu**); thus it was here that the earliest civilization on this planet was established. Tragically, the Maldek-Lemurians repeated their earlier nuclear mistake and destroyed Lemuria. The Lemurians then sought refuge on the other lost continent of Atlantis, but even here they had not learned from the past, and in a third nuclear war they also destroyed that continent.

According to King the cosmic masters decided to contact humanity through the establishment of the Aetherius Society in order to prevent still another disaster, which this time would destroy the whole planet. Such destruction will not be tolerated by the masters because the Earth is a Goddess (later known as the Gaia theory) and has already suffered enough at the hands of mankind. Instead, to prevent this from happening the masters, who are also known as the Supreme **Lords of Karma**, will guide mankind towards a "Millennium of Peace." Unfortunately, however, not everyone will benefit from this peace. Only those who have lived in accordance with the "Cosmic Principle," as taught by the society, will experience the rewards of this Millennium. Those who have not accommodated themselves to the Principle will be reincarnated on some un-named, and presently non-visible, extremely primitive planet to further their spiritual development.

The main purpose of the Aetherius Society, therefore, is to prepare the way for the arrival of the next "***Avatar***" who will be one of the Lords of Karma, and who will usher in the Millennium.

The Society has adopted a mixture of Christian, Hindu, and Buddhist practices, which include yoga and *prana* (breathing) exercises; the use of sacred chants (*mantras*), believed to give magical power to the one who recites them; a set of dietary rules, which encourage vegetarianism; and making pilgrimages to certain spiritually charged mountains.

See also **Ascended masters; Channeling; Planets, other; Ramtha; Unarius Academy of Science.**

Affect bridge. In psychological regressive therapy this is the return to the earliest memory of a traumatic situation or event that seriously affects the present mental health of the patient. In a number of cases the patient will locate that situation or event in what seems to be a past life. This happens even though neither the patient nor the therapist has any interest in reincarnation. The therapist without such interest will usually regard this as an example of a **screen memory**.

See also **Birth trauma; Blocked regression; Netherton Method; Scientology**.

A-field. Said to be the cosmic information field or the record of everything that happens in the universe. It is an updated (supposedly more scientific) version of the ***akashic*** **record**. According to Laszlo's *Science and the Akashic Field*, as individuals we are not immortal, but our individual experience is. When persons either are convinced that they are in communication with the dead, as in a typical séance, or are experiencing what they believe is a past life, they are really obtaining their information from the A-field.

Africa. Although a number of authorities have stated that the idea of reincarnation is found among various Sub-Saharan African peoples this statement has to be carefully qualified. What we would normally label as reincarnation is the passing of the complete vital essence of a person from one body into another, without any residue vital essence being left in some sort of afterlife world. This kind of reincarnation is not found in most traditional African societies. Instead, most African peoples accept a kind of partial reincarnation. Partial reincarnation occurs when only some of the characteristics of a deceased ancestor are reborn into one or more descendents. The main part of the deceased, however, retains a separate existence in the world of the ancestors, at least until the memory of that ancestor fades away among his or her descendents; and at which point the deceased goes through a second and final death. This idea of partial reincarnation also applies temporally. The usual belief is that an ancestor may be a part of a receiving descendent only for the first few years of the child's life, after which it withdraws and may reincarnate in another newborn descendent. This is obviously a very different concept from what we normally think of as reincarnation, and for this reason a number of scholars on African religion have been opposed to labeling this process as reincarnation. In this case, the process might actually be better labeled as a kind of highly benevolent ancestral **possession** rather than reincarnation. This is one reason why a tribal African is not likely to ever refer to having lived a previous life.

Among some African peoples partial reincarnation can also include ancestral spirits assuming the form of a visiting animal. However, full animal rebirth of an ancestor (**transmigration**) is extremely rare among Africans.

Among the African cultural groups that believe in some form of partial reincarnation are the Ga of Ghana, the **Benin**, the **Igbo**, the Urhobo, and the **Nupe** of Nigeria, the Beng of the Ivory Coast, the Nandi of East Africa, the Ovimbundu (Umbundu speakers) of Angola, the Ndembu of Zambia, and the **Zulu** of South Africa. For more on this subject see works by Heijke, Mbiti, and Oneywuenyi, listed in the "Sources Consulted" at the end of this work.

Among the West African **Akan**–speaking peoples, especially the Ashanti of Ghana and neighboring areas; and the **Yoruba** of Nigeria a more complete reincarnation view appears to be held.

See also **Ancestor worship; Animals and rebirth, Western view; Birthmarks; Karma and justice; Proximity burial; Rastafarians; Rebirth, cross-species; Rebirth, proximity; Repeater children (Ogbanje); Second death**.

Afro-American religions. This term covers non–Christian folk religions that have developed mainly in the Caribbean region and in Brazil. The most well known of these religions is the Voodoo (Voudou) in Haiti, **Santeria** in Cuba, Obeah in Jamaica, Shango in Trinidad and Grenada, and Candomble, Catimbo, Macumba, and **Umbanda** in Brazilian. The religious practice of the **Rastafarians** falls into a separate Afro-American category in that there is an extensive use of the Bible as a source of that group's beliefs. Of the various Afro-American religions Santeria and Umbanda have been highly influenced by the reincarnation teachings of **Kardecismo**. This is especially true for Umbanda which has adopted the Kardecismo doctrines of both reincarnation and karma.

See also **New Testament and Reincarnation; Possession**.

Afterlife (survival) by default *see* **Logic and pseudo-logic and the afterlife**.

Agasha Temple of Wisdom. This body of teachings was founded by Richard Zenor in 1943. Zenor believed that he was a medium (channeler) of a master teacher called Agasha, as well as a medium of the souls of the more ordinary deceased. The temple teachings include a belief in the universal consciousness of God, **pyramidology**, reincarnation, and karma. According to these temple teachings most people reincarnate 800–1200 times, with the **interim period** being about 150–300 years. As the **soul**, which in its early development state is shaped like an egg, spiritually grows throughout the reincarnation and interim periods it expands and unfolds like a lotus flower to eventually take its most perfect shape as a pillar of light.

The name Agasha is the Russian version of *agatha* which comes from old Greek meaning Good.

See also **Ascended masters; Channeling; Lazaris; Ramtha; Seth.**

Age factor and rebirth. One question regarding reincarnation that has been asked in the West at least since the time of **Tertullian** is, "Why is a person who has died as an adult not reborn with adult memories; indeed, in most cases with no memories at all?" This has lead to the idea that there is a distinction between the **soul** and the personality, or metaphysical soul and the empirical soul. It is the latter that in theory would hold the age-related memory and this, in accordance with **body-brain (mind) dependency**, would die with the body. The true or metaphysical soul, on the other hand, would experience no normal aging process. Since this soul would have no personal memories attached to itself, it would be more or less identical to every other such soul. This lack of individuality would be very similar to that of the Hindu *atman*.

A major problem with this solution is that it should totally negate the idea that some persons do remember past lives either, spontaneously or through **hypnotic age regression**. A particularly Buddhist problem with the age factor and rebirth is that Buddhism, at least in theory, can not accept any kind of metaphysical soul due to its *anatman* doctrine.

See also *Akashic Record*; **Individuality and rebirth; Karma and justice; Mental plane; Memories, reasons for Loss of past life; Resurrection individual age discrepancy issue.**

Age regression *see* **Hypnotic age regression.**

Agent detection factor *see* **Soul, psychology of.**

Agra-sandhani (Assessors or Recorders). This term refers to either the record of the judgment of a person's most recent past life or to the supernatural recorders of the judgment of deeds of a person's most recent past life. In the latter case they are almost the same as the *lipika*.

See also *Chintra-Gupta*; **Lords of Karma; Yama.**

Ahankara. This term literally means "I [*Ahan*]-maker [*kara*]" and it refers to the little false ego that each of us is said to repeatedly create lifetime after lifetime, and which denies us the realization that the only true I is the universal one, **Brahman.**

See also *Atman*; **Ego; Hinduism.**

Ahimsa. In **Hinduism**, Buddhism, and especially **Jainism** the religious act of reframing (*A-*) from killing (-*himsa*) not only refers to killing human beings, but also animals. It is part of the belief of these religions that deliberately killing other sentient beings will, for the most part, keep one trapped in the cycle of birth and death. In the case of Hinduism intentional killing, to the degree that it is part of one's social (caste) duty, as in the case of a soldier or policeman, does not have the same disastrous karmic repercussions as killing outside of such duty, at least according to the ***Bhagavad-Gita***. In Buddhism intentional killing of any kind can not be justified. In Jainism even the most unintentional killing is regarded as having serious karmic results.

See also **Caste system; Return and serve argument for rebirth; Vegetarianism.**

Ahmadiyya. In a generic sense this designates a number of orthodox Sufi groups. In the more specific sense it refers to the messianic sect founded in 1889 by Mirza Ghulam Ahmed Qadiyani (1835–1908) in the Punjab. Raised as a Moslem, Qadiyani sought to counter the criticism from British Protestantism as well as the threat of the revitalizing Hindu movement. He not only came to regard himself as an *avatar* of the Hindu god Krishna (**Vishnu**), as well as the *Madhi*, or the future Messiah of Islam, but he and his followers regarded him as the reincarnation of Isa or Issa (Arabic for **Jesus**) the prophet. This latter identification was facilitated by Ahmed belief that the tomb of one Yuz-Assaf in the Kasmiri city of Srinagar was really the tomb of Jesus. This, at least, followed the standard Islamic belief that Jesus in some way escaped death on the cross. According to Ahmad, unbeknownst to his disciples Jesus fled to Kashmir where, at the age of 120, he died and was buried.

Despite the Ahmadiyya being declared heretical by Islamic authorities, both of the two branches of this sect, the Qadianis and Lahorites, has been very successful in their missionary activities.

See also **Aquarian Gospel of Jesus Christ; Church Universal and Triumphant; Judgment of the dead; Muhammad Ahmad; Notovitch, Nicholas; Nusayris (Nursaris); Resurrection of Jesus; Scheintod hypothesis.**

Ahriman. In Zoroastrianism this is the name for the evil cosmic principle who opposes the good cosmic principle (*Mazda*) or God. Some 19th century Euro-American theosophical and occult groups adopted this name for various demon-like agents. For example, in Jocelyn's *Citizens of the Cosmos* Ahriman is the name for the entity that tries to alienate the human **soul** from the spirit, which when successful, enslaves the soul to matter. Further, this entity encourages the soul during the **interim period** to strive for rebirth as soon as possible instead of using its full allotted time to purify itself of materialism.

See also **Lucifer**.

Ahtun Re *see* **Channeling; Egypt; Ryerson, Kevin**.

Ajivikas (Way of life[-*Jiva-*]). This is the name of an ancient Indian religious sect that associated karma and rebirth with such a rigid **determinism** as to be fatalistic. This fatalism was highly criticized by early Buddhism and **Jainism** and it was partially this criticism that lead to the Buddhist doctrine of **anatman** (denial of an unchanging **soul**).

Akan. This ethnolinguistic group of West **Africa** is known for a fuller reincarnational belief than found among other African peoples. In their belief system human beings, but not animals, have an individual and immortal **soul** (*kra*) that represents a part of God. Each time the *kra* (soul) is sent into the world it is given a specific destiny (*nkrabea*) by God. If it fulfills this destiny it returns to God and becomes an un-embodied ancestor. If it does not fulfill its destiny it will have to return to embodiment as a child of the family of which it previously was a part (consanguineous rebirth).

See also **Benin; Rebirth, consanguineous; Yoruba; Zulu**.

Akashic or *Akashik* **Record**. This term comes from the Sanskrit *akasha* meaning ether, the all prevailing invisible medium that was once thought to exist between the planets in place of empty space. Alternatively, as the *akashic* record it is said to be a universal medium upon which is imprinted all thoughts, words, and deeds that ever existed. It is believed that certain psychically sensitive persons can read this record. It is believed by many of its supporters that this is the real source of past life memories rather than any re-embodiment of a **soul**. The advantages of this *akashic* theory over any rebirth are (1) there is no necessary immaterial bodily existence; (2) it is not in conflict with a resurrection view; (3) it does not have to deal with the karma and the **memory problem**; and (4) it does not have to deal with the **population increase issue**. In other words, these supporters of the *akashic* record claim that this record is better than rebirth by itself or even rebirth in conjunction with the *akashic* record because that record obeys the Law of Parsimony. This law says that the simplest explanation for any phenomenon is the best explanation.

According to reincarnationists, however, a major problem with the *akashic* record, or for any related retrocognition theory, as the exclusive source for past memories is that while such a record could account for memories, it could not account for the dispositions, habits, skills, and personality quirks that are thought also to be shared by a past and present individual.

Also, reincarnation believers point out that an *akashic* record or retrocognitive ability as the sole source for recall of past life memories would result in frozen memories rather than the normal constantly edited ones that occur in living minds, and that are essential for updating of any personality. Instead of such normal "constructive recall" the *akashic* record would record both the unedited and the edited versions of memory. This would make for a very confused memory bank from which to draw. In response to this criticism the *akashic* record proponents argue that the record is really liken to a collective mind or over-soul which presumably could edit its memories.

According to the channeled material from the **Grace-Loehr Life Readings** the *akashic* record exists beyond the **astral plane**, but is mirrored by that plane and thus is available for reading.

One of the more intriguing books that deal with reading the *akashic* record is *Past Lives of Famous People: Journeys of the Soul* by David Bengtson. According to this book the author, having read extensive parts of the *akashic* record, has been able to trace the reincarnation links of about 140 individuals from the present as far back as ancient Egypt. For example, in one reincarnational line mentioned in the book the **soul** of the Pharaoh Psalmtic (c. 700 BCE) was reincarnated as the Roman Emperor Octavian (63 BCE–14 CE) which was then reincarnated as Oliver Cromwell (1599–1658 CE) which was reincarnated as Mohammed Anwar Sadat (1918–1981). Bengton believes that many souls reincarnate in accordance with the **repetition compulsion**.

According to Beredene Jocelyn (*Citizens of the Cosmos*) the *akashic* record or Cosmic Memory is held by the **Saturn** beings in the astrological Sphere of Saturn through which all souls must pass in their **planetary ascent and descent** between earthly embodiments.

The *akashic* record was initially introduced to the West by the **Theosophy** of Madame **Helena Blavatsky**, and has become a very widely accepted concept in reincarnationist circles. Some of the more pro–Christian reincarnationists, such as Levi H. Dowling, the author of the **Aquarian Gospel**, and **Edgar Cayce**, identify the *akashic* record with the "Book or Record of Remembrance" as mentioned at **Psalms** 56:8, 69:28, 87:6; Isaiah 4:3, 65:6; **Daniel** 12:1; Malachi 3:16, Philippians 4:3; and **Revelation of John** 20:12–15, 21:27 (or even 3:5).

The *akashic* record is also called the cosmic picture gallery.

See also **Aetherius Society; Age factor and rebirth; Alzheimer's Disease; Angels and rebirth; Astrology and reincarnation;** *Book of Life*; **Disease;** *Bhavanga*; **Casey, Edgar; Causal body; Karma and justice; Lords of Karma; Michael (2); Objective immortality; Rebirth, alternative explanations to; Retrocognition; Steiner, Rudolf.**

Akh see **Egypt.**

Alayavijnana. Alaya means womb or storehouse, while *vijnana* means consciousness and in the **Vijnanavada** (Way of Consciousness) **School** of Buddhist philosophy it is the eighth and highest level of consciousness. It is not consciousness in any ordinary sense as are the other seven. Rather it is the non-reflected or non-self-aware consciousness that underlines the other seven consciousnesses, and refers to where the seeds (*bija*) of good and bad karma reside or are stored.

Alayavijnana is also said to be the state of awareness which is beyond the idea of existence and non-existence; and in which one, in theory, can perceive ultimate reality.

See also *Anatman*; **Karmic seeds;** *Manas*; **Mind; Zen.**

Albigenses Crusade *see* **Cathars.**

Alevism *see* **Cult of Angels; Nusayris (Nursaris).**

Alexander the Great (356–323 BCE) *see* **Greeks and reincarnation; Home, Daniel Douglas; Julian, Flavius Claudius, or Julian, The Apostate; Napoleon Bonaparte.**

Alexandria, Egypt. For Christians who favor the idea that Jesus taught reincarnation, yet find "The Young **Jesus** in India Theory" unacceptable, Indian influence via Alexandria has been suggested.

Located on the Mediterranean Sea in the Nile delta, for centuries this city was the trade link between the Greco-Roman world and India. Due to the wealth this trade brought the city Alexandria also became the most important intellectual center of Greco-Roman society. There is no doubt that ideas that were similar to **Hinduism** and Buddhism were familiar to religious and philosophical thinkers in the city in the pre–Christian era; however, the degree to which these ideas could have had an effect on a Jewish peasant prophet (Jesus) in Galilee is very difficult to judge.

See also **Ahmadiyya; Ammonius Saccas;** *Aquarian Gospel of Jesus Christ*; **Ashoka, King; Church Universal and Triumphant; Egypt; Jesus; Notovitch, Nicholas; Resurrection of Jesus; Scheintod hypothesis.**

Altered states of consciousness (ASC). While a few psychologists deny that there are what is commonly thought of as altered states of consciousness, most psychologists accept the term and the concept. The deniers base their opinion on the idea that there is nothing a person can do in the so-called ASC that he can not do in a completely normal (unaltered) state of consciousness. On the other hand, for those who accept such altered states, one definition for them is that an ASC manifests itself when there is a significant interference with normal monitoring and control of the person's environment. Another way of saying this is an ASC is where there is a dramatic departure from normal mental functioning.

The most common and obvious ASC is, naturally, sleep with or without dreaming. Other ASCs would be hallucinations; **out-of-the-body and near-death experiences**; hypnotic and other kinds of trances, especially any in which past lives are remembered; and certain mystical states.

See also **Automatic writing; Channeling; Hypnosis; Hypnotic age regression; Medium.**

Altruism and rebirth. One of the arguments for rebirth is that since the average person is inherently quite selfish there must be an uncommon reason that a small minority of persons seem to be naturally possessed of extraordinary altruism. This argument says that these individuals can only have evolved this characteristic over many increasingly benevolent life-times.

See also **Rebirth and moral perfection.**

Alzheimer's disease and reincarnation. The existence of this and related memory loss diseases have been used to criticize the idea that memory can survive the death of the brain. It has been pointed out that Alzheimer's patients lose memories as their brain cells disintegrate. This can leave a person with a near total loss of their former self. If this is true while the brain is still alive, how much truer must it be when the brain completely dies. In other words, even if there were a surviving **soul** it could not carry any memory once separated from the body; or in the reverse if a soul could carry memory, then Alzheimer's disease ought not to exist. A response to this is that while the mind (soul) is dependent on the brain for expressing memories it also acts as a storage back-up for memories. Therefore, while the disease effects the expression of memories, it does not affect the back-up storage. When the body dies, these stored memories will remain inactive until reborn into a new body-brain complex. A problem with this response is that as the disease progresses the brain is still functioning and storing new "if confused" memories that would also be inherited by the brain of a reborn person. Even in the absence of any kind of dementia the average person's memory deteriorates with age and this should be reflected in any remembrances of a former life.

Besides Alzheimer's, other diseases, drugs, and even malnutrition can cause dramatic personality changes which ought to effect the rebirth factor. It also needs to be mentioned that all of these elements offer potential problems for a belief in the resurrection of the dead.

See also ***Akashic* record; Body-brain (mind) dependency; Mind; Resurrection, bodily**.

Ambedkar, Bhim Rao (1891–1956). Born into the untouchable caste, this charismatic Indian leader converted from **Hinduism** to Buddhism, and following his example, so did thousands of other untouchables. This was done to challenge the injustice of the caste system, with its entire basis dependent on the concept of karma, which Ambedkar denied although still affirming belief in rebirth.

See also **Weber, Max**.

Ambrose of Milan (339–397). This Christian bishop was known for his literary works that are considered masterpieces of Latin eloquence, but also for his intolerance of non–Christians (pagans, Jews, etc.). In his work *Belief in the Resurrection* (about 380) he specifically denounced the belief in reincarnation. With this in mind, it must have been with great satisfaction that he was able to convert **Augustine**, later bishop of Hippo, and eventually a saint, from **Manichaeism**, which had as a central tenet a belief in reincarnation.

See also **Christian fathers critical of reincarnation**.

American Indians and reincarnation. A large number of native North American tribal religions include a belief in rebirth. This belief is especially wide spread among Arctic **Inuit** (Eskimo), Subarctic (Aleut, Beaver, Dene-Tha, Dakelhnes or Carriers, Kutchin, etc), and the Northwest Pacific Coast (**Kwakiutl**, Tlingit, etc.) tribes. Indeed, such belief reaches an intense level among the Tlingit of the Alaskan panhandle. A belief in rebirth was less concentrated among California and Southwest tribes. With some exceptions such as the Lenapes of Delaware, a belief in reincarnation was even rarer among the Eastern and Southeastern Woodland, the Great Plains, and the Plateau tribes. It was almost non-existent among the Great Basin tribes.

A number of North American Indians believed in multiple souls; the most common being a belief in dual souls. The first of these was the "free soul," which might leave the body in a state of sleep or trance, and which was regarded as the source of consciousness. The second **soul** was the life-soul, which accounted for physical aspects of the self. In typical shamanic manner such phenomena as aging, sickness, and death were often believed to be the result of the loss or theft of the free soul. At death it was the free soul that abandoned the body first, followed by the life-soul. It was thought that one of these might travel to the afterworld, while the other might reincarnate.

The presence of a belief in rebirth among South American Indians is less well documented; nonetheless, a full rebirth belief appears to be present among the Sanema-Yanoama of Brazil, the Ava-Ciripa and Guayaki (Ache) of Paraguay, the **Paramacca Maroons** of Surinam, and the **Yanomamo** of Venezuela.

Partial reincarnation concepts are found among other tribes. Among the Amazonian Jivaro there is the belief that at least some of the dead are reborn as animals. For example, a great warrior is likely to be reborn as a jaguar. This is a form of restricted rebirth. Also, the Lengua people of the Paraguayan Chaco are said to have a belief that some souls seek to return to life by trying to push out the original soul of an infant and to take its place. This, however, is more related to **possession** than to authentic rebirth. Among the Tukano (Barasana Indians) of Colombian (Northwest Amazon) there seems to be a belief in some sort of reincarnation of patrilineal soul-matter.

See also **Animals and rebirth, non–Western view; Animals and rebirth, Western view; Aztecs; Cannibalistic reincarnation; Christian missionary influence and reincarnation; Deaths, violent and premature; Gender issue of the soul; Hunting cultures and reincarnation; Inca; Kwakiutl; Mayan; Proximity rebirth; Rebirth, restricted; Rebirth, simultaneous; Souls, fixed and free; Souls, multiple**.

American Society for Psychical Research (ASPR). Founded in 1884, this organization strives to use scientific methods to study paranormal phenomena, including reincarnation. It publishes the *Journal of the American Society for Psychical Research*.

See also **Associations and organizations; Society for Psychical Research**.

American Transcendentalists. This name refers to the American literary and mystical movement that was centered in New England and that was especially prominent in the 1840's to 1860's. It was highly influenced by Upanishadic (pantheistic) literature and many of its members also accepted reincarnation. Among those members were writers Bronson Alcott (1799–1888), Ralph Waldo Emerson (1803–1882), Charles Emerson (1808–1836), David Henry Thoreau (1817–1862), and Louisa

May Alcott (1832–1888). Walt Whitman (1819–1992) is sometimes included in this group.

See also *Ex Oriente Lux*; **Upanishads**.

Amitabha Buddha. This is one of the five mythological celestial Buddhas in **Mahayana Buddhism**. Because of his great surplus of merit this Buddha is believed to be able to neutralize much of the ill karma his worshippers have accumulated. In **Vajrayana Buddhism** the **Panchen Lama** is regarded as the *tulku* (divine incarnation) of this Buddha.

See also **Avalokiteshvara**; *Avatar*; **Christianity and reincarnation**; **Dalai Lama**; **Incarnation versus Reincarnation**; **Merit, transference of**; **Nine doors**; **Pure-Land or Blissful Land Buddhism**.

Ammonius Saccas (175–242 CE) This Alexandrian philosopher was originally a Christian, but converted to paganism. He was the teacher of **Origin** and **Plotinus**, and hence he can be considered as the founder of **Neoplatonism** with its doctrine of reincarnation.

See also **Alexandria, Egypt**; **Priesthood, lack of an organized**.

Amnesia *see* **Birth trauma**; **Body-brain (mind) dependency**; **Cryptomnesia**; *Déjà Vu*; **Hypno-amnesia**; **Karma and justice**.

Amrita/Amata (S/P). This literally means the deathlessness (*a-mrita*). In a Buddhist context it is closely associated with the idea of nirvana, the end of rebirth. Although it might be thought of in Western languages as the equivalent of the word immortality as derived from im- (not)-mortal (dying), it does not have this same connotation in Buddhism in that no **soul** is involved with this deathlessness.

The term *amrita* is also the name of the nectar that the Hindu gods drink to insure their immortality and is the equivalent of the ancient Greek *ambrosia*.

See also **Eternalism**; **Immortality**.

Anabios (Greek: to return to life). **Plato** used this term to mean reincarnation. It is perhaps for this pagan use that **Paul of Tarsus** and some other New Testament writers avoided the term. Instead, they used *anastasis* (rising up) or *egersis* (waking up). *Anabios*, however, was used in the Greek translation of 2 Maccabees 7:9, to mean resurrection.

Anagamin *see* **Buddhist stages of liberation**.

Anamnesis (Greek: to remember or recollect). **Plato**, in his *Phaedo* and *Memo*, was one of the earliest recorded authors to suggest that **metempsychosis** (reincarnation) was clearly indicated by the unusual ability of some persons, especially young persons, to easily understand or quickly comprehend complex concepts or to demonstrate exceptional talent in areas in which they had little education or training. According to Plato, and innumerable persons after him, such precociousness could best be explained as a residue of a past life in which the individual had spent much time learning and practicing what in the succeeding life appeared to be an innate understanding and ability; in other words, to some degree all learning is recollection.

The Roman philosopher and statesman **Cicero** also believed that the speed at which children learn is proof that they have lived before.

It must be noted that this kind of recollection supposes that the **soul** survives death without any memories of personal experiences. All that is remembered is impersonal universal truths. This comes closer to the Indian belief in the survival of an impersonal memory-less soul (*atman*) than it does to the usual Western belief that the soul must retain personal memories to qualify as surviving death.

See also **Body-brain (mind) dependency**; **Child prodigies**; **Karma and justice**; **Karma, vocational**; **Pythagoras**; **Reincarnation in the West**; **Soul mates**.

Anastasis (Greek: Rising up or Resurrection). From the earliest Christian period this term applied both to Christ as the first to experience resurrection and to all his followers who hoped in the future to be resurrected.

See also *Anabios*; **Resurrection, bodily**.

Anatman/Anatta (S/P). Literally meaning no (*an-*) self or soul (*-atman*), this Buddhist term applies to the denial of a metaphysically changeless, eternal and autonomous **soul** or self. To understand this denial a number of factors must be examined.

In India, during the Buddha's time, the traditional term soul or self (*atman* or *jiva*) automatically meant a metaphysically permanent or unchanging; indeed, eternal autonomous entity that was on some level independent of the body. It was this soul or self, and indeed the very concept of eternalism (S: *shashvata-vada*), that Buddhism came to deny.

In arguing for the absence of a soul, early Buddhism first pointed out that all of our senses are dependent on our physical sense organs. We see through eyes, hear through ears, we taste through a tongue, smell through a nose and feel through skin. Take any of these organs away and the sense associated with them disappears. For example, if the so-called soul could see without physical eyes, than those eyes ought not only to be superfluous, but blindness ought to be impossible. The same ought to equally apply in the case of deafness, muteness, etc. Early Buddhism further argued that it was just such sensibilities as sight, hearing, tactility, etc. which were an essential part of personal identify, as in the very act of thinking "I am" or "this is me."

This early Buddhist view was in diametric opposition to those who believed that the soul, not the sense organs, gave us our ability to experience the light, odor, sounds, flavors and tactility of the world. This, of course, meant that consciousness itself was centered in a non-material entity. Yet, Buddhists held that if this were the case than no one ought ever to experience a loss of consciousness as when a blow to the head occurred.

From the early Buddhist perspective all the senses were dependent on the body and not a so-called soul. If there was a soul it would have to be devoid of all of these sensibilities, with the result that such a soul would have nothing to identify as "I" or "me."

Early Buddhism's second argument against a soul was based on the impossibility of the soul being an autonomous entity. If an autonomous soul really existed it should be able to command itself never to get sick, never to age, and never to die. Buddhism likened this lack of autonomy to a king, who commanded his forces to do something only to have them ignore him. Thus, the Buddhists said that just as such a king was a king in name only; likewise a soul was such in name only.

The third early Buddhist anti-soul argument was that there was absolutely nothing in the world that could be shown to be unchanging, so to postulate that there was a thing called the soul that was unchanging was little more than unsubstantiated wishful thing.

None of the above arguments could absolutely disprove the existence of a soul, but they certainly forced the intelligentsia of the time to have grave doubts about it.

Reinforcing the three above anti-soul arguments, a fourth one was a deep suspicion in early Buddhism about the value of extreme asceticism. In fact, this suspicion as much as the more intellectual arguments may be credited with the early Buddhist conviction that it was spiritually more beneficial to deny a soul than to either affirm it or remain cowardly indecisive about it.

To understand this suspicion requires an understanding of the two main religious competitors of early Buddhism. These were the now extinct Ajivika and the still existing sect of **Jainism**. Both of these sects taught a mortal body–eternal soul dualism. The theory behind this dualism was that the soul, which was believed to be eternal, was trapped in a mortal body. Through various extreme forms of asceticism it was thought that one could become the absolute master of one's self or soul, and upon being released from its imprisoning body at death, the soul could gain freedom from all suffering, and dwell in an eternal state of blissful, isolated (*kaivalya*) consciousness. This dualism in itself may not have been so abhorrent to early Buddhism had it not been that the asceticism required for the soul to be eternally liberated from the body included starving oneself to death (*sallekhana*). It seems that for the early Buddhists the problem with this **body-soul dualism** and the ascetic practice that went with it meant that liberation was considered possible only after death. This brought up such crucial questions as, "How can anyone know the soul is released after death? Has any released soul come back and told us this is true? Once the so-called soul is no longer a part of the body it has no mouth to speak to us." Indeed, according to the "release of the soul from the body theory," once released the soul could have no contact with or interest in the world it left behind. In light of the suicidal practices associated with the eternalist teachings the next natural question was, "What if after all such excruciatingly painful suicidal asceticism the soul turned out to be a myth?" In other words, "How could one be sure that liberation was obtained or even obtainable, if it were not done so in this very life?"

The earliest Buddhist canon suggests that from its beginning Buddhism taught that assurance of liberation could and should come while the seeker was still alive, not after death; and that it had nothing to do necessarily with non-provable theories about an eternal soul. In fact, from the Buddhist view point the very idea of an eternal soul came to be seen as encouraging a sense of clinging to selfhood that was detrimental to liberation which was the end of all self-centeredness.

It should be noted that early Buddhism did not oppose religiously oriented suicide altogether. There are incidences recorded in the canon of monks "taking to the knife" after attaining enlightenment. What it did seem to reject was pre-mature suicide. That is suicide before one had an absolute assurance of one's enlightenment and liberation.

If, as seems likely, one of the primary reasons for the no-soul (self) doctrine can be traced to a Buddhist criticism of Ajivika and Jain teachings, it is possible that this doctrine did not reach its final development until the rise of the Upanishadic teachings of the Brahmans (priestly caste). Not only did the **Upanishads** teach about a permanent soul (self) or *atman*, but they also began to identify this *atman* with the belief in **Brahman** as the creator God. Since concurrent with the Buddhist denial of an eternal self went a morality based denial of a creator God, any possible residue of a belief in a soul (self) associated with that God would have been eliminated This would have been a fifth reason for a preference for an *anatman* teaching.

Still a sixth likely factor that would have influenced a Buddhist no-soul (self) teaching was that once Buddhism committed itself to the idea of the all prevailing unsatisfactory nature of life the concept of no-soul (self) must have been seen as weakening attachment to that life. This non-attachment would serve to alleviate some of the existential pessimism and anxiety caused by the belief in an unsatisfactory (***duhkha***) existence.

Yet a seventh source for the Buddhist teaching of no-soul (self) must surely have been those profoundly blissful meditative states in which the sense of self was so often lost. This, in turn, would have even reinforced the concept of the world in normal consciousness as primarily one of dissatisfaction (*duhkha*). In fact, that experience of meditative no selfhood would have encouraged the belief that individuality or personal uniqueness was a major source of suffering.

Of course, an experience which entails a sense of loss of self during meditation can just as easily be interpreted as being united with or absorbed into a universal self as it can of experiencing no self at all. In fact, most religions that validate such a mystical experience encourage the former interpretation, especially if the universal self is allowed at least a slight degree of personhood. Early Buddhism did not allow any degree of that.

The early canonical Buddhist view of **nirvana** sometimes suggests a kind of extinction-like (*kataleptic*) state that automatically encourages a metaphysical no-soul (self). Early Buddhism, by believing in the non-existence of a soul-self, was paradoxically able to acknowledge that in really there was nothing to be extinguished and, therefore, there was no reason for any anxiety concerning such extinction.

Closely related to a meditative weakening of attachment, an eighth soul denying reason would have been the element of religious humility. In any ideology where human nature is seen as impure, due either to karma (in Indian religions) or sin (in Christianity) the only true solution to liberation, salvation or freedom is through some form of extremely humbling self-denial. This may take the form of humbling the desires of one's own body and will (asceticism) and/or of the equally humbling denial of metaphysical selfhood altogether.

One aspect of the early Buddhist denial of a soul (self) that is often overlooked is that the Buddha's teachings at times actually seemed more interested in denying the "my," and "mine" more than the "I"

or "me." This is especially noticeable in that the Buddha's teachings never denied what can be called the "heroic I." This is the "I" that, realizing that nothing permanent belongs to or can be a possession of the self (including the body), strives for liberation from the delusion of "my" and "mine."

The above possible reasons for denying a soul (self) would seem to logically deny continuation of any aspect of personhood after physical death; and yet the early Buddhist canon tells us that death was sooner or later followed by some kind of minimal karmicaly charged factor passing from one life to another. For this reason, Buddhism has always preferred to use the more general and ambiguous term rebirth for whatever it is that is transferred from life to life rather than such terms as reincarnation, **transmigration**, and **metempsychosis** which commonly connote a soul, or something very much like a soul, continuing on. However, even using the less specific term rebirth still does not help to explain how there could be any kind of real link from one embodied life and another.

To try to explain soulless rebirth Buddhists have used a number of analogies. The most common of these is the flame analogy. If, just before you blow out the flame (life) from candle A, you transfer the flame of A to candle B are the two flames (lives) the same or different? A second analogy is that the karmic consciousness of the dying person acts like a stamp that impresses itself on the newly arising consciousness of a fetus and then the stamp dissolves. A third view calls for a temporary intermediate being or consciousness (***antara-bhava***); in this case the dying consciousness somehow gives rise to an intermediate consciousness that transfers its karma to a newly conceived being before that intermediate consciousness dissolves. A modern analogy that has been suggested is that of billiard balls. If one ball (life) is in motion until it hits another ball (life) which then picks up the motion, is the motion of the first ball the same or different from that of the second ball?

As imaginative as each of these analogies has been there still are major problems with each of them. In fact, the continuing problem of rebirth without a soul was a major reason for the development of several later schools of Buddhist thought such as the **Personalists** and the **Vijnanavada School,** both of which, to uphold the doctrine of karmic continuation, developed their own compromises between no-soul and soul.

See also **Ajivikas**; *Alayavijnana*; **Annihilationism, Biblical;** *Atman;* **Body-brain (mind) dependency; Buddhism, folk; Eternalism;** *Gandharva;* **Heaven, hell, and Buddhist no-self; Individuality and rebirth; Interim period; Psychophysical aggregates; Rebirth factor; Rebirth** in Buddhism; Reincarnation in the West; Rebirth and suicide; *Shunya*; Soul.

Ancestor worship. This is the belief that the deceased continue to participate in and influence the lives of their descendents. This is one of the elements that have given rise in a number of cultures to a belief in reincarnation.

See also **Ethicalized or karmic rebirth; Heaven; Hell; Hotoke; Rebirth, origin of; Urantia Book**.

Ancestral or genetic memories *see* **Memories, ancestral or genetic**.

Ancestral or original sin *see* **Original or ancestral sin and reincarnation; Original sin, Christianity, and reincarnation; Original sin versus karma**.

Andaman Islanders. These indigenous inhabitants of islands in the Bay of Bengal are racially classified as Nigritos (Pygmy Negroes). These people do not believe in general reincarnation; instead they believe that if an infant dies it will be reborn as the next child of the same parents.

See also **Rebirth, selective**.

Andrade, Hernani Guimarães. This Brazilian parapsychologist has made several studies of Brazilian children who spontaneously recalled past lives. He has written at least three books on the subject among which are *A Case Suggestive of Reincarnation: Jacira and Ronaldo* (1980); *Morte, Renascimento, Evolucão* (1983); and *Reencarnacão no Brasil* (1988).

See also **Children remembering past lives; Ten Dam, Hans**.

Angels and reincarnation. The term *angeloi*, from which we get angel, was originally the Greek translation for the Hebrew *malak*, and although in Genesis 6:1, 4 *malaks* are called the Sons of God (Hebrew: *Beni ha-Elohim*), the term usually meant simply a messenger.

In certain modern Western esoteric traditions *angeloi*, having the **moon** as their domain, are thought to be responsible for guiding individual souls through to their next rebirth. Though ideally such *angeloi* are inherently genderless, they are said to assume the gender opposite of the gender of the **soul** of which they are guardians.

See also *Akashic* **record; Aquarian Foundation; Astrology and rebirth; Celestial gates;** *Chakras***; Channeling; Cult of Angels;** *Daniel, Book of***; Eighth sphere; Ephesians; Gender of souls; Hermes; Kiramu'l katibin; Layela (Laila[h]); Lords of Karma; Lucifer; Moon; Morganwg, Iolo; Mormonism; Oahspe;** *Sephiroth***; Silent watchers; UFOism; Unarius Academy of Science;** *Urantia Book***; Yazidis; Zoroastrianism**.

Anima (Latin: Soul). Among classical Latin scholars and philosophers there were different levels of the **soul**. One view was that these were the *anima materia* (the soul of non-living mineral being); the *anima herba* (the soul of plants); the *anima bruta* (the soul of animals); the *anima humana* (the mortal human soul); the *anima ratione praedita* (the rational and immortal human soul); and *anima divina* (the divine soul or over-soul, also called the *anima mundi*). Another view was that every human being had all the three lower souls as well as the specific human soul. Some classifications included other names such as the *anima illuminata* (the illuminated soul) and the *anima immortalis* (the immortal soul). Whatever name is applied to the higher soul it was only this that would reincarnate according to classical thinking.

See also **Archetypes; Over-soul, Universal; Soul, tripartite**.

Animals *see* **Animals and rebirth, non–Western view; Animals and rebirth, Western view; Animals, domesticated;** *Bhavachakra***; Transmigration, alternating lives; Transmigration, lateral; Transmigration, progressive; Transmigration, regressive**.

Animals and rebirth, non–Western view. In **Hinduism**, Buddhism, **Jainism**, and some other non–Western rebirth systems it is considered quite possible for a present human being to be reborn as an animal (regressive transmigration) and vice versa (progressive transmigration). Among those few Westerners who accept human to animal rebirth it is often assumed that any belief in the possibility of cross-species rebirth would lead to a great deal more compassion to animals than would otherwise be the case. This in fact, does happen, but only in a minority of situations. The reason for this minority situation is that since such animal rebirths are considered to be the result of the former human being violating some very strongly held taboos, the animal deserves whatever treatment it receives as part of its karmic punishment and to show it undue compassion might be to interfere with its rightful punishment. This, of course, could also be a form of **blaming the victim** for its suffering.

In the Buddhist *bhavachakra* scheme of things, for example, among the reasons for being reborn into the animal (S: *tiryak*) realm is excessive sexual desire (S: *kama* or *raga*: lust). Among most Hindus there is no particular reason for being kind to animals other than to the cow, as a sacred animal, or to some temple monkeys. Nothing demonstrates this more than the decidedly cruel animal sacrifices in many Hindu temples. In fact, in India real care and consideration towards animals is essentially confined to the Jains.

While it is true that dropping down to an animal life and violating some taboo are closely associated, there are exceptions. Among these exceptions is obligatory cross-special rebirth. For example, among the Kwakiutl Indians of the American Northwest the human **soul** must be reborn as an animal for as long as it takes for its former human body to totally decompose. After this it may be reborn into human form.

The belief in animal rebirth, while widespread among Asian people and North American Indians, is rarely, if ever, found among peoples in **Africa**.

See also **Animals and rebirth, Western view; Animals, domesticated; Arguments supportive of rebirth; Aristotle; Aztecs; Dayaks; Karma, developmental; Kwakiutl; Mind, theory of; Origin of souls; Soul, collective; Time and consciousness; Transmigration, alternating lives; Transmigration, lateral; Transmigration, progressive; Transmigration, regressive; Vegetarianism**.

Animals and rebirth, Western view. While many religious traditions accept the idea that a person could be reborn as an animal (regressive transmigration) most modern Western advocates of rebirth argue against this cross-species idea. The first argument against such rebirth is part of the Western preference for understanding rebirth as exclusively part of an evolutionary spiritual process; therefore, rebirth or **transmigration** into a lower life form is regarded as an impossible form of devolution. As logical as this first argument is, it must not be forgotten that for those who have been raised in a Judeo-Christian environment the biblical doctrine that mankind has been made in the image of God can not be easily abandoned and this first argument against cross-species rebirth certainly reflects this biblical doctrine.

A second Western argument against human to animal transmigration is that animals do not understand right from wrong and, therefore, can not be held karmicaly responsible for their actions. Such responsibility only comes with being able to make moral, hence karmic, decisions. If this is the case, then a spider, for example, could never improve on its karma to ever be reborn as anything other than a spider or its equivalent. This argument is especially significant when it comes to the **population increase issue**. In fact, a major reason for supporting animal to human rebirth is to try to solve that issue; but it does not work for most Western reincarnationists because of the moral neutrality of animals.

A third argument against a human to animal rebirth is that if, for example, a person's **soul** were to be reborn as say a pig, that soul would not recognize itself as having been born into that state due to moral violations. In fact, as a pig it would not have any questions about rebirth. This means that life as an animal could hardly be perceived as a punishment by that animal; therefore, such cross-species rebirth is a waste of time and energy.

A fourth argument for questioning transmigration from man to animal is that there would be such a loss of anything that could possibly be identified as formerly being a human being, much less a particular human personality, that this transmigration could be considered the equivalent of extinction of the former human soul. This fourth, as well as the third argument, were major points used by the Church Father **Tertullian** in his attack against **metempsychosis**.

A fifth reason for rejecting cross-species rebirth is that during hypnotically induced past life trance states no subject has yet to claim a past animal life.

See also **Animals and rebirth, non–Western view; Animals, domesticated; Aristotle; Christianity and reincarnation; Day-aks; Karma, developmental; Mind, theory of; Ontological leap or ontological discontinuity; Origin or Origenes Adamanthus; Origin of souls; Rebirth, East and West; Rebirth and the scientific theory of biological evolution; Soul, collective; Soul Darwinism; Time and consciousness; Transmigration, alternating lives; Transmigration, lateral; Transmigration, progressive; Transmigration, regressive; Vegetarianism**.

Animals, domesticated. Some people have tried to answer the **population increase issue** through a modified **transmigration** process. Rather than suggesting that any kind of animal (i.e. a serpent or rat) **soul** could be reborn into a human body, they suggest that those higher animals such as dogs, cats, horses, etc., having been partially humanized by thousands of years of intimate association with us, are not only a natural bridge between humans and animals, but themselves the most likely to make the **ontological leap** from non-human to human (progressive transmigration).

See also **Animals and rebirth, Western view; Mind, theory of**.

Ankh or *Crux Ansata*. This is a cross with a circle above the horizontal bar. It was an ancient Egyptian symbol of life and resurrection. It is used by the modern **Rosicrucians** group called the Ancient and Mystical Order Rosae Crucis (AMORC) to symbolize reincarnation.

Annihilationism, Biblical view. Annihilationism is any general belief that holds that there is either no aspect of selfhood that continues on after the death of the body, or any more specific belief that if there is such a continuation it is only temporary for some or all souls. While the belief that in a minority of cases some souls might face annihilation (selective annihilation) is compatible with a belief in reincarnation, a general annihilationism is obviously incompatible with reincarnation. For most believers in reincarnation the issue of annihilation can simply be ignored, but for those Western reincarnationists who are determined to find support for reincarnation in the Old and/or the New Testament any casual dismissal of the issue is dishonest in that there is clear evidence for annihilationism in both Testaments.

The issue of annihilationism in the Bible is complicated by the fact that the Old Testament and New Testament, for the most part, deal with the post-mortem condition in very different ways. In the case of the Old Testament, there is very little hope about anything positive that might follow death until the very late composition of that text. With the New Testament just the opposite is true. However, most people in the Christian world are so accustomed to hearing about the main theme of this work, the bodily resurrection of the dead, that they are unaware that there are also clear annihilationist passages in the New Testament. Most of these passages imply that on the Day of Judgment God will grant eternal life to the good souls, while the evil souls will experience a second death, in which their souls will face obliteration. In fact, there have even been some Christian groups that have felt that such annihilation is more in keeping with a loving and just God than is eternal torture in hell.

The New Testament passages that suggest such annihilationism are John 5:29; 10:28; 17:3; **Romans** 2:7, 6:22–23; 1st **Corinthians** 15:53–54; **Galatians** 6:8; 1st Timothy 1:17, 6:16; and 2nd Timothy 1:10. Annihilation may or may not be implied in **Matthew** 7:13, 10:28; John 3:16; Romans 6:22–23, and James 5:20. The fact that 1st Timothy 6:15–16 states that God alone possesses immortality have been further used to defend annihilationism.

On the other hand, as a main argument against annihilationism, there are innumerable words in Matthew, **Mark**, and **Luke** attributed to Jesus that plainly speaks of a continued existence in a suffering hell. There is also a place of post-mortem suffering mentioned in James, 2nd **Peter**, and the **Revelation of John**.

See also **Annihilationism, Buddhist view; Christianity and reincarnation; Christian view of the afterlife; Conditional immortality; Ecclesiastes; Eighth sphere; Hell; James 3:6; New Testament and reincarnation; Old Testament and the afterlife; Psalms; Psychopannychy; Resurrection, bodily; Second death; Universalism**.

Annihilationism, Buddhist view. Annihilationism (S/P: *ucheda-vada*), or the belief that nothing about human existence continues on after death, is in Buddhism regarded as one of the two heretical philosophical extremes that Buddhism rejects. The other extreme is **eternalism** (*shashvata-vada/ sassata-vada*). In contrast, Buddhism advocates the **Middle Way** (*Madhyama-pratipad/Majjhima-patipada*) view of ***anatman.*** In Buddhism annihilationism has been criticized, much as it has been in Western religion, on a moral basis. This criticism says that if people do not believe in a "life after death," and the punishment and reward that tends to go with this belief, people will have no reason to live moral lives. However, annihilationism by itself need not be lacking in moral principles. Many people over the millennia have believed that there is nothing after death, yet they have lived very moral lives. This may not have been the case for annihilationism in India during early Buddhist times. In India it seems that it was a forgone conclusion that hedonism (S: *kama-sukkha-allikanu-yoga*) would be associated with an annihilationist view. The pessimistic attitude about life created by the 6th century BCE Indian ascetic movement left for the advocates of annihilationism the choices of stoically accepting worldly suffering, indulging in pain numbing hedonism, or suicide.

See also **Accidentalism;** *Anatman;* **Annihilationism, Biblical view;** *Book of the Dead* **(Egyptian); Buddha's Necklace; Determinism; Karma with minimal rebirth; Personalists; Rebirth, buddhist; Rebirth and suicide; Rebirth in Zen**.

Anniversary recall phenomenon. This is said to be the experiencing of a feeling of illness or depression in the present life on the same day or date that some tragic event occurred in a past life.

See also **Spontaneous recall**.

Antara-bhava (S/P) *see* *Anatman;* **Bardo; Interim period**.

Anthropopathism. This term means the ascription of human (anthrop-) feelings (-path-) to non-human entities or even inanimate objects. The assumption that the universe, as a whole, feels love or compassion to humanity is anthropopathic and is basic to the belief that the universe would not be so cruel as to "not" offer an afterlife such as rebirth or resurrection to humanity. Anthropopathism also accounts for the belief that the universe cares enough about human morality to punish and/or reward it.

See also **Karma and God**.

Anthroposophy *see* **Rudolf Steiner**.

Antimimon Pneuma. (Greek: Counterfeit spirit). In some forms of **Gnosticism** this was considered to be a spiritual entity that was an intermediary between the body and the **soul**. It was this entity that was responsible for the soul's reincarnation.

Antinomianism (Greek: Opposed to the law). The law in this case originally meant the laws mandated in the Old Testament, especially the **Torah**. Once the writings of **Paul of Tarsus** came to be regarded as foundational to the meaning of the coming of Christ, opposition in his letters to keeping all the Law of **Moses** was interpreted by some extremists as meaning that even the moderate morality supported by that Law was no longer necessary for salvation, and in some cases following such Old Testament morality was counter to salvation. Even Paul, at times, found it necessary to warn against misinterpreting his teachings and using them to justify antinomian or hedonistic extremes (1st **Corinthian** 6:9–10; **Galatians** 5:19).

A number of sects of **Gnosticism** advocated antinomianism of one kind or another, often based on the belief that the Old Testament laws were those of the *demiurge* (lesser or inferior God) as opposed to the greater or real God of **Jesus**.

One of the main criticisms of reincarnation by the early Christian Fathers was that the doctrine of multiple lives encouraged antinomianism, as exemplified by the heretical **Caropocrates**.

See also *Charvakas*; **New Testament; Tantrism; Vegetarianism**.

Apocatastasis, Apokatastasis. This Greek derived word means re-establishment. In Christian theology it refers to the belief that there will eventually be a re-establishment of the state of sinlessness that existed before the fall of humanity due to Adam's disobedience. In other words, it means universal salvation. This form of **universalism** was condemned as a heresy by the Church Council in 543 CE (Constantinople) and even later by most Protestant sects. Although some Christian pro-universalists, including most Christian reincarnationists, believe that **Romans** 11:25–32, and even Romans 14:9–12, may imply universal salvation. The only explicit reference to universalism in the New Testament is found in 1st Timothy 2:1–7 where, in the context of offering prayers, it says, "Such prayer is right, and approved by God our Savior, whose will it is that all men should find salvation and come to know the truth.... Christ **Jesus**, himself man, who sacrificed himself to win freedom for all mankind, so providing, at the fitting time, proof of the divine purpose." It is important to notice that these words in 1st Timothy counter the more often expressed **predestination** passages in the New Testament that clearly state that far from universal salvation, God has predetermined that only a spiritual elite is destined for salvation with the rest of humanity to be damned.

Even if the passages in Romans are ignored, and despite the extreme minority biblical position for universalism, some Christian reincarnationists still adamantly point to 1st Timothy in their argument that such universal salvation is not only valid, but indirectly supports reincarnation as the only logical way such salvation could occur.

See also **Christianity and reincarnation; Hell; Origin**.

Apollonius of Tyana. Apollonius was a famous Neoplatonic and Neopythagorean philosopher of the 1st century CE, who supported the teaching of reincarnation. According to *Life of Apollonius of Tyana,* his biography by his students, Apollonius traveled extensively from Spain to India and, in the latter, came into contact with Brahmanic reincarnational views. In some forms of **Theosophy** it is believed that the soul of **Jesus** attained ascended mastership by incarnating as Apollonius.

See also **Ascended masters; Neoplatonism; Priesthood, lack of an organized; Pythagoras**.

Aquarian Foundation. This Foundation was founded in 1955 by the Rev. Keith Milton Rhinehart. It combines aspects of **Spiritualism, Theosophy**, and an assortment of Eastern religious ideas. Unlike Spiritualism, and more like Theosophy, the Foundation focuses less on contacting the souls of the deceased, and more on making and keeping contact with what it calls the masters of the **Great White Brotherhood** of Cosmic Light. These masters not only include some of those from standard Theosophy but also the non-apocalyptic UFO beings called Ashtar and Clarion and the angel Moroni. This last figure is presumably the same angel that is said to have appeared to Joseph Smith, the founder of **Mormonism**. The doctrine of reincarnation is an important part of the Foundation's belief system.

See also **UFOism**.

Aquarian Gospel of Jesus Christ (1908). This book, by Levi H. Dowling (1844–1911), was stated to have been transcribed from the *akashic* **record** by the author via **automatic (type) writing** in 1907 with the help of a great being called Visel, the goddess of Wisdom. It purports to tell the story of the

18 years of **Jesus**' life before his time in Judea, as reported in the New Testament. According to this book Jesus spent a number of these pre–Judean years traveling in India, **Tibet**, Persia, **Egypt**, and Greece. Also, the book also says that as a result of these travels Jesus came to accept and teach the doctrine of reincarnation. Obviously, this Aquarian Jesus is not the divine member of the Christian trinity; instead he is a man who attained the seventh or the highest, degree of initiation into the gnostic mysteries.

See also **Ahmadiyya; Alexandria, Egypt; Cayce, Edgar; Channeling; Christianity, esoteric; Church Universal and Triumphant; Notovitch, Nicholas; Oahspe; Universal Church of the Master;** *Urantia Book*.

Aquinas, Thomas (1224–1274). This prominent Catholic philosopher and theologian, addressed the issue of **metempsychosis**, which he also called reincorporation, in a variety of his writings, including *Super Evangelium S. Matthaei, Aristotelis Librum De Anima Commentarium, Scriptum Super Sententiis*, and most extensively in *Summa Contra Gentiles*. Aquinas, like **Plato**, believed that the human **soul** had three levels to it. The first of these was the vegetative level having the faculties of nutrition, growth, and reproduction. This soul level was shared by all life forms from plants to human beings. The second level was the sensitive one having the faculties of sight, hearing smell, taste, and touch. Only animals and human beings shared this soul level. Finally, there was the rational level, which gave to human beings alone intellect and will. Despite this original Platonic view of the soul, Aquinas was extremely critical of a belief in multiple lives.

Aquinas's first critique of the metempsychosis issue revolved around Plato's analogies of the **body as a mere garment of the soul** or the body being like a ship on which the soul, like a sailor, embarks and disembarks. Aquinas pointed out that these are very false analogies because when a soul is said to remove itself from the body that body decays, but clothes removed and a ship left behind remain completely whole because they have an existence totally independent of the body or the sailor. Aquinas further argued that since the rationality or thinking process has developed and is sustained through the soul's interaction with the objective world via the body, without that body the interaction, and hence the rationality, of the soul would cease. Aquinas also challenged the possibility of a human soul entering an animal or plant and, on the same basis, the possibility of an adult soul entering an infant's body. Aquinas's argument goes on to the problem of not being able to remember a past life. One example he offers is that of a person born blind in the present life ought to be able to at least remember and understand colors from some past life on the presumption that in all of them he was not blind. Aquinas summed up these parts of his critique by saying that without question what makes a person a particular individual is as much the absolute uniqueness of his body, his experiences in life, and his memories. Without these the soul is so impersonal as to be no one.

Aquinas's second set of arguments concerned the justice and mercy of God with regards to the issue of metempsychosis. He noted that it is not in accord with the logic of justice or a just God to punish or reward a person in a future life for deeds that person can not remember having done in a previous life.

While some of Aquinas' views unrelated to metempsychosis were challenged by other intellectual elements in the church, his anti-metempsychosis arguments remained unchallenged. Also, once he was declared a saint in 1323 any challenges to his views were more or less suppressed. Finally, in 1950 Pope Pius XII declared the philosophical views of Aquinas as superior to all others and so constituted church doctrine.

See also **Christian fathers critical of reincarnation; Church Council of 553; Corinthians, 1st and 2nd; Individuality and rebirth; Karma and justice; Memories, reasons for loss of past life; Psalms.**

Arcane School *see* **Bailey, Alice A.**

Archetypes. This term refers to primeval contents of the **collective unconscious** that are said to have originated in pre-logical or mythical thought, and to consist of ideas and predispositions that have been genetically encoded in human ancestry, and which have been passed on to all succeeding generations. The similarity of many myths and religious ideas found among very diverse and unrelated cultures is said to be a manifestation of such archetypes. Among these archetypes are the *anima* (femininity), *animus* (masculinity), the *persona* (outer or public personality), the **shadow** (a collection of all the traits the conscious mind does not wish to acknowledge, especially the unconscious animal nature), birth, rebirth, death, magic, power, the self (striver for unity), the hero, the child, God, the devil (externalized shadow), the old wise man, the earth mother, the flood, and the cross. It has been suggested that at least some of the presumed past life memories are built up and around such archetypes. The most familiar name connected with this archetype concept is **Carl Jung**.

See also **Tarot**.

Archons (Greek: leaders, rulers). This term covers two distinct set of entities. First, there are the benevolent supernatural powers (ex. angels) that serve as mediators between God and mankind. Second, there are the demonic or hostile powers that were created by the ***demiurge*** and which are often identified with the seven visibly moving celestial bodies (the five originally known planets plus the sun and the moon) or with the twelve demons that are said to represent the zodiac signs. Either set of these entities may be in control of the destiny of the human **soul**, both embodied and disembodied. It was believed by gnostic Christians that the mission of Christ was to enable the soul of the believer, on its way back to God, to pass safely through the demonic *archons,* as mentioned in Ephesians 2:1–3 and Colossians 1:13–17, and thus never again to undergo metempsychosis.

See also **Gnosticism; Planetary descent and ascent of the soul.**

Archy and Mehitabel. Between 1916 and 1936 there appeared in the New York *Evening Sun* and its successor a column by the humorist Don Marquis about a cockroach named Archy and a cat named Mehitabel who are able to talk to one another since both were reincarnated human souls. Archy in his last life was a free verse poet (*vers libra* bard) who, by nature, was a world-weary skeptical and cynical philosopher. Mehitabel was a homeless self-centered lady-like *bon vivant* who lived in New York's Shinbone alley and claimed to be Cleopatra in one of her past lives. The popularity of this pair led to a stage play (1954) that was turned into a chamber opera (1954), an album *Archy and Mehitabel: A Back-Alley Opera* (1955), and an animated film *Sinbone Alley* (1971).

See also **Cleopatra Syndrome.**

Archytas of Tarentum (about 400 BCE). Archytas, a friend of **Plato**, was a Pythagorean philosopher, a geometrician (mathematician), a physicist, a Tarentum military commander, and has been credited with inventing the screw and the pulley. Like both **Pythagoras** and Plato he was a well known champion of **metempsychosis.**

Arcturus (Greek). This is the name of one of the five brightest stars in the night sky. It is also called Alpha Bootes because it is in the northern constellation Bootes. *Arcturus* is located in an almost direct line with the tail of Ursa Major (Great Bear) which accounts for its name, which is Greek for bear guard.

Arcturus, according to Violet M. Shelley, in her *Reincarnation Unnecessary,* has been described in the **Edgar Cayce** readings as the center of this universe and through which individuals souls pass as they choose whether they will return to the planetary system of our sun or pass on to other planetary systems. Shelley further states that Cayce, in one of his life readings, was once told that he had been offered the chance of leaving this solar system via *Arcturus* but he chose to return to earth. Shelley says that each of us will eventually have such a choice and that, despite what might be thought, a return to earth does not always mean attachment to materiality. We may choose to return in order to be of help to others; although we do so at the risk of once again being caught in the cycle of return engagements.

See also **Celestial gates; Fortune, Dion.**

Arguments against human to animal rebirth *see* **Animals and rebirth, Western view; Transmigration.**

Arguments pro and con on an afterlife in general.

(1) Pro: Phenomena such as **Spiritualism**, reincarnation memories, **out-of-the-body experiences** and **near-death-experiences** imply survival after death. Con: For almost all of these phenomena, many scientists believe that there are non-psychic or non-supernatural explanations that do not require any disembodied factor.

See also **Body-brain (mind) dependency; Rebirth, alternative explanations to.**

(2) Pro: A belief in an afterlife can reduce or even eliminate the fear of dying. Con: such a belief can also make death more fearful if one believes in **hell**.

(3) Pro: The self must survive to make life personally meaningful. Con: A number of cultures have existed in which no desirable afterlife is found and yet people in those cultures have led meaningful lives. Also, in our own culture many very ordinary people have no belief in an afterlife and also live meaningful lives.

See also **Greek afterlife, the ancient; Old Testament and the afterlife.**

(4) Pro: Faith in an afterlife allows people to believe that they will be rejoined with loved ones. Of course, this is only true if one thinks everyone goes to the same peaceful place such as **heaven**. Con: Perhaps fewer people would choose to believe in an afterlife if they were told that while they would go to heaven their loved one would go to hell.

(5) Pro: A belief in an afterlife is supportive of social morality especially when that belief includes a belief that God, the gods, the dead, particularly ancestors, monitor the behavior of the living and punish or reward as is appropriate. Con: This belief can also make for a very repressed society, especially if the religious authority is backed by the secular authority. Also, disputes on the nature of an afterlife it has been used to justify persecution and

killing of heretics, witches, homosexuals, and any other non-conformists. It also has justified holy war.

See also **Ancestor worship; Greek afterlife, the ancient; Old Testament and the afterlife; Pascal's wager; Shinto**.

(6) Pro: If there is a belief in a post-mortem punishment and reward the injustices in life are easier to tolerate, especially if there is the hope that a person's oppressors or enemies will be punished. Con: The belief that injustice experienced by self and others in this life will be remedied in a future life allows people to tolerate injustices in this life rather than opposing them; in short it encourages injustice to thrive.

See also **Blaming the victim vs. illusion of innocence; Caste; Heaven; Hell; Soul**.

(7) Pro: If there is a personal and loving God he would not have wasted his effort on creating beings as complex as humans only to allow them to exist for the short span that life provides. Con: This argument depends entirely on there being such a God and it is a very weak logic to try to argue for the truth or reality of one thing (an afterlife) on the basis of the truth or reality of another thing (God) which itself is not provable. This is especially the case, if it is thought that the belief in such a God is largely a hope that the universe cares enough about people to grant life after death simply because so many people fear death.

(8) Pro: If we share with God the characteristic of being rational (we are made in His image), why would we not share his characteristic of being immortal. Con: First, as just noted in (7) this depends entirely on there being such a God. Second, a number of religions, while accepting a belief in a human-divine shared rationality, have not automatically presumed a shared immortality.

See also **Old Testament and the afterlife**.

(9) Pro: The very fact that human beings have conceptualized an afterlife for thousands of years suggests that there is one. Con: People have conceptualized many things that do not exist. Also, the vast array of different afterlife concepts suggests that such conceptions are unreliable. It has been suggested that the eons-old belief in an afterlife is not only due to a strong fear of death, but to an equally strong fascination with death. The latter can be demonstrated by elaborate scenarios of heavens, hells, purgatories, limbos, reincarnated lives, etc.

(10) Pro: God and, life after death in general, should be accepted on the basis of **Pascal's wager**. Con: There are so many different versions of life after death that even if Pascal's wager was accepted people would have to choose one of these over the others. What if a person chooses the wrong version? For Pascal's wager to be practical there should only be one version of an afterlife on which everyone agrees. Pascal assumed that there was just such a single true afterlife and that it was the Roman Catholic version. If this, or any other single true afterlife, did exist humanity should have by now discovered it. The fact that it has not been discovered greatly weakens Pascal's wager.

See also **Logic and pseudo-logic and rebirth; Rebirth and the preponderance of evidence; Soul**.

Arguments specifically against rebirth. Beyond the above arguments pro and con on an afterlife in general the following more specific arguments against rebirth have been offered.

(1) Rebirth destroys the hope of recognizing loved ones and friends in the afterlife. This argument has been countered by the argument that unless there is immediate rebirth, versus one with an **interim period**, loved ones and friends can meet and interact in the afterlife until it is time for each **soul** to start on its journey back to life.

(2) Rebirth confuses relationships. For example, an individual soul might have had the role of mother of another soul in one life, but in still another life the roll of a wife or daughter. The counter-argument to this is that as people mature in this life their relationships to one another change for the better or worse and this does not lead to chaos so it should not be any different in the afterlife.

(3) From an orthodox Christian position the greatest weakness in the theory of reincarnation is that it is impossible to separate that theory from **possession**.

See also **Arguments that challenge rebirth on a logical basis; Child as its own reborn father or mother; Incest and reincarnation; Karma, family**

Arguments supportive of rebirth. Besides the **arguments pro and con on an afterlife in general** there have been many Western arguments of various degrees of sophistication and/or naiveté given in support of the concept of rebirth. These are designated as Western because most Eastern religions do not feel a need to intellectually explain, much less justify, rebirth. Part of the reason for this is because those Eastern religions do not view rebirth in any especially optimistic fashion as do most Westerners. It is this very Western optimistic approach which, more often than not, requires an intellectual explanation. A fairly exhaustive number of these explanations are briefly listed below followed by the title of the encyclopedia's entry that deals with each more thoroughly. It should be noted that some of these arguments are in conflict with one another. For example, some are only pertinent to a belief in God, while others are a challenge to such a belief. Because of such incompatibilities no one person can adopt all or even most of these arguments. It will also be noted that some of these arguments are only a shade different from some others, but these subtle variations seem to be important to different people.

(1) Since many famous people have believed in rebirth this ought to at least suggest the possibility of rebirth.

See **Rebirth and famous supporters**.

(2) Extraordinary religious and philosophical teachers have taught rebirth. Among two of the most prominent are the Buddha and Jesus.

See **Buddha and rebirth; Christianity and reincarnation; Christianity, esoteric; Church Council of 553; Clement of Alexandria; Essenes; False claims of support for reincarnation; Jesus; Karma; New Testament and reincarnation; Old Testament and the afterlife; Origin; Predestination; Purgatory; Rebirth and famous supporters; Resurrection, bodily**.

(3) Rebirth is suggested by the periodic birth of a group of extraordinary men and women at around the same time in the same area.

See **Collective birth of extraordinary men and women**.

(4) Major scientific studies have suggested the likelihood of rebirth.

See **Kubler-Ross, Elizabeth; Stevenson, Ian; Wambach, Helen**.

(5) There has been a number of highly respected **Psychics supportive of rebirth**.

(6) The ancient Egyptians and Greek believed in rebirth.

See **Egypt; Greek afterlife, the ancient; Karma; Pythagoras; Plato; Priesthood, lack of an organized**.

(7) **Child prodigies or geniuses** can be explained by rebirth.

See *Anamnesis*; **Soul mates**.

(8) Those persons naturally possessed of extraordinary altruism can best be explained by rebirth.

See **Altruism and rebirth**.

(9) Rebirth answers why seemingly innocent people suffer.

See **Blaming the victim vs. illusion of innocence; Karma**.

(10) Karma and rebirth are more logically consistent with a truly just God than the arbitrary nature of the Western theistic doctrine of justice.

See **Arguments pro and con on an afterlife in general (7) and (8); Creationism, soul; Karma and justice; Karma versus grace; Theodicy**.

(11) Karma and rebirth alone are consistent with a loving God. Whereas (9) only speaks of the justice of God, this tenth argument is directly related to the idea that God is the personification of divine love.

See **Arguments pro and con on an afterlife in general (7) and (8); Karma and justice; Creationism, soul; Karma versus grace**.

(12) Karma and rebirth make it unnecessary to postulate a supreme God.

See **Christianity and reincarnation; Karma and God; Karma and justice; Theodicy; Rebirth, Karma, and Atheism**.

(13) For those who do not believe that a non-corporeal heaven and/or hell are possible a comforting alternative is a belief in a corporeal rebirth.

See **Corporeal versus non-corporeal afterlife**.

(14) People can be freed from the oppressive belief in the Christian concept of Original Sin by a belief in rebirth.

See **Original sin, Christianity, and reincarnation; Original sin versus karma**.

(15) Rebirth explains Original Sin better than the standard or orthodox Christian doctrine explains it.

See **Original or ancestral sin and reincarnation**.

(16) General morality is encouraged by a belief in rebirth.

See **Rebirth and general morality**.

(17) Rebirth discourages prejudice towards others.

See **Blaming the victim vs. illusion of innocence; Rebirth and general morality**.

(18) There has always been a more tolerant religious environment among those who believe in rebirth than there has among the Western single life believers.

See **Rebirth and religious tolerance**.

(19) Karma and rebirth are a more mature belief than the Western belief in the resurrection of the dead.

See **Karma; Rebirth and maturity; Resurrection, bodily**.

(20) Rebirth avoids the **Resurrection individual age discrepancy issue**.

See **Age factor and rebirth**.

(21) Rebirth avoids the **Resurrection cultural and technological age discrepancy issue**.

(22) Rebirth avoids the logical problems of "very own present bodies" resurrection that have traditionally been favored by orthodox Christianity.

See **Resurrection of Jesus; Resurrection, bodily**.

(23) For human beings to perfect themselves they need more than a single life time. If there is an afterlife following just a single life time, the **soul** would drag all its negative propensities into heaven.

See **Rebirth and moral perfection; Resurrection or reincarnation; Theosis.**

(24) Rebirth gives an optimistic view of life.

See **Blaming the victim vs. illusion of innocence; Neo-pagan religions; Rebirth and cyclical time; Rebirth in the West; Rebirth, compensation and life fulfillment.**

(25) We can only be fairly compensated for our personal sacrifices by rebirth.

See **Rebirth, compensation and life fulfillment**.

(26) Rebirth means that in the end no one will ever be cheated of opportunities to gain what they believe is their due. This differs from (25) in that there is no claim to not having gained something due to personal sacrifice.

See **Rebirth, compensation and life fulfillment**.

(27) Rebirth allows for unfinished karmic business. For example, it gives a person or a couple that died childless another chance at parenthood.

See **Karma as unfinished business**.

(28) Closely related to (27), but different enough to be a separate argument is the **Return and serve argument for reincarnation.**

(29) **Dying in peace** is facilitated by a belief in rebirth.

(30) We are made more compassionate to animals because of rebirth (transmigration).

See **Animals and rebirth, non–Western view**.

(31) Analogies from nature clearly demonstrate the truth of rebirth.

See **Rebirth, analogies from nature**.

(32) The **Scientific theory of biological evolution** strongly suggests rebirth.

See **Body-brain (mind) dependency; Rebirth and science; Rebirth and the scientific theory of biological evolution.**

(33) The natural order of all living things suggests rebirth.

See **Rebirth as the natural order of all living things.**

(34) Karma and rebirth are the spiritual parallels of the natural law of cause and effect.

See **Karma as natural law**.

(35) Logical symmetry requires rebirth.

See also **Rebirth and logical symmetry**.

(36) Spontaneous past life memories of children and some adults prove rebirth.

See **Spontaneous recall**.

(37) Past life memories recalled under **hypnosis** demonstrates the reality of rebirth.

See **Artificial (past life) recall**.

(38) *Déjà vu* **experiences** can be explained by rebirth.

(39) The ability of people to speak languages that they have not learned in the present life can be explained by rebirth.

See **Glottologues; Language inconsistency; Xenoglossy.**

(40) Rebirth is an explanation for **reoccurring dreams.**

(41) **Out-of-the-body experiences** and **near-death-experiences** suggest rebirth.

(42) Many of the recently channeled beings teach rebirth.

See **Channeling**.

(43) The existence of many reincarnated lamas or "*tulku*" in Tibet should count for proof of rebirth.

See **Dalai Lama**.

(44) **Homosexuality and transsexuality** can be explained by rebirth.

(45) **Widespread and multi-cultural belief argument** supports rebirth.

(46) Rebirth may be indicated by certain **birthmarks.**

(47) Certain types of **psychosomatic illness** are pointers to rebirth.

(48) Long term strongly held and seemingly **irrational fears** can suggest rebirth.

(49) **Reoccurring patterns of behavior** may suggest rebirth.

(50) The personality of each human being, even at an early age, is too complex to be explained without rebirth.

See **Human personality complexity**.

(51) Identical, and especially conjoined (Siamese), twins are a strong argument for rebirth.

See **Twins, identical**.

(52) Rebirth is necessary to distinguish saintly from the diabolical persons.

See **Saintly versus diabolical persons argument**.

(53) The tragedy of very early childhood deaths can be explained by rebirth.

See **Child's Epitaph**.

(54) There seems to be evidence that the proportion of male births after wars is often greater than at other times which suggests rebirth.

See **Male births, greater proportion of**.

(55) The disproportionate past life reports of violent and premature deaths would seem to make sense of the rebirth concept.

See **Deaths, violent and premature**

(56) The law of cause and effect should logically require that what is physically caused should have physical effects.

See **Logic of physical cause and effect**.

(57) The rise and decline of nations can be explained by rebirth.

See **Nations, their rise and decline argument**.

(58) **National character reappearances** suggests rebirth.

(59) Rebirth should be accepted on the basis of **Pascal's wager.**

(60) The sense of immortality possessed by the **ego** is due to its vague memory of having lived in the past.

(61) While no one of the above arguments may be sufficient to prove rebirth, a combination of several compatible arguments is strong enough to make rebirth highly probable.

See **Cumulative argument; Rebirth and the preponderance of evidence.**

Arguments that challenge rebirth on a logical basis. The basic argument against any reincarnation belief is as follows. If I no longer have the same body, memories of the past, any recognition of my former environment, that would include family members, friends, and maybe even enemies, how can it be said that I continue to exist? Moreover, whereas I died as an adult, if this so-called continuation starts with a new-born infant, parented by parents other than the ones that I formerly had, how can this be a continuation of me? Would it not be just as logical, or even more logical, to say that upon my death any person or persons who continues to be alive somewhere in this world who happen/happens to be of the same age as I am at my death age, is/are of the same ethnicity, gender, religion, occupation, and political persuasion that I was, is/are more me than some baby with a blank slate? The fact that any of those contemporary adults do not have the same memories as I did is inconsequential since neither does some "I" as a newborn infant.

One major rejoinder to this argument against reincarnation has been that none of the above personal characteristics, including personal memories, is the true self. In fact, no individuality is the authentic self. Instead, the real self is a non-individualized, impersonal something that is reborn into an infant, similar to the Hindu **atman**.

A counter question to this rejoinder has been, "what in this 'non-individualized, impersonal something' is there that only a particular deceased person and a particular newly born person have in common?" If there is nothing unique that both share, then could not the newborn be considered the equivalent of any person who died before him or her? Individualized karma has generally been proposed to answer the first question. As for the second question, reincarnationist must fall back on the non-individualized *atman* as the answer.

Another major reason for challenging the rebirth concept, especially if it is tied to the concept of karma, is that no single life seems ideal enough to eliminate all negative karma, and since each future life would likely add to that life new negative karma, it is not likely that there would be a possibility of ever ridding oneself of such karma and, therefore, no liberation from it and from rebirth. This becomes an even greater problem if it is thought, as it is in most Eastern religions, that all positive karma must also be gotten rid of if liberation is to be achieved. If the issue of karma is dropped then at least that would eliminate any challenge to reincarnation because of karma.

Finally, while of all the Eastern religions, it is Buddhism that has had the greatest appeal in the West; it is Buddhism that has the greatest problem with the rebirth issue because of its belief in soullessness (**anatman**).

See also **Age factor and rebirth; Alzheimer's Disease; Artificial (past life) recall; Blaming the victim vs. illusion of innocence; Body-brain (mind) dependency; Blocked regression; Children remembering past lives; Christianity and reincarnation; Consciousness continuity, sleep versus death; Determinism; Dissociation; Divided consciousness; False claims of support for reincarnation; Honest lying; Human personality complexity; Hypermnesia; Hypnoamnesia; Hypnosis; Karma as natural law; Karma in the ancient and modern west; Language inconsistency; Leading question; Mind; Multiple personalities; Ontological leap or ontological discontinuity; Out-of-the-body experiences and near-death-experiences; Population increase issue; Rebirth and cultural conditioning; Rebirth, alternative explanations to; Rebirth in Buddhism; Rebirth, criteria for proof of; Resurrection cultural and technological age discrepancy issue; Resurrection individual age discrepancy issue.**

Arhat/Arahat, also spelled *Arhant/Arahant*. These Sanskrit and Pali terms can be translated as either worthy one or noble one and refer to the male or female practitioner who has attained freedom from further rebirth. The term is sometimes simply translated as saint.

See also **Buddhist stages of liberation; Fetters, the Ten;** *Jataka Tales.*

Aries *see* **Astrology and rebirth.**

Aristotle (384–322 BCE). This student of **Plato** is regarded as one of the half-dozen most influential philosophers of Western thought. Up to the present time there continues to be debate as to whether or not Aristotle accepted the possibility of an immortal **soul**. This is one of the reasons that Aristotle's *Physics* and *Metaphysics* were condemned by the Catholic Church in 1210. Nonetheless, some medieval theologians, such as **Thomas Aquinas**, claimed that Aristotle accepted such immortality, and sought to integrate his philosophy into Christian thought. However, the later Italian Renaissance philosophers, known as the Alexandrists, once more denied Aristotle favored an immortal soul.

In specific regards to the platonic concept of **metempsychosis** Aristotle criticized the idea that a human soul could be reborn as an animal (**transmigration**). In fact, despite Aristotle's ambiguity on the soul's personal immortality, it was his criticism of metempsychosis that allowed some of Aristotle's views to find more acceptance in the late medieval Church than were the views of Plato.

See also **Animals and rebirth, Western view; Gnosticism; Neoplatonism; Origin; Soul, tripartite.**

Arnobius the Elder (4th century). Although born a pagan, Arnobius converted to Christianity no later than 300. He is most famous for his defense of his new faith which he recorded in his seven volume *Adversus nationes* (*Against the Pagans*) about 303. In particular, Arnobius criticized the Neoplatonic teaching of metempsychosis. **Firmianus Lactantius** was his student.

See also **Christian fathers critical of reincarnation; Neoplatonism.**

Ars Moriendi (Latin: the Art of Dying) *see **Bardo*; Conscious dying**

Artificial (past life) recall. This is the assumption of the identity of someone else while under **hypnosis**. Its legitimacy has been highly criticized. This is because the moment the hypnotist tells the entranced person to go back to an life before the present one that person may subconsciously create an imaginary past life to satisfy the hypnotist's command.

Also, for whatever seemingly past life memories are retrieved under **hypnosis**, there are alternative explanations for these that can be attributed to the "living person" and not a deceased entity. Among these alternatives are the ***akashic* record, cryptomnesia, psychometry, retrocognition, screen memories**, and **telepathy**. Each of these seriously undermines the reliability of hypnosis for genuine recall of past lives.

The term artificial recall is often used in contrast to **spontaneous recall** of a past life.

See also **Artificial rebirth;** *Déjà vu*; **Leading question; Rebirth, alternative explanations to; Reverie recall.**

Artificial rebirth. This term has two separate meanings. (1) It is a less accurate term for what should be called **artificial (past life) recall**. (2) It refers to a process, probably pioneered in Russia during Soviet times by the researcher Vladimir Raikov, who tried to enhance the art work of a group of students by hypnotizing them and telling them that they were such famous artists as Raphael and Michelangelo. As a result of this the artistic talents of the students improved. The same method was used with music students with like results. It has been suggested that a similar process can account for the art and music talents of persons who believe that they are the reincarnations of famous artists. The persons, once leaving the hypnotized or passive trance state, appear to be in a fully functioning normal state of consciousness; however, they are actually still in what can be called an active or dynamic trance state.

See also **Leading question.**

Artificial insemination *see* **Rebirth and artificial insemination**

Ascended masters. A number of late 19th and 20th century new religions claimed to have been in contact with, and received inspiration from, various secret brotherhoods located in the Himalaya Mountains, or on a celestial plane of some sort, or even from extraterrestrials locations. Actually, the earliest group to propose such a brotherhood seems to have been the original seventeenth century **Rosicrucians**. In their literature there was the mention of such an illuminated brotherhood that was said to reside in a mystical city in Arabia called Damcar. While this early literature does not mention reincarnation, some modern Rosicrucian groups believe that that brotherhood of illuminated masters does encourage the teaching of reincarnation.

Without question, one of the earliest of the modern versions of the brotherhood of Masters came from the French Kabbalist occultist Eliphas Levi (1810–1875) whose main interests were ceremonial magic and the **tarot**.

Another source for the concept of ascended masters may have come from the Hermetic Brotherhood of Luxor, an obscure occult organization first founded in London in 1870 under the guidance of Max Theon (Louis Bimstein). Since **Helena Blavatsky**, the founder of **Theosophy**, seems to have been associated with this Hermetic Brotherhood for a short while, it is possible that it was from it that she borrowed what became her version of the ascended masters. This is made even more likely in that there is a great similarity in parts of the teachings of Blavatsky and Theon, especially regarding the series of planes and seven sub-planes of the **soul**.

For Blavatsky, the Brotherhood was a collective term for spiritual adepts who were also called *Mahatmas* (Great Souls), or ***dhyani chohans.*** These masters had liberated themselves from the cycle of reincarnation and ascended to a spiritual plane that still allows them to assist in the liberation of others. It was Blavatsky that located the masters first in the Punjab and Kashmir areas and later in Tibet.

Another name for this secret brotherhood, according to the theosophist **William Q. Judge**, in his *Ocean of Theosophy* (1893), is the Elder Brothers of Mankind, and they reside on the planet Venus.

The concept of extraterrestrial beings benevolently guiding or watching out for humanity would eventually be adopted by some modern UFO groups.

After the Theosophists the concept of the Brotherhood continued to be popularized by a number of other individuals and groups such as **Aleister Crowley** who, as a member of the **Hermetic Order of the Golden Dawn,** called them the Secret or Inner Chiefs.

Still another often cited name for these secret adepts is the **Great White Brotherhood,** and as either former terrestrial inhabitants or extraterrestrials many of the believers in these Masters or Brotherhoods consider them to be a kind of secret world government, which will fully reveal itself in the future.

See also **Aetherius Society; Apollonius of Tyana; Channeling; Church Universal and Triumphant; Dark Brotherhood; Eckankar; Egypt; Gnostic Order of Christ; Jesus; Mark-Age, Inc.; Planets, other; Saint Germain; Silent watchers; Sinnett, A.P.; Steiner, Rudolf; UFOism;** *Urantia Book*; **Zoroastrianism.**

Asceticism. Unlike in **Hinduism** and **Jainism**, in Buddhism the indulgence of extreme asceticism or self-mortification (*attakilamathaanu-yoga*) is regarded as an impediment to liberation from the dissatisfaction (***duhkha***) of life or the round of rebirth and re-death.

See also **Accidentalism; Annihilationism, Buddhist view; Determinism; Eternalism; Hedonism; Middle Way; Rebirth and suicide.**

Ashoka, King. This third century BCE monarch ruled most of what is now modern India, as well as Pakistan, and Afghanistan. Early Indian records state that after converting to Buddhism he sent "*Dharma*" ambassadors to the courts of Syria, **Egypt**, and Greece. Although the term *Dharma* has several meanings, it is most widely used to mean the teachings of the Buddha; however, there are no historical records from those courts of the presence of any such ambassadors. Despite the absence of Western historical records, the Indian records themselves have been used to justify the belief that Buddhist ideas, including that of rebirth, penetrated Greek, Egyptian and even Jewish thought via those ambassadors. Furthermore, some New Age groups have suggested that indirectly through these same ambassadors Buddhism influenced later Christianity.

Since the concept of rebirth was known to the Greek world at least two centuries before the time of Ashoka there is little reason to credit Buddhist influence for this concept in the West. This fact, however, is unacceptable to many of the New Age forms of esoteric Christianity; so, one way or another they are determined to find a more direct link between the Buddha and Christ since this would better justify some of their eclectic teachings.

See also **Alexandria, Egypt; Christianity, esoteric; Greeks and reincarnation; Jesus; Orphism; Manichaeanism; New Age religions.**

Asia. Without question the primary source for most Asiatic beliefs in reincarnation is India. With the spread of Buddhism and, to a lesser extent, **Hinduism** throughout the rest of southern and eastern Asia a belief in rebirth and reincarnation became the dominant ideology in these areas. This has made it difficult to ascertain which Asian cultures may have developed rebirth concepts independent of Indian roots.

See also **Indonesia.**

Asmi-mana (S. Pride or conceit of "I"). This is related to the Buddhist view of *anatman* or no soul (self). *Asmi-mana* is a false evaluation of the presumed self in relationship to others and can be found in three forms. These are a prideful thinking of oneself as better than another; an unjustified humbling or deprecating of oneself in relationship to another; and an arrogantly motivated attitude of being the equal of another. *Asmi-mana* is seen as especially unfortunate in that it reinforces the other fetters that keep the cycle of rebirth and re-death spinning.

See also **Buddhist stages of liberation.**

Assassins. This was the name of a renegade Nizari Ismaili sect of **Islam** in the 12th–13th century CE that controlled a set of fortresses in Syria and Iran, the most famous of which was named *Alamut* (eagle's nest). The name Assassins is believed to have been derived from the Arabic word *hashish* (*Cannabis sativa*), the drug said to be heavily used by this sect as an aid in attaining mystical consciousness. The name Assassin came to mean a murderer for political reasons because the leaders of this sect often sent their followers to murder a leader of any state that was dangerously hostile to the sect. Because of the secrecy in which the sect held their teachings, not a lot is unquestionably known about those teachings, other than the fact that they were a blending of **Neoplatonism** and Islam. It appears that, like some other Ismaili sects, the Assassins believed in **transmigration.**

The doctrine of the Assassins, minus the *hashish* and political murder elements, seems to have been closely related to the doctrine of the modern **Druzes.**

Association for Past Life Research and Therapies. This is former name of the International Association for Regression Research and Therapy.

See also **Associations and organizations**

Association for the Alignment of Past Life Experience *see* **Associations and organizations; Netherton Method.**

Association for the Study of Karma. An Oklahoma based organization, it published *The Inner I*. Its present status is unknown.

See also **Associations and organizations**.

Associations and organizations. This is a list of various associations and organizations dealing with past lives that have existed at some point. Many such associations and organizations do not have a history of lasting very long; and some have only continued after a name change: **American Society for Psychical Research (ASPR); Association for the Alignment of Past Life Experience; Association for Past Life Research and Therapies; Association for the Study of Karma; Atlantic Guild for Past Life Awareness; Awareness Research Foundation; Foundation for Reincarnation and Spiritual Research; Independent Spiritualist Association of the United States of America; International Association for Regression Research and Therapy; International Board for Regression Therapy; Last Word: Therapies, Inc.; Phoenix Rising; Psychical Research Foundation; Society for Psychical Research Society for Spiritual Regression.**

Assyria *see* **Mesopotamia.**

Astara. This group was formed in 1951 by former Spiritualists Robert and Earlyne Chaney. While Robert became interested in **Theosophy** and in reincarnation, Earlyne had discovered that she had been chosen by one of the Theosophical ascended masters, Koot Hoomi, to reveal the ancient wisdom for a new age. Astara's teachings are very eclectic in that they include elements of **Spiritualism, Theosophy,** Lama Yoga (chanting of the holy name *Om*) and Christianity. All of these are united under the umbrella of the occult teachings of Hermes Trismegistus (Thrice Great Hermes), the ancient Greco-Egyptian deified sage Hermes-Thoth. The name of the group comes from the Greek goddess of divine justice, Astraea, and was chosen to represent the renewal of the past Golden Age. In 1976 the headquarters of Astara were moved from Los Angeles to Upland, California. Both Chaneys have written a number of books about Astara's teachings.

See also **Egypt.**

Astral body. The astral body is said to be a duplicate of the normal physical body only composed of much finer invisible matter. According to some of its advocates it is identical to the **soul**, while for others it is a temporary sheath surrounding the soul until the soul takes rebirth. The astral body is sometimes called the dream body since it is believed that during sleep it can leave the physical body and travel to wherever it chooses. The astral body has also been called the desire body (S: ***kama rupa***) or emotional body and even a wraith that manifests itself near or at the time of death. This body is often said to be connected to the physical body, either at the head or navel, by a kind of astral umbilical cord called the **silver chord** which, if severed, will result in death. In fact, upon physical death this cord is said to dissolve.

The concept of the astral body seems to have been adopted into Western esoteric thought in the late 19th century from the Indo-Tibetan religious world through such figures as **Helena Blavatsky**, the founder of **Theosophy**; however, once it was it introduced its exact nature was disputed by its various Western advocates. In fact, the Russian mystic **G. I. Gurdieff** is said to have taught that everyone does not have an astral body because is only develops as a result of hard spiritual work and struggle.

The book *Reincarnation: A Critical Examination* (1996) by Paul Edwards provides a rather thorough critique of the astral body concept on pages 127–131.

See also **Astral plane;** *Cabales* **or** *Caballi*; **Causal body; Death; Etheric body;** *Linga*; **Mental plane; Out-of-the-body experiences** and **near-death-experiences; Soul and spirit levels, Theosophical; Vampires.**

Astral light. The astral light is a not a well defined esoteric and occult term. In fact, it has a number of different meanings which are: (1) the light from the astral body or an aura; (2) the same as the *linga sharia*; (3) the universal animating element and/or power, hence equivalent to the *anima mundi* (world soul); (4) the universe's storehouse of memory or ***akashic*** record, which can be re-embodied and reincarnated; (5) the medium through which thought can be transmitted, as in the ability to psychically read another person's mind; (6) the etheric energy or medium used by practitioners of magick and (7) the sidereal light in Hermetic philosophy.

Astral plane (1). In **Theosophy** and related systems this plane is said to be the invisible plane of existence in which the **astral body** travels during the dream state or the trance state called astral projection, and between death and rebirth from and back to the physical plane of existence.

When the astral plane is called the plane or realm of desire as in Theosophy, it is not to be confused with the Hindu-Buddhist *kama dhatu* (realm of desire) or *kama loka* (world of desire). In the Indian case the desire realm covers the six sub-realms mentioned in the **bhavachakra** which are the worlds of humans, animals, **hungry ghosts**, **hell** realm, *asura* realm, and *deva* realm.

The Theosophical meaning of astral plane is not only much narrower than the Hindu-Buddhist meaning, but essentially relates only to the third of the seven aspects of the human **soul**. According to Theosophy, after the physical body dies and leaves the **etheric body** behind, the soul will then experience existence in the astral plane in its astral body. In this plane the soul will re-experience all the hatred and love, the sorrow and joy that it has been responsible for while in the physical realm. If the person in life did not live much more than a grossly material and unloving existence it will be trapped for a long time in the lowest, or seventh, subdivision of the astral plane. While in this subdivision it will experience the results of only the grossest and most unpleasant of its life actions and will do so as long as it takes for these negative results to be thoroughly purged from the soul. This is what Theosophy regards as hell, or more correctly **purgatory**.

No soul, however, can remain indefinitely in the seventh, or any other, astral subdivision. In fact, every soul must past through the entire astral plane, although the soul may not be conscious of all the subdivisions through which it passes. The difference is that those who have little, if any good karma, after leaving the lowest subdivision, will quickly pass through the others experiencing few, if any, of the rewards of these subdivisions. Those who do have good karma will pass slowly through each of the subdivisions so that they can experience all of the progressively greater joys each higher subdivision offers. It is for this reason that the astral plane, for most souls, is one of considerable happiness. This happiness is especially prominent in the highest three astral subdivisions, which are sometimes called **Summerland**.

One important aspect of the astral plane is said to be that each soul will experience the plane in accordance with its religious expectations. This means that a Christian will experience the astral plane in accordance with Christian beliefs, while a Hindu will experience the same plane as a Hindu after-life. It is because of this sectarian perception that certain of the highly developed beings in the astral plane will appear as angels to some and as *devas* (gods) to others.

When the soul has passed through all the levels of the astral plane and is ready to enter the **mental plane** it must abandon its astral body and with it the last remaining emotional attachment to a sense of self. This is experienced as a **second death**. This new death, however, is different from the first or physical death in that the astral body, now the astral corpse, retains just enough vitality and lingering memories so that as a **shadow** or **shade** it can be summoned forth by a medium during a séance. Eventually even these lingering memories will fade away, but the then remaining empty shell-like astral corpse may still be taken over temporarily by one of the exclusively astral dwelling, playful or malicious spirits, who may then masquerade as the former owner during a séance. When identified with the **kama rupa** this malicious spirit is said to even become a kind of spirit or ghost **vampire** feeding on the vital life-force of those in the world of the living who overly desire its return to life.

This description is based on *A Textbook of Theosophy*, The Theosophical Publishing House (1954, originally 1912) by C. W. Leadbeater. It differs in some minor ways from the version offered by **Helena Blavatsky** in that it incorporates the views of **Annie Besant**.

See also **Astral plane (2); Attached entity; Etheric plane; Omega; Planes of existence, names of; Scientology; Sciomancy; Soul and spirit levels, Theosophical**.

Astral plane (2). In the Afro-Brazilian tradition of **Umbanda** this is the spiritual realm beyond the material world in which higher beings reside.

See also **Astral plane (1)**.

Astral soul. In **Theosophy** this is the lower *manas*, the higher *manas* being the **ego**. This is not to be confused with the **astral body**.

Astral travel. This is the more technical term for soul travel and usually means the act of traveling to distant places, either in the physical world or the astral world, while the physical body remains in one place in a dream, trance, or comatose state.

See also **Astral body; Eckankar; Kubler-Ross, Elizabeth; Silver Chord; Soul and spirit levels, Theosophical**.

Astrology and rebirth. Astrology is the belief that the positions and movements of the planets and the moon in relationship to the sun and each other can significantly influence the lives of individual persons and groups of people. This definition more precisely refers to what is called judicial or mundane astrology as opposed to natural astrology which eventually gave rise to, and thus has been superseded by, the science of astronomy.

Mundane astrology can be divided into the two categories of exoteric astrology and esoteric astrology. The exoteric form is concerned first with character analysis, and second with predicting or divining important future events. As a system of divination the exoteric form is sometimes called astromancy.

Esoteric astrology involves the study of more spiritual aspects, such as the development of the **soul**. There is a belief among some reincarnationists that esoteric astrological readings can aid one in discovering a past life, in which case this aspect of astrology may be called karmic astrology. For such past life reading purposes some karmic astrologers regard it as essential to study not only the common natal (birth moment) chart, but the conception chart and the soul chart. The last of these three charts is said to deal with the time the soul first attaches itself to the mother who would bear the soul's next body. This attachment might take place not only before birth, but even prior to conception.

According to Joan Hodgson in her *Reincarnation through the Zodiac* (1978), the time at which the soul will incarnate is chosen by the **spirit** (soul) so that the planetary and zodiacal conditions are such as to ensure that the raw materials for building the various (bodily) vehicles are supplied by the *devas* or angels.

According to **Edgar Cayce** the planets, rather than being just physical celestial bodies, really represent the other dimension of consciousness to which the soul goes after death; and it is those states of consciousness that are reflected in the natal chart upon its return to physical re-embodiment.

In the view of some astrologers the planet **Saturn** is connected to past karma and, therefore, called the ruler of karma, ruler of destiny, or even the lord(s) of karma. Saturn is also the dominant planet for the zodiacal sign of Capricorn in which one of the two **celestial gates** is located.

According to Beredene Jocelyn's *Citizens of the Cosmos* (1981) it is in the **interim period,** while the soul is sojourning in the zodiacal sphere, that the physical characteristics of our next body are determined. While in Aries the nature of our future head will be determined, in Taurus it will be our larynx; in Gemini it will be our lungs, arms, hands, and bodily symmetry; in Cancer it will be our rib cage, breast, and stomach; in Leo, our heart; in Virgo, our lower metabolic organs; in Libra, our kidneys; in Scorpio, our genitals; in Sagittarius, our hips and thighs, in Capricorn, our knees; in Aquarius, our calves and ankles; and in Pisces, our feet.

The astrologer Martin Schulman, in his *Karmic Astrology: Retrogrades and Reincarnation* (1977), states that the retrograde motion of inner planets point to previous lives.

It is to be noted that in the West the application of astrological principles to rebirth and karma only dates back to the late 19th century rise of **Theosophy** and related movements. As such Western karmic astrology is still very much in the process of development and many karmic astrologers are in disagreement as to the best way to approach rebirth and karma astrologically. This is in contrast to Indian astrology which, although partly derived from Hellenistic (Greek) astrology, very quickly integrated rebirth and karmic principles into its astrological system. Moreover, the Indian system adds to its seven moving celestial bodies (sun, moon, Mercury, Venus, Mars, Jupiter, Saturn) the southern and northern nodes of the **moon** which gives the Indian system nine bodies with which to work. That the Indian system has only seven celestial bodies is because, unlike Western astrology, Indian astrology has not made a concerted effort to integrate into its system the more recently discovered trans-saturnian planets.

In the integration of the trans-saturnian planets into Western astrology it has been suggested that the earlier known seven moving celestial bodies have the same effect today as they have always had, which is mainly to influence individual lives. The more recently recognized planets (Uranus, Neptune, and **Pluto**) are regarded as collectively effecting long term economic, social, and political events of mankind. The reason for this is that the more personal planets have a sidereal period of from 2.9 months with Mercury to 29.46 years with Saturn. Thus, even Saturn has at least two sidereal cycles during an average person's life time. In contrast, the last three planets with sidereal periods of 84 earth years for Uranus, 164 years for Neptune, and 248 years for Pluto, take so long to revolve around the sun that their cycles can have little effect on an average life span, and so as far as karmic astrology is concerned, these three planets could have little or no effect upon an individual's rebirth.

A major issue that karmic astrology must deal with is that astrology in any prediction of destiny has long been considered to be at odds with various religious views of free-will. In fact, one of the earliest Western theologians to deal with this conflict was the Syrian, possibly Gnostic-Christian, scholar Bardesanes (154–222 CE). He proposed that the motion of the stars governs only the elemental (material) world, leaving the soul free to choice between good and evil. **Priscillian** (died 385 CE), another Christian theologian, and/or some of his followers believed that the heavenly bodies merely manifested the will of God to those who were skilled in astrological interpretations.

Some of the more pessimistic believers of the Greco-Roman period, and in particular those who were involved in **Gnosticism**, were convinced that much of what was in the heavens, especially as represented in the zodiac, was considered a representation of the "Wheel of Fate." Moreover, because the constellations reside six months below the horizon and six above it they represented the cycle of birth and death (**metempsychosis**). At its most ominous it was thought that each heavenly body was the domain of a powerful spiritual force which, in general, was detrimental to higher human spiritual attainment, particularly during the ascent phase of the **planetary descent and ascent of the soul**. In other words, the seven celestial bodies were responsible for keeping the soul trapped in the embodied cycle of birth and death. This meant that the spiritual goal was to escape from the astrologically dominated world.

The concept of karmic astrology has not been universally accepted by reincarnationists. In fact, some reincarnationists are extremely opposed to the concept. They point out that the ancient belief that found a relationship between the planets and rebirth is entirely understandable given the world's limited understanding at that time of the true nature of the various heavenly bodies. That limited understanding, however, is in the past, and if there is too close an association of astrology with rebirth then any criticism made against the former could be easily applied to the latter.

Finally, as in the past, karmic astrology has been morally criticized as leading to a belief in **determinism**, if not fatalism.

For more details on astrology and rebirth see also *Reincarnation and Freedom* (1987) by Lauritsen; *Reincarnation Unnecessary* by Violet M. Shelley; *The Divine Plot* (1986), *The Eternal Return* (1993), and *The Elements of Reincarnation* (1995) by A. T. Mann; *The Forces of Destiny* by Penny Thornton; and *Zolar's Book of Reincarnation* (1996). Thornton's book is particularly informative on the subject. There is also a chapter on Astrology and Reincarnation in Bjorling's *Reincarnation: A Bibliography* (1996).

See also **Angels and reincarnation; Arcturus; Celestial gates; Collin, Rodney; Eighth sphere; Dweller on the Threshold; Embodiment, moment of; Lords of Karma; Mann, Tad; Moon; Pluto, the planet; Pyramidology;** *Sephiroth*; **Scrying; Steiner, Rudolf; Tarot; Yeasts, William Butler; Zodiac.**

Asuras (S/P). This term signifies *a*-(not) and -*sura* (benevolent lesser deities), in other words the *asuras* are anti-gods, since they are constantly fighting against the gods (*devas*). In the West these are usually equated with the Greek Titans.

According to Buddhism the world of the *asuras* is one of the six realms of **samsara** into which a sentient being may be reborn, especially due to an exaggerated amount of envy in the preceding life. As with all other samsaric realms, inhabiting the *asura* realm is not a permanent condition. Once sufficient unskillful karma has been used up an *asura* leaves that realm and is reborn into one of the other realms.

In **Jainism** the *asuras* delight in torturing the deceased in **hell**. It is also their function to insure that a soul's sins are sufficiently purged to allow it to reincarnate.

See also **Astral plane** *Bhavachakra*; **Heaven, Hell, and Buddhist No-Self; Mara.**

Atheism *see* **Brahma and rebirth in Buddhism; God and rebirth in the West; Karma and free will; Karma and God; Karma and the moral structure of the universe; Population increase issue and a theistic solution.**

Atlantic Guild for Past Life Awareness. This American organization was founded by Karl Schlotterbeck with the purpose of dispensing information about reincarnation and **past life therapy**. Schlotterbeck has written *Living Your Past Lives: the Psychology of Past Life Regression*. New York: Ballantine Books, 1987

See also **Associations and organizations; Past life therapist, finding a.**

Atlantis *see* **Aetherius Society; Cayce, Edgar: Current knowledge discrepancy; Fortune, Dion; Franklin, Benjamin (2); Grace-Loehr life readings; Himmler, Heinrich; Jesus; Karmic romances; Lost Continent(s); Phylos the Tibetan; Ramtha; Score, John; Seth;** *Timaeus*; **Unarius Academy of Science.**

Atma see **Soul and spirit levels, Theosophical.**

Atman. Originally derived from the Sanskrit word for breath, *atman* it is presently the standard word in **Hinduism** for **soul**. More specifically it is the Hindu metaphysical term for a changeless or eternal self. In place of any kind of personality or individuality, *atman* is characterized as having the nature of being (*sat*), consciousness (*chit*), and bliss (*ananda*). These same characteristics are, naturally, also assigned to Brahman as *sachidananda*.

While *atman* is usually translated into European languages as soul, it must be realized that it can also mean God. This is because *atman* is just Brahman as understood through the deluded human mind, while Brahman is *atman* understood by the liberated or awakened mind.

Atman is not influenced by either wholesome or unwholesome karma. Instead, what is affected by karma is ***kosha***, the set of sheath-like bodies (*sharias*) surrounding the *atman*. These bodily sheaths exist due to the delusion of individuality or belief in separation from **Brahman** (God). As long as these bodily sheaths remain reincarnation continues. It is only through profoundly liberating oneself of any thought that *atman* (self) is separate from Brahman that the end of rebirth is possible.

See also **Age factor and rebirth; Anatman; Brahman; Body-brain (mind) dependency; Guenon, Rene; Individuality and rebirth; Karma and justice;** *Kshetrajna; Linga Sharia;* **Memories, reasons for loss of past life; Monism; Pantheism and panentheism; Soul and spirit levels, Theosophical;** *Sutratman;* **Vedanta Society; Yogananda, Paramahansa**.

Atmic *see* **Soul and spirit levels, Theosophical**.

Attached entity. This phrase refers to a **soul** that, for whatever reason, has not transitioned properly through the **interim period** between lives. Instead, knowingly or unknowingly, it attaches itself to the soul of a living person until it makes the transition. Four degrees of such attachment have been proposed. The first and mildest, called shadowing, is where the alien entity has a very limited and occasional influence on its host. The second, called oppression is where the entity's influence is more noticeable and obviously annoying to the host. The third degree, called **obsession**, is a blending of the personality of the entity and the host, which causes great confusion and distress to the latter. The severest case of attachment, called **possession**, is where the entity tries to completely take control of the host's body and mind. This is thought to be the rarest of the four degrees of attachment.

Many anti-reincarnationists hold the view that most, if not all, experiences of a past life are related to one or more attached entity conditions.

See also *Ahankara*; **Automatic writing; Channeling; Diakka; Etheric body; Kabbalah; Karma and rebirth;** *Kama-Rupa*; **Multiple personalities; Vampire; Walk-ins**.

Augustine, Saint Aurelius (354–430). Augustine was for nine years a follower of **Manichaeanism**. However, by 387 he converted to the Christian religion of his mother and soon became, not only the Bishop of the North African city of Hippo, but one of the most influential theologians in Western (Catholic) Christianity. Although he freely used ideas from **Platonism** in his defense of Christianity, by the time he wrote his most famous work, *De Civitate Dei* (*The City of God*), he had rejected the belief in **metempsychosis**. According to Augustine's argument the Neoplatonists taught that while some souls could attain the supreme happiness of intellectual comradeship with God, the compelling nature of reincarnation would eventually draw even them back into earthly rebirths. Christianity, on the other hand, offered a one way journey to heaven for eternity.

Despite Augustine's clear-cut rejection of multiple lives some authors still try to claim him as a believer in metempsychosis (reincarnation) by taking out of context a single passage from his *Confessions*. The fact is that not only is *The City of God* a major defense of the view of the resurrection of the dead as taught by **Paul of Tarsus**, but Augustine eventually also wrote some thirteen anti–Manichean tracts, which included a critique of the Manichaean view of rebirth. Indeed, it is in the *City of God* that one of his attacks on the belief in reincarnation is the argument that it might be possible for a mother to return as a maiden and marry her own son.

Augustine was also a strong supporter of the Pauline belief in **predestination**.

See also **Ambrose of Milan; Christian fathers critical of reincarnation; Christianity and reincarnation; Incest and reincarnation; New Testament and reincarnation; Resurrection, bodily**.

Aum Shinrikyo (Japanese: Supreme Truth Sect). This is a Japanese version of a **New Age religion** which was almost unknown outside of Japan until March 20th, 1995. This is when the sect launched an attack on a crowded Tokyo subway with sarin nerve gas. The leader of the group, Matsumoto Chizuo, more well-known by his adopted name of Shoko Asahara, began his career as a yoga teacher in 1984. After traveling to the Himalayas in 1986 he established Aum Shinrikyo. Taking teachings from **Hinduism, Vajrayana Buddhism**, Christianity, and the prophecies of Nostradamus Asahara claimed that he had been charged by the Hindu deity **Shiva** to create a utopian society. The failure of the Japanese political establishment to embrace his messianic teachings caused him to redirect his teachings to a belief in an Armageddon-like destruction of the world. It was when his views of such a destruction changed from a passive watching of it to an active assisting it to happen that he crossed into a criminal mentality. Asahara justified the actions of his sect by the fiendish claim that to murder people was an act of mercy since it saved them from building up the kind of bad karma that would lead them to a miserable rebirth.

See also **Belgi Dorje**.

Aum Temple of Universal Truth. This temple was founded by Elizabeth Delvine King (1858–1932) as the Church Truth Universal-Aum in 1925 in Los Angeles. The Aum Temple taught Esoteric Christianity as given by the **Great White Brotherhood**, of which **Jesus** Christ is the active head. Truth is the light and wisdom divine that has been given to assist mankind reach the kingdom of God. To enter the kingdom the self must be cleansed and purified through scientific prayer, renunciation of carnal beliefs and meditation. According to Aum Temple it is by cleansing, not bodily death, that one escapes the cycle of rebirth in the dense material world and the karmic law of cause and effect. In the early 1980's, the Temple was disbanded.

Aumism of Mandarom. Aumism is a syncretism of Western and Eastern religions founded in France in 1969 by Gilbert Bourdin (1923–1998) who, under the name of his Holiness Lord Hamsah Manarah, claimed in 1990 to be the Cosmoplanetary Messiah (the Messiah for whom all traditions are waiting). Bourdin had a number of problems with the authorities due to sexual abuse and tax issues; nonetheless, his followers believe he will be reincarnated or again incarnated in the near future. Aumism is in no way related to the Japanese **Aum Shinrikyo Cult.**

See also **Incarnation versus reincarnation.**

Australian Aborigines. Among many of the Australian tribal people reincarnation is believed to occur either for all persons or at least for children who die at a young age. In some cases there is a belief in **dual or double souls.** One of these is the pre-existent eternal-dreamtime soul which may reincarnate and the free soul which may become a malevolent ghost. Protective measures are required against the latter.

Among some aborigines it is believed that children are not just born of parental sexual union, but by one or both prospective parents entering the dreamtime (trance) and contacting the soul that wishes to be reborn as their child. This has some of the quality of announcing dreams. In other cases, the soul of the child to be enters the mother when she is in the immediate area of a local totem center, where the soul of a deceased ancestor is waiting to be reborn. For example, among the Western Waripiri people, souls accumulate in certain trees where they wait for an unsuspecting woman to pass by so they can jump out and enter their future mothers.

It is said that many Aborigines believe that they will be reborn as White Australians if they are lucky. This is a sad comment on the way the first people of the continent have been treated by European settlers.

See also **Dreams, announcing; Reincarnation, origins of; Soul, Fixed and Free; Oceania.**

Automatic speech. This is the phenomenon of someone speaking seemingly without such speech being under the person's control. It is a common occurrence in mediumship and **channeling.**

Automatic writing (also called psychography and direct writing). True automatic writing occurs when the conscious mind and the unconscious mind are temporarily in a state of dissociation from one another. This can happen spontaneously or, as is more common, under self-suggestion or the suggestion of a hypnotist. In any case, sitting quietly with a writing-implement (pen, pencil, typewriter, or computer) and a piece of blank paper, the hand of the person will seem to write or type independently of the will of that person. Most products of automatic writing (psychographs) are incoherent or of superficial quality, however, some of them can be very sophisticated. Psychologists point out that this kind of writing is not as mysterious as it may sound. They note that a great many very ordinary activities, such as driving a car, is in fact largely a subconscious activity.

A variation on automatic writing is the use of an alphabet **Ouija board** with a planchette or pendulum substituting for the paper or the handheld pen in producing the psychograph. Works related to the reincarnation issue that have had their source in automatic writing include the **Aquarian Gospel of Jesus Christ;** the **Course in Miracles; Oahspe; Phylos the Tibetan;** and some works by **William Butler Yeats.**

See also **Channeling; Hypnosis.**

Avadana/Apadana (S/P). Meaning "a note worthy deed" this term refers to an ancient Buddhist collection of stories about the previous lives of saintly figures, both monastics and lay persons. The purpose of the stories is to show the working of karma, in that skillful deeds bring good results (***vipaka***) and unskillful deeds bad results. The stories avoid detailed doctrinal matters, thus suggesting that they were intended to be told to lay persons rather than monks. Although some of the stories involve the past lives of the Buddha Gautama most of the stories about his lives are found in the ***Jataka Tales.***

Avalokiteshvara (S. Looking-down Lord). This is the name of the most popular celestial ***bodhisattva*** (wisdom being) in **Mahayana Buddhism.** In Tibetan or **Vajrayana Buddhism,** however, Avalokiteshvara is considered to be much more than a celestial being; he is believed to be the divine entity which repeatedly incarnate or take **possession** of the person who will become the **Dalai Lama.** In other words, the Dalai Lama is an *avatar* of this *bodhisattva.*

See also **Amitabha Buddha; Incarnation versus reincarnation.**

Avatar (divine descent [into flesh] or an incarnation). This refers to any celestial being that incarnates into human or animal form. In Hinduism, it is the high god **Vishnu** that has manifested himself as various *avatars*, the most popular of which are Rama and Krishna. In Tibetan Buddhism it is various *bodhisattva*s who incarnate as various high lamas.

See also **Avalokiteshvara; Dalai Lama; Panchen Lama; Incarnation versus reincarnation.**

Avichi. This is the name for the lowest of the eight hot hells and the most terrifying of the 136 hells in the folk Buddhist cosmology. A being may remain here for millions of years before release and a new rebirth.

See also ***Bhavachakra*; Buddhism, folk; *Papa-purusha*.**

Awagaun (Sanskrit or Punjabi ?). In **Sikhism** this is the name for the cycle of death and rebirth and so is the equivalent of the Hindu-Buddhist *samsara*.

Awareness Research Foundation. This Brasstown, North Carolina, organization has published *Techniques of Past Lives Recall.*

See also **Associations and organizations.**

Awareness techniques. This is a method to visualize past reincarnations while fully conscious originally developed by William Swygard in the 1960s. The technique is fully explained in Swygard's *Awareness Technique.* Lakemont, GA: CSA press, 1970.

Aztecs. There seems to be some evidence that the Aztecs had a "restricted" belief in reincarnation. They believed that the souls of warriors who had either died in battle or had become sacrificial victims would first ascend to the eastern paradise or "House of the Sun." Here they would stay for four years after which they would return to earth as exotic birds, especially hummingbirds (*huitzilin*), which were sacred to the sun and war god, *Huitzilopochtli*. In contrast, the souls of those who died as babies and those of men waiting to be reborn upon the destruction of the present world went to the high heaven of the original creator god and goddess.

There are two reasons that the Aztec belief in reincarnation must be considered "restricted." First, in the case of the warrior-hummingbird reincarnations, the Aztec did not speculate on what happened after this initial rebirth to those souls; therefore, it can not even be considered an alternating lives form of **transmigration**. Second, many other souls did not necessarily reincarnate, as for example, women who died in childbirth. Their souls first went to the Western paradise or "House of Corn," and from there they too would eventually return to earth, but only as phantoms of bad omens called *Cihuateteo*.

Of the dead who died by drowning, lightning, or mash fever, all of which were associated with water, they simply went to the southern pleasant realm of the rain god *Tlaloc*. All the remaining dead went on a four year journey to the unpleasant northern realm called *Mictlan*. None of those in either the southern or northern realms returned to earth.

See also **Dogs; Kulkulcan; Maya; *Psychopomps*; Rebirth, restricted; Transmigration, alternating lives.**

Babbitt, Elwood (1922–2000). A well known channeler who, while in a trance state, stated that he channeled not only such human entities as Christ, Winston Churchill, Albert Einstein, Sigmund Freud, Abraham Lincoln, and William Wordsworth, but also the Archangel **Michael**, the Hindu god **Vishnu** and that gods *avatar*, Krishna. Babbitt further stated that while not in a trance, but quite conscious, he can read past lives.

See also **Channeling; Hinduism.**

Babism and Bahaism. Babism was founded in Persia in 1844 by Mirza Ali Muhammad (1819–1850). A native of Shiraz, Iran, Mirza Ali Muhammad became a follower of Shaykh Ahmad Ahsai, who was strongly influenced by the **cult of angels**, which in turn had a strong influence on Mirza Ali Muhammad. In fact, it was thought that after the death of the Shaykh's son Ali, his **soul** was reincarnated as Mirza Ali Muhammad, especially since Mirza was born very soon afterwards. The term *Bab* means "gate" (to the Divine) and is the title the cult of angels uses to refer to the major incarnations (*avatars*) of the Haq, or the Universal Spirit. After the martyrdom of Mirza (1850) his Babist movement split into two groups, those that continued to follow the exclusive teachings of Mirza Ali as the Bab, and those that became the followers of Mirza Ali Muhammad's disciple, Mirza Husayn Ali or Bahaullah (the Glory of God). It was the latter who founded Bahaism after much effort to divorce itself from the militancy of Babism, and to shed itself of the influences of both Shiite Islam and the cult of angels. This divorce involved dropping any reference to teachings about reincarnation. There still are Babists in Iran, but their numbers are unknown.

See also **Yazidis.**

Bailey, Alice A. (1880–1949). Bailey is the founder of the Arcane School, tenets of which included the belief in reincarnation and karma. Bailey was at first a member of the Theosophical Society, but after **Helena Blavatsky**'s sympathizers failed to support Bailey's claim that like Blavatsky she too received secret communications via mediumship trance from hidden ascended masters, Bailey left **Theosophy** and established her own order in 1923.

See also **Church Universal and Triumphant; Lord(s) of Karma; Mental retardation; Psychology, abnormal.**

Banerjee, H. N. (1939–?). Banerjee, a well known researcher into reincarnation, was the director of the Indian Institute of Parapsychology in New Delhi, as well as a professor of Humanistic Studies at Columbia Pacific University in California. He started studying the subject of reincarnation in 1962. He is the author of *Lives Unlimited: Reincarnation East and West.* Garden City, N.Y: Doubleday & Company, Inc., 1974; *The Once and Future Life: An Astonishing Twenty-five-year Study on Reincarnation.* New York: Dell Publishing Co., 1979; and *Americans Who Have Been Reincarnated.* New York: Macmillan and Co., 1980.

See also **Extra cerebral memory.**

Baptism and reincarnation. In orthodox Christianity baptism is regarded as both a cleansing of Original Sin and the incorporation of the baptized individual into the death and resurrection of **Jesus** Christ. In the most rigid form of such orthodoxy, no un-baptized individual has any chance of avoiding **hell** or of sharing in eternal (heavenly) life. This view is in keeping with **Romans** 6:1–11; **John** 11:17–27, 14:18–21; 1 John 3:14. In theory, even those Christians who accept reincarnation prior to and/or up to the final judgment would require baptism.

See also **Augustine, Saint Aurelius; Christian view of the afterlife; Judgment of the Dead; Limbo; Mark, Gospel of; Millennialism; New Testament and reincarnation; Original sin, Christianity, and reincarnation; Peter, 1st and 2nd ; Rebirth and moral perfection; Resurrection or reincarnation; Star of David or Sign of Solomon.**

Bardo [Tibetan: *Bar-do*, S: *Antarabhava* or *Anubhava*]. Among both Buddhists and **Bon-pa** followers in Tibet the *bardo* is considered to be, not a place, but the interim state of being between the death and rebirth of the conscious principle (*rnam-shes*).

According to the text called the *Bardo Thodol [Bar-do Tosgrol]*, *(Liberation by Hearing in the Interim State)*, more commonly translated as the *Tibetan Book of the Dead*, this interim state, which can last up to forty-nine days, is divided into three states of consciousness. These are the *Chikhai* [Tibetan: *Hchi-khai*] *Bar-do* (Transitional State of the Moment of Death), the *Chonyid [Chos-nyid] Bar-do* (Transitional State of the Experiencing of Reality) or death consciousness, and the *Sidpa [Sidpai] Bar-do* (Transitional State of Seeking Rebirth).

In the first of these states a cleric, by reading from the *Bardo Thodol,* guides the dying and the deceased through the death and after death process. This guidance is said to be necessary because the dying or dead consciousness does not at first understand that death is occurring or has occurred. If the dying and newly deceased consciousness is attentive the consciousness experiences as a clear light the intuition of the highest reality. Those individuals who, while embodied, sufficiently prepared themselves for this light will be able to use that preparation to liberate themselves from any further rebirths. The clerical reader, therefore, calmly encourages the deceased not to waste that preparation and instead to take this opportunity for liberation rather than seeking another rebirth. The overwhelming majority of the deceased, being unprepared, will allow ignorance and fear to posses them. In their confused state they will forego the opportunity for liberation and become desperate to return to bodily life. So, after three and a half to four days they pass into the second *bardo* level. Here the deceased will confront their past karma, first as something divinely pleasurable, but then as something demonically terrifying. Trying desperately to escape from their own karmic-caused demons they will pass into the third and last *bardo* stage, which is the rebirth consciousness state. In this state the deceased will usually make a hurried or not too thoughtful choice of a new body in which to be reborn, and so will not only return to *samsara* to begin the cycle all over again, but to do so in a less than optimum way.

There is no doubt here that the *Bardo Thodol* considers the **rebirth factor** (*rnam-shes*) of the deceased to have full consciousness, despite the original Buddhist **anatman** denial of this possibility. In fact, what the book describes is not the rebirth factor as just a minimal karmic factor of official Buddhist doctrine, but that of an **astral body** type of conscious principle that apparently can see and hear without the necessary physical sense organs to do so. In fact, this is how the *bardo* rebirth entity is able to see and hear the mourning of those it left behind, thus encouraging that entity to seek rebirth. To prepare the living to deal with the *bardo* states well before death, depictions of those states are painted on cloth (*tankas*) and exhibited during the performances of popular public ritual dances.

It should be noted that the *Bardo Thodol* text was unknown until the 14th century, when it was said to be magically uncovered as part of a larger long buried *terma* [Tibetan*: gTer-ma,* mother-treasure], which actually means spiritual treasures or revealed teachings. According to the *Nyingma-pa* [*rNying-ma-pa*] and *Kagyurpa* (*bka'brgyud-pa*) Schools of **Vajrayana Buddhism** *termas* are secret books that were hidden in various wild, out of the way, difficult to reach places by the great Indian Tantric teacher Guru Padmasambhava (8th century) before leaving Tibet and by his disciple and consort Yeshe Tsogyal (757–817 CE) during the Tibetan persecution of Buddhism. Through various psychic methods certain holy individuals were able to locate and then publicize these texts. These individual are called treasure revealers or *tertons* [Tibetan: *gTer-ston*]. The concept of such hidden works was borrowed from the general Indian Mahayana Buddhist School, where such texts were known by their Sanskrit name "*nidhi*."

The *Bardo Thodol* is actually just part of a larger work the full name of which is the *Zabchos zhikhro dgongs-pa rang-grol* (*The Profound Teaching of Self-liberation in the Primordial State of the Gentle and Fierce Deities*). This title is often abbreviated to the more manageable *Kargling Zhikhro*. It is sometimes considered the most complete of all the *zhikhro* (a synonym for *bardo*) teachings. Besides the *Bardo Thodol*, this larger text contains the *Rig-pa ngo-sprod gcermthong rang-grol* (*Liberation through Seeing with Naked Awareness, Being a Direct Introduction to the State of Intrinsic Awareness*). This second text is an introduction to **Dzogchen** thought, the most advanced teaching of certain Tibetan Buddhist Schools.

The uncoverer of the *Kargling Zhikhro* was the *terton* Karma Lingpa of the *Kagyupa* (*bka'brgyud-pa*) School of Vajrayana Buddhism, and even today the text is most closely associated with that Buddhist School, as well as with the older *Nyingmapa* Buddhist School, and the even older non–Buddhist Bon-pa School.

Under the title *The Tibetan Book of the Dead*, the *Bardo Thodol* was first published in English, in 1927, by its translator W. Y. Evans-Wentz.

See also **Belgi-Dorje; Conscious dying; Devachan; Electra/Oedipus Complex and rebirth; Interim period.**

Basil (Basilus) of Caesarea or **Basil the Great** (about 330–379). Basil, a Christian Church Father, bishop, and saint, was the brother of **Gregory of Nyssa** and a major critic of *metempsychosis* (transmigration).

See also **Christian fathers critical of reincarnation; Christianity and reincarnation; New Testament and reincarnation.**

Basilides. This is the name of an important Egyptian gnostic teacher (died about 140 CE) whose teachings included the doctrine of **transmigration** or cross-species reincarnation. The orthodox Christian authorities had a particular dislike for his teaching because he taught that the God of the Old Testament was one of the brasher of angels, and hence he was even of lesser status than a *demiurge*. The **Jesus** in the account of Basilides had a docetic nature, and so never really suffered crucifixion.

See also **Animals and rebirth, Western view; Doceticism; Gnosticism; Valentinus.**

Beans. These was a forbidden food among the Pythagoreans and followers of **Orphism** and the reason seemed to be that beans were used in the worship of the dead. Since beans were among the earliest crops to appear in spring they were regarded as the first gifts from the underworld. For those who believed in reincarnation this could mean that beans held the souls of the departed. To eat them would be the equivalent of cannibalism.

See also **Cannibalistic reincarnation; Eggs; Pythagoras.**

Behavioral memory. This kind of memory includes **phobias and philias** that are carried over from a past life.

Belgi Dorje [Tibetan: dpal-gyi-rdo-rje] (803–842 CE). Belgi Dorje is the name of one of the great hero monks of Tibetan Buddhism. Buddhism had been introduced into Tibet from India by the middle of the 8th century, and with support from the kings of that country it began to flourish. This situation changed dramatically when, in 836, King Lang Darma [Tibetan: Glang-dar-ma] took the throne. This king preferred to support the native shamanic religion, or **Bon-pa**, whose clergy felt very threatened by the foreign religion. According to pro–Buddhist records, Glang-dar-ma closed all the Buddhist monasteries and ordered all the monks to either return to lay life or leave the country. Those monks who resisted were executed. In 841–842 Belgi Dorje assassinated the king and escaped into the mountains. With the king's death, Buddhism once again began to flourish. Since the very first vow that every Buddhist monk takes is never to kill, this very un–Buddhist act required some justification before the monk could be regarded as a great Buddhist and Tibetan hero. The justification was that since the king was building up great ill karma by persecuting Buddhism, in killing the king the monk was saving the king from adding to that store of ill karma. This would at least shorten the king's stay in the **hell** in which he had already earned a place. Because of this act of "compassion" towards the king, and even though it might cause the monk himself some time in hell, Belgi Dorje is regarded as a ***Bodhisattva*** in Tibet.

See also **Aum Shinrikyo; Rebirth and religious tolerance.**

Benin. The Benin are a people of West Africa who believe that everyone is consanguineously reborn fourteen times, but no one can be sure in which of these life-times a person is at any one time.

See also **Rebirth, consanguineous**.

Beruchim, Abraham. Beruchim was a sixteenth century North African Jewish Kabbalist who was such a severe advocate of repentance that many Kabbalists believe him to be the reincarnation of the biblical prophet Jeremiah (698–642 BCE).

Besant, Annie (1847–1933). Besant, early in her career, was a very active feminist, socialist, and atheist. Upon her reading of the *Secret Doctrine* by **Helena Blavatsky,** she became a devoted Theosophist in 1888. Along with **Charles Leadbeater** she became the head of the Theosophical Society upon Blavatsky's death in 1891. Residing in India in the last years of her life, she was a major activist in the Indian independence movement. This earned her the reputation of being a saint and even an *avatar* (earthly manifestation of the divine). Besant was one of the main supporters of Jiddu Krishnamurti (1895–1986), as not only the reincarnation of the Hindu god Krishna and Christ, but as the prophesized future Buddha, Maitreya, and even as the (Judeo-Christian) Messiah.

Besant published over thirty of works supporting the doctrine of reincarnation.

See also **Steiner, Rudolf; Theosophy**.

Bhagavad Gita (*Song of the Lord*). This work is a book size poem, probably composed around 300 CE that has been inserted as chapter six into the still greater epic Hindu poem the *Mahabharata*. The importance of the *Bhagavad Gita* is that it teaches that liberation from reincarnation is possible even for the non-priestly (**Brahman**) caste, and non-ascetic (monk) devotees. What is required to be liberated from the cycle of birth and death is first, to perform one's caste duty faithfully (***karma yoga***); second, to have no concern for personal material benefits from this performance; and third, to have absolute faith (***bhakti yoga***) that, as a result of the first and second conditions, the grace of God (Krishna) will then liberate the performer. It is especially in chapter two, at verse thirteen, and chapter six, at verse forty-one, of this text that reincarnation is affirmed. For the above reasons, the *Bhagavad Gita* is the most revered text in Hinduism.

See also ***Ahimsa*; Caste system; India; International Society for Krishna; Jesus; Karma versus grace; Return and serve argument for reincarnation; *Upanishads***.

Bhaishajyaraja-guru (Medicine king teacher). This name is translated into Chinese Yaoshi fo (WG) and in Japanese as Yakushi Nyorai. Both of these mean the Medicine Buddha. Actually, the full designation in Sanskrit is Bhaishajyaguru Vaiduryaprabha Tathagata (Radiant Lapis-Lazuli Master of Healing Buddha). This Buddha is prayed to for various cures from illnesses and deformities, and to provide food for the hungry and clothes for the poor. He is also popular among women devotees because he is said to have the power to ensure that in their next life they will be reborn as men.

See also ***Bodhisattva*; Gender issue of the soul; Pure-Land or Blissful Land Buddhism**.

Bhakti Yoga (Devotional yoga). This is the practice of devotional worship of God in **Hinduism**. It is one of the four major practices that are believed to liberate the **soul** from rebirth. The major significance of this yoga is that it is regarded as the main vehicle for neutralizing bad karma and, thereby, avoiding one or more otherwise karmicaly deserved unpleasant reincarnations. This is possible because in Hinduism the grace of the gods is considered to be superior to the law of karma (*karmaniyama*).

See also ***Bhagavad Gita*; Karma versus grace; Karma yoga; *Vaikuntha***.

Bhava (Being or becoming). This is the standard Buddhist and Hindu word for rebirth or reincarnation. The term *punar-janma/puna-bhava* (S/P) meaning "again birth" is also used.

Bhavachakra (Wheel of Becoming). According to Buddhism there are five or six realms into which a sentient being may be reborn. These realms are graphically depicted as a circle (wheel) with five or six spokes that divide the ordinary world of desire (*rupa-loka*) into lower and higher realms. In the case of six sub-sections the lower realms are animals (*tiryak*), **hungry ghost** (*pretas*), and **purgatory** (*naraka*). The three higher realms are those of the human beings (*manusa*), anti-gods (*asura*), and gods (*devas*). In the case of the five sub-sections the *asura* and *deva* are grouped together.

In some Buddhist Schools these six realms are associated with particular negative mental states or poisons. The gods represent pride, the *asuras* are jealousy, animals are ignorance or delusion, hungry ghosts are greed and miserliness, hell is anger and hatred, and the human realm is desire or lust.

Since the *Bhavachakra* concept involves transmigration rather than just reincarnation many Western groups, that are otherwise pro–Buddhist, do not accept this cross-species wheel of becoming.

See also **Animals and rebirth, Western view; Astral plane; Buddhist stages of liberation; *Devaloka*; *Jataka Tales*; *Kyklos Genesion*; *Peta-***

vatthu; *Pritiloka*; Privilege of a human birth; Pure-Land or Blissful Land Buddhism; Rebirth, instantaneous; Swastika; *Vimanavatthu*.

Bhavanga or *Bhava-anga* (P). This term is used in early Buddhism in the sense of the foundation or condition of existence (***bhava***) and is sometimes stated to be the subliminal consciousness that carries karma from one life (embodiment) to another.

See also ***Abhijna***; Rebirth in Buddhism.

Bible and rebirth. Among many Western, and some Eastern, proponents of rebirth there has been a concerted effort to find in both the Old and the New Testament covert evidence for the teaching of reincarnation. In fact, R. F. Goudy, in his *Reincarnation, A Universal Truth* (1928), states that there are over fifty *bona-fide* [his italicization] quotations teaching reincarnation in the Bible. Actually, more than seventy quotations have been listed in this encyclopedia, but a close examination of each of these demonstrates a total lack of anything *bona-fide* about them. Of course, this brings up the question why would there be a number that large if there was no validity to them? The answer is simple. The Bible is not a single book, but a collection of sixty-six books of which thirty-nine comprise the Old Testament (*Tanach*) and twenty-seven the New Testament. Often added between these two testaments are the fifteen Apocrypha. Altogether these texts were written over approximately 1500 years by some 40 authors in three languages. As a result of this complexity the Bible is full of inconsistencies and contradictions. Over the centuries this has lead to people interpreting, or more correctly reading into, the Bible whatever teachings they have favored. This process of finding evidence for whatever one may want is almost always achieved by lifting passages out of their immediate context which automatically distorts them, and makes them available for any number of favorable, if not fanciful, interpretations.

See also **Jesus**; **Karma in the Bible?**; **New Testament and reincarnation**; **Old Testament and the afterlife**; **Peter, 1st and 2nd**.

Biblical deluge and reincarnation. One of the older arguments in favor of there being rebirth teachings subtly implied in the Bible is that before the flood that destroyed all of mankind, except for Noah and his family, the human life-span was very long which gave people sufficient time to repent of their sins. But, with the greatly shortened life-span of post-deluge individuals, there is not sufficient time for repentance, and since God is entirely just, He has made available the alternative of more than one life for repentance purposes.

Biblical references *see* Acts 2:39; Adam; Angels and reincarnation; *Akashic* Record; Annihilationism, Biblical view; *Apocatastasis*; Baptism; Bible and rebirth; Biblical deluge and reincarnation; Born again; Carpocrates; Cayce, Edgar; Christianity and reincarnation; 1st and 2nd Corinthians; Crowley, Edward Aleister; Daniel, Book of; Deuteronomy 5:2–3; Ecclesiastes; Ecclesiasticus 41:8–9; Ephesians; "every knee should bend ... every tongue confess"; Exodus; Gabriel; Galatians; Genesis; Harrowing of Hell; Heaven's Gate; Hell; James 3:6; Jesus; Job; John, Gospel of; John the Baptist; I Am Movement; Kabbalah; Karma in the Bible?; Karma versus grace; Kingsford, Anna Bonus; Lazarus; Limbo; Lucifer; Luke, Gospel of; Mark, Gospel of; Matthew, Gospel; Melchizedek; Millennialism; New Testament and reincarnation; New Testament sacrificial concept; Numbers; Old Testament and the afterlife; Old Testament and the soul; Original sin, Christianity, and reincarnation; Palingenesis; Peter, 1st and 2nd; *Pistis Sophia*; Pleiades; Possession; Predestination; Proof text; Proverbs; Psalms; *Psychopannychism*; Purgatory; Rebirth and moral perfection; Resurrection, bodily; Resurrection of Jesus; Resurrection or reincarnation; Revelation of John; Romans; Sciomancy; Second death; Seven Veils, Dance of; Silver Chord; Simon Magus; Star of David or Sign of Solomon; Theosis; Universalism; Wisdom of Solomon 8:19–20; Xenoglossy; Yogananda, Paramahansa.

Bija (S: Seed). This is the name for **karmic seeds** in the *Vijnanavada* (Consciousness only) **School** of Buddhism.

Biological evolution and the soul *see* Ontological leap or ontological discontinuity; Population increase issue; Rebirth and the scientific theory of biological evolution; Soul, collective.

Birds, soul. Although rejected by orthodox Christianity there was, at least up to the late 19th century, a long standing fishermen's folk belief that certain birds harbor former human souls. Such birds are always viewed as ominous. Among the British Islanders the storm petrel (*Hydobates pelagicus*) and seagulls (*Laridae*) was believed to have the souls of the dead, especially drowned, sailors and this is why they were helpful as signs of approaching storms. This belief meant that it was very unlucky to kill one of these birds. Western European land-based beliefs held that the crow or raven (*Corvus*) held human souls of un-baptized persons and wicked priests. Among the Muslims in the Mediterranean the shearwaters (*Puffinus*) were thought to be inhabited by the souls of the damned. Of course, all these are example of restricted rebirth rather than full rebirth.

See also **Hell; Rebirth, restricted**.

Birth trauma. One of the major suggestions as to why people do not remember their past life is that the trauma of being forced to leave a secure and comfortable womb for the insecure and discomforting world outside is sufficient to obliterate any former memories. Indeed, it is seen as the equivalent of the amnesia some people experience after an extreme traumatic injury to the body and or mind.

See also **Affect bridge; Blocked regression; Memories, reasons for loss of past life**.

Birthmarks. In some folk societies birthmarks are significant as indicators that a particular family member has been reborn. One example of this is among the Igbo of West **Africa**. However, it is mainly modern researchers, such as **Ian Stevenson**, who have been interested in using birthmarks in their reincarnation studies. These researchers have compared birthmarks on living persons with wounds or scars of a deceased person and have suggested that these marks are physical manifestations that connect to the two lives. There are three major problems encountered with birthmarks. First, if a child is born with a particular birthmark reminiscent in some way of a birthmark of a deceased person might not this be sufficient for the adults around the child to suggest to the child an identity with the deceased? This could encourage the child to pick up on enough related information from the adults to form a supposed past life memory. The second, though rarer, possibility is that pseudo-birthmarks may arise on the child under the influence of strong adult expectations. The psychosomatic ability to produce such birthmarks must be taken seriously in the light of the far greater ability of some individuals to psychosomatically manifest bleeding wounds, as in some stigmata cases. Also, related to this second possibility is the theory of **maternal impressions** (or **maternal pychokinesis**). Still a third possibility is that the birthmarks are due to some kind of **possession**. With regard to this possibility it is to be noted that Stevenson has focused heavily on birthmarks because he believes that such marks are a firm method of distinguishing genuine rebirth from possession by an alien spiritual entity. However, there is no real reason for any assurance that an entity that took pre-natal possession could not be responsible for such marks.

See also **Arguments supportive of rebirth; Facial architectural consistency; Maternal impressions; Natal defects; Rebirth, consanguineous; Rebirth, criteria for proof of**.

Bjorkhem, John. Bjorkhem is a Swedish parapsychologist who, after hypnotically regressing hundreds of individuals, concluded that all of their past life experiences could be explained by **obsession** (obsessing entities).

Black hole. This is a karmic dark area which tends to draw a person into necessary challenging situations similar to those which the person, over several past lives, has refused to accept.

Blaming the victim vs. illusion of innocence. One major criticism of the concept of karmic rebirth is that without any proof that karma and rebirth are true the claim that most human suffering is due to past life sins is equivalent to unfairly blaming the victim for his suffering. The supporters of karma and rebirth try to counter this by saying that not accepting past life guilt merely leads to an illusion of innocence.

This karmic justification may have been acceptable prior to the development of modern biological science, but this is no longer true. All too often one hears things like that child was born with a genetic or birth defect because of some past life sin. Unless it is proposed that a **soul** seeking rebirth has control over the genetic material in a fertilized egg and chooses to sabotage its coming life by purposely deforming that material it is difficult to see a relationship between karma and genetic defects. An alternative argument has been that the bad karma of the soul attracts it to embryos or fetuses that are already genetically deformed. In this case, however, that bad karma had nothing to do with the conception of the child so the child remains innocent.

Unfortunately, there can be little doubt that for many centuries in South and East Asia the karmic concept of blaming the victim has, in fact, allowed for the status quo, in which the rich and powerful remain rich and powerful while the poor and powerless remain poor and powerless. One of the results of this is that South and East Asian societies historically have found very little reason to ameliorate physical or social suffering. Nothing demonstrates this better than the social injustice of the Hindu **caste system**.

Despite the unfairness of blaming the victim a paradoxical defense of that unfairness has been offered. It argues that if such blame allows the victim to be more peacefully resigned to a situation that he or she has no real power to change the blame is to the victim's advantage. For example, when a child is born with a terrible deformity someone might account for that deformity by saying that the child in a past life did something evil which is in the present life manifesting itself as the deformity. In this way the child is lead to believe that the world is always a just place because karmic influences only bring misfortune on the guilty as punishment. In many situations if we have to suffer, we generally prefer that it is for a meaningful reason, rather than a matter of meaningless chance, even if that reason is false and means blaming ourselves for it. This makes the belief in karma a convenient fiction and/or a **noble lie**.

One major danger of blaming the victim is its potential racism. The fact that most affluent countries are Western European in origin and Caucasian in race, while most poor countries are populated by darker skinned Africans, South Asians, and Latin Americans, could suggest to some that light colored skin (Aryan) is karmicaly better than dark colored skin.

The concept of karma seems to have even more blaming the victim potential when it is applied to collectives, as it often is. Did the millions of Africans that where kidnapped and sold into slavery in the Americas deserve that condition? What collective wrong did they do? The very suggestion that they did anything, without real supporting proof, is karmicaly supported racism. Again, did six million Jews deserve the death camps; could karma be used to justify anti–Semitism? Did the American Indian deserve ethnic cleansing and genocide?

It is most interesting is that among many presumably educated Buddhists, as long as misfortune is meted out collectively to non–Buddhists, karma is freely acknowledged, but when it comes to Buddhists collectively there is a reluctance to apply karma. If Buddhism teaches that by becoming a Buddhist you gain certain karmic advantages, which even Buddhist ordination ceremonies specify, then why should such things as the Cambodian killing fields have happened? What collective wrong did those people do? Also, ignoring the questionable **dehiscent or seed-pod principle,** what did the Tibetan people do to suffer such brutal oppression at the hands of the Chinese?

The blaming the victim issue has been sufficiently condemned by orthodox Western religions that it has challenged Western reincarnationists to find something more than a punitive meaning in karmic rebirth. This has lead to the idea that some souls during the **interim period** voluntarily accept new embodiments in which adversity or some handicap will predominate. This is done not in order to atone for any past wrong doings, but as an act of service and/or as a way to accelerate spiritual growth. This very altruistic explanation then helps to counter the disrepute otherwise associated with the adversity implied in various types of handicaps. This is a very Western approach, which is clearly influenced by the Judeo-Christian concept of the suffering savior, but it also has a quality of the Eastern ***bodhisattva*** ideal to it.

In defense of the doctrine of karma by some in the East it has been pointed out that until the rise of more scientific thinking in the 18th century Western Christianity had its own version of keeping the status quo through blaming the victim. Those defenders argue that for centuries it was taught in the West that misfortune came upon people as the just punishment by God for individual and collective sin, especially original sin. In other words, these biblically based concepts were no less a blaming of the victim than is the concept of karma. The karma defenders go on to say that it was a biblical teaching that the secular ruler (king or emperor) was given his authority to rule, or misrule, by the will of God. This too supported the status quo. In some ways, the major offender along these lines was conservative Protestantism. The Protestant belief in predestination, for example, encouraged pride among the rich, powerful, and healthy, while encouraging shame among the poor, powerless, and sick.

Whether the Eastern karma concept is better than the Western God concept or vice versa, the bottom line is that it has only been the more modern one-life only view of Western secularism that has been at the forefront of progressive social action and human rights.

Finally, it must be remembered that "blaming the victim" is not a criticism of rebirth, but of karmic rebirth. Rebirth by itself is independent of any particular **theodicy.**

See also **Caste system; Christianity and reincarnation; Congenital retardation; Dehiscent or Seed-pod Principle; Individuality and rebirth; Karma and justice; Karma as natural law; Karmic diseases; Karma in the ancient and modern west; Limitation lifetime; Mental retardation;** ***Moksha*****; Natal defects; Nightmare of eastern philosophy; Nirvana and** ***Parinirvana*****; Original sin, Christianity, and reincarnation; Original sin versus karma; Rebirth and cyclical time.**

Blavatsky, Helena Petrovna (1831–1891). This Russian born self-proclaimed esotericist is most famous as having been one of the main founders of the Theosophical Society in 1875. Blavatsky was at first opposed to the whole idea of reincarnation; in fact, there is no mention of it in her first book, *Isis Unveiled* (1877). By the time she published her second book, *The Secret Doctrine* (1888), she had become a firm believer in multiple lives. Embarrassed by her earlier rejection of such lives, all later editions of *Isis* had an appendix claiming that there was no discrepancy between her earlier and later views. With this change of mind it can be said that it was she, more than any other single individual, who encouraged late 19th century Europe and America to take an interest in Eastern (Hindu and Buddhist) esotericism in general, and rebirth and karma in particular.

Blavatsky's most controversial claim was that there was a secret brotherhood of mystical Himalayan adapts, or *Mahatmas* (S: Great Souls), who had decided that it was time to teach humanity the highest level of spiritual truth and that they had chosen her as their agent for this purpose. The *Mahatmas'* teachings were said to have been passed on to Blavatsky through both mysteriously delivered physical letters and through psychic, or mental, transmissions. Eventually, one or more of her early supporters stated that at least some, if not all, of the letters were actually written by Blavatsky herself.

Blavatsky's conversion to a belief in reincarnation had a major impact on her earlier belief in **Spiritualism**. Not only did she accuse spiritualist mediums as being, for the most part, frauds, but she claimed that they were miserable instruments of undeveloped souls of the lower world (**Hades**) whose practice caused some souls to be enticed back (reborn) into the material world when they would otherwise have been free of it. In appraising this condemnation it must not be overlooked that Blavatsky was herself claiming to be a medium (channeler) of what she considered exclusively higher "embodied" *Mahatmas*. It has, therefore, been proposed that her real objection to Spiritualism was its unwelcome competition.

There has been much debate on the possible sources for Blavatsky's teachings. Among the theorized sources has been Ismaili (Muslim) gnosis; the occult organization called the Hermetic Brotherhood of Luxor; the **Kabbalah**; and without question, Buddhism and **Hinduism**.

Blavatsky, whose contemporaries regarded her as either a genuine charismatic teacher or as an exposed-convicted fraud, was a prolific author, and besides her many books on reincarnation and related subjects she published her own journal, *Lucifer*.

Rather paradoxically, the spiritualist **Carl August Wickland** later claimed that Blavatsky's spirit recanted her belief in reincarnation through the mediumship of Wickland's wife.

See also **Arcane School; Ascended masters; Astral body; Astral plane; Channeling; Church Universal and Triumphant; Diakka; Esotericism versus Occultism; Etheric body; Higgins, Godfrey; Kingsford, Anna Bonus; Leek, Sybil; Lords of Karma; Lost continents and reincarnation; Mental plane; New Testament and reincarnation; Race and rebirth; Rosicrucians; Sinnett, Alfred Percy; Soul and spirit levels, Theosophical; Steiner, Rudolf; Theosophy; Vampires; Vegetarianism**.

Bleed-over. This is believed to be a non-karmic situation that happens in one life which strongly affects a future life. For example, if in a past life one died due to drowning this may bleed-over to an otherwise seemingly irrational fear of anything related to deeper bodies of water.

See also **Philias** and **phobias**.

Bleed-through of lives. It is believed that a not uncommon situation is that current the life memories bleed into the past life recall, which can make such recall less reliable or even seem inauthentic.

Blocked regression. This is said to describe the situation where the age-regressed person can not go back in time any farther than the beginning of the present life. There are several different explanations given for this. (1) The age-regressed person is truly blocked from experiencing his or her past life because of a major traumatic experience in that life, which most commonly is related to the way the person died. (2) The personal beliefs of the regressed person are consciously or subconsciously resistant to accept the idea of a past life. (3) The inability to experience a past life is because the person's **soul** has not been previously embodied. This could mean that it is a soul from a large pool of souls that have been waiting for their first chance at earthy embodiment or that it is a newly created soul that has just entered the reincarnation process. (4) The inability to experience a past life is because no one has ever been previously embodied and the sub-conscience of this particular person is not willing to create a past life fantasy to satisfy the hypnotist.

See also **Affect bridge; Birth trauma; Cummins, Geraldine; Deaths, violent and premature; Fantasy versus past life regression; Fixed number or variable number of souls; Memory, suppressed; Population increase issue**.

Blood and the soul *see* **Genesis; New Testament sacrificial concept; Old Testament and the soul; Soul; Steiner, Rudolf**.

Blue Sisters *see* **Great White Brotherhood**.

Bodhisattva. A spiritual being who either is on his or her way to becoming a Buddha, or who has one foot in **nirvana and *parinirvana*** and the other foot still in *samsara* (the world of birth and death). It is due to the latter case that the *bodhisattva* is able to assist others in attaining liberation. In fact, as a savior figure, the self-sacrificing *bodhisattvas* of **Mahayana Buddhism** and **Vajrayana Buddhism**, by their very willingness to continue dealing with the impure world of suffering, and their freely sharing their enormous amounts of surplus merit, are believed to be able to negate much of the evil karma of a devotee and so insure a better rebirth for that devotee. In this saving regard the *bodhisattva* functions in some of the same ways that Christ does in Christianity.

In a number of **New Age religions** some of the teaching functions of the *bodhisattva* have been transferred to various groups of **ascended masters**.

See also **Amitabha Buddha; Bhaishajyaraja-guru; Chinese religion and reincarnation; Christianity and reincarnation; Dalai Lama; Heavens, Buddhist; Kshitigarbha; Lords of Karma; Merit, transfer of; Rebirth and maturity; Return and serve argument for reincarnation;** *Tulku*.

Body as a mere garment of the soul. In some reincarnationist circles it is said that the physical body is to the **soul** no more than clothing is to a body. Just as a person periodically changes worn-out clothes so the soul changes worn-out bodies. The problem with this simile is that first we do not change bodies on a daily basis like we do clothing; also, in the case of clothing we generally do not wear an outfit only once and discard it. Instead, we save it to wear again. The body would be far more like a garment of the soul if we could, with little effort, periodically change in radical ways our physical appearance, race, gender, nationality, etc. Moreover, a human being rarely holds the kind of identity-attachment to clothes that a soul would presumably holds to it body. This, in fact, is represented by the belief of some reincarnationists that the soul often remains near its deceased body because it so identifies with it.

Despite the logical weakness of this clothes equal body metaphor it retains strong appeal because Psalm 102 mentions the phrase, although not in any reincarnational way.

See also **Aquinas, Thomas;** *Bardo*; **Corinthians, 1st and 2nd; Psalms; Soul and spirit levels, Theosophical.**

Body-brain (mind) dependency. All current scientific understanding of the human organism suggests that both consciousness and the identity of an individual depend on memories, which in turn are dependent on the complex neurological structure that is the physical brain. In fact, probes placed at various locations on the brain can stimulate such feelings as fear, guilt, loneliness, and disgust. Even such a fundamentally desirable emotions as love is clearly dependent on the relationship between the drugs dopamine and serotonin in the brain. Also, it has been discovered that drugs such as **ketamine**, lysergic acid diethylaminde (LSD), mescaline, and methylenedioxyamphetamine (MDA) can stimulate what at least appears to be both **out-of-the-body experiences and near-death-experiences** and past life memories under certain conditions. MDA, in particular, stimulates the feeling of age regression so that long forgotten things are recaptured by the memory. The very fact that various psychoactive drugs such as mescaline, and even such a common drug as alcohol, can radically affect the human personality strongly suggests a body-brain dependency. Perhaps more surprising is that even an overdose of certain vitamins can interfere with the self-identity factor.

If these drug effects were not enough to demonstrate that the mind (human personality) is dependent upon the physical brain then certainly the fact that when the brain is damaged sufficiently memories and even the whole identity of a person can be lost proves such dependency. Moreover, this can happen irreversibly, within three minutes or less if the brain is deprived of oxygen.

In the case of damage to the rhinal cortex of both hemispheres of the brain there is such a severe loss of memory (amnesia) that all memories since the damage (retrograde amnesia) fail to be retained and the person may do such things as read the same newspaper over and over again. In short, the person exists only in the momentary present. Damage to the occipital lobes, instead, can result in prosopagnosia which means that a person can not recognize familiar faces, including his own, in a mirror.

Another example of the mind's dependency on the physical body is seen when we understand that the question "Who am I?" is co-dependent on a bodily question of "Where am I?" When proprioception, the mainly unconscious sense of where one's body parts are in space, is severely damaged there is a loss of body-ego (proprioceptive self); and as a result, the person feels disembodied.

If, while alive, the sense of identity is so dependent on the proper functioning of the brain this would give strong support for concluding that the death of the brain ought to mean death of any individuality that a **soul** might have. If someone argues for an independent-of-the-brain soul that also carries memory or identity, then the counter to this has been "why in that case would the brain need to store memories." Such a duplication of functions would seem to be existentially uneconomical. Also, science would suggest that even if there were such a thing as post-mortem existing entity it would be so totally different, if not alien, to normal physical existence that we could never really know about it until after death. This would certainly account for the failure to prove genuine contact between the living and the dead, despite the often intense emotional bond that the living and, presumably, the dead still have for one another. In fact, if there was some sort of disembodied survival the entity would have no sense of space (boundaries) to define itself as a separate self. It would probably be a phenomenon that would not qualify as a real person in the opinion of science.

On the other hand, if it is proposed that the real soul has nothing to do with individual memories or any individuality, such as in the Hindu *atman*, then a soul independent of the body could be valid. However, then one person's impersonal soul would be absolutely no different from someone else's impersonal soul. Again, this is the case with *atman*. There does not seem to be any popular objection to every soul being identical in Hindu culture, but the same can not be said of Western culture. We consider it a right to retain our individuality in death as much as in life. It is for this reason that some Western reincarnationists have suggested that the brain is more like a radio or television receiving station for the broadcastings of the soul. Just as those broadcastings continue on, even if the radio-television breaks down, so the soul continues on after the body-brain breaks down.

The body-brain (mind) dependency, while a major problem for reincarnationists, is actually less a problem for the Judeo-Christian-Islamic idea of bodily resurrection of the person, "provided" it is of the pre-resurrection sleeping in the grave kind (*psychopannychism*). The reason is that such a "hibernating" soul is not required to retain any personal identity before becoming body and brain resurrected, when presumably God will somehow also resurrect the individual's personal memories along with its new physical condition.

The materialist view that the brain alone can account for full consciousness will probably not be provable until a self-conscious machine can be created. However, even then there may be those that will argue that such consciousness, not being God-made, is soulless; therefore, it can not continue to existence after death.

See also **Age factor and rebirth; Alzheimer's Disease; Anatman; Body-soul dualism; Charvakas; Drugs; Ghost; Hypnotic age regression; Memories, reasons for loss of past life; Mind; Out-of-the-body experiences and near-death-experiences; Rebirth and science; Resurrection, bodily; Resurrection or reincarnation**.

Body is the hell of the soul. This was a dualist expression used by the Platonists to describe the body. In the *Cratylus* of Plato there is also the mention of an Orphic view of the body as the prison (*phroura*) and the tomb of the **soul**, or in short "*Soma* (the body) [is] *sema* (the tomb)." Derived from this Platonic view are the similar versions of **body-soul dualism** found in some forms of **Gnosticism**.

See also **Orphism;** *Phaedo*.

Body-soul dualism. This is the concept that in every way the physical body is ontologically (in its very being or essence) the opposite of the **soul**. Such **dualism** means that the body and soul have nothing in common, have no positive way of relating to one another or, in extreme cases, not even a negative way of relating to one another. Also, this dualism usually implies that human suffering is a result of the soul being trapped or held prisoner in the body. As a result, the only hope a person has of being free of suffering is for the soul to become liberate from the body. Body-soul dualism can be divided into two forms, the amoral and the moral. In the first, the body is not viewed as evil, but only as an insentient prison. In the second, the body is a major source of evil, usually due to it having been created by some evil force. Most forms of **Gnosticism** were based on body-soul dualism, and more often than not, of the moral variety. This is because they viewed the material world as the creation, not of the supreme God (Spirit), but of a lower, either less wise or deliberately evil being or demigod called the ***demiurge***. This view, therefore, has lead to body-soul dualism also being called matter-spirit dualism.

Modern versions of body-soul dualism are found in **Jainism, Samkhya Yoga**, and so some degree, **Theravada Buddhism**. All three of these may be considered forms of amoral body-soul dualism since they do not accept a creator God of any kind, good or evil.

Christianity has sometimes been accused of being a form of body-soul dualism because of its often puritanical or anti-body, especially anti-sexual, attitude. No matter how puritanical it may be, however, Christianity can "not" be considered a form of body-soul dualism because it acknowledges only a creator that is supremely good, and it teaches that the souls of the dead will eventually be re-embodied in some form at the time of the resurrection.

See also **Body is the hell of the soul; Body-brain (mind) dependency; Bogomils; Cathars; Paulicians;** *Phaedo*; **Plato; Resurrection, bodily; Resurrection or reincarnation**.

Bogomils. This was originally a ninth century anti–Christian, pro-ascetic gnostic group found in Bulgaria, Serbia, Bosnia, and later Italy, which taught a **body-soul dualism** and held to a belief in **metempsychosis**. The Bogomils seemed to have had their origin in a blending of native Thracian **Orphism**, the Christianity of **Paul of Tarsus**, and influence from the **Paulicians**. The Bogomils were brutally persecuted by both Eastern (Byzantine Orthodox) Church and the Western (Roman Catholic) Church. As a result, in the 16th century the remnants of the Bogomils allied themselves with the Ottoman Turkish conquerors of the Balkans and eventually converted to **Islam**. It was probably from the Bogomils that the French and Italian **Cathars** arose. Because of the Bogomils, Pope Urban V (1362–70) referred to Bosnia as "the cesspool of the world's heresy."

An interesting sideline to the Bogomils is that, according to *Slayers and their Vampires* by Bruce McClelland (2006), the earliest **vampire** legend is linked to this Bulgarian sect, not to the Romanians. The legend appears to have had its origin in part from the Orthodox Church's condemnation of the Bogomils for their rejection of any belief in the crucifixion of Christ and hence their lack of superstitious respect for the sign of the cross. The 19th century association of the vampire with the Romanian prince, Vlad III, the Impaler (Dracula), is entirely due to Bram Stoker.

See also ***Demiurge***; **Greeks and reincarnation**.

Bone, sacred *see* **Sacred bone**.

Bon-pa [po] religion. This is the non–Buddhist religion practiced in Tibet. It is descended from a synchronism of an ancient pre–Buddhist shamanism and Tantric Buddhism. With the introduction of Buddhism into Tibet in the eighth century CE the pre–Bon-pa shamanic tradition absorbed a great number of Buddhist traits, but Buddhism also absorbed a number of traits from Bon-pa. One trait borrowed from Buddhism was the belief in reincarnation. From the 13th century, with the assumption of secular power by the Buddhist hierarchy, up to more modern times, the Bon-pa followers were periodically persecuted by that hierarchy.

See also ***Bardo***; **Belgi Dorje**; **Swastika**.

Book of Life (Hebrew: *Sefer ha'Hayim*). According to Jewish (Kabbalic) mysticism this is a book in heaven which has recorded every human thought, word, and deed. Sometimes it is claimed that there actually are three such books: one for the righteous person (*tzaddik*), one for the completely evil person (*rasha*), and one for the person who is neither wholly righteous nor unrighteous (*benoni*). Another universal record book called the *Book of Memory* (*Safer ha Zicharon*), which may or may not be the same as the *Book of Life*, is mentioned in some Kabbalic works. An Islamic version of such a book is the *al-Kitab al-A'mal* (*Book of Human Actions*) as mentioned in the Quran at Sura 69:19–27 and possibly the *al-Kitabu l-Mubin* of Sura 6:59. Such books could be thought of as the equivalent of the *akashic* record and, therefore, the real source of past life memories.

See also ***Chintra-Gupta***; **Kabbalah**; **Lords of Karma**.

Book of Remembrance *see* **Akashic** Record.

Book of the Dead (Egyptian). This is a collection of ancient Egyptian tomb inscriptions that date from 2500 BCE to 200 CE. The actual Egyptian title is the *Reu nu per em hru* (*Chapters of the Coming Forth by Day*). Although there is no single extant papyrus that is all inclusive, there were originally about 190 independent chapters to the final compilation. The purpose of these inscriptions was to safely guide the **soul** to the underworld (*tuat, duat*) of the god Osiris, and to assist in convincing the judges of the dead that the soul was of pure heart and free of sin. In other words, the book's purpose was "*sakhu*," which meant "to enable a person to be become *akh* (ritually transfigured), and hence an *akhu* (ritually transfigured spirit)." If the spiritual heart (soul) of the deceased failed to prove worthy of eternal life, then that heart would be consumed by the terrifying underworld beast *Amemait* (the Devourer of hearts/Eater of the dead). This resulted in eternal extinction.

Despite concerted attempts to read the concept of reincarnation into this text, such a reading can only be done by taking certain passages in it out of context and distorting their meaning.

See also **Egypt**; **Hermetic philosophy**; **New Testament and reincarnation**; **Proof text**.

Book of the Dead (Tibetan) *see* ***Bardo***.

Boomerang karma *see* **Karmic boomerang effect**; **Karma in the Bible?**; **Karma, organic or organismic**; **Karma, symbolic**.

Borderline state. This is the mental state in which objective consciousness merges into subjective consciousness. This state may be self-induced or induced by **hypnosis**. It is thought by some that this state is also characteristic of the consciousness present in the initial transitional stage from physical embodiment to disembodiment of the **soul**. A return to this consciousness under hypnosis is believed to encourage past life recall.

See also **Out-of-the-body experiences** and **near-death-experiences (NDEs)**.

"Born again." This phase from **John** 3:3–4 and 1st Peter 1:23 have been repeatedly used to argue that a "secret or not so secret" reincarnation doctrine is to be found in the New Testament. However, this is only possible if the passages are read entirely independent of their greater context. The Christian "born again" experience follows the Christian experience of identifying with the dying of Christ and is an experience very much of this life time (**Romans** 6:3, **Galatians** 2:19–20).

See also **John, Gospel of; John the Baptist; New Testament and reincarnation; Palingenesis.**

Boulder Fellowship Foundation. This Colorado based group was initially inspired by the **Bridey Murphy case**. It produced the book *Many Wonderful Things* (Los Angeles, 1957) by Robert W. Huffman and Irene Specht.

Boullan, Joseph-Antoine (1824–1893). This defrocked French Catholic priest, and later magician (occultist), announced in 1875 that he was the reincarnation of **John the Baptist**. Boullan also believed that spiritual salvation could be attained through sexual intercourse with archangels and other celestial beings (*spectrophilia*). It was claimed that his eventual death was due to magical murder by some rival magicians.

See also **Stygian sexuality; Work of Mercy.**

Bowman, Carol (1950–). Bowman is an author of several books on the past lives of children through spontaneous recall and she maintains of a website dealing with such past lives. While Bowman adds to the work of Ian Stevenson she does not back this work up with the same kind of detailed documentation that Stevenson tries to supply.

Brahma and rebirth in Buddhism. Whereas in **Hinduism** Brahma is considered to be at the top of the heavenly hierarchy, in Buddhism this deity, of which there are said to be three forms, is considered to have only a mid-level heavenly status. The highest of these three Brahmas is of particular significance as far as the coming into existence of the universe is concerned. Buddhist cosmology says that ultimately, rather than there being a beginning and end to the universe, there is a beginningless and endless cycle of rebirths and re-deaths of universes. At the beginning of a newly arising universe, the very first being to arise is a *Maha-Brahma*. Following him the rest of the universe comes into being. This *Maha-Brahma*, failing to understand that the universe is actually self creating, mistakenly assumes that it is he that has caused of the rest of the universe to arise. This mistaken assumption has been passed on to lesser beings, including human beings and this is why people believe in a supreme creator as found in religions like Hinduism, Christianity, etc.

Unlike these theistic religions, Buddhism teaches that *Maha-Brahma*, like all other beings that have merely attained high rebirth because of good karma, especially the kind that results from the deepest form of meditation, will still have to be reborn into the samsaric world of ***duhkha*** (dissatisfaction) at the end of the current universe. In fact, as soon as all the beneficial karma of that Brahma and other high beings is used up they will again discover themselves reborn in a lesser state where once more they will have to strive for liberation and the complete ending of the rebirth cycle. In this sense then, it is better to understand Brahma, less as a being than as a temporary occupant of particular heavenly office in which different occupants take their place, serve their allotted time, and then leave office.

Devotionally-wise this has meant that while prayers for material blessings could be offered to the samsaric trapped occupants in the Brahma office, these occupants were incapable of supplying any spiritual blessings that would facilitate salvation from **samsara**. In order to attain such spiritual blessing the devotee had to turn to the Buddhas and **Bodhisattvas**.

See also **Heaven, Buddhist; Karma and free will; Karma and the moral structure of the universe.**

Brahmacharya see **Brahman;** *Ojas.*

Brahman. In **Hinduism** this refers to the Universal or World Soul (***anima mundi***), Over-soul, or God. In the ***Upanishads*** and in Advaita Vedanta Brahman is ultimately identical to the ***atman*** as *Paraatman* or *Parabrahma* (Beyond Brahma). The term Brahman is derived literally from the Sanskrit for "prayer." Brahman or *Brahmin* also refers to the Hindu priestly caste (one who prays). This is especially true when pluralized to Brahmans, or even Brahmins. This term as spelled *Brahmana(s)* also can mean a priest, but is more often used to refer to certain priestly literature composed shortly before the *Upanishads*. The term *Brahmanism*, therefore, refers to that stage in the development of Hinduism, in which both the *Brahmanas* and *Upanishads* were written.

Brahman the deity is said to be envisioned in either of two forms which are Brahman without qualities (*Nirguna* Brahman) and Brahman with qualities (*Saguna* Brahman). The first is the totally the impersonal deity, while the second is worshipped as one of the three major high gods (*Trimurti*) or more personal Lords (*Ishwara, Ishvara*) of Hinduism — Brahma, the Creator of the universe; Vishnu, the Sustainer of it; and Shiva, the Destroyer of it. Any one of the many sub-manifestations of these high gods, such as Krishna, is considered *Saguna* Brahman as well. The *Trimurti* is also considered a metaphor for the round of existence: birth (rebirth), life activities, and death (re-death).

When compounded with another word such as in Brahma-*charya*, the Brahma part is to be translated as "the highest" or as "the holy"; thus *brahmacharya* means the highest or holiest conduct, which is to say the ascetic or celibate life, so a *brahmachari* is an ascetic or monk. That this, in fact, is the highest way of conducting one's life is demonstrated by the belief that this is the only way to escape from rebirth according to **Jainism**, most forms of Buddhism, and at least a large minority in **Hinduism**.

See also **International Society for Krishna Consciousness; Karma versus grace; Monism; *Mula*; Old Brahmin moonshine; Pantheism and panentheism; Incarnation versus reincarnation; *Vaikuntha*.**

Bridey Murphy case. This is perhaps the most well known past life regression story. In 1952 an amateur hypnotist, Morey Bernstein, tried past life **hypnotic age regression** on a Mrs. Virginia Tighe (1923–1995), a twenty-three-year-old housewife (alias Mrs. Ruth Simmons). This resulted in the manifestation of an Irish woman who claimed her name was Bridey Murphy, and that she had lived between the years 1798–1864.

The tape recordings of these hypnotic sessions were published by Bernstein as the book *The Search for Bridey Murphy* (1956); and were made into a popular movie by the same name (1956).

The *Chicago American* newspaper investigation of the case claimed to debunk the Bridey Murphy story as a case of **cryptomnesia** rather than an authentic case of reincarnation. Since the newspaper was later found to have had a partial ulterior motivation for such a debunking claim, the question of the authenticity of the Bridey Murphy story is still being debated. Danelek, in his *Mystery of Reincarnation* (2005), and Ducasse, in his *A Critical Examination of the Belief in a Life After Death* (1961), cover aspects of this debunking and offer some counters to it. On the other hand, in order to distance **hypnosis** from what was regarded as the bad publicity associated with past life regression, an attempt to analyze the material in Bernstein's book produced *A Scientific Report on "The Search for Bridey Murphy"* (1956).

The Bridey Murphy case led to a number of other attempts at pre-natal regression. One of the more well known was by Robert Huffman, who hypnotized a group of people in his Boulder, Colorado, home in 1954. A woman named Irene Specht proved to be the best subject. The story of the group's experiments and Irene's channeling were published three years later (1957) as *Many Wonderful Things*, by Robert W. Huffman and Irene Specht through the **Boulder Fellowship Foundation, Inc.**

See also **Multiple personalities**.

Bridges. In some cultures it is believed that the souls of the dead at some point in the afterlife must cross one or more bridges that separate the good from evil doers. In the simplest Chinese version there are only two such bridges. The one for the good is wide and easy to cross, while the one for the bad is very narrow and difficult to cross. In the more complex version there are six bridges — a gold one, a silver one, a jade one, a stone one, a smooth wooden one, and a rough wooden one. In this case, the bridge over which the souls pass will determine into what circumstances they will be reborn. Once across these bridges all souls will partake of the drink of forgetfulness and then be thrust into the stream of red which flows under the Bitter Bamboo Bridge on to rebirth.

Some Western reincarnationists also refer to "Rebirth" bridges. There is the Bridge of Sighs, which spans the gap between animals and humans, and the Rainbow Bridge, which spans the gap between humans and trans-human beings.

See also **Drink or fruit of forgetfulness; Hell, the Chinese**.

Brotherhood of the White Temple. This Sedalia, Colorado, based brotherhood was founded in Denver in 1930 by M. Doreal, who claimed to have been in contact with the Great White Lodge or the Elder Brothers of man. The Brotherhood, in its emphasis on the "Original Gnostic Teachings of Jesus," also goes under the name of the White Temple Church. The Brotherhood's core teachings are from the Kabbalic tradition and regard mankind as having in it a spark of the divine. The soul is said to reincarnate in order to change dark and disorderly characteristics into light and orderly ones. The Brotherhood's teachings also include a belief in the occult **lost continents** (Atlantis and Lemuria), **pyramidology**, and a very allegorical reading of the Bible. Doreal has written a number of books on the subject of the Brotherhood's teachings.

See also **Ascended masters**.

Bruno, Giordano (1548–1600). Bruno, originally an Italian Dominican priest, abandoned the order in 1576 after being accused of heresy. A **Renaissance** believer in the **hermetic philosophy**, Bruno advocated a renewed study of the magical aspects of this ancient philosophy. Also, Bruno not only supported openly the Copernican heliocentric cosmology but went further in proposing that there were other inhabited worlds beyond our own. This was in keeping with his belief in the unity of all life and all worlds through the concept of the world soul (*anima mundi*). Although he did not goes as far as equating this unity with God, which would have made him a pantheist; nonetheless, he incurred the wrath of the Church. It did not help his case that in both his 1584 *Spaccio de la bestia trionfante* (*Expulsion of the Triumphant Beast*) and his 1592 testament before the Roman Inquisition, he acknowledged a belief in the **metempsychosis** of the world soul that while very different from the metempsychosis of individual souls was enough to convict him of a so-called Pythagorean heresy. Bruno spent the last seven or eight years of his life in an inquisitional prison, after which he was burned alive at the stake.

For a detailed understanding of Bruno's philosophy see *Giordano Bruno* edited by Hilary Gatti. Aldershot Hants, England: Ashgate, 2002.

Brunton, Paul (1898–1981). Brunton, the author of *Hermit in the Himalayas* (1927), was one of the first Westerners to write about specific techniques to access one's past lives as he claimed Easterner Yogis were able to do.

Buchan, Sir John (1875–1940). Buchan, a Scottish author and former Governor General of Canada, in his autobiography, *Pilgrim's Way* (1940) refers to what he believed to be his previous life.

Buddha. The word Buddha comes from the Sanskrit *buddhi*, which means "Awakened One." The title generally refers to the north Indian ascetic Siddhartha Gautama (6th to 5th centuries BCE) after his enlightenment. Gautama's teachings arose partially out of dissatisfaction with both anachronisms in the **Vedic religion** and with the arrogant pretensions of its priests, the Brahmans, who claimed a monopoly on spiritual truth.

Since the teachings attributed to Gautama were not written down until over two centuries after his death there has been considerable debate as to how much of what was written down can be unquestionably traced back to him. However, the main characteristic of the written record, which more than likely did originate with Gautama, is what is called the **Middle Way or Middle Path**. The unique aspect of this middle designation is the denial of a soul (self) or *atman* and the repercussions it had on the concepts of rebirth and karma.

As Gautama's teachings (Buddhism) became a popular religion a belief arose that there had been a whole series of other enlightened beings in the eons well before that of Gautama. Moreover, in time, to these past Buddhas were added still other mythological and even celestial (totally supernatural) Buddhas such as **Amitabha Buddha** and **Bhaishajyaraja-guru**.

See also *Abhijna*; *Anatman*; Heroic 'I'; Jainism; *Jataka Tales*; *Lucifer*; Rebirth in Buddhism; Shotoku Taishi; *Sutras*; *Tulku*; Women.

Buddha and rebirth see **Buddhism, folk**; *Gandharva*; Interim period; Karma with minimal rebirth; Rebirth in Buddhism.

Buddha's necklace. This is a name sometimes given to the string of 108 beads that make up a Buddhist meditation rosary. It is more commonly called a *mala* (garland). There are a number of interpretations for the number 108, but perhaps the most interesting is a Western esoteric one that states that this is the normal number of rebirths allotted to a human being for his or her spiritual evolution. If this number is exhausted prior to spiritual self-realization or enlightenment then devolution and an annihilating second death will follow.

See also **Finite or infinite number of rebirths**; *Jataka Tales*.

Buddhi (Enlightened or awakened mind) see **Buddha; Causal body; Soul and spirit levels, Theosophical.**

Buddhism. From the second to the sixth century CE the teachings of the **Buddha** (Buddhism) were introduced, along with the doctrine of rebirth, to China, Korea, Japan, and Southeast Asia. By the ninth century, Buddhism had spread to Tibet, and from the fourteenth through to the sixteenth century to Mongolia, Manchuria and parts of Siberia. Since the late nineteenth century it has been spreading into Europe and the Americas. Finally, in the late twentieth century it began to spread into parts of Africa.

Buddhism is divided into the three main schools of **Theravada Buddhism**, **Mahayana Buddhism**, and **Vajrayana Buddhism**. The first of these is the oldest and most conservative, especially when it comes to the working of karma. The second and the third are more flexible in their views of karma because of the ***Bodhisattva*** teachings.

The issue of rebirth and karma in Buddhism is very complex and also can be quite controversial as the number of related entries listed below might imply.

See also *Abhijna*; Age factor and rebirth; *Ahimsa*; Ajivikas; *Alayavijnana*; Amitabha Buddha; *Amrita*; *Anatman*; Animals and rebirth, non–Western view; Annihilationism, Buddhist view; Arguments that challenge rebirth on a logical basis; Ashoka, King; *Asuras*; Atheism; Aum Shinrikyo; Avalokiteshvara; *Avichi*; *Bardo*; Belgi Dorje; Besant, Annie; Bhaishajyaraja-guru; *Bhava*; *Bhavachakra*; *Bhavanga*; Blaming the victim vs. illusion of innocence; Blavatsky, Helena Petrovna; Body-soul dualism; Bon-pa [po] religion; Brahman; Brahma and rebirth in Buddhism; Buddha's necklace; Buddhism, esoteric; Buddhism, folk;

Buddhist stages of liberation; Cao Dai; *Chakras*; Chen-Dao; Chinese religion and reincarnation; *Chitta*; Christianity and reincarnation; Church Universal and Triumphant; Dalai Lama; Determinism; *Devachan*; *Deva-loka*; Dualism; Emma-o; Empire of Jade; Esotericism versus Occultism; Eternalism; Finite or infinite number of rebirths; *Gandharva*; Gender issue of the soul; Heavens, Buddhist; Heaven, Hell, and Buddhist No-Self; Hell; Hell, the Chinese; Heroic 'I'; *Hotoke*; Hungry ghosts; *Ichantika*; Incarnation versus reincarnation; Individuality and rebirth; Indonesia; Interim period; *Jataka Tales*; Jainism; *Jigoku*; *Jiva*; *Kama-dhatu*; *Kama-rupa*; Karma; Karma and God; Karma and justice; Karma and rebirth; Karma and the moral structure of the universe; Karma, classifications of; Karma versus grace; Karma with minimal rebirth; Karmic diseases; Karmic seeds; Kshitigarbha; Leadbeater, Charles Webster; Lenz, Frederick; Limbo; Lords of Karma; Mahayana Buddhist rebirth texts; Malaysia; *Mana*; *Manas*; Manichaeism; *Mara*; Metempsychosis; Middle Way or Middle Path; Milinda Panha; Mind; *Moksha, Mukta or Mukti*; Monism; *Mula*; *Naraka or Niraya*; Nine doors; Nirvana and *Parinirvana*; *Ouroboros*; Panchen Lama; Personalists; *Petavatthu*; Pilgrimage; Plants; Population increase issue; *Pratitya-samutpada*; Prayers for the dead; Predestination; *Pretas*; Privilege of a human birth; Psychophysical aggregates; *Purvanivasanusmrti*; Pure-Land or Blissful Land Buddhism; Questions of King Milinda; Rebirth or rebecoming; Rebirth and cyclical time; Rebirth and logical symmetry; Rebirth and maturity; Rebirth and religious tolerance; Rebirth and suicide; Rebirth, East and West; Rebirth factor; Rebirth in Buddhism; Rebirth, instantaneous; Rebirth in Zen Buddhism; Rebirth, non-backsliding; Rebirth, proof of (Western Buddhist); Rebirth, qualifications for; Reincarnation, origins of; Return and serve argument for reincarnation; Russia, reincarnation in; *Samsara*; Schopenhauer, Arthur; Shinto; Shotoku Taishi; *Shunya*; Sinnett, Alfred Percy; *Skandha*; Rebirth factor; Soul mates; Souls, origin of the; *Sutras*; Swastika; Tantrism; Daoism; Theodicy; Theosophy; Three refuges and five Buddhist lay precepts; *Tulku*; Vedic Religion; Vegetarianism; Vijnanavada (Consciousness only) School; *Vimanavatthu*; Women; Yama.

Buddhism and Rebirth *see* **Rebirth in Buddhism.**

Buddhism, esoteric. One must be very careful with this term since it can have two very different meanings. In modern scholarly works on Buddhism it refers to Tantric or **Vajrayana** Buddhism. In the late 19th and early 20th century it more often referred to the Hindu-Buddhist synthesis of **Theosophy**, as evidenced by the book *Esoteric Buddhism* (1973) by the theosophist **A.P. Sinnett**.

See also **Tantrism**.

Buddhism, folk. This is the form of Buddhism that is believed in and practiced by almost the entire Buddhist world. Folk Buddhism ignores most of the specific philosophical technicalities of orthodox Buddhism. For example, whereas orthodox Buddhism subscribes to the *anatman* (no soul) doctrine, it would be very difficult to distinguish the Folk Buddhist view of rebirth from the soul-belief (*atman*) of Hinduism or Jainism.

One important aspect of folk Buddhism to note is that, as in Hinduism and Jainism, karma is not regarded as the sole factor in anyone's personal destiny; quite separate from it there is also the influence of the benevolent and malevolent spirits, the influence of the stars (astrology), and even the possibility of witchcraft by hostile neighbors.

See also **Astrology and rebirth**; *Avichi*; Gender issue of the soul; Rebirth in Buddhism; Rebirth in the West; Rebirth in Zen Buddhism.

Buddhist stages of liberation. In the early Buddhist canon there are described four stages on the way to liberation from rebirth. In each stage one must eliminate, or at least weaken, a certain number of the ten fetters that keep a being trapped in *samsara*.

The person who has attained one or more of these four stages is called in **Sanskrit** an *arya-pudgala* or in Pali an *ariya-puggala* (noble person). The first stage of liberation is that of a stream enterer (*shrotapanna/sotapanna*) and designates any man or woman, whether lay person or cleric, who has destroyed the first three fetters (S/P: *Samyojana*) a belief in a real self (*satkaya-dristi/sakkaya-dithi*); doubt (*vichikitsa/vicikicha*) about the Buddhist teaching (*dharma/dhamma*); and any attachment to rites and rituals (*shilavrata-paramarsha*). Each of these fetters is actually a belief, practice, or mainstay of Brahmanic or **Vedic religion**, a major competitor of Early Buddhism. In the case of the first fetter the belief in a real self was the belief in *atman* and **Brahman**. In the second case, one was expected to have at least an initial respect for, if not absolute confidence in, the **Buddha** and his teachings as being in no way inferior to those of the Brahmanic priests. As for the third fetter, attachment to rites and rituals, this meant abandoning any trust in the blood sacrificial rites and rituals of the Brahmanic priests.

Early Buddhism taught that anyone who attained to this stream enterer stage was not only guaranteed never again to be reborn into a less than human rebirth, but, also was guaranteed that full liberation would be attained within a maximum of seven lifetimes. The irreversible power traditionally assigned to this first stage can be appreciated by the fact that one of the individuals who is said to have attained it is also said to have later died an alcoholic. [*Tipitaka. Suttapitaka. Sanyuttanikaya* (SN). V, 323-324].

The second stage of liberation is called that of the once returnee (*sakrdagamin/sakadagami*), and refers to one who has greatly weakened the next two fetters of sensuality (*kama* or *raga*) and hatred (*dvesa/dosa*) or ill-will (*vyapada*). This is mainly a stage for a monk or a nun, and it is believed, that from this practitioner will be reborn into this suffering world only one more time before attaining liberation.

The third staged is that of a never returnee (*anagamin*), which is the practitioner who has completely destroyed the above first five fetters, and so will attain liberation in a formless or heavenly world, rather than in this human world.

The last stage is that of a fully liberated saint (**Arhat**), which is the practitioner who has also destroyed the last five fetters, which are those of craving for material existence (*rupa-dhatu*); craving for immaterial (higher spiritual) existence (*arupa-dhatu*); pride or conceit of I (*asmi-mana*); restlessness (*uddhatya/uddhacha*); and ignorance (*avidya/avijja*). As a result he or she will never again experience the world of rebirth (*punarbhava/punabhava*) and re-death (S: *punarmrtyu*), but will attain **nirvana** (liberation) in this very life.

See also **Bhavachakra; *Mana*; *Mulas*; Rebirth in Buddhism; Return and serve argument for reincarnation.**

Butterfly. A number of cultures have associated the butterfly with the souls of the dead. The Greek word *psyche* means both **soul** and butterfly. In China, Japan, and Java the butterfly sometimes may carry the soul of a deceased or even of a sleeping person. The latter instant is the reason one should never kill a butterfly since it would mean that the body would lose its soul and die. The butterfly may also be considered the soul of an old friend visiting someone or trying to deliver a message to the living. Among the **Aztecs** the butterfly as the symbol of the soul was called *Itzpapalotl* (Obsidian Butterfly).

The butterfly in Christianity usually symbolizes resurrection instead of rebirth, especially when depicted iconographically on the finger of Jesus as a baby.

Cabales or **Caballi.** This is the name given to the astral bodies of those who have died by violence (external or self-inflicted). They are said by some to wander the earth until their originally destined time of life has been reached.

See also **Astral body.**

Cabbalah (Cabala) *see* **Kabbalah.**

Cancer (the Crab). This is the fourth sign of the zodiac and it is associated with one of the two **celestial gates.**

Candia Debate. This was an important debate between Jewish scholars on the Kabbalic doctrine of **metempsychosis** and **transmigration** held in the city of Candia on the island of Crete in 1460. This city was probably chosen because it was on the route from Europe to the Holy Land.

See also **Kabbalah.**

Cannibalistic reincarnation. Among some tribal people it is believed that eating certain body parts of a deceased person will allow the **soul** of the deceased to reincarnate through the eater. For example, among the South American Ache (Guayaki) people, if a woman eats the penis of the deceased person the *ove* (soul) of that person will reincarnate as the woman's child. The whole intent of this ritualized cannibalism is to ensure that the woman gives birth to a boy, but sometimes a girl is born instead. This example might be considered a specific form of mortuary or burial cannibalism which is an attempt to preserve the valuable spiritual essence of people from being lost. In most cases, burial cannibalism involves eating only the deceased within one's own family or tribe (endo-cannibalism), rather than from outside of one's own group (exo-cannibalism). In ancient times, and even more recently, cannibalistic reincarnation was probably more common than present day documentation suggests.

See also **American Indians; Beans; Christian missionary influence and reincarnation; Rebirth, consanguineous.**

Cannon, Alexander (1896-1963). This English psychiatrist, and later occultist, regressed hypnotically some 1400 volunteers according to his works *The Power of Karma in Relation to Destiny*, Rider, London (1936) and *The Power Within*, E.P. Dutton, New York (1953), he collected 500 cases of spontaneous past life recalls.

See also **Garden of Waiting.**

Cao Dai. This religion was established in Vietnam in1926. It worships *Tien-ong*, His Excellency the Grandfather Immortal, also called the Third Amnesty of God. Cao Dai is a syncretism of Buddhism, Christianity, Confucianism, **Daoism**, and the **Spiritism** of Allan Kardec; as such it includes a belief in rebirth and karma.

Capricorn (the Goat horn). This is the tenth sign of the zodiac and is associated with one of the two **celestial gates**.

See also **Astrology and rebirth**.

Carpocrates. This gnostic Christian sect of the 2nd–3rd century CE taught that the **soul**, which was an incorruptible element of life, was trapped in a bodily form created by an evil *demiurge*. Since this *demiurge* had also created all the moral laws in order to keep souls captive, the only way to gain liberation was to defy these laws by experiencing everything that a body could experience. After this the soul would be released from the misery of further rebirths and be able to return to the true God. To accelerate the process the individual was expected to live as hedonistically as possible. According to the critics of the Carpocrates this included orgiastic activities and spousal swapping. This hedonic aspect distinguished the Carpocrates from most other dualist sects, which were usually more puritanical and ascetic. The fact that the Carpocrates related their belief in reincarnation to their antinomian hedonism only further served to discredit that belief among the far more conservative orthodox Christians.

Also, according to the Christian father **Tertullian** it seems that the Carpocrates were among the first to use the biblical passages **Matthew** 11:13–14; 17:12–13; **Mark** 9:13; and **Luke** 1:17 in which **John the Baptist** is said to have the spirit of **Elijah** as proof that the New Testament acknowledged reincarnation.

See also **Antinomianism; Dualism; Gnosticism; Irenaeus, New Testament; New Testament and reincarnation**.

Cartomancy (divination by cards) *see* **Phoenix Cards; Tarot**.

Caste system. This is the Indian system of rigid social ranking of people according to their birth.

Most Westerners have never seen the subhuman conditions in which some lower castes, and worse, the untouchables, are forced to live. Not only do the often very well off highest castes feel no responsibility to improve the lives of those beneath them, but look down contemptuously on the lower castes, and oppress them. They justify this by the claim that lower caste birth is a result of sinful karma, and so they deserve what they get. In other words, reincarnation not only justifies the economic and political status quo, it encourages a process of karmicaly **blaming the victim**.

See also **Ambedkar, Bhim Rao; Karma; Karma and faith; Karma and justice; Noble lie; Rebirth and cyclical time; Return and serve argument for reincarnation; Roy, Raja Ram Mohan; Weber, Max; Women**.

Cathars or **Cathari** (Greek: Pure). This was the name applied to a 12th and 13th century anti–Catholic, pro-ascetic, gnostic Christian group in Northern Italy, Southern France, and parts of Germany that almost certainly was an offshoot of the **Bogomils**.

The Cathars actually called themselves *Ecclesia Dei* (Church of God), and while acknowledging **Jesus** Christ as a divinely sent angel, they rejected the Old Testament as being the record of an inferior, even evil, deity or *demiurge*. They also rejected the Catholic sacraments of baptism, marriage, and Holy Communion. The main reason for these rejections was that the Cathars believed strongly in a **body-soul dualism**, which regarded marriage and sexual reproduction as a further trapping of souls into bodies.

Cathar society was divided into the ordinary believer and the celibate clergy or "Pure Ones"; hence the name given to them by outsiders. It was held that those members who sincerely took and kept their ascetic vow, the *consolamentum*, could gain liberation from the misery of **metempsychosis**. This vow was of such importance to the Cathars that it was thought better to choose deliberate **suicide** (*endure*) than to break it. This act of taking one's own life might be done by starving oneself to death or opening a vein and bleeding to death while lying in a hot bath. The Cathars did not regard such suicide as cowardly, because they believed that by choosing their own time of death they were snatching this choice away from Satan, the evil material creator.

The threat of the Cathars to the Church of Rome can be measured by the fact that the first known mention of the Cathars is in 1140, yet by 1179, during the third Lateran Council, the Church was already condemning the Cathars as heretics and in 1209 Pope Innocent III called for a crusade against them. This crusade came to be called the Albigensian crusade because the main Cathar center was in and around the city of Albi in Languedoc, southern France.

The anti–Cathar crusade was just the start of the attempt to exterminate these people and it was in order to finish their extermination that the Catholic **Inquisition** was originally established. This was initiated by Pope Lucius III in 1184 when he ordered bishops to make inquisition for heresy in their diocese and hand over to the secular authorities for punishment those who did not recant. This order was strengthen in1232 by Pope Gregory IX who appointed full-time inquisitors, at first mainly from the Dominican (the *domini canes*: hounds of the Lord), but then from the Franciscan orders.

Finally, in 1252, Pope Innocent IV authorized

the use of torture against the most recalcitrant of the heretics.

The last Cathar to be burnt in Languedoc was as late as 1330, some 100 years after the start of the persecution.

See also **Church Council of 553; Fortune, Dion; Guirdham, Arthur; Kabbalah; Rebirth and suicide; Rebirth, group; Resurrection, bodily; Soul groups.**

Cats. Besides the general reputation of cats as creatures with easy access to the occult world, one kabbalic legend says that the **soul** of a person who misuses the Divine Name is reborn into the body of a cat.

Causal body. In Theosophy, along with the **astral body, etheric body,** and **mental body** surrounding the soul sheath-like is the causal body. The main purpose of this body is to store or carry the past life karma of an individual. Also, in some Theosophical systems the causal body is what the **ego** (individuality) takes on once it no longer inhabits the mental body. Still others associate this body with the spiritual soul or *buddhi.* This is not to say that *buddhi* alone is the causal body, but it becomes that in alliance with the *manas* (mind). The causal body is, therefore, considered to be what is most commonly called the reincarnating soul. The causal body is also sometimes identified with the *akashic* record. In Sanskrit this causal body is called the *karana sharira* or **linga sharia.**

See also *Kosha;* **Mental plane; Soul and spirit levels, Theosophical.**

Cave. In many ancient cultures a cave represented either the entrance to the underworld, the underworld itself, or the tomb. Among some gnostic groups the cave also represented the womb into which the **soul** was reborn. While it is mere coincidence that tomb and womb rhyme in English, even without such rhyme, the ancient Greeks used the cave metaphor in a **tomb to womb** manner to describe reincarnation.

See also **Gnosticism; Orphism.**

Cayce, Edgar (1877–1945). Born on a farm near Hopkinsville, Kentucky, as a youth Cayce was known to believe that he could speak to angels and receive visions of his deceased grandfather. At about 20 years old he is said to have experienced a gradual paralysis of his vocal center which no doctor could explain, much less cure. This led Cayce to enter a self-induced trance in which he discovered a cure. In 1901 Cayce began to give thousands of what were thought to be clairvoyant medical diagnoses while in a similar self-induced trance state and as a result he became a specialist in what is called **trance therapy.** Then, starting in 1923, these diagnoses were expanded to include *akashic* record past life readings, of which there were some 2,500 by his death. Through some of these readings he came to believe that he himself had lived many lives before. Among these was a celestial life prior to **Adam** and Eve, a life on the **lost continent** of Atlantis, a priest in **Egypt** of the 11th millennium BCE, a Trojan soldier, a life as a disciple of Jesus, etc. According to Cayce it was not the apostle Luke (Lucus) who wrote the **Acts of the Apostles;** it was he (Cayce) as Lucius, the Bishop of Laodicea who wrote it.

Cayce, along with some new age groups, went so far as to propose that **Jesus** himself had several reincarnations prior to being the figure mentioned in the New Testament. The first of these was as the pre-embodied first expression of Divine Mind (the Logos) named Amilius. This being lived on the lost continent of Atlantis and was responsible for creating the present human physical form as a replacement for the ape-like human form in which the earliest fallen intelligent souls had entangled themselves. The second reincarnation of the historical Jesus to be was as Adam. This belief probably comes from an extremely liberal reading of those New Testament letters of Paul that connect the birth of sin through the old Adam with the death of sin through the New Adam (Christ), as in 1st **Corinthians** 15:22, 45.

According to Cayce, the biblical Enoch, the Old Testament patriarch who journeyed to heaven to receive mysteries, was also a previous embodiment of Jesus. The fact that, according to **Genesis** 5:3–22, the lives of Adam and Enoch overlapped by half a century seems to have been overlooked by Cayce. Then there followed incarnations as Hermes (the Egyptian Thoth), who was said to be the architect of the Great Pyramid, as well as the sage who began the **Hermetic philosophy** tradition; **Melchizedek**, the mystical high priest and king of Salem (ancient Jerusalem); Joseph, son of Jacob (Israel); Joshua, the leader of Hebrews into the Promised Land; Asaph, who was the music director and seer who served under King David and King Solomon; Jeshua, who was the high priest who helped organize the return from exile and the rebuilding of the temple, according to the biblical books of Ezra and Nehemiah, and who Cayce believed to have compiled the books of the Old Testament; and the last of the pre–Jesus embodiments was Zend, the man who Cayce claimed to have compiled and translated the books of the Zoroastrians. This last name was presumably taken from the name of the holy scripture of **Zoroastrianism**, which is the Zend Avesta. Cayce further believed that there will be one more reincarnation of the Logos-Jesus who will usher the world into in the kingdom of heaven on Earth.

Although Cayce continued to regard himself as a full Christian, it was not only his acceptance of reincarnation, but especially concepts such as Jesus having had former lives that allowed Cayce's ideas to be thoroughly criticized by orthodox Christian groups. Lynn Elwell Sparrow, however, in her *Edgar Cayce and the Born Again Christian* attempts to defend Cayce's Christian orthodoxy. Certainly, some degree of Christian orthodoxy ought to acknowledged Cayce, if for no other reason than he accepted uncritically the Old Testament mythology of the Garden of Eden, Babel, and the Flood sufficiently to claim that the children of Adam and Noah have even reincarnated as more recent persons.

Critics of Cayce's teachings were certainly not confined to Christian groups. Non-Christian skeptics readily criticized the fact that Cayce's past life readings included far too many lives of high status to be statistically valid. This, of course, is in contrast to more recent past life readings which involved a far greater number of low status individuals in every society in every historical period. There has also been some questioning why Cayce's past life readings are so overwhelmingly Western. Very few of these readings include past lives in Sub-Sahara Africa, China, Russia, or Latin America.

In response to this criticism it has been pointed out that few of his clients had ancestral roots in these areas; and with the exceptions of Atlantis and ancient Egypt, the past life ethnicity of his clients tended to closely match that of their present life.

Cayce was further criticized as sometimes assigning the same past life to more than one living individual. It has also been noticed that Cayce's Essene material seems to have diverted little from the views of the 1911 *Aquarian Gospel of Jesus Christ* by Levi H. Dowling and the work by H. Spencer Lewis, *The Mystical Life of Jesus* (1926).

Cayce's conviction that human souls were reborn on the non-physical planes of all the other planets in between earthly rebirths was thought to considerably stretch his credibility, and some of his many future predictions, such as the 1998 destruction of California and New York, which clearly proved to be wrong, did not help matters.

Despite these questionable issues, Cayce's writings probably have done more to promote past life readings and later **past life therapy** among the general population than any other author's writings and he continues to have many faithful followers.

Cayce's work is promoted by the Association for Research and Enlightenment which was found in 1931 and is located in Virginia Beach, Virginia.

Recently there has been the claim that Cayce has been reborn as a certain **David Wilcock**.

See also *Akashic* Record; Astrology and rebirth; Egypt; Essenes; Fellowship of the Inner Light; Hermes; Mayans; Melchizedek; Rosicrucians; Social status in past lives; Swarm of bees theory.

Celestial gates. These are two mythical heavenly gates, one of which is in the constellation of Cancer, and the other in Capricorn. The earliest reference to these two gates comes from Homer's *Odyssey* (book 13) in which Cancer is considered the gate through which men are born, and Capricorn the gate through which the gods are born. By the time of the philosopher **Porphyry** (234–305 CE), in a revised view of the gates, it was through Cancer that the souls passed to rest in a peaceful state and through Capricorn that the souls returned to earth to be reborn. The first, and most obvious, significance to these signs is that their arrival in the evening sky mark the summer and winter solstices. Secondly, the concept of these as gates of death and birth came from the belief that the planet **Saturn**, the most distant of the visible planets in pre-telescopic astronomy, was the ruler over Capricorn; while the **moon**, the closest to the earth, ruled over Cancer. Thirdly, the Cancer-Capricorn axis was used to determine the antiscion of a planet in astrology. In other words, as far as the ancients were concerned, these two planets and their signs marked the boundaries of time; and this was the main reason for their religious importance, especially for the followers of **Mithraism,** and, later, Christianity. December 22nd (the winter solstice) was regarded as the birthday of the Sun God Mithra and, until the Gregorian calendar reform moved this to the 25th of December, it was also the original date chosen for the birth of Christ.

A more modern, modified version of the celestial gate concept is mentioned in Jocelyn's *Citizens of the Cosmos* (1981), where it is stated that it is only during the three months ruled by the Archangel of the moon, Gabriel, that is from the end of December to the beginning of Spring, that the souls can re-enter the sphere of the earth to eventually be reborn.

There are two problems with these traditional astrologically related associations with reincarnation. First, because of the advance of the signs eastward the winter and summer solstices no longer astronomically occur under Capricorn or Cancer, but under Sagittarius and Gemini. Second, it must be understood that both the Capricorn and Cancer constellations are only visible in the northern hemisphere, so it would be unknown as to what the souls in the southern hemisphere did at death and rebirth. Perhaps it is just assumed that they simply reversed the process, exiting December–February (southern summer) and returning in June–August (southern winter).

See also *Arcturus*; Astrology and rebirth; Gnosticism; Interim period; Planetary descent and ascent of the soul; Planets, other; Pluto, the Plane; Zodiac.

Celestine Prophecy (1992). This best-selling book was said to have been channeled through James Redfield. Although it avoids words like karma and reincarnation, it apparently accepts both beliefs. The book mentions **soul groups** which are beings who, in the afterlife, offer support to others in obtaining a rebirth vision or what those souls wish to accomplish in their next life.

Celibacy and Reincarnation *see* **Chinese religion and reincarnation; Esoteric Fraternity; *Fiat Lux*; Jainism; Manichaeism; *Ojas*; Orphism; Priscillian.**

Celts *see* **Druids.**

Chakras (wheels). In *kundalini* (Hindu) yoga there are believed to be seven main psychic centers in the human body, the constructive and systematic cultivation of which are believed to lead to a better reincarnation or even enlightenment. This is achieved by having a psychic or spiritually invigorating energy called *kundalini* (serpent energy) flow upwards through these *chakras*. While none of these centers or *chakras* corresponds literally to any physical organ, attempts have been made to symbolically associate the *chakras* with such organs. The most commonly accepted locations for these are as follows. The first, or the lowest, *chakra* is believed to be located near the coccyx or anus; the second is located at either the level of the genitals or, in some case, perhaps because of prudery, it is located at the spleen; the third is at the navel (stomach or solar plexus) level; the fourth is at the heart level; the fifth is at the throat (larynx) level; and the sixth is just above the brow, an area which is sometimes called the psychic or **third eye** and is associated with the pineal gland. It may be coincidental, but it was the pineal gland that the Western philosopher **Rene Descartes** (1596–1650) thought was the location of the **soul**.

The seventh, or highest, of these psychic centers is located at or just above the crown of the skull, and is technically not considered a *chakra*. This is because it is less a staging center on the journey to spiritual liberation or enlightenment than it is the point of liberation or enlightenment itself. Nonetheless, if a *chakra* is only thought of as a level of spiritual attainment then the seventh level could be considered a *chakra*. Despite the separation between the crown *chakra* and the pituitary gland, which is just in the back center of the brain, the two are sometimes thought to be associated with one another.

Esoteric (Tantric) Buddhism also acknowledges a set of four or five *chakras*. These are the same as the above, only with the two lowest generally ignored or deleted.

The relationship between the *chakras* and rebirth can be complex, but in general it is thought that upon death if the adept can release the soul or rebirth factor through the crown *chakra* then this will lead to the end of rebirth. In this sense there is a similarity to the **nine doors** in **Vajrayana Buddhism**.

See also **Angels and reincarnation; Astrology and rebirth; Kabbalah; Planetary descent and ascent of the soul; *Nirvikalpa Samadhi*; Ojas**.

Chalice of Oblivion (Latin: *Oblivionis Poculum*) *see* **Drink or fruit of forgetfulness; Lethe**.

Chan-ch'a sha-o yeh-pao ching, WG (*Book of Divining the Requital of Good and Evil Actions*). This is a Chinese Buddhist apocrypha that explains how, through spinning a set of wooden tops, based on the religious euphemism "turning the wheel of the Dharma," one can learn about one's previous life, and even whether the immediate future life is going to be fortunate or unfortunate.

See also **Mahayana Buddhist rebirth texts**.

Channeling. This is the process whereby deceased persons' spirits, celestial beings (**angels**, God, **ascended masters**), extraterrestrial beings, or even intelligent animals (porpoises, whales) are said to communicate to mankind important information by a telepathic process or through the temporarily "invitational" **possession** of a living person's body, mind, or voice.

Channelers can be grouped into two basic categories, conscious channelers and trance channelers. In consciousness channeling, the channeler will leave aside his or her judgmental mind to let the channeled entity communicate its message, but the channeler's normal voice and body language will at most undergo only slight modification. In trance channeling, the personality, voice, and body language of the channeler appears more or less to be temporarily displaced by the channeled entity.

Channeling is really as old as religion itself, especially of the trance kind under the name of shamanism; in classical times channeling was practiced under the title of theurgy (Greek, divine action). After being suppressed by the Christian churches for over a thousand years, channeling was revived in the last part of the 19th and early 20th century as the spiritualist movement. Most recently channeling, as an independent movement, arose in the 1960s and has tended to disassociate itself from all earlier aspects of the movement. Part of this disassociation is reflected by the fact that the most recent channeling has usually replaced the earlier spirits of the deceased or even angels, with those of interplanetary minds. As in the older theurgical sense, however, most of the latest channelers seek the help only of benevolent spiritual sources, which distinguishes them from occult or black magic practitioners. An example of the latter is the case of **Aleister Crowley** who is said to have channeled a more or less amoral Egyptian spirit name Aiwass, who in 1904 dictated the text *Liber Al vel Legis* (*The Book of the Law*) through Crowley.

If channeling is viewed as a continuation of the earlier 19th century Spiritualist movement then the large number of extraterrestrial communications in this late 20th century movement may be understood as just keeping up with the times in that it was not until the more recent century that people began to seriously accept the possibility intelligent extraterrestrial life.

According to Robin Western in 1988, at the time of the publication of his *Channelers: a New Age Directory*, there were at least 235 individuals or organizations doing channeling; however, by the 1990s channeling seemed to have lost some of its popularity.

Some of the prominent channeled entities that have supported the idea of reincarnation are **Ahtun Re; Equinox; Benjamin Franklin (2); Hilarion; Lazaris; Mafu; Michael (2); Phylos the Tibetan; Ra; Ramtha; Satya; Seth;** and **Torah**. One factor that has made the subject of channeling very confusing is that some of the above channelers have borrowed or stolen other channeler's entities and/or those entities periodically decide to change channelers.

It has been argued that since a great number of the entities being channeled at this time agree on the reality of rebirth and, for the most part, karma, this agreement should be added to any other validating evidence for rebirth. The first problem with this argument is that the authenticity of the channeled entities would need to be unquestionably established before their views on rebirth would be valid. The second problem is that there has been some channeling in which the beings deny the truth of rebirth and karma.

It can be no surprise that most orthodox religions regard channeling, at best, as examples of a multiple personality or fraud; and at worst some form of **sciomancy** or **possession**.

See also **Aetherius Society; Agasha Temple of Wisdom; Aquarian Gospel; Automatic writing; Babbitt, Elwood; Church Universal and Triumphant; Dissociative Disorder; Egypt; Esotericism versus Occultism; Grace-Loehr life readings; Maclaine, Shirley; Multiple personalities; Oahspe; Ouija Board; Phantasmata; Planets, other; Ryerson, Kevin; Sutphen, Richard (Dick); UFOism; Unarius Academy of Science; Urantia Book; Wilcock, David**.

Chari, Dr. C.T.K. (1909–1993). Chari was a well-known Indian parapsychologist who has written a number of significant works critical of reincarnation. Among these are *Regression Beyond Birth* (1956) in which he offers a critical estimate of hypnotic regression to uncover past lives; *Paramnesia and Reincarnation* (1962); *Paranormal Cognition, Survival and Reincarnation* (1962); and his articles in the *Signet Handbook of Parapsychology* (1978). In these publications Chari prefers to explain data interpreted as proof of reincarnation as, at best, due to various **extrasensory perceptions** of living minds.

Charvakas (S. Followers of the philosopher Charvaka). This is the collective name for the early schools of Indian materialists (S: Lokayatas). As deniers of God and the immortality of the **soul**, they were major critics of the concepts of **transmigration** and karma. However, contrary to what some of their critics claimed, all Charvakas schools did not teach antinomian hedonism (a lawless cult of pleasure) any more than do most modern day materialists. A number of Charvaka teachers, like many materialists of all eras, were perfectly aware of the need for both moral and sensual restraints in order for the individual to live a satisfying life within society. The Charvakas were early advocates of a thorough **body (mind) brain dependency**.

See also **Antinomianism**.

Chen-Tao *see* **Zhendao**.

Child as its own reborn father or mother. With regards to rebirth, one very interesting question has been asked: Could a child ever be his or her father or mother reborn? This should technically be possible if either there is no necessary **interim period** between death and rebirth or such a period is no greater than the time between physical conception and the soul's entrance into the body of the infant. For example, in the most extreme case, if the **soul** enters into an embryo at physical conception and the father died immediately after ejaculation into the mother's womb, then the father's soul could enter into the embryo it had just fathered. Indeed, in the case where a soul does not take on re-embodiment until hours or even days after physical birth, as some people believe, the new born could have its own mother's soul if she had died in or immediately after childbirth. Most believers in reincarnation, perhaps embarrassed by these possibilities, tend to ignore them; however, those possibilities are becoming more difficult to ignore due to modern artificial insemination. Since it is now possible for a baby to be conceived from the sperm stored in a sperm-bank after the death of the donor, technically, the soul that at some point enters the womb could be that of the donor, which means the infant has his or her father's soul. The Electra/Oedipus Complex aspect of rebirth would be a logical solution to this problem.

See also **Electra/Oedipus Complex and rebirth; Incest and Rebirth; Mother, mule, and son; Rebirth and artificial insemination; Rebirth, instantaneous.**

Child prodigies or geniuses. Young children that exhibit extraordinary ability or talents far beyond what their age might otherwise expect of them have been repeatedly claimed as proof of reincarnation. Wolfgang Amadeus Mozart (1756–1791), who, at the age of five, wrote a piano concerto that was too difficult for anyone else to play, is the most often noted example of a child prodigy. But even more impressive was Jean-Louis Cardiac (1719–1726) who could recite the alphabet at age 3 months; read Latin and translated it into French and English at 4 years; was proficient in Greek, Hebrew, arithmetic, history, geography, and genealogy at 6. Unfortunately, like a number of such children, he died very early, in his case, at the age of 7.

That rebirth could account for the talents of such extraordinary children is not an unreasonable idea. There are, however, two main questions that arise if rebirth is used to account for such geniuses. First, if everyone, or at least the overwhelming majority of persons, has lived many previous lives why are such prodigies so rare? They ought to be quite common. Second, if a child can remember the complex details of playing a musical instrument, and even more so of reading and writing music, why can those same children not remember more personal details concerning a past life? The answer to the question has been that a person has to have a series of lives that involve the same skill before it can imprint sufficiently and manifest as a child genius; and the ability to have such a series might be very difficult to come by. The answer given to the second question has been that most personal memories are unique to each life and are not going to be imprinted repeatedly in the subconscious like a talent or skill might be able to imprint.

On the other hand, using reincarnation to explain child prodigies has been challenged as a **supernatural-in-the-gap process**, which is where a non-scientific explanation is inserted in a present-day gap in scientific knowledge. The progress that is being made in genetics studies is occurring so fast that it may soon give us a more scientific answer to such prodigies.

See also *Anamnesis*; **Arguments supportive of rebirth; Karma, vocational; Soul mates.**

Children remembering past lives. Far more children than adults are said to have **spontaneous recall** when it comes to remembering past lives. Several hypotheses have been offered for this.

First, children are closer in time to their former life than are adults; therefore, it is easier for them to remember what older people gradually forget. Second, some children who are not old enough to have developed a full and secure sense of present selfhood seek security by trying to hold on to their past selfhood until it can safely be replaced by a present version. Third, as children acquire memories in the present life, which are necessary for every day functioning, the past life memories must be suppressed so as not to interfere with the present life. Fourth, children, especially very young ones, are more psychically gifted than are adults, but as children grow older they gradually lose this gift. Of course in this fourth case the children may be experiencing the past through **retrocognition** rather than being a reincarnate **soul**. Fifth, recently deceased souls, unaware that the body they inhabited has died or are resistant to that death, take **possession** of a child as an easy target to try to continue in an embodied state. As the child gets older and asserts his own personality and/or as the possessing entity gradually accommodates to the idea that its original body died, the possession fades away. Obviously in this fifth case, reincarnation is being mistaken for possession.

The phenomenon whereby the memories of past lives held by young children fade as they get older is called retroactive inhibition. This fading begins as the child approaches school age, which is about 4–6 years old. By the age of 10 years most children do not even remember having had such memories.

Besides the above explanations offered for this retroactive inhibition phenomena there are three others, all of which are critical of rebirth. The first is that the child's memories were never authentic, but part of a game the child was unintentionally creating to gain attention. Once the children began going to school and/or taking on more responsibility for their lives they no longer find the game meaningful, and so it is abandoned. The fact that most of the cases of spontaneous recall occur in cultures that doctrinally accept rebirth, such as in India and among the **Druzes** of Lebanon, has made such an attention getting game seem quite possible.

In particular, credence has been given to this "game" explanation for the cases examined by **Ian Stevenson** in the northern Indian State of Uttar Pradesh. This is one of India's poorest states, yet at least 60 percent of the children he investigated claim to have formerly been of a higher caste than in their present life. Since lower castes form the overwhelming percentage of the population it would be statistically expected that the children would remember past lives mostly in lower castes. The children's claim to a former higher caste tends to elicit more adult attention towards them than if the same or a lower caste were involved.

The second critical explanation for some children, both to claim a past life and for their future retroactive inhibition, deals with temporary "negative *déjà vu*." This is where familiar people, places and things start to feel strange. This can lead to a child regarding his or her family as strangers and, in their place, regarding a strange family as his or her real one. In fact, a number of cases have been reported in which just such rejection of the present family and attachment to a strange family has occurred both in India and Lebanon.

The third critical explanation for the retroactive inhibition phenomena has to do with cultures that do not doctrinally accept rebirth. In these cultures the few children who do claim to remember past lives usually give far fewer details about the past lives then do children in pro-rebirth cultures. This suggests that in cultures that are supportive of rebirth the adults around the children may be intentionally or unintentionally adding to the children's memories.

Whether or not there is adult involvement in past life recall by these children it does tend to be the case that the more details the children give about the past lives the more the number of errors there are in the children's recall.

The major problem with accepting the memories of very young children is that it has been repeatedly documented that they unintentionally mix fact with fantasy. For example, a number of children when asked under pressure about possible sexual abuse have created false scenarios about being involved with abusively satanic sexual rituals. Also, in one experiment, a Finnish psychiatrist, Dr. Reima Kampman, had the opportunity to hypnotize a number of children and suggest to them that they had lived before the present life. The children came forth with some very elaborate and consistent past life scenarios. On a follow-up investigation, however, Dr, Kampman was able to uncover **cryptomnesia** sources for many of these scenarios. This implied to the doctor that the children were exhibiting the equivalence of hypnotically induced **multiple personalities**.

In fact, one of the critiques leveled at Stevenson's cases is that he has not allowed for the possibility that some of his subjects may be exhibiting multiple personality syndromes.

Finally, the question has been asked, "How much of past life memory is need to qualify as proof of rebirth?" None of the children have demonstrated more than a very limited partial memory of the presumed past life. Does the mere ability to recognize some previous family members and/or the way the previous person died constitute enough memory to qualify as the previous person reborn? It has been argued that every human being far more than this minimal memory?

See also **Child prodigies or geniuses; Deaths, violent and premature; Extrasensory perception; Fantasy versus past life regression; Honest lying; Katsugoro case; Leading question; Mental plane; Multiple personalities; Rebirth and cultural conditioning; Rebirth, proximity; Rebirth, qualifications for; Retrocognition; Shanti Devi case; Stevenson, Ian.**

Child's Epitaph. "If so soon I must be done for,/ What on earth was I begun for?" This rhyming couplet is sometimes used to exemplify some arguments for rebirth. One argument says that some souls only need to return to life for a very short time before leaving the cycle of rebirth and redeath. Another argument is that soon after birth a **soul** realizes that it either was embodied in the wrong body or it made a mistake in the parents it chose. In either case, the soul seeks to escape through some self-generated early death.

Chimeras see **Embryonic fusion.**

Chinese religion and reincarnation. In earliest folk Chinese religion there was no clearly delineated orthodox belief system about the **soul** since there was no formal religious authority to dictate such orthodoxy. However, the general consensus, which goes back to pre–Buddhist times was, and to some degree still is, that each person has two souls. These are the *yin*, the feminine, earth or blood soul called *p'o* (WG); and the *yang*, the masculine, heavenly, or breath soul called *hun*. The *p'o* is associated with the emotions and senses, and so it is the sentient or animal soul. The *hun* is associated with intelligence and reason, and so it is the human soul. While the *p'o* is a part of the body from conception, the *hun* does not enter the body until either the first breath of the infant or, according to some sources, not until a month after birth.

At death these two souls are said to leave the body, each by a different aperture; the *hun* leaves first by way of the upper part, especially the top of the skull (fontanelle), and then the *p'o* leaves from the lower part of the body. On rare occasions, such as avenging its murder or some other serious wrong to the deceased, the two souls may stay together and possess another body. Normally, however, the p'o is thought to survive in or near the grave until its former body decays, which may take up to three years; but if the disembodied *p'o* becomes offended, as in the case of an improper burial of its former body, then it survives for a long time as a maliciously haunting and **hungry ghost** (*kuei/gui*). After this the *p'o* goes to the **Yellow Spring** (purgatorial hell). A proper burial, and hence release of the *p'o* from the body is one way to ensure that the body, with only the *p'o* animating it, does not become a flesh eating **vampire**. On the other hand, for whatever reason, the one way of keeping the *p'o* from leaving the corpse is to stop up each of the orifices of the body with jade. In older times, among the rich and powerful, the corpse was completely clad in a suit of jade pieces sewn together with gold wire.

The *hun*, after proper burial rites, ascends to heaven to become an ancestral spirit (*shen*), where it survives only up to five generations or up to the time that no living family members feels any more connection to it. At this point it merges into a kind of impersonal collective ancestral element.

It should be clear that nothing in this traditional Chinese view of the afterlife had anything to do with reincarnation. It was not until the introduction of Buddhism into China around the 2nd century CE, that the Chinese were exposed to the concept of reincarnation and even though **Daoism** eventually adopt a reincarnation doctrine, it took several centuries to do so. The Confucianists, on the other hand, not only didn't adopt such a belief, they did every thing in their power to oppose it. The reason for this opposition was that the Confucian ethos was, in most cases, the exact opposite of the Indian Buddhist one.

Confucius's teachings have always been almost exclusively concerned with the establishment of proper economic, social, and political conditions, and hence are mostly this-world oriented. Not only were his teachings not based on the supernatural, he considered much of the religion of his time to be sheer superstition. Confucius is said to have summed up his religious views with the statements "If you are not able to serve men (in this world), how can you serve the spirits (in the next world)," and "If you do not understand life, how can you understand death." Even later on, when his teachings became the state ideology, there never developed any priesthood around an otherwise considerable cult of the man Confucius.

One result of the Confucianist this-worldly attitude was that the Chinese, as a whole, believed that there could be no greater good than a long life in this body involved in productive labor as a social obligation to one's family and the state.

Buddhism, in contrast, viewed life as full of suffering and its pleasures as deceptive; moreover, the Buddhist ideal was one of leaving one's family for a homelessness and mendicant lifestyle. From the Confucianist view this was seen as a show of ingratitude to, and disrespect for, the parents, who had given one life and, who in return, were entitled to support in old age. Indeed, the Buddhist ideal of monastic **celibacy** was in violent opposition to the Chinese imperative to have children to keep the treasured family line going and the ancestors forever worshiped. In fact, as mentioned above, the Chinese believed that as long as the name and memory of one's ancestors was memorialized their spirit would continue to exist, but if ignored those ancestors would experience a kind of secondary and permanent death. However, even without this ancestral obligation, just the idea of suppressing normal human sexual desires was looked upon by the Confucianists as rather ridiculous, if not unhealthy.

If celibacy was judged as unhealthy, even more so was the repulsive Buddhist encouragement to achieve this suppression of normal human desires by such activities as cemetery or charnel ground meditation.

There were, also the more extreme ***bodhisattva*** vows, one of which was the altruistic (from a Buddhist perspective) willingness to sacrificing pieces of one's own flesh for the sake of saving others. The Confucianists considered this a violation of the filial rule not to deliberately harm the body that one's parents gave to you.

Equally shocking was the Buddhist rebirth story, as told in the ***Jataka Tales,*** of the *bodhisattva*, as a sign of his spiritual unattachment, giving away, not only all his family possessions, but even his wife and children.

Also, there was the Buddhist teaching that one's parents could end up in a **hell** or be reborn as animals, due to their bad karma. Even the suggestion that this could happen, violated the Chinese sense of filial piety and ancestor veneration.

Perhaps most horrifying of all, was the possibility, no matter how remote, that one's mother or father, brother or sister in an earlier life could become one's wife or husband in a later life due to karmic ties. From the Confucianist view point, with its extreme filial piety, such role reversals amount to the hideous crime of incest. In short, the entire Buddhist doctrine of rebirth was insulting to Confucian sensibilities.

Despite the anti-rebirth theory, and indeed, at times the virulent anti–Buddhist attitude of the upper class Confucianists, Buddhism and its rebirth doctrine did have a great appeal to the Chinese lower classes. Considering that the lives of the lower classes were mostly drudgery and there was little hope of changing this, the Buddhist teachings about the rewards of a better future life (rebirth) for the poor and the powerless offered something that none of the native traditions could offer. Furthermore, the teaching that the rich, the powerful, and the oppressive landlords and tax collectors were likely headed for hell doubled Buddhism appeal. As if this were not enough, within a very short time the teachings about the **Pure-Land**, with it promise of rebirth in the heavenly paradise of **Amitabha Buddha**, gained enormous popularity not only among the lower classes but even among some of the upper classes, especially women.

See also **Bhaishajyaraja-guru; Child as its own reborn father or mother; Deaths, violent and premature; Empire of Jade; Hell, the Chinese; Incest and reincarnation; Karma, family; Mu-lian, The Story of; Pure-Land or Blissful Land Buddhism; Rebirth in Zen; Second death; Souls, multiple;** *T'ai-Yueh-Ta-Ti.*

Chintra-Gupta (Manifold-Secret). In **Hinduism** this is the name of the scribe in the realm of the dead who records in the registry called the *Agra Sandhani* the virtues and vices of human beings for **Yama**, the god of the dead. This record will then be used to help decide reincarnational destinies.

See also *Book of Life;* **Lords of Karma.**

Chiromancy. This is divination by reading the lines in the palms and fingers of the hands. It was believed by some Kabbalists that clues to a person's past life could be read in these lines. Although Jewish sources before the *Sefer ha-Zohar* mention the practice, it seems that it was only its inclusion in that text that introduced it into Kabbalic thought. Chiromancy is not to be confused with palmistry, which must include chirognomy or chirology, the study of the shape of the hand; nor with chirosophy, which is the study of the comparative value of hand forms.

See also **Kabbalah.**

Chit (Consciousness). This term is not to be confused with *chitta* (mind).

See also *Atman.*

Chitta (Mind). In early Buddhism *chitta* was more or less synonymous with *manas* (mind) or *vijnana* (consciousness), but in later Buddhist schools *Chitta* was distinguished from *vijnana* as it came to be associated with rebirth (linking) consciousness (P: *patisandhi vinnana*).

This term is not to be confused with *chit* (consciousness).

See also **Original sin, Christianity, and reincarnation; Psychophysical aggregates; Rebirth in Buddhism.**

Chnoumis, Chnouphis. In **Theosophy** this Greek name is said to refer to the creative force or unmade and eternal deity in ancient Egyptian religion which, as the dual *Chnoumis-Kneph*, is the pre-eminent god of reincarnation.

See also **Egypt; Khepra.**

Christ *see* **Adam; Aetherius Society; Ahmadiyya;** *Apocatastasis; Aquarian Gospel of Jesus Christ;* **Baptism; Cayce, Edgar; Christian atonement theories; Christian view of the afterlife; Christianity and reincarnation; Jesus; John, Gospel of; New Testament and reincarnation; Resurrection of Jesus; Zhendao.**

Christian atonement theories. One of the reasons standard Christian doctrine gives for rejecting reincarnation is that the multiple-lives concept is incompatible with the concept of the atonement of Christ. Actually there has not been just one, but three main theological views as to why Christ, either as man or God, had to suffer and die on the cross as atonement for mankind's sins.

The earliest of these atonement theories is the "Ransom to the Devil and Death Theory." In this, the fall of **Adam** (mankind) automatically gave the devil the legal right to man's **soul**. God, as the upholder of cosmic legality, was forced to pay the devil a price if he wanted to liberate man from his legal masters. The crucifixion and resurrection of an innocent or sinless being alone was that price. Such Church Fathers as **Augustine** accepted this view.

The second atonement concept was the "Subjective (Abelardian) Theory." According to Peter Abelard (1079–1144) the contemplation of a sinless being on the cross causes the believer to appreciate how sinful he really is and to recognize the power of sacrificial-love needed to overcome sin. This would cause the believer to be morally transformed and motivated to follow Christ's example as best he can. This view found only minority support in the Middle Ages; but it has been revived and enjoyed greater support in modern times.

The third atonement concept was the "Objective (Anselmic) theory." Saint Anselm (1033–1109) modified the earlier Ransom Theory, in his *Cur Deus Homo?* (*Why the God-man?*). In this work the price that had to be paid for human sinfulness and mortality did not need to be offered to the devil but to God. For God's own justice to be satisfied He could not freely forgive mankind since no amount of mere human suffering could repay Him for the indignation He had suffered from human willfulness. Therefore, it was up to God himself to pay for the redemption of humanity. This was done through the suffering and death of Christ (the divine Son). This third atonement view partially replaced the earlier "Ransom" view, and was adopted as orthodox by the Western Churches from the Middle Ages up to the present. This last theory is more closely related to the **New Testament sacrificial concept**.

Of these three atonement theories, the first may or may not be incompatible with reincarnation;

the second does not seem to offer any incompatibility; but the third and most orthodox, definitely would seem to be incompatible with reincarnation.

See also **Christianity and reincarnation; Emanationism; Karma and forgiveness; Original sin, Christianity, and reincarnation; Original sin versus karma**.

Christian fathers critical of reincarnation. The first few centuries of Christian history witnessed a major battle between what became the more orthodox view that rejected any belief in reincarnation and what came to be regarded as the heretical view that supported reincarnation in some manner.

See also **Aeneas of Gaza; Ambrose of Milan; Aquinas, Thomas; Arnobius the Elder; Augustine, Saint Aurelius; Basil of Caesarea; Clement of Alexandria; Gregory of Nyssa; Irenaeus; Jerome; Justin Martyr; Lactantius; Nemesius; Origin; Tertullian; Theophilus**.

Christian missionary influence and reincarnation. Christian missionary activities among tribal peoples in medieval Europe resulted in a major demise of the belief in reincarnation among these people, and a similar demise has occurred in other places more recently dominated by such missionary activities.

See also **American Indians; Cannibalistic reincarnation; Lapps (Saami)**.

Christian view of the afterlife. Other than to say that the Christian view of the post-mortem state does not include reincarnation it is difficult to specifically say what that state is. On the one hand, a belief in Christ's sacrifice and resurrection is said to offer the believer eternal life. This would seem to imply that the non-believer experiences annihilation, to which some, but not most, of the biblical letters of **Paul of Tarsus** allude. In fact, the dominant biblical view is that those who do not accept Christ will suffer eternal damnation. The eternity of such damnation would then imply that believing in Christ was not originally necessary for eternal life "in **hell**," only for it in heaven. This would be supported by the Christian teaching that Christ, upon his death, entered hell, **purgatory**, or **limbo** to preach to and presumably liberate the Old Testament prophets and saints from which ever of those places their souls dwelled. The confusion as to which of these afterlife realms Christ entered depends on whether one is Roman Catholic, Eastern Orthodox, or Protestant.

Finally, there is the issue of whether the **soul** enters heaven or hell immediately upon death of the body or enters into a dreamless sleep-like condition until awakened at the future general resurrection, in which the old body will be recreated.

See also **Annihilationism, Biblical view; Aquinas, Thomas; Baptism; Christianity and reincarnation; John, Gospel of; Judgment of the Dead; Millennialism; New Testament and reincarnation; New Testament sacrificial concept;** *Psychopannychism;* **Resurrection, bodily; Resurrection of Jesus**.

Christianity and reincarnation. Despite efforts by Christian reincarnationists standard Christianity can not easily accept a belief in reincarnation. By standard I refer to those religious traditions that hold three main beliefs. First, they regard the figure of **Jesus** of Nazareth as the anointed Messiah, or Christ, and the son of God. This means he is regarded as the most complete revealer of sacred truth ever to have lived or who will live. It should be noted that this does not automatically mean that Jesus must be accepted as fully divine. A number of smaller, but still standard, Christian groups do not accept his full divinity. Second, standard Christianity regards the crucifixion and death of Jesus as essential to the salvation of mankind. Third, it regards both the Old Testament and New Testament together as the only authentic sacred canon.

Standard Christianity rejects reincarnation and karma for a multiplicity of reasons. (1) Traditional readings of both the Old and the New Testament books offers no irrefutable evidence that the doctrine of reincarnation was part of the teachings of the prophets or of Jesus. (2) The New Testament clearly teaches that there is an eternal hell. In fact, in several passages it is Jesus who is credited with teaching it. Among these passages is **Matthew** 8:12, 13:42, 25:30, and especially 25:41 and 25:46; also, **Mark** 9:45–48; **Luke** 16:22–29. (3) A multiple life concept is clearly denied by the author of Hebrews 9:27–28, "And as it is the lot of men to die once, and after death comes judgment, so Christ was offered once to bear the burden of men's sin." (4) Excluding the element of original sin, which is a collective guilt, not an individual one, **Romans** 9:12 declares that children, before they are born, are innocent of both good and evil. (5) The doctrine of **metempsychosis** was clearly opposed by the early church fathers. (6) It is thought that reincarnation would weaken, or even make unnecessary, the suffering, dying, and **resurrection of Jesus** as atonement for humanity's sins. (7) For some Christian Churches reincarnation would call into question both the Old Testament and **New Testament sacrificial concept**, including the theophagic **Eucharist** as an absolutely necessary means to salvation. (8) Reincarnation distracts from the urgency of salvation that is implied with a single life and encourages procrastination as far as salvation is concerned. (9) Reincarnation is in competition with the general resurrection of the dead. (10) Both reincarnation and karma imply that salvation can be gained, either mainly or exclusively, through good works rather than through the Christian belief in the unearned grace of God. (11) Christianity teaches that God has the power to forgive even the most heinous of sins, provided that the sinner sincerely repents. With karma, technically, there is no such forgiveness or escape from the consequences of any ill-performed actions. This is especially true for the non-theistic karma-acknowledging religions. The major exception is **Pure-Land Buddhism**. (12) The impersonality of karma is vastly inferior to the personal and loving concern of God. (13) When cross-special (animal-human) reincarnations is accepted, the ennobling fact that mankind was made in the image of God is denied. (14) It is possible to dispense altogether with a belief in God through a belief in reincarnation and karma. (15) Reincarnation and karma offer no satisfactory "ultimate explanation" for evil in the world. (16) Reincarnation and karma discourage working towards a more economically and politically just society and thus lessens the dignity of every person; instead it contributes to a **blaming of the victim** for his own suffering without proof of guilt. (17) Karma is another name for a fatalistic **determinism** which denigrates humanity. (18) Reincarnation is far too compatible with the hubris idea that mankind can become like, is identical to, or eventually is reabsorbed back into God. (19) Because of the lack of any remembrance of any past life, reincarnation and karma can not be considered morally valid, much less just. (20) The **population increase issue** makes nonsense of reincarnation, especially if cross-special reincarnation is denied. (21) Reincarnation claims to be based upon natural laws, but unlike all other natural laws reincarnation can not be scientifically proven.

It should be noted that of these arguments, 1–18 are specifically religious arguments, while 19–21 are non-sectarian arguments. As such the non–Christian can more or less ignore the first eighteen, but must take into account the last three.

Although the above reasons for the Christian rejection of reincarnation, both sectarian and non-sectarian, are sufficient to convince the majority of Christians that reincarnation is incompatible with Christianity, a minority of Christians believe that the two are compatible. For these pro-reincarnation Christians one of the most popular arguments is that all souls reincarnate until *"every knee should bend ... [and] ... every tongue confess"* (Philippians 2:9–11) and so make Christ as their personal savior. Those souls that have already accepted Christ leave the cycle of rebirth for a heavenly existence. Of course, the conservative Christian response to this is that considering that a majority of the world's population has been Christian for several centuries and that a goodly percentage of them have over those centuries accepted Christ as their personal savior, the population of souls in the world should be dramatically decreasing, not increasing.

See also **Aeneas of Gaza; Animals and rebirth, Western view;** *Apocatastasis*; **Aquinas, Thomas; Arguments that challenge rebirth on a logical basis; Aristotle; Augustine, Saint Aurelius; Baptism; Basil of Caesarea; Bogomils; Cathars; Christian atonement theories; Christian fathers critical of reincarnation; Christian missionary influence and reincarnation; Christian view of the afterlife; Christianity, esoteric; Christianity, lost chord of; Church Council of 553; Church Council of Lyons and Council of Florence; Clement of Alexandria; Elijah (Elias); Emanationism; False claims of support for reincarnation; Gnosticism; Gregory of Nyssa; Hell; Helmont, Franciscus Mercurius van; Irenaeus; Islam; John, Gospel of; John the Baptist; Judgment of the Dead; Justin Martyr; Karma and forgiveness; Karma and God; Karma and justice; Karma as natural law; Karma versus grace; Lactantius; Limbo; Millennialism; New Testament and reincarnation; Old Testament and the afterlife; Original sin, Christianity, and reincarnation; Original sin versus karma; Predestination; Population increase issue and a theistic solution;** *Psychopannychism*; **Purgatory; Rebirth and cyclical time; Rebirth and general morality; Rebirth and moral perfection; Rebirth in the West; Resurrection, bodily; Resurrection or reincarnation; Sacred Bone; Seventeenth century renewed interest in rebirth; Synesius of Cyrene; Tertullian; Theodicy; Theophilus**.

Christianity, esoteric. This is any one of a variety of teachings that consider the standard doctrines of both Catholicism and Protestantism as exoteric (outer) teachings and, therefore, as either inferior to or a conscious distortion of the true teachings of **Jesus**. The esotericists further believe that those true teachings had been concealed, suppressed, lost, or only much later revealed. This description of esoteric Christianity, in its broadest sense, includes both ancient and modern sects; for example, the ancient and medieval gnostic Christians, the Mormons, Christian Scientists, Jehovah's Witnesses, and various New Age Christian groups. A major difference separating these esoteric Christian is that some continue to reject reincarnation; while others accept it.

See also *Aquarian Gospel of Jesus Christ*;

Ashoka, King; Cathars; Christianity and reincarnation; Christianity, lost chord of; Church Council of 553; Church Universal and Triumphant; Eckankar; Esotericism versus Occultism; Hell; Mormonism; New Age religions; New Testament and reincarnation; Rosicrucians; Scientology; Steiner, Rudolf.

Christianity, lost chord of. This term, coined by **William Q. Judge** (1851–1896), is used by many people who are convinced that the Bible, or at least the New Testament, originally taught the doctrine of reincarnation, and that this doctrine was then "lost." Since the word lost usually implies a nondeliberate action, and since the advocates of the lost chord really believe that the doctrine of rebirth was deliberately suppressed by the early church, it would probably make more sense to speak of the "suppressed chord of Christianity" rather than the lost chord.

One of the weaknesses of this view is that if the church had gone to such effort to erase from the Bible compromising passages about reincarnation (**metempsychosis**), why did they keep those that are so often used to prove the Bible taught reincarnation?

See also **New Testament and reincarnation; Old Testament and the afterlife.**

Christos (anointing) **technique.** This is one method that is said to stimulate the remembering of events in a former life. It requires at least two individuals — the anointer and the anointed. In the first stage of the process the person who seeks to remember his past life lies down and tries to enter into a relaxed meditative state. The anointer then massages an oil or balm into the forehead (**third eye** area) and then on the ankles of the anointed person. A strong mentholated ointment is thought to work best. In the second stage, the anointer verbally encourages the anointed person to visualize a progressively deeper state of relaxation. Soon the anointed reaches a point where he or she is ready for the suggestion to mentally travel back in time to childhood and then further back to before the start of the present life. The mind traveler is then instructed to tell what he or she is experiencing.

It seems that no one is absolutely sure who first developed this Christos technique, but the name most closely associated with it is G. M. Glaskin. He wrote *Windows of the Mind* (1974); *Worlds Within* (1978); and *A Door to Eternity* (1979).

See also **Past life regression and suggestibility.**

Christward Ministry. This group was founded by Flower A. Newhouse (1909–1994), a self-proclaimed Christian mystic and clairvoyant. Its teachings are a blend of Christianity, Jungian psychology, meditation, astrology, angelology, and the concept of reincarnation and karma. The headquarters of the sect is a retreat called Questhaven, which is near Escondido, California.

Chronoportation. This is an elegant word for "time travel," either physically or mentally. An ability of the mind to break through the time barrier and experience the past as a passive viewer has been suggested as an alternate explanation for past life memories.

See also **Rebirth, alternative explanations to; Retrocognition.**

Chuan-lun wang (WG). In Chinese mythology this is the tenth king of hell. He is not responsible for any kind of punishment like the other kings, but for preparing the souls leaving hell for their rebirth. It is he that decrees the form into which one will be reborn in accordance to the soul's karma.

See also **Hell, the Chinese; Yen-lo.**

Church Council of 553. This was also called the Fifth Ecumenical Council and the Second Council of Constantinople. Many reincarnationist advocates point to this Council as being the first Christian Council to condemn reincarnation or **metempsychosis** as a heresy. At this Council, however, the doctrine of metempsychosis was not directly mentioned. Instead, it was the doctrine of the pre-existence of souls that was declared heretical, especially as that doctrine was taught by **Origin**. Moreover, pre-existence was condemned in the context of universal salvation, not in the context of any multiple life theory. The mistaken belief that this council condemned metempsychosis comes from the fact that, while a pre-existence does not automatically equate with metempsychosis, metempsychosis does depend on the pre-existence of souls. So for all practical purposes the doctrine of metempsychosis was "indirectly" declared heretical.

The doctrine of metempsychosis was not explicitly condemned until the Church Council of Lyons (1274) at which time the Papacy's condemnation was specifically directed against the teachings of the **Cathars**. This Papal condemnation was then repeated at the Council of Florence (1439–1441).

The reason for the very late official condemnation of metempsychosis was that the Church, up to that time, took it so much for granted that any multiple-life teaching was incompatible with Christianity that there was no reason for condemning the obvious. After all, some of the most important early Christian Fathers such as **Augustine, Gregory of Nyssa, Irenaeus, Justin Martyr, Tertullian, Theophilus,** and even **Origin** had, in no uncertain terms, attacked metempsychosis.

See also *Apocatastasis*; Christianity and reincarnation; Christianity, esoteric; False claims of support for reincarnation; Neoplatonism; Soul's existence prior to embodiment; Universalism.

Church Council of Laodicea. This Christian council met in 364 CE in the western Asia Minor city of Laodicea, which today is called Denizli, in Turkey. It was here that the decision was made as to which books to include in, and excluded from, the Christian Bible. With the one exception of the **Revelation of John**, all the books presently found in the Bible were accepted at this time. Revelation, while rejected for inclusion at this council, was shortly afterwards also accepted. There were approximately forty other texts that were rejected for one reason or another.

While none of the accepted books were supportive of **metempsychosis**, there is no "concrete" evidence that reincarnation was a concern with regards to the rejection of the other books; however, considering the possible gnostic influence on some of those excluded texts, positive attitudes towards metempsychosis may have been a factor in their rejection.

See also **New Testament and reincarnation**.

Church Council of Lyons (1274 CE) and **Council of Florence** (1439). These were the two church councils at which the Papacy specifically condemned a belief in metempsychosis. It was also at these Councils that the concept of *psychopannychism* was rejected in favor of immediate transportation of the **soul** to heaven or hell

See also **Cathars; Church Council of 553**.

Church of the Divine Man. This religious sect was founded in 1973 by Lewis S. Bostwick (1918–1995) as a spiritual healing church based on the idea that one must have faith in oneself as God. Bostwick was originally associated with **Scientology**, but in the late 1970's he broke with that organization and established his own church. The church includes in its teachings a belief in reincarnation, karma, spirit guides, **chakras, psychometry**, telekinesis, and auras. Bostwick is also the founder of the Berkeley Psychic Institute (1975).

Church Universal and Triumphant. This is a controversial **New Age religion**. It was found by Mark Prophet (1918–1973) in 1958 under the original name of Summit Lighthouse. Following Prophet's death in 1973 his wife, Elizabeth Clare Prophet (1939–2009) announced that Mark had left this world to become one of the **ascended masters (Great White Brotherhood)**. Mrs. Prophet, then having been secretly anointed by the ascended master **Saint Germain**, took over the leadership of the church. The Church's teachings were modeled on one of the splinter groups of the **I Am Movement**, of which Mark Prophet was at once a member. The Church's beliefs are a syncretism of Esoteric Christianity, **Theosophy**, Buddhism, Western alchemy, catastrophic millenarianism, and **channeling**. The Church teaches that ascended masters such as **Jesus**, the **Buddha**, Mahatma Morya, Master Djwal Khul, and Master Koot Hoomi (Kuthumi) all taught the doctrine of reincarnation. It will be noted that the last three names were also associated with **Helena Blavatsky** and **Alice Bailey**.

Elizabeth Prophet is a supporter of "The Young Jesus in India (and Tibet) Theory" as originally espoused by **Nicholas Notovitch**.

See also **Ahmadiyya;** *Aquarian Gospel of Jesus Christ*; **Christianity and reincarnation; Christianity, esoteric; New Testament and reincarnation; Psychology, abnormal; Sinnett, Alfred Percy; White Lodge**.

Chukchi. These native people of the far northeast corner of Siberia, like their neighbors the **Koryaks**, traditionally believe in some form of reincarnation.

See also **Hunting cultures and reincarnation; Lapps (Saami); Yukagir**.

Cicero, Marcus Tullius (106–43 BCE). As suggested by some of his writings, this Roman statesman, orator, and philosopher, relying mainly on earlier Greek works, seemed to have accepted **metempsychosis** as a real possibility.

See also *Anamnesis*; **Greek afterlife, the ancient; Planetary descent and ascent of the soul**.

Circle of Necessity (Greek: Kuklos Anagkes). This is another term for the duration between death and rebirth. Anagke or Ananke was the name for the goddess of Necessity, who, according to one myth, was the mother of the three Fates (Moirai).

See also **Ouroboros; Plato**.

Clairaudience. This is the psychic ability to discern sounds that are far beyond the normal range of hearing. It is thought to be one of the possible psychic alternative explanations for experiencing a **past life recall**.

See also *Abhijna*; **Rebirth, alternative explanations to**.

Clairvoyance. This is the psychic ability to visually discern what is far beyond the normal range of sight. It is thought to be one of the possible psychic alternative explanations for experiencing a **past life recall**.

See also *Abhijna*; **Rebirth, alternative explanations to**.

Clement of Alexandria (About 155–220 CE). This Christian church father, and teacher of **Origin**, is another figure that some reincarnationists have mistakenly tried to make one of their own. This identification has apparently been made on the very slim basis of a passage in the first chapter of his work *Exhortation [Protrepiticus] to the Heathen* which, while making no reference to **metempsychosis**, seems to support the pre-existence of the **soul**. The passage reads, "But before the foundation of the world were we, who, because destined to be in Him, pre-existed in the eye of God before, — — we the rational creatures of the Word of God, on whose account we date from the beginning; for "in the beginning was the word." This passage deals with two issues. First, there are the pre-existent human souls, not as already created, but only as a thought [in the "eye"] of God. Second, there is the very substantial pre-existence of the Word [Logos] of God as stated in Gospel of **John** 1:1.

There is little doubt that Clement's Neoplatonic approach to Christian doctrines brought his orthodoxy under some suspicion, but only as a possible *pre-existiani*, not as a believer in *metensomatosis*. Those who would use this meager example of Clement's writing to claim him as a reincarnationist forget that if there were even the slightest suspicion of Clement as a supporter of **metempsychosis** he would never have been considered a church father in the first place.

See also **Christian fathers critical of reincarnation; Christianity and reincarnation; Church Council of 553; New Testament and reincarnation; Origin; Soul's existence prior to embodiment.**

Cleopatra Syndrome. The question might be asked: Why have so many people at one time or another claimed to be figures like Cleopatra or Marie-Antoinette, as opposed to Zenobia of Palmyra, Elizabeth I, Katherine the Great, etc? The answer would seem to be that the first two died tragically, while the rest died naturally of old age. A tragic premature death seems to call out for compensation that a more normal death does not, and this encourages identification with such tragic figures more than with the others.

Cloning *see* **Rebirth and artificial insemination.**

Coffin to cradle. Like **death to breath** and **tomb to womb**, this is a metaphor for reincarnation.
See also **Crypt.**

Collective birth of extraordinary men and women. This is one of the arguments supportive of reincarnation. This argument states that throughout most of human history there has been only a very few, if any, extraordinary men and women born in any one period. However, in a few periods, such as 6th and 5th century Greece and in the 15th and 16th century **Renaissance** there were a disproportionate number of intellectually exceptional persons born. This, it is claimed, can best be accounted for by a group of like-minded souls choosing to be reborn very close to one another in time and space. The fact of the matter is that there are other reasons that can just as easily account for such phenomena. For one thing, 6th and 5th century Greece did not have a monopoly on extraordinary persons. There were more or less as many great minds all the way up to the end of the Roman Empire. The following European Dark Ages was as much an anomaly as anything else, but during that time the neighboring Islamic civilization was producing an equal number of great intellects. The Renaissance, which was partially stimulated by that Islamic influence, was simply a recovery of European greatness and has continued to produce great minds up to the present.

Collective guilt *see* **Blaming the victim vs. illusion of innocence; Christianity and reincarnation; Exodus; Original sin versus karma; Resurrection of Jesus.**

Collective karma *see* **Karma; Karma, group.**

Collective soul issue *see* **Soul, collective.**

Collective Unconscious. This is said to be a part of the unconscious which contains memories common to humanity. It is distinctive from the personal unconscious, which develops from the unique experiences of the individual.
See also **Ancestral Memories.**

Collin, Robert (1956–1956). This British astrologer was a follower of **P. D. Ouspensky** and **G. I. Gurdjieff**. In Collin's best known work, *The Theory of Celestial Influence* (London: Vincent Stuart, 1954) he attempts to unite the sciences and world history by way of the planetary influences. Of Collin's other works his *The Theory of Eternal Life*, (London: Vincent Stuart, 1956) uses some of the ideas of *The Theory of Celestial Influence* to formulate a theory of the cycles of rebirth and re-death. Collin attempted to demonstrate through a logarithmic time scale that an astrological mechanism exists for understanding the reincarnation process.
See also **Astrology and rebirth; Mann, Tedd.**

Colton, Ann Ree (1898–1984). Along with her husband Jonathan Murro (1927–1991), Colton was the co-founder of The Ann Ree Colton Foundation of Nescience, a non-profit religious and educational foundation located in Glendale, California (1953). Colton is the author of *Draughts of Remembrance: Memories of Past Lives, The Seven-Year Etheric Cycles of the Soul* (1959).
See also **Body-brain (mind) dependency.**

Come-as-you-were parties. These are modified costume parties in which everyone comes dressed in the manner of one of their past lives. They were marginally popular in the late 20th century.

Committee for the Scientific Investigation of the Paranormal (CSIOP). This organization, especially through its journal *Skeptical Enquirer*, has been a major critic of reincarnation claims.

Compensatory justice *see* **Karma and justice**.

Conception and the soul *see* **Creationism, soul; Embodiment, moment of; Generationism and Traducianism; Infusionism; Rebirth and abortion; Rebirth and artificial insemination; Soul's existence prior to embodiment**.

Conditional immortality. This is the belief that the **soul** is not inherently immortal, but must earn immortality or at death it will be annihilated. The ways of earning such immortality have been thought to include pious or holy living, heroic actions, magical rituals, and favoritism from a deity.

See also **Annihilationism, Biblical view**.

Confucianism versus Buddhism *see* **Chinese religion and reincarnation**.

Congenital retardation. Reincarnationists have suggested two separate, yet closely related, reasons for this condition. The first is that a person is born this way because he or she is finishing some past life unfinished karma business that does not require anything more than a minimal mental capacity to complete. In fact, more than this minimum capacity would interfere with the completion of such business. The second reason offered is that the **soul** of that person in a past life committed some unskillful act that in this life requires the soul to learn to cope with a mentally retarded brain. A criticism of both these theories is that they involve **blaming the victim**.

See also **Deaths, violent and premature; Karma as unfinished business**.

Conscious dying. This is the process whereby a trained guide encourages the dying person to remain in a relaxed, but conscious, state as long as possible so that the transition from life to death is free of all anxiety and confusion. This way the deceased will be fully aware of his or her new disembodied state and will be able to either choose the best route to rebirth or even attain final liberation from the cycle of birth and death. In the West this practice was modeled on the Tibetan *Bardo* procedure.

Conscious dying is not to be confused with "submissive death," which is when a person has given up any hope of having their desired quality of life, and so "passively" wills themselves to death.

See also *Ars Moriendi*; **Pure-Land or Blissful Land Buddhism**.

Consciousness continuity, sleep versus death. This is the belief that rebirth of the consciousness of self after death is analogous to going into a deep dreamless sleep and awakening from it with full consciousness of being a self as before. This is a very naïve analogue. When a person awakes from even the deepest sleep he or she has the same body as before, is only a few hours older, is in the same location as before, is in the society as before, has the same relatives, friends, and enemies as before, etc. In other words, consciousness of self is very much related to all of its external elements. After death any so-called awakening of a consciousness through a rebirth is not going to have any of the above factors for that re-embodied consciousness to be able to regard itself as a continuation of a former self. This is especially true in that the re-embodied consciousness is usually that of an infant.

See also **Altered states of consciousness**.

Consciousness or awareness *see* **Mind**.

Convenient fiction *see* **Noble lie**.

Cooke, Grace (1892–1979). A well known British Spiritualist who, in her later years, claimed that with the aid of the *akashic* **record** and her spirit guide (control), the Amerindian White Eagle, she was able to recall past lives as a Mayan, and as an Egyptian priestess and queen. The story of these lives is found in Cooke's book *The Illumined Ones*, White Eagle Publication Trust, Liss (Hants.) 1966. Cooke's (White Eagle's) teachings are continued through the Church of the White Eagle Lodge founded in 1934 in England.

See also **Egypt; Grant, Joan; White Lodge**.

Coptic Fellowship of America. Founded in 1937 in Los Angeles, California, by the Egyptian born Hamid Bey (?–1976), the Fellowship acknowledges the existence of hidden masters who teach esoteric Christianity that includes the concepts of reincarnation and karma.

See also **Ascended masters; Egypt**.

Cordovero, Moses. This sixteenth century Kabbalic teacher of **Isaac Luria** is believed by some Kabbalists to have been the reincarnation of the biblical Eliezer, the servant of Abraham. On the other hand, in a different kabbalic legend it says that this same Eliezer is one of nine persons who entered paradise without first having to die.

See also **Kabbalah**.

Corelli, Marie (1855–1924). Along with H. Rider Haggard, Corelli was one of the two most widely read Victorian novelists to bring the concept of

Corinthians   68

reincarnation and karma to popular British awareness. Corelli's works with these themes include *A Romance of Two Worlds* (1886), *Ardath* (1889), *Ziska* (1897), and *The Life Everlasting* (1911).

See also **Karmic romances**

Corinthians, 1st and 2nd. It is in 1st of these two New Testament letters by **Paul of Tarsus** that the earliest extent mention of the **resurrection of Jesus** is found; assuming that part of this letter, 1st Corinthians 15:3–7 is not a later interpolation. 1st Corinthians also mentions Jesus as a kind of second **Adam** who died to overcome the death that the first Adam's sin brought into the world (1st Corinthians 15:22, 45). 1st Corinthians 3:1–2, along with **Mark** 4:10–12, are often used to imply that there was an early Christian secret teaching that might have included the doctrine of **metempsychosis**. Trying to justify the presence of either a reincarnational or karmic view in this letter would seem to require a major revision of the meaning of Paul's words. Whatever so-called secret teaching Paul may have implied by these verses could only have included metempsychosis if one disregards all the numerous passages in which he repeatedly focuses on the resurrection of the dead.

2nd Corinthians 5:2–4 uses the metaphor of the body as clothes (of the **soul** or spiritual person) to be put on and taken off. This wording of the **body as a mere garment of the soul** has encouraged some people to read into these passages a suggestion of reincarnation.

See also **Annihilationism; Aquinas, Thomas; Christian atonement theories; Cayce, Edgar; Ephesians; Jesus; Karma in the Bible?; New Testament sacrificial concept; Old Testament and the soul; Patton, George S; Psalms; Resurrection, bodily; Resurrection of Jesus; Romans.**

Corporeal versus non-corporeal afterlife. Most people want to believe that death is not the end of their existence, yet find the whole idea of a non-corporeal state of being, where souls are presumably rewarded or punished, to be an unreasonable concept. For some of these people the idea that death, with or without a non-corporeal **interim period** between death and rebirth, is an acceptable alternative.

In fact, many who favor such a re-embodiment process also believe that it offers a less supernatural explanation of an afterlife than does any eternal non-corporeal existence. Since there is still the problem of how to account for the transference of consciousness from a deceased body to a newly conceived or newly born body it is questionable whether such rebirth is any less supernatural than a non-corporeal alternative.

See also **Rebirth, instantaneous**.

Cosmic memory *see* **Akashic Records**.

Cosmic picture gallery *see* **Akashic Records**.

Course in Miracles. In 1965 a university professor and psychologist, Helen Schucman (1909–1981), began to have visions and hear the voice of an entity that called itself **Jesus**. This entity told Schucman to write down what he was to teach her. It was this **automatic writing** that eventually was published in 1975 as the three volume book titled *A Course in Miracles*, (Foundation for Inner Peace, Glen Ellen, CA.) While the book quotes passages from the Bible, its over all teachings are a mixture of Christian Science–like mental or faith healing and a New Age version of Hindu-Buddhist beliefs.

When it came to the issues of reincarnation and karma, Schucman apparently had a very ambiguous view of them. On the one hand, according to her biography, *Absence from Felicity* (1991) by Kenneth Wapnick, she appears to have believed that she had experienced a number of often traumatic past lives, including one involving the crucifixion of Jesus; but on the other hand, Jesus is quoted as telling Schucman that most theories of reincarnation and karma are essentially magical and the whole question is not really necessary to religion at all. *Absence from Felicity* goes on to say that although the concept of reincarnation is inherently illusory it can serve a helpful purpose of helping people to counter the idea of hell, a belief that is hard for the ego to relinquish. In the end, however, beliefs in reincarnation and karma must be discarded, as they are still linked to a linear view of time, which is one of the ego's magic tricks to obscure the reality of eternity.

Schucman goes on to speak of the "genetic fallacy," a belief the ego eagerly holds on to and which reduces all current behavior and feelings to the past, whether these are attributable to former lives, genetic make-up, or early developmental experiences. The truth is that everything we do, think, or feel comes only from a decision made in the here and now.

It should be obvious that the Jesus channeled through Schucman is not considered to be the divine incarnation of orthodox Christianity; instead he is a man who attained Christ-consciousness.

See also **Noble lie**.

Creationism, soul. This is the belief that each **soul** is individually created by God at the moment of conception. Creationism denies any kind of **soul's existence prior to embodiment**. It is also in opposition to **infusionism, emanationism,** and **generationism and traducianism**.

For many reincarnationists there is a moral problem with soul creationism. They question the idea that a morally perfect and all loving God would automatically create a new soul to implant into a womb regardless of the conditions under which conception occurred. It is acceptable to them that God should create and implant a new soul in a newly conceived fetus, if such conception were in the context of the sexual intercourse of a married couple or, at least, a mutually desiring unmarried couple, but should God do the same in the case of a rape victim? This leads to the question can an embryo develop into a fully formed and functioning infant without the implantation of a soul by God? If no; then God is a criminal party to any conception due to a rape.

There is also a problem for those soul creationists who also accept the standard Christian belief that all human beings are punished for the sin of **Adam** and Eve. If new souls are created by God every time embryos are produced by human beings, why should these sinless souls suffer, when technically only the bodies in which God puts them would share anything with Adam and Eve as the physical ancestors of humanity? Does this not make God morally a sadist? To save God's moral reputation it could be proposed that God is some how forced to create a new soul for every body human beings conceive, in which case, God is partly controlled by the actions of mankind. This of course, reduces the omnipotence of God.

Rebirth avoids this creationist moral problem by placing the ultimate responsibility for a soul's womb implantation on the soul itself or its karma. Christian traducianism also offers a more logical, though not necessarily more just, explanation for the inheritance of original sin.

In all fairness to the Christian creationist perspective, however, the Christian response should be noted. According to this, since all human conceptions are a continuation of original sin there is only a matter of degrees of sinfulness between the lust of a mutually consenting couple and that of a non-mutually consenting couple. Furthermore, it might be argued that since sexual intercourse is a part of the human freedom to do good or evil, for God to interfere by granting or withholding souls would be to interfere with this freedom.

It is to overcome the problem of the transmission of original sin that some Christian traditions have favored generationism or traducianism, in contrast with creationism alone as orthodox.

See also **Arguments supportive of rebirth; Emanationism; Gender issue of the soul; Generationism and Traducianism; God and rebirth in the West; Karma and justice; Ontological leap or ontological discontinuity; Original sin, Christianity, and reincarnation; Original sin versus karma; Population increase issue and a theistic solution; Soul, origin of the.**

Cremation and rebirth. In Eastern religions it is believed that cremation of the deceased body aids the **rebirth factor** in detaching itself from being earth-bound so it can more easily and quickly achieve whatever it needs to prior to its next rebirth. The opposite is thought to occur with any kind of elaborate embalming.

See also **Critical time periods; Egypt; Ganges River.**

Criteria for sincere claims to rebirth *see* **Rebirth, criteria for proof of.**

Critical time periods. Some religious traditions believe that the deceased follow, or should follow, a fairly rigid schedule between the moment of death and whatever comes after that. In the first **Bardo** (of the *Tibetan Book of the Dead*) the deceased has only three and a half to four days to pass from the first level of the **interim period** into the second level. Moreover, the entire process from death to rebirth is said to be forty-nine days, which is seven weeks of seven days.

According to one Hindu view the journey of the **soul** to the underworld takes 4 hours and 40 minutes, so the body of the deceased must not be cremated before this time.

See also **Cremation and rebirth; Interim period.**

Cross-species rebirth *see* **Animals and rebirth, Western view; Christianity and reincarnation; Rebirth, cross-species; Transmigration, progress; Transmigration, regressive.**

Crowley, Aleister, originally Edward Alexander (1875–1947). Crowley was a notorious English occultist who practiced sexual magick and founded a religious cult called Thelema after the Greek word for "will." This represented his axiom "Do as you will, shall be the whole of the Law." Crowley began his occult interests after reading *The Book of Black Magic and of Packs* (1898) by Arthur Edward Waite (1857–1942), which led to Crowley's joining the **Hermetic Order of the Golden Dawn** in 1898, with the magical name of Perdurado. After a rapid rise in the order he came into conflict with its leader **W. B. Yeats** and was either pressured to leave or was expelled, which soon lead to his decision to seek his mystical fortune independently. It was in 1904 that Crowley had his major magic(k)al breakthrough. While visiting Cairo, **Egypt**, Crowley's wife entered into a trance and channeled an entity called Aiwass, who was said to be a representative of the ancient Egyptian god Horus. Crowley, who after this took the new magic(k) name The Master Therion (Greek: Beast), identified himself with the

Great Beast 666 or Anti-Christ in the biblical **Revelation of John**. It was also during this time that Crowley became convinced that he was the reincarnation of Ankh-fn-khonsu, an Egyptian priest of the XXVI dynasty (663–525 BCE). Later he identified his other former lives as the Ko Hsuen, a disciple of Lao Tzu; the Borgia Pope Alexander VI (1492–1503), who was infamous for his indulgence for physical pleasures; as the scryer Edward Kelley, who was the assistant to the Elizabethan occultist John Dee; as the charlatan alchemical occultist (Count) Alessandro di Cagliostro (1743–1795); and finally as the famous French occultist Eliphas Levi (1810–1875).

Crowley's new inflated image of himself led in 1906 or 1907 to his forming his own occult and sexual magick order, the Argenteum Astrum (Silver Star, i.e. Sirius), which functioned only until 1914. In the mean time, in 1912, he also joined the British section, the Mysteria Mystica Maxima, of the German sexual occult and magick group Ordo Templi Orientis (Order of the Oriental Templars). By 1922 he became the head of the British section.

Much of Crowley's extreme magical interests and practices can be partly explained by his long desire to somehow become a member of the **Great White Brotherhood**.

In later years Crowley's continuing reputation as a self-declared Beast 666 black magician gradually isolated him from society and by the time he died he was not only addicted to alcohol and drugs, but, according to some accounts, he had come to the belief that he was a **vampire**.

It is in Crowley's book *Magick in Theory and Practice*, chapter VI, The Magical Memory (1929) that the author affirms his belief in reincarnation. In fact, the opening line of that chapter states, "There is no more important task than the exploration of one's previous incarnations." Also, in Crowley's *The Equinox*, the official organ of the Argenteum Astrum, Liber Thisarb, CMXIII p. 105, Crowley gives a procedure for remembering one's past embodiment.

Although not considered a Neo-Pagan, Crowley's *Book of the Law* (*Liber Al vel Legis*) initially influenced the *Book of Shadows* (unpublished text) of Gerald Gardner, a major founder of the modern **Wicca** movement. This Neo-Pagan movement, however, later expunged most of Crowley's satanic views and practices from Wiccan literature. A number of modern Satanist groups, on the other hand, regard Crowley as a prophetic ancestor. Finally, Crowley's teachings appear to have had an influence on L. Ron Hubbard, the founder of **Scientology**.

See also **Ascended masters; Channeling; Esotericism versus Occultism; Fortune, Dion; Neo-pagan religions; Solar Temple, Order of; Spare, Austin Osman; Steiner, Rudolph; Templars.**

Crux Ansata see Ankh.

Crypt. Into one crypt, out of another. This is a metaphor for entering the first, or burial, crypt and exiting from the second (the womb). It's a variation on **tomb to womb, coffin to cradle;** and **death to breath.**

Cryptesthesia. This is an alternative term for psychic or extrasensory perception. It was coined by Dr. Charles Richet (1850–1935), a Nobel prize-winning physiologist and prominent researcher of psychic phenomena.

See also **Rebirth, alternative explanations to.**

Cryptomnesia. This is the sudden remembering of something long forgotten in one's life. The human subconscious accumulates an enormous amount of information to which the conscious mind has forgotten that it was ever exposed. Since innumerable cases of past life memories, including the famous **Bridey Murphy case**, have been shown to be entirely the result of cryptomnesia most critics of the rebirth concept point to this form of amnesia to account for all sincere past life memory cases.

In the opinion of some past life recall supporters some aspects of cryptomnesia can actually be used in support of genuine past life recall. The theory behind this is that if a person's present-life memory has gone to the trouble of abducting a present-life memory and applied it to a past life it may be because there was something about the abducted memory that was of real significance to the past life.

See also **Hypermnesia; Past life memory recall; Rebirth, alternative explanations to.**

Crystal gazing see Scrying.

Cult of Angels. A majority of non–Muslim Kurds practice one of several indigenous Kurdish pre-Muslim faiths that can loosely be labeled the "Cult of Angels" (Yazdanism), from *yazdani* (angel) in Kurdish. There are three extant branches of the Cult, namely **Yarsanism**, Yezidism, and Alevism. The latter are also known as Aliullahi or Ahl-i Haqq meaning "deifiers of Ali" who was the cousin and son-in-law of Mohammed, and became the fourth Caliph.

All forms of the Cult, past and present, hold a fundamental belief in luminous, angelic beings of ether, numbering seven, which protect the universe from an equal number of balancing dark forces of matter. Another shared belief, and a cornerstone of the Cult, is the belief in the reincarnation of souls along with incarnations of the deity constituting major and minor *avatars*.

Several now extinct religious movements may have their origin in some early version of the Cult of Angels. Among these could be one or more forms of **Gnosticism**; **Manichaeism**; and even **Mithraism**. Somewhat later it may have given rise to **Khurramiyya** and Druzism, and in still more modern times to Babism. In its present form the Cult shows many accommodations to **Islam**, with which over the past 1,400 years it has often had an antagonistic relationship. It is thought that perhaps 30–35 percent of all present-day Kurds follow various forms of the Cult.

See also **Babism and Bahaism; Druzes; Nusayris; Yazidis**.

Cummins, Geraldine Dorothy (1890–1969). This renowned Irish automatist medium had as her spirit control E.W.H. Myers, the co-founder of the (British) Society for Psychical Research. According to her control a new **soul** is born within a group, and has to take an earth pattern (karma) already laid down by the thoughts and actions of the soul's group predecessor.

Cummins claimed that people do not reincarnate hundreds of times or more; in fact, the majority reincarnate only a very few times. Cummins wrote *The Scripts of Cleopha*s, Rider and Company, London (1928), *Road to Immortality*, The Psychic Book Club, London (1947, originally 1932); *Beyond Human Personality*, Ivor Nicholson & Watson, London (1935), *They Survive*, Rider and Company, London (1946), *Mind in Life and Death*, Aquarian Press, London (1956); and *Swan on a Black Sea: A Study of Automatic Writing: The Cummins-Willet Transcripts*, Routledge & K. Paul, London (1965).

Cummins was very interested in practicing **psychic archaeology**. In particular she sought to obtain unknown or lost information regarding the early history of Christianity, especially of the time of the Apostles.

See also **Blocked regression; Finite or infinite number of rebirths; Group soul**.

Cumulative argument. This argument in support of rebirth states that while any single isolated argument used to justify the doctrine of rebirth may seem without convincing weight by itself, adding together a number of compatible individual arguments increases the probability of the truth of rebirth. This method of proof has been used time and time again because on the surface it seems logical and so has a certain popular appeal. However, despite its popularity the cumulative argument is not necessarily any stronger than any of the individual arguments of which it is made.

See also **Rebirth and the preponderance of evidence**.

Current knowledge discrepancy. This is a well-documented factor in many presumed past life memories. It is when a person describing a life in the past uses data that is commonly or currently assumed to be correct, but which an expert knows is incorrect or which a later discovery proves it to be incorrect. Examples of this are to describe camels in Old Kingdom **Egypt**, when they were not introduced until centuries later; to give a date such as 100 BCE for a past life when this Christian dating system did not exist until the early Medieval period; to state one had a life in the **lost continent** of Atlantis when modern science has shown its existence as a near impossibility; to remember a life as an intelligent being on a planet that could not possibly have evolved such a being.

See also **Past life memory recall; Planets, other; Rebirth and science; Rosemary case; Supernatural-in-the-gap process**.

Cycle mates. According to the **Grace-Loehr life readings** these are two or more souls that, more often than not, re-embody at the same time to interact with one another for certain cycles of those souls' development. Cycle mates are not as strongly bound as are **soul mates**, instead they are more like soul twins; in fact, **soul twins** are often cycle mates.

Cyclical time *see* **Rebirth and cyclical time**.

Dabistan. In this Persian Sufi manual of mystical lore, various forms of *tanasukh* (reincarnation) are mentioned, such as rebirth as a human being (*naskh*), as an animal (*maskh*), as a plant (*raskh*), or even as a mineral (*faskh*).

See also **Yarsanism**.

Daimones. This Greek derived term in Homeric times (12th century BCE) meant a supernatural power in its anonymous, unpredictable, and frightening form. By the time of the Greek philosopher, biographer, and priest of Apollo at Delphi, Plutarch (1st–2nd century CE) the term *daimones* referred to highly developed, blessed human souls which existed to guide recently deceased virtuous souls to heaven. The souls of the non-virtuous simply refused to accept the *daimones* assistance and so once again fell into repeated earthly rebirths.

As early as the Septuagint, the 2nd century BCE Greek translation of the Old Testament , the term came to mean, not a benevolent or deified spirit (*eudaimon*), but only an evil one (*kakodaimon*). This greatly altered meaning for *daimon* was continued by Christian authors.

The Septuagint-Christian meaning of *daimones* should not be confused with the later 16th century list of seven *daimones* associated with the then seven known celestial bodies.

See also **Angels and reincarnation; Lucifer**.

Dalai Lama. This title (Mongol: oceanic lama) was first given to Snam Gyatsho [Tibetan: bsod-nams rgya-mtsho] (1543–1588) the third supreme leader of the *Gelug-pa* [Tibetan: *dGe-lugs-pa*] School of Tibetan Buddhism by the Mongol ruler Altan Khan. It was then applied retrospectively to the two previous *Gelug-pa* leaders. It was also Altan Khan who originally installed the Dalai Lamas as the supreme temporal rulers of Tibet, a position which they held until the Chinese Communist seizure of Tibet in the 1950s.

The Dalai Lama is actually not considered a reborn **soul** in the sense that an ordinary person is thought to be. Rather he is considered by his followers to be the *Tulku* (incarnation) of **Avalokiteshvara** (Tibetan: Chenrezi) the **bodhisattva** of compassion. In other words, the Dalai Lama is an *avatar*, an incarnation of a being that has an exclusively celestial or divine origin, rather than any ordinary earthly origin.

When a Dalai Lama dies his successor must be discovered through a number of ritually required processes. First, before the old Dalai Lama dies he is expected to tell approximately where he will choose to be incarnated again. Second, the names of all children born in Tibet immediately after the death of the Dalai Lama are obtained by the abbots of the great monasteries throughout Tibet. Third, the college of lamas examines the astrological signs, consult the Shamanic *Lhamoi Latso* **Oracle**, and check other auspicious signs and omens for clues as to the place and family of the next Dalai Lama. Fourth, the names of three prospective children are drawn from the abbot's lists. Fifth, lots are drawn, more signs and omens checked and the chosen child is put to a test which consists of picking out the rosary, drinking cup, shawl, and other possessions of the late Dalai Lama from among similar objects never belonging to him. Finally, the successful candidate must have one or more auspicious marks on his body.

The Dalai Lama is not alone in the claim to be an incarnation of Chenrezi. The Gyalwa Karmapa Lama of *Kagyu-pa* [*bKa'brgyud-pa*] School of **Vajrayana Buddhism** is also so identified.

See also **Panchen Lama; Possession; Incarnation versus reincarnation; Russia, reincarnation in.**

Dali, Salvador (1904–1989). This famous Spanish painter apparently attributed his interest and ability to paint mystically luminous works to his having been in a past life the Spanish mystic Saint John of the Cross (1542–1591).

Damanhur. This is a spiritual community in northern Italy founded by Oberto Airaudi in 1977. The members of this community believe that there are certain lines of energy (synchronic lines) found all over the world which represent the nervous system of the earth. These lines converge in two significant places. One is in Tibet and the other is in the Piedmont valley just north of the city of Turin where Damanhur is located. Damanhur teachings include the belief that human beings share a divine nature and that through both reincarnation and an understanding of the Damanhur philosophy the realization of that divine nature can be fully gained.

Daniel, Book of. This last book of the Old Testament claims to have been written in the 6th century BCE, but was really a product of the 2nd century BCE. The book is theologically most significant for its unequivocal acknowledgement of a physical resurrection at the apocalyptic end of time. As such it is a direct challenge to any attempt to claim that the Old Testament clandestinely supports the concept of reincarnation.

See also *Akashic* **Record; Angels and reincarnation; Church Council of Lyons and Council of Florence; Hussein, Saddam; Old Testament and the afterlife;** *Psychopannychism*; **Resurrection of Jesus; Revelation of John.**

Daoism/Taoism. This native Chinese religious tradition did not originally include any concept of reincarnation; however, with the introduction of Buddhism into China, some forms of folk Daoism eventually adopted this belief.

See also **Chinese religion and reincarnation; Empire of Jade;** *Lingbao [Numinous Treasure] Scripture*; **Rebirth and cyclical time.**

Dark Brotherhood. This is said to be the opposite of the **Great White Brotherhood**. The Dark Brotherhood, according to the **Dhyani Chohan's Hilarion**, is not specifically evil since they are responsible for assisting the less spiritually developed persons for whom the Great White Brotherhood have no time; but they do have the adversary role of testing those who might may be candidates for the attention of the Great White Brotherhood. In some Theosophical groups this brotherhood is called the Black Brotherhood or the Brothers of the Shadow.

See also **Ascended masters.**

David, the Biblical King *see* **Adam; Frank, Jacob; Kabbalah; Koresh, David.**

David, Star of *see* **Star of David** or **Sign of Solomon.**

Davis, Andrew Jackson (1826–1910). This famous American spiritualist trance medium believed that he was channeling **Emanuel Swedenborg**, and claimed that he had received several spirit communications that stated that "reincarnation was nonsense" and at best was "a magnificent mansion built on sand."

See also **Diakka; Home, Daniel Douglas; Morse, J.J.; Spiritualism; Wickland, Carl**.

Dayaks. A native people of Sarawak (Western Borneo), some of whom believed that ancestors are reincarnated as **serpents**, therefore, serpents ought not to be killed.

See also **Indonesia; Rebirth, restricted**.

Dead Sea Scrolls *see* **Essenes**.

Death. Technically, this is the condition in which an organism can no longer be considered alive. Before modern medical technology was able to keep a human being's heart and circulatory system functioning despite irreversible damage to the person's brain, death was simply defined as the cessation of coronary functioning. Today brain death is considered a more practical indicator of death. No matter what the criterion for death is, it must be regarded as an irreversible process. This is the main reason why a so-called near-death experience can not be considered a case where the person's brain has died, and his consciousness left his body (the corpse), but then returned to the body and to life. This applies regardless of how short the period between the so-called death and return was; therefore, what are called near-death experience can not be used to prove that a soul or state of consciousness can exist independent of the body, which is an essential for any kind of reincarnation.

See also **Alzheimer's Disease; Astral body; Body-brain (mind) dependency; Eighth sphere; Kubler-Ross, Elizabeth; Mind; Out-of-the-body experiences** and **near-death-experiences; Second death**.

Death as punishment *see* **Original sin, Christianity, and reincarnation**.

Death panorama. This is said to be the experience of the recently deceased in which he or she views the whole of his/her most recent life as a timeless panorama rather than sequentially as would normally be the case. Some theories of reincarnation include this panoramic experience as part of the **interim period**.

Death posture *see* **Spare, Austin Osman**

Death, second *see* **Annihilation; Eighth Planet; Second death**.

Death to breath. Like **coffin to cradle** and **tomb to womb**, this is a metaphor for reincarnation.

See also **Crypt**.

Death trauma *see* **Birth trauma; Memories, reasons for loss of past life**.

Deathlessness *see* **Amrita**.

Deaths, violent and premature. The research on past life memories by **Dr. Ian Stevenson** has suggested that there are far more claims of rebirth for individuals who died prematurely and/or violently than for those who died under more normal circumstances. In general, 60–75 percent of his cases fit this category. In fact, some cultures that accept reincarnation believe that rebirth only happens to individuals who experience such deaths; all other people are born with new souls. These cultures suggest two main reasons for such selective rebirths. The first is that suddenness of the death left the deceased so disoriented that he or she was desperate to return to a normal embodiment. The second is that the suddenness left the deceased with "unfinished business" that required re-embodiment.

The fact that a claim to a violent death may elicit more attention towards a child supposedly remembering a past life has added to the belief that the child's memories may be more an attention getting mechanism than genuine memories. Also, the idea that violent and premature deaths may soon lead to a rebirth is an emotionally soothing factor for the average adult, especially one who has suffered a loss.

Stevenson, in fact, believed that people who died violently underwent quicker rebirths than those who died more naturally. He stated that he noted that children who recall having died violently start to verbalize about their former lives at a slightly younger age than do other children.

A different statistic comes from the psychologist **Helen Wambach** (1978, 1979). Out of a sample of 1,100 adult subjects she found 62 percent claimed natural deaths, 18 percent violent deaths, and 20 percent were of unknown causes. This would probable match the historical situation rather closely.

Among the Inuit (Eskimo) and other native people of Alaska and Canada rebirths are said to be far more common for individuals who died prematurely and/or violently.

On the other hand, the Chinese have a far different take on certain violent deaths. They believe that, at least, in the case of persons who have been hanged or drowned, their souls can not be reborn until they have arranged for another person to be hanged or drowned in the same place.

See also **Blocked regression; Children remembering past lives; Deaths, violent and premature; Karma as unfinished business; Old souls; Parents in the next life; Rebirth, selective; Rescue circles; Social Status of Past Lives**.

Deciduous trees. A tree's seasonal loss of leaves and seemingly winter death, followed by spring rebirth, is one of the analogies in nature that has suggested the concept of rebirth to ancient peoples *see* **Rebirth, analogies from nature.**

Deferred payment plan for the soul. This is an irreverent description of the Western belief in the general resurrection by some reincarnationists. The faithful die, but then they must wait until some distant future time to receive their reward. The advertised selling point for this is that compared to the joyful eternity with which those souls will be rewarded, even a relatively long, yet finite, wait is worth it.

See also **Resurrection, bodily; Theodicy.**

Dehiscent or Seed-pod Principle. This is the idea that a plant has to die in order to release its seeds and live again in a new manifestation. It may seem a great jump from the this seed-pod principle to Tibetan politics; nonetheless, this principle has been applied by some reincarnationists metaphorically to explain why a culture with such supposedly great spiritual adapts as Tibet could so easily be overwhelmed militarily by a materialistic China.

According to those reincarnationists two factors were at work here. First, the Tibetan Buddhist hierarchy was karmicaly punished for trying to hold on to their power by keeping Tibet an isolated backward feudal state. Second, compassionate cosmic forces (perhaps anonymous **bodhisattva**s) had finally decided that it was time for the rest of the world to be offered the profound teachings of **Vajrayana Buddhism**, but in order to do this those forces had to pry the reluctant lamas and *tulkus* loose from their mountainous monasteries and shove them out into the rest of the world. Although this meant great suffering for the possibly innocent Tibetan people, their sacrifice would eventually be rewarded in future-lives.

Actually this approach to the Tibetan tragedy was originally developed by Western theorists to counter the **blaming the victim** criticism.

See also **Ascended masters;** *Bardo*; **Blaming the victim vs. illusion of innocence; Bon-pa [po] religion; Dalai Lama;** *Tulku*.

Déjà vu (French for "already seen"). This is an impression of having seen or experienced something before. Advocates of rebirth regard certain *déjà vu* experiences as proof of reincarnation. However, there are a number of non-paranormal explanation for *déjà vu* that need to be examined before using it as any kind of proof of a past life.

First, while there can be a genuine sense of familiarity about just part of some stimulant, the mind often attributes this familiarity to the entire stimulant. Second, the *déjà vu* experience can be due to paramnesia, the subconscious combination of two or more authentic memories that suddenly enter consciousness. This gives the false belief that what should normally be experienced as something new is experienced as something familiar. Third, there is experience of double exposure. In this, the double functioning of the two hemispheres of the brain causes the subject to see something twice with only a fraction of a second between the two sightings. The mind interprets this as having seen something for a second time. Fourth, a trick of the mind can occur when a blinking of the eyes causes a distorted sense of time, which the mind again interprets as seeing something for a second time. Fifth, the mind, when encountering an unfamiliar and possibly threatening situation, reduces its level of anxiety by causing the situation to seem familiar and unthreatening.

The terms paramnesia and pantomnesia are the more scientifically psychological names for *déjà vu*, but when applied specifically to past life recall *déjà vu* is referred to as "intuitive past life recall."

When a *déjà vu* experience refers only to something that one believes he or she has heard before it is technically called a *déjà entendu* (already heard). An example of this would be when one travels to a place with an unfamiliar language and one feels that the sounds of that language are somehow familiar. Also, there is *déjà eprouve* (already experienced), *déjà senti* (already felt), even *déjà aime* (already loved). This last word would fall under the category of **Karmic romances.**

See also **Arguments supportive of rebirth; Children remembering past lives; Cryptomnesia; Olfactory psychic experience.**

Demiurge (Greek: craftsman). Originally used by **Plato** for the supreme creator, by the time of the rise of **Gnosticism** and **Neoplatonism**, it had come to mean an inferior, sometimes evil, deity that was responsible for the creation of the material world versus an all good, nearly unknowable higher deity who sought to liberate human souls from reincarnation into the this-worldly domain of the *demiurge*.

See also **Antinomianism; Archons; Basilides; Body-soul dualism; Bogomils; Carpocrates; Cathars; Gender issue of the soul; Manichaeism; Paulicians; Valentinus.**

Demonomancy. This is the practice of using demons for divinatory purposes. Conservative Christian and other religious groups regard **spiritualism, channeling**, and sometimes even delving into past lives as forms of demonomancy or demonic **sciomancy.**

See also **Angels and reincarnation;** *Daimones*; **Old Testament and the afterlife.**

Demonic possession *see* **Possession**.

Dependent causality *see* ***Pratitya-samutpada***.

De Rochas, Colonel Albert (1837–1914). This French psychical investigator seems to have been the first person to attempt age-regression under **hypnosis**. De Rochas describes his early work in such regression by magnetic sleep (hypnosis) in his *Les Vies Successives* (1911). De Rochas' first experience with regression was an accidental event in 1893, but it was not until 11 years later (1904) that it occurred to him to continue such regressions. One criticism of Rochas' regressions was that almost all of them claimed past lives as French men and women, which would be expected for his subjects who, for the most part, were not too educated and had little experience with travel abroad, and could not imagine lives elsewhere.

See also **Hypnotic age regression; Rebirth, proximity**.

Descartes, Rene (1596–1650). Descartes, philosopher, scientist, and mathematician, after starting with the premise "Doubt Everything" in order to arrive at an ultimate truth or reality, finally concluded that the only thing that could not be doubted was the doubting mind. As a result he was able to state "I think, therefore I am (Latin: *Cogito, ergo sum*)." From this basic premise Descartes claimed that one could logically believe in God and, by extension, the reality of the **soul**, which he also believed to be located in the human pineal gland.

The much earlier founders (4th–5th CE) of the **Yogachara School of Buddhism** began with the same basic premise "the questioning mind itself can not be doubted" premise to, by extension, affirmation of the reality of rebirth and karma.

See also **Astrology and rebirth;** *Chakras*; **Mind; Pineal and pituitary gland**.

Descent into hell (Christian) *see* **Harrowing of Hell; Limbo**.

Destiny *see* **Determinism; Karma and free will; Predestination**.

Determinism. This is the general belief that, to one degree or another, forces or powers outside of a person's individual control determines that person's life. Materialist determinism suggests that physical and historical events more or less determine the lives of people as groups and even as individuals. Added to this can be psycho-biological determinism that suggests that our behavior is far more determined by individual genetic and biochemical forces than most people realize.

General determinism should be carefully distinguished from **predestination,** which is the form of determinism that states that God has determined the ultimate destiny of people. A more extreme form of predestination is fatalism, which is the belief that all, or almost all, of the most important events in a person's life are predetermined or predestined by the powers that be (gods, God, the stars, etc.). Related to the issue of determinism is the issue of **karma and free will**. Some critics of the karma theory accuse it of leading to fatalism. While some ancient proponents of karma, such as the **Ajivikas,** were fatalists, **Hinduism, Jainism**, and Buddhism have always support free will to one degree or another.

A rejection of determinism (*ishvaranimmaanavada*) is essential to the **Middle Path** of Buddhism because without it one is incapable of escaping from the cycle of rebirth and re-death.

See also **Accidentalism; Asceticism; Astrology and rebirth; Eternalism; Hedonism**.

Deuteronomy 5:2–3. This is one of the passages that are sometimes used to argue that reincarnation is implied in the Old Testament. In this passage Moses is speaking to the Israelites. He says to them, "The Lord our God made a covenant with us at Horeb. It was not with our forefathers that the Lord made this covenant, but with us, all of us who are alive and here this day." Horeb is another name for Mount Sinai, and the covenant Moses is referring to was actually made with the generation of grandparents of those to whom he is speaking. In fact, the complete text implies that of those forefathers only three individuals are still alive. The usual and orthodox interpretation of this passage is that in making the covenant with the forefathers God was making it just as strongly with their descendants (grandchildren). The reincarnational interpretation of this passage is that the souls of the forefathers have been reincarnated into the bodies of their descendants; therefore, Moses is simply reminding those reincarnated forefathers of their earlier covenant. However, since, there must have been considerable generational overlap between grandparents and grandchildren this reincarnation interpretation is illogical. Also, the Israelite population of the later period was greater than of the earlier period, and this interpretation, naturally, is problematic in light of the **population increase issue**.

See also **Ecclesiastes; Exodus; Forty; Genesis; Kabbalah; Karma in the Bible? Old Testament and the afterlife; Old Testament and the soul; Psalms;** *Torah*.

Devachan (Dwelling of the gods). In **Theosophy** this is an **interim period** state between lives in which the **ego**, after leaving behind its lower sheaths (**astral body**, etc.) has time to peacefully or even blissfully contemplate its past and future.

The prominent theosophist James S. Perkins, in his book *Experiencing Reincarnation* (1977), states that spiritually advanced souls spend 1,000 to 2,000 years in *devachan*; that the souls of cultured self-disciplined people and those who have professional pursuits spend about 1,000 years there; that well-meaning and dutiful people spend 600–1.000 years there, and so forth, with the most primitive human beings spending only 30–40 years in *devachan*.

In **Vajrayana Buddhism** *devachan* can mean the **Pure-Land** paradise of **Amitabha Buddha**.

See also *Devaloka*; **Heaven**; *Kamaloka*.

Devaloka (World of the gods [*deva*]). In Buddhism this is one of the five or six worlds into which an ordinary human being can be reborn as a reward for wholesome karma. Although an extremely blissful state, it is just as impermanent as in all the others *kama-rupa* realms. Just as a **rebirth factor** is born into this realm due to virtuous karma, as soon as all that virtuous karma has been exhausted the rebirth factor must be reborn into one of the other four or five realms of *samsara*, and continue to be reborn and re-die until finally attaining **nirvana**. For this reason heavenly rebirth is not the highest goal in Buddhism.

It needs to be noted that all the entities in the *deva* realm are not benevolent beings. For example, the god **Mara**, the evil one, dwells in the *deva* realm.

Finally, among some Western reincarnationists the term *devas* is equated with the term angels.

See also *Abhavya*; **Astral plane**; *Asuras*; *Bhavachakra*; **Brahma and rebirth in Buddhism**; **Heaven**; **Nine doors**; **Pure-Land or Blissful Land Buddhism**; *Vimanavatthu*.

Devas (S. Gods) *see* ***Devachan***; ***Devaloka***.

Devil *see* **Lucifer (1)**.

Dharma Shastras (Law Commentaries). These are Hindu texts which outline the various rules (*dharmas*) for the establishment of a harmonious society. It was mainly through these texts, compiled from about 200 BCE onwards, that a widespread acceptance of reincarnation was established in **Hinduism**.

Dhyani chohans. This is a Sanskrit-Tibetan compound name used in **Theosophy** to mean meditation lords, and it refers collectively to former human beings who have become the **ascended masters** or Masters of the **Great White Brotherhood** (Lodge). These *dhyani chohans* are divided into three levels. The lowest consists of those who are still incarnated in human form; the second are those who, while disincarnated, are still accessible to human beings; and the third are those far too advanced for human consciousness to completely comprehend. Among these *dhyani chohans* are El Morya, **Hilarion**, **Jesus**, Kuthumi, **Saint Germain**, Venetian, and Serapis (otherwise an Egyptian god).

See also **Church Universal and Triumphant**; **Dark Brotherhood**; **Sinnett, Alfred Percy**.

Diakka. In Spiritualism this is said to be a sizable group of morally unclean souls that reside in their own part of **Summerland** and who deliberately seek to misguide poorly skilled mediums and others who try to investigate the afterlife. This would presumably include the subject of reincarnation. It may have been just this group of malicious souls that **Helena Blavatsky** included in her rather excessive condemnation of spiritualism after her very short interest in the subject. The name *diakka* comes from the work of the famous Spiritualist **Andrew Jackson Davis** (1826–1910) who wrote *The Diakka and their Earthly Victims*, (A. J. Davis Company, New York, 1873).

See also **Vampires**.

Diathanatic (Greek: carried through death). This term refers to whatever it might be that carries over from one life to another. For example, *diathantic* memory would be whatever memory one had in this life about a past life.

See also ***Psychophore***.

Dibbuk, Dybbuk (Hebrew: to cling, cleave). This is a form of malevolent **possession** described in the **Kabbalah**. Some sources state that a wicked **soul** (*nefesh*) becomes a *dibbuk* either because its sins block its journey into the afterworld and/or if the soul has not reformed after three lives (embodiment).

See also **Attached entity**; *Karet*.

Dichotomy. In reference to reincarnation, this refers to a view of the human being as a two part entity of the body and the **soul**, as opposed to a trichotomy of the body, the soul, and the **spirit**. While a dichotomy seem to be justified by some New Testament passages, a trichotomy is more commonly implied. In either case, if reincarnation is accepted it is the soul that would reincarnate, not the spirit.

Diogenes Laertius (2nd century CE). In his work *Lives and Opinions of Eminent Philosophers* (c. 220 CE) this classic author tells us that **Pythagoras** was able to remember a series of past lives beginning with Aethalides, the son of the god Hermes, who while denied god-like immortality, was granted the ability any lives he would live.

Dionysus. This ancient Greek deity is most commonly thought of simply as the god of wine and ecstasy; and this is exactly what he was, except when he is referred to as Dionysus Zagreus. In the Zagreus form he was the patron god of **Orphism**, a reincarnation believing sect that actually advocated abstaining from wine. There is nothing unusual about any Greek god having such opposite associations. The Greeks, like most pagan people, were not greatly concerned about keeping their theology neatly organized. Such organization is of concern only to a highly institutionalized priesthood, which the Greeks did not have. In accordance with any lack of consistency in most ancient mythology, in Orphism the mother of Dionysus Zagreus is the goddess Persephone, while outside of Orphism the mother is the mortal Semele. However, even in the non–Orphic myth Dionysus had a connection to death and immortality due to the story that he retrieved Semele from the underworld and guided her to the abode of the immortals.

See also **Double torches; Greeks and reincarnation; Priesthood, lack of an organized; Rebirth, analogies from nature; Theophilus.**

Disincarnation. This is the same as disembodiment; and as such it is the opposite of reincarnation.

Dissociation. This is a psychological process whereby there is a sudden, temporary alteration in the usual integrative functions of consciousness, identity, or motor behavior. If this alteration impacts consciousness, significant personal situations are not remembered. If this affects one's personal identity, either the individual's normal identity is temporarily lost to a new identity, or one's normal sense of reality gives way to a sense of unreality. This condition has been suggested as one way of explaining **channeling**.

See also **Multiple personalities; Trance states.**

Divided consciousness. This is the condition in which two streams of consciousness are present at the same time. It is a frequent condition during **hypnotic age regression** (past life regression). The person in this state is able to relive what is thought to be a past life while at the same time being completely aware of the present time and their identity. Divided consciousness is sometimes referred to as dual consciousness.

Divining past lives *see* **Dreams, announcing; Lhamoi Latso Oracle; Sciomancy; Scrying; Tarot.**

Doceticism. This term comes from the Greek meaning "to seem" and refers to an early Christian gnostic concept that denied that **Jesus** was born, crucified, and died in a real physical body. This denial was necessary for most Christian gnostics in that Jesus could not be trapped in matter and still be expected to be able to liberate others from such matter. This left Jesus as a pure spirit who created a kind of phantasmal or illusory embodiment in order to communicate his saving truth to embodied (entrapped) souls.

Some docetic Christians even used the gospel story at **Matthew** 27:32; **Mark** 15:21; and **Luke** 23:26 to argue for their view. In those passages Jesus was too weak to carry his cross so the Romans pressed into service the bystander Simon of Cyrene to carry the cross for Jesus. The docetic believers then argue that, through some clever, if not miraculous exchange, it was Simon, not Jesus who was crucified. This docetic down-playing of the resurrection allowed some gnostic Christians to replace the orthodox resurrection doctrine with a belief in reincarnation. To say the least, orthodox Christianity regarded doceticism as a damnable heresy.

The docetic view apparently was still strong enough in the late 6th century that it was able to influence Mohammed's view of the fate of Jesus. In the Quran, at *Sura* 4:157–158, it is stated, "They [the Jews] slew him not, nor crucified him, but it appeared so unto them; ... they slew him not for certain, But Allah took him up unto Himself."

The usual reason given for an original Moslem preference for a docetic view had nothing to do with favoring reincarnation; instead, it is an orthodox Islamic belief that a true prophet of God, which Jesus is considered to be in Islam, is sufficiently under divine protection so that no human action can ultimately harm him.

See also **Basilides; Emanationism; Gnosticism; Islam; Paulicians; Resurrection of Jesus.**

***Dor deah*.** This the Hebrew for "Generation of Knowledge" and is a reference to the Kabbalic idea that as a group the generation of the biblical flood reincarnated at the time of the Tower of Babel, and again at the Exodus, and now or very soon at the Age of Aquarius.

See also **Kabbalah; Rebirth, ethnic; Rebirth, group; Karma, racial.**

Double, The *see* **Shadow body.**

Double torches. In some Greek pottery the god Dionysus is flanked by two Maenads (frenzied female devotees) each of which carries a torch, one held up and the other held down. These are thought to represent the ascent (*anodos*) and rebirth or descent (*cathodes*) of the **soul**.

See also **Orphism.**

Dpal-gyi-rdo-rje *see* **Belgi Dorje.**

Dreams. Some people believe it is possible to recapture past life memories from the subconscious during sleep because of the temporary disengagement from the more critical elements of the conscious mind. Having a re-occurring dream of parts of a life in some past time has been interpreted as spontaneous recall of past life memories. Consistent daydreams are sometimes also thought to be related to past life memories.

The idea that dreams have deep psychological meaning has been around for a very long time. It was given some scientific validity by early depth psychologists, such as Freud and Jung. However, psychoanalysis, for the most part, eventually found dreams to be too unreliable for therapy in this life. This was reinforced by modern psychology which has done, and continues to do, a very good job of showing that most, if not all, of our dreams are related to working out problems in our present-day every day life, not in some past one.

See also **Arguments supportive of rebirth; Astral body; Silver Chord; Soul and spirit levels, Theosophical; Soul, psychology of; Souls, fixed and free.**

Dreams, announcing. These are dreams had by a parent or a close relative of a yet to be born child, which suggest to the dreamer that the child will be a reborn family member or friend. Such dreams are not uncommon among cultures that traditionally accept reincarnation. This foretelling of the future through dreams (oneiromancy), however, complicates any scientific investigation of the case since the child, if recalling a past life, may have memories influenced by the adult dreamer's expectations. Most serious past life researchers, therefore, do not give much credence to such dreams.

See also **Australian Aborigines; Consanguious Rebirth.**

Dreams, lucid. This is the dream state in which the dreamer knows he is dreaming. It has been suggested that some past life scenarios experienced while in a hypnotic state may be related to lucid dreaming. Lucid, or even just ordinary, dreaming of deceased persons has been proposed as one of the sources for a belief in an afterlife.

See also **Soul, psychology of.**

Drink or fruit of forgetfulness. In a number of mythologies the souls of the deceased, before being reborn, travels to a place where they are told to drink or eat a substance which will cause all memories of their former life to be lost. This is then said to be the reason that people can not remember past lives. In rare cases some individuals are believed to have avoided such consumption which accounts for their ability to remember parts of a past life. Some ancient Latin sources refer to this forgetfulness as drinking from the Chalice of Oblivion (Latin: *Oblivionis Poculum*).

Kabbalic literature has a slightly different take on this forgetfulness. It says that the night-angel Layela (Laila[h]) gives the about to reincarnate **soul** a pinch on the nose and a light push on the upper lip of the astral face of the soul that causes it to forget its past. The indentation on everyone's upper lip is believed to be the proof of this angelic touch.

See also **Hell, the Chinese; Kabbalah;** *Lethe*; *Mnemosyne*; *Nepenthean* **veil; Plato; Right-hand path and left-hand path.**

Drugs *see* **Body-brain (mind) dependency; Kingsford, Anna Bonus; Moore, Marcia.**

Druids. The Druids were the priesthood of the Celtic speakers of Gaul (ancient France) and the British Isles. The majority of evidence points to a belief in **transmigration** among at least the Celtic peoples of Gaul. The earliest known mention of the Druids of Gaul was by the Greek historian Timaeus (mid 4th–mid 3rd century BCE). This was followed by mention of them by the Greek Stoic philosopher Posidonius (about 135–51 BCE). However, neither of these men mentions anything about Druid beliefs. It was not until the Greek writer Diordus Silculus (60 BCE–30 CE) that there is a mention that the Druids of Gaul believed that the **soul** was immortal and passed from one body to another.

Julius Caesar, who conquered Gaul between 58 and 50 BCE, states in *book VI* of his *De bello galico (of the Gallic War)* that "They [the Druids] are chiefly anxious to have men believe the following: that souls do not suffer death, but after death pass from one body to another: and they regard this as the strongest incentive to valor, since the fear of death is disregarded."

No classical figure gives us any information about the beliefs of the Druids of the British Isles, therefore whether the belief on the continent also applied to the insular Druids is still under debate.

Under the modern name Druidry there was been a revival of what was thought was the ancient religion of the Celtic Druids, of course, minus the original Druid practice of human sacrifice and enemy head-hunting.

See also **Higgins, Godfrey; Morgannwg, Iolo; Neo-pagan religions; New Age religions; Spiritism; Summerland; Wicca.**

Druzes. This is a religious sect in Syria, Lebanon and Israel named after one of its founders, Al Darazi. It evolved out of a medieval heretical form of Shiite Islam which regarded one of the Fatimid caliphs of Egypt, al Hakim Bi-Amr (985–1021?), as an earthly manifestation or incarnation of God. Eventually abandoning the main requirements of

Islam, including observing Ramadan and the pilgrimage to Mecca, orthodox Muslims consider the Druzes to be apostates. The sect also adopted the non-orthodox Neoplatonic belief in the reincarnation (Arabic: *tanasukh*) of souls. The Druze community is divided into the majority of uninitiated lesser knowing believers and the minority of initiated sages.

The Druzes believe that everyone must undergo reincarnation into different life situations in order to attain purification and perfection. It is for this reason that everyone must experience a life of health and sickness, of wealth and poverty, etc. They further believe that when one of their ordinary members dies he or she is always reborn as a Druzes and always as the same sex, while when one of the perfected sages dies he or she ascends to heaven to live with God as a star. The Druzes do not have a belief in karma, since it is a personal God, not impersonal law that passes judgment. Therefore, for all those in the world who have not gained such astral immortality by the time of the Day of Judgment they will be sorted out and destined to either an eternity in heaven or in hell. For the Druzes there is no **interim period,** there is only instantaneous rebirth.

The world's highest percentage of **past life recall** is found among the Druzes. This gives rise to the issue of how much their religious belief itself influences such recall.

See also **Assassins; Children remembering past lives; Judgment of the Dead; Neoplatonism; Nusayris (Nursaris); Rebirth, instantaneous; Rebirth, ethnic; Sufism; Yazidis.**

Dual consciousness *see* **Divided consciousness; Multiple personalities.**

Dual or double souls *see* **American Indians; Australian Aborigines; Hunting cultures and reincarnation; Rebirth, simultaneous.**

Dual personality *see* **Multiple personalities**.

Dualism. This is the belief that reality comes in two irreconcilable forms. Among the major forms of dualism the following are most common:

(1) There is the belief that there is a fundamental opposition between the physical (bodily) realm and the spiritual (**soul**) realms. A large number of traditions that believe in reincarnation are dualist in this sense. Among these are **Jainism** and **Samkhya Yoga** practitioners; however, while both of these are forms of **body-soul dualism,** they are ontologically forms of pluralism because there is no attempt to find a single common ultimate source for all souls.

(2) There is the belief that the individual soul and God are separate and distinct from one another and, therefore, the human soul can never merge into the being of God. All orthodox Western forms of monotheism, as well as certain dual forms of **Hinduism**, are in this group.

(3) There is the belief that there is a fundamental or absolute opposition between good and evil. This absoluteness allows for no real moral compromising, hence any idea of the relativity of good and evil is regarded as heretical. **Zoroastrianism**, Christianity, and to a lesser degree Judaism and Islam are examples of such moral dualism in that what God demands is good and everything else is evil.

In each of these three forms of dualism there are to be found some traditions that accept reincarnation and some that do not.

Platonism, some forms of **Neoplatonism** and **Gnosticism, Manichaeism, Bogomils, Cathars, Patarines**; and **Paulicians** were generally of both the first, third, and in even some cases the second kind of dualism.

Reincarnational teaching traditions such as Hindu Advaita Vedanta and **Mahayana Buddhism** totally reject any kind of dualism for a non-dual or monistic ontological view of reality; nonetheless, both of these accept reincarnation.

See also **Brahman; Essenes; Fall of the Soul; Monism; Pantheism and panentheism; Pluralism.**

Ducasse, Curt John. Ducasse is the author of *Is a Life After Death Possible?* (1948); *Nature, Mind, and Death,* (1951); and *A Critical Examination of the Belief in a Life After Death* (1961). In each of these he gives his arguments for rebirth.

Duhkha/Dukkha. This term means "dissatisfaction or worrying" in life. In Buddhism, **Jainism**, and **Hinduism** the reality of *duhkha* is the main motivation for wanting to eventually escape from rebirth. The term *duhkha* too often is translated into English as "suffering, pain, ill, unhappiness, anguish," etc., but this suggests something akin to the opposite of, or the lack of, physical and mental comfort. The original meaning of *duhkha* seems to have been "a wheel with an off-center axle hole" hence "off kilter, always jolting or troublesome." The early Buddhist canon describes *duhkha* in the following context: Birth, sickness, old age and death are *duhkha*; union with persons we do not love is *duhkha*; separation from ones we do love is *duhkha*; not to obtain what we want is *duhkha*; and the **psycho-physical aggregates** that make up our being are *duhkha*. In other words, *duhkha* clearly stands for everything displeasing to us from a minor annoyance to a catastrophic event. The presence of *duhkha* does not deny the existence of pleasure or happiness in life, rather it suggests that no matter how much pleasure or how little pain there is, we can never truly find life satisfying or fulfilling. Of course, a major reason for this *duhkha* is due to the very weariness and tedium of rebirth itself.

See also ***Adhi-daivika duhkha; Anatman;*** Annihilationism, Buddhist view; ***Samsara; Shunya.***

Dweller on the Threshold. This phrase refers to the karmicaly produced astral remnants of a former life of a hedonistic or materialistic person. It is said that the Dweller, while residing on the **astral plane**, continues to influence physical re-embodiment in the next life as a kind of evil genius who inspires a life of suspicion, fear, and a continuation of self-destructive indulgence.

It is unclear if the Dweller on the Threshold is to be considered the same as, or different from, what is called the Guardian of the Threshold. Under the latter name the definition incorporates the residue of all of the unresolved negative karma, which can take on the externalized form of a demon that confronts a **soul** at the threshold to the higher spiritual world. This demonic form will prevent entry into that world by forcing the soul back into the round of reincarnation. When the karmic debt no longer blocks the way the soul will at last be able to enter into, and presumably remain in, the higher spiritual world forever. The term Guardian of the Threshold, with little doubt, arose from the frightening figures placed at the entrances of East Asian temples and on the borders of *mandalas*.

The astrologer Liz Greene, in her book *Saturn: A New Look at an Old Devil* (New York: Samuel Weiser, 1976), refers to **Saturn** as the Dweller at the Threshold, the keeper of the keys to the gate through which self-understanding is achieved and freedom won.

Under still a third name, Watcher on the Threshold, there is what has been identified as the ego's fear of growth and change, which must be faced and conquered. In the English Hermetic magical order, the *Aurum Solis* (Gold of the Sun), which was founded in1897, the Watcher is regarded as a misunderstood reflection of the higher self that has been molded into a fearful figure by the lower self's ignorance. In the view of **Alice Bailey**, the Watcher is the sum of all the distorted thoughts, feelings, and actions that a person has built up over past lives, which matches the above definition of the Guardian of the Threshold.

The modern concept of the Dweller, Guardian, or Watcher is said to have been at least popularized by, if not originated with, the mystical novel *Zanoni: A Rosicrucian Tale*, (Philadelphia: Wanamaker, 1842), by the occultist Sir Edward Bulwer-Lytton (1803–1873). The protagonist in *Zanoni* was loosely based upon the life of Comte de **Saint Germain**. Lytton was a Patron of the Societas Rosicruciana in Anglia (**Rosicrucian** Society in England), and was on friendly terms with the French occultist Eliphas Levi.

See also **Etheric body; Saturn; Silent watchers.**

Dying in peace. One argument in support of rebirth is that it allows a person to die peacefully. Actually this is only true if the dying individual believes he or she will attain a better, not a worse, rebirth. Peace can also come with the Western concept of the resurrection of the dead and of heaven. This suggests that, as far as a peace inducing belief, one after-life concept may be no more valid than the other.

See also **Rebirth, compensation and life fulfillment; Resurrection, bodily.**

Eady, Dorothy (1904–1981). This English Egyptologist became well known through her claim that she remembered a past life in ancient **Egypt**, where she was a priestess named Bentreshyt, who served at the temple of Abydos and was the lover of the 19th dynasty Pharaoh Seti I (1306–1290 BCE). In 1933 the psychic connection of Eady with Egypt caused her to move to Abydos and work for the Egyptian Antiquities Service. Eady co-authored, with Hanny El Zeini, *Abydos: the Holy City of Ancient Egypt* (1981). Eady's life story was published by Jonathan Cott under the title *The Search for Om Sety: A Story of Eternal Love* (1987).

Earth-bound. This usually refers to the **soul** of a recently deceased person that is having great difficulty divorcing itself from either its former body and/or from those persons left behind to which it has very strong emotional ties, positive and/or negative. It is said in some religious traditions that a show of excessive grief on the part of the living can encourage the earth-bound condition. In **Theosophy** earth-bound usually refers to a soul that is unable or unwilling to pass from the **etheric body** into the **astral body**.

See also **Creationism, soul; Etheric body; Jainism.**

East-West traveling. In some symbolic systems traveling east to west (rising to setting sun) means birth to death, while traveling west to east is death to rebirth.

See also **Sheep.**

Ecclesiastes. There are two passages from this Old Testament book that some reincarnationists believe helps prove that parts of the Bible clandestinely teach rebirth. Two such passages are found at Ecclesiastes 1:4 and 1:9–11. The first of these reads, "Generations come and generations go, while the earth endures forever." In this passage the word 'generations' is taken to mean a series if life-times for each person, especially by some Kabbalists. The second passage reads, "What has happened will happen again, and what has been done will be done again, and there is nothing new under the sun." Both passages, read in their proper context, show that they refer to an attitude of pessimistic world weariness. The earlier verse, 1:2–3, tells us, "Emptiness, emptiness, says the Speaker, emptiness, all is empty. What does man gain from all his labor and his toil here under the sun?" This is reinforced at verse 1:8a, "All things are wearisome: no man can speak of them all."

Like almost any passage in the Bible, if taken out of its greater context it can be distorted to mean anything someone wants it to mean. Any belief that reincarnation is implied in Ecclesiastes would certainly have to explain away Ecclesiastes 9:5–6, and 10, which are among the most explicit nearly annihilationist set of passages in the Old Testament. In fact, as a whole, Ecclesiastes is the most pessimistic, indeed, cynical, book in the Bible. Its main theme is the ultimate vanity and emptiness of life in the face of either near or full obliteration at death. The only other book that comes close to this cynicism is that of **Job**.

See also **Annihilationism, Biblical view; New Testament and reincarnation; Old Testament and the afterlife; Peter, 1st and 2nd; Silver Chord**.

Ecclesiasticus or the Wisdom of Jesus Son of Sirach. Verses 41:8–9 in this apocryphal book read, "Woe to you, godless men who have abandoned the law of God Most High! When you are born, you are born to a curse, and when you die, a curse is your lot." The reincarnational argument for this passage is that the reason men would be born to a curse as stated in line 2 is because they had been the godless men in line one. This should logically mean that they had been godless before birth, hence, in a previous life. Furthermore, they would not in their new life be able to overcome their godlessness sufficiently to escape punishment in the future. However, the emphasis in the following passages on a person of good reputation out living a god-fearing person and the reputation of a bad person ending in ruin would seem to negate any reincarnational meaning to the original passage.

See also **Deuteronomy 5:2–3; Ecclesiastes; Old Testament and the afterlife**.

Eckankar. The name Eckankar is derived from the modified spelling of the Hindi-Punjabi words for one (*ek*) and God (*onkar*). As the name of one of the **New Age religions** it was founded in 1965 by Paul Twitchell (1908–1971). In 1950 Twitchell joined the Self Revelation Church of Absolute Monism under Swami Premananda, but under controversial circumstances left to become the student of a Hindu-Sikh teacher, Kirpal Singh, who taught the Divine Science of the Soul. Also, for a short time he was a member of **Scientology**. Most of the Eckankar teachings seem to be derived from these sources. However, according to the official Eckankar position Twitchell received the teachings from a secret line of celestial masters or adepts, who initiated Twitchell into their order in 1956. Since 1981, their spiritual leader has been Harold Klemp.

A major teaching of Twitchell was that the **soul** can leave the body at will, especially during sleep, and travel to wherever it chooses. For this reason the Eckankar movement at first designated itself as the teaching of "The Ancient Science of Soul Travel." This was later replaced by the slogan "The Religion of Light and Sound."

Reflecting this new designation, Eckankar teaches that after a series of reincarnations the ultimate goal is to realize God in his dual nature of light and sound and so to became a co-worker with God. To facilitate this goal one is to undertake the practice of chanting the sacred Sufi word "*Hu*."

See also **Ascended masters; Astral travel; Sikhism**.

Eclesia Catolica Cristiana. This is a religious organization founded in Puerto Rico in 1956, originally under the name Spiritualist Cristiana Church, by Delfin Roman Cardona. It changed to its present name in 1969. It is a mixture of Roman Catholicism and the Spiritist teachings of **Allan Kardec**, which include a belief in reincarnation.

Edwards, Paul. Edwards is the author of *Reincarnation: A Critical Examination* (1996). While the argument of the book is very thorough, the sarcasm of the author towards genuine believers is extreme. It is no wonder that this book has made him a primary antagonist to believers in reincarnation. A major critique of this book can be found in *A Critique of Arguments Offered Against Reincarnation* (1997) by Robert Almeder.

See also **Astral body; Minimalist Reincarnation Hypothesis; Ransom Report**.

Eggs. In **Orphism** eggs were a symbol of rebirth and since the goal was to escape rebirth any association with eggs, including eating them, was to be avoided. In contrast to this eggs are a Christian symbol of resurrection, which is one justification for their use at Easter.

See also **Beans**.

Ego (Latin: I). In common speech this is the sense of I-ness or selfhood. The word is most closely associated with the depth psychologies of **Sigmund Freud** and **Carl Jung;** however, in the context of theories of reincarnation ego means something very different from those of **depth psychology.**

In Western philosophy and religion the ego is thought of as the fundamental aspect of personal or individual reality. In fact, there is usually thought to be very little, if any, difference between the ego and the **soul.** This positive view is followed by **Theosophy.** Among some Theosophists the term ego may be used to mean the permanent element of personhood, in which case it is similar to the Hindu *atman*. However, in other cases the term ego is used as the collective name for the immortal mental, intuitional and spiritual bodies. In still other cases, the ego is the storage place for all positive memories from one or more past embodiments and experiences all the rewarding thoughts from one or more past lives after the dissolving of the **astral body** and any negativity in it.

In theosophical views it is generally agreed that if the ego in its previous life has not developed the necessary virtues and wisdom to avoid reincarnation, which is the case for the overwhelming majority of egos, then once it has sufficiently reflected on its past merits it will form around itself a new **astral body** and **etheric body** and so be drawn back to a new embodiment.

On the other hand, if the ego has developed sufficient wisdom and virtue then it too will dissolve, like the previous non-corporeal bodies, which makes it part of the "mortal" soul. This leaves only the "immortal spirit," with its three upper levels (***manas, buddhi, atma***), of which no part ever enters into the materiality of the physical body but remains forever uncontaminated in the world of pure spirit.

In **Hinduism** the ego in the sense of a personal self is *ahankara* (the I-maker) and is considered to be an inferior or false aspect of one's true or ultimate impersonal self (*atman*). In Buddhism this *ahankara* is considered little more than insubstantial mental delusion (*anatman*).

See also **Causal body;** ***Devachan;*** **Id, Ego, Superego; Individuality and rebirth; Mental plane; Soul and spirit levels, Theosophical.**

Egypt. Since the Egyptian civilization is the second oldest in the world it has seemed very important to some reincarnation advocates to prove that the ancient Egyptians not only believed in reincarnation but exported that belief to the rest of the ancient world. However, despite the many attempts of ancient, medieval and modern reincarnationists, as well as of Hollywood popular entertainment, there is no indication that ancient Egyptian religion included the concept of reincarnation. This fact should be obvious. Since reincarnation minimizes attachment to or identity with one's current body there would have been no reason for the Egyptian obsession in preserving the corpse (*khat*) as properly prepared (*tut*), especially a properly ritualized or sanctified mummy (*sah*). Even more to the point, the costly building of pyramids to protect the deceased body would have made no sense if the Egyptians believed in reincarnation. A better corollary between a belief in reincarnation and an attitude towards a deceased body is found in the Indo-Buddhist world were cremation is the standard practice.

References to the surviving elements of a person are not consistent in Egyptian literature; nonetheless, the following concepts about those elements seem fairly common. The Egyptians believed in a kind of spiritually entombed "resurrection," which involved the existence of up to eight factors beyond the body. The precise meaning of some of the names of these factors is still in doubt, but the current consensus is as follows. The physical body (*khat* or *kha*) was subject to death and decay, unless preserved by mummification. The vital force (the *ka*) upon leaving the body brought about death. That which made an individual a unique personality (the *ba*), like the *ka*, would live after the body died. Priestly ceremonies were conducted to allow the *ba* to be united with the *ka*, creating an entity known as an *akh* (effective one). This *akh* (*akhu, khu,* or *ikhu*) lived on in the intellect and moral intentions of the person (the *sahu*), and it was this *sahu* which lived in the heavens with the gods or the permanent stars. However, *sahu* only came into being after the "judgment of the dead" was successfully passed. There was also the incorporeal personification of the life force of a person (the *sekhem*) which also lived in heaven with the *akh.*

A person's shadow (*khaibit, haibit,* or *sheut*) was also always part of the **soul.** It was believed a person could not exist without this in this life or the next. For this reason statues of people and even deities were sometimes referred to as their shadows.

There was also the true name (*ren*), as a part of the soul; a deceased person could continue on in the afterlife only as long as his or her *ren* was spoken, and so to avoid obliteration after death efforts were made to sustain it by placing it in numerous writings.

Finally, there was the heart (*ab* or *ib*) which was thought to be the most important part of the soul because after death it would give evidence for, or against, its formerly alive self when the gods conducted "the weighing of the heart" (***psychostasis***) ceremony.

If the care taken to preserve the material body through mummification was not enough to counter any belief that the ancient Egyptians believed in reincarnation then certainly that soul weighing ceremony should make it clear; because standing next to the balance that weighed the *ab* to determine its virtues versus its vices was the monster goddess Ammut (Ammit or Amemait) which meant the devouress [of souls]. If the *ab* weighed more than the feather of Maat (goddess of truth), the *ab* would be immediately consumed by the demon, thus ceasing to exist, rather than dwelling in the house of eternity (*hut en neheh* or *per-djet*).

That the Egyptians had no belief in reincarnation can also be demonstrated by one of their creation myths. In this it was believed that the creator god Khnum or Path, after creating the essence of a person inserted it into women's womb. In short, there was no place here for reincarnation.

Perhaps no modern esoteric tradition has made more of an effort to assign a reincarnationist belief to pre–Hellenistic Egypt than has **Theosophy**. In that tradition it has been claimed that of the fifteen gates of the Egyptian underworld of Osiris (*Amenti*) there were two chief ones. These were the entrance gate of death (*rustu*) and the exit gate of reincarnation (*amh*). Furthermore, it has been claimed that the Egyptian scarab god, **Khepra**, was the presiding deity over reincarnation. In fact, that god symbolized resurrection, not reincarnation.

When the historical records are carefully checked they show without any ambiguity that the concept of reincarnation did not enter Egypt until the later Hellenistic (Greek) period (2nd century BCE to 3rd century CE) when elements of Greek **Orphism** became popular in Egyptian gnostic circles.

The tendency to try to associate rebirth with pre–Hellenistic Egypt is partially a carry over from the 17th–18th century heliocentric theory. This was the belief that if the Egyptian civilization was earlier than any other ancient civilization it must have been the ultimate source of all spiritual wisdom. Actually, the ancient Greeks seem to have been an even earlier proponent of this theory. They and the later Romans did not realize that the ancient Egyptians never thought of their own religion as particularly mysterious. Instead it was always outsiders who mistook as esoteric what was to the Egyptians just a strong attachment to their own gods.

A more modern form of heliocentrism arose in the early19th century and influenced a number of Western religious and quasi-religious movements. This heliocentrism was boosted by the attempt to connect Mesoamerican (Toltec, Aztec, and Mayan) pyramid building cultures with their Egyptian counterpart.

The heliocentric theory continued to be popular in some esoteric quarters even throughout the 20th century despite the fact that Western archeologists had clearly acknowledged that even older than the Egyptian civilizations was the Sumerian civilization.

Also, during the late 19th and early 20th century those Western occultists who wished to try to harmonize their occultism to some degree with Christianity tended to favor Egyptian esoteric teachings over oriental ones because they believed that Egyptian esotericism was more compatible with Christianity. For example, the oriental emphasis on karma seemed to interfere with the Western occult emphasis on spiritual perfection through alchemy. Nonetheless, most of these pro–Egyptian occultists still favored the idea of reincarnation which, of course, meant that they would have to go out of their way to impose that belief on the ancient Egyptians. This association of reincarnation with ancient Egypt for the past century and a half has only been strengthened by the large number of individuals who have claimed past Egyptian lives.

The real issue concerning claims of having had a past Egyptian life is not necessarily the large number of people that have made the claims. The fertility given to Egypt by the Nile River has for thousands of years allowed for that country to sustain a vastly greater population than many other parts of the world. In fact, ancient Egypt may have had a greater population than all of Europe before the rise of Greek civilization.

The Egyptian civilization also covered a period of nearly three thousand years. This alone could account for the number of claimed past Egyptian lives. The real issue is that most of the claimed Egyptian lives are of rulers, priests, temple dancers, and other high status or exotic professions. In particular, many past life recallers have claimed to have had a past life in some relationship to the heretic Pharaoh Akhenaton, the female pharaoh Hapshepsut, and at least one of the Pharaohs mentioned in the Old Testament. Yet, since 90 percent of the Egyptian population would likely have been peasants and/or slaves it seems strange that these social classes are missing in most past life claims.

Another weakness of these claims is often demonstrated by the **current knowledge discrepancy** factor. This means that those individuals often use names or terms to describe the Egyptian scene that would not have been used by an ancient Egyptian. For example, numbering pharaohs as in Ramses I, Seti II, Amenhotep III, etc. are designations only applied to Egyptian rulers by 19th century Egyptologists. Also, an ancient Egyptian would never refer to the great religious center of Egypt as "Thebes" since this is a much later Greek name for the Egyptian "Weset or Newt."

Most recently, the ancient Egyptian connection is notable among channeled beings. The majority of them seem to have either Egyptian or Egyptian sounding names; for example, one is named **Ra** who was also the Egyptian supreme sun god, another is named **Seth** who was the dark brother of the god Osiris, and there are the Egyptian sounding names of **Ahtun Re, Mafu** and **Ramtha**.

See also **Alexandria, Egypt; Arguments supportive of rebirth; Book of the Dead (Egyptian); Channeling; Chnoumis; Crowley, Aleister; Dhyani Chohans; Eady, Dorothy; Esotericism versus Occultism; Essenes; False claims of support for reincarnation; Fluorite; Gnosticism; Grant, Joan Marshall; Greeks and reincarnation; Hawkman; Hermetic philosophy; Hermetic Order of the Golden Dawn; Herodotus; Hollywood and reincarnation; Kubitschek, Juscelino; Mormonism; Mummy, The; Phoenix; Rosemary case; Second death; Social status in past lives; Solar Temple, Order of; Soul; Steiner, Rudolf; Tarot cards; Theophilus;** *Thoth, Book of*.

Eighth sphere. In Hermetic works the eighth sphere is identified as the **Milky Way**, a reaching of which was the ultimate goal of the **soul**.

In **Theosophy**, however, the eighth sphere is also called the planet of death. As such it is the place or state of being where lost souls pass into non-existence. This is due to their evil having made them so unredeemable that they can not be reborn even into the worst of conditions. When it is thought necessary to assign a physical site to this state it is usually the **moon** that is chosen and which is then given the name the dark satellite.

This eighth planetary aspect is not to be confused with the eighth zodiacal house in astrology which is also associated with death.

See also *Abhavya*; **Angels and reincarnation; Annihilationism, Biblical view; Astrology and rebirth; Gabriel;** *Ichantika*; **Planetary descent and ascent of the soul; Second death.**

Elect or chosen of God. This is a concept found in the New Testament that only a select few men and women will eventually be chosen by God to be saved and share in the messianic kingdom. It is specifically mentioned at **Matthew 24:22, Romans 8:33,** and **Titus 1:1.** Since such a concept is at odds with most ideas about the reason for **reincarnation** those who try to impose a reincarnationist teaching on the Bible find it convenient to ignore this election concept.

See also **Karma and free will; Karma versus grace; Predestination.**

Electra/Oedipus Complex and rebirth. According to a number of rebirth schema a **soul** that is to be reborn in a female body will, upon being attracted to a copulating couple, experience a great lust for her father to be, while the souls of a future son will lust for his future mother. This does not seem to give much credit to the sperm and egg in the fertilization process. One question that needs to be asked is what happens if the soul of a perspective female embodiment finds only that a genetic male embryo have formed in the womb, or vice versa for a male oriented soul faced with a female embryo? Is this what causes **homosexuality and transsexuality**? If so one would expect a much larger homosexual percentage in the general population. Perhaps the assumption is that these minority or atypical orientations develop sometime after conception.

Another question is what happens if the male is using a condom, if the woman is using a birth control pill, or if one of the copulating pair is sterile. Does the **soul** enter the womb only to need to exit it? Also, if copulation is oral or anal does the soul ever get confused and try to enter the wrong orifice? It would seem far simpler just to assume that the soul becomes embodied only after the embryo has been conceived. Unfortunately, however, such post-conception embodiment creates its own set of problems with regard to **karma and rebirth**.

See also **Child as its own reborn father or mother; Embodiment, moment of;** *Gandharva*; **Gender issue of the soul.**

Elementary *see* **Kama-rupa.**

Elijah/Elias. One of the main arguments given for the claim that the earliest Christian community believed in **metempsychosis** is that there are passages in the New Testament that "supposedly state" that the 9th century BCE Old Testament prophet Elijah was reborn as **John the Baptist**. According to biblical legend Elijah was one of the very few individuals said to have been assumed into heaven in body as well as **soul**. This saved him from a dismal ghostly existence in *Sheol*. The reason for this miraculous event apparently was so that when it is the time for the Messiah to arrive, Elijah will be sent ahead to herald this arrival. This being the case, it might be wondered how Elijah could reincarnate if he had not first physically died.

Among the passages cited by reincarnationists in support of their view of Elijah's **reincarnation** is **Mark 9:13; Matthew 11:13–14; 17:12–13;** and **Luke 1:17.** Mark reads, "However, I tell you Elijah has already come and they have worked their will upon him [persecuted and killed him], as the scriptures say of him." Matthew, borrowing from Mark, reads, "For all the prophets and the Law [Torah] foretold things to come until John [the Baptist] appeared, and John is the destined Elijah, if you will but accept it." "I tell you Elijah has already come and they failed to recognize him, and they worked their will upon him, in the same way the Son of Man [Jesus] is to suffer at their hands." Luke, also borrowing from Mark, reads, "He [John] will go before him [the Messiah] as a forerunner, possessed of the spirit and the power of Elijah, to reconcile, father and child, to convert the rebellious to the ways of the righteous, to prepare a people that shall be fit for the Lord." To further add support to this claim of John as a reincarnated Elijah some have cited Malachi 4:4–5, "Look, I will send you the prophet Elijah before the great and terrible day of the Lord comes."

If taken out of context, these passages, especially Luke, do sound as if Elijah was reborn as John, but when they are examined in context it becomes clear that John is being spoken of only metaphorically as a prophet "in spirit and power" like Elijah. In fact, in the Gospel of **John** 1:21 the personal (reincarnational) identity between Elijah and John is clearly denied. The passage reads, "'Are you [John] Elijah?' 'No,' he replied."

That reincarnation is not implied in the Gospels is further shown by Mark 8:27–28, and the corresponding passages in Matthew (16:13–14) and Luke (9:18–19). In these **Jesus** asks his disciples who the people think he [or he as the Son of Man] is? They answer, "Some say John the Baptist, others **Elijah**, others Jeremiah, or one of the prophets [come back to life]."

It can be argued that by saying that Jesus was thought of as possibly the returned Elijah, Jeremiah, or another prophet that the people are possibly acknowledging the doctrine of reincarnation which was at that time known from the Greeks; but since John the Baptist had only been executed shortly before Jesus' question, to have an authentic reincarnationist implication one would have to eliminate John the Baptist from this list. With John included, some sort of **possession** would be more likely implied. Such a possible possession is reiterated when King Herod, having murdered John, was also afraid that Jesus was possessed of John's spirit as in Mark 6:14–16, Matthew 14:1–2, and Luke 9:7–8.

Also, any idea that either Mark or Matthew implies a reincarnational connection between Elijah and John the Baptist should be negated by the accounts of the "Transfiguration" given by Mark (9:2–5), Matthew (17:1–4), and Luke 9:30. In these, Jesus has gone up to a high mountain in the company of three disciples, Peter, James, and the disciple John. There they see a transfigured Jesus conversing with Elijah and Moses. If the disciples had believed that Elijah had reincarnated as the Baptist, then considering that John had been executed by that time, it can be argued that it would be more natural for the two figures conversing with Jesus to have been a recognizable John and Moses.

Obviously none of these arguments against a biblical interpretation of an Elijah to John reincarnation have convinced major supporters of a pro-reincarnationist view; in fact, such a major figure as **Rudolf Steiner** continued to support the "out of context view" of Elijah as the Baptist. Indeed, Steiner even added to the issue by claiming that the Elijah as the Baptist was later reborn as the Renaissance painter Raphael (1483–1520), and still later the German poet Novalis, the pseudonym of Fredrich Leopold Freiherr von Hardenberg (1772–1801). This all seems rather strange if Elijah is supposed to wait in heaven to herald the Messiah.

Leaving Christian views aside, kabbalic Jewish sources have their own view of Elijah and reincarnation. According to one of these, before becoming Elijah, his soul had multiple lives, the most famous of which was Pinehas, the grandson of the priest Aaron, brother of Moses.

See also **Carpocrates**; **Kabbalah**; **New Testament and reincarnation**; **Origin**; **Son of Man**; **Vintras, Eugene**.

Elysium Fields *see* **Grant, Joan Marshall**; **Greek afterlife, the ancient**; **Moon**; **Right-hand path and left-hand path**; **Soul, tripartite**; **Virgil**; **Y**.

Emanationism. This term refers to the Neoplatonic explanation of the origin of the universe in general, and of the human **soul** in particular. It taught that in the primordial past, from the One (God) emanated divine *nous* (pure intelligence) from which, in turn, emanated the world soul (*anima mundi*). It was from this single divine soul that all individual souls emanated and they, either mistakenly or foolishly, produced the matter that made up the physical bodies into which those souls became trapped. In the Neoplatonic-gnostic schema of salvation it was, therefore, the goal of all those individual souls to try to regain their freedom from this entrapping matter and to merge back into the world soul, and eventually even back into the One. This concept of the soul's origin was rejected early on by orthodox Christianity on the basis that it both destroyed the separation between perfect God and imperfect humanity and that it was generally associated with gnostic **doceticism**, that denied that **Jesus** was born into, suffered, and died in a physical body.

See also **Creationism, soul**; **Gnosticism**; **Infusionism**; **Neoplatonism**; **Traducianism**.

Embalmment of the dead *see* **Cremation and rebirth**; **Egypt**.

Embodiment, moment of. A major argument among reincarnationists concerns at what point in time the deceased entity (**soul**) takes on a new body. There are those that argue for an entrance into the womb some time before conception, or fertilization of the egg cell; others argue for entrance into the womb at the exact moment of such fertilization. Still others argue for a post-conception, but a pre-birth entrance. Lastly, a very few reincarnationists argue for a post-birth, or extra uterine, rather than any intrauterine re-embodiment.

Considering that between two-thirds and three-fourth of all embryos that are naturally conceived spontaneously abort it would seem more efficient for souls to become embodied at later point in a pregnancy than an earlier one.

According to the teachings in *Earthly Cycles* (1994) by the channeled entity Alexander as channeled through Ramon Stevens, no soul fuses with the embryo within the first three months of its intrauterine life, except in the case where a mother-child relationship was established before the mother's birth due to some karmic link. The reason for the wait is avoid as much as possible the chance of spontaneous abortion.

Wagner Alegretti, in his *Retrocognitions* (2004), states that the reincarnating entity aligns itself for the first time to its new body as soon as the infant takes its first breath and the umbilical chord is cut, normally about nine months or 36 weeks, unless it is prematurely born. However, this is initially a tenuous alignment that will have to grow stronger as the child matures into an adult; and will not be completed in most cases until around the age of 26, when the body stops growing.

One medically determined suggestion is that the rebirth occurs about the time that a fetus could survive outside the womb with proper medical care, which is about 175 days (25 weeks) after conception; although in rare cases the fetus might be able to survive and develop outside the womb as early as 20 weeks. The 20 week stage is the earliest that the neurological development of the fetus can be thought to experience distress (*samsara*). For this reason it has been suggested that this is a likely time for the soul to undergo embodiment.

Another indicator for the embodiment moment is said to be related to the factor of identical twining or other multiple birthing. If it is assumed that each twin, triplet, etc. has received a totally separate soul then embodiment ought to come only after the fertilized egg cell from which all the siblings will be produced has fully divided into separate embryos. Of course, one could always propose that the twining, etc. was itself due to the earlier presence of two or more souls having entered the womb and that multiple identical children are due to soul influence upon the original single fertilized egg cell. The only other alternative would be that of **soul-fission**.

Finally, the more embryologically sophisticated reincarnationists believe that any concept of how early a soul seeks embodiment must to take the following timing into consideration. Technically, embryo formation does not occur right after the sperm fertilizes the egg. This is because the egg is not yet prepared to fuse with the sperm's genetic material (DNA). This fusion process actually takes about twenty-four hours. Until that happens one ought not to think of the embryo as a genetically complete organism.

See also **Astrology and rebirth; Creationism, soul; Electra/Oedipus Complex and rebirth; Emanationism; Embryonic fusion; Genesis; Hovering of the soul; Infusionism; Magnetic attraction metaphor; Possession;** *Pratitya-samutpada;* **Soul's existence prior to embodiment; Rebirth and abortion; Rebirth and artificial insemination; Rebirth in Buddhism; Scientology; Soul twins; Stake a claim; Traducianism; Welcomers.**

Embryonic fusion. This is the rare process in which two non-identical fertilized eggs or pre-embryos fuse and produce one single individual which is technically referred to as a *chimera*. The result can be a single fetus having two different blood types, some cells that have XX chromosomes and others that have XY chromosomes, or even a full set of female and male sexual organs. When the last of these occurs the individual is genuinely a hermaphrodite. This fusion is, obviously, the direct opposite of the production of identical twins by the separation of a single fertilized egg. Embryonic fusion must not be confused with conjoined twins.

When dealing with the issue of **soul** embodiment the development of such *chimeras*, naturally, gives rise to the question of whether or not soul fusion can also occur. Since it is currently thought that this bodily fusion can occur up to sixteen days after fertilization, any souls that were embodied before this time would either have to fuse or one of them would have to voluntarily withdraw or involuntarily be expelled. To avoid such an inconvenient situation it could be that souls instinctively do not seek embodiment until after such time that such fusion is possible.

Note that embryonic fusion is not to be confused with the process of conjoined twinning which is when two entirely separate individuals happen to be physically attached to one another by one or more bodily organs.

See also **Arguments supportive of rebirth; Soul twins; Twins, identical.**

Emma-o. This Japanese Buddhist name is ultimately derived from the Sanskrit name **Yama** the god-ruler of the underworld (*Jigoku*). Upon the dead being presented to Emma-o the god holds in front of the **soul** a magic mirror which discerns all the virtues and vices of the deceased. These are recorded by two secretaries, the female Miru-me and the male Kagu-hana, which are often depicted as two disembodied heads. It is these records that will determine whether the dead must spend time in **purgatory** or be reborn into one of the other realm of existence on the wheel of becoming (*bhavachakra*).

See also **Heaven, Buddhist; Hell, the Chinese; Kshitigarbha; Yen-Lo.**

Empedocles of Acragas (495–435?). This Greek philosopher firmly supported the idea of **metempsychosis** as suggested by **Pythagoras**. In fact, he believed that he could remember past lives as a plant, a fish, a bird, and a woman. In his work *Purifications*, of which only a part has survived, Empedocles describes the descent of the **soul** from an original state of unity and blessedness into the rebirth cycle due to sin and the lengthy process of purification needed for it to ascend back to life among the gods. This process begins with the soul first going through many lives in the vegetable realm until it is reborn as a laurel, the highest form in that realm. From this tree the soul goes into the animal realm until it is reborn as a lion and from there it can be reborn into a human form.

Empedocles understood corporeal existence as punishment for the original sin of killing for food or sacrificial rites. Such killing, according to Empedocles, was the equivalent to murder because human souls were reborn into animals and vice versus, therefore, in killing animals, sooner or later, we would kill (murder) a body inhabited by a human soul. Also, according to Empedocles, as well as the later Platonists, the soul could only be liberated from this bodily rebirth by living a pious, philosophical, and vegetarian life style. It seems that Empedocles may have become convinced of metempsychosis later in life since his earlier work *On Nature* appears to deny the immortality of the soul.

See also **Fall of the Souls; Greeks and reincarnation; Magna Graecia; Priesthood, lack of an organized; Vegetarianism.**

Empire of Jade. In **Daoism** this is a celestial paradise ruled over by the Jade Emperor (Yu-hang, WG) or the August Personage of Jade, the first and highest of the three heavenly deities. This ruler has the power to admit souls to his empire or condemn them to further reincarnations in accordance with their karma.

An alternative Chinese heavenly concept is that of the palace of the immortals. In this Daoist influenced Buddhist belief the virtuous souls may go to this enchanting pagoda-like palace administered by the god of happiness, Fu-Hsing (WG), where they will enjoy themselves until it is time to return to a new embodiment.

See also **Bhaishajyaraja-guru;** *Bodhisattva*; **Chinese religion and reincarnation; Hell, the Chinese; Yen-Lo.**

Empty Tomb of Jesus *see* **Daniel, Book of; Resurrection of Jesus**.

Engrams (From German: *Engamm*, a memory trace) *see* **Scientology**.

Ennius, Quintus (239–169 BCE). One of the greatest and most versatile of the early Roman poets and a great admirer of Greek culture and literature, Ennius is said to have introduced the idea of **metempsychosis** to the Romans. It is said that he regarded himself as a reincarnate of the Greek Poet Homer.

Enoch, Third Book of. Also called the *Sefer ha-Hechalot*, the *Sefer Chanoch*, or *Hebrew Enoch*. The last name, in particular, is given to distinguish it from three other *Books of Enoch — Enoch I, II, and IV*. This kabbalic text includes a description of reincarnation.

See also **Cayce, Edgar; Gabriel;** *Guf ha-Briyot*; **Kabbalah; Melchizedek; Mormonism;** *Tzror ha-Chayyim*; **Unarius Academy of Science.**

Ensomatosis (from the Greek soma: body, hence "embodiment") *see* ***Kyklos Genesion*; Metempsychosis.**

Ephesians. Some reincarnationists believe there is a subtle teaching of reincarnation at Ephesians 1:4–5, and 9. This reads, "In Christ He [God] chose us before the world was founded, to be dedicated, to be without blemish in his sight, to be full of love; and He destined us — such was his will and pleasure — to be accepted as his sons through Jesus Christ...." Like so many other biblical passages taken out of their context, this one can be used to say what anyone wants it to say. However, a proper reading of the passage in context, especially as it continues in verse 9, shows that the author is acknowledging the doctrine of **predestination**, not of **a soul's existence prior to embodiment** that could favor a reincarnation reading. That verse reads, "He has made known to us his hidden purpose — such was his will and pleasure determined beforehand in Christ —." In other words, even before the creation of the world, God already knew that man would fall, and determined in his own mind which of the souls that he would create in the future that he would save and damn. This predestination concept is reinforced at **Romans** 8:29; 9:10–24; 2nd Timothy 1:9.

See also **Angels and reincarnation; Christian atonement theories; Christianity and reincarnation; Corinthians, 1st and 2nd; Galatians; Gnosticism; Karma versus grace; New Testament and reincarnation; New Testament sacrificial concept; Peter, 1st and 2nd; Romans.**

Equinox. This is the name of an entity channeled through a woman by the name of Jonee Scibienski beginning in 1984. Equinox is a channeled entity that supports the concept of reincarnation.

See also **Channeling; Crowley, Aleister; Franklin, Benjamin (2); Hilarion; Lazaris; Mafu; Michael (2); Ra (1); Ra (2); Ramtha; Ryerson, Kevin; Satya, Seth; Torah (2).**

Eschatology *see* **Karmic eschatology; Rebirth eschatology; Soteriology.**

Eskimos (Inuits) *see* **Hunting cultures and reincarnation.**

Esoteric Buddhism *see* **Buddhism, esoteric.**

Esoteric Christianity *see* **Ashoka, King; Church Universal and Triumphant; Christianity, esoteric; Esotericism versus Occultism; Steiner, Rudolf.**

Esoteric Fraternity. An American occult organization begun by Hiram E. Butler and originally named Genii of Nations, Knowledge and Religion. In 1887 it became the Esoteric Fraternity and relocated its headquarters from New England to California. It taught **New Thought, Esoteric Christianity**, reincarnation, and **celibacy**.

Esotericism versus Occultism. The terms "esoteric" and "occult" are often treated as synonyms, especially in New Age literature. This is because the two do overlap to some degree. However, one can speak of esoteric Buddhism or esoteric Christianity, but not occult Buddhism or occult Christianity. The term esoteric comes from the Greek "*esotero*" meaning inside, inner, or within; whereas occult comes from the Latin "*occuere*" and means to conceal. Both terms imply something secret, but not for the same reason. Esoteric usually signifies a secret or mysterious truth which leads to a higher spiritual level and that while this is currently known only to certain initiated persons ultimately it should be open to all. Occult implies a secret that excludes most people because it is oriented to a dangerous and/or self-enhancing power or ability to control parts of the physical world, which usually includes control over other people. The term occult, but rarely esoteric, is also used in reference to dealing with the dead, for either benevolent or malevolent reasons. In this same regard, occult is more often found in association with the word 'supernatural' than is esoteric. In modern times the less sinister and, indeed, more mentalist term "psychic" seems to have replaced, to a large degree, the word supernatural with its occult association and in doing so psychic is more acceptable in esoteric circles.

Modern reincarnationists were among the first to refer to some of their views as esoteric versus occult, and psychic versus supernatural.

See also **Buddhism, esoteric; Channeling; Egyptian versus Oriental Occultism; Theosophy.**

Essene Center. The Center was founded in 1972 by Walter Hagen in Hot Springs, Arkansas. Hagen taught that **Jesus** was an **Essene** and that, as the modern-day representative of that ancient order, it was from Jesus' followers that the Messiah would eventually come. A belief in reincarnation was an important part of the Hagen's teachings. The Center appears to have been defunct by 1980.

Essenes. This 1st century BCE and 1st century CE millennialist Jewish ascetic sect has been credited with teaching metempsychosis. This mistaken idea is due to the writings of the very controversial Jewish historian Joseph ben Matthias (37–93 or 100 CE), more commonly known by his Latin name, Flavius Josephus. This author, who was originally considered to be the most reliable source of the information known about this sect, claimed that the Essenes were very close to **Platonism** in many of their teachings, including that of the bodily changing of the **soul**. The mistaken idea that bodily changing means **metempsychosis** is actually based on a misreading of a passage in his *Jewish Wars*. It reads, "(It is said that) on the one hand all souls are immortal; but on the other hand, those of good men only are changed into another body [*metabainein eis heteron soma*] but those of evil men are subject to eternal punishment." The distinction made in this passage between the fate of the good and evil matches that of the "resurrection" of the good into a new heavenly body and damnation of the evil in hell. In contrast to these words of Josephus, metempsychosis concepts have both the good and the evil take on new bodies, and any talk of eternal damnation is minimized or shifted to a time after a series of re-embodiments.

The 20th century discovery of the Dead Sea Scrolls also has supplied enough information to challenge the mistaken view of Josephus' work. We now know that the Essenes considered themselves to be among the most orthodox of all Jews and since, in their time, the idea of metempsychosis was associated with pagan Greek thought, the Essenes would have most likely rejected it. Instead, it appears that the Essenes believed in some sort of resurrection of the dead.

One of the *Dead Sea Scroll* texts often mentioned as supposedly acknowledging metempsychosis is the *Qumran Melchizedek* or *I IQ Melchizedek*. Within this text there is the sermon called "The Last Jubilee" which identifies the future King of Righteousness, or Messiah, with the ancient legendary pre–Israelite priest-king of Jerusalem, **Melchizedek**. According to one translation of this sermon it is written that the King of Righteousness will be the "revival" of Melchizedek.

If, in giving the benefit of the doubt to a metempsychosis-favored reading of Josephus we must ask why would Josephus attributes metempsychosis to the Essenes if they didn't believe in it? The reason would be that he was writing shortly after the brutal suppression of the great Judean revolt against Roman rule in 70 CE, after which Judaism throughout the empire was looked upon with great suspicion and even contempt. Josephus could have been trying to rehabilitate and enhance the reputation of Judaism by associating it with highly respected Greek teachings, one of which was **Orphism**.

Despite the present new understanding of the Essenes and of the possible motives of Josephus a number of modern believers in reincarnation have continued to insist that the Essenes were reincarnationists. To add further credibility to their insistence many of these supporters claim that **Jesus** was a member of the Essenes. However, there seems no real evidence for this claim other than the desire to connect Jesus to the sect on the assumption that he also accepted reincarnation.

If any orthodox Jewish sect of this time was more intellectually open to Greek thought it would have been an Essene-like sister ascetic sect in **Egypt** called the Therapeutae. Although there is even less accurate information on this sect then there is on their Judean counterpart, it does seem that the Therapeutae took a more allegorical approach to Jewish scriptures than did the Essenes. One item that both the Judean and Egyptian sects seem to have held in common was a somewhat scripturally unsanctioned belief in **body-soul dualism**. Such an unorthodox Jewish dualism might have been more open to a metempsychosis belief in Hellenized Egypt, under a possibly Orphic influence.

Finally, in a remaining attempt to prove that the Essenes, as well as Jesus, were supporters of metempsychosis it is argued that since the Kabbalists teach reincarnation it must be a very ancient Jewish belief. The fact that no Kabbalist teachings can be identified until the twelfth century CE is either ignored or denied.

See also **Cayce, Edgar; False claims of support for reincarnation; Greeks and reincarnation; Resurrection, bodily**.

Essenes of Arkashea. This group claims a heritage dating to an ancient order founded by Pharaoh Akhenaten in the year 1354 BCE. The modern Essenes of Arkashea claim that the original Egyptian order has survived secretly over the centuries and that they are part of it; however, they became publicly known only in 1993 by finally publishing their teachings. The term Arkashea refers to the history of what each individual has done as he or she reincarnates from life to life. The Essenes attempt to explore this history as it is written within each member in order to become free of maya (illusion) and gain self-realization. In other words, the resident members of the Essenes' monastery in Alabama study themselves.

See also **Egypt**.

Eternalism. (1) This is any general belief in the immortality of the **soul**. (2) More specifically, eternalism (S/P: *shashvata-vada/sassata-vada*) is one of the two philosophical extremes that Buddhism rejects as heretical. The other extreme is annihilationism (*ucheda-vada*). Buddhism, in contrast, advocates the **Middle Way** view of *anatman* or no-soul (self). It might be thought that because Buddhism teaches a post-mortem existence through rebirth that it qualifies as a form of eternalism. This would only be true if Buddhists taught that rebirth was endless or that upon liberation from the cycle of rebirth something still identifiable as a self (*atman*) continued on forever. Whereas **Hinduism** positively acknowledges the latter, Buddhism refuses to do so. This does not mean that Buddhism denies such continuation, which would make it a kind of delayed annihilationism, but it simply refuses to speculate on the fate of the deceased enlightened person.

See also **Accidentalism;** *Amrta;* **Annihilationism, Buddhist view; Determinism; Hedonism; Soul; Immortality**.

Etherian Religious Society of Universal Brotherhood. This Society was formed in 1965 in California by its director, the Rev. E. A. Hurtienne. The Society teaches that all forms of life on all planes of existence are related; that love, which is the unifying force of life, must become a living reality, for only through this love can eternal life be achieved; that karma and reincarnation are universal laws; and that man is a spiritual being with seven complete bodies. The purpose of the Society is to minister through love so as to insure dignity, equality and justice for all; to help establish the future root races (developmental stages) of humanity upon earth; and to assure the entrance of earth into the Planetary Federation of Light of our solar system.

Etheric body. In metaphysical terms this is the psychic body double that is responsible for the life or animation of the physical body. It is the separation of the etheric body from the physical body that is said to bring about death. In some esoteric systems the etheric body is called the *prana* (breath) body.

According to **Theosophy** once the physical body dies the soul's consciousness is centered on the etheric body and, depending on how materialistic the deceased individual was while still in his physical body, this etheric (**earth-bound**) state can last anywhere from a few moments to several weeks. For the truly materialistic deceased his or her attachment to the former physical realm keeps the etheric body in a state of miserable turmoil. Sooner or later, however, sheer exhaustion in this **limbo** state will force the dissolution of the etheric body, in most cases, and the deceased will then experience existence in his **astral body.** This dissolution is only prevented if the etheric body in desperation manages to take **possession** of some physical body, especially that of a psychically innocent infant, or in rare cases the body of an animal.

This view of the etheric body is taken from *A Textbook of Theosophy* (1912) by C. W. Leadbeater who differs in some minor ways from the version taught by **Helena Blavatsky**, in that Leadbeater incorporates the views of **Annie Besant.**

See also **Attached entity; Ghost;** *Kama-rupa*; *Linga Sharia*; **Sensation body; Soul and spirit levels, Theosophical.**

Etheric Cycle *see* **Colton, Ann Ree.**

Etheric plane. This is the realm of the **etheric body** and is said to both exist between the physical and **astral planes** and yet to interpenetrate the world of ordinary physical experience. It is believed that, like the oceanic tides, it is powerfully influenced by the **moon** and other celestial bodies.

See also **Mental plane; Planes of existence, names of.**

Etheric revenant. This is an entity in which the **soul** of a recently deceased has failed to separate itself from the **etheric body** (and or **astral body**) in the **second death** as it is expected to do and which naturally delays its eventual rebirth. If this etheric revenant entity survives too long it may become a haunting **ghost** or a psychic **vampire.**

See also *Kama-Rupa*; **Soul and spirit levels, Theosophical.**

Ethicalized or karmic rebirth *see* **Karmic eschatology.**

Eucharist, Christian *see* **Christianity and reincarnation; Lucifer; New Testament sacrificial concept; Rebirth and moral perfection.**

Europe and reincarnation. While at times the doctrine of reincarnation seemed to have been lost in Europe, in fact, from the time of the Greek Pythagoreans and Ophics and of the Celtic Druids, there was in every period at least a small minority of Europeans that did believe in it. Among these were some **Romans,** Gnostics, Manicheans, **Paulicians, Bogomils, Patarines, Cathars,** Kabbalic Jews, Renaissance Platonic and Pythagorean revivalists, **Rosicrucians,** Theosophists, and Spiritist.

See also **Gnosticism; Kabbalah; Manichaeism; Orphism; Pythagoras; Renaissance; Spiritism; Theosophy.**

"Every knee should bend ... every tongue confess." This biblical phrase is found at Philippians 2:9–11 in the context of "Therefore God raised to the heights and bestowed on him [**Jesus**] the name above all names, that at the name of Jesus every knee shall bend — in heaven, on earth, and in the depths — and every tongue confess, Jesus Christ is Lord, to the glory of God the father."

Some pro-reincarnationist Christians use this passage to support the idea that reincarnation is implied in this biblical passage. According to their thinking, since "every tongue" must include all the languages that have become extinct, and every knee must refer to the speakers of those languages, this literally means that every **soul** that has ever been embodied on earth must not only be evangelized, but truly converted to Christ; and the only way this could happen is if every soul has had whatever number of lives necessary for it to be evangelized.

The more traditional or orthodox Christian explanation of these verses is that by the time these passages were written the faithful needed some explanation for the delay of the Second Coming of Christ (the *Parousia*) and the establishment of the Kingdom of God; therefore, the passages meant that that Christ will not return until every living person of every language has, at the very least, had a chance to be evangelized, even if some of this must be done in **hell** (the depths). This explanation receives strong support from **Mark 13:11,** "But before the end [presumably the end of the corrupt world and the coming of Christ and the kingdom] the gospel must be proclaimed to all nations." This is repeated at **Matthew 13:10.**

It should be noted that almost identical to the phrase in Philippians is that found at **Romans** 14:11–12, "For Scripture says, 'As I live, says the Lord, to me every knee shall bow and every tongue acknowledge God.'"

See also **Christianity and reincarnation; Peter, 1st and 2nd.**

Evil and karma *see* **Karma and the moral structure of the universe.**

Evolution, material and spiritual *see* **Ontological leap or ontological discontinuity; Population increase issue; Soul, collective.**

Evolutionary transmigration of souls. This is the doctrine that human souls were first embodied in mineral form, then for various reasons were able to transmigrate into plants, then into animal bodies, and from there into human forms. From here these souls move on to trans-human bodies such as angels, and in time will evolve into still higher levels of being. The **Yazidis** (Yezidis) seem to hold to evolutionary transmigration.

See also **Dabistan; Morganwg, Iolo;** *Tanasukh*; **Yarsanism.**

Ex Oriente Lux (Latin for "Out of the East, Light"). This is a belief which developed in the 19th century that there was a greater spiritual wisdom to be found in India, eastern Asia, and even in the Middle East than in the progressively industrializing, materialistic West. In Europe among the names most closely associated with this belief were Sir Edwin Arnold, **Helena Blavatsky,** and **Arthur Schopenhauer,** while in America it was R.W. Emerson and the other **American transcendentalists.** The *ex oriente lux* view has continued into the 21st century and has been a major contributor to the still growing Western acceptance of a belief in rebirth. The problem with *ex oriente lux* is that no society, culture or group of cultures has a monopoly on wisdom, much less truth. The followers of this idea generally prefer to ignore the fact that many in the East believe in *ex occidente lux*. Anyone who has had contact with Korean Christians, for example, can attest to their belief in the superiority of Western religious wisdom over that of the East.

Existential seriality. This is a supposedly more scientific name for the theory of reincarnation. It is equivalent to the term seriate-lives.

See also **Hetero-retrocognition; Somatic rebirth.**

Exodus. This Old Testament book has as its main themes the revelation of God to **Moses** on Mount Sinai; the liberation of the Israelites from slavery in **Egypt**; and of their **forty** years of wandering in the desert. However, at least one Jewish gnostic group used the Exodus story to suggest that the Israelite escape from Egypt was analogous to the **soul** escaping from its bodily entombment.

For modern reincarnationists there are two closely related passages in Exodus that are believed to teach reincarnation. The first of these 20:5 reads, "I [God] will punish the children for the sins of the fathers to the third and fourth generations of those who hate me. This is repeated at Exodus 34:7 as, "Jehovah, the Lord, a god ... who punishes sons and grandsons to the third and fourth generation for the iniquity of their fathers!" The reality is that when these passages were originally written the Jews still believed in the primitive tribal morality of collective guilt. In typical tribal based mentality there is little or no emphasis on the individual responsibility of a particular member. This means that if any tribal or clan member commits a crime against another tribe or clan it is unimportant to the offended group which particular person in the offending group committed the crime. The whole tribe or clan of the offender is held responsible and, therefore, demanding retribution from the whole group is considered valid.

This collective guilt concept is also behind the case in **Genesis** 3:17–19 where all of Adam's descendents were considered as responsible for his offense against God as was **Adam** himself. It is also behind such thinking as in Leviticus 10:6 where it is said that God would be angry with all of the community for a misdemeanor by one of God's priests.

Recognizing this collective guilt concept as unjust, some reincarnationists, especially Kabbalists, claim that these passages actually refer to third and fourth soul reincarnation generations, not biological descent ones.

See also **Deuteronomy 5:2–3; Exodus;** *Gilgul* **or** *Gilgulim*; **I AM Movement; Jesus; Kabbalah; Old Testament and the afterlife; Original sin, Christianity, and reincarnation; Sciomancy.**

Extinctivist. This is a person who believes that personal consciousness at death simply becomes extinct; hence it is a synonym for an annihilationist.

Also see **Annihilationism, Biblical view; Annihilationism, Buddhist view.**

Extra cerebral memory. This is a term used by Dr. **H. N. Banerjee** for memories that seem to be independent of the cerebrum, the main repository of normal memory. It would be the equivalent of memory retained by a **soul.** It is to this extra-cerebral memory to which Banerjee attributes past life recall.

Extrasensory perception. It has been proposed by a number of critics of reincarnation that all so-called past life recalls that can not be explain by normal sensory ability can be explained by a variety of extrasensory or psychic abilities, none of which require any kind of afterlife state. **Ian Stevenson** in his General Discussion section of *Twenty Cases Suggestive of Reincarnation* (1966), gives a rather extensive review of extrasensory perception as one possible source for past life recall. However, he generally rejects extrasensory perception as a real source for past life recall. He states that if past life recall is due to extrasensory perception then such extrasensory perception must be limited or exclusively connected with past life recall. Such extreme tunnel focus of any extrasensory perception he regards as highly unlikely. Also, Stevenson points out that while such extrasensory perception might account for even most of the memories that the recallers claim, it would not account for some of the behavior similarities (emotional responses, mannerism, habits, skills, etc.) between the deceased and the recaller, which Stevenson believes can only be best explained by the recaller having inherited such behavior from the deceased.

See also *Akashic* **Record; Clairaudience; Clairvoyance; Cryptesthesia; Medium; Psychometry; Rebirth, alternative explanations to; Retrocognition; Telepathy (telegnosis) with the living.**

Ezekiel *see* **Karma in the Bible?; Old Testament and the afterlife; Resurrection of Jesus.**

Facial architectural consistency. This is the theory that the shape and proportions of the face are more or less consistent from one life to another. Walter Semkiw, in his *Return of the Revolutionaries* (2003) and *Born Again: Reincarnation Cases Involving International Celebrities ...* (2006), offers what he regards as considerable proof of such consistency.

See also **Birth marks; Kevin Ryerson.**

Facial blank. This is the temporary total loss of expression, and sometimes other signs of life, that often occurs while a subject is in deep trance. It also occurs when a subject is going from one presumed past life to another such life. On the other hand, this state is also especially noticeable when a person suffering from **multiple personalities** switches from one personality to another. This has been used by some anti-reincarnationists to suggest that past life recall is just a form of multiple personality syndrome.

Faculty X. This refers to the psychic ability to experience places and times other than the here and now. This faculty has been suggested as the real source of past life recalls.

Faith and rebirth *see* **Karma and faith; Mind; Proof for and against reincarnation argument.**

Fall of the Souls. This is a widely spread belief that before the birth of mankind souls existed in a non-material state, and as such they were without defilements; in short, sinless. Due to some tragic event this state of purity was lost and souls fell into the material world and were trapped into bodily forms. In accordance with this belief the goal of all souls is to escape from this entrapment and regain their non-bodily purity.

According to various ancient and modern gnostic groups, for such a goal to be achieved each **soul** must pass through an ever more purified, less materialistic series of lives until they are reborn into a life that will permit an escape.

A variation of the Fall of Souls is the "fall upward" or the "happy or blessed fall" (*Felix Culpa*). This is the idea that souls had to fall from a state of "immature innocence" into a state where, through moral struggle, they would gain the maturity and higher wisdom that would qualify them for various divine states or other rewards. This more optimistic version of the fall is not only the one that most modern reincarnationists prefer, but the one even some liberal Jewish and Christian thinkers employ in their interpretation of the fall of **Adam** and Eve, along with a standard belief in the resurrection of the dead.

See also **Empedocles; Morganwg, Iolo; Orphism; Original sin, Christianity, and reincarnation; Original sin versus karma; Paulicians;** *Qlippoth;* **Ramtha; Resurrection, bodily; Scientology.**

False claims of support for reincarnation. It is unfortunate that far too many supporters of reincarnation consistently depend on false claims regarding historical individuals and events concerned with reincarnation. While some of these inaccuracies smack of deliberate falsifications by over-zealous reincarnationists, most of them can be attributed to sloppy historical research. In the latter case, most of these supporters have simply relied on previous information that was originally inaccurate, and which has been repeatedly passed on so many times that the resulting impression is that there is a consensus that the information is true.

See also **Christianity and reincarnation; Church Council of 553; Clement of Alexandria; Egypt; Essenes; Franklin, Benjamin; Fraud; Justin Martyr; Rampa, Lobsang Tuesday; New Testament and reincarnation; Origin; Past life fakery.**

False-memory syndrome. This is the condition in which a person remembers something about their past in this life that never really existed. This condition is far more common than most people believe. Critics of past life recall point out that if we can not trust our memory in this life, how much less ought we to trust it in a so-called past life.

See also **Hypnosis**.

Falun Gong. Founded in 1992 this organization teaches a form of Qi Gong (Chinese yoga) but also the concepts of reincarnation and karma. In 1999 the Chinese Communist government launched a new campaign against what it regarded as religious superstition with Falun Gong as one of its targets. This lead to a massive demonstration of Falun Gong members which considerably unnerved the government and in reaction the government intensified its effort to suppress the group, but this has only succeeded in driving the group underground.

Famous supporters and rebirth *see* **Rebirth and famous supporters**.

Fantasy and reincarnation *see* **Children remembering past lives; Fantasy prone personality; Fantasy versus past life regression; Hypnosis; I, William the Conqueror; Rebirth, proximity**.

Fantasy prone personality. This refers to a person who is highly imaginative and spends a fair amount of his or her time fantasizing a life or lives different from his or her real life. A hypnotist finds such a person easy to hypnotize, not to mention to age regress to another life.

See also **Hypnotism; Fantasy versus past life regression**

Fantasy versus past life regression. It is held by some psychologists that the difference between fantasy and past life regression is that in regression the individual experiences strong emotions while involved in the past life scene, which in a daydream or other fantasy is lacking. Also, any fantasy is easily open to modifications, minor or radical, at a moments notice. Past life recall during regression is far more stable and consistent.

See also **I, William the Conqueror; Past life memory recall**.

Far memory. This is a general term for remembering very distant past lives.

See also **Grant, Joan Marshall**.

Fatalism *see* **Determinism**.

Fellowship of the Inner Life. The Fellowship was founded in 1972 by the self-proclaimed psychic Paul Solomon who through trance sessions received messages from a voice simply called "The Source." These sessions eventually offered a complete spiritual philosophy which included a belief in the **lost continent** of Atlantis, information on the treatment of diseases, and certain prophecies. Reincarnation is believed to allow time for the soul's spiritual growth. In 1978 the Fellowship headquarters were moved from in Atlanta, Georgia to Virginia Beach, Virginia, where **The Association for Research and Enlightenment** is also located.

See also **Edgar Cayce**.

Fetters, the ten (S: *Samyojana*) *see* **Buddhist stages of liberation**.

Fiat Lux. This is a small monastic religious community in Southern Germany founded in 1980 under the directions of Christ as channeled through Erika Bertschinger Eike, who goes under the name of Uriella. Besides advocating celibacy and **vegetarianism**, a belief in reincarnation and apocalyptic UFOism are important teachings of the community.

Finite or infinite number of rebirths. In **Hinduism**, Buddhism, and **Jainism** it is presumed that the number of reincarnating entities are so astronomically great that any finite guess as to that number would be useless. Western reincarnationists, for the most part, reject this "infinite" view mainly because Westerners still hold on to a Judeo-Christian concept of linear time which expects a finite number. Among Western groups or individuals, however, there is no consensus on the number of times a **soul** may or must be reborn.

Among the earliest Westerners to suggest a finite estimate of rebirth were some of the Theosophists. According to one of their reckonings the soul went through no more than about 800 reincarnations. This number was arrived at by taking into account the need for each soul to be reborn into each of seven branch races multiplied by each of seven subdivisional races multiplied by each of seven main races multiplied by two necessary rebirths in each branch race. This gave a minimal figure of 686, to which was added 100 or so as a variable, which was then rounded off to 800.

Noreen Quinn, the writer for the **Grace-Loehr life readings**, gives the minimum and maximum figures of 60 to about 200 lives. Goudey, in his *Reincarnation: A Universal Truth* (1928), mentions the theory that each soul is required to live 777 lives, 700 of which are in ignorance, 70 in culture, and 7 in wisdom. **Rudolf Steiner**, on the other hand, suggests a minimum of 24 lives, 12 of which are male and 12 female, over a minimal period of 25,920 years. Some Kabbalic traditions allow for no more than three lives.

These figures do not exhaust the various estimates of finite rebirths, but provide a good example of the lack of agreement on this issue.

See also **Aztec; Buddha's necklace; Buddhist stages of liberation; Cummins, Geraldine; Dayaks; Fixed number or variable number of souls;**

Gender issue of the soul; Genesis; Herodotus; *Jataka Tales*; Kabbalah; Rebirth in the West; Rebirth, restricted.

Finland. There seems to be some evidence that the pre–Christianized peoples of Finland believed that the dead could reincarnate in the bodies of grandchildren and other future generations.

See also **Lapps (Saami)**.

Fixed number or variable number of souls. Among religions such as **Hinduism**, Buddhism, and **Jainism** the number of waiting rebirth factors that are in the cycle of rebirth is so astronomical that for all practical purposes there will never be an end to the rebirth process, even if this has to occur in a succeeding universe after the death of the present universe. This view does not deny that souls periodically leave the round of rebirth, but it simply states that there is a quite adequate supply of souls present elsewhere, including in animals, that are waiting to replace the exiting souls.

Among most Western proponents of reincarnation such an endless process is usually disregarded in favor of a time limit when reincarnation comes to an end. Also, unlike most Eastern views the more personal monotheism of Western religion leaves open the likelihood of the periodic creation of new souls to both replace the ones that leave the system as well as to account for the **population increase issue**. This seems especially necessary if, as in the West, there is a general objection to animals acting as a pool for human souls.

See also **Blocked regression; Finite or infinite number of rebirths; Kabbalah; Population increase issue; Rebirth and cyclical time.**

Fixed or free souls *see* **Souls, fixed and free.**

Fluorite. Chemically, this is calcium fluoride and it has many standard usages. For example, it is used for opalescent glass and in its clear, colorless form of optical quality it is used for apochromatic lenses. In the New Age crystal movement it is used in all three of its forms — clusters, octahedrons, and pyramids; however, using it in the pyramid form during a specific kind of **past life recall meditation** is said to assist in experiencing, not only the past, but even future lives, and especially as to how karma affects such lives. Of course, regardless of what power fluorite might have in its own right, the emphasis on the pyramid form is one more manifestation of the mistaken belief that the shapes of the pyramids of **Egypt** were related to a belief in reincarnation.

See also **Pyramidology**.

Folk Buddhism *see* **Buddhism, folk.**

Forgiveness and karma *see* **Christianity and reincarnation; Karma and forgiveness; Karma versus grace; Pure-Land or Blissful Land Buddhism.**

Fortune, Dion (1890–1946). This was the pseudonym for Violet Mary Firth, the famous Anglo-American esotericist. Fortune derived her esoteric name from a shortening and anglicizing of the magick motto (name) *Deo non fortuna* (by God, not chance). Fortune began her esoteric career in 1919 when she joined the Alpha and Omega Lodge of the Stella Matutina and the outer order of the **Hermetic Order of the Golden Dawn**. She left the order in 1929 to establish her own order, the Community of the Inner Light, later renamed the Fraternity of the Inner Light, which still later became the Society of Inner Light. This last named society included a subdivision called The Guild of the Master **Jesus** which Fortune established for those who wishes to consider themselves both esotericists and Christians.

Fortuna is said to have remembered a nearly unbroken series of lives as a priestess going back as far as one on the **lost continent** of Atlantis. She believed that to understand the purpose of one's life required understanding the nature of past lives, and in particular the **archetype** of the Great Mother, a symbolic embodiment of the universal memory or *akashic* **record**. A number of members of the Society of Inner Light claimed past lives as **Cathars,** and were said to have brought Cathar elements into the Society.

Although Fortune never claimed any connection to the **Wicca** movement, many in that movement use her writings, both fictional and non-fictional, in their practice.

Finally, Fortune's book *Psychic Self-Defense* (1930) was a seminal work on the subject of magical attacks.

See also **Crowley, Edward Aleister; Richardson, Alan; Vampires; Yeats, William Butler.**

Forty. The importance given to the number forty in the Bible has encouraged some Christian reincarnationists to suggest that there is a relationship between this number and the **interim period** similar to or even related to the forty-nine days in the *bardo*. The fact that the word quarantine, which comes from the Italian quarantine (forty days), and was thought to symbolize a cycle of being or of non-being seems to have further encouraged a mystical significance to this number.

Actually, the original interest in forty may have come from the importance in Mesopotamia of the forty day disappearance of the **Pleiades**, a period of rains, storms, floods, etc. The return of the star cluster was a time of celebration, and a bundle of forty reeds was burned to commemorate the passing of the forty days of bad fate.

Forty-nine days *see* **Bardo; Critical time periods; Forty; Gandharva/Gandhabba; Hell, the Chinese; Interim period; Matthew, Gospell**.

Foundation for Reincarnation and Spiritual Research. This organization was founded in 1985 to focus empirical research on reincarnation as developed by **Ian Stevenson**. However, the foundation's goal also included finding correlations between its presumed scientific research and Vedic and yogic literature.

See also **Associations and organizations**.

Frank, Jacob (1726–1791). This Polish Jew was one of the most notorious of the false messiahs to arise in Eastern Europe. He claimed that he was the reincarnation of the patriarch Jacob, King David, as well as the previous false messiah, Shabbettai Tzevi (1626–1676). Frank, basing his teachings on the *Zohar*, rejected rabbinical Judaism, and for this reason his followers were called the Frankists or Zoharist sect. As part of his attempted to weaken rabbinic Judaism he advised his followers to embrace Christianity and about 1,000 of them were baptized. Frank himself abandoned Judaism for Catholicism in 1759 but later his insincerity was exposed and for a while he was imprisoned as a heretic. After his death his movement totally disappeared.

See also **Adam; Kabbalah; Koresh, David**.

Franklin, Benjamin (1706–1790). This signer of the *America Declaration of Independence* certainly seemed to have some belief in an afterlife but, despite attempts by authors of books on reincarnation, the claim that he believed in reincarnation can not be supported by a close reading of any of his works. Instead, the claim rests on an epitaph for his tombstone that he was said to have written in his youth. "The body of B. Franklin, Printer; like the cover of an old book, its contents torn out and stripped of its lettering and gilding, lies here, food for worms. But the book shall not be lost, for it will as he [Franklin] believed appear once more in a new and more elegant edition, revised and corrected by the author." The problem with this epitaph as proof of a belief in reincarnation is that it could also describe a belief in a resurrected body in the Christian sense.

See also **American Transcendentalists; False claims of support for reincarnation; Rebirth and famous supporters**.

Franklin, Benjamin (2). According to the channeler Mark Victor Venaglia, the entity that has been channeled through him by this name is the same as the American Founding Father. This entity, usually described simply as Ben, has a particular fondness for Manhattan, New York. According to Ben this fondness is related to the fact that it is in New York that all those alive on the **lost continent** of Atlantis before its sinking have reincarnated. Ben has a particular message for those inflicted with AIDS. He claims that it is an ancient disease that has manifested itself in the modern world to teach people to care about one another. Those individuals inflicted with AIDS once inhabited the island of Crete and a small island off the southwest coast of Atlantis and belonged to a civilization of nobles and healers. Ben claims that in time a cure for this disease will be discovered by a women doctor whom Ben calls Beth.

See also **Channeling; Equinox; Grace-Loehr life readings; Hilarion; Lazaris; Mafu; Michael (2); Ra (1); Ra (2); Ramtha; Ryerson, Kevin; Satya; Seth; Torah (2)**.

Fraternity of Light. Likely founded in Philadelphia by a group of kabbalic magicians, it follows certain teachings of **The Hermetic Order of the Golden Dawn**. The Fraternity believes in an *atman*-like divine consciousness in everyone which must reincarnate until it evolves spiritually enough to no longer need a physical body. Also included in the Fraternity's teachings is Celtic magic (or the Coven of Diana).

Fraud. While there undoubtedly are numerous deliberately fraudulent claims of having experienced past lives, these can not account for the very sincere experiences of many others. Even if innocent fraud, as in **honest lying** or holy lying, is taken into account there still remains sufficient cases that must be accounted for by means other than fraud.

See also **Cryptomnesia; *Déjà Vu*; Multiple personalities; Past life fakery; Past life memory recall; Rampa, Lobsang Tuesday; Rebirth, alternative explanations to**.

Free-association. This psychoanalytic technique is said to be useful at times and under certain circumstances to provide clues to past lives.

From tomb to womb. Like **coffin to cradle** and **death to breath**, this is a metaphor for reincarnation.

See also **Crypt**.

Frozen or unedited past life memory problem *see* **Akashic Record; Retrocognition**.

Full participation. A full participation past life scenario can be experienced in two ways. One is when a person sees it projected before him like a movie. The other is when a person feels physically and mentally as if he had returned to the past and is fully participating in that life once more.

See also **Trance states**.

Future lives *see* **Christos** (anointing) **technique; Dreams, announcing; Fluorite; Grant, Joan Marshall; Seth**.

Gabriel (Hebrew: Man of God). Although Gabriel is mentioned in the Gospel of **Luke** 1:19, 26, he is never specifically called an archangel. He is also mentioned in **Daniel** 8:17, not as an angel, but as "one with the semblance of a man," and at 9:21 as "the man, whom I had already seen in a vision."

In the Kabbalic and gnostic systems this planetary angel or archangel, ruling over the **moon**, is the final guide of the **soul** to its next rebirth. In all forms of orthodox Christianity it is Gabriel who will trumpet in the Day of Judgment after the general resurrection of the dead.

See also **Angels and reincarnation; Celestial gates; Planetary descent and ascent of the soul**.

Galatians. In this New Testament letter there is found the major theme that will be later emphasized in some of the other letters of **Paul of Tarsus**, which is that no one can be saved by the righteous moral behavior of the Old Testament Law (*Torah*), but only through faith that **Jesus**, through his death, took on the curse of the Law (Galatians 3:13) and in doing so freed the faithful from the Law's impossible requirements (Galatians 2:15–3:14). With this in mind it is difficult to imagine how some one could find support for a **soul's existence prior to embodiment**, much less than for reincarnation in this letter, but the attempt has been made.

Galatians 1:15–16 states that, "...God, who has set me apart from birth and called me through his grace, chose to reveal his Son to me and through me, in order that I might proclaim him among the Gentiles." A very similar statement is found in the Old Testament at Jeremiah 1:4–5, "The word of the Lord came to me: 'Before I formed you in the womb I knew you for my own: before you were born I consecrated you, I appointed you a prophet to the nations.'" These two passages are often cited together as having a reincarnationist meaning.

However, for both of these passages the same argument against a reincarnationist view can be made, namely that they mean that "before birth" God had "predetermined" the "destiny" of Jeremiah and Paul even without their souls necessarily already being in existence.

Also, Galatians 6:7–8 at times has been regarded as a pro-rebirth verse. It reads, "Make no mistake about this: God is not to be fooled; a man reaps what he sows. If he sows seed in the field of his lower nature, he will reap from it a harvest of corruption, but if he sows in the field of the Spirit, the Spirit will bring him a harvest of eternal life."

This is actually only one of several "reap and sow" passages that are cited by reincarnationists to suggest that there is also the doctrine of **karma in the Bible**, yet here again the orthodox view that "with in a single life time one receive after death what one deserve" fits better with the rest of the text than does a reincarnation view.

Still another reincarnationist claim is made for Galatians 4:19 where, in the second part of this passage, Paul is speaking to his followers and says, "For my children [followers] you are, and I am in travail with you over again until you take the shape of Christ." This passage has been use by some reincarnationists to claim that Paul was claiming that he would keep returning to earthly life [be reborn] until all his following was redeemed. Obviously it is the words "over again" that might seem to give this passage a reincarnational meaning. That no such meaning is likely can be seen by what he writes next, at 4:20, "I wish I could be with you now; then I could modify my tone [voice]; as it is, I am at my wits' end about you." What Paul is referring to is that his followers are regressing back to a belief that they must obey the Old Testament Law [Torah], he is worried sick about this and wishes he could be with them now to change their misdirection.

See also **Angels and reincarnation; Annihilationism; Christian atonement theories; Christianity and reincarnation; Corinthians, 1st and 2nd; Ephesians; Gnosticism; Karma in the Bible? New Testament and reincarnation; Romans**.

Galya Raza (Hebrew: Revelation of a Secret). This sixteenth century kabbalic work by an anonymous author has an elaborate theory of creation and the origin of evil as a framework for its reincarnational teaching.

See also **Kabbalah;** *Sefer ha-Gilgulim*.

Gandharva/Gandhabba (S/P). This is a term for the presumed **rebirth factor** mentioned in the early Buddhist Canon. In early Buddhism it is regarded as the karmic causative aspect of rebirth. However, in **Vajrayana Buddhism** it is regarded as a temporary intermediate being that exists in the **interim period** between lives, and as such it acts as a bridge between the old embodied being and the new embodied being. Such a temporary intermediate being is technically made necessary by the Buddhist doctrine of no-soul (self) or *anatman*.

In the *Abhidharmakoshabhasya* (*Treasury of the Abhidharma*), by the famous fifth century Buddhist teacher Vasubandhu, the *gandharva* is described as a very subtle mental body which exists for a **forty-**

nine day period between death and rebirth, and which feeds on odors, hence the literal meaning of its name "that which eats (*arvati*) odors (*gandham*), or odor-eater. This intermediate being is said to become attracted to a new life in accordance with **the electra/oedipus complex**.

See also **Karma and rebirth; Mahayana Buddhist rebirth texts; Rebirth in Buddhism**.

Ganges (Ganga: Swift-goer) **River**. To Hindus this is both the name of the most sacred of all rivers and the name of the goddess that personifies it. It is believed that pilgrims bathing in the Ganges at the city of Varanasi (Benares), despite its modern industrialized pollution, cleanses them from sin and thus will insure themselves a more fortunate rebirth. Also, having a person's cremated remains thrown into the river at this site will improve the next life of the deceased even up to liberating the **soul** from rebirth altogether. Even committing **suicide** by drowning oneself in the Ganges will also improve ones next life; otherwise, only the un-cremated body of holy persons should be released into the river. This is because the corporeal forms of holy persons do not need to be first purified by fire.

See also **Hinduism; Karma versus grace; Pilgrimages**.

Gap in current knowledge *see* **Current knowledge discrepancy; Science and pseudo-science**.

Garden of Waiting. According to one of the subjects of hypnotic regression by **Dr. Alexander Cannon**, this is the name of the realm where souls are prepared for their rebirth descent.

See also **Great White Brotherhood**.

Gates of death and rebirth *see* **Celestial gates**.

Gaulle, Charles-Andre-Marie-Joseph de *see* **Napoleon Bonaparte; Patton, George S.**

Gehazi. According to one kabbalic source this servant of the prophet Elisha was reincarnated as a dog for the sin of aiding King Jehoboam in that king's efforts to establish worship of the golden calf in the northern kingdom of Israel.

See also **Kabbalah**.

Gehenna or Gehénnon. From the Hebrew *Ge-Hinnom*. It means hell in general, but more specifically it refers to the first of the seven hells in Kabbalic Judaism that a soul may spend time in before reincarnating.

See also **Hell; Old Testament and the afterlife**.

Gender issue of the soul. There is an on going debate in various reincarnationist circles as to whether the **soul** is genderless, androgynous, or has inherent gender. This is closely related to the debate as to whether or not a soul is consistently reborn into the same physical gender or periodically changes genders.

In the case of **creationism** of the soul, God creates an individualized soul to insert into each conceived embryo; but whether He has given it a gender already or leaves that to be determined by the biology of the embryo is open to further debate. In **traducianism**, the soul, like the body, is formed from the union of the parents which leads to the conclusion that either the soul is genderless or takes on the gender of the embryo.

In **infusionism**, where the soul pre-existed, gendered, genderless, or androgynous may be the case. **Plato**, in his work the *Symposium*, gives details of a myth told by the playwright Aristophanes. In this myth the original human beings existed in a double form. Each had two faces looking in opposite directions, four arms and four legs, and a pair of genitals. One group of these beings had one male and one female genital, another group had two male genitals, and a third group had two female genitals. This double genital nature allowed human beings a level of sexual freedom that contributed to making them so proud of themselves that they angered the gods. In order to punishment humanity the gods split each person in half. According to Aristophanes this explains why the souls of human beings are so drive by passion, each human being is not only looking for its other physical half, but its other soul half in order to be whole again. Obviously, this myth also conveniently explains why there is both heterosexuality and homosexuality.

A later view of the soul and gender found in Plato's *Timaeus*, is far less romantic and, in fact, is misogynous. In this the female body was not only created after the male body, but existed only out of the unfortunate necessity to house "fallen" male souls. Presumably, then there were only male souls and these could only escape rebirth from a male body, with those male souls in a female body needing to reincarnate.

In some ancient gnostic sects it was believed that the reason that the original androgynous souls were divided was because the lesser, and evil, creator (***demiurge***) wanted to keep souls trapped in bodily form for as long as possible.

The Kabbalah teaches that the pre-existent soul, as in the *Symposium*'s platonic system, is androgynous and that it splits into separate male and female parts during its original descent from the celestial paradise to the earth for embodiment. Also, as in the *Symposium*, the reason that souls undergo reincarnation is because they are searching for their **soul mates**; and no soul can or will be liberated from continued embodiment until it finds its original other half.

Modern support for an original bisexual soul comes from the **Grace Loehr Life Readings**. According to these readings when the soul undergoes its first earthly embodiment it is divined or polarized in masculine and feminine halves which will not be reunited until all of its numerous earth embodiments have been completed. In the mean time each half will taken on bodily forms of both sexes. In other words, the male soul half will experience many lives as both male and female, as will the female soul half. This is considered necessary for the full development of the soul as a whole.

R. F. Goudey, in his *Reincarnation: A Universal Truth* (1928), says that ordinarily it is thought that not less than three and not more than seven lives of the same sex are followed before changing to a different one.

The gender issue of the soul in Buddhism should technically be meaningless, since the *anatman* teaching denies the very existence of a soul. It should even be nonsensical to suggest that there is even a vague gender related aspect of any kind to the **karmic carrier** that official Buddhist doctrine regards as passing from one life to another. If it should do so, it automatically would be giving a personal quality to that carrier, and such a quality at least borders on the idea of a soul. This, of course, has not stopped folk Buddhism from assigning gender and various other personal aspects to the karmic carrier. In fact, folk Buddhism is as fully soul-accepting as is **Hinduism, Jainism**. This becomes especially obvious in the Buddhist **Pure-land** scriptures where one of the reasons that Buddha land is pure is because there is no women's **rebirth factor** in it. This means that all must enter it only via a male body.

Among the **Nusayris** the gender issue is made even simpler. Women do not have souls; therefore, it is only male souls that reincarnate.

A fact to be noted is that in those cultures where gender change during reincarnation is not expected, or in some cases not even considered possible, no such changes are reported. This is one of the elements that have encouraged the claim that reincarnation is a culturally determined fantasy. One response to this has been that the soul understands what the expectations are of the culture into which it is to be reborn, and re-embodies according to the rules of that culture.

In a small study in England of some twenty-two age-regressed individuals mentioned in Penny Thornton's 1990 *The Forces of Destiny* (page 138), women are much more likely to acknowledge having gender changed in the past than are men. This probably reflects the status of men in still patriarchal Western society continues to be higher than that of women.

A few reincarnationists have acknowledged that gender without physical sexual organs and the accompanying secondary sexual characteristics is a logically meaningless concept.

See also **American Indians; Angels and reincarnation; Bhaishajyaraja-guru; Buddhism, folk; Electra/Oedipus Complex and rebirth; Fantasy versus past life regression; Finite or infinite number of rebirths; Generationism and Traducianism; Grace-Loehr life readings; Homosexuality and transsexuality;** *Jataka Tales*; **Kabbalah; Moon; Mormonism; Pure-Land or Blissful Land Buddhism; Rebirth in Buddhism; Seth; Soul twins; Stygian sexuality; Yanomamo**.

Generationism and Traducianism. Both these terms refer to the belief that each person's soul is brought into being along with the person's body through the sexual union of the person's parents. In generationism the "souls" of parents give rise to the soul of the child in an "analogous" manner to the parents physically conceiving the child.

Traducianism, on the other hand, denotes a "materialistic" belief that the "physical body" of the parents gives rise to the soul in a fashion similar to producing the physical body of the child.

While no Christian denominations favor traducianism some are willing to accept generationism in place of soul **creationism**. In a Christian context, generationism has the advantage of explaining how everyone is born with "original sin" which soul creationism has a moral problem justifying. On the other hand, if the human soul is a product of both the parents' souls then the human soul of **Jesus** might not be free of original sin, which Christianity requires it to have been. This would also apply to the Virgin Mary, despite the any doctrine that she was conceived immaculately (without original sin). An attempted compromise has been to state that original sin is passed on only through the father, not the mother. In a context in which Jesus had only a human mother, not a human father, this would solve the problem of original sin for Jesus, but not for Mary. Another form of uni-parental soul generation would be that only the mother contributes to the soul, either via her egg cell or into the fetus via the umbilical chord, but this brings back the possibility of Jesus inheriting original sin from Mary. Obviously, no form of or generationism, much less traducianism is acceptable to reincarnationists.

See also **Creationism, soul; Emanationism; Embodiment, moment of; Soul's existence prior to embodiment; Gender issue of the soul; Infusionism; Original sin, Christianity, and reincarnation; Soul, origin of the**.

Genesis. This is the first book in the Old Testament and the first of the five books of the *Torah* (Hebrew: Law). It is the first to mention the underworld (*Sheol*), often translated as simply "the grave" (37:36, 42:38). This book also is the first of several Old Testament books in which the **soul** is directly equated with blood (Genesis 4:10, 9:4). Also, some literalist interpretations of Genesis 2:7–8 are said to mean that the soul's entrance into the body, and hence authentic life, does not begin until the newly born infant takes its first breath. That passage reads, "The Lord God formed a man (Hebrew: ***adam***) from the dust of the ground (Hebrew: *adamah*) and breathed into his nostrils the breath of life. Thus the man became a living creature (living soul)."

Some reincarnationists believe that they can find disguised support for reincarnation in Genesis. First there is Genesis 4:24 which concerns Lamech, a fifth generation descendent of Cain, who was the first man to have two wives. The passage reads, "Adah and Zillah [name of the wives], listen to me; wives of Lamech, mark what I say: I kill a man for wounding me, a young man for a blow. Cain may be avenged seven times [for the murderer of his brother Abel], but Lamech seventy-seven." This very mysterious passage has sometimes been used to claim that the Old Testament here is implying multiple life-times, in fact, 7, 77, or 777, depending on who cites it. How this passages might refer to past life times is open to serious question. It is possible that some Christian reincarnationists are interpreting at least 77 in light of the 70 times 7 in **Matthew** 18:21–22 and/or vice versa.

Second, there is Genesis 28:12, 17, and 19. The first verse reads, "He [Jacob] dreamt that he saw a ladder [Hebrew: *sullam*], which rested on the ground with its top reaching to heaven, and angels of God were going up and down upon it." The second reads, "This [dream site] is no other than the house of God, this is the gate of heaven." The final reads "He named that place Beth-El (House of God)." Actually, the original word for ladder can be translated as "ramp" or "stairway" which, from an archeological point of view, probably implies that the dream involved a *ziggurat* (stepped tower) which had both ramps and stairways and which was regarded by the Mesopotamians as a "gate of heaven" or "house of god."

According to a reincarnationist interpretation, these three passages should not be understood as God promising to Jacob that his innumerable descendents would be the future owners of the land. If such a traditional interpretation were valid then the process in which the angels moved from one end of the ladder to the other, would be for them to descend from heaven to earth and then ascend from earth to heaven, and not the other way around as stated in the text. This according to a reincarnationist interpretation, must mean that the angels were, in fact, souls which first ascended to heaven at death and then descended again at rebirth. Moreover, "rested on the ground" means that the ladder is based on earth, which is a metaphor for the earthly body.

Finally, there is Genesis 9:6, which is reinforced by **Revelation of John** 13:10. The Genesis verse reads, "He that sheds the blood of a man, for that man, his blood shall be shed." Revelations reads, "Whoever takes the sword to kill, by sword he is bound to be killed." Persons such as **Paramahansa Yogananda** have argued that since many killers die natural deaths the only way these biblical statements could be fulfilled would be for the killer to be reincarnated and himself be killed."

See also **Adam; Angels and reincarnation; Exodus; Finite or infinite number of rebirths; Forty; Jesus; Job, The Book of; Kabbalah; Melchizedek; Old Testament and the afterlife; Old Testament and the soul; Plato; Psalms; Serpent; Seven; Soul mates; Spiritism.**

German supporters of reincarnation *see* **Goethe; Herder; Lessing; Richter; Schiller; Schlosser; Schopenhauer; Wieland.**

Gilgul **or** ***Gilgulim*** (Hebrew: Turning over or rolling over). This became the standard Hebrew term for reincarnation. It replaced the somewhat earlier *ha'takah* (transference) or *ibbur* (impregnation) with *ibbur* taking on the special meaning of benign **possession**. In its more extensive form the Hebrew word for reincarnation is *gilgul neshamot* (wheel of the **soul**).

Although most Jewish traditions do not accept reincarnation the Hasidic sect uses reincarnation in its interpretation of Torah, as with the punishment to third and fourth generations mentioned in **Exodus**.

See also **Deuteronomy 5:2–3; Hasidism; Holocaust, Jewish; Job, Book of; Kabbalah; Karma, racial; Old Testament and the afterlife;** ***Qlippoth*****; Rebirth, ethnic; Rebirth, selective;** ***Tanya.***

Gilgulim, Sefer ha- (Hebrew: *Book of Transmigration*). This Kabbalic text by Hayim (Chayyim) Vital (1543–1620), a disciple of the renowned Kabbalic mystic **Isaac Luria**, is not to be confused with the *Sha'ar ha-Gilgulim* which is also by Vital and also deals with reincarnation. Vital believed he had undergone a variety of lives.

See also ***Galya Raza*; *Hezyonot, Sefer ha-*; Kabbalah.**

Glossolalia. This is speaking in a pseudo-language while in some degree of altered state of consciousness. The most well known manifestation of glossolalia is the Pentecostal "speaking in tongues," which the New Testament regards as one of the gifts of the Holy Spirit (Acts 2:3–12, 10:46, 19:6; 1st **Corinthians** 12:10, 31; 1st Corinthians 13:8; 1st Corinthians 14 [throughout]; and **Mark** 16:17–18). The church in medieval times and some churches in modern times have viewed both glossolalia and **xenoglossy** as signs of **possession** by evil spirits. It is xenoglossy, and not glossolalia, that is sometimes offered as proof of reincarnation.

See also **Muller, Catherine Elise.**

Glottologues. This is a person, such as a medium, who speaks in a language unknown to others. Glottologues must be clearly distinguished from those practicing the more past life-related **xenoglossy**.

See also **Muller, Catherine Elise**

Gnostic Order of Christ. This Order came into existence in 1988 as an offspring of the **Holy Order of Mans**. The Gnostic Order regards itself as following the Path of the Western Tradition of the Priesthood after the Order of **Melchizedek** of the Order of the Holy Cross. According to the teachings of this Order **Jesus** was a man who, having reincarnated through many lives, finally realized the secret gnostic or hermetic knowledge necessary for liberation and who is now one of the **ascended masters.**

Believing that all religions teach some form of truth the Order acknowledges the value of such Western religious literature as the Bible, the **Nag Hammadi Texts**, and a variety of Eastern texts.

See also **New Testament and reincarnation**.

Gnostic Orthodox Church of Christ in America. This church was founded in 1984 by George Burke (Swami Nirmalananda Giri), a western member of the Hindu monastic order of Shankaracharya. The Church is in communion with the **Liberal Catholic, Province of the U.S.A.** which allows it to integrate the doctrine of reincarnation with Eastern Orthodox mysticism.

Gnosticism. In the broadest sense of the term this is any spiritual teaching that says that spiritual knowledge (Greek: *gnosis*) or wisdom (*sophia*), rather than doctrinal faith (*pistis*) or some ritual practice is the main route to supreme spiritual attainment. In a more narrow sense Gnosticism is a designation for a very diverse group of religious sects which appeared in the first through third century CE. Each sect was to one degree or another, a syncretism of Iranian **Zoroastrianism** and Zurvanism; Greek **Orphism** and **Neoplatonism**; Egyptian religion; Judaism; and Christianity. Some forms of Gnosticism were very ascetic, while other forms were extremely libertine. The very diverse sources from which these sects borrowed their teachings usually meant that many of their teachings were not well integrated. Some gnostic groups considered themselves Christian while the more orthodox Christians considered them all to be heretics. A number of both Christian and non–Christian gnostic groups accepted the doctrine of reincarnation. The most successful non–Christian gnostic sect was **Manichaeism**. A strong element of gnostic mythology also entered into the **Kabbalah.**

See also **Body is the hell of the soul; Carpocrates; Cave; Doceticism; Emanationism; Hermetic philosophy; Karma versus grace; Mark, Gospel of; Neoplatonism;** *Pistis Sophia*; **Planetary descent and ascent of the soul;** *Qlippoth*; **Resurrection, bodily; Resurrection or reincarnation; Right-hand path and left-hand path; Simon Magus; Valentinus; Zodiac.**

God and karma *see* **Karma and God.**

God and rebirth in the West. For most people it is very common to associate a belief in a **soul** and some form of an afterlife with a belief in God.

With the increased discovery by Westerners of Eastern religions, such as Buddhism and **Jainism**, the ability for some to believe in a soul and an afterlife without having to believe in God accounts for some of the growth of an interest in rebirth by Westerners. However, to state that religions like Buddhism and Jainism do not believe in some form of deity must be clarified. The term atheism can only applied to these two religions to the degree that they reject the concept of a supreme creator deity. In that these religions accept the reality of lesser or non-supreme deities (*asuras, devas*) they are quite theistic.

The fact that Buddhism technically denies the existence of a soul while acknowledging the concept of rebirth is more or less as consistently ignored by Western Buddhists as it has always been by Eastern Buddhists. It is clearly the idea of rebirth that takes priority.

See also **Arguments pro and con on an afterlife in general (6 and 7); Arguments supportive of rebirth;** *Bhavachakra*; **Brahma and rebirth in Buddhism;** *Devachan*; *Devaloka*; **Karma and God; Karma as absolute or relative; Karma versus grace; Ontological leap or ontological discontinuity; Population increase issue and a theistic solution; Rebirth and religious tolerance; Soul, origin of the.**

God as creator and reincarnation *see Anatman*; **Arguments pro and con on an afterlife in gen-**

eral; Body-soul dualism; Brahman; Brahma and rebirth in Buddhism; Creationism, soul; Demiurge; Gender issue of the soul; Gnosticism; God and rebirth in the West; Jainism; *Jiva*; Karma and free will; Karma and God; Karma as absolute or relative; Karma versus grace; Lucretius; Ontological leap or ontological discontinuity; Plato; Population increase issue and a theistic solution; Rebirth and logical symmetry; Soul, origin of the.

Gods, cyclically dying and rising. Many reincarnationists assume that those ancient people who believed in a god or goddess that dies and come back to life would automatically believe in rebirth of the believer; however, a close examination of this assumption shows otherwise. In the earliest recorded belief about such a god, the Mesopotamian Tammuz, while he died each autumn-winter only to live again each spring-summer; his worshippers, upon death, simply went to a dismal **Hades** or **Sheol** type underworld where they would never again see the light of day. This same afterlife situation applied to all the other Middle Eastern and earliest Greek dying-rising god traditions. It was not until the development of the later Greek **Orphism** that a cyclical dying and reviving god included the believer in that cycle.

See also **Rebirth, analogies from nature; Resurrection of Jesus.**

Goethe, Johann Wolfgang von (1749–1832). This famous German poet and dramatist had a strong belief in reincarnation as did his brother-in-law, J. G. Schlosser. Goethe's fascination with everything Roman made him suspect that he was the reincarnation of Julius Caesar.

Going lilac. This term is found in Brennan's *The Reincarnation Workbook* (1989) and is credited to one Margaret O'Donnell. It refers to those persons who have an interest in esoteric studies, including rebirth, who are inclined towards vagueness, impracticality, theatrics, a pseudo-sweet spirituality, and who have a liking for showy lilac colored robes. Taking on several of these elements would qualify one as a lilac person. Lilac persons supposedly have a tendency to become so focused on their reincarnation interests that they spend more time caring about one or more of their past life personalities than their present one.

See also **Life script problem.**

Gorgias see **Plato.**

Grace, divine see ***Bhagavad Gita***; **Bhakti Yoga; Christianity and reincarnation; Colton, Ann Ree; Gnosticism; Id, ego, and superego; Jerome, Eusebius Hieronymus; Karma versus grace; New Testament and reincarnation; Origin** or **Origenes Adamanthus; Original sin, Christianity, and reincarnation; Plato; Pure-Land or Blissful Land Buddhism; Purgatory.**

Grace-Loehr life readings. Grace Wittenberger Loehr was the wife of the Reverend Franklin Loehr, the founder of Religious Research Foundation of America. In the early 1950's Mrs. Loehr discovered that she was an especially adept past life reader via the channeled entity which called itself Dr. John Christopher Daniels who, in turn, stated that he had been a research librarian in the ***akashic*** records for some 4,300 earth years. By the time that Mrs. Loehr left the foundation in 1979 she had given several thousand readings. The channeling of Dr. Daniels was then continued by Franklin Loehr until his death in 1988.

According to Dr. Daniels the **soul** is not a single unity, but a many-faceted, corporation-like grouping that is also an individuation of cosmic beingness. Because of this complexity, which implies a size too big for any single personality to contain, a soul is able to send only a portion of itself into an earth embodiment. This allows for other parts of the soul to function independently of its earth part in non-terrestrial areas. At death the personality may survive for some time, but it will eventually cease to exist and the soul will create a new personality to be reborn, perhaps even before the extinction of the old one.

The life readings channeled through Dr. Daniels, some going back as far as lives on the **lost continent** of Atlantis, insist that the human soul never assumes anything less than a human personality, thus excluding animal (regressive) transmigration.

See also **Channeling; Finite or infinite number of rebirths; Gender issue of the soul; Solity; Transmigration, regressive.**

Grant, Joan Marshall (1907–1990) Grant was a British author who claims to have remembered a number of past lives, some going back to ancient times. She wrote a number of books which she regarded as a chronicle of these lives. Among these, several deal with ancient **Egypt**, one with a 16th century Italian lute player, one with an American Indian female warrior; and one with a Greek priestess of a mystery cult. Grant's ***Far Memory***, which is her most recent life autobiography, was published by Ariel Press, Columbus, Ohio (1956).

Some skeptics of Grant's claims point out that her father had an interest in Egyptology and that as a child she may have assimilated information about Egypt and other past civilizations from him. On the other hand, it has been argued that her **soul** may have deliberately chosen to reincarnate as the daughter of a man interested in Egypt.

Grant had an interesting way of viewing the time factor of her various lives. Instead of envisioning them sequentially, or from past to present, she envisioned them as existing simultaneously. The best way to understand this is to think of an orange with a number of sections or segments surrounding a central core. Each segment represents one life. The individual actually exists in the central core. The individual normally focuses all his attention on a single segment which he then considers to be the present life. In remembering a so-called past life the individual is just temporarily shifting his focus to a different segment which he then considers to be a past life. Theoretically this same model could be used to explain the so-called glimpse into the future. Here the individual is shifting his focus to a life he is simultaneously living, but from the perspective of the so-called present life he considers to be a future life.

See also **Cooke, Grace; Future-lives; Kelsey, Denys; Lazaris; Ouspensky, Parallel lives; Plurality of existences; Pyotr D; Seth; Rebirth, simultaneous; Stevenson, Ian.**

Great White Brotherhood. This is an often cited alternative name for the secret adepts called the **ascended masters.** This name seems to have originally come from a text called *The Cloud on the Sanctuary* (1800) by Karl Von Eckartshausen. This work deals with inner spiritualism or the interior church and, despite the word "white," has no relationship to any kind of racism. The Brotherhood is sometimes also referred to as the Great White Lodge, the Occult Hierarchy, or even the Illuminanti.

While a belief in this Brotherhood does not automatically implies a belief in reincarnation, the overwhelming majority of Brotherhood believes are also reincarnationists.

The term Great White Brotherhood should presumably not be confused with the White Brothers. According to one of the subjects of hypnotic regression by **Dr. Alexander Cannon**, those souls in the **garden of waiting** that are prepared for their rebirth descent are guarded and protected during this preparation by those called the White Brothers and Blue Sisters.

See also **Aetherius Society; Aquarian Foundation; Ascended masters; Aum Temple of Universal Truth; Crowley, Aleister; Dark Brotherhood; Holy Order of Mans; I Am Movement; Pythagoras; Rosicrucians; Solar Temple, Order of; White Lodge.**

Greek afterlife, the ancient. The earliest Greek concept of an afterlife was associated with the god of the underworld, **Hades** (Greek: the unseen). This god's realm, which eventually was also called Hades, was a dim and sad ghostly place, to which all of the dead went regardless of their virtues in life or lack thereof. In other words it was, like the original *Sheol*, neither a place of punishment nor reward. Later Greek thought began to make a moral differentiation between the afterlife of the person of virtue and that of the person without virtue. For the virtuous there was a paradise which was thought of as either the Isles of the Blessed or the Elysium Fields.

The Isles of the Blessed were at first considered an afterlife paradise for especially heroic persons. Later on it became less elitist and was considered the destination of all who had lived a moral life. **Pythagoras** located the Isles on the **moon**, while **Plato** and **Cicero** placed them somewhere beyond the stars. This change from an earthly paradise to a celestial one was probably influenced by Babylonian astrological arts of the time.

The Elysium Fields or Plain was a paradise that was of special importance in the later Greek Elysium mystery religion. Like the Isles of the Blessed the exact location of this paradise was also in question. While some authorities also placed this paradise on the moon other authorities placed it beneath the earth in a special section of Hades and still other thought of it as being in the far west where the sun set.

For all those who died without gaining the right to paradise their fate was to remain in Hades, only now it was mostly a place of punishment. For the truly wicked, however, there was **Tartarus**. In earlier Greek mythology, except for the river of fire (*Phlegethon*) on one side of it, this was a totally lightless place beneath Hades where the gods sent their enemies, especially the Titans, for punishment. By the time of Plato it had come to mean a general place of punishment for all general evil doers.

The major exception for the later view of Hades as a place just of punishment was when it was thought of as the place where souls resided prior to being reborn into another earthly body. By Christian times Hades was simply equated with **Hell** as the realm of Satan.

See also **Greeks and reincarnation; Hermes;** *Kyklos Genesion*; **Old Testament and the afterlife; Second death; Shadow** or **shade; Shinto; Virgil.**

Greeks and reincarnation. The ancient Greeks never formulated a consistent concept of an afterlife. However, there is no mention, or even a hint, of a belief in **metempsychosis** or transmigration in the oldest Greek literary works, the Homeric epics. The earliest known clear-cut mention of the doctrine of metempsychosis among the ancient

Greeks has been attributed to the 6th century BCE philosopher Pherecydes of Syros and his student **Pythagoras**.

It has been theorized that the belief in metempsychosis entered the Greek world from **Egypt**, or even India, but these beliefs are almost certainly wrong. While it was easy enough for Greeks to travel to Egypt, the doctrine of metempsychosis was simply not taught there. While India would not have been impossible to reach, it would have been nearly impossible for a Greek speaker to have communicated with Indians in the 6th century BCE. It was not until the conquests of Alexander the Great in the fourth century BCE that Greek and Indian cultures and languages were in direct contact with one another. Moreover, it was not until the discovery of the monsoon winds in 47 CE that a major increase in the exchange of goods and ideas began to affect the Greco-Roman world from the East.

Another suggested source for the Greek doctrine of metempsychosis has been from the shamanic people of Thrace (Bulgaria) or even Scythia (Ukraine). The shamanic people of both these areas had direct relations with the Greeks through the Greek trading colonies around the Black Sea. Moreover, this possibility is supported by the fact that the cult of Dionysus, the god at the center of the **Orphism**, seems to have originated in Thrace. On the other hand, Jan N. Bremmer, in his *The Rise and Fall of the Afterlife* (2002), questions a Thracian origin and suggests a more indigenous Greek source. This would make sense in that more recent research has indicated that the Greek belief in metempsychosis made its first appearance in **Magna Graecia** (Southern Italy and Sicily), a region closing associated with Pythagoras.

See also **Arguments supportive of rebirth; Ashoka, King; Bogomils;** *Book of the Dead (Egyptian);* **Butterfly; Cave; Creationism, soul; Empedocles; Greek afterlife, the ancient; Hermes; Hermetic philosophy; Herodotus;** *Kyklos Genesion;* **Plato; Priesthood, lack of an organized; Second death; Right-hand path and left-hand path; Virgil; Zodiac.**

Gregory of Nazianus (329?–389 CE). This bishop of Constantinople, in his *On the Soul and the Resurrection*, declared the idea of reincarnation as incompatible with Christian resurrection.

See also **Christian fathers critical of reincarnation; Christianity and reincarnation; New Testament and reincarnation.**

Gregory of Nyssa (332–398 CE). This Christian bishop of Nyssa, in his *On the Making of Man*, criticized both the idea of the **soul's existence prior to embodiment** and its reincarnation. Gregory was the brother of **Basil (Basilus) of Caesarea**.

See also **Christian fathers critical of reincarnation; Christianity and reincarnation; New Testament and reincarnation.**

Grey occultists. According to Eklal Kueshana, in *The Ultimate Frontier* (1963), these occultists are the majority of the world's clerics in that they try to control humanity by teaching the false doctrines of original sin, hell-fire, eternal damnation, the resurrection of the dead, and an eternally indolent heaven, instead of the doctrines of universal salvation through reincarnation and spiritual growth to divinity. The grey occultists are, unknowingly or knowingly, in the service of the demonic powers called the Black Mentalists.

See also **Esotericism versus Occultism; Stelle Group.**

Grief and rebirth *see* **Earth-bound.**

Griffin, David Ray (1939–). Griffin, a contemporary Whiteheadian scholar, has dealt with the body-mind relationship issue and reincarnation in several of his books. Griffin suggests that the human **soul** can function independently of the body and even reincarnate into other bodies. Griffin also believes that Alfred North Whitehead's notion of "prehension" (meaning the ability to include past events and memories into one's interior being) may exist.

See also **Body-soul dualism; Objective immortality.**

Grof, Stanislav (1931–). This co-founder of transpersonal psychology and LSD researcher has written or co-authored a number of books dealing with reincarnation.

Group karma *see* **Karma, group.**

Group reincarnation *see* **Karma, family; Rebirth, group; Soul groups.**

Group soul. This describes a situation where three or more former discernibly separate entities to some degree unite or merge with one another to form a larger more efficient entity. The term **group soul** should not be confused with either the terms collective soul or **soul groups**.

The concept of a group soul has sometimes been used to explain past life recall without any kind of rebirth doctrine. According to this explanation every soul belongs to a group that can number in the twenties, hundreds, or thousands. Since there is a natural psychic connection between all the souls in the group there is a great deal of shared memories. Therefore, when a currently living individual recalls aspects of the life of a person who died before the birth of the individual, or even as recent as his infant years, those recalled memories really belong to a separate soul, but one that is in the same group as the soul of the living person.

The 19th century psychic researcher **F.W.H. Myers** had his own concept of a group soul which was a number of souls united in a single spirit, acting and reacting upon one another in the ascending scale of psychic evolution.

See also *Celestine Prophecy*; **Cummins, Geraldine; Karma; Karma, racial; Lazaris; Michael (2); Ra (2); Rebirth, alternative explanations to; Rebirth, group; Seth; Wilcock, David.**

Guardian of the Threshold *see* **Dweller on the Threshold.**

Guenon, Rene (1886–1951). Guenon, was a French philosopher who, unlike most modern esoteric writers, strongly argued against reincarnation. Guenon took the position that all personal characteristics of a person, including memories, have nothing to do with the real **soul**. He believed that the real soul has many levels of existence to pass through before fully realizing that it is part of a single universal being. Because the soul has so many forms of existence through which it must pass it can not afford to repeat any one of them. Any one soul, therefore, will take on human form only once, regardless of how short or long that form lasts. Guenon further suggests that any memories of a past life are but the psychic residue shed by the soul at death and somehow picked up by a living person. Such shed memories, he believed, may also account for **possessions**, hauntings, and the séance phenomena. In his *Introduction to the Study of the Hindu Doctrines*, (1945) Guenon labeled reincarnation as metaphysical nonsense because it limits universal possibility: yet, despite this, his concept of the soul is very ***atman***-like.

Guf ha-Briyot (Hebrew: the Body or Vessel of Creatures). This is said to be the celestial reservoir (*guf*) from which souls enter the cycle of bodily existence. Until the *guf* is emptied, the Messiah can not come. After death souls go on to the ***tzror hachayyim***.

See also ***Enoch, Third Book of*; Kabbalah.**

Guided imagery. In this method for recalling past life memories, the conscious self is encouraged to relax and visualize images from the subconscious with the understanding that whatever images arise are not without some significance in either the present or past life. Sometimes in certain kinds of guided imagery music can accompany and facilitate this process.

Guirdham, Arthur (1905–?). Dr. Guirdham, a British psychiatrist, was consulted in 1962 by a Mrs. Smith who was suffering from persistent nightmares. She said that these dreams involved images of the 13th century **Cathars** of Languedoc (Southern France). In particular, the dream involved a man by the name of Roger, who she came to regard as her past life lover. In fact, as her therapy continued under Dr. Guirdham she came to identify Roger with the doctor. Whether by coincidence or not it turned out that Dr. Guirdham himself already had an interest in the Cathars; therefore, it is not entirely surprising that the doctor himself soon acknowledged that he was Roger. These Cathar connections did not stop with the doctor and Mrs. Smith, however. 1968 an acquaintance of the doctor, a Miss Miles, by what was said to be pure chance, admitted to Dr. Guirdham that she also experienced memories of a Cathar past life. More remarkably, still three other individuals by 1971 came forth to the doctor with Cathar past memories.

This seeming group, or collective, reincarnation phenomenon soon took on another dimension when it was claimed that all these individuals also remembered past lives together as far back as the fourth century C.E. and as recently as the Napoleonic era.

The validity of this case was put into question by the fact that Dr. Guirdham refused to permit independent investigators to interview any of the other above mentioned individuals. Furthermore, it was discovered that the events in the Cathar past of Dr. Guirdham had many parallels to the 1945 novel *High are the Mountains* by Hannah Closs. (London: A. Dakers limited.)

Nonetheless, according to Guirdham the following books are a documentation of his past life experience as a Cathar: *Cathars and Reincarnation* (1970); *A Foot in Both Worlds* (1973); *We are One Another* (1974); and *The Lake and the Castle* (1976).

Of course, since the publication of these works it has been very fashionable for past life recallers to discover a life as a Cathar.

Guirdham also wrote under the pseudonym of Francis Eaglesfield.

See also **Honest lying; Memory contamination; Past life fakery.**

Gurdjieff, Georgi Ivanovitch (1872–1949). Gurdjieff, a well known and often controversial Russian spiritual teacher, was the founder of what is sometimes called the Fourth Way. The Fourth Way is what his followers consider the integration of the older emotional path of the monk, the physical path of the *fakir*, and the intellectual path of the *yogi*. The greatest influence on Gurdieff seems to have been **Sufism**. According to Gurdjieff, human beings are not born with souls, but must develop or earn them. As for Gurdjieff's views on reincarnation, it can be summed up in the words "reincarnation is such a misunderstood and misrepresented concept that it is useless to talk about it."

See also **Astral body; Collin, Robert; Ouspensky, Pyotr; Russia, reincarnation in**.

Gwenved. According to some ancient Celtic beliefs if the **soul**, going through many rebirths, was able to purify itself sufficiently it would eventually find itself in the eternally peaceful White Heaven or *Gwenved*.

Hades (Greek: most likely meaning "invisible" or "unseen"). This name for the ancient afterlife world in Homer's time (12th century BCE) was thought of as being in the far west, beyond the mythic river Oceanus, which was thought to surround the earth. Later it was placed beneath the earth. By the time of the Greek poet Hesiod (8th century BCE) Hades was divided into two regions of darkness, the shallower Erebus and the deeper **Tartarus**. Eventually, the gloomy fields of Asphodel were also added.

Hades was also at times the name of the god of the underworld; however, since it was thought that to say his name could bring upon oneself misfortune, he was given the euphemism **Pluto**, meaning "Wealth." This renaming was justified on the basis that the underworld was also the source of precious metals and gems. Another euphemism for this god was Zeus of the Underworld.

In at least one theosophical understanding of Hades, it is a metaphor for womb into which the **soul** descends in order to be reborn.

See also **Greek afterlife, the ancient;** *Lethe*; **Orphism; Pluto, the God; Theosophy**.

Haggard, H. Rider (1856–1925). Along with **Marie Corelli**, Haggard was one of the two most widely read Victorian novelists who brought the concept of reincarnation and karma to British popular awareness. His works with these themes, sometimes called the Ayesha series, include *She* (1886), *Ayesha, the Return of She* (1905), and *She and Allen* (1920). Haggard also makes reference in his autobiography to his experiences in previous lives.

See also **Karmic romances**.

Hall, Manly Palmer (1901–1990). Hall, a Canadian-American esotericist, showed an interest in exotic knowledge at an early age. He became a member of the Theosophical Society and the Rosicrucian Fellowship of Max Heindal while in his teens. In the fall of 1920 he gave a lecture on reincarnation in Santa Monica, California which began his career as an esoteric lecturer. In 1922 he began to write his magnum opus *The Secret Teachings of All Ages: An Encyclopedic Outline of Masonic, Hermetic, Qabbalistic and Rosicrucian Symbolical Philosophy*, which was published in 1928 and earned Hall a world-wide reputation. In 1923 he received ordination as a minister in the Los Angeles based metaphysical Church of the People. In 1934 Hall developed plans for what soon became the Los Angeles Philosophical Research Society where he taught up to shortly before his death. Hall has over 200 books on esoteric subjects to his credit; a number of these deal with reincarnation.

See also **Midnight; Rosicrucians; Theosophy**.

Hamsa. Sanskrit for crane, swan, or goose, especially as the *vahana* (vehicle) of Brahma. It is also a Hindu symbol for reincarnation.

Harrowing of hell (Also Descent into Hell). This refers to the Christian belief that during the time between the death of **Jesus** on the cross on Good Friday and his resurrection on Easter Sunday his spirit descended into hell to liberate the souls of the just, especially the Old Testament patriarchs and prophets, something that could not be done until Christ's sacrifice purged them of the sin of **Adam**. This descent into hell by Jesus became an official part of Christian orthodoxy at the Fourth Council of Sirmium (359 CE) and was reaffirmed in the final form of the Apostles' Creed (1216).

The notion of the harrowing of hell is not specifically found in the New Testament, but is justified on the very questionable basis of **Acts** 2:27–31 "...for thou will not abandon my soul to death, nor let thy loyal servant suffer corruption. Thou has shown me the ways of life, thou will fill me with gladness by thy presence" ... "he spoke with foreknowledge of the resurrection of the Messiah." Acts here is actually quoting **Psalms** 16:10, "...for thou will not abandon me to *Sheol* nor suffer thy servant to see the pit." On more secure grounds the Harrowing could be based on 1st **Peter** 3:19, and 4:6. In 1st Peter 3 it states, "And in the spirit he [Christ] went and made his proclamation to the imprisoned spirits...," while 1st Peter 4 states, "Why was the Gospel preached to those who are dead? In order that.... They might in the spirit be alive with the life of God." There seems to be some difference of opinion as to whether the "place of imprisonment" and/or *Sheol* in these particular passages referred to hell proper (Hades) or to the **limbo** of the Fathers.

Christian orthodoxy has used the Harrowing to argue against reincarnation on the basis that there would be no need for the Harrowing if all souls reincarnated.

See also **New Testament and reincarnation; Old Testament and the afterlife; Purgatory**.

Hashimiyya. This rather obscure 8th century CE Iranian gnostic group seems to have believed in reincarnation (*tanasukh*).

See also **Islam; Kanthaeans; Khurramiyya.**

Hasidism (Hebrew for "pious ones"). In its most common usage this term refers to the Jewish mystical movement that began in the 18th century Russian controlled part of Poland. This movement was strongly influenced by the Kabbalic teachings of **Isaac Luria**, which included a belief in reincarnation.

See also **Holocaust, Jewish; Kabbalah; Karma, racial; Old Testament and the afterlife;** *Qlippoth*; **Russia, reincarnation in.**

Hauntings. The common concept of a haunting involves the restless spirit of a deceased person; however, for some reincarnationists it can mean the spirit of someone who was so attached to materiality that they are delaying the natural reincarnation process.

See also **Guenon, Rene; Kabbalah.**

Hawkman. This is a superhero in the DC Comics universe, who first appeared in *Flash Comics #1* (1940) and was a featured character in that title throughout the 1940s, but the title disappeared from print after World War II. Although several incarnations of Hawkman have appeared in DC Comics, the original Hawkman was Carter Hall, an archeologist who was the reincarnation of an ancient Egyptian prince, Khufu. In the original series Hawkman was accompanied by his reincarnated bride, Shiera Sanders, who was the crime fighter Hawkgirl. In the 1950s a new version of Hawkman and Hawkgirl was introduced, but here they were from another planet instead of earthly reincarnates. Since 1985 Hawkman's history has become a very mixed affair with new versions of the character appearing sometimes as an ancient Egyptian reincarnate and other times as an extraterrestrial.

See also **Egypt.**

Heaven. In Western religion this is both the dwelling place of God and final goal of the morally worthy dead. This is actually in contrast to most non–Western cultures where the dwelling place of God and the dead are separate from one another. Most folk cultures have some version of a paradise for the deceased, but in the majority of cases it does not depend on moral worth. Instead, heaven is a pleasant realm for all of one's deceased kin since all are regarded as worthy of it, regardless of their moral qualities. To view it any other way is impious. In other words, in these traditions an afterlife has no soterial (**soul**-saving) significance.

The Kabbalists maintain that there are seven heavens with the highest, called *Elyon*, being the dwelling place of God and the most exalted angels. In **Islam** there are also said to be seven heavens, the highest of which is called Illiyum, and is formed of divine light. In Theosophy there are seven level of the ***devachan***.

In religious systems which acknowledge both a heavenly realm and the rebirth-karma complex or **karmic eschatology** such as **Hinduism**, Buddhism, and Jainism the heavenly realm is just one of several possible realms other than an earthly one into which a person can be reborn. In these religious systems any birth into a heavenly existence is usually not permanent. In time the heaven dweller must pass out of that realm and re-enter the rebirth cycle.

See also **Astral plane;** *Bhavachakra*; *Devaloka*; **Ethicalized or karmic rebirth; Greek afterlife, the ancient; Heavens, Buddhist; Hell; Kabbalah; Mental plane;** *Moksha*, *Mukta* or *Mukti*; **Nine doors; Old Testament and the afterlife; Paradise; Pure-Land or Blissful Land, Buddhist; Summerland.**

Heaven, hell, and Buddhist no-soul (Self). It has often been noted that the Buddhist teaching of no-soul (self) or *anatman* is at odds with the traditional Buddhist belief that a being can be reborn into a metaphysical state, the purpose of which is to reward or punish the "self." The fact of the matter is that traditional Buddhism has more or less ignored the teaching of no-soul (self) in order to satisfy the average believer's desire to hold on to a self. The average Buddhist, like the average person of most other religions, wants to believe that if he or she has not gained what he or she either desired or felt entitled to in this life then he or she would be pleasantly compensated for this lack in some way, in one or more future lives. Also, that same person usually wants to believe that those who did not deserve to enter heaven ought to experience painful deprivation (**hell**) in some way in one or more future lives. This view can only be described as an intense belief in the reality of selfhood.

See also *Bhavachakra*; **Heavens, Buddhist.**

Heavens, Buddhist. In traditional Buddhist mythic cosmology the concept of heaven, or more correctly of the heavens, is nothing like the Western Judeo-Christian one. To simplify a rather complex scheme it can be said that all the various levels and sub-levels of the Buddhist heavens fall into three groups. The lowest of these is the realm of desire (*kamaloka*) which has six sub-levels. The first sub-level is inhabited by (deities) that have bodies and emotions similar to those of human beings, especially in that these deities come in either male or female forms. Here are found the four heavenly kings that guard over the four cardinal directions; and above them is the sub-level of the thirty-three deities who are ruled over by the god Indra. Above this is the sub-level of **Yama** (Japanese **Emma-O**), originally the ruler of the ordinary dead, but who later was said to be the ruler of the **hungry ghost** realm and still later the ruler of **hell**. The next sub-level is the *Tushita* **Heaven**, which is where the ***bodhisattva*** Maitreya dwells. The last two sub-levels of the *kamaloka* are the *nirman-rati* and the *para-nirmita-vashavartin*. The only significance to these two realms seems to be that **Mara,** the god of Death, resides in the latter one.

The second group of heavens is called the realm of form and is also divided, in this case into four sub-levels, each of which is named after one of the *rupa* (form) *dhyanas* (meditations). Of these the only one of any significance is the heaven of the first *dhyana*. It is here that the Brahma deities reside. These beings differ from the lower deities in that they are genderless and rule in solitude.

All of the heavenly dwellers above Brahma deities, including those in the *arupa* (formless) *dhyanas* (meditation) realms, are so immersed in their states of sublime meditative bliss that they are totally divorced from all states of existence below them.

The most important fact about all these heavenly realms is that, although they are where human beings may go who have built up a large treasury of karmic merit, they are not the best of all possible realms in which to be reborn. The reason is that the very blissful nature of even the lowest of these realms leaves their denizens with no motivation to seek enlightenment and liberation from **samsara** (world of birth and death). The result of this is that as soon as these deities use up their store of karmic merit they must fall back into one of the non-blissful states of existence. If they are fortunate they will return to a human birth, which is the best of all the realms of *samsara*, because only in the human state is there the required balance of joy and sorrow to allow for one to realize the value of seeking enlightenment.

Finally, none of these Buddhist heavens must be confused with any of the Buddha-fields or **Pure-Lands**. These are traditionally considered totally independent states of existence.

See also **Animals and rebirth, non–Western view;** *Asuras; Bhavachakra;* **Brahma and rebirth in Buddhism; Hungry ghosts**.

Heaven's Gate. This is the name of a group of thirty-nine people who believed in apocalyptic **UFOism** and who committed mass suicide at their southern California Rancho Santa Fe headquarters in 1997. The group was founded by Marshall Herff Applewhite and Bonnie Lu Nettles in 1975. These two believed that they were reincarnated beings sent from heaven to restate the message of **Jesus**. They also believed that they were the two witnesses prophesied in Revelation 11:3–12 who would be killed by the enemies of God, but who in three and a half days would be brought back to life and would be taken to heaven in a cloud. This cloud, they believed, was actually a space ship of some kind. With the unexpected natural death of Bonnie Lu Nettles in 1985 the ideology of the group changed somewhat, but it continued to believe that Earth was a place of great misery due to souls being trapped in the cycle of reincarnation. With the arrival of the 1997 Hale-Bopp comet and the belief that a spaceship was concealed in its tail, the members of the group were convinced that this was the ship to heaven for which they had been waiting. Since the ship could only transport disembodied souls it was thought necessary for its passengers to release themselves from corporeal existence, which they did.

See also **Koresh, David; Solar Temple, Order of the**.

Hebrews *see* **Christianity and reincarnation; Melchizedek; New Testament sacrificial concept; Old Testament; Rebirth and moral perfection; Seventeenth century renewed interest in rebirth**.

Hedonism (S: *kama-sukkha-allikanu-yoga*). In Buddhism hedonism or the over indulgence of worldly pleasures, is a major impediment to the goal of escaping from the inevitable dissatisfaction (*dukkha*) of life or the cycle of rebirth and redeath.

See also **Accidentalism;** *Amrta;* **Annihilationism, Buddhist view; Asceticism; Determinism; Eternalism; Middle Way**.

Heimarmene (Greek: fate). As an ancient Greek goddess, fate was in charge of the ***kyklos genesion*** (cycle of becoming, i.e. **Metempsychosis** or **Transmigration**). The Greek *moira* was a synonym of *heimarmene*.

Hell. This word commonly refers to a place or condition of punitive suffering, especially in an afterlife. In examining cultures world-wide, ancient and modern, it is to be noted that in comparison to the number of cultures that believe in some form of afterlife paradise or **heaven**, those that believe also in an afterlife place of punishment are far fewer. In fact, the entire idea of hell is absent in most folk societies since the whole concept of one's deceased kin going to a place of punishment is irreverent. This is especially true of cultures that practice **ancestor worship**. Instead, in these folk societies punishment for breaking taboos or other undesirable behavior is thought to result in illness or misfortune in this life. This anti-hell view precludes a meaningful place for a fully developed **karmic eschatology**.

In most religions that teach rebirth and accept a hell the soul is usually said to abide there only temporarily, which actually makes hell much more like the Western **purgatory** (*naraka*) than a true hell. This temporary or purgatorial idea has been adopted by Christian reincarnationists who believe that the orthodox Christian view of an eternal hell makes a mockery of God's justice and love. In fact, most Western reincarnationists who accept a hell or purgatory state go one step beyond the Eastern view of purgatory in that they regard it as, not only temporary, but as a remedial or purgative state rather than a retributive state. This, in turn, is part of the whole Western view of reincarnation as an optimistic, necessary spiritual growth process towards enlightenment versus the Eastern view of reincarnation as an exclusively punitive process that is necessitated by the failure to attain enlightenment.

In the New Testament hell is referred to as everlasting which might seem an insurmountable objection to any temporary stay in hell, but for the less orthodox this is not the case. They point out that while hell itself may be ever lasting, this does not necessarily mean that those sent there must remain there forever, for the mercy of God would not require that. This view, obviously, is compatible with reincarnation.

Regardless whether it is the Eastern or Western view of purgatory, it is important to understand that in the context of rebirth and karma any idea of an other than this-life punishment system, or for that matter a reward system (heaven), must be very carefully balanced with a this-life karma punishment and reward system if rebirth is to have soterial (soul-saving) significance. It is, in fact, for this reason that in such religious systems as **Hinduism**, Buddhism, and **Jainism**, the stay in the hell realm can not be permanent. In time the hell dweller must pass out of that realm and re-enter the rebirth cycle and at some point must complete its punishment in the earthly realm.

See also **Annihilationism, Biblical view;** *Apocatastasis*; **Astral plane;** *Avichi*; *Bhavachakra*; **Christianity and reincarnation; Christianity, esoteric; Eighth sphere; Greek afterlife, the ancient; Harrowing of Hell; Heaven; Hell, the Chinese; Hungry ghosts; Karma in the ancient and modern west; Limbo; Myers, F. W. H.; New Age; Nine doors; Old Testament and the afterlife; Rebirth, instantaneous; Rebirth in the West; Resurrection, bodily; Romans.**

Hell, the Chinese (Chinese: *Yi/Di Yu*, Earth Prison). Due to the custom of **ancestor worship** the Chinese had no real concept of hell, or even **purgatory**, until the arrival of Buddhism. Once Buddhism became popular a specifically Chinese folk version of hell, much influenced by **Daoism**, came into being. The Chinese folk hell, or more correctly purgatory, is divided into the Ten Palaces of Hell (*Shih Tien-yen-wang*, WG). Each of these is administered by one of the ten kings (*shih-wang* WG) of hell, with each king having a specific function with regards to punishing the evil souls (*hun*).

The **soul** upon death leaves the body and journeys to hell. Upon reaching it there is a demon gate keeper who demands payment. The reason given for this demand is that in one's previous death and journey to hell one borrowed extensively from the Bank of Hell (*Yen-lo*, WG) and the debt has not yet repaid. This payment is supplied by the family of the deceased in a number of ways, especially by the burning of special funeral money. If no payment is forthcoming, a rare event thanks to family deposits in the Bank of Hell, the gate keeper beats the arriving resident for the whole of the first week. Once past the gatekeeper there is a preliminary sorting out of the good from the evil souls by way of a scale (*psychostasis*). Those souls that are too heavy due to their vices are marked for punishment. This takes up the second week in hell. Next, the souls go to the Village of Bad Dogs where the demon dogs perform a further, more refined sorting in the third week. The fourth week finds the souls facing the Mirror of Retribution (*Sie-kang tai*, WG) which shows the condition into which souls will be reborn, either as human beings or animals. In the fifth week, the souls will be taken to a terrace where they will have one last chance to see their former home, family, and have a chance to reflect on the life they have left. In the sixth week, all the souls will have to cross, by one of two **bridges**, a great watery chasm inhabited by monsters. The bridge for the evil doers, the Bridge of Sighs, is very thin and dangerous to cross, while the one for the virtuous, the Fairy Bridge, is wide and comfortable to cross. At the seventh week the souls reach the rotating Wheel of the Law (or Wheel of the King) of rebirth. However, before any souls climb on to the Wheel, however, they must drink a bitter-sweet brew, or liquor of forgetfulness, which is given to them by the Lady Meng (*Meng-Po Niang-Niang*, WG), goddess of the underworld. This drink will vanquish all memory of their past lives.

The Chinese have conceived an interesting reason for such forgetfulness. This forgetfulness was made necessary because in ages past unscrupulous men would claim that in a past life they had been the legitimate husbands of some women and so they had this-life sexual rights to those women. To end such skullduggery the gods instituted the drink of forgetfulness so that everyone who claimed that they could remember a past life would be known as a liar.

Once souls are on the Wheel their future will be determined by the point they are permitted to drop from it. If souls are permitted to leave the Wheel near the top right they will be reborn into wealth and power; if near the top left, as the poor and miserable; if at the middle right, as a viviparous animal; if at the middle left, as an oviparous animal; if at the lower right their rebirth is as a creature with a shell or scales; and at the lower left rebirth is as an insect. These seven weeks make for the forty-nine days that some consider the standard **interim period** time between death and rebirth

A simpler competing Chinese schema of hell states that the first king receives the deceased and judges whether or not they deserve punishment. If the soul is innocent of any major vices it will be immediately sent to the hall of the tenth king. If guilty of one or more major vices or crimes the souls will be sent to the second through to the ninth kings, who will administer specific punishments for specific crimes. The tenth king determines the kind of life into which the soul, upon being released from hell, will be reborn and here too this rebirth will occur only after taking the drink of forgetfulness.

In some versions of this Chinese hell schema suicide victims went to the "City of the Dead by Accident (*Wang-si ch'eng*, WG)" where they were doomed never to be reborn, but to remain there forever.

Much of the information about the Chinese versions of hell can be found in the *Precious Records* (*Yu Li,* WG), popular Daoist and Buddhist texts which describe in grizzly detail the torment of the dead.

See also ***Bodhisattva***; **Chinese religion and reincarnation; Chuan-lun wang; Daoism; Drink or fruit of forgetfulness; Emma-o; Empire of Jade;** ***Naraka***; **Vegetarianism**.

Helmont, Franciscus Mercurius van (1618–1699). This author of *Two Hundred Queries* (1640 is perhaps best known for having argued against the orthodox Christian claim that Hebrews 9:27–28 does not deny the possibility of multiple life-times (reincarnation). That passage reads, "And as it is the lot of men to die once, and after death comes judgment, so Christ was offered once to bear the burden of men's sin,"

See also **Christianity and reincarnation; New Testament and reincarnation; Seventeenth century renewed interest in rebirth**.

Heracleides of Ponticus (b. about 390 BCE). A student of Plato and Aristotle, Heracleides was at once a philosopher, psychologist, and astronomer. He understood that the earth rotates, an idea not commonly accepted until 1800 years later and that both the inner planets, Mercury and Venus revolve around the sun. His interests in the mind-**soul** (*psyche*) lead him to study trance, visionary, and prophetic states of consciousness. He sought to prove the existence of the gods, divine retribution, and **metempsychosis**. He believed that the original home of the soul was in the **Milky Way**.

See also ***Kyklos Genesion***; **Planetary descent and ascent of the soul; Poimandres; Priesthood, lack of an organized**.

Herder, Johann Gottfried von (1744–1803). This famous German philosopher and man of letters wrote "Dialogues on Metempsychosis." In *Prose Writers of Germany,* translated by Frederic H. Hedge. New York: C.S. Francis and Company, (1856).

Hermes. This ancient Greek god was originally an ithyphallic (erect penis) fertility deity. By the time of the composition of Homer's *Odyssey,* however, he had become the messenger of the gods and protector of travelers in foreign lands. As such, Hermes in time took on a dual function. In the first of these he was the patron deity of commerce, science, and invention. In the second he was *Hermes Chthonius* (Hermes of the underworld), the one who guided the souls of the dead (hence also *Hermes Psychopompos*) to the underworld (Hades). In one version of the Orpheus story it was Hermes who guided Orpheus into and out of Hades. In some other myths Hermes also helps judge the dead and so was partially responsible for guiding them on to their next rebirth.

Hermes was early on depicted as a fully grown, bearded man, clothed in a full tunic. Later on he was portrayed as a beardless naked youth. This later image may have been encouraged by the Hermai, who were two boys whose function was to act as guides to enquirers of the dead at the oracle of Trophonius.

It is of some interest that **Edgar Cayce** considered this mythological figure to be an embodied celestial **soul** sent from on high to help redeem mankind from bodily entrapment, while at the same time helping Cayce, in his former life as Ra Ta, an Egyptian high priest, build the Great Pyramid.

See also **Angels and reincarnation; Egypt; Greek afterlife, the ancient; Greeks and reincar-**

nation; Hermetic philosophy; *Iliad and Odyssey*; Orphism; Planetary descent and ascent of the soul; *Poimandres*; *Psychopomps*; Pythagoras.

Hermetic Order of the Golden Dawn. This was an occult society founded in England in 1888, initially based on Masonic and Rosicrucian concepts, but soon expanded to include alchemical, Kabbalic, ancient Greco-Egyptian Hermetic, Theosophical beliefs, astrology, **Tarot**, and ritual magick. After the Theosophical Society, it was from this order that some of the most influential modern Western advocates of reincarnation came.

While the order survived for only fifteen years it gave rise to a number of daughter esoteric groups, but since none of these claimed the original name, any of those modern groups that use the Golden Dawn title and claim direct descent from the older order are making a very questionable claim.

See also **Ascended masters; Astrology and rebirth; Crowley, Aleister; Egypt; Fortune, Dion; Kabbalah; Kingsford, Anna Bonus; Rosicrucians; Sinnett, Alfred Percy; Theosophy; Yeats, William Butler.**

Hermetic philosophy. This is a diverse set of esoteric or mystical beliefs supposedly based on the Alexandrian writings of **Hermes** Trismegitus (Thrice-greatest). This synchronistic figure was a merging of the Greek god Hermes with Thoth, the Egyptian god of wisdom, inventor of writing, and judge of the dead. This Hermes Trismegitus was then humanized into a mythical king that ruled Egypt for 3,000 years and wrote 30,000 books. The literature embodying this philosophy, the *Corpus Hermeticum*, is essentially a blending of **Neoplatonism**, alchemy, medicine, astrology, and magic, and as such there is no uniform creed or dogmatic orthodoxy to it. In general, the aim of Hermetism was akin to its contemporary, **Gnosticism**, which was the spiritual transformation or deification of man through superior (esoteric) knowledge of mankind, the world, and a transcendental God. In fact, the hermetic philosophy was very much drawn upon by Gnosticism. While the surviving corpus of Hermetic writing date back to the end of the third centuries CE, some of its teachings may date further back. The sections of the Hermetic writings that most explicitly deal with metempsychosis are the *Poimandres* and the *Asclepius*.

See also ***Book of the Dead*** (Egyptian); **Bruno, Giordano; Egypt; Esotericism versus Occult; Greeks and reincarnation; Hermetic Order of the Golden Dawn; Herodotus; Jesus; Kingsford, Anna Bonus;** *Nag Hammadi Texts*; *Pistis Sophia*; *Poimandres*; **Priesthood, lack of an organized; Rosicrucians; Sallustius.**

Hermetic Society for World Service. Founded in 1947, the Society teaches that through its various spiritual techniques it can liberate the souls of its members from the cycle of reincarnation and the return of those souls to God. The Society also believes that there will be a biblical battle of Armageddon, which will occur on "the inner planes," but will, nonetheless, manifest through a series of wars on the outer earthly plane.

Herodotus (484–430 or 420 BCE). It is probably to this Greek historian that we first owe the mistaken belief that the Egyptians believed in reincarnation. In his *The Histories, Book 2* he says of the Egyptians that "They were the first to broach the opinion that the **soul** of man is immortal and that, when the body dies, it enters into the form of an animal which is born at the moment, thence passing on from one animal into another, until it has circled through the forms of all the creatures which tenant the earth, the water, and the air, after which it enters again into a new human frame, and is born anew. The whole period of the transmigration is (they say) three thousand years." Herodotus then goes on to say, "There are Greek writers, some of an earlier, some of a later date, who have borrowed this doctrine from the Egyptians, and put it forward as their own. I could mention their names, but I abstain from doing so." This second quote presumably referred to **Pythagoras** and his followers.

This view of an Egyptian origin for **metempsychosis** by Herodotus was not necessarily an innocent mistake. Even for the Greeks the ancient nature of Egyptian civilization was enough to credit all wisdom to **Egypt**.

See also **Empedocles; Greeks and reincarnation; Plato.**

Heroic "I." In Buddhism the normal concept of a permanent and autonomous factor or entity called "I" is thoroughly denied. Indeed, when it comes to the process of fully realizing that there is no such permanent and autonomous factor there is liberation from all future rebirths. However, there must be some since of "I" want to strive for liberation for liberation to occur. This striving "I" is the heroic "I."

See also ***Anatman***.

Heschel of Opatov, Abraham Joshua. This 18th–19th Russian Hasidic Kabbalist rabbi, not only taught about reincarnation (***gigul***), but believed that in one of his past lives he was a High Priest of ancient Israel.

See also **Kabbalah; Russia, reincarnation in.**

Hetero-retrocognition. This is a supposedly more scientific name for the remembrance of past lives.

See also **Existential seriality; Somatic rebirth.**

Hezyonot, Sefer ha- (Hebrew: *Book of Visions*). This diary of the Kabbalist Chayyim Vital contains his teachings on reincarnation, **possession**, and other mystical phenomena.

See also ***Gilgulim, Sefer ha-***; **Kabbalah**.

Hidden observer. This is the part of the mind behind normal consciousness that has access to every one of our memories, including all of the otherwise forgotten ones. This part of the mind is said to have an extraordinary creative ability of it own. Also, this part of the mind is considered to be so independent of our normal consciousness that when it projects itself into ordinary consciousness it is not recognized as a part of oneself. A number of psychologists attribute both **multiple personalities** and past life personalities to this hidden observer.

See also **Honest lying; Past life fakery**.

Higgins, Godfrey (1773–1833). This British writer was the author of two books. The first was *The Celtic Druids* (London: R. Hunter, 1827), which became a fundamental source for the contemporary revival of Druidism. The second was *Anacalypsis*, which became a major source for *Isis Unveiled* by **Helena Blavatsky**. The entire title of Higgins' book was *Anacalypsis: An Attempt to Draw Aside the Veil of the Saitic Isis: or, an Inquiry into the Origin of Languages, Nations, and Religions*. vol. 2 (London: Longman, Rees, Orme, Brown, Green, and Longmen, 1836)

Anacalypsis presents an esoteric history of the human race in which, during an ancient golden age, humanity was of one language, one color (black), and one religion. That religion was Buddhism with its belief in **metempsychosis**, and which according to Higgins was far older than believed to be today.

See also **Druids; Theosophy**.

Hilarion. In 1977 an entity by this name began to channel through Maurice B. Cooke nearly a dozen science-like metaphysical books. One of Hilarion's messages deals with "the Tribulation" which is described as the catastrophic alteration of this world in which mankind will be divided into two groups. The first is those who already have attained to a certain spiritual maturity and who will remain on an earth that has shifted into a higher spiritual plane; and the second is those who, needing more growth, will be relocated through reincarnation to another planet on a less spiritual plane.

Hilarion is also the name of one of the **Dhyani Chohan** in **Theosophy**. Whether the two Hilarion are the same or not is difficult to ascertain.

See also **Channeling; Dark Brotherhood; Equinox; Franklin, Benjamin (2); Iamblichus of Chalcis; Jesus; Lazaris; Lords of Karma; Mafu; Michael (2); Ra (1); Ra (2); Ramtha; Ryerson, Kevin; Seth; Torah (2)**.

Himmler, Heinrich (1900–1945). Himmler was the German Nazi Reich Fuhrer who, although technically a Roman Catholic, believed in reincarnation. In fact, he was sure that he was the reincarnation of the German King Heinrich I (918–1024). Through Himmler's semi-secret occult society, *Ahnenerbe*, he authorized searches for Christian relics, such as the Holy Grail, which supposedly were hidden away by the **Cathars**. To find the original homeland of the Aryan race he also sent expeditions to Tibet as well as to the American tropics in the hope of discovering remnants of the **lost continent** of Atlantis, which some Nazi believed was the original homeland of a pure Aryan race.

See also **Moltke, Helmuth Graf von**.

Hinduism. This term describes the religion of the overwhelming majority of the people of India and Nepal. Hinduism evolved out of a blending of the old **Vedic religion** with one or more pre–Vedic religious traditions. Modern Hinduism is more like a family of closely related religions, rather than a single religion, which is why there is no single orthodox theology in Hinduism. What gives a moderate amount of unity to this family is a respect for Vedic literature and a fundamental belief in the doctrines of both reincarnation and karma.

As far as the popular Hindu belief in karma is concerned it is not regarded as the sole factor in anyone's personal destiny. Lawrence A. Babb, in his *Destiny and Responsibility: Karma in Popular Hinduism* (1983), has noted that quite separate from any influence of karma on one's life that there is also the belief in the influence of the grace or anger of the gods, the influence of the stars (astrology), and even malice of other human beings as sometimes channeled through witchcraft.

While the issue of rebirth and karma in Hinduism is more consistent and less controversial than in Buddhism, that issue is still quite complex as the number of related entries noted below suggests.

See also **Age factor and rebirth;** *Agra-sandhani*; *Ahimsa*; **Ahmadiyya; Animals and rebirth, non–Western view; Astrology and rebirth;** *Atman*; **Besant, Annie;** *Bhagavad Gita*; **Bhakti Yoga;** *Bhava*; **Brahman; Buddhism; Caste system;** *Chakras*; **Critical time periods; Determinism;** *Dharma Shastras*; **Dualism;** *Duhkha*; **Ego; Eternalism; Finite or infinite number of rebirths; Fixed number or variable number of souls; Ganges; Guenon, Rene; Heaven; Hell; Immortality; Incarnation versus reincarnation; India; Individuality and rebirth; Indonesia; International Society for Krishna Consciousness; Jain-**

ism; *Jivakosha*; *Jivanmukta*; Karma; Karma and free will; Karma and justice; Karma and rebirth; Karma as absolute or relative; Karma, classifications of; Karma, origins of; Karma versus grace; Karma yoga; *Linga-Sharia*; Lords of Karma; *Mandara*; Madhva; *Manu-Sanhita*; *Maya*; Memories, reasons for loss of past life; *Moksha, Mukta* or *Mukti*; Monism; Moon; *Naraka*; *Ouroboros*; Pantheism and panentheism; *Patala*; Patanjali; Pilgrimages; *Prakriti*; *Prarthana*; *Pretaloka*; *Pritiloka*; *Puranas*; Ram Dass, Baba; Rebirth and cyclical time; Rebirth and logical symmetry; Rebirth and religious tolerance; Rebirth, East and West; Return and serve argument for reincarnation; Roy, Raja Ram Mohan; Shiva; *Shunya*; Sikhism; Rebirth factor; Soul mates; Soul, origin of the; *Suryamarga*; *Swarga*; Tantrism; Theodicy; Theosophy; *Upanishads*; *Vaikuntha*; Vedanta Society; Vegetarianism; Vivekananda, Swami; Yama; Yogananda, Paramahansa.

Hitler, Adolf. According to the book *The Spear of Destiny: The Occult Power behind the Spear which Pierced the Side of Christ* (1973) by Trevor Ravenscroft, a well informed acquaintance of Hitler claims that in 1911 Hitler, during a peyote-induced hallucination, experienced a past life regression drug trance. Hitler had hoped that his former existences would include an early incarnation as a powerful German ruler; instead, it showed him to have been the historical personage behind the evil sorcerer and villain of von Eschenbach's Parzival (Parsifal), Klingsor. This personage was Landulf II of Capua-Langobardi of Benevento (915–961 CE), the ninth century tyrannical Lord of Terra di Labur. Landulph's insatiable grasping for power led him to study the black arts and to a traitorous link to the Islamic forces threatening Italy. It was for these reasons that he was excommunicated in AD 875 and was forced to flee to Sicily, then a Moslem stronghold. Part of Hitler's identification with Landulf may have come from the fact that Hitler apparently had only a single testicle and it was claimed that the Landulf-Klingsor figure had been partially or fully castrated by the relatives of a noblewoman he had raped. Also, it was possibly because the island of Capri was associated with the principality of Capua that Hitler appears to have believed that in a still earlier life he was the Roman emperor Tiberius Claudius Nero Caesar (14 CE–37 CE), who spent the last ten years of his life in seclusion on Capri.

Dietrich Eckart, the man that introduced Hitler to his peyote experience, came to believe that he also was the reincarnation of a ninth century character. In his case it was Bernard of Barcelona, another notorious betrayer of Christianity to the Arabs and a black magician who was said to use thaumaturgy to hold off Carolingian (French) armies in Spain.

The prominent theosophist James S. Perkins, in his book *Experiencing Reincarnation* (1977), believed that in 1938, through sequence of dreams, he had a recollection of a past life during the time of Alaric, King of the Visigoths (ruled 395–410 CE), and he recognized that German ruler had been reincarnated as Hitler. In fact, Perkins believed that the reason Hitler did not try to invade England by sea was due to a subconscious memory of the disastrous sinking of Alaric's fleet in his attempt to invade North Africa from Italy.

See also **Moltke, Helmuth Graf von; Nero Claudius Caesar Drusus Germanicus.**

Hollywood and reincarnation. Movies and television have at various times taken advantage of the reincarnation theme. There are more than sixty movies, some dating back to 1916; many of these are demeaning to real believers. Wagner Alegretti, in his *Retrocognition* (2004), lists some 31 movies or television shows, dealing with reincarnation which were made from 1922 to 1998 in various European languages, 22 of which are in English. Also, a number of movie stars have publicly stated their belief in rebirth, none more so than **Shirley Maclaine** who has written several books on **channeling** and reincarnation.

See also **Egypt; Karmic romances; Mummy, the; Vampires.**

Holocaust, Jewish *see* **Jewish Holocaust.**

Holy lying *see* **Honest lying.**

Holy Order of Ezekiel. This Order was founded in 1969 by Dr. Daniel Christopher. The Order's basic teachings centered upon the knowledge of God's power and the techniques of achieving personal success and fulfillment through that power. The Divine Life lessons distributed by the Order prepared the seeker to receive the power promised by Christ. These included instruction in meditation, yogic breathing, the use of "Aum" (a mantra), the meaning of mystical symbols, spiritual healing, and numerology. There was a strong belief in reincarnation and karma. In the 1970's the headquarters of the Holy Order were in Glendale, California, but sometime after that the Order ceased to function.

Holy Order of Mans. The name "Mans" in this order is taken from the first letter of the Greek words *Mysterion-Agape-Nous-Sophia* (Mystery-Love-Intelligence-Wisdom). This order was founded in 1968 by Earl W. Brighton, a student of the

AMORC **Rosicrucians**. In its original form it blended biblical themes with Eastern religion, belief in the **Great White Brotherhood**, and reincarnation. After Brighton's death the order broke up with the main body abandoning eastern thought and converting to Eastern Orthodox Christianity under the name of Christ the Savior Brotherhood. Those who chose to continue the original teachings formed several new groups including the **Gnostic Order of Christ**, Science of Man, and the American Temple.

Home, Daniel Douglas (1833–1886). This world famous British psychic medium's attitude towards reincarnation can be summed up in the words, "I have met a dozen Marie Antoinettes, six or seven Marys of Scotland, a whole host of Louis and other kings, about twenty Great Alexanders, but never a plain John Smith. I would like to cage the latter curiosity."

Home, also claimed that the spirit of Allan Kardec, the founder of **Spiritism**, regretted having taught the doctrine of reincarnation.

See also **Cleopatra Syndrome; Soul-fission; Swarm of bees theory**.

Homosexuality and transsexuality. Many believers in reincarnation say that it can explain both same-sex gender attraction as well as the feeling that one is the opposite gender to one's present biological gender (gender *dysphoria*). These reincarnationists suggest that if there has been an unbroken series of past lives in which a soul was embodied as a woman with a natural attraction to men; but then is embodied as a man, there may still be a strong residue of sexual attraction to men. The reverse of this would account for lesbians. Transsexuals, on the other hand, may still strong identity with the former gender itself.

According to the teachings of channeled entity **Ra (2)**, as recorded by Don Elkins in part II of the book *Law of the One* (1981) a person becomes homosexual when 65 percent of their past lives have been of a gender opposite to the present life.

Not only is the existence of homosexual and transsexual people suggested as proof of reincarnation, but it has been further suggested that at least the very belief in such cross-gendering reincarnation would make societies more tolerant of such individuals. This, however, does not seem to have lessened the distain for such people in South Asia or East Asian societies. The major difference between those Eastern and Western societies is that the former have rarely persecuted, much less executed, such people in the fashion that Western societies have.

See also **Arguments supportive of rebirth; Electra/Oedipus Complex and rebirth; Gender issue of the soul; Plato**.

Honest lying. Many psychologists who are skeptical of past life recall do not believe that most persons who recall a past life are consciously lying. The psychologists believe that there is sufficient proof that the individual, especially under **hypnosis**, truly believes those memories to be authentic. Moreover, in those cases where the memories could be verified as having come from a normal or non-psychic source, the individual is honestly surprised at his or her self-deception. In cultures that regard rebirth as a sacred teaching this honest lying can also be called holy lying.

See also **Fraud; Hidden observer; Past life fakery; Past life memory recall**.

Hosea *see* **Karma in the Bible?; Old Testament and the afterlife**.

Hotoke (Japanese: A Buddha). The Sino-Japanese term, although meaning *Butsu* (fully self-attained enlightened being) is actually used for any ancestral spirit who, after a certain period of time and the proper rituals, automatically becomes a kind of honorific Buddha. *Hotoke ni naru* (to become a Buddha) is a polite term for having died. It is believed that if the proper "becoming a Buddha" ritual is not performed the spirit may become an *onryo* or angry ghost. This is a uniquely Japanese tradition and almost certainly is derived from the parallel **Shinto** custom of regarding one's deceased ancestors as *kami* (divinities). Of course, the concept of *hotoke* leaves the Westerner, at least, with the question of how such an ancestral status fits in with the Buddhist rebirth concept. Two answers can be given to this question. The first and religious one is that all ancestors are reborn in the **Pure-Land** which ends any further rebirths. The second, and perhaps more realistic, is that for centuries many Japanese have not taken the concept of rebirth very seriously when it comes to their own ancestors.

Despite the terminology, Japanese Buddhists still recognize a difference between a *hotoke* and a true *Butsu*.

See also **Ancestor worship; Animism; Karma and justice**.

Hovering of the soul. This is the concept that the soul does not enter the womb to be reincarnated right away but hovers around its prospective mother for a longer or shorter period between embryonic conception and birth itself.

See also **Embodiment, moment of**.

Hubbard, Ron L. *see* **Scientology**.

Hulul (Arabic: descent or incarnation) *see* ***Tanasukh***.

Human embryo stem cell uses and rebirth. In an article by John Tierney *"Are Scientists Playing*

God? It Depends on Your Religion" (2007) it is pointed out that based upon the belief in a single God-given life in Euro-American society there is naturally major religious opposition to the use of human embryo stem cell; however, there is little or no opposition in those Asian societies where the majority of the population believes in multiple rebirths.

See also **Rebirth and abortion**.

Human personality complexity. One of the **arguments supportive of rebirth** is that the personality of each human being, even at an early age, is so complex that trying to explain that complexity as having entirely developed during the present life is unreasonable. For this reason alone rebirth makes sense.

Two possible responses to this argument are commonly presented. The first is a biological one which states that the genetically determined complexity of the human brain is quite sufficient to explain human personality; for example, one of the most complex aspects of human beings is their linguistic ability, and most scientists now accept that the human brain is genetically hard-wired for language.

The second response is a metaphysical one which suggests that each person, through some subconscious ability, is individually connected to a **group soul**. While the individual members of this greater soul experience only one embodiment period they have at their disposal the accumulated experience of the group to use for individual development.

Hungry ghosts. In the general eschatology of Buddhism the realm of hungry ghosts (S/P: *Preta/Petas*) is one of the mildest of the three negative purgatorial states of rebirth. Whereas the very evil would go to **hell** (*naraka*) to undergo horrible suffering, those less evil could be born either into the animal or hungry ghost state. In the hungry ghost state one has an extensive appetite but an extremely miniscule mouth. Thus, no matter how much one tries to eat one is always painfully hungry. Greed, miserliness, envy and jealousy are among the reasons for being reborn into this state. The *pretas* will eventually be able to leave their miserable starving existence to be reborn into some more material form so they can try to improve the future.

Pretas are not to be confused with *Priti*, which are the ancestral spirits.

See also **Astral plane; Bhavachakra; Chinese religion and reincarnation; Karmic eschatology;** *Linga*; **Moon;** *Petavatthu*; *Pritiloka*; *Puranas*, **Rebirth eschatology**.

Hunting cultures and reincarnation. In a variety of hunting cultures it is believed that a certain part of the slain animal must be left behind to ensure its eventual **transmigration** into a future body to be hunted. In fact, it is believed that if the hunter does not assist his prey in being reborn he will experience personal ill fortune.

Among the examples of this practice are those of the Inupiaq of Northern Alaska who believe that the souls of sea mammals (seals, walrus, and whales) are attached to their bladders or heads. When a hunter kills one of these animals it is essential that he return that body part to the sea so that the **soul** may be reborn as a new animal. Unless this is done there will be no renewal of the food source. Among the Northwest Pacific Coast Indians it is the bones of the salmon are returned to sea.

See also **American Indians; Chukchi; Deaths, violent and premature; Koryaks; Lapps (Saami)**.

Hussien, Saddam (1937–2006). The deposed and executed leader of Iraq regarded himself as the reincarnation of the greatest of the ancient Babylonian (Chaldean) kings, Nebuchadnezzar II (r. 605–562 BCE). This was the king who conquered Judah and took the Jewish elite into captivity and is written about in the book of **Daniel**.

Hutin, Serge (1929–). This French occultist has published extensively on a great number of esoteric subjects including reincarnation.

Huxley, Thomas Henry (1825–1895). This famous British biologist regarded the concept of reincarnation as equally valid as the doctrine of evolution.

Hypermnesia. This is the condition of heightened recall. The unusual ability to remember otherwise forgotten material may occur under both **hypnosis** and free association. It is thought by many that it can account for most cases of past life recall.

See also **Hypnotic age regression; Cryptomnesia**.

Hypnoamnesia. This is the inability of the hypnotized subject to remember what happened while in the trance state, unless ordered to remember by the hypnotist. It accounts for much of the surprise by a person who has for the first time recalled a past life.

See also **Hypnotic age regression**.

Hypnosis. This is one of several states of altered consciousness to the degree that it differs from the normal everyday consciousness. In this altered state the normal consciousness mind gives way to the subconscious mind which then permits, among other phenomena, both positive and negative hallucinations, a remarkable control over the organic processes of the body such as an indifference to pain, and a high susceptibility to suggestion. In the latter case no suggestions, however, will be accepted that conflict either with the normal will for self-preservation or with strongly held moral values. Hypnosis can be self-induced or induced by another (a hypnotist). Among the features of the deeper levels of a hypnotic trance state are dissociation and time distortion. In the latter case the person entranced has a less than normal ability to accurately estimate the passage of time. Also, under certain circumstances, hypnosis can result in fragmentation of the personality which can encourage parts of a seemingly secondary personality to manifest itself.

According to some hypnotic practitioners the hypnotic state is characterized by alpha brain waves as opposed to the beta waves evidenced in normal consciousness, **theta waves** evidenced in light sleep, and delta waves evidenced in deep sleep. The alpha wave condition is presumably true whether the hypnotic state is of a light, medium or deep (somnambulistic) level. It has been estimated that at least 95 percent of the population can be hypnotized into the first of these three levels, 70 percent in the second level, but only about 5 percent in the third level. This deepest level is what a stage hypnotist requires. Breaking these percentages down to a division between adults and children, about 10–15 percent of the adult population is highly hypnotizable, while 80–85 percent of children up to the age of 12 are highly hypnotizable. It is in this deep state that **hypnoamnesia** occurs. It is also only in this third hypnotic level that the subject can experience positive hallucinations of seeing, hearing, etc. unreal objects and negative hallucinations of not seeing, hearing, etc. real objects.

It is sometimes thought that there are two different types of hypnosis, authoritative and permissive. In the first the hypnotist (operator) will begin with an authoritative statement such as "you will" or "you are." It works well with subjects used to obeying orders, but it also encourages the subject to meet the expectation of the hypnotist, for example if a past life is called for. If the subject has a **fantasy prone personality** he or she may satisfy the operator's expectation with a made-up past life.

Permissive hypnosis begins with words like "you may" and encourages far more self-directedness while under hypnosis, in which case there may be a much smaller percentage of past life recall.

It should be noted that just as some people under hypnosis remember past lives, others under hypnosis have been known to remember being victims of kidnapping and physical examinations by space aliens in their spaceships before being released. It also appears that a hypnotic trance state gives an adult permission to return to a childhood fantasy world. This is part of the reason that the reliability of memory under hypnosis is sufficiently in question for it not to be accepted in most law courts.

See also **False-memory syndrome; Hypnotic age regression; Leading question; Past life regression and suggestibility; Progression therapy; Proof for and against reincarnation argument; Soul fragmentation; Trance states; Wambach, Helen.**

Hypnotic age regression. According to some age regression hypnotists there are two types of age regression trance. The first is revivification, in which the subject relives, or re-experiences, the events of a past life. While in this state the subject is totally unaware of his or her present life. His or her speech will match that of the presumed former life as will any handwriting sample. Persons capable of this deep trance state are called *somnambules* since it is similar to the trance state of a sleepwalker.

The second type of age regression is called pseudo-revivification. Here the subject, while in the trance state, can review scenes from a presumed past life, but, at some level, retain an awareness of their present life. His or her speech and handwriting will match that of the present life. In both kinds of age-regression there is found **hypermnesia** or heightened recall.

Ian Stevenson, the best known researcher of past lives, in his *European Cases of the Reincarnation Type* (2001), states that he thinks that all but a very few cases of claimed previous lives induced by hypnosis are worthless. His justification for this view is that subjects mingle confabulated details with accurate memories; the previous lives generated are nearly always those whose existence can not be traced; and that investigators had often shown the origin of the details of those previous lives to be from normal sources available to the hypnotized subject prior to age regression.

The earliest record of attempts at age-regression under hypnosis appears to be from 1904 by the French psychical investigator, Colonel Albert de Rochas.

See also **Artificial rebirth; Bridey Murphy case; Fantasy versus past life regression; Hidden observer; International Association for Regression Research and Therapy; Netherton Method; Past life regression and suggestibility; Rhine, J. B; Trance states.**

I Am Movement. This politically conservative offshoot of **Theosophy** was founded by Guy Warren Ballard (1878–1939) and Edna Ballard (1886–1971). According to Guy Ballard, while hiking in the forest around **Mount Shasta** in Northern California in 1930, he met the ascended master Le Comte de **Saint Germain,** who informed Ballard that he had been chosen as an "Accredited Messenger" to restore the truth about the re-embodiment of the divine "Mighty I Am Presence" or divine inner reality within everyone. This term "I am" as a name of God is found in the Old Testament at Exodus 3:14 and Isaiah 41:4. In the first of these, Moses, upon being told by God (Yahweh) to go liberate the Israelites, asks God by what name shall he refer to Him. God answers, "I am; that is who I am. Tell them that 'I am' has sent you to them." Also, according to Ballard, Saint Germain revealed to him many of Ballard's previous lives, including the one as George Washington.

Ballard is said to have later received more revelations when he joined the Master and an assembly of others, including some Venusians, in a cave in the Grand Teton Mountains. All of these experiences are recorded in Ballard's books *Unveiled Mysteries*, (Chicago: Saint Germain Press, 1934) and *The Magic Presence*, (Chicago: Saint Germain Press, 1935). Ballard also wrote under the pseudonym Godfre' Ray King.

The death of Ballard created a crisis in his I Am Movement since he had taught that the ascension, the liberation from the physical body and future reincarnations would happen without undergoing physical death. Nonetheless, some members remained faithful accepting Mrs. Ballard's claim that Guy had become one of the **Ascended masters** or had joined the **Great White Brotherhood**. A financial scandal and a later dropped government prosecution further weakened the Movement until the death of Edna Ballard left it with few members. The I Am Movement was influential in the rise of the **Church Universal and Triumphant**.

See also **Jesus; Phylos the Tibetan; UFOism; Venus**.

I, William the Conqueror: a meditation on an improbable past life. While doing research for this *Encyclopedia of Reincarnation and Karma*, and without undergoing a formal hypnotic past life trance, I entered into a private meditative state with the self-suggestion that I regress in time to find a life I might have once lived. After a short while the name that entered my mind was William, the French-Norman Conqueror of England (1066 CE). Not taking this seriously, I tried to push this name out of my consciousness and search for another possibly less grandiose identity. No matter what I did, however, the name William always re-imposed itself. To discover why this particular name might have insisted on appearing I analyzed my present life to see if there was any connection to that name. The results of that analysis came up with the following particulars.

My father's first name was "William" and his second name was "Norman," which is my first name. My mother's maiden name was "Williams" and I am of British descent. It was only a few days before my birth that my mother was in Montreal, French-speaking Canada, and crossed the border into English-speaking America to ensure my birth as an American citizen. Similarly, William had crossed the Channel from French-speaking Normandy to invade English (Anglo-Saxon) speaking England. I was born in the French Hospital in New York City in October under the sign of Libra, in the same month and under the same sign in which William landed in England (Sept. 27) and won the decisive Battle of Hasting (Oct. 14), which assured him the English crown. The year of my birth, 1944, was also the year that the Allied military forces invaded Normandy from England in order to defeat the Nazis. The first foreign language I was exposed to in my New England elementary school was French and the European language I always wanted most to learn was French. William's immediate heir was his son William II, who ruled for only 4 years, only to be succeeded by his brother Henry, the fourth son of William I. After my father's war-time disappearance, my mother's lover, who was the only father figure I ever knew, was named Henry. Even when it came to the last name of my father and my last name I found correlations. My father was actually born with the clan name of Campbell, which is actually French for beautiful field. His stepfather was a McClelland and this name was added on to Campbell, which is how I ended up with McClelland and not Campbell as my last name. Also, the Campbell clan in Scotland is one of the few remaining clans to have as its official leader a Duke, in this case the Duke of Argyll. William the Conqueror held the title Duke of Normandy before seizing the English throne. William and I have the same numerological breakdown to our names. McClelland is 4-3-3-3-5-3-3-1-5-4 which adds up to 34 which is then reduced to 7, while William is 5-9-3-3-9-1-4 which also adds up to 34, reduced to 7. A number of years before this meditation I had a past life reading via the **tarot** at a psychic fair at which time I was told that I had once lived as a Danish fisherman and it so happens that the Normans, French for Norsemen, were descendents of Danish Vikings. I have always had a fascination with ancient and medieval history and have studied it extensively. This fascination has motivated me to collect swords and armor. I have visited England four times, and France once. Finally, it is interesting to fantasize having been a king rather than a peasant.

I concluded, that despite these seemingly numerous direct and indirect associations between William and myself that this was most likely a good example of how these facts about my present life encouraged my subconscious to choose to identify with William rather than there being any real connection between him and me. Of course, some rebirth proponents would suggest that all of these present life facts were not just coincidental, but actually represented my past life as William manifesting itself in the present through **synchronicity**.

See also **Fantasy prone personality**; **Fantasy versus past life regression**.

Iamblichus of Chalcis (260/70–325/30 CE). This Neoplatonic and Neopythagorean philosopher taught that the soul's main task was to escape the round of **metempsychosis** by practicing five kinds of virtue: paradigmatic, political, priestly, purificatory, and theoretical. Imblichus was also regarded in his time as a major theurgist (practitioner of white magick). One of the written works of Iamblichus was *Peri Psyches* (*About the Soul*). Iamblichus was also a teacher of **Sallustius the Neoplatonist**; while **Flavius Claudius Julian** studied under one or more students of Iamblichus.

In the modern theosophical and occult traditions Iamblichus is said to have been in a former life **Hilarion**, the *Dhyani Chohan*.

See also *Kyklos Genesion*; **Neoplatonism**; **Priesthood, lack of an organized**.

Ibbur. This is a form of benevolent **possession** described in the **Kabbalah**.

See also *Dibbuk*; *Gilgul*.

Ichantika. In general this refers to a hedonist or materialist, and in **Theravada Buddhism** it means a being that is so spiritually degenerate that it has lost all ability to escape from the karmic wheel of birth and death.

See also *Abhavya*; **Eighth sphere**.

Id, ego, and superego. In Freudian depth psychology the id is the subconscious part of the mind in which all of our natural (animal) wants and desires are contained. The id has no sense of what society regards as right and wrong (morality). It is the responsibility of society to tame the id by creating the ego and superego. Too great a taming, however, can lead to repression of certain essential natural needs which can lead to mental illness (neurosis or psychosis).

The ego is the fully conscious part of the mind. For the most part, it is where all of our rational thinking takes place. The ego must constantly try to balance the needs of the id with those of the superego. A failure to do this can also result in mental illness.

The superego is that part of the mind that has adopted all or most of the moral views of society. If the superego is allowed to irrationally (too extensively) suppress the needs of the id mental illness will result.

In modern times the psychological concept of the id has to some degree replaced the religious concept of the devil, and the inherently sinful **soul**; the superego has replaced God given conscience, divine grace, or the Holy Spirit; and the ego has replaced the religious man caught between sin and God. From a Freudian (psychoanalytical) perspective this leaves little space for a soul to be reincarnated.

See also **Ego**; **Mind**; **Unconscious, the**.

Idolatry of the brain. This is a phrase used by B. Alan Wallace and refers to the view of those cognitive psychologists and neuroscientists who assume the mind is merely the product of the physical mechanics of the brain. Wallace is an American Buddhist, who was a monk for 14 years, during part of which he was mentored by the **Dalai Lama**. He then went on to get a doctorate in religious studies at Stanford and still later to become the president of the Santa Barbara Institute for Consciousness Studies. Wallace has written and edited a number of books, and is a strong supporter of the rebirth theory.

See also **Body-brain (mind) dependency**.

Igbo of Nigeria. This is one of the African peoples who have a belief in a form of reincarnation or "Returning to the World (*Llo Uwa*)." The Igbo believe in a multiple **soul** with three aspects which are called *obi* (breath, vital force, animation, consciousness), *chi* (emanation of the supreme god, one's personal destiny), and *eke* (reborn spirit of an ancestor, a guardian spirit).

See also **Africa**; **Repeater children (Ogbanje)**; **Soul, tripartite**.

Iliad and *Odyssey*. In the schools of **Pythagoras** and **Orphism** these two epics were regarded metaphorically as representing the descent and return of the **soul**. In the first, the soul leaves its heavenly home to struggle (go to war) in earthly life until, as in the *Odyssey*, it must leave that struggle and journey through the underworld, before at last finding its way back home (be reborn). It is in book XI of the *Odyssey* that Odysseus journeys to the underworld (**Hades**) to consult the seer Teiresias about returning home and the dangers involved in such a journey.

See also **Hermes**; *Nepenthean* **veil**.

Immortality. This term should not be confused with the idea of eternal life. The latter implies the former, but the former does not necessarily imply the latter. Immortality should be reserved to mean that a certain life is not subject to the "normal age limits" or to the normal means of death. For example, the Greek gods were called immortals, but their immortality depended on their taking the food and drink, ambrosia and nectar, of immortality. This same concept can be found in **Hinduism** where the gods, to survive, must consume the drink *amrita* (immortality) which the gods and demons produce by churning the cosmic ocean. Legend says that this drink is stored in the **moon**, the periodic empting and the refilling of which account for the moon's waning and waxing.

Also, certain Daoist sages are called immortals, but this too depends on their eating the fruit of immortality, in this case, the heavenly peach. Likewise, immortality is usually associated with such supernatural beings as **vampires**, yet as any horror story fan knows, not only must they sustain themselves on fresh blood, but they can die killed by special means.

Reincarnation, like-wise, should not be assumed to mean eternal life. Indeed, even if souls pass from life to life this does not automatically mean that this passing will continue into eternity because once the **soul** is liberated from the rebirth process there is no guarantee that liberation is not synonymous with extinction.

It is to be noted that the Sanskrit term for immortal is *a-mara* (death-less).

See also **Annihilationism, Biblical view; Eternalism; Mara; New Testament and reincarnation; Objective immortality**.

Important person criticism. One often heard criticism of reincarnation is that most persons who claim to have had a past life claim that it was of some important or famous person. The critics then usually add that such a claim to past fame is a way to compensate the claimant for a present humdrum life. To the degree that this is still assumed to be the case, it is a valid criticism against reincarnation. However, in the past few decades the overwhelming majority of reported past lives describe what could only be called quite ordinary lives; therefore, the important person criticism is far less valid than it use to be.

See also **Social status in past lives**.

Inca Indians. According to some 16th century Spanish records the Incas, although believing in an afterlife, did not have a clearly delineated concept of what that afterlife was like. The Spanish sources state that reincarnation was merely one of several possible options the Inca had available to them. Other old Spanish sources say that neither the Inca proper nor most other peoples of Peru believed in the reincarnation: however, such a belief was mentioned for the Cavina, who lived in the Vilcañota Valley in the neighborhood of Quiquijana, and who considered themselves to be "Inca by privilege." Since the Spanish views of the Indians were rarely positive there does not appear to be any conclusive evidence as to what the Inca believed or did not believe.

See also **Unarius Academy of Science**.

Incarnation versus reincarnation. The term incarnation in its broadest meaning can refer simply to an ordinary soul entering a new body and is, therefore, synonymous to reincarnation minus to the "re-" prefix. In the term's narrower meaning it refers to a non-ordinary soul or divine being entering or assuming bodily form. In this sense Christ is said to have incarnated into flesh, but not reincarnated. Likewise, the Saguna **Brahman** god Vishnu in **Hinduism** is said to have periodically incarnated or descended (hence an *avatar*) into the world. In **Mahayana Buddhism**, but not **Theravada Buddhism**, the historical Buddha Gautama is regarded as a descendent (*avatar*) or incarnation of the celestial Buddha **Amitabha**. Among Tibetans the **Dalai Lama** and other great religious figures (*tulkus*) are regarded as repeated incarnations of various celestial beings. Since such Tibetan figures repeatedly incarnate it could be said that they reincarnate, but if the emphasis is placed on their presumed divine origins they are repeated (serial) incarnations, rather than ordinary reincarnations.

See also **Avalokiteshvara; Panchen Lama; Possession**.

Incest and reincarnation. One criticism made against the idea of reincarnation is that in theory it might be possible for a mother to return as a young woman and marry her own son, or for a father to return as a young man and marry his own daughter. Of course, the probability of such situations would decrease if there was a significant **interim period** between death and rebirth.

See also **Augustine, Saint Aurelius; Child as its own reborn father or mother; Chinese religion and reincarnation**.

Inconsistent views and reincarnation. One of the arguments against the reincarnation concept is that people, supposedly knowledgeable about reincarnation, have such varying views on major parts of the concept that the whole concept is suspect. The following entries attest to this inconsistency: **Akashic Record;** *Anatman*; **Animals and rebirth, non–Western view; Animals and rebirth, Western view;** *Atman*; **Causal body; Children remembering past lives; Cryptomnesia; Current knowledge discrepancy;** *Déjà Vu*; **Egypt; Embodiment, moment of; Gender issue of the soul; Interim period; Language inconsistency; Lost continents and reincarnation; Multiple personalities; Old souls; Parents in the next life; Planets, other; Population increase issue; Rebirth, qualifications for; Rastafarians; Rebirth in the West; Rebirth, East and West; Rebirth, simultaneous; Roberts, Jane; Screen memories; Soul, collective; Soul, origin of the; Supernatural-in-the-gap process; Rebirth and cyclical time; *Urantia Book*.

Incremental change of identity. From the moment a person is born he or she starts the process of changing identity. By the time one reach the age of ten he or she no longer identify closely with his or her former infant stage, especially since most of that stage can not be remembered. Likewise, when a person is twenty he or she has only minor identification with that former ten-year-old. By thirty, one is an almost totally different person from the ten-year-old and certainly from the infant. By fifty it becomes even more difficult to relate to any part of one's childhood personality, and by senior citizenship it can be said that the senior is only vaguely the same person as the youth. This is the incremental change, or very slow change of identity, from one age to another, and it is only because there are so many intermediate stages that an older person can say he or she was born at such a place and such a time. If there was a significant loss of memory of one or more of those stages it is questionable whether a person could, with full confidence, accept that continuity from childhood to late adulthood.

Critics of reincarnation argue that if the above is true for this life, how much truer should it be for two lives between which physical death intervenes. For example, if in one life I am a white male, heterosexual, upper class, Christian American and in the next life I am a black lesbian, lower class, Muslim Tanzanian could it really be said that I can logically identify with both? If over a series of six lives only one of the original factors changed, then incremental transformation might allow for a sense of continuity of identity, but otherwise it is very questionable to suggest such continuity. However, even a one factor per-life at a time change would not necessarily constitute a continuity of identity in the absence of all memories of the previous life or lives.

See also **Rebirth, proximity**.

Independent Spiritualist Association of the United States of America. This association was founded in 1924 by Amanda Cameron Flower (1863–1940). Flower was at first associated with the National Spiritualist Association of Churches, but separated from them because of their opposition to a belief in reincarnation.

See also **Associations and organizations; Spiritualism**.

India. The one doctrine that every religion that has arisen in India has accepted is some form of rebirth and karma as absolute truths.

See also **Ajivikas; Alexandria, Egypt; Ambedkar, Bhim Rao; Ashoka, King; Astrology and rebirth; Besant, Annie; Buddhism; Caste system;** *Ex Oriente Lux*; **Hinduism; Jainism, Kabirpanthi; Priesthood, lack of an organized; Ram Dass, Baba; Rebirth and cyclical time; Rebirth, East and West; Reincarnation, origins of; Sathya Sai Baba; Sikhism;** *Upanishads*; **Uttar Pradesh; Vedic Religion; Weber, Max**.

India, Jesus in *see* **Ahmadiyya;** *Aquarian Gospel of Jesus Christ*; **Church Universal and Triumphant; Jesus; Resurrection of Jesus**.

Individuality and rebirth. All Indian based religious traditions, be they Hindu, Jain, or Buddhist, have emphasized the ideal of an impersonal, or a depersonalized selfhood to one degree or another.

In **Hinduism**, especially Advaita (Non-dual) Vedanta, this emphasis takes the form of the *atman* (soul). Since each *atman* is a part of the undifferentiated **Brahman** (God) all *atman* are ultimately identical. In other words, they lack uniqueness or individuality, which means they are all impersonal. The individuality of a soul is considered to be a part of the sheath (*linga sharia*) that surrounds the soul and it must dissolve away if liberation from rebirth is to occur. Also, in **Jainism** the soul seeks to divest itself of all individuality so as to experience impersonal transcendental bliss. In Buddhism this same idealization of impersonality over individuality is found in the concept of there ultimately being no intrinsic reality to selfhood (*anatman*) for all is emptiness (*shunyata*). In other words, each of these traditions regards "individuality" as not only an impediment to liberation, but as the very source of suffering and the real barrier to liberation.

Even if not rejected by the Hindu and Jain concept of a totally impersonal self or the Buddhist concept of no-soul (self) or emptiness the value of individuality would still be reduced by their concepts of innumerable rebirths. If one's present life is just one in a series of thousands of lives that a person has lived and will live, then no one of those lives can be more valuable than any other life. The result is that none of those lives have anything but a temporary value.

The pan–Indian tendency to devalue individuality is in great contrast to the Western religious attitude of the personal individuality of everyone due to a belief in a single unique life. This Western attitude has had a profound influence on the rest of Western society; for example, the modern concept of democracy, of human rights, of women's liberation, gay liberation, and to some degree even animal rights are all a by-product of the Judeo-Christian emphasis on the importance of the individual.

The Eastern devaluation of individuality resulting from a belief in rebirth has given rise to the important question of does the Eastern de-emphasis of individuality help account for the long history of Eastern indifference to social reformation or even the well documented willingness of the religious establishments to support even the most despotic government regimes?

In several modern Western reincarnationist schools the natural depersonalization factor that goes with a belief in multiple lives has been countered by viewing reincarnation as a spiritual evolutionary process, a view that is alien to the Eastern ideal of escaping from the cycle of rebirth and redeath.

See also **Blaming the victim vs. illusion of innocence; Body-brain (mind) dependency; *Kosha*; Monism; Personality versus individuality; Rebirth and cyclical time.**

Indonesia. In this Southeast Asian country the majority of the population is Muslim, yet despite the rejection of reincarnation in orthodox **Islam**, many Indonesians accept the doctrine of rebirth. This is due to **Hinduism** and Buddhism having preceded the arrival of Islam in the area as well as possible pre–Indian influenced native traditions. The continued belief in rebirth is especially strong among Javanese Muslims. This includes a belief that certain types of souls are reincarnated as monkeys. Among the Minangkabau of central Sumatra there is the belief that God may allow a dying sinner to return to this world to do penance, but in the form of a tiger. Of course, to the east of Java is Bali, which is the last area of Indonesia to fully retain the Hindu-Buddhist tradition with its official doctrine of reincarnation.

See also **Asia; Butterfly; Dayaks; Malaysia; Sufism.**

Infusionism. This is the belief that souls pre-exist and enter the body at some point. It is in opposition to both **soul** creationism, **generationism, and traducianism**. Infusionism is a pre-requisite for a belief in reincarnation.

See also **Creationism, soul; Emanationism; Gender issue of the soul; Ontological leap or ontological discontinuity; Soul's existence prior to embodiment; Soul; Soul, origin of the.**

Inquisition, Catholic. This Roman Catholic organization was originally established in the 12th century to eliminate the reincarnation believing group called the **Cathars**, but it was eventually used to arrest and try those accused of witchcraft, and any suspected deviation from orthodox Catholic teaching, such as pseudo–Jewish or pseudo–Muslim converts, and especially Protestants.

See also **Bruno, Giordano; Karma; Rebirth and religious tolerance.**

Interdependent Origination *see Pratitya-samutpada.*

Inter-human reincarnation. This refers to reincarnation that is exclusively between one human being and another human being; in short, it is synonymous to lateral transmigration.

See also **Evolutionary transmigration of souls; Transmigration, lateral.**

Interim period. This is any period, short or long between death and rebirth. In **Jainism** the interim period is though to be about nine months, which matches the average gestation period. Among the **Druzes** immediate reincarnation is the expected situation. Among Western supporters of rebirth there is no agreed upon view of an interim period. Some follow a modified **Theravada Buddhism** view of no interim, while others have suggested a period of 400–600 years, and still others following a platonic lead, have suggested that there could be one to three thousand years between some rebirths.

One reason Theravada Buddhism discounts any interim period (*antara*) is that the more one suggests that a **rebirth factor** can exist independent of a physical realm or semi-physical realm the more the rebirth factor would seem to take on the characteristics of a permanent entity or **soul**. The Theravada rejection of an interim does not mean an immediate rebirth into another human form, since rebirth could occur in the animal, **hell, hungry ghost** (*pretas*), or the heavenly realm (*devaloka*). Some forms of **Mahayana Buddhism** are less concerned about the implications of an interim period and suggest an interim existence (*antara-bhava*) of seven weeks or forty-nine days. Of all the schools of Buddhism it is **Vajrayana Buddhism** that most elaborates on the interim, which it calls the *bardo*.

In Japan it is thought that the intermediate period between death and rebirth is thirty-three years, which is the reason for a full cycle of thirty-three annual memorial services for the deceased. When it comes to opinions on an interim period among Western believers there are a number of differing opinions. In the first Western writing on the issue of the interim period, the *Phaedo* of **Plato**, there it is said to be a period of seven generations between each rebirth.

Rudolf Steiner, the founder of Anthroposophy, believed that the longer one lived in the most recent embodiment, the longer might be the interim (*pareschaton*) state or rest period before rebirth. This would mean that death during infancy or childhood would require a shorter interim than death during adulthood. A number of other reincarnationists appear to support this view, especially with regards to childhood.

Again, according to Steiner, the soul in its **etheric body** uses the first three to three and a half days after death to review its past life before abandoning this body for the interim period **astral body**. It has been suggested that this three to four day period is derived from either the fact that this is the longest most human beings can function without sleep, or that there are three nights of the dark of the **moon**. Steiner further claimed that the soul must reside in the astral world the equivalent of one third of whatever number of years it most recently spent embodied. For example, if the person died at seventy five it needs to spend twenty-five years in its astral body. This number was taken from the fact that most people spend a third of their lives in sleep.

Irving Cooper, in his *Reincarnation: The Hope of the World* (1964), agrees with Steiner that the longer one lived in the most recent embodiment the longer might be the interim state, but he adds that the intensity of, or greater amount of experience in, the most recent life makes for a longer interim period. Also, the greater the level of intellectual or spiritual development one has reached in life increases the time between rebirths. Cooper says that while the interim period can be as short as five years it can be as long as three thousand years, with the average being about five hundred years.

R. F. Goudey, in his *Reincarnation: A Universal Truth* (1928), claims that among the factors influencing the length of any one interim period are (1) the demands of others for joint relationships on earth; (2) the need of taking into account premature or delayed rebirths so that a suitable physical body with proper environment and heredity can be provided which will best suit the needs of the new incarnation; (3) the race and era in which experiences are gained; and (4) the need to sacrifice individual development for the grouping of souls during national crises so that racial consciousness can be properly molded to assist nations towards their development. In particular, Goudey implies that the interim period is likely shortened immediately after major wars to relieve the sudden increased overpopulation of the heavenly world.

It has been suggested in some **Rosicrucian** sources that the soul must have a combined embodiment period and an immediately following post-disembodiment period that must add up to 144 years for each reincarnation cycle. In other words, if the soul was embodied for 84 years it must remain in the disembodied interim for 60 years before it can begin a new embodiment.

In the past life reports collected from the numerous patients of **Dr. Helen Wambach** the interim period is said to have averaged about 52 years.

No matter how long or short the interim might be, it has been suggested that the function of an interim is to give the soul a resting period, not only between the traumas of death and rebirth, but a rest after the exhausting nature of bodily life as a whole.

The interim period has also been proposed as an aid in explaining the **population increase issue**.

See also **Agasha Temple of Wisdom; Ahriman; Angels and reincarnation; Animals; Astral plane; Astrology and rebirth; Attached entity;** *Bhavachakra*; **Birth trauma; Celestial gates; Child as its own reborn father or mother; Critical time periods; Death trauma;** *Devachan*; **Etheric body;** *Gandharva*; **Incest and reincarnation; John, Gospel of; Karma, racial; Mahayana Buddhist rebirth texts; Moon; Plato; Psychology, abnormal; Romans; Soul, origin of the; Stygian sexuality; Summerland.**

Interlife. This is another term for **interim period**.

Internal-external rule. This is the idea that internalized factors in one life will in the next life manifest as external factors. For example, just the desire to be a great painter in the past life will be achieved in the present life. Also, the moral qualities of the past life will manifest themselves as physical qualities in this life, such that a past deformed moral nature will result in a present deformed body.

See also **Blaming the victim vs. illusion of innocence.**

International Association for Regression Research and Therapy. This California based association and was originally established in 1980 as the Association of Past life Research and Therapy. The Association is less interested in proving reincarnation than it is in using past life regression as a therapeutic tool. Since 1986 the Association has published the *Journal of Regression Therapy*.

See also **American Society for Psychical Research; Associations and organizations; Hypnotic age regression; Society for Psychical Research; Theta (1).**

International Board for Regression Therapy. This New York based organization was founded by Russell Davis. It is an independent examining and certifying board for past life therapists.

See also **Associations and organizations.**

International cases. This is a term used by **Ian Stevenson** to describe cases where a child recalls a life in a very different culture from the one in which he or she presently lives. In particular, Stevenson has used the term to refer to those Burmese children that recall past lives as Japanese soldiers who died in Burma (Myanmar) in the Second World War.

International Society for Krishna Consciousness. This is a controversial and updated form of Hinduism carried to the West in 1965 by its founder A.C. Bhaktivedanta Swami Prabhupada (1896–1977). Its teachings are based upon the *Bhagavad Gita*. Like all Hindu sects it is grounded in a belief in reincarnation and karma.

See also **Brahman**.

Internet and reincarnation. Search "reincarnation" in any internet search engine and more information will be retrieved than one can possibly digest.

Intrauterine factor and rebirth *see* **Electra/Oedipus Complex and rebirth; Embodiment, moment of; Soul twins.**

Intuitive past life recall *see Déjà vu*; **Reverie recall; Spontaneous recall.**

Intuitional plane *see* **Mental plane; Soul and spirit levels, Theosophical**

Inuits *see* **Hunting cultures and reincarnation.**

Iran (Persia) *see* **Assassins; Babism and Bahaism; Gnosticism; Hashimiyya; Islam; Kanthaeans; Khurramiyya; Manichaeism; Mithraism; Rawandiyah; Yarsanism; Yazidis; Zoroastrianism.**

Iraq *see* **Mesopotamia; Yarsanism; Yazidis.**

Irenaeus (about 130–180/200 CE). This Christian bishop of Lyons (Gaul), in his major work *Adversus omnes Haereses* (*Against the Heresies*), sought to refute **Gnosticism**, especially the teachings of **Valentinus**. Also, he criticizes the **Carpocrates** teaching of the reincarnation of souls, especially on the grounds that there is no memory of the past life.

Irenaeus was the first known Christian authority to decide that the Gospels of **Matthew, Mark, Luke,** and **John** alone were orthodox. All others at his disposal he regarded as heretical. This suggests further that the early Church Fathers saw nothing in these four gospels that would give biblical support to the doctrine of reincarnation.

See also **Christian fathers critical of reincarnation; Christianity and reincarnation; New Testament and reincarnation.**

Irrational fears. It has been claimed that certain types of long and strongly held fears that seem to have no present life rational explanation are attributable to a past life. There is no doubt that during **hypnotic age regression** procedures a past life rational explanation is sometimes offered for the fear.

See also **Arguments supportive of rebirth; Cryptomnesia; Psychosomatic illnesses; Screen memories.**

Isaac, Jacob, the Seer of Lublin (18th–19th century). Isaac was a celebrated Hasidic master who was said to be able to recount the past lives of the people he met. Unfortunately for him, he was thrown out a window and killed for incorrectly predicting that the Napoleonic Wars signaled the End of Days.

See also **Kabbalah.**

Isaac the Blind *see* **Abraham of Posquieres, Isaac ben.**

Isaiah *see Akashic* **Record; Angels and reincarnation; I AM Movement; Jesus; Lucifer; Mark, Gospel of; New Testament sacrificial concept; Old Testament and the afterlife; Resurrection of Jesus; Sciomancy.**

Islam. This third of the great monotheistic religions arose out of a synthesis of Judaism, Christianity, and Arab paganism. It is divided into two major groups: the Sunni and the Shiite. The former has remained closer to the earliest views as presumably taught by the prophet Muhammad/Mohammad, while the latter has been more influenced by the esotericism of **Neoplatonism** and even **Zoroastrianism**. Both forms of Islam reject the concept of reincarnation and, like orthodox Christianity, affirm the future Resurrection (*Qiyama*) of the Dead. In fact, in the Quran, at *Suras* 2:62; 5:69 and 22:17, it is stated that only those people who believe in God and the Day of Judgment (*Yawm al-Din*: literally, Day of the Religion) shall have nothing to fear and will not grieve [their fate].

Despite doctrinal acceptance of resurrection, this has not prevented some otherwise orthodox Moslems/Muslims, especially those in India and Indonesia, from accepting the concept of reincarnation (Arabic: *tanasukh*), stemming from the wide spread belief in it in pre–Islamic times. Also, some Islamic groups whose orthodoxy is either suspect or considered heretical accept reincarnation unapologetically. Among these are various Sufi groups and the *Ahl-I Haqq* or *Ali Ilahis* (Deifiers of Ali).

The early Islamic movement was actually very familiar with the concept of reincarnation because a significant percentage of the people conquered by that movement in its first hundred years were followers of Manichaeism which accepted reincarnation. However, after the first few decades of tolerating this religion the Caliphs turn to a major persecution of it to the point of its extermination in Islamic territory. In contrast, the Caliphs continued to tolerate the religions of both their Jewish and Christian subjects, who, with few exceptions, rejected reincarnation.

Reincarnation, heretical or not, is probably easier for some Moslems to accept than for most Christians because in the Quran, at *Sura* 4:157, it is denied that Jesus was crucified unto death, and so Islam has no place for his personal resurrection, which orthodox Christianity has traditionally used to counter reincarnation.

On the other hand, *Sura* 23:99–100 would seem to be very specific in its rejection of a second, much less greater number of chances to live a righteous life. This reads, "…when death comes to one of them [disbelievers], he says, My Lord, send me back that I might do righteous in that which I left behind. No! It is only a word he is saying: and behind them is a barrier (Arabic: *barzakh*) until the Day they are resurrected."

Despite the Quranic rejection of reincarnation, some Western and even Eastern reincarnationists have made considerable effort to draft the Quran into supporting a pro-reincarnation position, but like the effort to do the same with the Bible this only works if one takes passages out of context, in which case one can distort those passages into meaning anything one wants them to mean as noted below.

According to **H. N. Banerjee,** in his *The Once and Future Life* (1975), there are at least two citations from the Quran that support reincarnation. He gives neither the name of the translation he is using, nor the chapter and verse number he is quoting. Nonetheless, some searching through various translations indicates that, at least for his first (mis-) quotation, he has chosen *Sura* 71:17–18. Banerjee's wording is (1) "from it (i.e, earth) have we created you, and into it we will return you, and out of it we will bring you forth a second time." Banerjee's second quote reads, "say, go through the earth, and see how he hath brought forth created beings, Hereafter, with a second birth will God cause them to be born again: for God is Almighty." Even as Banerjee has given both citations, they can equally, if not better, be interpreted as support for the orthodox Islamic teaching of the resurrection of the dead. For example, the translation by Unal (2007), compared to Banerjee's first quote reads, "And Allah has produced you from the earth growing, And in the end He will return you return into (it), and raise you forth." In two other translations of the Quran (Saheeh 1997, The Institute 1997), like Unal, the phrases "second birth" or "born again" are not used and two of the four translations specifically include the word "resurrection."

Another Quranic passage single out for a reincarnation meaning is *Sura* 2:28. Using the translation by Pickthall (no date) it reads, "How disbelieve you in Allah when you were dead and He gave you life! Then he will give you death, then life again, and then unto Him you will return." Once again it is just as easy to read the standard orthodox Islamic teaching of the resurrection in this verse as it is a reincarnationist reading if the first reference to being dead is metaphorical for not yet having been created while the second death mentioned is the return to non-existence until the second resurrectional life.

A third so-called reincarnation passage is the very ambiguous *Sura* 7:172 which, at the very most, might prove the pre-existence of all the human souls to eventually be embodied. To make sure that all humanity, from the creation of Adam onwards, would have no excuse for not accepting the rule of God, God calls forth from Adam's loins all the souls of his descendents to be and makes them acknowledge that rule. Since there is no other even vaguely possible mention in the Quran of the pre-existence of souls, it can best be argued that pre-existence is not really the theme in this *Sura*.

If one should think that that pro-reincarnation passage hunting in the Quran is a recent activity one merely has to read *Reincarnation in Islam* (1927) by Nadarbeg K. Mirza, who includes as proof that the Quran teaches reincarnation the following *Suras:* 3:26; 4:56; 12:57; 16:65, 70; 17:49–51; 22;5–6; 30:19; 46:17, 19; 57:17, 22; 84:6–19. But again, the problem with almost all of these is that they can just as easily be interpreted to mean a future resurrection of the dead. Mirza, however, goes one step beyond most passages hunters in that he also cites the following *Suras* to show that even karma is taught in the Quran, 6:79; 10:44; 30:41; 42:30–31. As far as Mirza's contribution to the idea of reincarnation in the Quran issue is concerned, it must be noted that he was a supporter of **Theosophy**.

In one of the most recent efforts to read reincarnation into the Quran there is Walter Semkiw's *Return of the Revolutionaries* (2003), pages 28–29. Here Semkiw sites *Suras* 2:28, 287; 3:30; 5:69, 171; 6:95; 11:38; 21:47; 36:12. However, even with the translation he is using, *The Essential Quran* by Thomas Cleary, only five of the cited nine verses "might imply" reincarnation versus a simple end-of-time resurrection.

No matter how one reads any of these reincarnational arguments the fact is that they pale when compared with the overwhelming number of

Quranic passages that "aggressively" teach a single life followed by a future resurrection.

Finally, if there was still any hope that a pro-reincarnationist teaching is found in Islam this should be countered by the teaching about the two blue-eyed black angels Munkar (the Unknown) and Nakir (the repudiating). These two visit the dead in their graves and interrogate them as to their belief in the true religion (Islam). If the deceased is a true Muslim they are ordered to sleep in the grave until the resurrection. If they are found to be unbelievers the ground will open to receive the soul where it will be constantly crushed until the final Day of Judgment.

See also **Ahmadiyya; Assassins; Birds, soul; Christianity and reincarnation; Cult of Angels; Doceticism; Druzes; Ismailis; Judgment of the Dead;** *Kiramu'l katibin; Madhi,* **The; Malaysia; Monism;** *Nafs* **and** *Ruh;* **Nusayris; Peter, 1st and 2nd; Resurrection, bodily; Sikhism; Sufism;** *Yarsanism.*

Isles of the Blessed *see* **Greek afterlife, the ancient.**

Isma'ilis. This radically gnostic influenced subsect of Shiite **Islam**, unlike most other forms of Shiite, much less Sunni Islam, accepted the doctrine of reincarnation (**tanasukh**). According to Ismaili doctrine, upon death everyone would be asked by angels the question, "Did you recognize who was the (rightful) *imam*?" If you answered correctly your soul was free to go to heaven; but if you answered incorrectly your **soul** would have to return to earthly re-embodiment repeatedly until eventually you gave the correct answer.

Israel, Manasseh ben (17th century). This Kabbalic leader taught a popular version of the mysteries of the soul and reincarnation. He was the author of the occult text *The Soul of Life* (Hebrew: Nishmat Chayyim).

See also **Kabbalah**.

Ivanova, Barbara. Ivanova is the first person in the former Soviet Union to do research on reincarnation as well as conducting **past life therapy**. A collection of her works in English is titled "*The Golden Chalice*" (1986).

Jacob (Israel) *see* **Adam; Cayce, Edgar; Genesis; Kabbalah; Romans.**

Jainism. This is a non–Vedic **Religion** in India that can be traced back to at least the 6th century BCE. The term Jainism comes from the Sanskrit "*Jina*" meaning the victorious one or conqueror; and in this case it means the religion of the spiritual conquerors of the passions. Jainism had its historical beginnings in the teachings of the northern Indian religious ascetic (*Jina*) Vardhamana, also called the Mahavira (Great Soul), who was a slightly older contemporary of the Buddha Gautama. Jains, however, do not actually regard Mahavira as the founder of their religion in the same way Buddhists regard Gautama as their religious founder. Instead, the Jains believe that Mahavira was the latest of several great reformer or revitalizers of a much older religion and there is some evidence that this Jain view is correct. An earlier form of the religion may even pre-date the Vedic Aryan settlement in India, in which case the concept of rebirth may have begun with some form of proto–Jainism and later have been picked up by nascent Buddhism and proto–**Hinduism**.

Jainism regards all animate and inanimate phenomena as possessing souls (*jivas*). These reincarnate up and down the various levels of existence until they are able to burn off all karma, both positive and negative, thereby liberating themselves from further rebirth. From the Jain perspective, the only chance for liberation (*kevala*) to occur is for a **soul** (*jiva*) to be reborn in the body of a potential Jain ascetic.

The Jain understanding of karma that must be burned off is quite different from the understanding of karma in Hinduism and Buddhism. Whereas, Hindu and Buddhist karma is primarily psychological in nature karma in Jainism is seen as subtle matter that attaches itself to the soul (*jiva*) and weighs that soul down. It is this weight that keeps the soul **earth-bound**. Only by ridding the soul entirely of such weight can the soul, shedding its material individuality, eventually ascend to the heavenly top of the universe where it will remain as an impersonal entity absorbed in eternal bliss.

The Jain concept of karma must be considered not only far more rigid than the Buddhist, or even Hindu concept, but the asceticism needed to eliminate karma is far greater or more extreme in Jainism than it is in at least, Buddhism. This extreme can even include a painful ritual suicide by slow self-starvation (*sallekhana*).

In Jainism there are five vows that must be taken and uncompromisingly observed in order to escape from rebirth. These are absolute non-violence (*ahimsa*) to all life forms, truthfulness (*satya*), not stealing (*aseteya*), having no possessions (*aparigraha*), and complete **celibacy** (*brahmacarya*).

See also *Abhavya; Ahimsa;* **Ajivikas; Animals and rebirth, non–Western view;** *Asuras;* **Blaming the victim vs. illusion of innocence; Body-soul dualism; Brahman; Determinism; Dualism;** *Duhkha;* **Finite or infinite number of rebirths; Fixed number or variable number of souls; Gender issue of the soul; Hell; Individuality and rebirth; Interim period; *Jiva*; *Jivanmukti*; *Kaivalya*; Karma; Karma and free will; Karma and God; Karma and rebirth; Karma as absolute or relative; Merit, transfer of; *Nirjara*; Plants; Rebirth and cyclical time; Rebirth and religious tolerance; Rebirth and suicide; Rebirth, East and West; Rebirth factor; *Samkhya* Yoga; *Samvara*; Soul mates; Soul, origin of the; *Swastika*; *Upanishads*; Vedic Religion; Vegetarianism.

James 3:6. This passage is imbedded in a warning against the dangers of improper speech. It reads, "It [the tongue on fire] represents among our members the world with all its wickedness; it pollutes our whole being; it keeps the wheel of our existence red-hot, and its flames are feed by **hell**." The phrase 'the wheel of our existence' has been interpreted by some supporters of **reincarnation** to mean a reincarnational cycle. However, what precedes and what follows this passage does not support that interpretation.

See also **Annihilationism, Biblical view; Hell**.

Janua Coeli, Janua Inferni (Latin: Gate of Heaven, Gate of Hell). These names were derived from the Roman god Janus, who, as keeper of the gate, had two faces, one facing right and the other left. In other words, he was the god of beginnings, looking to the past; and of endings, looking to the future. This dual positioning has made him a symbol of past and future lives.

Japan *see* **Animism; Buddhism;** *Emma-o*; *Hotoke*; *Kshitigarbha*; **Pure-Land or Blissful Land Buddhism; Shinto;** *Tama*.

Jataka Tales (Birth (*jataka*) Stories). This is a collection of 547 tales which illustrate moral or virtuous acts supposedly performed by the Buddha as a *bodhisattva* in his past lives, either as a human being or as an animal. Many of the stories, minus the figure of any specific *bodhisattva*, probably predate the rise of Buddhism.

Western critics have pointed out several inconsistencies with these stories. The first is with those *Jataka Tales* that claim that the *bodhisattva* experienced previous lives as an animal. For example, he is said to have been an antelope, buffalo, deer, dog, elephant, hare, horse, lion, monkey, and rat; several kinds of birds, including a vulture; a variety of reptiles, a frog, and a fish. Orthodox Buddhism, however, makes it very clear that rebirth as an animal of any kind is the result of bad karma and the idea that the Buddha had lived so many animal lives would technically imply that he had a lot of bad karma, which is in Buddhism a heretical belief. Perhaps this is one of the reasons that only the verses parts, not the prose parts, of the *Tales* are considered canonical.

A second inconsistency has to do with the gender issue. In none of these tales is there ever found the possibility of the *bodhisattva* being female, either as a human or an animal. While this belief may be due to the patriarchal sexism of both Indian society and Buddhism, it has been justified on the basis that rebirth entities rarely, if ever, change their gender. However, this attempt to deflect a sexist charge is futile in that another Buddhist doctrine states that while a being in a female body can attain the enlightenment level of a saint (S: *Arhat*), no one in a female body can ever become a fully self-enlightened Buddha. In other words, one sexist statement is reinforced by another sexist statement.

In spite of these arguments Buddhism claims that rebirth is based upon karmic actions and not on the gender of the actors. The logic of this would seem to mean that since women are treated as inferior to men in most societies, it is more likely that one would be reborn as a female for karmic punishment and as a male for karmic rewards. In this case, there should be a lot of inter-life gender changes unless just being a woman is a forever unchangeable karmic obstacle and just being a man is a forever karmic advantage.

Some Western Buddhists use the fact that there are only 547 birth stories to mean that the number of average rebirths is probably no more than 550 to 600 spaced out over about 25,000 years; however, no such limited number has ever been proposed by orthodox Asian Buddhists. Even if the Buddha may be a special case, other beings are expected to have thousands or more rebirths.

See also ***Abhijna***; ***Avadana***; ***Bhavachakra***; **Buddha's necklace; Buddhist stages of liberation; Fetters, The Ten; Finite or infinite number of rebirths; Pure-Land or Blissful Land Buddhism**.

Jeremiah *see* **Beruchim, Abraham; Karma in the Bible?; New Testament and reincarnation; Old Testament; Sciomancy**.

Jerome, Eusebius Hieronymus (about 345–419 CE). This Catholic saint, and most learned of the Roman Catholic fathers, was commissioned by Pope Damasus to revise the Latin translation of the Greek New Testament as well as a Latin translation of the Old Testament from the Hebrew. It was Jerome's translations that became the orthodox text of the Western Christian (Roman Catholic) church throughout the Middle Ages.

At first an admirer of **Origin**, Jerome translated a number of Origin's Greek writings into Latin; however, he eventually became a party to an early criticism of the **soul's existence prior to embod-**

iment in the works of Origin. This criticism, it is important to note, made it clear that he regarded Origin as innocent of any belief in **metempsychosis**. Oddly, this has not prevented some supporters of **reincarnation** for claiming Jerome as one of their own.

See also **Christian fathers critical of reincarnation; Christianity and reincarnation; Church Council of 553; New Testament and reincarnation.**

Jesus (Hebrew: Yeshu from Yeshua from Yehoshua (Greek: Joshua) meaning God Saves), approximate dates 4 BCE–29 CE.

Among many Western, and some Eastern, reincarnationists there is the belief that Jesus taught the doctrine of **reincarnation** and to prove this they have cited numerous passages from the New Testament. There are two major problems with this belief. First, as innumerable biblical scholars will admit the only record of Jesus' so-called teachings come exclusively from Christian texts, either orthodox or non-orthodox. In other words, we have no evidence from an outside unbiased objective source as to what Jesus really taught. Second, since each Christian source has a separate bias or highly personal agenda in its claim as to what Jesus taught, and many of these claims are in considerable conflict with one another, we can not be sure which, if any of them, may have truly reflect the real teachings of Jesus. In view of these facts, all anyone can absolutely claim is that a number of what are considered Gnostic Christian writings contain indisputable reincarnational teachings; but when it comes to the orthodox or canonical texts of the New Testament any claim that such a teaching is found there is extremely questionable. Every one of the biblical passages that supposedly quote Jesus' own words and that have been interpreted to suggest reincarnation can be so interpreted only if taken out of context as **proof text**.

In addition to reading canonical passages out of context, some reincarnation advocates have turned to extra-canonical sources, both ancient and more modern to support their view of Jesus as a teacher of reincarnation. Among these sources are a variety of old Christian gnostic works such as the ***Nag Hammadi Texts*** and the ***Pistis Sophia***, while among modern works are the ***Aquarian Gospel of Jesus Christ*** and the writings of **Edgar Cayce**.

Many Western advocates of reincarnation not only believe that Jesus taught reincarnation, but that he acquired this belief during his youth while traveling in the northern Indian region of Kashmir or Ladak (western Tibetan speaking area). This is called "The Young Jesus in India Theory." However, if Jesus had lived outside of the Palestinian-Judea area as a youth the silence about this in all of the Gospels is difficult to fathom. There is also "The Post-crucifixion Jesus in India Theory." According to this theory Jesus only appeared to die (scheintod hypothesis) on the cross, but actually survived and escaped to India afterwards; in which case, there was no real **resurrection of Jesus**. Naturally, none of the "Jesus in India" advocates accept the orthodox Christian view of Jesus as part of a divine trinity, but instead regard him as having been one of the great **ascended masters**, the ***Dhyani Chohan***, or a ***tulku*** (reincarnated masters) who attained to that status by a series of ever perfecting reincarnations or **avatar** incarnations.

Among the various proposed previous lives of Jesus are Horus, the Egyptian son of the god Osiris; Krishna, the divine manifestation of God (**Brahman**) in the ***Bhagavad Gita***; Mithra, the Romanized Iranian solar deity; and the **Buddha**.

Most recently the founder of the Unification Church, Sun Myung Moon, is said to believe he himself to be the reincarnation of Jesus as the returned Messiah.

See also **Acts of the Apostles; Aetherius Society; Ahmadiyya; Alexandria, Egypt; *Apocatastasis*; Apollonius of Tyana; Ashoka; Baptism; Christianity and reincarnation; Church Universal and Triumphant; Course in Miracles; Emanationism; Essenes; Fortune, Dion; Generationism and Traducianism; Gnostic Order of Christ; Gnosticism; Harrowing of Hell; Heaven's Gate; Hilarion; I Am Movement; Islam; John, Gospel of; Kingsford, Anna Bonus; Lazaris; Liberal Catholic Church; Lucifer; Luke, Gospel of; Mark-Age, Inc; Mark, Gospel of; Matthew, Gospel of; Melchizedek; Mithraism; New Testament and reincarnation; Notovitch, Nicholas; *Oahspe*; Paulicians; Peter, 1st and 2nd; Pluto, the planet; Rastafarians; Rebirth and moral perfection; Rosicrucians; Sathya Sai Baba; Scientology; Soul twins; Steiner, Rudolf; Unarius Academy of Science; *Urantia Book*; Zhendao.**

Jesus in India *see* **Alexandria, Egypt; Church Universal and Triumphant; Jesus; Notovitch, Nicholas.**

Jewish Holocaust. This was the racially motivated collective murder of six million Jews by the Nazi regime during the Second World War (1939–1945). This "Time of Desolation" (Hebrew: *Shoah*) has elicited innumerable deeply thought out responses from both Jews and Christians. Perhaps none of these were as radical, or morally questionable, as the one suggested by the ultra-orthodox Rabbi Ovadia Yosef, the leader of the *Shas* (political) Party in Israel. In August of 2000 the Rabbi made the very controversial statement that the Holocaust victims were reincarnated Jewish sinners who had to suffer as atonement for their transgressions. Jewish authorities forcefully criticized Yosef for this **blaming the victim** view, for heartlessly deprecating the memory of the Holocaust victims, and cruelly disregarding the feelings of the surviving families of those victims. In a subsequent speech the Rabbi tried to calm the outrage of his earlier Holocaust statement by the indirect apology of saying that he was only trying to provide a theological explanation for the Holocaust and he really regarded all of the Jewish victims as pure and completely pure saints.

A very different view of the relationship between reincarnation and the Holocaust is taken by Rabbi Yonassan Gershom, in his book *Beyond the Ashes: Cases of Reincarnation from the Holocaust* (1992). Gershom, who as a self-identified reincarnation believing Neo-Hasidic, states that he has been contacted by more than 250 individuals, most of whom were not Jewish in this life, but who in each case believe strongly that he or she was Jewish in his or her immediate past life and lived through or died in the Holocaust.

Gershom believes that the there are at least two legitimate reasons that more non–Jews than Jews contact him about former Jewish Holocaust lives. First, in the case of Jews who have sudden recall episodes or flashbacks about the Holocaust no identity crisis usually arise for them; but the same is not true for non–Jews who have such flashbacks. The second reason is that those who remember dying as terrified children, died fervently wishing that they were not Jewish and that it may have been this wish that helps account for the fact that a high percentage of those people were reborn as blondhaired, blue-eyed non–Jews in this life. At the same time, Gershom acknowledges the theory that some of those with "Aryan looks" could be people that fantasized being reincarnated Jewish Holocaust victims in order to relieve some sort of guilt feelings that develop due to being identified with the Nazi oppressors as a result of having such Nazi ideal master-race looks.

Any attempt to use Gershom's material as proof of rebirth is very difficult as Gershom is the first to admit. He states that the Holocaust has so permeated modern Jewish culture that stories by Jews that seem to recall lives in the concentration camps are easily open to explanation of **cryptomnesia**. On the other hand, Gershom believes that while non–Jewish clients would be a less culturally biased sample, as noted above, such issues as guilt might negate their reliability; moreover, even without a guilt factor almost every person in the United States in the last half of the 20th century has been exposed to Holocaust information of some kind which is apt to contaminate any otherwise reliable data.

Although not mentioned by Gershom, there is also the possibility that some of his non–Jewish subjects wish to share in the considerable sympathy directed towards most former concentration victims, if not from this life, than at least from a past life. Still another explanation that has been suggested is that such Holocaust memories are actually **screen memories** for suppressed childhood abuse.

The idea that non–Jews in the present life were Jews in any past lives has been challenged by the orthodox Hasidic community. This is because it contradicts the opinion of many Hasidic teachers, present and past, including the great 16th century Kabbalic mystic **Isaac Luria**, that once a Jew, always a Jew, and so rebirth into a non–Jewish family is impossible. Naturally, this ethnic rebirth belief creates a specifically Jewish version of the **population problem issue**.

See also **Hell; Kabbalah; Karma, racial; Lost continents and reincarnation; Metagenetics; Old Testament and the afterlife; Olfactory psychic experience; Rebirth, criteria for proof of; Rebirth, ethnic; Resurrection, bodily**.

Jews, Ashkenazic and Sephardic. Historically the Jewish people whose ancestors lived for generations in Central and Eastern Europe are known as Ashkenazic Jews, while those whose ancestry can be traced back to pre-sixteenth century Spain and Portugal are called Sephardic Jews. However, according to Rabbi Berg, in his *Wheels of a Soul* (1984), these terms when used correctly refer to one who studies the **Kabbalah** (a Sephardic Jew) and one who does not study the Kabbalah (an Ashkenazic Jew). Moreover, Berg states a Jew born to study the Kabbalah and who either ignores it or opposes it will be reborn as an Ashkenazi.

Jigoku (Japanese: Purgatory or Hell) *see* **Emma-o; Kshitigarbha;** ***Naraka***.

Jiva. This is the preferred term for the life *monad* (**soul**) in **Jainism**. This is because the common term *atman* in **Hinduism** implies a belief in the supreme creator God (**Brahman**), which Jainism denies. In the Advaita Vedanta form of Hinduism, however, *jiva* refers to the empirical, but ultimately illusory, self that reincarnates.

See also ***Jivanmukta*; Monism; *Purusha*; Soul and spirit levels, Theosophical**.

Jivakosha. In **Hinduism** this is any of the sheaths that surround the **soul** (*jiva*).

See also ***Kosha***.

Jivanmukta. This is a person who has attained full liberation (***moksha***) in this very life time and who will not be subject to further rebirth. In other words, this is a person whose karma has been reduced to what can be burned off in this life (*prarabdha karma*) with none left that would force that person into a new rebirth.

See also **Buddhist stages of liberation; Karma, Prarabdha**.

Jizo *see* **Kshitigarbha**.

Job. In this Old Testament book the God-fearing, virtuous and prosperous Job is described as a man who has set his face against all wrong doing. God tests Job's faith in Him by striping him of his prosperity and inflicting him with great miseries. At first Job justifies the ways of God by saying, "If we accept good from God shall we not accept evil?" As his suffering goes on, however, Job wishes for death (to sleep in ***Sheol***) and then does question the justice of God, not just for himself, but for all mankind. Job notes how the wicked often prosper while the innocent suffer; nonetheless, Job never questions the existence of God, so finally Job concludes that God's justice is a mystery and inscrutably beyond human understanding. With this he accepts that God's actions are justified on the basis that whatever God does is right, whether it meets the human standards of fairness or not. Job then meekly submits to this argument in total humility, repenting of any doubt.

Through all of this it is notable that compensation after death for the innocent and/or punishment for the guilty is never mentioned or even indirectly implied. The good and evil, will share a common end in either the shadowing underworld of *Sheol* or endless rest in the grave. Since there is no mention of possible compensation for Job's suffering in a future afterlife it is clear that the book was written before the Jews developed a compensatory concept of heaven.

Despite the clear lack of a satisfactory **theodicy** in this book, some Kabbalists have actually read a reincarnation theme into Job 1:20–21. These Kabbalists regard Job as the reincarnation of the father of Abraham, Terah, who had sinned by worshipping other gods. These two verses in Job read, "Naked I came from womb, naked I shall return whence I came." To suggest that the word "womb" refers to reincarnation does not take into account that in the Old Testament the "womb" is periodically used as a metaphor for the earth or dust out of which God is said to have created man and to which man returns upon death. This is first stated in Genesis 3:19, "...until you return to the ground: for from it you were taken. Dust you are, to dust you shall return." Further proof that there is no reincarnation implied in Job 1:20–21 is found in the passages following Job 1:20–21. They make it quite clear that all of Job has the one theme that God, not man, has absolute control over life and death.

Some reincarnationists, rather than citing Job as having to do with reincarnation, prefer to hold it up as proof that the biblical view of God is morally inadequate in comparison to a doctrine of karma.

See also **Ecclesiastes; Kabbalah; Karma in the Bible? Old Testament and the afterlife; Theodicy**.

John Chrysostom (347–407). This Archbishop of Constantinople, in his *Homilies on the Gospel of John* (about 391), criticized the Pythagorean and Platonic doctrines of **metempsychosis** as shameful, especially the idea that a human soul could enter an animal's body.

See also **Christian fathers critical of reincarnation; Transmigration, regressive**.

John, Gospel of. This New Testament book was the last of the four gospels to be written and the last to be accepted as canonical.

John was written in at least three stages by three different hands, one of which was pro–Gnostic, while the last was anti–Gnostic. Along with these two perspectives there are both pro–Jewish and anti–Jewish sentiments in the Gospel. This conflicting authorship makes it even more possible to read reincarnational passages into this Gospel than is possible with the other three gospels. For this reason, John is the favorite gospel for those who argue that the New Testament at least alludes to an original teaching of reincarnation by **Jesus** and/or the earliest church.

The first of these favored passages is John 3:3–4. Jesus states, "In truth, in very truth I tell you, unless a man has been born (from Greek *gignesthai*, to be born) over again (*anothen*) he can not see the Kingdom of God." Naturally, orthodox Christianity claims that this passage refers to the need to be reborn spiritually, not physically. In other words, it is to have a profound spiritual conversion (*metanoia*) from the doubting mind to a mind grounded in unquestioning faith. That this orthodox interpretation is far more likely to be accurate than a reincarnationist one can be seen from verses John 3:4–7, where one Nicodemus asks, "But how is it possible for a man to be born when he is old? Can he enter his mother's womb a second time and be born?" Jesus clarifies his statement with the words "...born from water (baptism) and spirit (of God). Flesh can give birth only to flesh; it is the Spirit (of God) that gives birth to spirit."

The idea that the term "born again" refers to reincarnation has also been challenged by the fact that the Greek word *anothen* can mean both "again" and "from above." While Nicodemus interprets it more in the first meaning, Jesus interprets it more in the second meaning. 1st **Peter** 1:23 also refers to being born again, but in the same way as John 3:3–4.

The second passage that reincarnationists cite is John 5:14 which reads, "A little later Jesus found him [the cripple recently cured by Jesus] in the temple and said to him, 'Now that you are well again, leave your sinful ways, or you may suffer something worse.'" To make this command have a reincarnation interpretation the "...you may suffer something worse" is said to automatically mean "in a future life-time." However, there is no justification of any kind, other than wishful thinking, to add to this phrase such a post-mortem meaning.

John 8:58 is the third passage that has been used to claim one or more past lives for Jesus. Here Jesus is quoted as saying, "In very truth I tell you, before Abraham was born, I am." This major **proof text** might sound pro-reincarnationist, but only when taken out of its context, and when done so can it be made to say something it does not say. In its full context the quote is being used to deny the charge that Jesus is possessed, and to affirm that he is the supernatural "pre-existent," not "reincarnated," Son of God. If Jesus was really trying to convince his hostile listeners of the doctrine of reincarnation the text should logically read, not "I am," but I was, or even better, "we were." In the first case he would be acknowledging a unique reincarnation, not necessarily shared by others, while in the second case, he would be acknowledging a general doctrine of reincarnation.

If John 8:58 is not read out of context then it is first understood as a deliberate reinforcement of the prologue of the gospel, "When all things began, the word [Christ] already was" (John 1:1); and second, like all the many "I am" phrases in John, it is meant to refer the reader back to Exodus 3:14 where God (Yahweh) answers the question of Moses with the words, "I am, that who I am" and Isaiah 41:4, "It is I, the Lord, I am the first, and to the last of them, I am He." Indeed, the most obvious proof of this is found at John 13:20 where Jesus more or less repeats Exodus with the words "I am what I am." The other "I am" phrases that also emphasize that Jesus is in some manner as much God as is Yahweh are where Jesus refers to himself as the bread of life (John 6:35, 41, 48); the light of the world (John 8:12); the door of the sheepfold (John 10:7–9); the resurrection and [the] life (John 11:25); the way, the truth, the life (John 14:6); and the real vine (John 15:1). In none of these is there any possible reinforcement for a reincarnationist view.

John 9:2–3 is the fourth, and perhaps the most often cited, New Testament passage used to suggest that Jesus and the disciples not only knew about but even accepted the belief in reincarnation. It reads, "His [Jesus'] disciples put the question, "Rabbi, who sinned, this man or his parents? Why was he born blind?" If the reading of this passage stops here it certainly suggests that since the man was born blind, the disciples, in asking whether the man had sinned, must mean "sinned before he was born"; in other words, in a previous life. Since the Greek concept of **metempsychosis**, especially as mentioned by **Plato** and in **Orphism**, was widely known in the greater Mediterranean world in the 1st century, there is no reason not to believe that Jesus and the disciples were familiar with the concept, but familiarity and acceptance are not the same. In fact, there are several other passages in the gospels that imply a familiarity with the concept of reincarnation most, if not all, of which are connected with the **Elijah** and **John the Baptist** issues.

That John 9:2–3 does not mean reincarnation is made clear by the next passage (9:4). This passage goes on to say, "It is not that this man or his parents sinned," Jesus answered: "he was born blind so that God's power might be displayed in curing him." Following this Jesus then cures the man's blindness and the resulting publicity from this reaches the ears of the Pharisees, their intended audience. In other words, to read an acceptance of reincarnation in John 9:2–3 is only possible if the passage is taken out of its greater context.

The fifth passage cited by reincarnationists is John 11:25. It reads, "I [Jesus] am the resurrection and I am life. If a man has faith in me, even though he dies, he shall come to life; and no one who is alive and has faith shall ever die." A reincarnational reading focus on the "even though he dies, he shall come to life." At the same time, this is one of the main passages that orthodox Christians cite to try to repudiate any claim to a New Testament support for reincarnation. The argument is that Jesus promises his followers a future eternal life that does not require any other lives between this one and the promised one.

In the sixth passage favored by reincarnationists, John 14:2, Jesus, speaking to Peter, says, "There are many dwelling-places [rooms] in my Father's house; if it were not so I should have told you: for I am going there on purpose to prepare a place for you." To make the passage read reincarnationally, the term "dwelling places" (*monai* in the Greek) is interpreted as many different **interim period** realms. In fact, this passage was perhaps made most famous to reincarnationists through Gina Cerminara's book *Many Mansions* (1967), which is one translation of the above "many dwelling places."

It might be noted that the Mormons interpret this same passage to mean that there are four different destinations for **soul**. First, there is the mansion with the greatest glory, known as the Celestial Kingdom; second is the Terrestrial Kingdom, which is a kind of secondary heaven; third is the Telestial Kingdom, which is a kind of purgatory; and the fourth is the kingdom without glory, the Outer Darkness, **Hell**.

Still another, and very liberal, interpretation of John 14:2 is that it means that there is some place in heaven even for those who have followed a religious tradition that has nothing to due with the biblical God. This interpretation, however, would seem to clash with the passage in the verse below it, at John 14:6. In fact, it is John 14:6 that is often cited by orthodox Christianity in its claim that any compromise, such as a belief in reincarnation, with a belief in the exclusive power of Christ as one's savior is unchristian. This passage reads, "I am the way; I am the truth; I am the life: no one comes to the Father except by me."

The last of the Johannine passages to be offered as "possibly" implying reincarnation are John 16:12 and 16:25. Both of these imply that Jesus has a secret truth or secret teachings which pro-reincarnationist assume could only be about reincarnation.

John 16:12 says, "There is much that I could say to you, but the burden would be too great for you. However, when he comes who is the Spirit of Truth he will guide you into all truths." John 16:25 says, "Till now I have been using figures of speech [some translations say proverbs]; a time will come when I no longer use figures, but tell you of the Father in plain words."

See also **Annihilationism, Biblical view; Baptism; Born again; Clement of Alexandria; Gnosticism; Hell; Irenaeus; Jesus; John the Baptist; Karma versus grace; Lazarus; Mark, Gospel of; Mormonism; New Testament and reincarnation; New Testament sacrificial concept; Origin** or **Origenes Adamanthus; Peter, 1st and 2nd; Predestination; Soul's existence prior to embodiment;** *Psychopannychism;* **Resurrection of Jesus; Romans.**

John, Revelation of *see* **Revelation of John.**

John the Baptist *see* **Boullan, Joseph-Antoine; Carpocrates; Elijah; John, Gospel of; New Testament and reincarnation; Work of Mercy.**

Jonah *see* **Resurrection of Jesus.**

Jonathan Livingston Seagull (1970). This delightful and extremely popular novel by Richard S. Bach offers a beautiful description of reincarnation as the necessary process whereby all seagulls, and presumably other species, learn that there is more to life than eating, fighting and flocking. Reincarnation allows for learning that there is such a thing as perfection, and that our purpose for living is to discover that perfection and personally manifest it. Bach has written a number of other books with reincarnation themes. One of these, *The Bridge Across Forever* (1984), describes his three-year search for his soul mate.

Joseph of Genesis *see* **Cayce, Edgar; Psalms.**

Josephus, Flavius *see* **Essenes.**

Judaism and the afterlife. Present day Judaism has a variety of views about life after death. The liberal, or Reformed School, more or less leaves it up to the individual member to accept or reject a post-mortem state. The more conservative, and especially the more mainstream, Orthodox School expect its members to believe in a future resurrection of the dead. The esoteric orthodox, or Hasidic School, champions a belief in **reincarnation** (Hebrew, ***gilgul*** or *gilgulim*) as found in the Kabbalah.

Perhaps the earliest well-known Jewish teacher of reincarnation or transmigration was Anan ben David, the eighth century founder of the Jewish sect called Karaism. Most of his followers, however, did not accept the teaching. In fact, the tenth century Karaite author Kirkisani, in his *Sefer ha-Orot,* condemned the teaching of reincarnation, particularly transmigration. Nonetheless, the teaching continued in some circles until it was adopted by the authors of the **Kabbalah.**

Just as passages in the New Testament have been taken in a **proof text** manner out of context and used to support the idea that parts of New Testament teach reincarnation, so the same thing has been done in the case of the Old Testament.

See also **Old Testament and the afterlife.**

Judas Syndrome. Quite a number of past life recallers have suggested that they were Judas, the betrayer of Jesus. To account for such multiple claims more sophisticated reincarnationists have acknowledged that most people have had some experience at either being betrayed or betraying and that the subconscious mind uses the biblical story as a kind of psycho-drama to resolve their personal betrayal aspect.

Jude *see* **Predestination.**

Judge, William Quan (1851–1896). Judge was one of the original founders of the Theosophical Society in 1875. He was also responsible for the revival of the American branch of the Society during his presidency of it, partially by choosing to separate from the mother movement in 1895. This separation was due to the increasing Hinduization of the teachings of **Helena Blavatsky** and Henry S. Olcott's once they moved the international headquarters to India in 1879. Judge also became president of the American Society for Psychical Research in 1895. He is the author of a number of books and articles on reincarnation and karma.

See also **Blavatsky, Helena; Christianity, lost chord of; Theosophy.**

Judgment of the Dead. This concept is found in Orthodox Judaism; Christianity, and **Islam**. The general judgment of the dead at the end of time (Hebrew: *acharit hayamim*), along with the resurrection of the dead (*tehiyat ha-metim*), in Judaism is not envisioned as clearly or dogmatically as it is in Christianity or Islam and most present-day forms of Judaism seem content to leave at that.

In standard Christian thought the judgment of the dead can be listed under either "particular judgment," in which each individual is judged immediately upon death or "general judgment" in which all humanity is to be judged at the end of time. In Roman Catholicism the distinction is necessary in that the souls of some sinners may be sent to **purgatory** at their "particular judgment" so as to attain heaven at the final judgment; also that saintly souls, especially martyrs, can immediately upon death go to heaven were they can intercede between the faithful and God.

To the degree that Protestantism rejects purgatory and the cult of saints this distinction between particular and general judgment is of no importance. Instead, for those Protestant sects that accept *psychopannychism* (pre-resurrection sleeping in the grave) there would be no particular judgment, only a final one.

For some Christians who accept the orthodox belief in the final judgment of the dead, but also believe in reincarnation, the above particular judgment takes the form of reincarnation up until the second coming of Christ, at which point the final judgment and the resurrection of the worthy dead will occur.

In Islam the Day of Judgment (*Yawm ad-Din*, literally the Day of Religion) is more precisely envisioned. According to major Islamic traditions that Day will be preceded by the rising up of the False Messiah (*Masih ad-Dajjal*, literally, the Lying Messiah) which will require the true Messiah, who is the prophet **Jesus** (*Isa 'l-Masih*) to return from heaven (*Sura* 4:159), in part to defeat his false counterpart. Another apocalyptic figure involved with this Judgment Day is the *Madhi* (Arabic: *al-Madhi*, literally, the Director), which one Islamic tradition claims must be a descendant of the family of the Prophet Mohammed. At some point, after much struggle between the true believers and the unbelievers, the resurrection of the dead (*Yaumu 'l-qiyamah*, literally the Standing up) will occur with the good inheriting paradise and the evil being sent to a fiery hell. This orthodox final judgment view has not prevented many South and East Asian Muslims from believing in pre–Judgment Day reincarnation.

See also **Ahmadiyya; Doceticism; Druzes; Millennialism; Muhammad Ahmad; Resurrection, bodily; Resurrection or reincarnation; Sikhism.**

Julian, Flavius Claudius or Julian, The Apostate (reign 361–363 CE). Julian was the last pro-pagan Roman emperor. Although raised as a Christian, he tried to reverse the pro–Christian policies of the previous three emperors, which earned him the title the Apostate.

Julian was killed on the battlefield during a futile attempt to conquer the Persian Empire. It has been said that he believed that such a conquest was possible because he, like the earlier emperor Caracalla (188–217), considered himself to be the reincarnation of Alexander the Great.

Julian, in his defense of paganism wrote a book called *Against the Galileans* (Christians) all copies of which were ordered destroyed by one of his Christian successors, Theodosius II.

See also **Mithraism; Porphyry Malchus; Priesthood, lack of an organized; Romans, Ancient; Sallustius the Neoplatonist;.**

Jung, Carl. Jung is most famous for his ancestral memory or **collective unconscious** concept, in which universal symbols called **archetypes** are stored. At no point in his professional career did Jung make a clear statement in support of a belief in reincarnation. There is some fleeting evidence that he may have taken this belief more seriously as he approached death, but even this, if true, was disguised under terms "ancestral souls," "ancestral components," and "psychic ancestors." This has not stopped some supporters, such as Michael Talbot, in his *Your Past Lives: A Reincarnation Handbook* (1987), from trying to take Jung's words out of context to prove he was a believer in reincarnation.

After Jung's death a hearsay source implied that Jung suspected that he had once been the 4th century Egyptian hermetic alchemist Zosimus of Panopolis, not to be confused with the later 5th century pagan anti–Christian Greek historian Zosimus. A more a detailed investigation of Jung's views is found in *Soul Journey: A Jungian Analyst Looks at Reincarnation* (1991) by John A. Stanford.

See also ***Anima***.

Justice, rebirth and karma *see* **Karma and justice.**

Justin Martyr (About 100–163/7 CE). This early Christian philosopher and Roman Catholic martyred saint seemed to have been the first Christian authority to mention **metempsychosis**. In his defense of Christian teachings, in his *Dialogue with Trypho*, he especially criticizes the idea of human souls being reborn into animal bodies. At the end of the dialogue Trypho says, "Therefore souls neither see God nor transmigrate into other bodies: for they would know that so they are punished, and they would be afraid to commit even the most trivial sin afterwards. But that they can perceive that God exists, and that righteousness and piety are honorable, I [Trypho] also quite agree with you [Justin], said he.)" "(You [Trypho] are right," I [Justin] replied.)" Despite this Dialogue some pro-reincarnationists have actually listed Justin on their side. The very fact that he was orthodox enough in his views to be a Catholic saint should be sufficient proof that he was opposed to reincarnation.

See also **Christian fathers critical of reincarnation; Christianity and reincarnation; New Testament and reincarnation.**

Kabbalah, also spelled Kabala, Kabbala, Qabbalah, Qabbala, Cabbala, Cabbalah, and Cabala. The Kabbalah is an esoteric theosophical or mystical interpretation of the Old Testament, which includes a belief in reincarnation. In Hebrew "Kabbala" means "tradition" and it more specifically refers to a collection of mystical Jewish texts, some elements of which may go back to the 1st century CE, but most of which are heavily dependent on later **Neoplatonism**.

The earliest mention of the doctrine of reincarnation in medieval Judaism is connected with the name Anan ben David, the late 8th century founder of a break-away Jewish sect called the Karaites. Karaite belief in reincarnation, however, was eventually abandoned under criticism from such figures as the 10th century Karaite teacher Jacob al-Kirkisani in a special chapter of his book *the Kitab al-Anwar* (*Book of Lights*).

The next indication of a major Jewish interest in reincarnation is around 1180 by way of a text called the *Sefer ha-Bahir* (*Book of Brightness*). This text first appeared in southwest France and was written in a mixture of Hebrew and Aramaic. It may only be coincidental, but it was in this same area of France, in the 12th century, that was the main center of the reincarnation believing **Cathars**.

The *Bahir* is the first of many books to be considered a part of the *Kabbalah*. In this text the idea of reincarnation is supported in five separate passages, even though *gilgul*, the later specific Hebrew term for reincarnation, is not used. Also, in this text the category of souls undergoing reincarnation is limited to those who have committed certain sexual sins that, except for God's mercy, should result in the extermination of those souls (Hebrew: *keret*). In general, these sins meant any deliberate act that caused the persons to fail in their obligation to procreate. The reason for non-procreation being a sin was due to the Jewish belief that prior to procreation a **soul**, or person bearing it, was incomplete in its life function. Only upon a person having a child did he or she attain completeness. For this reason if a couple died childless it was thought they would not only reincarnate, but be united again to fulfill their parental obligation.

The second major Kabbalic text is the *Sefer ha-Zohar* (*Book of Splendor*). It was produced in late 13th century in Spain. This is basically a mystical commentary on the *Pentateuch* (*Torah*), the first five books of the Old Testament. It was mostly written in Aramaic. While the doctrine of reincarnation was taken up by it, like the *Bahir*, it also taught that *gilgul* was simply a punishment for certain sexual sins. Significantly, with the expulsion of the Jews from Spain in 1492, the *Zohar* was not only carried to other lands, but became a popular text in Christian, as well as Jewish, mysticism, especially after the invention of printing in the 15th century.

One name that stands out in the early history of the Kabbalah is Nahmanides (c. 1194–1270). This great scholar was the highest Jewish legal and religious authority of his time in Spain. It was his positive reception of the Kabbalah that permitted its spread throughout the Spanish Jewish community. Several of Nahmanides' works reflect a Kabbalic point of view, in particular his commentary on the Old Testament *Job*. Without mentioning the term *gilgul* he interprets the suffering of the seemingly innocent Job to a past life in which Job must have committed sufficient wrongs to deserve his later punishment. Indeed, some Kabbalists even identified Job's former life and sin as being that of the idolatrous father of the patriarch Abraham. This of course, was a very logical way of settling the problem that Job always had in terms of **theodicy** (divine justice).

As the concept of *gilgul* evolved, it gradually went from one of being just a condition of punishment to also one of an opportunity to overcome past failures. In this case the number of persons involved in the *gilgul* process increased. For example, *gigul* was used to explain such biblical obligation as levirate marriage (Hebrew: *Yibbum*), as in Deuteronomy 25:5–10. This is the form of marriage where a surviving brother of a deceased man is required to marry the deceased's surviving widow if the deceased husband had no children. In the reincarnationist context it was even thought that the first born son of such a marriage was actually the deceased brother reborn.

The use of *gilgul* to explain a Biblical issue that had hitherto gone either unexplained or unsatisfactorily explained, lead individuals such as Joseph ben Shalom Ashkenazi, a 14th century immigrant to Spain, to expound an extreme version of the *gilgul* theory that changed it into a cosmic law which affected every part of creation. However, even more important than Shalom Ashkenazi, for the increasingly official acceptance of *gilgul*, was the book, the *Sefer ha-Gilgulim (Book of Transmigration)*, by Hayim Vital (1543–1620), a disciple of the renowned Kabbalic mystic **Isaac Luria**.

Shortly there after, there evolved the Kabbalic theory of reincarnational chains of biblical figures. For example, this takes into consideration the fact that, with the exception of an initial vowel sound, only consonants are give value in written Hebrew. So, in accordance with the Kabbalic mystical letter substitution system called the *notarikon*, the letters A-*d*-*m* in the name Adam indicated that the first man Adam was reborn as (King) *D*avid, who in turn would be reborn as the *M*essiah (Hebrew: *Mashiah*). This theory could not be universally accepted since in other Kabbalic texts the soul of the future Messiah, like that of a few other high ranking souls, was immune from *gilgul*. Also, some Kabbalists held that all the souls of human beings that have been or will be embodied were contained in Adam, because when he sinned his soul fragmented into all subsequent souls. Also, due to influence from the *Zohar*, some Kabbalists believe that Adam may have even reincarnated as the biblical patriarch Jacob (Israel).

Despite some more orthodox challenges to the *gilgul* system it proved too logically convenient to be marginalized, and so according to it, not only was David, the reborn Adam; but Bathsheba was the reborn Eve; and Uriah, Bathsheba's husband, was the serpent in Eden. This rebirth scenario was used to explain and justify David's sin of having Uriah killed in battle in order to steal his wife. While in the Old Testament itself this act is vehemently condemned by Nathan the prophet, the Kabbalists actually give it a metaphysically based moral justification.

Again, Abel, the son of Adam, was regarded as having been reborn as Moses, while Abel's brother, Cain was reborn as Jethro, the father-in-law of Moses; and the daughter of Jethro, or wife of Moses, was the twin sister of Abel. This group reincarnation was said to be necessary to atone for the murder of Abel by Cain.

The ultimate expansion of *gilgul* was the inclusion of animal **transmigration** into the process. Although mentioned as early as the 13th century in the *Sefer-ha-Temunah*, a later addition to the Zohar, (the *Tikkunei Zohar*), and in the *Ta'amei ha-Mizot*, such non-human re-embodiments were of little importance at first. Also, while a minority of some late Kabbalists spoke of the *gigul* even of plants and minerals this was much farther than mainstream Kabbalists were ever prepared to go. Even with a wider acceptance of animal *gilgul*, a clear distinction, nevertheless, was kept between true animal souls being reborn as humans and true human souls being reborn as animals. In the latter case, it was accepted that the truly wicked among men might be reborn as an animal one or many times as punishment, but not without a human rebirth in between animal rebirths. This allowed for the person to repent and avoid another animal rebirth. If such repenting did not occur the soul would be reborn into an even lower animal form than previously. This acceptance of transmigration was not universal among Kabbalists, many of which preferred to confine themselves to a belief in reincarnation (lateral transmigration) alone.

For those Kabbalists that did acknowledge such animal *gilgul*, no specific limitations on the number of such regressive transmigrations were given. The same was not true for human *gilgul*. The *Bahir* states that the soul of a sinner can reincarnate in human form up to a thousand times, but made no mention of the number of times for the righteous reincarnating. Some later authorities, however, applied to the righteous the "three times only rule." This number was based on the passage in the Job 33:29, "Behold, God does all these things, twice, three times, with a man." Also used were such passages as ***Exodus*** 20:5 which reads, "I [God] will punish the children for the sins of the fathers to the third and fourth generations of those who hate me. This is repeated at *Exodus* 34:7 as "Jehovah, the Lord, a god ... who punishes sons and grandsons to the third and fourth generation for the iniquity of their fathers!" The reality is that when these passages were originally written the Jews still believed in the primitive tribal morality of collective guilt. Nonetheless, for those teachers who accepted the "three times only rule" any soul that did not succeed by the third time went to hell or, for a murderous soul, it might reincarnate into an animal, plant, or even an inanimate object such as a stone. In those cases, the souls so embodied were said to be able to act as haunting agents called *ubar*.

The early Spanish Kabbalic literature, on the other hand, reversed these numbers. They limited reincarnation of sinners to no more than three times after the soul first entered a body, while the thousand times was applicable to the righteous, who would return to benefit mankind. Besides the number of possible rebirths there were several other important conflicting rebirth related views in Kabbalic literature, among which is the view on the exact nature of the soul that reincarnates.

The most commonly accepted view of the soul

was that it was a triad. There was the life, or vegetative soul (*nephesh*), with which everyone was automatically born; the animal or vital soul (*ruah*); and the rational or holy soul (*neshamah*). One major deviation from this schema was that the *nephesh* is given vegetative, animal and ordinary cognitive (*medabber*) abilities and called the speaking soul (*ha-nephesh ha-medabberet*). The *ruah* supplies the ethical ability or power to distinguish between good and evil. The *neshamah* was equated with the rational soul (*ha-nephesh ha-sikhlit*), which in this case meant the higher cognitive ability of being able to contemplate God, since this soul level was itself a part of God. A second major deviation schema simply recognizes a two part division of the soul into the vital (*ha-nephesh ha-hayyah*) and the *neshamah*.

In the first, or most commonly accepted, tripartite schema the *ruah* and *neshamah*, while assigned to a specific *nephesh*, were not automatically embodied with it. Instead, they resided in the paradise where their descent into the embodied world occurred only as an individual developed. It was thought by the majority of authorities that while the *ruah*, along with the *nephesh*, could be defiled by the actions of the person, the *neshamah*, being of a holy nature, could not be so contaminated. In fact, some Kabbalic literature held that upon any person's actions becoming too wicked the *neshamah* would abandon the individual and return to paradise. This, of course, would exclude the *neshamah* from any belittling reincarnation. A dissenting view assumed that the *neshamah*, while retaining its purity, would be forced into *gilgul* along with its partner souls. Another dissenting view held that all three souls could be involved with sins specific to their nature. Thus, sins of the body belonged to the *nephesh*, sins of speech belonged to the *ruah*, and sins of thought belonged to the *neshamah*.

In later Kabbalic literature the tripartite soul schema was altered to include two still higher souls, the *hayah* and the *yehidah*. This pentad of souls, however, was not as popular as the earlier threefold version.

Regardless of whether it was a triad or a pentad of souls participating in *gilgul*, an eschatological problem arose about them, based upon the fact that all Kabbalic authorities continued to hold on to the orthodox Jewish belief in a future final resurrection of the dead. Orthodoxy held that at the resurrection the soul, in all its parts or levels, would be reunited with its body. If a soul, over a few or many reincarnations, had possessed more than one body, the question became which body was to be resurrected for its eternal habitation? One answer was that each time reincarnation is required the soul acts like a lit candle lighting another candle, such that only an exact copy of the first soul takes on a new body. This meant that at the resurrection there would be any number of identical souls, but each of these would be reunited only with its own unique body.

Another solution to this resurrection based eschatological problem was that each person actually has more than one soul inhabiting him or her. Each time a new body is born, God sends a pre-existing, but a never having been embodied pure soul from "The Treasure-house of Souls (*Ozar ha-Neshamot*)," which is in the blissful celestial paradise (*Gan Eden shel ma'alah*), to dwell in that body. This new body, however, attracts up to three old (formerly embodied) souls whose natures, sins, and needs for redemption are sufficiently similar to one another to allow them to function as a whole. This arrangement of a host soul and several guest souls was permitted only for the relatively good guest souls. Evil souls had to reincarnate in far less desirable ways. The advantage to this arrangement was that each soul, as host to others, original had only a single unique body which would be reassigned to it at the resurrection.

The issue of souls entering into hell (*gehinnom*) was another point of contention between Kabbalists. Some Kabbalists argued that a punishable soul simply reincarnated instead of spending time in hell, while others insisted that souls must first be purged of their major faults before reincarnation. Still others assigned souls to a purgatory-like state called the "Vale of Weeping (*Emek ha-Bakha*)," which it clearly distinguishes from *gehinnom*.

According to still another Kabbalic view, when a soul is first about to descend into the world it visits the terrestrial Garden of Eden and sees there the glory of the righteous souls, then it visits *gehinnom* and sees the unrighteous souls. After this the soul, originally hermaphroditic, divides into it male and female parts to enter their respective bodies. This, naturally, brought up the issue of the gender of reincarnating souls, which was also in dispute. It was agreed that each soul prior to the first embodiment was both male and female and split apart as it descended from heaven to earth for embodiment. Yet some Kabbalists argued that only male souls could undergo *gilgul*. In fact, it was partly this situation that was thought to account for barrenness among some women. Such women were believed unfortunate to have had a male soul reincarnated into female bodies.

On the other hand, according to the book *Wheels of a Soul* (1991), by Rabbi Berg, the *Sefer ha-Gilgulim* teaches that a woman has an easier time in fulfilling her *tikun* (cosmic repair) than a man because she has more spiritual understanding (*binah*) and as a result may have to experience only a single embodiment. However, she may voluntarily reincarnate more than once to help her male soul mate fulfill his *tikun*.

The category of persons who could ultimately be saved was another bone of contention. The broadest view was that both those from the other side (*sitra aha*) or Gentiles, and those from the holy side (*sitra di-kedusha*) or Jews would be saved. Another opinion allowed for only the inclusion of *Noahides* to be saved. These were Gentiles who followed the seven pre–Mosaic (*Noachian*) laws as found in **Genesis** 2:16; 9:4 that God gave to Noah as the new father of all mankind after the biblical flood. A more radical view was that only Jews could be saved and a still more radical and exclusionary opinion was that only those Jews that fully understood the Kabbalah could be saved.

One other concept found in the Kabbalah related to *gilgul* was that of *ibbur* (Hebrew: embryonic development, pregnancy or impregnation). In the main part of the *Zohar* and other early Kabbalic but latewritings, this term overlaps with *gilgul* in meaning, on it has a separate though related meaning. *Ibbur* came to signify the entry of a soul into an alien body, not at the time near birth like a regular reincarnation, but sometime well after that.

Certain limitations were believed to apply to this form of **possession**. First of all, only relatively virtuous souls would seek such *ibbur* and then they would do so only for a certain required time. The purpose of such an *ibbur* (possessing) activity was either to fulfill a certain action or commandment that was not fulfilled by the time of the death of the soul undergoing *ibbur*, or for the entering soul to give encouragement to, or guide, the host soul in the performance of some righteous action. For example, this *ibbur* might take only the few moments necessary to perform a single ritual act or it could reside in with its host for several years, perhaps even up to the host's death, if the host spiritually benefited from the *ibbur*.

While originally there was an acceptance of only such righteous *ibbur* there soon arose the idea of an unrighteous *ibbur*. A bad *ibbur* would be one that gained entrance into its host because of some evil the host had committed prior to the *ibbur's* entry. Once within the host an evil *ibbur* would seek to further corrupt the host, even to the point of destroying the host's own personality.

Since using the term *ibbur* for both benevolent and malevolent purposes was soon thought undesirable a new term was adopted to characterize an evil *ibbur*. This term, not found in the Kabbalah but taken from a Yiddish folk tradition, was ***dibbuk***, and literally meant an attachment from the outside and was really the shortened form of *dibbuk me-ru'ah ra'ah* (an attachment of an evil spirit).

According to at least one Kabbalic view there were not enough bodies for all souls to reincarnate at the same time. But instead of rotating, once souls enter the rebirth cycle they continue in it until finally liberated. This means that there was a pool of souls, namely those in the treasure-house of souls that have not yet reincarnated, and they must wait there until surplus bodies are available to enter. This is said to explain why there are some very **old souls** and some very new ones.

What has been covered in this entry does not include all Kabbalic teachings, most which have little to do with the issue of reincarnation. For this reason many Jewish and non–Jewish practitioners are involved in Kabbalic work that has nothing to do with reincarnation. This is particularly true of what has been called Christian Kabbalah, most of which became the Occult Kabbalah, more often spelled Qabalah. Such Occult Qabalah, which often did re-adopt a belief in reincarnation, was at the heart of the magical systems associated with Eliphas Levi, and S. L. MacGregor Mathers, the co-founder of **The Hermetic Order of the Golden Dawn**, and its many offshoots.

See also **Ascended masters; Attached entity; Blavatsky, Helena; Candia Debate;** *Chakras;* **Chiromancy;** *Dibbuk;* **Elijah;** *Enoch, Third Book of;* **Fall of the Souls; Finite or infinite number of rebirths; Frank, Jacob;** *Galya Raza; Gehazi;* **Gender issue of the soul; Gnosticism;** *Guf ha-Briyot;* **Heschel of Opator, Abraham Joshua;** *Hezyonot, Sefer ha-;* **Jewish Holocaust; Job, Book of; Karma, racial;** *Karet; Layela;* **Levirate marriage; Moses, the Old Testament prophet; Numbers 16:22; Numerology and rebirth; Old Testament and the afterlife; Philo Judaeus; Population increase issue; Population increase issue and a theistic solution; Psalms;** *Qlippoth;* **Rebirth, ethnic; Rebirth, group; Rebirth, selective; Resurrection, bodily; Soul; Soul, tripartite;** *Tanya;* **Tarot cards;** *Tzror ha-Chayyim;* **Virgo** (*Elul*).

Kabirpanthi (followers of the path of Kabir). Kabir (1440–1518) was an Indian mystic who sought to unite Hindu and Muslim teachings in the hope of bring the antagonistic followers of those faiths in a peaceful unity. In this regard he was the forerunner of **Sikhism**, which was established by a disciple of Kabir, Nanak. Kabir took from Islam the belief in one God, the equality of all people before God, and a rejection of idolatry, asceticism, and the **caste system**. He took from Hinduism the belief in reincarnation and karma. There are presently two main sects of Kabirpanthi, one is more Muslim, the other more Hindu. The sacred writings of Kabir are found in the *Bijak* (*of Kabir*).

Kaivalya. (Isolation). This is the ideal state of the **soul** (*jiva*) in *Jainism*. It signifies complete and eternal separation from further rebirth into a material body.

See also **Buddhist stages of liberation;** *Jivanmukta*; *Moksha*; **Nirvana and** *Parinirvana*.

Kama dhatu, also ***kama-loka*** (Realm of Desire). In Buddhism this consists of the six sub-realms of rebirth (*sad-gati*) into **samsara**. These are the realms of human beings (*manusya*), animals (*tiryak*), gods (*deva*), anti-gods (*asura*), **hungry ghosts** (*preta*), and **purgatory** (*naraka*).

See also **Astral plane;** *Bhavachakra*; *Kamaloka*; **Mara;** *Tri-dhatu or Tri-loka*.

Kamaloka. This is the first and lowest of the six heavens of the realm of desire
in the traditional Buddhist mythological cosmology. In **Theosophy** and the Anthroposophy of **Rudolph Steiner** it is a post-mortem period of sometimes purgatorial-like recollection which proceeds entering the ***devachan*** and finally rebirth.

See also ***Devaloka***; **Heaven, Buddhist.**

Kama rupa (Body of Desire). In the book *Esoteric Buddhism* (1973), by A.P. Sinnett, the term *kama rupa* is translated as the animal soul, but later Theosophical works usually drop this translation. Instead, in some Theosophical teachings the *kama rupa* seems to be equated with the **etheric body**, especially as it is thought that a distraught etheric body (*kama rupa*) can turn into a harmless or harmful ghost-like figure (an elementary). In still other Theosophical views the *kama rupa* is equated with the *astral body*.

See also **Astral plane; Attached entity; Buddhism, esoteric; Etheric revenant; Soul and spirit levels, Theosophical; Vampire.**

Kampman, Reima *see* **Children remembering past lives; Multiple personalities.**

Kant, Immanuel (1724–1804). This preeminent German (Prussian) was perhaps the most important European philosopher of modern times. Kant's main goal was to establish, once and for all, the authority of pure reason. In doing this he was forced to admit that not only God, but also the **immortality** of the soul and free will could not be demonstrated through reason. However, to avoid being labeled an atheist by the Lutheran state church, Kant declared that the mind must inevitably accept the existence of all three of these religious phenomena because they were a necessary basis for virtue or morality. Kant's compromise of his "truth based on pure reason" has opened him up to the criticism of betraying his own goal. While Kant would only have been thinking of such immortality in the context of the Christian resurrection, his argument of "a necessary basis for virtue or morality" has been used by reincarnationists as well.

Kanthaeans. This little known Mesopotamian (Iraq) gnostic religious group may have originated as early as the late 5th century CE, but was first reported on in the late 8th century. According to the Arabic heresiographer Al-Shahrastani, at least one of the three branches of this religion believed in **reincarnation** (*tanasukh*).

See also **Hashimiyya; Islam; Khurramiyya; Rawandiyah.**

Kardec, Allan *see* **Spiritism.**

Kardecismo. This is a Brazilian religious movement that incorporates the **Spiritism** of Alan Kardec with elements from the Afro-Brazilian mediumship religion of Candomble and Macumba and especially from **Umbanda**.

See also **Afro-American religions; Santeria.**

Karet (Hebrew: Cut-off). According to the famous Spanish Kabbalist Nahmanides (1194–1270), the term refers to a **soul** that, due to sin, must reincarnate into a degraded body. On the other hand, according to the 16th century Kabbalist Isaac Luria *karet* means being block from entering the afterlife and so becoming a ghost or ***dibbuk***.

See also **Kabbalah.**

Karma/*kamma* (deed or action). In traditional Indian religions karma is regarded as part of the universal or cosmic law of cause and effect. This means that we reap the fruit (***vipaka***) of what we sow (karma). If we sow what is constructive or skillful (*kusala*) we will reap what is constructive or skillful, if we sow what is destructive or unskillful (*akusala*), we will reap the same.

The starting point for understanding the theory of karma is to recognize that it has a primary and a secondary function. The primary and more general function is to explain why there is such inequality of poverty and wealth in the world as well as why seemingly good and/or innocent people appear to suffer unfairly, while bad, and presumably guilty, people remain unpunished or even gain rewards.

The secondary and more personal function of karma is to convince individuals that, despite the obvious inequality and unfairness in the world, bad deeds are eventually punished and good deeds are eventually rewarded, if not in this life then in a future life. This secondary function is obviously in the service of the primary function. It says that one's present day rebirth into an undesirable state is usually a punishment for past unskillful or unmeritorious actions (S: *akusala* or *papa karma*), while one's rebirth into a desirable state is usually a reward for past skillful or meritorious actions (*kusala* or *punya karma*). In other words, these two related functions of karma teach that there is a logical, non-arbitrary reason for human suffering and as a result it implies that the world is ultimately a just place.

In actuality, in **Hinduism**, Buddhism, and *Jainism*, it is the passing on of karma, rather than the rebirth of a soul, that assumes priority. **Soul** rebirth is primarily the vehicle for manifestations of karma. Indeed, even spiritual liberation is subordinate to karma. For all practical purposes karma replaces the judging, sentencing, and rewarding power of a Western style personal God.

In India both the primary and secondary functions of karma have also been used to justify the **caste system**.

See also **Blaming the victim vs. illusion of innocence; Karma and faith; Karma and forgiveness; Karma and free will; Karma and God; Karma and justice; Karma and rebirth; Karma and the moral structure of the universe; Karma as absolute or relative; Karma as natural law; Karma as unfinished business; Karma, bodily; Karma, classifications of; Karma in the ancient and modern west; Karma, delayed; Karma, developmental; Karma, family; Karma, global (planetary); Karma, group; Karma in the Bible; Karma, origins of; Karma, racial; Karma, retributive; Karma versus grace; Karma, vocational; Karma with minimal rebirth; Karmic bankbook; Karmic boomerang effect; Karmic carryover; Karmic diseases; Karmic eschatology; Karmic script; Karmic seeds; Karmic ties; Lords of Karma.**

Karma and faith. While some people can accept rebirth as real based on the ambiguous evidence in the various arguments offered in support of it the same can not be said of the belief in karma. No concrete evidence for or against karma seems to be obtainable. It does little good even to try to prove its existence from rebirth itself, especially in the light of the lack of provable memories of past lives. A belief in karma, therefore, must ultimately be on the basis of faith alone. This faith alone aspect is very important because rebirth is a meaningless concept in Eastern religion without the ethical continuity of karma. In short, it is karma and not rebirth that is at the eschatological heart of Eastern religions.

See also **Arguments supportive of rebirth; Ethicalized or karmic rebirth; Karma and justice; Karma and rebirth; Karma in the ancient and modern west; Karma with minimal rebirth.**

Karma and forgiveness. It has said that one of the most important differences between karma as the impersonal judge of human transgressions, and a personal God as a judge of such transgressions, is that the karma can not forgive these transgressions while a God can. This is only partially true. Karma, unlike God, can not arbitrarily forgive, but forgiveness within the law of cause and effect is very possible. To gain forgiveness as part of the fruit (***vipaka***) of karma simply requires one to make forgiving karma by freely forgiving others their transgressions against you. In short, to karmicaly give forgiveness, in *vipaka* terms, is to receive such forgiveness.

See also **Karma versus grace**.

Karma and free will. In the West the doctrine of karma has often been criticized as being a fatalistic form of **determinism**. That there is a determinist aspect to karma can not be denied; nonetheless, Buddhism, **Hinduism**, and **Jainism** teach free-will and are technically opposed to determinism. One way of understanding this is to view karma as a kind of leash tied to a pole in the ground by which one's life is held. While one can not act outside of the radius of that leash, within the radius of it one has complete freedom to act. This, at the most, makes karma a weak form of determinism verses the stronger form associated with fatalism which allows no freedom for moral actions or responsibilities. A further indication that karma is not a kind of fatalism can be seen in the form of *ahosikarma* (karma that is ineffective). In order for karma to produce an effect several auxiliary causes, such as circumstances, surroundings, etc., are required. If those requirements are lacking, as sometimes happens, karma does not produce any effective results.

For Buddhism, in particular, karmic fatalism is again further weakened by the Buddhist insistence that there are, besides karma, four other non-karmic causal constraints (*niyama*) that can influence a person's life for better or worse. These are physical inorganic constraints such as seasonal phenomena of winds and rains, heat and cold (*utu niyama*); physical organic constraints such as germs and seeds, which today would include the scientific theory of cells and genes (*bija niyama*); constraints of mind or psychic law, which would include all psychic phenomena (*citta niyama*); and constraints of what Buddhism regards as natural religious laws, as well as such laws of nature as gravity (*dharma niyama*). These four constraints, along with karma, embrace everything in the world, and every mental or physical phenomenon can be explained by them. In that karma and the four constraints are considered part of natural laws, there is no necessity for a supreme lawgiver. In fact, the opposition to viewing karma as fatalism has always been a reason that Buddhism has opposed acknowledging any kind of supreme lawgiving-creator. According to Buddhist logic, such an omnipotent deity would automatically predetermine everything.

Despite the clear anti-determinist teachings in Eastern religions, many Christian sources continue to label karma as deterministic, if not fatalistic. The more sophisticated pro-karma response to this label has been to point to the far more obvious and absolutist Christian determinism implied in the New Testament letters of the apostle **Paul of Tarsus**. In some of these letters Paul teaches that God chose who to save and who to damn even before the world was created. In fact, this Pauline view on predestination became the bedrock of later Calvinist Protestantism. It is true that most modern Christian groups today more or less ignore, or in a few cases completely repudiate this teaching, however, this does not change the fact that in orthodox Christian belief the Bible is the Word of God and can only be ignored or repudiated at the risk of damnation.

See also **Ajivikas; Karma and God; Karma and justice; Karma as absolute or relative; Karma in the ancient and modern west; Karma versus grace; New Testament and reincarnation; Population increase issue and a theistic solution; Rebirth, East and West.**

Karma and God. When it comes to the issue of karma and God religious opinion generally has divided along a theistic and non-theistic line. In the East this divide has traditionally been between theistic **Hinduism** and **Sikhism** and non-theistic Buddhism and **Jainism**. However, for the most part, between these two groups a belief or non-belief in God has not made much difference in terms of karmic rebirth. The reason is that in both theistic and non-theistic Eastern religions the function of rewarder and punisher of behavior, as technically performed by the impersonal law of karma (*karmaniyama*), is thought of as independent of God.

If this independence has rarely been a topic of debate in Eastern religions the same can not be said of Western groups that support a belief in rebirth and karma. In fact, these groups have used the karmic issue to strongly argue for either the theist's or the atheist's view.

The theistic view is that rebirth and karma allows for a just and loving personal God to give evil doers more than one chance at redemption rather than sending them to an eternal hell after only one lifetime. However, one major problem with this belief in a personal caring God and karma-rebirth is that such a God would most likely allow people to remember at least the most immediate past life so they could benefit from their mistakes; therefore, the absence of such remembrance has been used to challenge a belief in such a God.

Another karmic challenge to a belief in God has been that a belief in karma serves one of the main purposes for a belief in God, in that it assures people that the universe cares enough about them morally to bother to be a cosmic judge, punisher and rewarder of human behavior. Of course, this "karma as a substitute for a judging God view" itself has provoked a challenge from the "extreme atheistic camp." This camp argues that, first, a belief in karma and rebirth is not only a belief in a just God under another name, but that it is human hubris to believe that the universe cares enough about mankind to ensure justice and, second, from the perspective of human responsibility any type of an after-life punishment or reward simply relieves people of opposing injustice in the world since karma will presumably deal with this.

See also **Anthropopathism; Arguments pro and con on an afterlife in general (6 and 7); Arguments supportive of rebirth; Atheism; Brahma and rebirth in Buddhism; Christianity and reincarnation; Creationism, soul; God and rebirth in the West; Karma and free will; Karma and justice; Karma and the moral structure of the universe; Karma versus grace; Population increase issue and a theistic solution; Rebirth and religious tolerance; Theodicy.**

Karma and intentionality (S/P: *Cetana*) *see* **Karma as absolute or relative; Restitution negates retribution.**

Karma and justice. Most supporters of rebirth and karma, in both the East and the West, believe that these two concepts help to make sense out of the seeming judicial contradiction that good people frequently suffer while evil people often prosper. This judicial or moral contradiction is resolved by stating that the present good person is working off some past bad behavior, and the evil person is experiencing the benefit of some past good behavior. This simplistic view, however, does not take into consideration the "karma and memory problem."

Throughout human society, past and present, it is usually assumed that a direct and provable relation should be made between a crime and the punishment in order for the punishment to qualify as just. In fact, to punish someone for a crime that not even circumstantial evidence can link to that person is universally considered an act of grave injustice. Equally, to reward a person for an action that can not be proven to have been performed by that person, if not unjust, is at least unfair. With the exception of a few people who claim to remember one or more past lives, no memory from one life to another is retained; therefore, there can be no proof that a person, in misfortunate or fortunate circumstances, deserves what is assumed to be punishment or reward for past actions. In other words, this lack of memory puts the whole concept of karma as a source of justice in doubt. Indeed, in the absence of past life memories, even if karma has something to do with unfortunate or fortunate circumstances, it might be considered morally meaningless.

On the other hand, in defense of the meaningfulness of karma, even without a memory of the past, the following analogy has sometimes been offered. What if a year old child finds some matches and in the process of playing with them severely burns his face, such that he is disfigured for life. By the time he is ten years old he will have no memory of that tragic action; nonetheless, he is responsible for his condition. The weakness of this argument is that while the child has no memory of the cause of his disfigurement, his parents do have such a memory and can attest to the child that he is the cause of his own condition. Nowhere in the concept of karma is there the equivalent of the parents to certify the claim that everyone is in some way responsible for their present condition.

Despite the apparent incompatibility of memoryless rebirth and karmic justice it should be noted that the memory and justice issue is essentially a Western problem. This is because of the Western (Judeo-Christian) view that personal memory is required for individuality and hence for genuine individual moral responsibility. This is in sharp contrast to the Hindu and Buddhist view that individuality, with all its attachment to personal memories, is not only illusory in nature, but is the initial cause of all moral or judicially wrong thoughts, words, and deeds. The very fact that most people do not retain personal memories from one life to another is regarded, less as a justice issue and more as proof of how insignificant such memories are. In these Eastern religions it is simply the impersonal delusion of individuality itself that passes on from one life to another. Therefore, there is little reason to expect, much less morally demand, that personal memories be retained.

The problem of past life memory and karmic justice is also less of a problem for Eastern religions, in which there either is no supreme God (Buddhism, Jainism) or there is, ultimately, only an impersonal supreme God (Hindu **Brahman**), than it is for Western religions with their very personal God.

On the one hand, for a just and very personal Western God to send even the most evil of persons to an eternal hell has often be criticized as unjust. Therefore at most, a temporary **hell** followed by rebirth might be a more logical extension of God's justice. This gives sinners all the necessary chances to reform that they need. However, this still leaves the previously stated problem of how can real justice, divinely controlled or not, be based on an unprovable link between present life misery and past life wrong doings? Is this still not unjust punishment without proof of guilt? Also, if there is a just personal God should He or She not offer unquestionable proof of the link between guilt and punishment? Obviously, this creates a problem for those Westerners who wish to harmonize a belief in rebirth with the lovingly just side of God.

If we dispense with the personally divine and return to a non–God oriented religion, such as Buddhism, then it is really an inconsequential matter that there can be rebirth without past life memories. This is because karma is viewed as an impersonal natural law that will function, as would any natural law, without the proof that would satisfy the normal human demand for justice or fairness.

The belief in karma, with or without God, for all of its logical problems has clearly served some purpose for at least the 2,500 years or more that it has dominated Indian religious thought. If nothing else, belief in karma in the face of human suffering has made hundreds of millions of people believe that there is justice in the world. Whether karma is true or false, if people believe in it this means that they have convinced themselves that the world would not make them suffer if they were not guilty of something in the past. They can then regard their suffering as justified, and through such psychological rationalization lessen their misery. In this sense, at a minimum, karma and rebirth function as a convenient fiction and/or **noble lie**.

Everything said so far has to do with a belief in individual karma. Another way of viewing karma and justice is to view it collectively rather than individually. In this case, since according to the Buddhist law of interdependent causality or origination (***pratitya-samutpada***) all beings are interdependent; every individual, past, present, and future, is part of every other individual, past, present, and future, and karmic rebirth is a part of this interdependency. Therefore, it can be argued that it might not matter who sowed a deed and who reaps the resulting punishment or reward.

Finally, it should be noted that the issue of karma and justice is only important to those cultures that relate to rebirth as some form of punishment or reward. In cultures where an ancestral **soul** is thought to be reborn back into his or her family or clan there is no concept that this is a punishing or rewarding event. In such cultures it is totally unimportant that the past or ancestral life be remembered and the question of justice is immaterial.

See also **Age factor and rebirth**; *Akashic* **Record**; *Anatman*; **Aquinas, Thomas; Arguments supportive of rebirth;** *Atman*; **Creationism, soul;**

Blaming the victim vs. illusion of innocence; Caste system; Individuality and rebirth; Karma; Karma and faith; Karma and free will; Karma and God; Karma as natural law; Karma in the ancient and modern west; Karma in the Bible?; Karma, retributive; Karma versus grace; Kubler-Ross, Elizabeth; Limitation lifetime; MacTaggart, John Ellis; Memories, reasons for loss of past life; Natal defects; Past life memory categories; Predestination; Purgatory; Rebirth and cyclical time; Rebirth and unilinear descent; Rebirth, East and West; Rebirth in the West; Chinese religion and reincarnation; Theodicy.

Karma and logic. Critics of the concept of karma have argued that the concept has failed to give logically consistent answers to the following questions. If karma is true what registers and administers it? Does each rebirth factor carry its own positive and negative karmic points so that it automatically chooses a new life that will punish or reward it? Does some collective intelligence such as the so-called **Lords of Karma** (*Lipikas*) perform this function? Does some universal mind or consciousness such as the impersonal Mahayana Buddhist *alaya-vijnana*, or personal God administer it?

If these questions can not be answer with some logical consistency, and still people believe in karma then it must be asked, why? At least three major reasons seem to be behind such a belief each of which has its own logical problems. First, millions of people have accepted karma for thousands of years; therefore, it is probably true. People believed for thousands of years that the sun revolved around the earth, yet that did not make it true. Second, an important teacher such as the Buddha is said to have taught it; therefore, it should be true. According to the Buddhist canon the Buddha also taught a mythic geography with a flat earth, and four continents with Mount Meru in the middle. If the Buddha, in fact, taught these things as fact he was clearly wrong so how can we be sure he was not equally wrong about karma. Third, people want desperately to believe in an ultimately just world. As desirable as such justice is, just because people want it does not make it true.

See also **Arguments supportive of rebirth; Karma; Resurrection or reincarnation.**

Karma and memory problem *see* **Karma and justice.**

Karma and rebirth. If karma is to be considered part of a just existence it must be one of the causative factors in the rebirth process. For example, if rebirth can not occur without some karmic aspect partaking in the rebirth process then karma is an integral part of being. On the other hand, if the fruit (*vipaka*) of karma attaches itself to the reborn entity independent from the rebirth process itself then, being unrelated to the reborn entity, karma would act as a kind of a parasitic factor, like an **attached entity**. In this latter situation, *vipaka* might still be justified as long as it was a universal and not a selective attachment. In other words, it could be that every newborn inherits the *vipaka* of another person unrelated to the newborn, but which the new being must work out. In this case it would presumably be pure chance who inherited good *vipaka* and who inherited bad *vipaka*, but at least in terms of the initial odds everyone would be karmicaly equal. This would actually account for what is sometimes suggested in Buddhism as no-soul (self) being reborn and only *vipaka* passing from one life to another. This would also satisfy the "primary" function of **karma**, namely an explanation of why some people have fortunate lives while others have misfortunate lives. It would not, however, satisfy the "secondary" function of karma, the giving assurance that good people end up being rewarded and bad people punished, even if this happens in another lifetime.

A problem with the inheritance of unrelated *vipaka* is that in an ever expanding population some people would inherit another's *vipaka* while some would not. This would make the system unfair. Of course, just because it is unfair does not mean it could not be true. In this universe fairness may be just wishful thinking or at best a **noble lie.**

See also **Blaming the victim vs. illusion of innocence; Electra/Oedipus Complex and rebirth; Ethicalized or karmic rebirth;** *Gandharva*; **Karma and faith; Karma and justice; Karma with minimal rebirth; Karma, with and without Rebirth; Karmic eschatology; Population increase issue; Possession; Rebirth in Buddhism.**

Karma and the moral structure of the universe. When any "religion" asks about the origin of the universe it is not really asking out of scientific curiosity but out of moral concern. In other words, it is really asking about the origin of good and evil.

In Buddhism the question as to the origin of the universe is usually stated to be logically unanswerable and any discussion or debate on the subject as a waste of time and effort. This might seem to be a weakness on the part of Buddhism in relationship to some forms of theism since the theist can easily answer that the origin of the universe is in the creative act of God. The Buddhist counter to this is that if God created the universe who or what created God? The standard theistic answer is that no one or nothing created God, since God has always existed. The Buddhist response becomes "Why not just say that the universe has always existed? Why add God to the eternity of existence if He is not necessary?" To do so is to make God simply a logical redundancy. If a knowledgeable Buddhist is pushed for an answer to the origin of the universe the best possible answer he can give is that each new universe comes into existence due to fruition (*vipaka*) of unresolved karma from the previous universe.

Unresolved karma, rather than a Creator Deity, as the origin of the present universe has been counter criticized by Western religions as simply pushing the origin one step back from God; hence, not really answering the question of its origin any more than Western monotheism does. In other words, "the infinite regression or beginningless" of both Buddhism and Western monotheism are no real explanation of the origin of the universe and hence of evil.

On the other hand, unlike Western religion, Buddhism has an alternative explanation for evil (*papa*) in the world. Since Buddhism is not dependent on belief in an all good God who logically should have created only an all good world, Buddhism can acknowledge that the root of evil is inherent in the very present nature of the world, especially as it is understood as being in a constant state of flux or impermanence. For mere mortal human beings to cope with this impermanence satisfactorily requires great skill. Some people attempt to cope by making choices that seem beneficial to them in the long term, even if not in the short term. This, more often than not, is called skillful (*kusala*) behavior. Other people choose what seems beneficial to them only in the immediate future and ignore the more distant future. This more often than not is called unskillful (*akusala*) behavior. One skillful choice often leads to another skillful choice, and so making skillful choices becomes habitual. These habitually skillful choosers are usually thought of as doers of good and builders of positive karma which eventually can lead to liberation from the cycle of birth and death. Similarly, several unskillful choices usually lead to more unskillful choices until unskillful choices become habitual. These habitually unskillful choosers build up very negative karma which pulls them farther and father away from escaping the cycle of birth and death.

See also **Karma and God; Karma-*vipaka* as a long term moral tendency; Rebirth and logical symmetry; Soul, origin of the; Tetralemma or Fourfold Negation.**

Karma and the origin of evil *see* **Karma and the moral structure of the universe.**

Karma as absolute or relative. There has been a long standing argument among traditional Indian religious systems as to how rigid or flexible karma is. In general this argument comes down to the degree to which intentionality is or is not of major significance. In **Jainism** karma is thought to be more or less inflexible or absolute, since it is considered to be a form of matter similar to "clay particles." For this reason Jains believe less in developing good karma and avoiding bad karma; instead, Jains try to avoid creating any kind of new karma and getting rid of all past karma. In Jainism an action has more of a life of its own which means one must experience the *vipaka* (karmic consequences) of the action regardless of intentionality. In Buddhism and Hinduism it is intentions that count more than the action itself, which makes karma far more relative. In Buddhism, and to a lesser degree in Hinduism, to be subjected to *vipaka* for an action one does, there must have been conscious intent to perform that action followed by the consequence of the action.

If intentionality (*cetana*) is the dominant determiner of whether an action is good or bad, then moral precepts must have a certain degree of relativity to them. For example, it is not merely a matter if one person kills another intentionally and a different person kills someone unintentionally, the motivation behind the intentional killing would have to be added to the issue. If I intentionally kill someone trying to kill me or someone I love this is not the same intentionality as if I intentionally kill some one out of vengeance. In the case of the person I kill in self-defense, given different circumstances, I would have had no intention whatsoever to kill him. In short, the intentionality to kill was forced upon me; whereas, the revenge killing was entirely intentional.

The intentionality aspect of karma-*vipaka* should also make it culturally relative. For example, in certain Middle Eastern societies if an unmarried woman has a sexual affair that brings dishonor to her family then it is considered, not only acceptable, but mandatory that her family should kill her. Two variables are present here. First, the woman presumably knew the rules and customs of her society, which meant she understood the danger of her action and its probable consequences; in this sense, whether she admits it to herself or not, she is intentionally disgracing her family. Second, the family had no prior desire to harm the woman; in fact, she may have been a much loved member of the family. This means that the family's intention has less to do with killing the woman and more to do with preserving its honor. This ought to mean that the family is being forced by the customs of its society to kill the woman. There is no question that a lot of very complicated, perhaps even contradictory karma-*vipaka* is involved here, because at least half of the wrong is with the woman.

If, prior to the sexual affair, we now have this family immigrate to America the entire dynamic of intentionality changes. Regardless of the mores and customs of their former society, both the young woman and her family, in immigrating to a new country, are expected to accept the rules and customs of that country. First among these is that in America an unmarried adult woman is free to have a sexual affair if she chooses to do so and her family has no right to interfere. Second, if the woman has an affair it does not shame the rest of the family in the eyes of American society in general. Third, if the family killed the women that would disgrace the family and the killers would be severely punished which would add to the family's disgrace. In this new scenario the intentionality factor has completely changed. The woman, if she accepts American mores unconditionally, does not have any intentionality to disgrace her family and the family has no honor to protect. On the other hand, the woman ought to take into account the possibility that her family might act "in the old way," if which case she can not be entirely innocent; however, even in this case, any killing by the family is still entirely voluntary and intentional, which means the wrong continues to be more with the family. Thus, the bad karma-*vipaka* of the family is going to be greater in America than it would have been in the old country.

The relativity of karma-*vipaka*, especially the social relativity aspect, may be difficult for Westerners to relate to since it also means that there can be no justification for a "majority of one" as in the more absolutist Western case. Western (Judeo-Christian) morality is presumed to be based on the will of a personal God. This in theory means that it does not matter what society accepts as right, but what God accepts as right. This is clearly reflected in the Old Testament where the people of ancient Israel often had one set of standards while the prophet or mouthpiece of God, "the majority of one," had another set of standards that took priority over that of society. It is for this reason that the Judeo-Christian view might find the killing of the young woman in either social situation as equally wrong.

Intentionality in the Buddhist understanding of karma-*vipaka* is important also in that it counters the commonly heard Western view that karma is ruthless and, therefore, unjust and far inferior to the love based justice of God.

See also **Ahimsa; Blaming the victim vs. illusion of innocence; Karma and God; Karma and justice; Karma in the ancient and modern west; Karma versus grace; Restitution negates retribution; Return and serve argument for reincarnation.**

Karma as natural law. It is often claimed that karma is the spiritual parallel of the natural law of cause and effect. When people speak of karma in such causal ways they are implying that there is an empirically based causal connection between the observable phenomena of suffering and happiness, and the unobservable phenomenon of a past life. However, this is not true.

The first problem with karma as a natural law is that, unlike all true natural laws, karma has no predictable value to it. In other words, the claim to karmic causality is completely *post hoc* (after the fact). A predictability requirement can be explained by the following example. If a person's present life is a disaster one may be able to look back at incidents in that present life and say that it could have been predictable that his future would be a disaster. But there is nothing in the theory of karma that allows us to predict anything on a similar empirical level. Any predictability in karma is entirely speculative and dogmatic. As a result of this, the greatest criticism that can be made against the concept of karma is that it involves **blaming the victim.**

The second problem with karma as natural law arises when karma is said to be true because it is "simply an extension" of the natural law of cause and effect. The use of the word "extension" in this supposition is very questionable. All scientifically verifiable laws of cause and effect are totally amoral whereas, good and evil, justice and injustice, fairness and unfairness, reward and punishment are all subjective moral concepts that have no place in the natural law of cause and effect. Nature is amoral or indifferent to human morality. This might suggest that karma is little more than a desire by human beings for a cosmic support for human morality. If there is any karmic-like law in nature it is that the strong will be rewarded by survival, and the weak will be punished by extinction.

See also **Karma-*vipaka* as a long term moral tendency.**

Karma as unfinished business. A number of Western supporters of rebirth and karma object to any punitive aspect to them. This is generally related to an objection to a monotheistic style judgmental God and hell. These Westerners, while accepting the cause and effect nature of karma, prefer to view what might seem to be punishment as the soul's own need to expiate the unfinished business of its past unskillful actions. Karma as unfinished business, however, does not always imply trying to make up for past mistakes. It can also refer to trying to fulfill a personal goal or social obligation that one was not able to fulfill in a former life. For example, according to certain Kabbalists, one of the main reasons for rebirth is to gives a person or couple that died childless another chance at fulfilling their obligation of parenthood.

.See also **Arguments supportive of rebirth; Deaths, violent and premature; Kabbalah; Karma, developmental; Karma in the ancient and modern west; Kubler-Ross, Elizabeth.**

Karma, attitudinal. This term describes deeply ingrained attitudes and emotions from a past life which are said to manifest themselves in the present life in some physical manner. For example, a former strongly held feeling of anger or resentment may manifest itself as heart, lung, liver disease, or if one felt constantly weighed-down with problems in the past it might result in shoulder or back problems in the present.

Karma, bodily. This term covers cases where a person is born with or soon develops some physical characteristic that can be traced back to a former life. This is said to account for some **birth marks**, **natal defects**, and **physical handicaps** that do not respond to normally successful therapy. Unfortunately, it also provides an opening for **blaming the victim**.

See also **Karma, organic or organismic.**

Karma, Buddhist *see* ***Anatman*; Karma as absolute or relative; Heaven, hell, and Buddhist no-soul (Self).**

Karma, classifications of. Karma, from an Indian perspective, has been classified in a number of different ways. While the following is the classification according to Buddhism, a very similar classification can be found in **Hinduism**. The following classifications come from the Pali canon. The first is *sanchita* karma, which is unresolved karma accumulated from past lives. This can be altered to some degree, especially through spiritual practices. The second is *prarabha* karma, which is karma that is inherited from past lives. This can not be altered within the present life, so it must simply be accepted as it is. The third is *agami* or *kryamana* karma, which is created in the present life and over which one has complete control. This must be resolved in a future life.

A second classification of karma is based on karma's particular function. Thus, there is regenerative (*janaka*) karma, which conditions the future birth; supportive (*upattham-bhaka*) karma, which assists or maintains the results of already-existing karma; counteractive (*upapidaka*) karma, which suppresses or modifies the result of the regenerative karma; and destructive (*upaghataka*) karma, which destroys the force of existing karma and substitutes its own results.

A third classification of karma is according to the priority of the results. There is serious or heavy (*garuka*) karma, which produces its results in the present life or the next and which can be subdivided into positive and negative forms. In the positive form there is highly skillful karma that is associated with very refined mental ecstatic trances states (*jhanas*) and which are considered heavy because they produce results more speedily than ordinary unrefined mental states. On the negative side there is the highly unskillful karma that results from any of the five serious crimes: killing one's mother, killing one's father, killing a saint (*arhat*), wounding a Buddha, and creating a schism in the monastic order (*sangha*).

There is also death-proximate (*asanna*) karma, which is the action one does at the moment before death, either physically or mentally. In the case of consciousness, this is thinking of one's own previous good or bad actions or having good or bad thoughts. It is this karma which is said to determine the conditions of the next birth, if there is otherwise no positive or negative *garuka* karma. In the absence of either *asanna* or *garuka* karma, what determines the conditions of the next birth is habitual (*acinna*) karma. Finally, in the absence of *acinna* karma, the rebirth determining karma is reserved (*katatta*) karma, which is the unexpended karma of a particular being.

While all of the above kinds of karma are associated with a specific individual some believers, especially Western ones, also acknowledge collective karma. This is the idea that karma can affect not only individuals, but also groups of people. Various authors have suggested the existence of such collective forms as family karma, geographic karma, place or site karma, global (planetary) karma, marital karma; national or state karma, and racial karma.

It should be carefully noted that while karma and ***vipaka*** are generally thought of as part of a moral law, they technically are not. Karma itself is often said to make no clear and unambiguous declarations as to what is good and/or bad. In fact, in its nature as a so-called impersonal law of cause and effect, it should have no ability to make such moral distinctions. It is this morally neutral factor that makes karma morally relative rather than absolute, at least from a Hindu and Buddhist perspective, although not from a Jain perspective.

See also ***Alayavijnana*; Arguments supportive of rebirth; Astral body; Buddhist stages of liberation; Jainism; Karma as absolute or relative; Karma, delayed; Karma, developmental; Karma, family; Karma, geographic; Karma, global (planetary); Karma, group; Karma, marital; Karma, national or state; Karma, place or** site; Karma, racial; Karma, retributive; Karma, vocational; Karma with minimal rebirth; Stevenson, Ian.

Karma, collective *see* **Karma, classifications of**.

Karma, delayed. This is karma that is not expected to manifest itself for resolution either in this life or in the very next one. It is thought that since the accumulation of karma can be very complex any one rebirth may not be suitable for the resolution of all of it; therefore, some karma may have to wait several lifetimes before it can be suitably resolved.

Karma, developmental. Developmental karma is that which is thought to exclusively encourage spiritual grow. If there should be some degree of suffering involved in such growth that suffering is not to be considered punishment of the individual; instead, it is a way to give the person the insight that will help him or her continue to advance spiritually.

This is a fairly new concept of karma suggested by those Westerners who reject the standard Eastern idea of retributive karma. One of the major points of developmental karma is the opposition to any kind of human rebirth (**transmigration**) into an animal existence

See also **Animals and rebirth, non–Western view; Animals and rebirth, Western view; Karma as unfinished business; Karma in the ancient and modern west; Karma, retributive; Kubler-Ross, Elizabeth; Rebirth, East and West; Roberts, Jane; Soul, collective; Transmigration, lateral**.

Karma, family. This is said to apply to groups of people who reincarnate together as families, often taking different familiar rolls. For example, a mother in one life may be a wife or daughter in another life, while the former husband may be a son or brother, etc. It is also believed that it is possible that gender role reversals may occur such as a former father being a daughter or sister, etc.

See also **Karma, group; Karma, relationship; Rebirth, consanguineous; Rebirth, group; Polarities; Soul family**.

Karma, geographic. This is a collective karma that is related to a wide geographic area. As such it would cover an area smaller than a global or planetary area, but much larger than an individual place or site.

Karma, global (planetary). This is the idea that the whole of humanity builds up a karma that must eventually be resolved.

Karma, group. This is karma that is said to be shared by a group of people such as a family or a community. It is a form of collective karma, but on a very limited or small scale.

See also **Karma, family; Rebirth, group**.

Karma in the ancient and modern west. A very major, but often forgotten, point in a strong karmic belief system is that any concurrent belief in an other-worldly heaven or hell must not be allowed to weaken the secondary function of **karma** (support for morality) to such an extent that it negates karma's primary function (explaining social inequities). This is to say that if a time spent in either hell or heaven is sufficient to satisfy justice then the inequities of the world would no longer be explained by the deeds of a past life; hence, the primary function of karma would be undermined. For this reason, a belief in any other-worldly or **interim period**, **hell** or heaven becomes an unnecessary, or merely optional, belief along side a karmic belief.

The fact that there was no strong karmic component associated with the classical Western concept of metempsychosis partially helps to explain the failure of the Greek (Hellenistic) culture and even later Western civilization to adopt metempsychosis as a major religious belief. This is in spite of the widespread acceptance of that belief in **Platonism** and **Neoplatonism** in pre–Christian and early Christian times.

It is true that some of the classical philosophers, such as **Plotinus**, were experimenting with a karmic-like belief, but it was not until such religions as **Manichaeism** developed that a fully **karmic eschatology** was adopted; however, by that time Christianity was ahead of all other religions in the competition for converts.

The absence of a karma concept in the ancient Western world is not surprising. In fact, the concept of karma is not found in most non–Indian influenced cultures that otherwise have **rebirth eschatology**. Even today, a number of Western supporters of reincarnation, such as **Ian Stevenson**, either reject the karma concept altogether or rejects at least its retributive aspect. In fact, Stevenson states that none of his extensive research on rebirth suggests retributive karma. He believes that at the very most rebirth might include developmental karma.

Another major reason for a lesser acceptance of the karma concept in both the ancient and modern West has been the argument that no single life could eliminate all negative karma and since each future life would usually build up its own new negative karma, there is never likely to be a time when all negative karma could be eliminated. In fact, it is argued that since the standard Eastern goal of *moksha* or **nirvana** requires liberation from both negative and positive karma, such liberation would be close to impossible. Obviously, Eastern religions do not accept this argument, believing as they do that it is possible to eliminate all karma.

Finally, both the Platonist and Neo-Platonist supporters of metempsychosis were blatantly elitist in that they taught that salvation (freedom from rebirth) was only available to an intellectual minority, primarily philosophers.

See also **Blaming the victim vs. illusion of innocence; Buddhism; Caste system; Christian Objections to Reincarnation and/or Karma; Christianity and reincarnation; Karma; Karma and faith; Karma and free will; Karma and justice; Karma and rebirth; Karma as absolute or relative; Karma as natural law; Karma as unfinished business; Karma, Buddhist; Karma, developmental; Logic of physical cause and effect; Natal defects; Parents in the next life; Plato; Plotinus; Priesthood, lack of an organized; Rebirth, qualifications for; Rebirth, East and West; Rebirth in the West; Stevenson, Ian; Theodicy; Unity School of Christianity.**

Karma in the Bible? Many reincarnationists who wish to keep some ties to Christianity have sought to prove that the Judeo-Christian scriptures acknowledges reincarnation, at least furtively, and in some cases they believe that the scriptures also acknowledges the doctrine of karma.

There is not the slightest doubt that many passages in the both the Old Testament and the New Testament teach that what a person sows, so shall he reap, as the following passages demonstrate. **Deuteronomy** 24:16, "A man shall be put to death only for his own sin." **Job** 4:8, "This I know, that those who plough mischief and sow trouble reap as they have sown." **Psalm** 9:16, "Now the Lord makes himself known. Justice is done: the wicked man is trapped in his own devises." Psalm 62:12, "Thou dost requite a man for his deeds." **Proverbs** 17:5, "A man who sneers at the poor insults his Maker, and he who gloats over another's ruin will answer for it." Proverbs 24:12, "God, who fixes a standard for the heart, will take note. God who watches you — be sure he will know; he will requite every man for what he does." Jeremiah 17:10, 32:19, "I, the Lord, search the mind and test the heart, requiting man for his conduct, and as his deeds deserve." "Thine eyes watch all the ways of men, and thou rewardest each according to his ways and as his deeds deserve." Ezekiel 18:20 & 30, "It is the **soul** that sins and no other then that shall die: a son shall not share a father's guilt, nor a father his son's. The righteous man shall reap the fruit of his own righteousness, and the wicked man the fruit of his own wickedness." "Therefore, Israelites, says the Lord God, I will judge every man of you on his deeds. Turn, turn from your offences, or your iniquity will be your down fall." Hosea 8:7 and 10:13, "Israel sows the wind and reaps the whirlwind." "You have ploughed wickedness into your soil, and the crop is mischief; you have eaten the fruit of treachery." Obadiah 15, "...you shall be treated as you have treated others, and your deeds will recoil on your own head." In this final Old Testament citation is one example of what has been interpreted as a statement of the **karmic boomerang effect**.

The sowing and reaping metaphor continues in the New Testament. Among these is **Matthew** 7:1–2, "Pass no judgment, and you will not be judged. For as you judge others, so you will yourselves be judged, and whatever measure you deal out to others will be dealt back to you;" Matthew 16:27, "For the son of man is to come in the glory of his father with his angels, and then he will give each man the due reward for what he has done;" **Romans** 2:5–6, "In the rigid obstinacy of your heart you are laying up for yourself a store of retribution for the day of retribution, when God's judgment will be revealed, and He will pay every man for what he has done;" 2nd **Corinthians** 5:10, "For we must all have our lives laid open before the tribunal of Christ, where each must receive what is due to him for his conduct in the body, good or bad;" **Galatians** 6:7–8, "Make no mistake about this: God is not to be fooled; a man reaps what he sows. If he sows seed in the field of his lower nature, he will reap from it a harvest of corruption, but if he sows in the field of the Spirit, the Spirit will bring him a harvest of eternal life;" 1st **Peter** 1:17, "If you say 'our Father' to the One who judges every man impartially on the record of his deed, you must stand in awe of him while you live out your time on earth," **Revelation** 2:23, "This will teach all the churches that I am the searcher of men's hearts and thoughts, and that I will reward each one of you according to his deeds," and Revelation, 22:12, "Yes, I am coming soon, and bringing my recompense with me, to requite everyone according to his deeds!"

It should be noted that the closest a sow and reap pair that can be attributed to Jesus is found in the Gospel of Matthew 6:26 where Jesus says, "Look at the birds of the air: they do not sow or reap and store in barns, yet your heavenly Father feeds them." Since these words of Jesus have nothing to do with moral cause and effect they can not support a karmic teaching.

In the Gospel of **Luke** 13:2–5 words specifically attributed to Jesus imply that he did not recognize the kind of impersonal cause effect that karma implies. In reference to a seemingly unprovoked attack by Roman soldiers on Jewish worshippers in Galilee he says, "Do you imagine that, because these Galileans suffered this fate, they must have been greater sinners than anyone else in Galilee? I tell you they were not." Following this Jesus gives a second example of the lack of any relationship of guilt and tragedy. He says, "Or the eighteen people who were killed when the tower fell on them at Silaom — do you imagine that they were more guilty than all the other people living in Jerusalem? I tell you they were not."

Not a single one of the above passages, unless extracted and isolated from the surrounding context, can be read in any way other than in standard Judeo-Christian future resurrectional terms.

See also **Christianity and reincarnation; New Testament and reincarnation.**

Karma, justice, and infancy. A particular Western criticism of the concept of karma is that it would be unjust to make an infant suffer for the sins of a former adult. One response to this Western criticism has been that the fruit (*vipaka*) of the sins (karma) of the previous life may not mature until the karmic inheritor has reached adulthood. But if this is the case why do infants suffer at all?

Karma-less rebirth *see* **Karma in the ancient and modern west; Rebirth eschatology.**

Karma, marital. This is a form of collective karma that is built up by a married couple and may come to fruit (*vipaka*) during the marriage and/or in a future life.

See also **Karma, family; Karma, classifications of.**

Karma, national or state. As the name implies this is the karma that citizen of nations collectively build up and with which future citizens must deal.

See also **Collective Karma; Karma, geographic; Karma, global (planetary) Karma; Racial Karma.**

Karma-nemesis. This is a term used by **Helena Blavatsky** to refer to karma as a punishing agent.

Karma, organic or organismic. It has been suggested that whatever one did excessively, with one's body in a past life, will result in a greatly diminished capacity to do the same in the present or some later life. For example, if in a past life you were a total glutton you may be born in this or a future life with severe digestive problems. If in a certain past life you were obsessed with having sexual intercourse, then in this or a later life you might be either impotent or frigid.

See also **Blaming the victim vs. illusion of innocence; Karma, bodily; Karmic boomerang effect; Karma, symbolic.**

Karma, origins of. The concept of karma, without doubt, had its origin in India, or more specifically, in northern or northwestern India, as two factors prove. First, it is in India, and those cultural areas directly influenced by Indian culture, that the idea of karma as a moral element is inextricably bond up with the rebirth concepts. Outside of Indian influenced cultural areas this linkage generally does not exist. Secondly, the word 'karma' is of Sanskrit derivation and means 'action' and in its earliest usage referred to the action required to perform the Vedic sacrifices. As such, in this earliest use karma had a purely ritual meaning and had nothing to do with the belief in rebirth. In fact, the overwhelming majority of Western scholars, though agreeing that the concept of karma arose directly from Vedic thought, find no evidence of a rebirth-karma association anywhere in the earliest Vedic literature. It is a mostly pro–Hindu minority of scholars who argue for such an early Vedic based belief in both rebirth and an association of rebirth with karma as a moral principle.

Exactly how rebirth and karma became associated with one another will probably never be fully known; however, it is possible to speculate that in the very late Vedic period, as tribal oriented village units were brought together into larger governing units (small kingdoms) social disruption of urbanization began to occur. With the resulting greater sense of individual alienation social conformity could no longer be justified on the basis of tribal or family ties.

In a tribal system the behavior of the individual is more or less the responsibility of the kinship group. If a member of the tribe commits a crime his family, clan, or even the whole tribe may be held equally guilty. With the breakdown of such a kinship group, a new, more individualized basis for moral responsibility had to be found. Karma fulfilled this need.

The idea that one's current misfortune was due to one's "own" past mistakes, and that one's future condition depended on one's present behavior provided such moral responsibility in the new social milieu. In other words, the concept of karma was a socio-politically useful doctrine and it was this concept that became the main ideological support for India's prevailing social organization, the **caste system.**

Evolution of the karma concept appears to have come about through two developments. First, rather than good or bad karma being the proper or improper performance of any one Vedic sacrifice itself, it came to be interpreted as the cumulative actions of a lifetime of performing proper or improper sacrifices. Such cumulative karma would then determine whether or not the individual, at death, was blessed with the right to join the ancestors or experience a less desirable fate. Second, there seems to have been a reinterpretation of the Vedic sacrifice as an internal rather than an external action. This meant that one's inner actions or deeds became the source of one's success or failure in life. At first, this inner sacrifice concept applied only to the Vedic ascetics with their sacrificial-like self-torturing activities. At some point, however, this more moralized karmic idea apparently merged with the prevailing belief in rebirth. With this merger karma would come to encompass everyone's actions, which completed its development as a moral system.

The completion of the karmic concept most likely developed in the new urban environment because this is where it was needed the most. Not only was this environment the place where kinship ties were the weakest, but in the cities the idea of karma would have appealed to the rising merchant class and somewhat later to the governing bureaucrats. Karma, as a pan-ethnic moral ideal, in particular, was useful for those doing business with strangers. Right and wrong, truthfulness and honesty in business transactions and negotiations could not depend on the capricious morality of "my group" has the right to cheat "yours." Also, karma holds that moral value, like a merchant's wealth, depends on a willingness to work hard for it; it is achieved, not ascribed. Therefore, the merchant who was ranked low in the caste hierarchy could regard himself as morally equal even to a Brahmin. The Indian kings similarly found karma a useful idea for uniting gradually detribalized and ethnically diverse people.

While the concept of karma as associated with rebirth, was probably initially looked upon suspiciously by the more conservative priestly circles, eventually no group came to benefit from this concept more than the Brahmins. Their position at the top of the social hierarchy came to be totally justified by the concept of karma. Indeed, as the caste system continued to evolve into an increasingly more socially inflexible and morally questionable system it would have needed some morally justifiable dogma to support it.

Finally, there can be no doubt that the doctrine of karmic rebirth is one answer to the universal questions of: Why I am here, what is the purpose of my life, and what happens after death? The belief in one's individual pre-birth karma clearly gives meaning to suffering in life by explaining that one must pay for my bad actions committed by me in past lives. Post-mortem karma also gives meaning in the form of hope that one's present condition may improve in the next life.

See also **Bhagavad Gita**; Reincarnation, origins of; Upanishads; Vedic Religion.

Karma, parental. In some of the Hindu *Puranas* there is a vague reference to the idea that the karma of parents can affect the karma of the child. The same idea is also found in some Tibetan texts.

Karma, place or site. This is the belief that certain places such as homes, or even cities, have their own karma connected to the actions of their inhabitants. If this is true, then whenever someone is planning on moving from one city or home to another they might want to study the background or history of that new place in relationship to their present place of residence to judge whether they are making a move to a karmicaly better or worse site.

The most karmicaly charged places would presumably be holy sites; for example, to move to Varanasi, Jerusalem, or Mecca would be a good karmic decision because of the amount of holy feelings that have, over the centuries, been attached or imprinted in that place.

The logical problem with this "off to a holy land" concept would be that in the case, at least, of a sacred place like Jerusalem, which has for centuries experienced sectarian violence of titanic proportions, might not that city have been imprinted also with an immense amount of negative karma. Thus, it might be impossible to judge whether its holy nature is sufficient to counter that negativity.

See also **Karma, geographic; Karma, global (planetary); Karma, national or state**.

Karma, *Prarabdha*. This is the residue karma that an otherwise liberated saint has and which will be fully resolved in this life thus not causing any further rebirth.

See also *Jivanmukti*.

Karma, primary and secondary functions *see* **Karma; Karma in the ancient and modern west**.

Karma, racial. This term can mean one of two things. First, that a person born into a particular race will share the collective karma of that race. Second, that a particular racial group will always, or almost always, have the same set of souls born into it for some karmic purpose. If just rebirth, as opposed to rebirth and karma, is involved in this second situation then it is simply called ethnic reincarnation. The prominent theosophist James S. Perkins, in his book *Experiencing Reincarnation* (1977), believed, that for different reasons, **Australian Aborigines**, Japanese, and Jews were predominantly racial karmic people.

Although there is no official acceptance of the Indian concept of karma in Hasidic Judaism there does seem to be what amounts to the equivalent of karma in determining how a Jewish **soul** will be reborn. Since the 16th century Hasidic mystic **Isaac Luria** apparently believed that Jews remained Jews throughout all reincarnations, this would be a form of racial karma of the second kind.

The **Rastafarians** have a similar belief that Black people are more or less always reborn as Black people and since Rastafarianism teaches that the plight of Black people today is due to sins of the distant past, this also would fall under the first definition of racial karma of the first kind.

See also ***Dor deah***; **Kabbalah; Karma; Metagenetics; Rebirth, ethnic; Rebirth, proximity.**

Karma, redemptive. This form of karma is said to develop between lives and is caused by either a decision to make reparations for harmful acts made in the past or by the deliberate desire to become reembodied to help others gain redemption.

Karma, relationship. This is karma that is believed to be specifically related to the relationships people have had in the past. It starts in childhood with family interaction and continues throughout one's life. It is said to operate even with the most tenuous of such relationships.

See also **Judas Syndrome.**

Karma, retributive. This refers to karma that, at some point, will function as a form of punishment for past bad and unskillful actions, words, and thoughts. This is part of the boomerang karma version of justice. If you hurt someone in this life you will be hurt by someone in another life. This karmic boomerang effect is part of the traditional Eastern view of karmic justice as primarily a punitive phenomenon.

Among Western supporters of karma there has been an ongoing argument as to how valid retributive karma is. A minority accepts the standard, very punitive Eastern view, but the majority of Western reincarnationists prefer to view karma as a more compensatory justice phenomenon. This is where if you hurt one in this life you will be required by karma to counter this in a future life, perhaps by saving or healing another. This is more in keeping with the Western preference of viewing karma as more of a developmental factor in which any retributive-like aspects of karma are entirely in the service of the moral maturation of the individual.

See also **Karma; Karma and justice; Karma, developmental; Karmic boomerang effect; Rebirth, East and West.**

Karma, symbolic. This is karma that a person experiences in a more symbolic fashion than would be the case in boomerang karma. For example, if in a past life you purposely ignored the cries for help of another then in this or a future life you may experience being deaf and/or a mute. If in a past life you watched another person drown and did not try to help, then you might be reborn with a debilitating fear of water.

See also **Karmic boomerang effect; Karma, organic or organismic.**

Karma versus grace. In Christianity there has been a two thousand year old, often quite violent, debate as to whether salvation is entirely dependent on God's grace (monergism); or whether human good works also contribute to salvation (synergism).

Christianity defines grace as the undeserved gift or favor of God. It is considered undeserved because original sin is said to have so debased human nature that nothing a human being can do can cause him to be seen as worthy in the eyes of God. In the most conservative biblical sense this means that no matter how virtuous a person's life is, or how many good works he does, he can not contribute to his own salvation. Instead, it is only through grace, or rather through faith in the grace of God through Christ, that salvation (eternal life) from sin is possible (**John** 3:16; 2nd **Corinthians** 5:19, 17:3; **Ephesians** 2:8–9; Titus 3:5; Jude 21). In fact, this conservative biblical position of justification by grace alone (*sola gratia*) is based upon the belief that all mankind's virtues and good works are contaminated by self-centeredness or pride (1st Corinthians 1:30). In other words, the Christian does not become perfect so that he may be saved, but is saved so that he can be perfected in his glorification of Christ.

In the few Christian denominations that hold to the extreme grace-only view of **Paul of Tarsus**, such as standard Calvinism, it is claimed that while salvation is open only to one who demonstrates a virtuous life, the virtue in that life does not really arise from the self-effort of the virtuous person, as it is only an outer sign of the grace that God has imposed upon that person. This divine imposition then has divided humanity into a predestined majority that will be eternally damned and a predestined minority which will be eternally saved (**Romans** 8:29–30, 9:12; Ephesians 1:4–10; 2nd Timothy 1:9–10). In short, Calvinism precludes the existence of free-will.

The opposite of this orthodox grace alone view is called the Pelagian heresy, which minimized the role of salvation by divine grace in order to maximize the role of human effort via good works in the salvation process. This heresy, despite Paul, has penetrated almost all present day mainstream Christian churches to the degree that while grace is the main vehicle for salvation human good works count for some worth.

If karma is defined as the actions of a person, and good karma is the virtuous actions of a person that works towards salvation, it can be seen that karma would seem to make the Christian scheme of salvation through grace unnecessary. This is one of the major reasons that mainstream Christianity rejects the notion of salvation through karma.

A clear distinction between Christian grace and non–Christian karma is found in their respective attitudes towards moral perfection. A karma-good works view justifies the idea of multiple lives, since it is obvious that few, if any, persons can attain to moral perfection in one life time. The Christian grace view holds that no such moral perfection is necessary for salvation because Christ's atoning sacrifice on the cross completely makes up for the lack of moral perfection of all those who, in faith, accept this atonement. For this reason more than one life is unnecessary for salvation.

Of course, a number of Christian reincarnationists, such as Lynn E. Sparrow in her *Reincarnation: Claiming Your Past, Creating Your Future* (1988), believe that karma and Christian grace are entirely compatible. Some Christian reincarnationists even believe that a life with faith in Christ might actually be liberating in that very life, while a failure to have such faith forces one back into the multiple life cycle until such faith is eventually acquired.

While the association of divine grace with Christianity is very well known, it is far less well known that such grace can be found in certain forms of Buddhism. In a predominantly non-theistic religion such as **Theravada Buddhism** no god can interfere with karma; hence, grace of any kind would seem to be out of the question. On the other hand, **Mahayana Buddhism**, which is also technically non-theistic in that it rejects a supreme creator deity, is theistic in that it accepts that the great divine *bodhisattvas* can, under certain circumstances, significantly reduce a devotee's karma because of the *bodhisattva*'s own great surplus of karmic merit. That surplus is believed to act as a kind of unearned saving factor or grace. Of course, such reductions of karma would mainly apply to personal failures to keep the Buddhist precepts as long as there was no strong intentionality or desire to break those precepts. This *bodhisattva* grace, to a great degree, is said to prevent karma from becoming an absolutely ruthless law of cause and effect.

Of all the forms of Mahayana Buddhism, it is the Japanese Jodo Shin Shu (True **Pure-Land** School), with its worship of Amida (S: Amitabha) Buddha, that comes the closest to a Christian-like "grace alone" concept. This is because Amida Buddha, in the distant past paid for the sins of his past, present, and future devotees. But even here, as in all forms of Buddhism, a doctrine of predestination is regarded as a form of fatalistic determinism and as such must be totally rejected. None of Amida's followers have ever been pre-chosen; each one of those followers must make the minimal effort of asking Amida for salvation.

In the case of **Hinduism** the grace of the gods can neutralize karma through a devotee's practice of *bhakti* (devotional) *yoga*. Such karma negating grace is found in all three of the dominant Hindu cults: Shaivism, Shaktism, and Vaishnavism; but it is most pronounced in the last of these.

There are two main sects of Vaishnavism, the Northern School (Vatakal or Vadagali) and the Southern School (Tenkalai or Tengali). These schools are also at times referred to respectively as the path of the monkey (*kapi marga*) and the path of the kitten (*narjara marga*). These animal designations come from the fact that in the northern sect the relationship between God (Vishnu) and his followers is said to be like that between a baby monkey and its mother. While the baby is dependent on its mother for milk and protection, at least it has the ability to cling to its mother's back when she wants to moves around. In this sense the devotee of God (Vishnu) can, and must, make some minimal good karma producing self-effort in order to receive the grace of the deity.

In the southern sect, the relationship between Vishnu and his followers is like that between a kitten and its mother. Not only must the baby depend on the mother for milk and protection, but even for it to be moved from place to place the mother must pick it up in her mouth and carry it. In this sense the devotee of Vishnu is considered so dependent upon God's grace that not even the most minimal self-produced good karma could add anything significant to the devotee's salvation.

See also *Bhagavad Gita*; Ganges; Jerome, Eusebius Hieronymus; Karma and free will; Karma and God; Karma as absolute or relative; New Testament and reincarnation; Original sin, Christianity, and reincarnation; Original sin versus karma; *Palingenesis*; Pilgrimages; Rebirth and moral perfection; *Theosis*; Unity School of Christianity; *Vaikuntha*.

Karma-*vipaka* as a long term moral tendency. This concept is a response to the various weaknesses of karma-*vipaka* as a perfect system of reward and punishment or **karma as a natural law**. It implies that those **rebirth factors** that developed beneficial moral character had a greater tendency to be attracted to positive rebirth conditions, and those rebirth factors that developed malevolent moral character had a greater tendency to be attracted to negative rebirth conditions. This would acknowledge that mistakes or mismatches were very possible in the short run, but that over many rebirths, or the long run, moral justice would be served.

Karma as more a rule of chance rather than perfect efficiency is also more in keeping with what is acknowledged as true of everyday life. People take chances throughout their lives that if they do the right thing they will reap a proper reward, but the sensible and mature person does not demand guarantees of those rewards before doing what may bring them about.

The argument goes that if people automatically function in this way now, why is it not logical to assume and accept that if there is something called rebirth and karma that the same rules of chance apply to it? To expect some immutable law to pay for being virtuous and punish for being less so is to be just as immature as the person who says I will not bother to try to invest in working for the good life unless someone can guarantee it.

A view of karma-*vipaka* as long term chance allows for plenty of room to accept that in any one lifetime an individual is not necessarily responsible for their misfortune. This then avoids the morally unacceptable outcome of **blaming of the victim**.

See also **Karma and the moral structure of the universe**.

Karma, vocational. This form of karma-*vipaka* manifests itself when people enter into vocations in which they seem to need little or no training, and which seems completely natural to them. This is said to indicate that they gained their training in a previous life.

See also *Anamnesis*; **Child prodigies or geniuses**.

Karma with and without rebirth. While the concept of karma has traditionally been closely associated with the concept of rebirth, this association is not an absolute requirement since there are four ways of viewing karma. First, there is "present collective" karma, which means that presently we are all collectively responsible for the good and ill in this world. Second, there is "present individual" karma, which means that a persons past actions in this very life have resulted in their present condition. Third, there is "non-present (past/future) collective" karma, which means that we are but the continuation of all the generations that have lived before us and those in the future will be our continuations. In this case, we must take responsibility for the past just as the future must take responsibility for the present. Fourth, there is "past/future individual" karma, which means that each of us has been, is, and will be an "isolated entity" that alone is responsible for the good and ill in all our multiple lives. Only the last of these requires an individual rebirth, and in turn, it alone blames the suffering, the poor, and the powerless for their own condition while granting the healthy, the rich, and the powerful all respects. Standard Hindu, Jain, and Buddhist sacred texts more or less ignore all but the fourth view of karma.

Karma with minimal rebirth. This is the idea that what is truly reborn is karma-*vipaka* itself. This idea has been proposed by some Buddhists as a way of resolving the apparent contradiction of rebirth without a **soul** (*anatman*). Western critics of this proposal have often seen it as a semantic trick to avoid annihilationism.

See also **Annihilationism, Buddhist view; Atman; Heaven, hell, and Buddhist no-soul (Self); Interim period; Karma and faith; Karma and rebirth; Rebirth in Buddhism; Rebirth, qualifications for; Schopenhauer, Arthur**.

Karma yoga. This is the yoga of social duty. It is first mentioned in the ***Bhagavad Gita***. In that text the god Krishna teaches that any person who performs his caste obligations, be it that of a high caste or of a low caste, with complete detachment (*vairagya*) will acquire merit sufficient to end the cycle of rebirth and enable the performer to attain liberation. Unfortunately this teaching has been conveniently used justify the inequities of the **caste system**.

See also **Bhakti Yoga; Return and serve argument for reincarnation**.

Karmic astrology. This is astrology specifically applied to rebirth and past life karma.

See also **Astrology and rebirth**.

Karmic bankbook. This metaphor is used to suggest that release from the cycle of rebirth and redeath (closing one's account) will not occur until every bit of one's karmic credits and debits have been balanced. This is more a Western view than an Eastern one in that in the latter all karma, good and bad, must be dissolved before release from the cycle of birth and death.

Karmic boomerang effect. It is assumed that that karma-*vipaka* (deed and its fruit) function as the law of what one sows, one will reap. In other words, it is a form of moral reciprocity or retributive justice which is said to act in the manner of a boomerang. If one throws evil at another person in this life the evil will circle around and hit the thrower either in the same life, but more often in the next life. The question that must be asked is why this is necessarily so? It can not be presumed that karma-*vipaka* is just as people want it to be, such that in the end bad people get their deserved punishment and that good people get their deserved reward. Without having any memory of past lives how can anyone be sure that karma-*vipaka* does not really function so that a person who harms others builds up the kind of karma-*vipaka* behavioral habit that forces him to continue to harm others indefinitely. Likewise, the person who is victimized in one life may develop a karma-*vipaka* behavioral habit that attracts more victimization in succeeding lives. This is, in fact, a not uncommon phenomenon in society where an abusive husband and father produces a son who will become an abusive husband and father. Likewise, some women are repeatedly attracted to relationships in which they are abused and victimized. In fact, some claimed past life scenarios seem to suggest the working of just such a **repetition compulsion.**

See also **Karma and justice; Karma in the Bible?; Karma, organic or organismic; Karma, retributive.**

Karmic carrier *see* **Buddhism, folk;** *Gandharva;* **Interim period; Karma with minimal rebirth; Rebirth in Buddhism.**

Karmic carryover. This is the concept that the carrying over of an unwanted and unhealthy memory from a past life to the present-life can greatly interfere with that present life. The memory of a certain trauma, in particular, could be such a carryover.

See also **Affect bridge; Blocked regression.**

Karmic diseases (Japanese: *Gobyo*). Until the advent of modern medicine, throughout those parts of Asia where rebirth was the standard belief it was always assumed that some illnesses or diseases are due to a person's past bad karma. In Japan this was an especially widespread belief when faced with a difficult to cure (*nanbyo*) diseases. In the most popular Buddhist text, *the Lotus Sutra,* there are passages that equate illness, especially leprosy, with having spoken offensively against that *sutra* in a past life. In such presumed karmic disease cases, the services of a Buddhist priest were sought rather than those of a doctor.

See also **Blaming the victim vs. illusion of innocence; Psychosomatic illnesses.**

Karmic eschatology. This term is in contrast to the simpler **rebirth eschatology.** Whereas karma depends on some sort of rebirth, rebirth does not depend on karma. In karmic eschatology rebirth is understood primarily as merely a vehicle for karmic continuation. This is to say that any undesirable condition in one's present life is probably a punishment for past wrong actions.

Outside of Indian and late ancient Greek cultures rebirth had little to do with moral or ethical behavior. Instead, it was mainly a process that allowed ancestors to be repeatedly reborn into the same family. It was only in more sophisticated urbanized cultures that an ethical component was added to rebirth. While the Greeks never developed a specific word for such ethicalization the Indians did, and that word was karma. Once rebirth came to be seen as the result of individual moral behavior, rebirth as a recycling of ancestral souls was greatly weakened. This was obvious since the new born in a family would possess some **soul** that needed that particular family situation for its punishment or reward. A major psychosocial result of this was that a person was no longer just part of a family collective personality. Every person was now a separate individual, morally responsible only for him or her self, who now was in need of salvation, unlike in simple rebirth eschatology.

See also **Heaven; Hell; Karma and faith; Karma and justice; Karma and rebirth; Karma in the ancient and modern west; Karma, origins of; Karma with minimal rebirth; Priesthood, lack of an organized; Rebirth, consanguineous; Rebirth, proximity.**

Karmic romances. These are stories that originated in the late Victorian Era in which the main characters were reincarnated either in search of their **soul** mate and/or to atone for some sin committed in a past life. In these stories the most popular sources for reincarnated souls were the **lost continent** of Atlantis and ancient **Egypt.** Among the most popular writers of this genre were **Henry Rider Haggard** (1856–1925), **Marie Corelli** (1855–1924), Edwin Lester Arnold (1857–1935), and more recently Katherine Kerr (1944–). The three-volume novel *Transmigration,* by Mortimer Collins, published about 1874, is probably the oldest of these romances.

In the section on reincarnation in the book *Historical Fiction: A Guide to the Genre* (2005), by Sarah L. Johnson, the author suggests that there are far fewer novels of reincarnation featuring a man with past life experiences than there are those featuring a woman with past life experiences.

See also **Hollywood and reincarnation.**

Karmic script. This is the term for a karmic pattern that is said to cover several embodiments. This can manifest as bodily karma, vocational karma, and karmic ties. It is sometimes referred to as karmic themes.

See also **Karma, bodily; Karma, vocational.**

Karmic seeds (Skt. *Bija*). This is a term used by the **Vijnanavada** (Consciousness only) **School** of Buddhism to try to describe the way that karma was stored in the universal mind, or consciousness (*alayavijnana*), and which eventually gives rise to the entire phenomenal world. One of the reasons for the development of this school was to try to explain how rebirth could occur without a soul (self) or *anatman.*

See also *Manas.*

Karmic ties. These are believed to develop when two or more persons in the same life-time have an intense relationship that requires some sort of closure or resolution, but which does not take place before the death of one or more of the persons. This then requires that those persons in another lifetime re-establish a relationship of some kind to resolve the issue. It is further believed that the roles in the earlier life may be reversed in the later one.

See also **Chinese religion and reincarnation; Karma, family; Rebirth, group; Soul groups.**

Katsugoro case. This case is cited in the *Gleanings in Buddha Fields* (1897) by Lafcadio Hearn who states that the story is a translation of a Japanese document.

According to the story, Katsugoro was a boy born in 1815 who, at about the age of seven, asked his elder sister if she could remember where she came from before her present birth. Thinking the question silly, she asked him if he could remember anything before he was born. He said that he could and that his name use to be Tozo and that he was the son of a man from another village. He said that when he had been five years old his former father had died and that he himself had died of smallpox at the age of six. After relating all this, Katsugoro asked to be taken to his former home to visit the tomb of his former father, which his family agreed to do. When he arrived there it was determined that what Katsugoro had said was correct and that, in fact, the child Tozo had been born in 1805 and had died thirteen years before in 1810 at the age of six. (Hearn states that the year of birth of a Japanese child is counted as one year of his age.)

This case is of interest in that the Japanese, at least since the 17th century, have held to the Buddhist belief in rebirth only in a very nominal fashion and certainly have had no expectations that someone might actually remember a past life. However, since there was no objective (scientific-like) investigation of this case its usefulness in supporting any reincarnation theory is extremely weak.

See also **Children remembering past lives; Possession; Shanti Devi case.**

Kelipoth see Qlippoth.

Kelsey, Denys (1917–2004). This British psychiatrist could be considered the founder of modern **past life therapy**. He began his interest in this in the 1950s, well before there was any real interest in it such therapy in America. Kelsey co-authored with his wife, the psychic **Joan Grant**, *Many Lifetimes*. London: Gollancz, 1968. Kelsey's book *Now and Then: Reincarnation, Psychiatry and Daily Life* was published posthumously in 2007 by Trencavel Press, Folkstone, Kent.

Kennedy, John F. (1917–1963). There are an extraordinary number of shared personal traits that President Kennedy shared with President Abraham Lincoln which included familiar, spousal, career, assassination, funeral, and Vice-Presidential choices. These shared traits have convinced many people that Kennedy was the reincarnation of Lincoln. What is not explained by those so convinced is why such traits and events in Kennedy's life should mimic those of Lincoln because of reincarnation. Very few other lives that are thought to share the same **soul** show such **synchronicity**.

Ketamine *see* **Body-brain (mind) dependency; Moore, Marcia.**

Khepra (Khepera, Khepri, Kheper, or Khefer). This is the Egyptian scarab god which **Theosophy** tries to assign the role as the presiding deity over reincarnation. Khepra is the scarab or dung beetle which rolls before it a ball of dung in which to lay its eggs. Ancient Egyptians believed a divine version of Khepra brought the sun god, Ra (Re), out from the underworld each morning and rolled him across the sky. As such the scarab beetle was associated with the daily rebirth of the sun. Also, because of this sun association beetle amulets were regarded as protectors against evil and placed in the wrappings of mummies to ensure the latter's safety as well as to guarantee a favorable judgment in the Hall of Osiris. None of this, however, was ever associated with the reincarnation of individuals since immortality in ancient **Egypt** meant continued life in the realm of Osiris.

Khurramiyya. According to the Arabic heresiographer Al-Shahrastani, this little known Iranian, largely Kurdish, gnostic religious group believed in reincarnation (***tanasukh***).

One branch of this group was situated in Azerbaijan while another was in southern Kurdistan. The latter was involved in an uprising, which was finally put down under the Abbasid caliph Mutasim in AD 833. The Khurrami were also known for their revolutionary practice of communal ownership of all properties and means of economic production and lack of social distinctions.

See also **Cult of Angels; Gnosticism; Hashimiyya; Islam; Kanthaeans; Rawandiyah.**

Kingsford, Anna Bonus (1846–1888). This remarkable feminist not only wrote her first book at the age of thirteen but was later to be the first woman to become a medical doctor in Great Britain. While seeking for higher truth she encountered **Spiritualism** in 1867 and, despite being married to an Anglican clergyman, she converted to Roman Catholicism in 1870. Sometime between 1875 and 1878 she began to have a series of what she called "received illuminations," which occurred chiefly during sleep and which were possibly influenced by her reported use of nitrous oxide, the most popular consciousness-expanding drug of the time. These illuminations formed the basis of her many writings.

Kingsford believed that truth was not confined to any one religion. This can be seen in her works that constitute a synthesis of the sacred mysteries of the Egyptians, Greeks, Hebrews (Kabbalists), and Christians. Perhaps her most famous work is *The Perfect Way, or the Finding of Christ* (London: Watkins, 1882). This was republished after her death in a more fragmentary and yet personal form under the title *Clothed with the Sun: Being the Illuminations of Anna (Bonus) Kingsford* (London: George Redway, 1889).

The title of this second work is presumably taken from the **Revelation of John** 12:1–2, which reads, "Next appeared a great portent in heaven, a woman clothed in the sun, beneath her feet the moon, and on her head a crown of twelve stars." *Clothed with the Sun* supports the belief in reincarnation (in obvious disregard of her Catholicism) and in chapter XXXIV there is a recording of an illumination regarding the previous lives of **Jesus**. In this illumination Jesus was said to have acknowledged that womanhood is superior in form to manhood and that he himself had a former life as a woman. When asked why he came the last time in the inferior form of a man he stated that he was a man only outwardly and that actually he was a woman in all but body. This superficial appearance he said was due to the necessities of that particular time.

The standard theological understanding of "the woman clothed with the sun" is that she represents the 12 tribes of Israel, as made clear by the 12 stars in the her crown, so how this could be interpreted as part of a belief in reincarnation requires a certain leap beyond logic.

Kingsford was such an impressive figure that, although technically not a member of the Theosophical Society, she became the President of its London Lodge in 1883 at the personal request of **Helena Blavatsky**. After finding the direction of the Society moving more towards Eastern thought, Kingsford co-founded the Hermetic Society, which was more oriented towards the esoteric Christian traditions. Some of this may have been due to the influence of the writings of the rather infamous magus Eliphas Zahed Levi. Due to her death from a lung disease at age 42 Kingsford did not live to see that her works would serve as a major inspiration for the formation of the famous occult society, the **Hermetic Order of the Golden Dawn**, founded in the same year as her death.

Kingsford was also a strong advocate for **vegetarianism** and an ardent anti-vivisectionist.

See also **Hermetic philosophy; Steiner, Rudolf; Theosophy; Woman.**

Kipling, Rudyard (1865–1936). This famous British author wrote a short story entitled *The Finest Story in the World* (1899), in which the main character can remember a series of past lives or, as Kipling says, a case of true **metempsychosis**.

Kiramu-l-katibin (Arabic: Guardians and Noble Scribes). These are two angels mentioned in the Quran (*Sura* 82:10–11). The one on the right of each deceased person contemplates and dictates to the one on the left all the good and evil deeds of a person until the record is finally given to the angel of death (Azra-il or Izra-il). The Muslim daily closing prayer (*salat*) acknowledges the presence of these angels along with the acceptance that everyone has only one pre–Judgment Day life.

See also ***Akashic*** **Record, Islam; Lords of Karma.**

Kline, Milton V see **Multiple personalities; Bridey Murphy case.**

Koans see **Mahayana Buddhist rebirth texts; Rebirth in Zen Buddhism.**

Koran see **Quran.**

Koresh, David (1959–93). Born Vernon Wayne Howell, Howell became a member, and later leader, of the Branch Davidian Seventh-Day Adventist religious cult in Waco, Texas. In 1990 Howell legally changed his name to David Koresh, partly because he became convinced that he was the reincarnation of both King David and King Cyrus of Persia and that he had been appointed by God to rebuild the Temple and destroy Babylon. In other words, Koresh claimed to be the Messiah. The Bureau of Alcohol, Tobacco, and Firearms learned that the Branch Davidians had failed to pay taxes on a hoard of machine guns that they possessed and fearing another Jonestown incident, mounted the now-infamous raid on the Mount Carmel complex outside of Waco in February 1993. This resulted in a 51-day siege, and ended in the death of numerous Branch members and government agents.

See also **Adam; Frank, Jacob; Heaven's Gate; Kabbalah; Solar Temple, Order of the.**

Koryaks. This tribal and shamanic people of the far eastern part of Siberia, including the Kamchatka peninsula, believe that every person is the reincarnation of one of his or her ancestors and that a newborn must be given his or her former name. To divine just who the ancestor is a stone is placed in a leather pouch which is suspended from a small tripod. The eldest family member pronounces names of deceased ancestors in succession until the stone shakes at the sound of a particular name. It is this name that is then given to the newborn.

See also **Chukchi; Eskimo; Lapps (Saami); Rebirth, consanguineous; Yukaghir.**

Kosha (sheath or covering). In the Vedanta School of Hinduism this designates the layers or bodies that surround the personality-less **atman** and hence make up the human personality. There are five of these and they range from the most outer and most material to the most inner and most spiritual in nature. The first of these is the *anna-maya* (food-made sheath) or the physical body (*sthula sharia*). The second is the *prana-maya* (breath, life-force, vital or subtle-made sheath) which gives basic animation to the body and mind; and the body will remain alive only as long as this *kosha* remains with it. The third sheath is the *mano-maya* (mind-made) which functions as the receiver of all sensory impressions. The fourth is the *vijnana-maya* (consciousness-made) sheath which supplies intelligence, discrimination, and will to a person. The last is the *ananda-maya* (bliss-made) sheath which is responsible for the blissful experience of union with God while the person is still embodied. It should be noted that sometimes only three sheath (*sharias*) are said to surround the *atman*. From outer to inner these are the physical (*sthula*) *sharia*, the subtle (*suksma*) *sharia*, and the causal (*karana*) *sharia*.

All these *kosha* must dissolve before the **soul** (*atman*) can be re-absorbed into **Brahman**. These *kosha* are described in the *Taittiriya-Upanishad*. The second, third, and fourth *kosha* are also collectively called the **linga-sharia**.

See also **Causal body; Individuality and rebirth; Maya; Monism; Personality versus individuality; Soul.**

Krishna, the God *see* **Aetherius Society; Ahmadiyya; Babbitt, Elwood; Besant, Annie;** *Bhagavad Gita*; **Brahman; International Society for Krishna Consciousness; Jesus; Karma yoga; Steiner, Rudolf.**

Kshitigarbha (S: Earth-womb) *Bodhisattva*. This is the name of one of the most important *bodhisattva*s in **Mahayana Buddhism**, particularly in East Asia. In China he is known as Ti-ts'ang (WG), and in Japan as Jizo. In his Japanese form, as an extension of his function as the protector of travelers, Jizo is said to travel by himself to the underworld, *Jigoku*, to rescue the souls of aborted fetuses.

See also **Emma-o.**

Kubitschek, Juscelino (1902–1976). This former president of Brazil (1956–1961) instituted the building of the new capital of the country, Brasilia, in 1956. According to some Brazilians he was a reincarnation of the 14th century BCE Egyptian pharaoh Akhenaton and Brasilia was viewed by them as the modern version of the new capital (*Amarna*) built by that pharaoh.

Besides both men being innovative leaders and builders of new capitals, what is said to have linked these two is the fact that both died 16 years after inaugurating their cities, both cities are know for their pyramidal or triangular buildings; and Brasilia is laid-out in the form of a flying ibis-like bird, the ibis being a sacred bird in Egypt. This belief in the Kubitschek-Akhenaton link is further encouraged by the fact that Brasilia, from the start, became the New Age and occult center for the country.

See also **Afro-American religions; Egypt; Kardecismo; Umbanda.**

Kubler-Ross, Elizabeth (1926–2004). This well-known psychiatrist began the serious study of the end stages of life and inspired the hospice movement around the world. Her most famous book, *On Death and Dying* (1969), identified the five stages of the average dying experience: denial, anger, bargaining, depression, and acceptance.

Dr. Kubler-Ross eventually came to believe that **out-of-the-body experiences** and **near-death-experiences** proved post-mortem existence and that travel in the **astral body** proved reincarnation. Kubler-Ross was, however, very critical about the concept of karma, believing that everyone is reborn with a clean slate. Kubler-Ross also came to acknowledge the **channeling** of some spirit guides. Two of Kubler-Ross' books that specifically deal with post-mortem survival are *On Life After Death* (1991) and *Death is of Vital Importance: On Life, Death and Life After Death* (1995).

See also **Karma as unfinished business; Karma, developmental.**

Kulkulcan. This is the Yucatec Mayan name for the original Toltec-Aztec (central Mexican) cultural hero god Quetzal-coatl, the Feathered-Serpent. This same deity is called Gukumatz in Guatemalan Mayan. Kulkulcan was associated with the planet Venus as the morning star, while his alter-ego, or twin, Xolotl, patron of magicians, was identified with Venus as the evening star.

Some sources state that among the ancient Mayan people this cultural hero was the patron deity of the afterlife, but whether this was of a new life in the spirit world or reincarnation into this world is open to debate.

See also **Aztecs; Lucifer.**

Kuthumi, Master *see* **Church Universal and Triumphant; Dhyani Chohans; Pythagoras; Sinnett, Alfred Percy**

Kwakiutl. According to this Northwest Coast Indian culture when people die they must be reborn first as animals, at least until their former human body is fully decomposed, and only then is the **soul** free to be reborn as a human being. This alternating life **transmigration** process is not the case if the person is unfortunate enough to have died at sea. In this case the soul belongs to the animals, especially the sea otters, and can never return to the human world. The Kwakiutl also believe the animal into which a soul will be reborn depends partly on the occupation of a person. For example, a sea hunter becomes a killer whale and a land hunter becomes a wolf. One can also be reborn as the totem animal of one's clan. Twins, it seems, are always reborn as salmon and, like shamans, have supernatural powers which include remembrance of their past life.

See also **American Indians**.

Kyklos Genesion (Cycle of Becoming). This is the ancient Greek term for the repeated cycle of birth and death (**metempsychosis**).

See also **Greeks and reincarnation; Orphism;** *Pneumatikoi*; *Samsara*.

Lactantius, Lucius Caelius Firmianus (about 250–325). This Christian Father rejected the Pythagorean doctrine of **metempsychosis**, in his *Divine Institutes*, as unchristian.

See also **Arnobius the Elder; Christian fathers critical of reincarnation**.

Ladder. Coming down and going up a ladder is a metaphor for death and rebirth.

See also **Genesis; Planetary descent and ascent of the soul; Seven rungs of the heavenly ladder**.

Lama [Tibetan: *bla-ma*] *see* **Avalokiteshvara;** *Avatar*; **Dalai Lama; Lhamoi Latso Oracle; Panchen Lama; Possession;** *Tulku*; **Vajrayana Buddhism**.

Language inconsistency. It has been suggested that a person who recalls a past life with a linguistic environment different from the present one should be fluent in the language of that former environment if the recall is genuine. This fluency should be independent of the subject ever having learned the former language in the present life. So far no such fluency has been proven for any subject. In every case studied there remains some suspicion that any foreign language fluency has been learned through normal channels during the present life.

One fairly consistent linguistic factor has been noticed in subjects who give evidence of languages skills from their past lives. There is very minimal verb usage in their utterances. This is undoubtedly because verbs and their conjugations are the most difficult elements of a language to learn or to falsify. It is far easier to unconsciously acquire and remember nouns and noun phrases and this is what most unfamiliar past life language utterances involve.

One response by pro-reincarnationists to this is that nouns are also the first elements of language learned by an infant, which means the most deeply encoded on the mind. Following the principle of "first learned last forgotten" it would be logical that a remembrance of nouns would be greater than a remembrance of other linguistic forms. Another pro-reincarnationist response to past life language skills is that recalled memory involves mental imagery more than verbal associations; therefore, a lack of linguistic consistency may not be proof of a pseudo-recall.

Only a few individuals have explored the issue of reincarnational language recall, one of whom is Thorwald Dethlefsen, the director of the Institute of Extraordinary Psychology in Munich. His research has been published in his books *Voices from Other Lives: Reincarnation as a Source of Healing* (1977) and *The Challenge of Fate* (1979). There is also the work by **Ian Stevenson**, *Unlearned Languages: New Studies in Xenoglossy* (1984).

See also **Muller, Catherine Elise; Rebirth, criteria for proof of; Rosemary case; Xenoglossy**.

Lapps (Saami). These people of northern Scandinavia have been Christianized to one degree or another for several centuries which makes it difficult to know what their original belief system entailed. However, according to Frazer (*Golden Bough*), when a pregnant Saami woman was near the time of delivery the mother would have a dream of a deceased ancestor or other relative who was to be reborn as her baby and whose name the child should receive. If the woman did not have the appropriate dream the child's father or other relatives would make the necessary determination by consulting a shaman for divination. Also, one custom reported among some Saami entailed the use of an idol or image which represented a departed person and was evidently looked upon as that person's second self. As a receptacle for that person's **soul** it could help to render the person's rebirth in the future possible.

See also **Old Norse**.

Last judgment *see* **Islam; Judgment of the Dead;** *Nafs* **and** *Ruh*; **Rebirth and the scientific theory of biological evolution; Sikhism**.

Last thought. Some reincarnationists believe that the very last thought one has just before the moment of death is a major factor in determining the nature of one's next life. However, other reincarnationists challenge this idea on the basis that a whole life can not be summed up in one last thought. Moreover, what if a person has had an exemplary life and yet, due to the trauma of dying has a less than exemplary last thought? If the last thought proponents are right then the negative karma resulting from that last thought could make a mockery out of the person's entire life.

See also *Bardo*; Death trauma.

Last Word: Therapies, Inc. This California based organization was formerly the Association for Past Life Research and Therapies.

See also Associations and organizations.

Law of parsimony *see Akashic* Record; Rebirth, alternative explanations to.

Layela or **Laila[h]**. This is the night-angel who, according to the *Zohar*, a major Kabbalic text, is the angel appointed to guard souls at the time of their rebirth.

See also Drink or fruit of forgetfulness; Kabbalah.

Lazaris. This is the name of an entity that is said have been first channeled through Jach Pursel in 1974. This entity, rather than being human-like, described itself as a group being that exists in another dimension. According to Lazaris there are no past or future-lives because what we think are past and future lives exist simultaneously with our so-called present life. In fact, some of these simultaneous lives even seem to overlap in time. For example, in a so-called present life one believes he that he was born in 1960, but then there may be another one of his lives in which he believes he did not died until 1980. The conflict that is perceived here is only the result of my having been conditioned to think of time in an exclusively linear manner.

The name Lazaris is not to be confused with the biblical Lazarus, the man whom **Jesus** is said to have raised (revivified, not resurrected) from the dead after four days (**John** 11:41–44).

See also **Channeling; Equinox; Franklin, Benjamin (2); Grant, Joan Marshall; Group soul; Hilarion; Mafu; Michael (2); Ouspensky, Pyotr D; Parallel lives; Plurality of existences; Ramtha; Rebirth, simultaneous; Ryerson, Kevin; Satya; Seth; Torah (2); Wilcock, David**.

Leadbeater, Charles Webster (1847–1934). At one time a curate in the Church of England, Leadbeater later joined the Theosophical Society (1884) and became one of its leaders after the death of **Helena Blavatsky**. He is perhaps best known from his *A Textbook of Theosophy* (1912). Along with **Annie Besant** he supported the candidacy of Krishnamurti as the reincarnation of Krishna and Christ, and hence, as the prophesized future Buddha (Maitreya) and the returning Messiah. After leaving the leadership of the Theosophical Society to Annie Besant, Leadbeater went on to help establish the **Liberal Catholic Church, Province of the United States**. Both as co-author, with Besant, and independently, Leadbeater published a number of works on reincarnation published by the Theosophical Publishing House, Adyar, Madras in India.

See also **Astral plane; Etheric body; Mental plane; Theosophy**.

Leading question. This is any question that encourages a response that the questioner desires. In any investigation of rebirth claims, not only must the investigator avoid leading questions, but he must ascertain whether such questions were asked of the person by earlier questioners. Most reported claims of past life memories have, to one degree or another, been either contaminated by, or suspected of, contamination by such questions.

In the case of **hypnotic age regression** a closely bound issue to leading questions is the factor of transferential relationship which, like the relationship between patient and psychiatrist, tends to cause the hypnotic subject to fall in line with the expectations of the hypnotist.

The most blatant form of leading questions is when a hypnotist chooses a time and place, such as Paris in 1905, and then instructs the hypnotized subject to recall a past life there and then. The subject will generally accommodate the hypnotist by "recalling" a life to suite that place and time even if the subject knows nothing about the place and period. In other words, the subject will employ whatever material he can image that might be seem to be appropriate for Paris in 1905.

See also **Artificial rebirth; Hypnosis; Proof for and against reincarnation argument**.

Leek, Sybil (1917–1982). This well known author and media celebrity was foremost associated with astrology and promotion of the **Wicca** movement in both England and the United States. Guided by the spirit of **Helena Blavatsky**, as she believed, Leek wrote and lectured extensively about reincarnation. Her main book on the subject was *Reincarnation: The Second Chance* (1974).

See also **Astrology and rebirth**.

Leibniz, Gottfried Wilhelm von (1646–1716). This famous German philosopher and mathematician, in his *Philosophische Schriften,* offered a very often repeated quote concerning reincarnation, namely "Of what use would it be to you, sir, to become king of China, on condition that you forgot what you have been? Would it not be the same as if God, at the same time he destroyed you, created a king in China?" Despite this statement attempts have been made to associate Leibniz's theory of eternal monads (souls) with a belief in reincarnation.

Leland, Charles Godfrey (1824–1903). This American folklorist and occultist claimed to have discovered the survival in Italy of a pagan cult that still worshipped the goddess Diana. According to Leland one of the witches (*stregha*) of the cult that he befriended gave him a copy of their cult book, which he published in 1899 under the name *Aradia, the Gospel of the Witches*. This book became a primary source for the later **Wicca** tradition. It was in an earlier book by this author, *Etruscan Roman Remains in Popular Tradition* (1892), in which he detailed an Italian witch family tradition in which one generation of male and female witches would be later reborn among their own biological descendents.

See also **Rebirth, consanguineous**.

Lemuria *see* **Aetherius Society; Lost Continent(s); Phylos the Tibetan; Ramtha; Unarius Academy of Science**.

Lemurian Fellowship. The Fellowship was founded in 1936 by Dr. Robert D. Stelle, who claimed to be operating under the direction and guidance of the Lemurian Brotherhood, one of the original mystery schools. According to the fellowship, the Great Being, Christ, in order to help humanity recognize its true purpose, first appeared to humanity as **Melchizedek** on the **lost continent** of Mu (Lemuria). Christ appeared for a second time as Poseidonis, many thousands of years later on Atlantis, again as a guide to humanity. The Fellowship, in its dedication to the teachings of Christ, seeks to build a nucleus of the Kingdom of God (the New Order) on earth, which can be facilitated by the spiritual progress of humanity through many reincarnations. The fellowship was first formed in Chicago, but established its permanent headquarters in Ramona, California, in 1941.

See also **Stelle Group**.

Lenz, Frederick (1950–1998). In 1985 this disciple of Sri Chinmoy took on the title Zen Master Rama (incarnation of the Hindu god Vishnu) and claimed to teach Tantric Zen. The fact that up until that point there had never been such a tradition either in Zen or in Tantrism was of little concern to Rama since he further claimed to have discovered this teaching by himself. This self-discovered "Tantric path" apparently allowed him to justify his right to sexually exploit a number of his female students. Lenz died from drowning, while apparently under the influence of a drug overdose.

For someone who claimed to have been a master of "Eastern Thought" Lenz had a surprising misunderstanding of Buddhism and, to a lesser degree, of **Hinduism**. For example, on page 83 of his book *Lifetimes: True Accounts of Reincarnation* (1979) he states, "There is very little difference between the Buddhist and Hindu versions of the death and rebirth process we call reincarnation." On page 74 he states, "The Hindus and Buddhists believe that when the **soul** is first created it is not fully developed." On page 106 he again implies that Buddhists believe in a soul and the goes on to imply that Buddhists believe in a creator God. As noted in many instances in this encyclopedia there are great differences between the Hindu and Buddhist notions of death and rebirth and Buddhists certainly do not believe in either a soul or in a creator God. On page 107 Lenz writes that Hindus believe that God personally interviews each soul before allowing it to reincarnate. This ignores the standard Hindu belief in the totally impersonal workings of karma. On page 114 Lenz continues with his misinformation by stating that the Hindu and Buddhist theories of how karma operates are basically the same. This is followed up on page 116 with the absurd statement that Hindus and Buddhists believe that there is no such thing as evil. Finally, on page 124 Lenz makes the illogical statement that the purpose of karmic retribution is not to make the individual suffer but to teach him. In saying this he completely ignores the question of how karma can teach anyone when the overwhelming majority of even the strongest believers in karma and rebirth have no remembrance of their so-called past life mistakes from which to learn.

In *Lifetimes: True Accounts of Reincarnation* Lenz states, on page 19, that he did not remember any of his own past lives, yet in his later book, *The Last Incarnation* (1983) he detailed several of these lives.

See also **Fraud**.

Leo, Alan (1870–1917). Leo was an early 20th century astrologer, whose original name was William Frederick Allan and who took the name Leo from his birth sign. Leo joined the Theosophical Society in 1890 and founded the Astrological Lodge of that Society in 1915. Leo was one of a handful of persons who incorporated rebirth, karma, and Jungian psychology into his astrology.

See also **Astrology and rebirth; Collin, Rodney; Mann, Tad; Theosophy**.

Lessing, Gotthold Ephraim (1729–1781). This German man of letters, in the final chapter of his 1780 *Erziehung des Menschengeschlechts* (*Education of the Human Race*) initiated a public debate on reincarnation. However, while supporting the concept of lateral transmigration he rejected regressive transmigration.

See also **Transmigration, lateral; Transmigration, regressive.**

Lethe (Greek: Oblivion). According to Greek and Latin poets Lethe was a spring or river in **Hades**. When the deceased drank from it they lost all memory of their past lives. The Greeks located the spring at the subterranean oracle of Trophonius near Lebadeia (Leivadia) in Boeotia. This was thought to be the entrance to the underworld. Virgil, in his Aeneid, wrote that Aeneas saw ghosts drinking at the Lethe before their rebirth.

Directly opposite of Lethe is the river or lake or marsh of Mnemosyne (Memory), drinking from which would allow the **soul** to retain its memory of a past life.

See also **Drink or fruit of forgetfulness; Greek afterlife, the ancient; Greeks and reincarnation;** ***Nepenthean*** **veil; Orphism; Plato.**

Levirate marriage. In its standard, or exoteric, meaning this is where a man is obligated to marry the widow of his brother, if the brother died without having a son. Such marriages are mandated in the Old Testament. In post-biblical Judaism this practice was abandoned as no longer appropriate. However, the Kabbalists, rather than just declaring the practice no longer in force, gave such a marriage an esoteric meaning. They claimed that its original purpose was to allow the **soul** of the deceased man to be reborn through his former wife.

See also **Kabbalah.**

Lhamoi Latso Oracle. In the traditional process of determining the whereabouts of the latest incarnation of the **Dalai Lama**, this oracle uses a lake high in the Tibetan mountains, whose water is remarkably clear, for **scrying** purposes. This oracle is not to be confused with two other major Tibetan oracles, the first of which is the Nechung State Oracle that advises the Dalai Lama on issues of state via the spirit Nechung, a protector of the Dalai Lama. This spirit is channeled through a specially trained monk called a *kuten* (physical base). The other oracle is the Gadong State Oracle, the *kuten* of which comes from a family lineage of lay mediums.

See also ***Tulku.***

Liberal Catholic Church, Province of the United States (LCC). Like its sister church, the Liberal Catholic Church International (LCCI), this is a descendent of the Old (Dutch) Catholic Church, which separated from Rome in 1870. The separation was caused by the Dutch church's refusal to accept the new Roman doctrine of Papal infallibility. The LCC was founded between 1916 and 1918, mainly by **Charles Webster Leadbeater**. A major difference between the two liberal churches is that the LCC is a form of Christian **Theosophy**, and as such its teachings include reincarnation and the belief that **Jesus** was one of the great **ascended masters**, as opposed to the standard Christian view of him as the Son of God. The LCCI, on the other hand, holds to more standard Christian teachings.

See also **Gnostic Orthodox Church of Christ in America.**

Life script problem. This refers to a condition in which a few rare individuals who, having discovered what they believe to be a past life, tend to model the present life on the past one. This can go so far as allowing the problems of the past life to be acted out or repeated in the present life.

See also **Going lilac.**

Limbo. Limbo is generally defined as a place where souls go which do not qualify for **heaven**, yet do not deserve **hell**. In some religions souls reside in limbo only temporarily; while in other religions they remain there indefinitely.

A number of pro-reincarnationist Christian writers have claimed that limbo is not a place but rather is the passing through a series of rebirths until one is qualified to enter heaven. The problem with this non-standard Christian view is that it can not be justified biblically or by any orthodox Christian tradition which, until recently, has had a very different understanding of limbo.

As formulated in the medieval church, the orthodox view was that there were three states of limbo. These were the limbo of the fathers; the limbo of the children; and the limbo of the fools. The first was the state of detention for the biblical prophets and heroes who died before the atonement of Christ. This limbo was thought to have been emptied when the saintly dead arose from the grave after the crucifixion (**Matthew** 27:52–53) or when Christ descended into the world of the imprisoned dead (**harrowing of hell**) to preach his atonement (1st **Peter** 3:19; 4:6; 1st Peter 4:6). The second limbo was a place for children who either had died before baptism, hence were not cleansed of original sin, or who had died before they could become personally responsible for sin. According to some authorities this second limbo was also the realm for adult souls who had lived moral lives but for whatever reason had not received the gift of supernatural grace necessary to enter heaven. The medieval churchmen were less sure about the third limbo, also called Fool's Paradise. This was for those who were born mentally incapacitated; hence, not fully responsible for their sins.

The existence of limbo as a neither heaven nor hell state was originally considered a necessary part of God's loving and just nature by the Catholic Church, but most Protestant groups rejected the concept of limbo as biblically unjustified. In fact, this weak biblical justification for limbo, plus the modern opposition to the idea of un-baptized children never entering heaven, recently caused even the Catholic Church to reevaluate the very existence of limbo. In the early 1990's reference to it was dropped from the Catholic catechism and in April 2007 Pope Benedict XVI signed a theological edict effectively eliminating it from Catholic teachings.

From a Buddhism perspective a temporary reincarnation into the animal realm might be thought of as a form of limbo in that it does not have the soterial advantages of a human birth, but is also not as condemning as hell. In **Theosophy** being stuck in the **etheric body** for too long is being in a kind of limbo.

See also **Baptism and reincarnation; Christianity and Original Sin; Predestination; Purgatory.**

Limitation lifetime. According to Dr. John as channeled during the **Grace-Loehr life readings**, this is where a **soul** purposefully chooses to take upon itself a life of major limitations or of great adversity. This is done so the soul can acquire a level of strength and development not otherwise attainable. In this voluntary undertaking karma is of little importance; therefore, it was wrong to assume that all lives of great hardship are due to past life detrimental karma, which equated with **blaming the victim.**

It is important to note that this voluntary undertaking is exclusively a Western concept, since in the East a life of hardship is always attributed to detrimental karma from the past. It might be thought that the ***bodhisattva*** vow to renounce fully entering **nirvana** might be a kind of limitation lifetime, but this would be incorrect. None of the official *bodhisattvas* reincarnate into the human realm, but serve humanity from a blissful otherworldly state, which is devoid of any limitations or adversity.

Limited life or **soul substance.** Many folk religions teach that there is only a limited amount of life or **soul** substance in the world; therefore, that substance must constantly be recycled. Reincarnation is obviously one form of such recycling.

See also **Reincarnation, origins of.**

Lincoln, Abraham *see* **Kennedy, John F.**

Linga Sharia (Body of Characteristics). The Sanskrit word *linga* originally meant only a phallic shaped object worshipped as a fertility symbol, especially by the worshippers of the Hindu god Shiva. By the fourth century CE the term *linga* also came to mean a subtle body, which some consider to be the carrier of karma from one rebirth to another. Such a body is necessary since the **soul** proper (*atman*), which is enveloped by the *linga sharira*, can not be contaminated by karma. The *linga sharira* is also called the *sukshma* (subtle) *sharia* and the *karana (*causal*) sharira*. The *linga sharia* is also the collective name for the second, third, and fourth *kosha*.

In modern **Theosophy** and kindred systems the *linga sharira* is also equated with the causal body in some texts; although, in other texts it is often regarded as the equivalent of the more inferior **astral body**.

See also **Individuality and rebirth; Maya; Soul and spirit levels, Theosophical.**

Lingbao [Numinous Treasure] ***Scripture of the Most High Concerning Karmic Retribution*** (Py: *Taishang dongxuan lingbao yebao Yinyuan jing*). This Daoist text dates from the sixth or the beginning of the seventh century CE. Among its unique elements is its view that the seven stars of the *Beidou* (Py: Big Dipper or Ursa Major) serve as the awakeners of prenatal life. In the seventh month in the form of seven divine boys (Py: *qi shentongzi*) or young lords (*jun*) the influence of these stars descends into the womb, enters the fetus to open its seven orifices, and infuses into it seven celestial souls (*hun*). Only then can the fetus be considered human enough to be entered into the celestial registry, which then affords control and protection of the destiny of the soon to be born.

This text also introduces, perhaps for the first time, the Daoist deity of the Heavenly Venerable Savior from Suffering (Py: Jiuku Tianzun) who is obviously modeled on the earlier, and highly popular, Buddhist *bodhisattvas* **Avalokiteshvara** and as **Kshitigarbha**. Like the second of these *bodhisattvas*, Jiuku Tianzun has the ability to grant merit to the deceased which allows them to escape from karmicaly deserved **hell** and to enter **heaven**.

See also **Bodhisattva Daoism.**

Logic and pseudo-logic and rebirth. Challengers of an afterlife have criticized some supporters of an afterlife for what the challengers regard as a number of pseudo-logical tenets or ploys in support of an afterlife.

The first of these ploys is to surround the claim with scientific terminology; however, such terminology alone does not make the claim scientifically valid. A second is to swamp the public with masses of anecdotal cases devoid of any real corroborative evidence. The fact is that a single fully scientifically corroborated case of reincarnation would be worth much more than a hundred uncorroborated anecdotal ones.

A third ploy is to play on the fact that many people are convinced that if something can not be explained by current scientific means that it just might be mysterious enough to qualify as beyond normal explanation (i.e. supernatural in nature). A fourth ploy is the *ad ignorantiam* practice, where it is argued that if you can not disprove a claim it must be true. An example of this is that since no one can disprove an afterlife, an afterlife must be true. Once again, many surprisingly intelligent people succumb to this fallacy. A fifth ploy is to make such bold claims that the public is sure that no one would do that if the claims were not true. A sixth ploy is the "fallacy of negation" or "false dilemma" thinking. This is where pseudo-science tries to discredit its opponents by dichotomizing an issue into an "either-or" situation. For example, any weaknesses in an otherwise perfectly logical argument is distorted all out of proportion by the attempt to force the argument into either it must be a logically flawless proposition or the opposing argument must automatically be closer to the truth. An example of this is "all cases of past life recall can not be accounted for by alternative explanations; therefore, those past life recalls must be authentic." Unless one is willing to closely investigate the therefore clause for its own flaws this is a very successful ploy. A seventh ploy is the fallacy of redundancy (begging the question, tautological thinking). This can best be seen in the very widespread tautology "How do you know there is an afterlife? I know because the Bible says so. How do you know the Bible is dependable? I know it is because the Bible is a revelation from God. How do you know there is a God? I know it because the Bible says so." It may seem ridiculous that anyone would be convinced by this circular thinking, yet millions of biblical Fundamentalists are convinced by it. An eight ploy, called the "slippery slope argument," goes as follows. "Believing in an afterlife can help make people be more moral. Not believing in an afterlife can help people be more immoral. Morality is better than immorality; therefore, it is better to believe in an afterlife than to disbelieve in it." Of course, what this conclusion fails to acknowledge is that plenty of believers have been and are very immoral (e.g. those who ran the Inquisition, the Crusaders and other holy war fighters) and that plenty of disbelievers have been and are very moral; in the past some of these became the victims of the first group. A ninth pseudo-logical ploy almost everyone unconsciously plays is "An Afterlife (Survival) by Default." Because no one really knows what it is like to be dead we attribute to the deceased mental traits without which we can not imagine existing. This default pseudo-logic is why it is often perceived as counterintuitive to deny an afterlife and it is one reason why the belief in an afterlife is so strongly held world wide. A tenth ploy is an over dependency on authoritative individuals. If a dozen well known and or admired people believe something is true it must be true. The weakness of this reason is that with a little more effort the potential believer could probably find another dozen well known or admired people who do not believe that same thing is true.

See also **Current knowledge discrepancy; Perception and reality; Rebirth and famous supporters; Stevenson, Ian**.

Logic of physical cause and effect. This argument for rebirth says that if there is a reward and punishment process after death for actions done in this bodily existence, then it only makes sense, and is only fair, if the rewards and punishments are experienced similarly in bodily form. In other words, reward and punishment lose their significance in a non-material heaven, purgatory, or hell. The real heaven, purgatory, and hell must be found in the physical conditions of the next physical life.

The logic of this argument works best if any concept of an **interim period** reward and punishment process (heaven or hell) is eliminated; and just such elimination is favored by many Western reincarnationists. The logic of this argument is weaker in **Hinduism** and Buddhism where it is believed that there is both an **interim period** and this world reward and punishment.

See also **Arguments supportive of rebirth; Karma in the ancient and modern west; Rebirth, East and West; Rebirth in the West**.

Lords of Karma. In Hindu mythology there is a group of beings or supernatural forces known as the Lipikas or "Lords of Karma." Karma is technically an impersonal law of cause and effect and as such should have no personified aspect to it. Most believers, however, hope that a more personal aspect to karma will take into consideration the, at times foolish and unintentional, mistakes of individual human beings. This has given rise to the idea that intelligent and sympathetic beings are either ultimately in charge of karma or that they have the power to modify karma to the advantage of individual human beings. These Lords can be thought of as either high-level angels, gods (*devas*), or more abstract forces of nature. The concept of these Lords is also said to be necessary to prevent karma from being understood as a fatalistic denial of human free-will.

Some Western theosophists believe that it is the Lipikas that keep the *akashic* **record** updated. This would be logical since the term lipikas comes from the Sanskrit "*lip*" meaning to write, and "Lipi-devi" is the Hindu goddess of the alphabet or, as Saravasti, she is the goddess of speech.

In modern **Theosophy** the Lipikas are frequently mentioned, with the number of them given as four or seven. In the first case, they seem to be loosely associated with the four kingly guardians of the cardinal directions. In the latter case, they are associated with the heptad of planetary spirits, but whether this means the planetary angels (archangels assigned to ruler the planets) is difficult to determine. In the *Secret Doctrine* of **Helena Blavatsky** the Lipikas are mentioned many times, but the closest description of them is found in the ambiguous sentence, "The Swift Son of the Divine Sons, whose sons are the Lipikas, runs circular errands." Blavatsky gives no further explanation than this.

The theosophist **Alice Bailey,** in her *Treatise on the Seven Rays: Esoteric Astrology* (1951), relates the term Lord of Karma to **Saturn,** the planet which is said to impose retribution and which requires that all karmic debts be paid.

In *Karma in Motion* (1990), by the theosophist Felix Layton, it is stated that the Lords of Karma may function at great sacrifice to themselves to temporarily store in their own consciousness some of the worst or most destructive of humanity's karma until a future time when humanity will have grown mature enough to deal with it constructively.

There are no specific "Lords of Karma" in **Mahayana Buddhism** because here the Buddhas and ***bodhisattva***s, such as **Amitabha, Kshitigarbha,** and **Bhaishajyaraja-guru** function to ameliorate the fruit of karma (*vipaka*).

See also **Aetherius Society;** *Agra-sandhani*; **Astrology and rebirth;** *Bhavachakra*; *Book of Life*; **Karma versus grace; Theosophy; UFOism.**

Lost continents and reincarnation. In the late 19th and early 20th century there was a revived interest in two supposedly lost continents, Atlantis and Lemuria (also called Mu). The belief in such lost continents has allowed for the romantic idea that there were many past lives or **old souls** from these continents that could be said to have reincarnated into modern day bodies. This idea was well nurtured by **Helena Blavatsky, Edgar Cayce, Rudolf Steiner,** and many other less well known figures. According to Edgar Cayce, 1910 and 1911 were years in which there was a great influx of technically advanced re-embodied Atlantian souls and this helps explain the technological progress of the early 20th century.

The problem with any continued attachment to either of these submerged continents on the part of some more recent reincarnationists is that it simply gives the critics of any belief in reincarnation more reason to discredit that belief as a whole. This unfortunately has not stopped some late 20th century reincarnationists from remaining loyal to these hypothetical continents. This is especially true of adherents of a number of UFO religions.

See also **Aetherius Society;** *Akashic* **Record; Current knowledge discrepancy; Egypt; Franklin, Benjamin (2); Phylos; Planets, other; Ramtha; Rebirth and science; Supernatural-in-the-gap process; UFOism.**

Lost soul. In modern **Theosophy** this is a **soul** that over many lifetimes has become progressively more degenerate until it can no longer even attain a rebirth, but instead will fade out of existence.

See also **Eighth sphere.**

Lotus Ashram. Founded in 1971 in Miami, Florida by Noel and Coleen Street, the Ashram follows the healing tradition of Noel's Maori (New Zealand) ancestors while teaching yoga, vegetarianism, and a belief in reincarnation.

Lucian (Lucianus, or Loukianos 115–200 CE). This major Greek satirist made a particular effort to ridicule the myths and religions of his time. This ridicule was also directed at the doctrine of **metempsychosis,** especially in his *The Cock [Gallus] of Micyllos the Tanner.* Here the talking rooster mentions his previous lives as **Pythagoras** and the famous courtesan Aspasia, and instructs his owner, Micyllos, in the virtues of poverty over riches.

Lucifer (1). This is Latin for "Light Bearer" and refers to the morning star, or the planet **Venus,** as the brightest pre-dawn celestial body after the moon. The name Lucifer was not synonymous with the term devil or Satan until sometime after the 13th century. In fact, it is even a title for **Jesus** in the New Testament (**Revelation of John** 22:16 and 2nd **Peter** 1:19).

As the planet Venus, the name Lucifer in some reincarnationist circles is considered an ideal symbol of rebirth because it is the morning (birth) star rising in the east only to disappear in the glare of the sun, and then to reappear as the evening star descending (death) in the west.

On the other hand, according to Beredene Jocelyn in her *Citizens of the Cosmos* (1981), Lucifer is a cosmic agent that encourages pride, egotism, illusion, and spiritual alienation, also one who encourages the **soul** during the **interim period** to selfishly "drop-out" of returning to re-embodiment.

See also **Ahriman; Arcane School; Daimones; Kulkulcan; Planetary descent and ascent of the soul; Trance states.**

Lucifer (2) *see* **Helena P. Blavatsky.**

Lucretius, Carus Titus (99–55 BCE). This Roman philosopher, in his epic book length poem *De Rerum Natura* (*On the Nature of Things*), used twenty-eight arguments against the immortality of the **soul** and was the first recorded critic of **metempsychosis**. His stated purpose for the poem was to liberate mankind from religious fear and false promises. Lucretius argued that the soul has two parts: the *anima* which is distributed throughout the body and is responsible for sensation and the *animus,* which is located in the breast (heart) and is the source of consciousness. Both soul parts are as material as the body, only they are of a finer matter and both die with the body.

Lucretius, while acknowledging the existence of the gods as immortals, denied that they had any power to help or harm mankind because they were not the creators of the world. Instead, the world came into existence through natural laws governing the atoms out of which the world was made. The gods only function was to be examples of the ideal life, which above all includes living without any fear of death.

Lucretius regarded the Pythagoreans, the Platonists, and the Stoics as false philosophers since they encouraged the myth of immortality, and even worse, the belief in **heaven** and **hell**.

According to Lucretius "Death being nothing to man, man is lord of himself."

See also **Pythagoras; Plato**.

Luke, Gospel of. This New Testament book is less often cited for a supposed hidden doctrine of reincarnation than is the case for the other three gospels. In fact, there are only two such passages in this text. in Luke 20:29–33 Jesus is asked a trick question by some Sadducees, who intrinsically rejected any belief in the resurrection of the dead. The passage reads, "Now, there were seven brothers: the first took a wife and died childless; then the second married her, then the third. In this way the seven of then died leaving no children. Afterwards, the woman died. At the resurrection whose wife is she to be, since all seven had married her?" Assuming she was not a "black widow wife" it is clearly rather absurd that any woman would even have the opportunity to be the widow of seven brother serially due to some strange death pattern; thus, it has been possible for some reincarnationists to interpret this passage to mean that the woman really had seven different husbands over seven life-times.

The only other Lucian passage favored by reincarnationists is Luke 17:3–4 which is more or less identical to **Matthew** 18:21–22.

See **Annihilationism, Biblical view; Carpocrates; Cayce, Edgar; Christianity and reincarnation; Doceticism; Elijah; Hell; Irenaeus; Jesus; John the Baptist; Mark, Gospel of; New Testament; New Testament and reincarnation; New Testament sacrificial concept; Paulicians; Possession; Rebirth and moral perfection; Resurrection, bodily; Resurrection of Jesus; Steiner, Rudolf**.

Luria, Isaac (1534–1572). This founder of one of the main schools of the Kabbalah, not only taught the doctrine of metempsychosis, but some of his followers believed he was the reincarnation of the great 2nd century mystic Shimon (Hebrew: Shimon) bar Yochai.

See also **Fall of the Souls; Gnosticism; Hasidism; Karma, racial; Qlippoth; *Sephiroth***.

Maccabees, Book of *see **Anabios**;* **Old Testament and the afterlife**.

MacGregor, Geddes (1909–1998). MacGregor is one of the most distinguished Christian theologians to defend the reincarnation concept. In his *Reincarnation in Christianity: A New Vision of the Role of Rebirth in Christian Thought* (1978), Macgregor deals with the standard question of why we do not remember past lives if we lived them. He believes that, first, if we were to remember those lives, the burden of all those memories would be such that we might become paralyzed by them; therefore, it is a mercy that we start each new life without those memories. Second, we all know how difficult it is for most very old persons to be open to radically new ideas and values that might conflict with all the ideas and values with which they have grown old. This would doubly apply to people if they remembered the ideas and values of past lives. These two answers have been adopted by most reincarnationists. MacGregor is also a proponent of summation memory. MacGregor has written a number of other books on Christianity and reincarnation and is the editor of *Immortality and Human Destiny: A Variety of Views* (1985).

See also **MacTaggart, John Ellis; Memory, summation**.

MacIver, Joanne (1948–). The father of Joanne, Ken MacIver, had learned hypnosis while serving with the army and was an avid believer in reincarnation. In 1962 Mr. MacIver tried in vain to hypnotize a friend of his but failed to do so. Instead his 14 year old daughter, Joanne, fell into a hypnotic state. Under hypnosis Joanne began to describe a former life as a girl named Susan Ganier who was born in 1833 and lived on a farm in Ontario, Upper Canada.

In 1966 **Jess Stearn**, deciding to research the case, went to the area in which "Susan Ganier" said she resided, which was near Owen Sound and Meaford. Unfortunately, it was impossible to obtain a death certificate for Susan or any "official" documents of her existence. Some evidence seemed to indicate that Susan had existed and one must take into account that in the early and mid–nineteenth century, communications and proper statistical keeping were not very efficient. Nonetheless, the lack of proper documentation makes this an easily suspected case of hypnotically encouraged **honest lying**. On the other hand, if Joanne and/or her father were either trying to prove reincarnation and/or seeking publicity they did a poor job of it by choosing someone so obscure and difficult to document.

Since both Joanne and Susan Ganier were said to have blue eyes Stearn's research ended with the well-known book *The Search for the Girl with the Blue Eyes* (1968).

See also **Past life memory recall**.

MacLaine, Shirley (1934–). Perhaps no Hollywood star has shown as much interest in the paranormal then Ms. MacLaine. She has written a number of books about her past lives and about **channeling**.

See also **Hollywood and reincarnation**.

MacTaggart, John Ellis (1866–1925). MacTaggart was an important British Hegelian philosopher who wrote *Human Immortality and Pre-existence* (1915) and *The Nature of Existence* (1921). He offered a solution to the criticism that rebirth without retention of memories of the past life was morally meaningless. MacTaggart's theory was that memory is significant in the following ways. First, through memories acquired from the trials of life we become intellectually more sophisticated and hopefully more virtuous in our behavior. Second, memory allows us to be attached to those whom we love and to avoid those we dislike. When a person dies his or her knowledge dies also, but neither the intellectual nor virtuous strength the **soul** gained from the now extinct memories would be lost. Similarly, the soul will have an intuitive attraction in its next life to sympathetic souls from the previous life. These factors are what make for a soul's intellectual, moral, and spiritual progress.

A problem with McTaggart's view is that if intellectual and virtuous strength is totally independent of knowledge, much less memories, than what he means by such strength is unclear. Common sense would normally make it fully dependent on knowledge and/or memories.

See also **MacGregor, Geddes**; **Memories, reasons for loss of past life**.

Mafu. This is an entity channeled through a woman by the name of Penny Torres Rubin starting in 1986. After a visit to India Rubin took on the name Swami Paramananda Saraswatti and upon returning to the United States established the Foundation for the Realization of Inner Divinity. The Foundation disseminates the teachings of Mafu who claims to be a 32,000 year old enlightened being from the Brotherhood of Light, and who supports the concept of reincarnation. In fact, he says that his last life on earth was as a first century BCE Greek.

See also **Channeling**; **Equinox**; **Franklin, Benjamin (2)**; **Hilarion**; **Lazaris**; **Michael (2)**; **Ra**; **Ramtha**; **Ryerson, Kevin**; **Satya**; **Seth**.

Magna Graecia. In ancient times Magna Graecia (Greater Greece) was the name for the entire coastal region of southern Italy because of the large number of Greek colonies there. It was here that **Pythagoras** settled and established the first Pythagorean communities. As such the region became a fairly concentrated center of ancient reincarnationist thought, some of which spread to the nearby Greek colonies on Sicily, one of which was Agrigentum, the birth place of **Empedocles**. Recent research would seem to suggest that it was from Magna Graecia that the idea of reincarnation spread through out the rest of the Greek world.

See also **Archytas of Tarentum**; **Greeks and reincarnation**.

Magnetic attraction metaphor. To explain how a **soul** or rebirth entity might be reborn to the right parents it has been suggested that, like a magnet drawn to an iron surface, each soul is magnetically drawn to just the right genetic heritage of the parents and/or to the genetic code of the embryo or fetus.

Maha Bodhi, The. This is the English language journal of the Maha Bodhi Society in India, publication of which began in 1892 and continues up to the present. Over the years it has contained numerous articles on rebirth and karma.

See also *Open Court*.

Mahayana Buddhism. This is the form of Buddhism practiced in the East Asian countries of China, Korea, Japan, and Vietnam. Unlike **Theravada Buddhism** it usually acknowledges an **interim period** between rebirths.

See also *Bodhisattva*; **Buddhism**; **Merit, transfer of**; **Vajrayana Buddhism**.

Mahayana Buddhist rebirth texts. While there are far too many Mahayana texts dealing with rebirth and/or karma to list here the following are among some of the most well known or important.

Diamond Cutter Sutra's Revilement. This Zen Buddhist encounter dialog is found in two koan collections, as case 97 of the *Blue Cliff Record* and as case 80 in the *Book of Serenity*. It reads, "*The Diamond-Cutter Sutra* says, 'If someone is reviled by others, this person has done wicked acts in previous ages and should fall into evil ways, but because of the scorn and revilement of people in the present age, the wicked deeds of the past ages are dissolved.'"

Fox Koan. This is a famous Zen Buddhist story about a Chinese Buddhist monk who was reborn time after time in the form of a fox as punishment for having denied the Buddhist doctrine of causality. In East Asian lore foxes are regarded as having magical shape-changing abilities. Therefore, it was not too difficult for this monk-fox to temporarily take on human form and appear before one of the great Zen masters and beg the master to show him how to gain liberation from his vulpine life. The master, taking pity on the poor creature, magically liberated him by reversing the monk's original heretical denial. This would seem to be a clear "doctrinal (teaching Buddhist doctrine) koan" in that it states the standard Buddhist teaching of karma and **vipaka**.

Garbhavakranti-nirdesha-sutra and *Saddharmasmetyupasthana-sutra*. These are two Sanskrit Mahayana Buddhist texts in which the nature of the **interim period** is outlined. The first of these texts, the *Sutra of Entering the Womb*, details the progression of the interim period entity from the last moment of death to its conception in the womb and through each week of its fetal development. The second text, the *Sutra on Stability in Mindfulness of the True Dharma*, describes an elaborate set of up to seventeen individual interim period states.

Sutra of Perfect Enlightenment. This is an apocryphal Chinese Buddhist text, the full Chinese name is *Ta-fang-kuang Yuan-chueh-hsiu-to-lo-liao-i-ching*; while the abbreviated name *Yuan-chueh-ching*. In this text each of twelve **bodhisattvas** asks a question of the Buddha with regards to the issue of perfect and immediate enlightenment. What is of special interest is that one of the *bodhisattvas* mentioned is that of "Clean Karma."

Finally, there are two especially important texts that give detailed arguments for rebirth. These are the *Tarkajvala* by Bhavaviveka (5th century CE) and the second chapter of the *Pramanavarttika* by Dharmakirti (7th century CE).

See also **Blaming the victim vs. illusion of innocence**; *Chan-ch'a sha-o yeh-pao ching*; **Gandharva**; **Rebirth in Buddhism**; **Rebirth in Zen Buddhism**.

Maher Baba (1894–1969). This Indian holy man was the first important *guru* to gain a following in the West. His name, which means "Loving Father," was born into a Zoroastrian family, was a student of a Sufi, and taught a synthesis of various religions which included the doctrines of reincarnation and karma.

See also **Sufism; Zoroastrianism**.

Maiden embodiment or incarnation. This refers to a **soul** that has never before experienced embodiment in human form.

Malachi *see* **Akashic Record; Elijah; Old Testament and the afterlife; Sciomancy**.

Malaysia. This Southeast Asian country is divided into two geographical regions. The western part takes up the southern portion of the Malay Peninsula, where the majority of the population is Muslim, but with significant Hindu, Buddhist, and Christian minorities. The other region takes up the western third of the island of Borneo. This part of the country has a very large number of people of Chinese descent, most of whom are Buddhists and Daoists. Despite Islamic unorthodoxy the belief in reincarnation and karma is widespread among Malaysian Muslims.

See also **Indonesia; Islam**.

Male births, greater proportion of. According to **Ian Stevenson** there is evidence that the proportion of male births after wars is often greater than at other times. This could suggest that due to the large number of military (male) fatalities there are more male souls to be reborn than female souls, assuming that most of these souls did not change gender between the two lives. On the other hand, this more than normal number of male births could have something to do with the fact that in time of war there is a higher incidence of delayed marriages which could ultimately affect this gender condition. Some have also claimed that there is a greater frequency of sexual intercourse during home leaves and after demobilization which tilts the sex ratio towards boys.

See also **Arguments for Rebirth; Gender issue of the soul**.

Malkula. It is generally believed among these people of Vanuatu (New Hebrides) that once the correct funeral rites have been performed for the spirit of the dead (*nimwinin*) the spirit departs to take up its abode in the Land of the Dead. However, sometimes it is reborn into a human body. For example, if a child shows a striking resemblance, facially or in character, to some deceased relative such as a grandparent it is said that the *nimwinin* of this relative has become reincarnated in the child. When such a reincarnation is believed to have taken place the child is generally called by the name of the person of whom he or she is the new manifestation.

See also **Oceania**.

Mana (pride or conceit) *see* ***Asmi-mana***.

Manas (mind). In early Buddhism *manas* was more or less synonymous with *vijnana* (consciousness) and *chitta* (mind), but in the later **Vijnanavada** (Consciousness only) **School** of Buddhism *manas* was distinguished from the latter two. In both early and later Buddhism *manas* is where the seeds of past karma are activated and call for rebirth.

In **Theosophy** *manas* is the equivalent of the higher mind or ego if it is used by itself. As *kama-manas* it refers to the lower mind. As the ego it is the reincarnating entity.

See also **Astral soul; Causal body; Mental body; Mental plane; Soul and spirit levels, Theosophical.**

Mandara. This is the coral tree *(Erythrina indica)* which is found in the paradise of the Hindu god Indra. When the inhabitants smell its fragrance they can remember their past lives. This tree is also known by the name *parijata*.

Manichaeism. A dualist religion founded by the Iranian (Persian) prophet Mani (216–274 CE), it was a syncretism of **Zoroastrianism,** Buddhism, **Orphism, Neoplatonism**, and Christianity. This syncretic approach technically qualified Manichaeism a form of **Gnosticism,** but it was Mani's teaching that was the first major religion to knowingly unite Western and Indian thought. Manichaeism may have even been the ancestor of the **Paulicians.**

According to Manichaeism in the distant past there was a great battle between the forces of good, or light, and the forces of evil, or darkness. While the forces of light won the battle they did not do so before the dark forces had captured some of the light elements. These elements, as souls, were trapped in matter (bodies) which were part of the evil creation. The religious goal was to liberate this trapped light, and that could only be done through such ascetic practices as absolute non-violence, **celibacy,** and **vegetarianism**. Manichaeism adopted from Buddhism, and possibly Orphism, the belief in **transmigration** and karma.

At first Manichaeism was a strong competitor to Christianity, but with the establishment of the latter as the state religion of the Roman Empire Manichaeism was treated as a heresy and ultimately suppressed in the Mediterranean world. Manichaeism, however, spread east as far as China and for a short time became the state religion of the Uighur Turks in Western China. Due to Islamic persecution Manichaeism eventually died out in West and Central Asia. In China it was outlawed in the 9th century but became an underground religion, possibly surviving there until the 17th century.

See also **Ashoka, King; Augustine, Saint Aurelius; Body-soul dualism; Bogomils; Cathars; Cult of Angels;** ***Demiurge;*** **Dualism; Islam; Priscillian.**

Mann, A. Tad (1943–). This major astrologer believes that he has found a way of locating past lives. To do this he has developed what he calls the Astrological Reincarnation Time Scale (ARTS). Mann calls his uniquely developed astrological system Life Time Astrology. The system uses a logarithmic time scale adapted from one developed by **Rodney Collin**. According to Mann his system has shown that the same entity that was Alexander the Great (336–323) was later Charlemagne and then **Napoleon Bonaparte**.

Mann is the author of *The Divine Plot* (1986), *The Eternal Return* (1993), and *The Elements of Reincarnation* (1995).

See also **Astrology and rebirth; Leo, Alan.**

Manson, Charles Willie (1934–). This Charles Manson is the leader of the infamous Manson Family who, in 1969, ordered his disciples to murder some of his enemies. Altogether there were eight people killed, most of whom were Hollywood celebrities. As the Family guru Manson tried to take on the appearance of, claimed to be, and was accepted by the Family as, the reincarnation of **Jesus**.

Manu-Sanhita (*Laws of Manu*). This highly regarded Hindu text is ascribed to a legendary figure named Manu and rather than being a well planned systematic code it is a collection or digest of the laws and beliefs that were current during the time of its compilation, which probably covered a period ranging from 600 BCE to 300 CE.

Although called a book of law, besides what is normally thought of as law the text also contains an outline of the ultimate goal as salvation through union with **Brahman** (God) by means of one's full acceptance of **caste system** duties.

The text is very explicit about what happens to those who ignore or violate such duties, or otherwise performs ill deeds. For example, if a man steals grain he will be reborn as a rat; if honey — a bee; if milk — a crow; if meat — a vulture; if a cow — an iguana. An adulterous woman will become a jackal; the violator of a teacher's (guru's) bed will be reborn a hundred times as grass or a creeping vine; and a Brahman (priest) who deserts his caste duty will be reborn as a vomit eating ghost (*ulkamukha*). This is, of course, only a partial list. The *Manu-Sanhita* is also called the *Manu Smrti,* or *Manavad-harma-shastra.*

See also ***Dharma-Shastras;*** **Hinduism.**

Mara. In Buddhism this is the name for the personification of death or entrapment in the round of rebirth and re-death (*samsara*). In the West it is sometimes thought that Mara is the equivalent of the Christian devil, but this is only partially the case. Mara, as the personified natural phenomenon of death, does not have the connotation of a sinfully rebellious figure opposing God as the devil does in Christianity. Since in Buddhism it is ignorance that keeps us trapped in our suffering, Mara is rather consistently equated with ignorance, not sin. This nondemonic view of Mara can also be appreciated by the fact that Mara is sometimes used as an appellation for Kama, the god of love (lust) who is responsible for keeping people attached to each other and so trapped in the cycle of birth and death.

Finally, Mara should not be equated with the Western devil because Mara is not regarded as one of the ***asuras*** (anti-gods). Instead, he is one of the gods (*devas*) who is on par with all the other gods. It is for this reason that Mara inhabits the heaven of the gods, not **hell** (**purgatory**).

See also **Immortality**.

Marie Antoinette *see* **Cleopatra Syndrome**.

Mark-Age, Inc. This organization originated in 1960 under the direction of Nada-Yolanda, the pseudonym for Pauline Sharpe, who the organization regards as a prophet for the new age and the "messianic second coming." The name of the organization comes from its belief that the years from 1960 to 2000 marked the age in which the Earth would be entering a period when mankind would realize a new brotherhood of humanity. The teachings of Mark-Age are a blending of Western and Eastern traditions, as exemplified by its teachings of reincarnation and karma as well as its reference to the **Jesus** as Sananda (S: He who has ascended) the Christ, the name of Jesus as an **ascended master**.

Mark, Gospel of. This is the earliest of the four canonical gospels to be written, the date of its composition is about 70 CE. The priority of Mark can be demonstrated by the obvious fact that both the Gospels of **Matthew** and **Luke** were dependent upon Mark for much of their material.

As the earliest gospel Mark is the first to mention the empty tomb story. Whether the author of Mark invented the story of the empty tomb or found it already in development remains a mystery, but the reason for the story, of which the pre–Marcan Paul seemed to know nothing, was to make what might otherwise have been thought of as a purely spiritual resurrection into an unquestionably non-gnostic or non-docetic physical one. Since then it has been this physicality that has been used by orthodox Christianity to exclusively support the concept of resurrection against reincarnation and to declare the latter belief heretical.

Since many present-day Christians more or less ignore the idea of heresy it should not be surprising that those Christians who wish to find biblical support for reincarnation believe they can find it in at least the three following sections of Mark.

First there is Mark 4:10–12. Here the disciples have asked Jesus why he teaches in parables. **Jesus** answers, "To you [the disciple] the secret of the kingdom of God has been given; but to those who are outside everything comes by way of parables, so that, as the Scriptures say they may look and look, but see nothing; they may hear and hear, but understand nothing; otherwise they might turn to God and be forgiven." These words are actually lifted right out of Isaiah 6:9–10, and Mark used them to imply that Jesus' teachings are for a (hidden) elect, not for the masses, who are to be left in confusion.

This idea of a secret teaching has been picked up by some pro–Christian reincarnationists to suggest that among those secret teachings is the doctrine of reincarnation. However, Mark's real motivation for implying a secret teaching is less to support a secret teaching factor itself than to support his whole idea of a Messianic secret which he hopes will explain to his readers why the Jewish and Roman authorities put Jesus to death instead of hailing him as the Messiah.

The Gospel of Matthew 13:10–15, despite dropping the Messianic secret theme of Mark, borrowed these secret or elect passages without much alteration. However, in the Gospel of Luke, at the place where Mark's passages should appear (Luke 10: between 22 and 23) the whole idea of a secret teaching has been dropped.

The second section of Mark to be given a reincarnational interpretation is Mark 2:22 is repeated Matthew 9:17 and Luke 6:37–38. These passages refer to "not putting new wine into old skins (containers) but new wine into new skins." The wine skins are regarded by some as a biblical metaphor for reincarnation.

The third so-called reincarnationist passage is Mark 10:29–30. Here Peter has claimed that he and the other disciples have given up everything to follow Jesus. "Jesus said, 'I tell you this: there is no one who has given up home, brothers or sisters, mother, father or children, or land, for my sake and for the Gospel, who will not receive in this age a hundred times as much — houses, brothers and sisters, mothers and children, and land — and persecutions besides: and in the age to come eternal life.'" To make this passage supportive of reincarnation it is claimed that no one in a single life could be as spiritually self-sacrificing as required by Jesus.

So if the disciples had met the demand it implies that they had perfected themselves over multiple lives to do so. Furthermore, the promise that they will receive in return everything a hundred-fold, including a hundred mothers, must imply a hundred life-times to come.

See also **Carpocrates; Christianity and reincarnation; Corinthians, 1st and 2nd; Doceticism; Elijah (Elias); "every knee should bend...; Forty; Gnosticism; Hell; Jesus; John the Baptist; John, The Gospel of; New Testament and reincarnation; New Testament sacrificial concept; Old Testament and the soul; Resurrection of Jesus.**

Marlowe, Christopher (1564–1593). This English dramatist, in his *The Tragedy of Doctor Faustus*, has Faust invoke **Pythagoras** in his final moments on earth (scene XIV, 116–121): "Ah, Pythagoras' **metempsychosis**—were that true, this soul should fly from me, and I be changed unto some brutish beast. All beasts are happy, for when they die their souls are soon dissolved in elements, but mine must live still to be plagued in hell."

Masefield, John (1878–1967). While many of the poems of this poet Laureate of England (1930–1967) are well known, this is less true of his poem *Creed*.

> I hold that when a person dies
> His soul returns again to earth:
> Arrayed in some new flesh disguise
> Another mother gives him birth.
> With sturdier limbs and a bright brain
> The old soul takes the road again.

See also **Patton, George; Poetry on reincarnation.**

Maternal impressions or maternal psychokinesis. This refers to the possibility that a pregnant woman may some how impress on the body of her fetus minor physical characteristics that were possessed by another person with which the mother was familiar. The idea of "maternal" impressions provides an alternative explanation for those that doubt that a newly embodied "soul" could cause **birthmarks**, nevi (moles), etc. on its new body as a physical manifestation of a wound or defect inherited from its former body.

Mathesis. This Greek word means the ability to remember a previous life.

See also **Pythagoras.**

Matthew, Gospel of. As in the other Gospels there has been a variety of attempts to find support for reincarnational teachings in this gospel. The first section suggested for this support is Matthew 5:26. It reads, "I tell you, once you are there [in jail] you will not be let out till you have paid the last farthing." A reincarnational reading of this passage is that the jail refers to the entrapment in the round of birth and death and until you have paid out (eliminated) all your karma, or at least bad karma, you can not be freed from jail.

The second favored section is Matthew 9:16 which reads, "No one sews a patch of un-shrunk cloth on to an old coat; for then the patch tears away from the coat, and leaves a bigger hole." This passage is immediately followed by Matthew 9:17 which is the passage about put new wine into old wine-skins that is also found in **Mark** 2:22 and taken directly from there. It should be no surprise that the contrasting of old and new in 9:16 and 17 would be used in attempting to imply the soul goes from an old body to a new one.

The final favored section is Matthew 18:21–22. This reads, "Then Peter came up and asked him [Jesus], Lord, how often am I to forgive my brother if he goes on wronging me?" Peter then asked, "As many as seven times?" **Jesus** replied, "I do not say seven times; I say seventy times seven." It should be mentioned that some New Testament translations instead say seventy-seven times. What follows these verses is statement that such multiple forgiving is how a believer should think of the forgiveness of the Kingdom of Heaven. However, since the idea of forgiving someone seventy-seven times, much less four hundred and ninety times in the same life time seems such a superhuman requirement that some reincarnationists believe that Jesus did not really mean to forgive that many times in a single life. With this in mind the passage can be esoterically interpreted to mean that the forgiving nature of **Heaven** (God) offers at least seventy-seven and maybe even up to four hundred and ninety lifetimes for individuals to work out their karma. The supporters of this multiple lifetime interpretation often use the last two lines of **Genesis** 4:24 as parallel. This reads, "Cain may be avenged seven times, but Lamech seventy-seven."

In **Luke** 17:3–4, on this same issue of forgiveness, it is advises that only seven-fold is sufficient, so Luke is not considered as supportive of a reincarnation interpretation as is Matthew.

See also **Annihilationism, Biblical view; Astrology and rebirth; Augustine, Saint Aurelius; Carpocrates; Christianity and reincarnation; Doceticism; Elect or chosen of God; Elijah; Exodus; Forty; Hell; Irenaeus; Jesus; John the Baptist; Karma in the Bible?; Limbo; New Testament and reincarnation; New Testament sacrificial concept; Origin or Origenes Adamanthus; Palingenesis; Possession; Predestination;** *Psychopannychism;* **Purgatory; Rebirth and moral perfection; Resurrection of Jesus; Seven.**

Maya (S: illusion, magic). In **Hinduism** *maya* signifies the activity of **Brahman** in producing an illusory or magical world in which nothing is as it seems. *Maya* is the mind of Brahman playing a hiding, seeking, and finding game with himself. The hiding is the illusion of birth and death. The seeking is the illusory act of striving for liberation from birth and death. The finding is the realization that there was never any birth and death or need for liberation from it in the first place.

See also **Monism**; ***Prakrit***; ***Shunya***.

Mayan Indians. During the first half of the 20th century the assumption, as reflected by scholars such as J. Eric Thompson, was that the Classic (prior to the Toltec warring kings' influence) Maya culture (250–900 CE) was a society ruled by peaceful, indeed benevolent, astrologer-priests. This idealistic view led to all sorts of romantic speculation about Mayan higher wisdom and a number of metaphysical groups were certain that this wisdom must have included a belief in reincarnation. However, the latter half of the same century provided extensive evidence that the earlier picture of Mayan society was wrong and that well before the arrival of the Toltec the Mayan culture included the brutal ritualized warfare and human sacrifice that was characteristic of other Mesoamerican people, such as the Toltecs and **Aztecs**. Despite this new evidence, many new age individuals and groups continue to believe in the advanced cosmological prophetic abilities of a reincarnation believing Maya society. Among the more bizarre beliefs is that Mayan culture was descended from Atlantis. This belief, In particular, was encouraged by the writings of **Edgar Cayce**. The fact is that for the ancient Maya there is no secure evidence of a belief or non-belief in reincarnation.

During the 1930's Protestant missionaries began seeking converts among the Maya so the current beliefs of these people may now be very different from their ancestral beliefs. On the other hand, according to research in 1930–31 by the anthropologist Robert Redfield, the Mayan speaking people of the village of Chan Kom, in the state of Yucatan, believed that the souls of good people, after spending some time in heaven, were reincarnated into newborn infants. This was necessary because God did not have sufficient souls to continuously repopulate the world. The souls of the wicked, in contrast went to the lowest level of the underworld (*Metnal*) which was ruled over by the Lord of Death.

See also **Christian missionary influence and reincarnation**; **Kulkulcan**; **Lost continents and reincarnation**; **Mayan Order**; **Mayan Temple**.

Mayan Order. This San Antonio, TX, based Order has existed since at least 1944. It claims to have been founded by some individuals who rediscovered the teachings of an ancient group of Mayan Indian holy men who were in possession of great astrological, mathematical, medical, and occult knowledge, which included a belief in reincarnation. Only a few of these holy ones survived the attempt by the Spanish to destroy them and their wisdom literature. The wisdom that has survived is now said to be preserved by the Mayan Order. A major source of information about the Order's teaching can be found in *The Miracle Power* by Rose Dawn. (San Antonio, TX: Mayan Press, 1959).

See also **Mayan Temple**.

Mayan Temple. This was the name of a San Antonio based organization that prospered from the mid–1930s to the early 1960s. It offered correspondence lessons in an eclectic mixture of Kabbalic, Esoteric Christian, and Buddhist teachings, which included the doctrine of reincarnation. Very little of these teachings had anything to do with actual culture of the **Mayan Indians**.

See also **Mayan Order**.

Meditation. Some authorities believe that certain types of meditation can be instrumental in retrieving past life memories.

See also ***Bardo***; **Yoga**

Medium. In **Spiritualism** this is any person who acts as an intermediary between the spirit world and the ordinary material world. From the middle of the 20th century on the term medium has largely been replaced by the term channeler. At times it has been suggested that all authentic past life recalls are the result of unconscious mediumship abilities on the part of the recaller.

See also **Automatic writing**; **Channeling**; **Extrasensory perception**; **Necromancy**; **Ouija Board**; **Sciomancy**.

Melchizedek or **Melchisedec** (Hebrew: King of Righteousness [Tzedek] or Righteousness is king). This is the ancient legendary pre–Israelite priest-king of ([Jeru]-salem [peace]). He is described as a priest of "God the Most High" (Hebrew: El Elyon) in Genesis 14:18–20, and is even more cryptically mentioned in Psalm 110:4. The name Melchizedek is also found in the Slavonic apocrypha's *Second Book of Enoch*, and in one of the *Dead Sea Scrolls*, where as a nephew of Noah, Melchizedek was taken to heaven before the Flood to serve as a priest until the Messianic age.

In the New Testament Melchizedek is mentioned in Hebrews 5:6–10; 6:20; and 7:1–20 where, referring back to Psalm 110, Christ is called a priest forever in the succession of Melchizedek. Hebrews says that Melchizedek "has no father, no mother, no lineage; his years have no beginning, his life has no end. He is like the Son of God: he remains a priest for all time." The author of Hebrews clearly wants to make **Jesus** a priest, but the author knows that according to Jewish law a priest must come from the line of Levi-Aaron and Jesus is supposedly of the line of Judah-David, so the author finds a separate priestly lineage in Melchizedek into which he can fit Jesus. Hebrews then regards the priesthood of Melchizedek, not only as prior to Levitical priesthood, but more perfect than it. The connection between Christ and Melchizedek is further strengthened, according to Hebrews, by the fact that Genesis mentions that Melchizedek offered "bread and wine" to the patriarch Abraham.

Considering the mystical aura that Hebrews gives to Melchizedek it is no surprise that **Edgar Cayce** and some of the **New Age religions** regarded Jesus as the "successor" of Melchizedek in a reincarnational sense.

See also **Enoch, Third Book of; Essenes; Gnostic Order of Christ; Lemurian Fellowship; New Testament and reincarnation; New Testament sacrificial concept; Stelle Group;** *Urantia Book*.

Melville, Herman (1819–1891). In his most famous work, *Moby Dick* (1851) [chapter 119], Captain Ahab, talking to himself, declares that in a former life he was a fire-worshipping Persian (Zoroastrian) who was burned during a sacrifice and in his current life still bears the scar.

Memories, ancestral or genetic. It has been theorized that part of what may be called a past life is actually memory that somehow has passed down from one generation to another through common genetic material. Of course, such memory, should it be valid, has very limited expressiveness. First of all, such memory would have to be from someone in the direct ancestral line. For example, it would have to be from a parent or grandparent that died before the birth of the person claiming the memories, not from a cousin, aunt or uncle. Second, the memories of a grandparent, for instant, passed on to a grandchild would be limited to those that existed before the conception of the grandchild's parent. Altogether, the idea of genetic memory does not have a great deal to offer on the issue of reincarnation.

See also **Archetypes; Collective Unconscious; Jung, Carl.**

Memories, reasons for loss of past life. There are a number of reasons suggested for the fact that everyone does not retain the memories of a past life or lives. One reason is that the conditions of both death and birth are traumatic enough to wipe these memories away. A second reason is that if we remembered even one of our past lives, much less many of them, we would be so bogged down in these memories that we would have difficulty in living the present life. This is especially true if any of the most recent lives were extremely unflattering to our present egos. A third reason is that by not having past life memories we have the opportunity to start each life afresh. This third reason is far more popular among Western reincarnationists than it is among Eastern ones because it is often thought to weaken, or even discount, any karma factor. The fourth reason is that our more distant memories in this current life are often flawed and it is very common to fill in any forgotten elements with imagined information. This being the case, how much more true must it be for memories of a past life.

There are four additional reasons for not remembering a past life all of which are closely related to one another. First, since the immortality of the souls does not allow it to relate to time sequencing, memories are not stored in the soul sequentially. Instead, memories are stored in like-nature clusters. For example, there are separate clusters for memories dealing with love, hatred, sadness, grief, etc. Second, the soul, being immortal naturally, has no understanding of time in the sense of past, present, and future, since these divisions are exclusively related to the concept of mortality. Since memories are organized sequentially if the soul should store them they would be of little use to anyone. This also gives the soul an impersonal *atman*-like nature. Third, just about every memory a person has acquired in a particular life is of relevance to that life alone. When reborn into a new body, there will be a new set of relatives, a new set of friends, possibly a different gender, race, socio-economic situation, and culture, etc. none of the memories of the past life are going to be of much use in the new life. In fact, from the point of view of the eons old soul, each set of memories related to a specific life is merely a set of short term memories. As in the preceding reason this one would also be characteristics of an *atman*-like impersonality. Fourth, memory is a factor of **body-brain (mind) dependency** and the **soul** does not participate in those memories, so the memories are lost at death rather than being carried over into the new birth. This reason also makes the soul relatively impersonal or *atman*-like.

In an attempt to bring modern science into the explanation for past life memory loss note has been taken of the relationship between memory and the hormone oxytocin. It seems that this hormone, when given to laboratory animals, causes a memory loss in them and it is also this identical hormone that controls a pregnant woman's rate of labor contractions. It has been suggested, therefore, that a large amount of oxytocin passes into the fetus during the birth process and this washes away the past life memories of the newly born child. An opposite effect of an enhancement of memory is linked to the chemical adrenocorticotrophin (ACTH), which is released by the body under stress. So it has been suggested that this chemical in the womb allows some children to remember a past life.

It might be noted that oxytocin is also the hormone that is needed in sufficient amounts in the human body to ensure social bonding. Children raised in orphanages often fail to develop normal oxytocin levels and as a result have life-long social bonding problems. Of course, this and other hormonally determined mental states have been used to support the idea that the mind (soul) is simply a product of brain chemistry and when the brain dies so does the mind or soul and any possibility of reincarnation.

With the possible exception of the ACTH factor, the preceding reasons for the absence of past life memory seems to negate the possibility of authentic past life recall. This conclusion is not acceptable to those, mainly Westerners, who believe that some form of authentic past life recall is essential to sustain their belief in reincarnation. That this is far more a Western issue than an Eastern one is demonstrated by the fact that Eastern believers seem content to accept that most, if not all, such recall is the exclusive privilege of enlightened sages. Indeed, it is even thought that such recall or remembrance (*purvanivasanusmrti*) develops only as a necessary pre-condition to liberate the sage from any remaining hidden karmic causes or roots that otherwise would keep the sage still bound to the cycle of rebirth and re-death.

Finally, it must be remembered that the "retention of memories issue" is of real significance only if the concept of karma is also involved. If the situation into which one is reborn is in no way related to the moral behavior of the past life, that is without punishment or reward, then the critical argument that it is unjust to be born without knowing (remembering) why becomes a non-issue.

See also *Abhijna*; **Age factor and rebirth; Birth trauma; Child prodigies or geniuses; Death trauma; Future-lives; Karma and justice; Mac-Taggart, John Ellis; Mental plane; Past life memory categories; Vegetarianism.**

Memory alone critique. This is a criticism of the idea that having a memory of a past life is proof of rebirth. The criticism is based on the idea that human personhood constitutes not only memories, but personality traits, emotions, intellectual capacities, likes and dislikes, and even a particular or unique bodily form.

See also **Karma and justice; Personality versus individuality.**

Memory categories and past lives *see* **Diathanatic; Past life memory categories.**

Memory contamination. This occurs when a person hears something from a trusted source about which that person had no previous knowledge, but soon becomes convinced that he or she also remembers that same something. In a significant number of cases of past life recall such contamination has been documented.

See also **Guirdham, Arthur; Resurrection of Jesus.**

Memory, summation. This refers to the theory that while each of us loses our memories of specific events of past lives, we are influenced by the sum of all of the character, disposition, and innate talents we have had in those lives.

See also **MacGregor, Geddes.**

Memory, suppressed. This is any memory that has not been allowed to enter the conscious mind, but has been pushed into the subconscious mind. Such suppression is usually due to some traumatic event associated with the memory which would be too painful or disturbing to the conscious mind to acknowledge. Some psychologists believe that such suppressed memories in the form of **screen memories** can account for at least some of what are otherwise considered memories of a past life.

See also **Blocked regression.**

Mental body *see* **Astral body; Causal body; Etheric body; Soul and spirit levels, Theosophical**

Mental plane. In **Theosophy** and related systems this is one of the six spiritual planes of existence; it is the next highest after the **astral plane**. The experience of the **soul**, in its mental body form, on the mental plane is unlike the experience of the astral body on the astral plane because the soul has left behind every negative or stressful aspect of consciousness, after which it will work out all of its positive memories in the mental plane. This, according to Theosophy, is the reason why most people have no personal memories remaining to be passed on into the next embodiment.

The mental plane can be considered as offering a more heavenly experience than the astral plane and most souls remain here longer than in either the earthly physical or astral planes. This mental plane is of great significance because it is here that the **ego** or true individuality is established, which retains a permanency until that future time in which it can be reunited with the divine primordial. This view of the mental plane is taken from *A Textbook of Theosophy* by C. W. Leadbeater. It differs in some minor ways from the version suggested by **Helena Blavatsky**, in that it incorporates the views of **Annie Besant**.

See also **Individuality and rebirth; Karma and justice; Memories, reasons for loss of past life; Second death; Soul and spirit levels, Theosophical; Planes of existence, names of.**

Mental retardation. According to such figures as Alice A. Bailey, a soul that had in a past life become morally degenerate, if reborn into a life of mental retardation could avoid any further retribution in the next life or lives. This, of course, is a prime example of **blaming the victim**.

Merit, transfer of. In **Hinduism, Mahayana Buddhism**, and **Vajrayana Buddhism** there is the belief that the karmic merit accumulated by one entity can be transferred to another entity. For example, in Hinduism the merit produced by the proper performance of certain sacred rituals by a son can help the deceased parent(s) gain a better rebirth. Similarly, in Mahayana Buddhism the offering of alms to monks is believed to produce sufficient merit that can be used to redeem a parent from **hell** or the **hungry ghost** realm. It is also a Mahayana teaching that those beings who, after eons of having spiritually perfected themselves and become ***bodhisattvas*** or Buddhas have accumulated so much surplus karmic merit that they can transfer this to their worshippers for better rebirths.

The status of merit transference in **Theravada Buddhism** is somewhat controversial. Some texts seem to deny it while other texts affirm it. In **Jainism** it is most clearly denied.

See also **Amitabha Buddha; Karma versus grace; Pure-Land or Blissful Land Buddhism.**

Mesoamerica *see* **Aztec; Maya.**

Mesopotamia (Iraq). This area included the ancient cultures of Sumer, Babylonia, and Assyria. There is no evidence of any belief in reincarnation in this region until two or more centuries after the Greek conquest of the area in the 4th century BCE and the later development of **Manichaeism**.

See also **Greeks and reincarnation; Yarsanism; Yazidis; Forty; Genesis; Gods, cyclically dying and rising; Kanthaeans.**

Messiah. According to some Kabbalic traditions the Messiah will be the reincarnation of the biblical King David.

See *also* **Ahmadiyya; Besant, Annie; Christianity and reincarnation; Essenes; Frank, Jacob; Harrowing of Hell; Jesus; Judgment of the Dead; Kabbalah; Koresh, David; Leadbeater,** Charles Webster; Mark-Age, Inc; Mark, Gospel of; Melchizedek; New Testament and reincarnation; Old Testament and the afterlife; Paul of Tarsus; Rebirth and cyclical time; Steiner, Rudolf; Zoroastrianism.

Metagenetics. This is the idea that genetically related people share spiritual links that can not be shared by those who are genetically unrelated. One or more Nordic deity oriented **Neo-pagan religions** advocate a metagenetic view. This has lead to accusations that their followers are disguised Neo-Nazi sympathizers. Clearly, expressed in the wrong context metagenetics can be a dangerously misunderstood belief. Metagenetics is also a part of the reincarnation theory of the **Rastafarians**.

See also **Jewish Holocaust; Kabbalah; Karma, racial; Rebirth, ethnic.**

Metempsychosis. The term is derived from the Greek, meaning to animate over again the **soul**, or the changing (meta-) of the soul (psyche). Alternative names for this term are ***palingenesis***, rebirth, reincarnation, and **transmigration** and with the exception of the first of these, all are more commonly used today than metempsychosis. Metempsychosis is actually somewhat of an inaccurate term because it implies changing souls rather than bodies. For this reason the alternative term of ***metensomatosis*** (changing of bodies) has been proposed, but this is almost never found in modern writings. Even rarer is the term *metacosmesis*. Metempsychosis generally shares with transmigration the idea of cross species reincarnation and as such is rejected by most pro-reincarnationist Westerners.

Although some older English translations of Buddhist literature used the term metempsychosis it is avoided today for the same reason transmigration is because, from a Buddhist view point, both terms have the same connotation of a permanent and autonomous soul (*atman*) entering a new body. This leaves "rebirth" as the most acceptable English term for translating Buddhist material.

In this encyclopedia the term metempsychosis is primarily used when referring to the issue of multiple embodied lives in the Greco-Roman, early Christian, and **Renaissance** periods.

See also ***Anatman***; Animals and rebirth, non–Western view; Animals and rebirth, Western view; Animals, Domestic; *Ensomatosis*; Greeks and reincarnation; Introduction; *Kyklos Genesion*; Ontological leap or ontological discontinuity; Origin or Origenes Adamanthus; Orphism; Rebirth, cross-species; Rebirth, non-backsliding; Theophilus.

Metempsychosis, or the Transmigration of Souls, Systematically Considered, and Rescued from

Obloquy and Contempt by the Joint Authority of Reason and Revelation; the Whole Comprehending a Complete Body of Animation, Scientifically Investigated and Impartially Revised, by the late Lord (the name has been deleted here), in the Probationary Character of a Post-Horse. This ambitious title is found on a fifty-four page book published in 1781 in London by an unknown author. In the introduction to the book it states, "The succeeding pages furnish authentic proof in favor of a system long since exploded with derision. The doctrines it inculcates will be exposed to the objections of the learned, perhaps to the contempt of the ignorant. The writer will endeavor to obviate the former with all the assiduity he is master of; the latter must, in consequence remain unnoticed."

Considering the renewed interest in reincarnation in seventeenth century England, as measured by the number of books on the subject published there at the time, it is somewhat surprising that the above book was one of only a few books on metempsychosis or transmigration published in the 18th century. It was not until the 19th century that a renewed interest in the subject occurred.

See also **Seventeenth century renewed interest in rebirth.**

Metensomatosis. This Greek derived term means "Changing of Bodies" and is not only a more accurate term than **metempsychosis** or **transmigration**, but it is the term most often used in ancient Greco-Roman and early Christian sources. For reasons that are not too well understood the term *metensomatosis* fell out of favor and is almost never used in modern writings. It is because of the modern rarity of this word that in this encyclopedia the less rare metempsychosis is substituted for it when referring to the issue of multiple embodiments or multiple embodied lives in the Greco-Roman to **Renaissance** period.

Michael (Hebrew: Who is like God) **(1)**. In traditional Christianity the archangel Michael acts as a *psychopomp*, or carrier of souls to the afterlife state. In fact, the gospel song "Michael Row the Boat to Shore" suggests that he replaced the classical Greek underworld figure Charon, in whose boat the dead were rowed across the river Styx.

See also **Babbitt, Elwood; Work of Mercy.**

Michael (2). This is the channeled entity of *Michael's Teachings* (1979). Contact with this entity was first reported in 1970 when Jessica and Walter Lansing (pseudonyms), both of whom had a long interest in the paranormal and parapsychology, began using the **Ouija Board**. The collective entity that manifested called itself Michael and at some point during its channeling it explained that each individual **soul** is actually part of a larger body or **group soul** of approximately a thousand members. Each individual member enters into the physical plane (is reincarnated) as many times as is necessary to experience all aspects of life and to achieve full human understanding. At the end of a cycle of such reincarnations all members of the group reunite, on what it called the causal plane, in order to combine their knowledge, skills, and wisdom as had the Michael group. Such a collective of souls then acquires lucidity and benevolent karma by ministering to those still on the physical plane of existence. Michael, itself, is a group soul of 1,050 such former human souls. The teachings of Michael have been documented by Chelsea Quinn Yarbro, a popular writer of occult fiction.

See also **Akashic Record; Angels and reincarnation; Babbitt, Elwood; Causal body; Franklin, Benjamin (2); Gabriel; Hilarion; Lazaris; Ra; Ramtha; Ryerson, Kevin; Saint Germain; Seth; Stygian sexuality; Wilcock, David.**

Middle Way or **Middle Path** (S/P: *Madhyamapratipad/Majjhima-patipada*). This is one of the most important terms in Buddhism, since it is believed that only by following such a path is a person capable of gaining liberation from *samsara* (the continued cycle of birth and death). The use of middle in this term signifies an avoidance of extremes while seeking liberation. Actually this avoidance entails three pairs of extremes. The first pair is the extremes of **hedonism** (*kama-sukkha-alikanu-yoga*) and extreme **asceticism** or self-mortification (*attakilamathaanu-yoga*); the second pair is **accidentalism** (*ahetu-apachaya-vada*) and theistic **determinism** (*ishvaranimmaana-vada*) and past-action determinism (*purvaketa-vada* or *purvekatahetu*); and the third pair is **annihilationism** (*uccheda-vada*) and **eternalism** (*sasvata-/sassata-vada*). Sometimes the term middle path is assigned to what is more commonly and more correctly called the Eight-fold Path, which are right views, right intentions, right speech, right action, right livelihood, right effort, right mindfulness, and right concentration.

Midnight. According to **Manly P. Hall,** in his *The Secret Teachings of All Ages* (1928) it was believed in the ancient Greek Eleusian Mystery Cult that at midnight the invisible (spirit) world closed to the terrestrial world and that the souls to be reborn had to slip into their new bodily forms just before the midnight hour.

Milinda Panha (Pali: Question of Milinda). This is a text that reports to be a series of questions asked by a king of a Buddhist monk. The king was Milinda, the mid 2nd century BCE, Hellenized (Greek) ruler of Bactria (modern Pakistan-Afghanistan), whose name in Greek was Menander. The monk was the very learned *Thera* (monk-elder) Nagasena. The whole purpose of the dialog was to clarify certain puzzling aspect of Buddhist doctrine. Among the most important of these doctrines was how it was possible to have rebirth without a soul (*atman*). Nagasena uses a variety of metaphors and similes to justify this Buddhist teaching of **anatman** (soullessness), as well as other controversial elements of Buddhist teachings. The *Milinda Panha,* which was not actually written down until about 100 BCE, is today an extra-canonical text of **Theravada Buddhism.**

See also **Ashoka, King; Rebirth in Buddhism.**

Milky Way. To the ancient Greco-Romans this celestial band of presumably unmoving stars, or a place just beyond this band was regarded as a realm that souls would ascend to at their final liberation from further bodily rebirth. This same belief was revived in more recent times by some Spiritualists.

See also **Heracleides of Ponticus;** *Ogdoad*; **Planetary descent and ascent of the soul; Poimandres;** *Sephiroth*; **Summerland.**

Millennialism (also Millenarianism). In Christian resurrectional belief this is the idea that a thousand-year period (Latin: millennium; Greek: Chiliasm) of the Kingdom of Heaven will be established either immediately before (pre-millennialism) or immediately after (post-millennialism) the second coming (*Parousia*) of Christ.

In the case of "pre-millennialism," as found at **Revelation of John** 20:1–21:5, the world will experience extraordinary tribulations and the appearance of the Anti-Christ (Satan). This tribulation will call forth the true Christ to defeat Satan, who will be chained up. The loyal Christian, and perhaps other "redeemable," dead will be resurrected to participate in the millennium. At the end of this time Satan will be let loose, the forces of evil will again challenge the forces of good, the "unredeemable" dead will resurrect, and the final judgment of the living and dead will occur in which Satan and his unredeemable following will be consigned forever to eternal punishment.

In the case of "post–Millennialism" the millennium will precede the *Parousia* which will be followed by a single, or undivided, great battle between good and evil as well as a general resurrection of all the dead and the final judgment. In 1944 post-millennialism was declared unorthodox by the Roman Catholic Church; but continues to be advocated by some Protestant groups.

While Christian millennialism may seem in opposition to any form of reincarnation, some Christian supporters of reincarnation believe that it is possible to harmonize them. In this harmonized version people will remain in the cycle of rebirth "only" until a future point when the general resurrection, followed by the final judgment, will occur.

See also **Judgment of the Dead; Peter, 1st and 2nd; Resurrection, bodily; Resurrection or reincarnation.**

Mind. In psychology mind or consciousness can generally be defined as awareness; however, in some religious views mind or consciousness are each considered either identical to, or a function of, the **soul** or **spirit**. Making mind, soul, and spirit synonymous with one another can lead to considerable confusion. To avoid this it is best to regard mind and consciousness as religiously neutral terms, while soul and spirit should be seen as exclusive religious terms.

The mind is most consistently thought of as that which contains memories. Even as far back as Old English the ancestor of the term mind meant memory, to remember or to warn. That it had the same meaning even farther back is demonstrated by the Sanskrit cognate *manas*, which also means the mind. The word mind also commonly refers to the intellect and reason. In dualistic systems of thought it can be placed in opposition to the body, but rarely to the extent that the soul or spirit is often placed in opposition to the body.

In the West in the late 17th century there began a gradually greater understanding of the functions of the brain, and with this a progressive distinguishing of the mind from such metaphysical concepts as the soul and spirit. The issue of mind as the real essence of the individual can be traced back at least as far as **Rene Descartes** (1596–1650) and his famous formula of "I think, therefore, I am" (*Cogito, ergo sum*). In the following century the rise of capitalism for the first time allowed the more materialistically viewed mind, under the term "psyche," to take the place of the soul as the repository of memory and, hence, as the basis of the real self.

There is, of course, a certain humorous incongruity in applying a word that has the Greek root *psyche* (soul) to mean something that pertains to the mind as a non-metaphysical factor. Nonetheless, it was the early 20th century science of the *psyche* (psychology), especially in the form of depth psychology, that more than anything else encouraged replacing the soul with the mind. It was furthermore with such non-supernatural concepts as the **id, ego**, and **superego**, libido (sexual desire), *thanatos* (death wish), and the Electra/Oedipus (child and parent or God conflict) complex of Freudianism that revolutionized our perception of selfhood as mind-hood. The success of depth psychology in replacing certain religious views, however, must be partially credited to the fact that depth psychology itself adopted mythic, even semi-religious, vocabularies, doctrines, and attitudes. This can best be understood in that, at least for the earliest depth psychology advocates, it seemed justified that if the mind took the place of the soul, then the psychiatrist could take the place of the priest. This replacement of the specialist of the soul by the specialist of the mind was also evident in Jungian depth psychology, which actually was more sympathetic to religion than was Freudianism.

Even before depth psychology traded in the word soul for mind, a number of late 19th century teachers and groups offering new esoteric doctrines were active in this trade; a major leader in this effort was **Theosophy**.

Replacing the term soul with the supposedly less metaphysical term mind has not been universally accepted. Many Western philosophers and psychologists have concluded that the term mind is actually no less metaphysical and possibly no more real than the term soul. These philosophers and psychologists have regarded both terms as simply similes we have created for behavior that we are at present unable to explain in more concretely scientific ways. In support of their opposition to regarding mind as more scientific than soul these opponents can easily point to the fact that in a number of metaphysical systems consciousness, as the Divine Mind, is considered synonymous for Universal Soul, spirit, or God. Furthermore, any attempt to replace the soul with the mind as the object of rebirth does not, in the least, make rebirth a more scientific concept.

See also **Body-brain (mind) dependency; Body-soul dualism; *Chitta*; Ego; Electra/Oedipus Complex and rebirth; Guenon, Rene; *Skandha*; Soul; Soul and spirit levels, Theosophical; Willis, Thomas; Vijnanavada School of Buddhism.**

Mind (soul)-body relationship *see* **Body-soul dualism.**

Mind, theory of. The "theory of mind" is the term used to mean that one individual can infer the perceptions and motivations of another individual. There is considerable controversy as to how much evidence there is of "theory of mind" in non-human species. Great apes and porpoises, and sometimes elephants, are thought to have this ability to some degree; however, it is this unquestionable ability on the part of human beings that is often used to distinguish humans from other animals.

When it comes to the issue of reincarnation and animals, the logical approach would seem to be that to show that if any animal has an individual versus just a collective soul, then that animal should first be able to exhibit "theory of mind."

See also **Animals and rebirth, non–Western view; Animals and rebirth, Western view; Animals, domesticated; Soul, collective; Soul, psychology of.**

Mindstream Church of Universal Love. The Church began in 1979 with a charter from the Universal Life Church of Modesto, California; however, it has no set doctrine. Its prime mission is to assist members in discovering their own path in life. This assistance is through classes, individual sessions on dream study, development of psychic skills, meditation, spiritual healing, relaxation, goal setting, and reincarnational age regression that is done without hypnosis.

Minimalist Reincarnation Hypothesis. This hypothesis is found in Robert Almeder's essay *A Critic of Arguments Offered Against Reincarnation* (1997). Almeder believes that there is something essential to some human personalities, which we can not plausibly construe solely in terms of brain states, and which survives after biological death in some manner. Almeder further states that this essential trait is the repository of certain memories and dispositional factors and that after some time this essential trait, by some mechanism, comes to reside in other human bodies either some time during the gestation period, at birth, or shortly after birth. Also, Almeder says that this minimalist hypothesis does not commit anyone to know why or how this re-embodiment occurs, or for how long, or for what end. He also does not speculate on any so-called **interim period**, how frequently reincarnation occurs, or whether reincarnation occurs for all persons, after every death. Finally, the minimalist hypothesis does not require any commitment to a belief in karma. In short, the minimalist reincarnation hypothesis just says that "at least some human personalities reincarnate."

One thing Almeder does not mention is that his hypothesis could as easily be applied to **possession** as it could to reincarnation. The rest of *A Critic of Arguments Offered Against Reincarnation* offers a counter argument to the scathing and often sarcastic criticism of reincarnation by **Paul Edwards**, and includes a defense of the research of **Ian Stevenson**.

Minimal rebirth *see* **Karma with minimal rebirth.**

Mirror *see* **Emma-o; Hell, the Chinese; Scrying; Yama.**

Mithraism. This was a religion developed during the latter part of the Roman Empire and was based on the worship of the Persian (Iranian) sun god Mithra. It was especially popular with members of the Roman army. For a short time, it was even the more or less the official state religion under the emperor Aurelian (died 275 CE). Mithraism accepted the **Neoplatonic** concept of **metempsychosis** and the seven stage **planetary descent and ascent of the soul**; the latter were associated with the seven Mithraic levels of mystical initiation.

See also **Celestial gates; Cult of Angels; Julian, Flavius Claudius; Romans; Seven rungs of the heavenly ladder; Theophilus.**

Mnemosyne (Greek: memory). This was a female titan goddess who was believed to be the mother of the nine Muses (goddesses of the arts) by Zeus. A river or lake named for Mnemosyne was said to flow through **Hades**, the drinking from which would allow the soul to retain the memories of its previous life. Directly opposite this river was the river **Lethe**, the drinking from which would cause the soul to forget all memory of its past life.

Moksha, also **Mukta** or *Mukti* (S: Released). This term signifies that a person has been released from further rebirth. When used in **Hinduism** it means that the person will be united in some way with God (**Brahman**) at death. When used in Buddhism it is the equivalent of **nirvana** and *parinirvana.*

Moksha as an element of the word *mokkhassa maggam* means the way to full liberation, and as such it is considered far superior to the *saggassa maggam* which is merely the way to **heaven**.

See also *Jivanmukta; Kaivalya; Vaikuntha.*

Moltke, Helmuth Graf von (1848–1916). This Prussian Field Marshall and military genius not only had a great interest in the occult, but in particular he was interested in finding the Holy Grail, which some believed had been brought to Niedermunster, Germany, in the 9th century. His part in this belief was related to his conviction that he was the reincarnation of the 9th century sainted Pope Nicholas the Great, whose Papal reign was 858–867. After Moltke's death his spirit is said to have kept up a periodic communication with his wife Eliza von Moltke; through these communications a number of other individual's in the Field Marshall's life were credited with past lives. For example, Moltke's even more famous uncle, also named Helmuth von Moltke (1800–1891), was said to be the reincarnation of Pope Leo IV (r. 847–855); General Ludendoff (1865–1937) was once Pope John VIII (r.1003–1009), General von Schlieffen (1833–1913) was once Pope Benedict II (r. 684–685), and Kaiser Wilhelm II (1859–1941) was previously the Bishop of Rothard, the Fox of Soisson (9th century). Moltke, the nephew, was an acquaintance of **Rudolf Steiner**.

See also **Himmler, Heinrich; Hitler, Adolf.**

Monad. This term means "the one" or "the alone" and originated with the philosopher Gottfried Wilhelm Leibniz (1646–1716) who used it to describe an infinitesimal psychophysical entity which comprised ultimate reality. While all *monads* were unique and indestructible they were only distinguished from each other by their differing degrees of consciousness. Later uses of the term *monad* equated it with a part or aspect of the **soul**. **Theosophy**, in particular, used the term to mean either the unified triad of *Atma-Buddhi-Manas*, or just the *dyad* of *Atma-Buddhi*. In some esoteric and occult systems

Monism (Greek mono: one). This is the metaphysical concept that all of reality is ultimately one indivisible phenomenon. All that we perceive as separate and distinct is in the final analysis due to our misperceptions.

A major problem with most kinds of monism, especially Hindu monism, is that it leaves no "logical" place for either rebirth or karma except as an illusory factor. It is for this reason that in the chapter on karma in *Advaita Vedanta: a Philosophical Reconstruction* (1969), by Eliot Deutsch, the author notes that the necessity of karma is not logically implied by the metaphysical principles of *advaita* (non-dual), in which **Brahman** is the sole reality; hence, karma must have the logical status of a convenient fiction or **noble lie**. Although in theory the Mahayana Buddhist non-dualist position allows more room for both rebirth and karma, it must be noted that the pluralism of **Theravada Buddhism** is on even more secure grounds for these allowances.

See also **Body-soul dualism; Dualism; Pantheism and panentheism.**

Montgomery, Ruth Shick (1912–2001). This author has written some ten popular books relating to **automatic writing** (typing), **lost continents, spiritualism, walk-ins**, and reincarnation.

Moody, Raymond A. Jr. (1944–). Dr. Moody has written extensively on the subject of the afterlife, including reincarnation, as in his books *Life After Life* (1976) and *Coming Back: A Psychiatrist Explores Past Life Journeys* (1991). Moody is also well known for his research center, the Theater of the Mind, in which he has revived the ancient Greek practice of *psychomanteum*. For the ancients this meant looking into a pool or pan of water (hydromancy) in order to gain a vision of, or communication with, the deceased. In Dr. Moody's updated version the client, seeking to recall a past life, stares into a mirror (catoptromancy or enoptromancy) which is actually a form of **scrying**.

Moon. Because of the moon's waxing and waning cycles it has long been a common symbol in many traditions for the afterlife, and especially for rebirth.

Among the ancient Greeks the moon was regarded as one of the possible locations of the paradise called the Isles of the Blessed or the Elysium Fields (paradise for the worthy dead). Also, in certain esoteric traditions **purgatory**, especially that associated with the Indo-Buddhist *kama-loka* (world of desire), is considered to be located on the moon.

In very late **Vedic Religion** the dead were said to follow either of two paths. The souls of those who had performed perfectly the proper Vedic sacrifices while alive ascend along the solar path (*suryamarga*) never to return to earth. The souls of those who failed in their sacrificial duties went along the lunar path (*chandramarga*) to wait on the moon until time for their reincarnation on earth.

In present day Indian astrology the points at which the moon's orbit intersects with the ecliptic, called northern node and southern node, have an important reincarnation function. The northern node of the moon called *Rahu* (Dragon's head) is commonly accepted as an indicator of the individual's fate in a specific life, while the southern node or *Kethu* (Dragon's tail) is acknowledged as an indicator of an individual's unresolved karmic residue of earlier lives, most especially any unlearned lessons the individual failed to learn from one life to another. This association of the lunar nodes with fate and karma may have to do with the fact that the nodal axis is the point at which eclipses happened, and in ancient times eclipses were thought to signify dramatic events to come.

Beredene Jocelyn, in her book *Citizens of the Cosmos* (1981), states that souls upon descending back to earth for rebirth will become males if they approach at the new moon phase, which is when most of the light reflected from the moon is turned away from earth towards the outer universe. Those souls that approach at the full moon phase will become females.

The three nights in which the moon is dark (invisible), due to its location directly between the earth and sun, has also been thought important in some reincarnation traditions in that they consider these three days (nights) to be the **interim period** between death and rebirth. Some forms of modern **Theosophy** have also adopted the idea that the **soul** journeys to the moon as its first stop during the interim period between death and rebirth. In the Kabbalic magic tradition, the archangel **Gabriel**, who is assigned to ruler over the moon, is regarded as the final guide of the soul to its next rebirth.

See also **Angels and reincarnation; Astrology and rebirth; Celestial gates; Eighth sphere; Gender issue of the soul; Greek afterlife, the ancient; Immortality;** *Pritiloka*; **Rebirth, analogies from nature.**

Moore, Marcia (1928–1979). Besides *Reincarnation: Key to Immortality* (1968), this author has written several other books on the subject of past lives. However, what is of most interest in her approach to reincarnation is the suggestion, in *Journey into the Bright World* (1978), that the anesthetic agent "ketamine hydrochloride" can be used to recall past life memories. Moore mysteriously vanished from her home in 1979 and it was not until two years later that her lower jaw alone was found in a local forest and identified through dental records. The cause of death is not known.

See also **Body-brain (mind) dependency.**

Moral perfection *see* **Rebirth and moral perfection; Resurrection or reincarnation;** *Theosis*.

More, Henry (1614–1687). Although the essay *The Immortality of the Soul* (1659) by this English philosopher was primarily concerned with proving the **soul's existence prior to embodiment** he did deal with the issue of reincarnation. While rejecting both regressive and progressive transmigration, Moore was willing to accept lateral multiple lives as a real possibility.

See also **Transmigration, lateral; Transmigration, progressive; Transmigration, regressive.**

Morganwg, Iolo (1747–1826). This was the pen name of Edward Williams and meant Iolo of Glamorgan, Glamorgan being William's birth place. Morganwg was a major figure in the revival of the Welsh bardic tradition and of the **druids**. According to Morganwg, the ancients believed that all souls passed through an evolutionary process that started with the mineral world, which he called the Cauldron of *Annwn*. From here souls were born into the first world or circle of existence called *Abred*. This was the common world of plants and animals, including humans. From here enlightened human souls could reincarnate into the second world, or circle of existence, called *Gwynfydd*. This is the realm of angels and was the intended ultimate goal of mankind. In this angelic world souls could remember all of their past lives and incarnate into any form of life they wished. The third world or circle of existence was called *Ceugant* and was the exclusive realm of the divine infinity.

A modified version of Morganwg's scheme was that all souls were once in *Gwynfydd*, but fell into the mineral world because of their prideful attempt to enter *Ceugant*. This is a modified version of the **fall of the souls.**

See also **Evolutionary transmigration of souls.**

Mormonism. Because Mormonism teaches the **soul's existence prior to embodiment** it is sometimes mistakenly believed that this highly Freemasonic and Kabbalic influenced form of esoteric Christianity teaches reincarnation; but it does not. In fact, orthodox Mormonism regards the teaching of reincarnation with even more repugnance than does more orthodox Christianity. Nonetheless, there seems to be some indirect evidence that Joseph Smith (1805–1844), the scrying, and possibly sciomancing, founder of Mormonism may have at one time speculated on the belief in reincarnation. This may have been encouraged by a mistaken belief that the Egyptians taught reincarnation.

While the mainstream Latter Day Saints (LDS) of Salt Lake City, Utah, and even most splinter Mormon groups reject reincarnation, at least one splinter group, The True and Living Church of Jesus Christ of Saints of the Last Days (TLC) located in Manti, Utah accepts reincarnation. This church teaches about "multiple mortal probations (MMPs)," which are said to be similar to Eastern reincarnation concepts; however, in the TLC's multiple mortal probations, the person always returns with the same gender and personality. Also, the more righteous a person is the fewer the probations (lives) he or she will have to experience.

See also **Aquarian Foundation; Christianity, esoteric; Egypt; Gender issue of the soul; Lost continents and reincarnation; Sciomancy.**

Morning Star *see* **Lucifer; Yeats, William Butler.**

Morse, J.J. (1848–1919). This communications famous trance medium declared that he had received several spirit that stated that "reincarnation was nonsense."

See also **Davis, Andrew Jackson; Spiritualism; Wickland, Carl A.**

Moses, the Old Testament prophet. According to both the *Zohar* and the Kabbalic thinking of the school of **Isaac Luria**, Moses was the reincarnation of the patriarch Noah due to the fact that Noah, as the second father of humanity, had failed to guide his generation to repentance.

See also **Deuteronomy 5:2–3; Grant, Joan Marshall; I Am Movement; Jesus; Kabbalah; Matthew, Gospel of; New Testament and reincarnation; Numenius of Apamea; Old Testament; Philo Judaeus or Philo of Alexandria; Psalms; Resurrection of Jesus; Serpent.**

Mother, mule, and son. This grouping of terms made up a little known criticism of **metempsychosis** by some early Christians. They suggested that if a human **soul** could return as an animal then it was theoretically possible for a mother to be reborn as a mule which her son might some day ride. This idea then was ridiculed as violating the biblical commandment to honor one's parents.

See also **Child as its own reborn father or mother.**

Mount Shasta. This volcanic mountain some 14,162 feet high in northern California has been linked to the subject of reincarnation through such works as *A Dweller on Two Planets* (1894) by Frederick Oliver; *Lemuria: The Lost Continent of the Pacific* (1931) by W.S. Cerve and James Ward; and *Unveiled Mysteries* (1934) by Guy Ballard, the founder of the **I Am Movement**. The mountain's mysteriousness was further reinforced by E. L. Larkin (d. 1924), who ran the Mount Lowe Observatory and claimed to see strange lighting effects coming from the mountain.

See also **Cayce, Edgar; Phylos the Tibetan; Saint Germain; Rosicrucians.**

Movement of Spiritual Inner Awareness. Founded in 1971 by the ex–Mormon John-Roger Hinkins (1934–), the Movement's teachings derive mainly from Buddhism, Hinduism, and particularly the Sant Mat (Radhasoami) tradition of **Sikhism**. The Movement emphasizes gaining the assistance of Mystical Traveler Consciousness which is done through initiation and meditating on the mantra "Hu." With the assistance of this Consciousness and taking responsibility for one's own karma the individual can be liberated from the cycle of birth and death.

Muhammad Ahmad (1834?–1885). In Islam it is believed that in the future there will come a divinely sent man (Arabic: al-*Mahdi*, the Guided One) to purify Islam and the world prior to the Last Judgment. Throughout Islamic history there have been a number of individuals who have claimed to be *al-Mahdi*, but perhaps the most famous of these was Muhammad Ahmad, from the then Anglo-Egyptian Sudan.

The full name of this Sudanese messianic leader was Muhammad Ahmad ibn Sayyid 'Abd Allah. A charismatic figure and founder of his own dervish order (religious fraternity), Muhammad Ahmad declared a holy war (*jihad*) against the British and their Egyptian allies and succeeded in temporarily driving both out of the country. Although he claimed to be descended from the prophet Muhammad, Ahmad did not object to being also considered the reincarnation of the Prophet.

See also **Ahmadiyya; Islam; Judgment of the Dead.**

Mula (S/P: Root). In Buddhism there are said to be three great negative or unskillful (S/P: *akushala/*

akusala) root factors that keep entities trapped in the round of birth and death (*samsara*). These are sexuality (*kama*) or lust (*raga*), hatred (*dvesa/dosa*), and ignorance (*avidya/avijja*). Sometimes the word greed (*lobha*) or thirst (*trishna/tanha*) replaces lust and the word delusion (*moha*) replaces ignorance in this triple root concept. At the same time there are the three positive or skillful (*kushala/kusala*) or opposite root factors that aid in liberating beings from samsara. These are contented sexual abstinence (*brahmacharya/brahmachariya*), friendliness (*maitri/metta*) or charity (*alobha* or *dana*), and knowledge (*vidya/vijja*) or right apprehension (*amoha*). The term thirst (*trishna/tanha*) is particularly important in Buddhism because in the absence of a soul (*atman*) to pass from one life to the next what really causes rebirth is the thirst for being or existing.

See also ***Anatman***; **Brahman; Buddhist stages of liberation; Schopenhauer, Arthur.**

Mu-lian, The Story of. This popular Chinese story tells of a boy that was sent by his poor parents to a monastery where he worked diligently to become a monk. When he grew up he went to visit his parents only to find that his father had died and his mother had abandoned the Buddha's teaching and had become very hard-hearted and cruel. She was unkind to her servants, animals, and had taken to meat eating. Mu-lian tried to reform her, but to no avail. When the mother died she went to one of the lowest hells. Mu-lian realizing her condition wished to save her and, being a devoted monk, he gained the assistance of **heaven** to do so. After many trials during his journey through the various levels of **hell** Mu-lian finally found the spirit of his mother. However, his mother's sins had been so great that even heaven could not freely absolve her of them. Instead, Mu-lian was told to return to the world and acquire enough merit to pay for his mother's redemption. This he did and finally his mother was released to be reborn again in the world. This story is obviously one of great filial piety, and as such, it serves to reinforce belief in that virtue in Chinese society.

See also **Chinese religion and reincarnation.**

Muller, Catherine Elise (1861–1929). This French medium was one of the earliest to claim not only past lives but an ability to carry on inter-planetary communications. She was studied by the early multiple-personality researcher and French physiologist Theodore Flournoy. Muller claimed to have previously lived over 500 years, from life as the daughter of an Arab Sheik to, more recently, as Marie Antoinette. Furthermore, Muller claimed to be in communication with beings on Mars and, to even speak their language. Not surprisingly, an analysis of her Martian speech turned out to be characterized as a strange vocabulary with a very French grammar. Flournoy published his study on Muller, using the pseudonym Helene Smith for her, in his book *From India to the Planet Mars: A Study of a Case of Somnambulism with Glossolalia* (1963).

See also **Cleopatra Syndrome; Glossolalia; GloLanguage inconsistency; Planets, other.**

Multiple personalities. This describes a form of mental illness in which two or more seemingly distinct personalities are said to share the same body. Over the centuries two main theories have been given for this phenomenon. The first, and oldest, theory is that it is a case of **possession** by a malevolent spirit. While most people in the modern industrialized world have ceased to believe in this possibility, the present day belief in channeling could be considered a modern variation of such possession. In this case, however, the possession is generally thought to be for the good of the recipient and society at large.

The second, and more modern, theory is that a split or multiple personality disorder (MPD) is a type of schizophrenia in which the normally integrated personality fragments into two or more personalities, each which appear to be integrated personalities of their own, and which are relatively independent of one another. It has been thought that the reason for this split is to eliminate unwanted or painful memories from the original personality. This is why the original personality is usually unaware of the off splits. In rare cases an individual has been known to manifest more than twenty such personalities.

Both the old possession theory and the modern MPD theory have been used to try to explain past life recalls; however, since the possession theory is dealt with under the entries **attached entities** and **possession**, only the MPD theory will be deal with here.

A careful comparison of MPD with past life recall shows that there are at least four reasons for discounting past life recall as a form of MPD. First, many of today's psychiatrists deny the validity of MPD as a patient generated disorder. It has been suspected, due to some clinical evidence, that MPDs arise, not before therapy, but during therapy as a by product of a patient's fantasies that have been unintentionally encouraged by suggestions from the therapist.

Second, all the so-called separate personalities in MPD are contemporary with one another; whereas, the presumed past life personalities form a non-contemporary past timeline series. This means that the past and present personalities are not in competition with each other and so do not interfere with the present mental health of the present personality. This is in great contrast to MPDs where the various split personalities can cause dangerous interference with one another.

Third, when comparing past life recall with MPD there is usually no highly emotional or deep-seated traumatic element associated with the past life recall that would trigger the kind of mental conflict found in MPD. An exception to this could be in the case of some past life recall that is related to **screen memories.**

Fourth, in most cases, past life recall is manifested by very young children who have not had enough time to develop a MPD.

It should also be noted that there is growing evidence to suggest that even the most normal of individuals have benign multiple personality capacities. Unless exaggerated beyond a tolerable level, when manifested, these are not taken too seriously.

For an early investigation into the relationship of multiple personalities and past lives there are two papers found in *Hypnosis At Its Bicentennial: Selected Papers*, edited by Fred H. Frankel (1978). One is by Reima Kampman and Reijo Hirvenoja and the other by Milton V. Kline.

See also **Bridey Murphy case; Children remembering past lives; Christos** (anointing) **technique; Dissociation; Facial blank; Fantasy versus past life regression; Past life regression and suggestibility; Past life therapy; Possession; Psychosomatic illnesses; Retroactive inhibition.**

Mumukshatwa (S). This term means the desire for liberation from the cycle of birth and death (reincarnation).

Mummy, The. In many versions of *The Mummy* movies reincarnation has been part of the plot. The first, among the more noted ones, is *The Mummy* (1932, Universal) in which the female character, Anck-es-en-Amon, has had many lives over a period of four thousand years and now is embodied as the English woman Helen Grosvenor. As movie timing would have it, Helen just happens to be in **Egypt** when her ancient love, the mummy Imhotep, is mistakenly resuscitated as Ardath Bey. Between 1940 and 1945 Universal produced a series of four more mummy movies, each more preposterous than the other. In these, the mummy's name has changed to Kharis and his former love is Ananka.

The Mexican film industry produced its own series of mummy (*momia*)-past life regression movies starting with the *Aztec Mummy vs. the Robot* (*La Momia Azteka Contra el Robot Humano*, 1958, Cinematografica Calderon S.A*)*. Here the mummy is an ancient Aztec warrior, Popoca, and his love is the princess Zochi, reincarnated as Flora, the wife of a past life regression psychiatrist.

British cinema contributed to the mummy scene on several occasions, but in the 1971 *Blood from the Mummy's Tomb (EMI Films)*, an archeologist disturbs the tomb of an ancient Egyptian queen, while at the very same moment, thousand's of miles away, the archeologist's wife is giving birth to their daughter. This perfect timing allows the queen's soul to be reborn in (or take possession of) the daughter's body and the mayhem begins.

In the Canadian *The Mummy Lives!* (1993, Global) Kia, the ancient concubine of the god Zoth has reincarnated in modern times only to become the object, not of love, but lust of her ancient violator Azira, a resuscitated mummy.

In the 1999 Trimark Pictures mummy movie, *The Eternal*, the soul of a Druid witch, whose body has been preserved as an Irish bog-mummy, is reincarnated as a woman who has to struggle against her former evil self and her present good self.

There is also the 2001 *The Mummy Returns* (Alphaville Films) in which there are two modern day reincarnations; the first is of the daughter of the Pharaoh Seti I and the second is the Pharaoh's adulterous wife who was had him murdered by her priest lover, Imhotep. It is Imhotep who becomes the resuscitated mummy.

See also **Hollywood and reincarnation; Steiner, Rudolf.**

Myers, E.W.H. (1843–1901). This British classicist was the co-founder of the (British) **Society for Psychical Research**. According to at least one Spiritualist medium, Myers' post-mortem spirit explained that reincarnation was necessary for those souls that had sunk so morally low in life as to otherwise have no chance of spiritual redemption. He is said to have referred to these people as animal men.

See also **Cummins, Geraldine**.

Nafs and *Ruh* (Arabic: soul and spirit). *Nafs,* which corresponds to the Hebrew *nephesh*, is the general term in **Islam** for the human soul. It is the *nafs* of the individual that is subject to the Day of Judgment (*Yaum al-Din*).

Sometimes the term *nafs* is used to mean the lower spiritual self of a person, that which is possessed of passions and is easily incited to evil. Other times *nafs* is used reflexively to mean self or itself in which case it can refer to a person, animal, inanimate object, or even God. In other words, only the specific context can determine what exactly *nafs* means.

The *nafs* must be clearly distinguished from the *ruh* (spirit) which is what God breathes into human beings to give them life, and corresponds to the Hebrew *ruah*. The *ruh* is regarded as an intellectualizing element (*aql*) which raises each person above the animal level. *Ruh* is that part of each person that returns to God at death.

For the minority of Moslems who accept reincarnation it is difficult to know whether it is the *nafs*, the *ruh* or both that reincarnates.

See also **Muhammad Ahmad**.

Nag Hammadi Texts. This collection of 13 diverse gnostic and hermetic papyrus manuscripts, written in Coptic (old Egyptian), and dating from the 3rd-4th centuries, were discovered in a large clay jar in the upper (southern) Egyptian desert in 1941. Up until that time most of what was known about **Gnosticism** was culled from anti-gnostic material written by various early Christian authorities. The *Nag Hammadi texts* gave scholars their first substantial understanding of various forms of Gnosticism in the Gnostic's own words. In some of these texts, such as *The Secret Book of John* and *The Apocryphon of John*, reincarnation of at least a spiritual elect is mentioned.

See also **Gnostic Order of Christ; Hermetic philosophy;** *Pistis Sophia*.

Napoleon Bonaparte (1769–1821). According to the *Memoirs of Prince Talleyrand* (1892) Napoleon, whether he sincerely believed it or not, was said to have told his generals that in a past life he was the Frankish emperor Charlemagne (742–814 CE).

According to the calculations of the astrologer **A. Tad Mann** Napoleon was first embodied as Alexander the Great (356–323 BCE) and then as Charlemagne and it was as the re-embodiment of the latter that Napoleon believed he was justified in declaring himself Emperor of France in 1804, and subsequently refusing to recognize the legitimacy of the German office of Holy Roman Emperor with its claim to be the legitimate elected successor of Charlemagne. At the same time, some reincarnation authorities claim that Charles-Andre-Marie-Joseph de Gaulle (1890–1970), the French general and president, considered himself the reincarnation of Napoleon. This is said to account for De Gaulle's general dislike for the British. Reincarnation, however, is not needed to explain any French dislike of the British, since these two nations have felt enmity towards one another since the Middle Ages.

See also **Patton, George S; Repetition compulsion**.

Naraka or ***Niraya*** (Devoid of happiness). This is the general name for the Hindu and Buddhist **hell** or **purgatory**. In **Hinduism** it is sometimes divided into seven parts. The first part is reserved for childless persons, the second for those awaiting rebirth, and the third for general evil doers. It is the fourth and below that are places of torment. The last of these is *kakola* and is a pit from which there is no escape through rebirth.

See also ***Avichi;*** ***Bhavachakra;*** **Hungry ghosts**.

Natal defects. Many Eastern, and some Western, advocates of reincarnation believe that the reason that some children are born with a physical or mental defects is the result of bad karma. This **blaming the victim** is a morally questionable belief in that it has allowed many in Asian societies to offer no real sympathy, much less assistance, to these children on the basis that such assistance would be interfering in the children's well deserved karma.

See also **Birthmarks; Caste system; Death; Karma and justice; Out-of-the-body experiences** and **near-death-experiences**.

National character reappearances. One of the **arguments supportive of rebirth** is that certain current national characteristics closely reflect certain former national characteristics. This particular argument is almost exclusively an Anglo-American one. It says that 18th and 19th Britain, with its great empire mirroring the Roman Empire, strongly suggested that there was a mass rebirth of ancient Roman souls in Britain. This was followed by a gradual decline in that empire due to those souls next choosing rebirth in the United States in the 20th century. This same argument regards 17th and 18th century France as a recipient of a large influx of ancient Greek souls. This argument suffers from the same circular logical problem as the **nations, their rise and decline argument**.

See also **Renaissance**.

Nations, their rise and decline argument. One of the **arguments supportive of rebirth** is that rebirth explains the rise and decline of nations. This argument states that a nation rises to greatness because a very large number of advanced souls are attracted to it for rebirth. Likewise, a nation declines when the reverse situation occurs. The problem with this argument is that it does not state why a very large number of advanced souls are attracted to that nation in the first place. In short, the argument can only end up being circular in its logic.

Naylor, James (1618–1660). This prominent early Quaker leader was persuaded by some religiously overly enthusiastic Quaker women that he was a reincarnation of Christ. Tried for blasphemy he was imprisoned for three years and died a year or so after his release.

Near-death experience *see* **Out-of-the-body experiences** and **near-death-experiences**.

Necromancy. This is the practice of divination from corpses. The term is also commonly, but improperly used for the communication with the spirits of the dead for the purpose of divination. However, the proper term for such spirit communication is **sciomancy**. Many conservative Christian sects, making no distinction between these terms, accuse those who attempt to delve into past lives as necromancers (sciomancers) who are receiving information coming from lost souls, poltergeists, and/or demons.

Nemesius of Emesa (4th century). This bishop of Emesa (modern Homs), Syria is famous for his work *Peri Physeos Anthropou* (*On the Nature of Man*). This work is the first known Christian oriented compendium of inductive psychology and theological anthropology. In the book Nemesius criticized the views of the soul as taught by both **Plato** and **Aristotle**. Nemesius says that in Plato's view the soul was regarded as too independent of the body, while in Aristotle's view the soul was too dependent upon the body. Nemesius claimed that the Christian view was a proper balance between these two extremes. Nemesius apparently accepted the **soul's existence prior to embodiment**, but the attempts that have been made to claim him as a supporter of reincarnation are very questionable.

See also **Christian fathers critical of reincarnation**.

Neo-pagan religions. Neo-Paganism is often lumped together with **New Age religions**, and while there is a considerable overlap between the two, most Neo-Pagan groups consider themselves as a separate spiritual movement and several characteristics do differentiate the two. First, as worshippers of various phenomenon found in nature, Neo-Pagans rarely speak of realizing ones "Higher Self" as do most New Age groups. For Neo-Pagans the present, ordinary self, in harmony with the natural world, is perfectly acceptable. Second, there is no talk of any apocalyptic or new millennium era in the future in which many New Age groups believe. Third, Neo-pagans look back in history to develop their beliefs, rites and rituals; New Agers rarely do. Fourth, Neo-Pagans are generally very ritually oriented, unlike most New Age groups.

Some groups do bridge the separation between the New Age and Neo-Pagan groups such as the Neo-Shamanists. Still, even here there is a tendency to lean to a New Age side or a Neo-Pagan side. The former focuses on the self and personal development, while the latter focuses on community healing that may include a symbolic healing of nature.

One commonality that should otherwise unite the two groups, namely a preference for a belief in some sort of rebirth, reincarnation or **transmigration** actually serves to further separate them. New Age believers generally take a very gnostic attitude towards rebirth, seeing it as a condition from which to escape through developing one's higher self. Neo-Pagans, on the other hand, consider rebirth as something to repeatedly welcome.

See also **Druids; Gnosticism; Hell; Rebirth, East and West; Rebirth in the West; Summerland; Taylor, Thomas; Wicca**.

Neoplatonism. This school of philosophy, originating in Alexandria, Egypt, was most likely established by **Ammonius Saccas** (175–242). Although technically it was an attempt to revive and expand on the teachings of **Plato** Neoplatonism really grew out of the teachings of **Plotinus** (204–269), with Proclus (411–485) its last major teacher. As a formal school it lasted until the fifth century when, along with all other pagan philosophical and religious schools, it was closed by order of the Christian Roman (Byzantine) emperor Justinian I in 529 CE.

Despite its pagan origins, Neoplatonism had a major influence on later orthodox Christian, Jewish, and Islamic thought. Since many Neoplatonists accepted a belief in **metempsychosis** it was because of this influence that a number of unorthodox Christian, Jewish, and Islamic sects adopted the belief as well.

See also **Druzes; Emanationism; Gnosticism; Hermetic philosophy; Iamblichus; Julian, the Apostate; Kabbalah, Manichaeism; Nusayris; Platonism; Priesthood, lack of an organized: Sallustius the Neoplatonist; Sufism; Synesius of Cyrene; Theosophy**.

Nepenthean veil. This means the veil of forgetfulness. The word *nepenthe* or *nepenthes* comes from the Greek *ne-*(for not), and *-penthos* (for grief); and is traced back to the Odyssey of Homer where it is the name of an Egyptian drug believed to make one to totally forget all one's troubles or miseries and as such it is a synonym for the waters of **Lethe**.

See also **Drink or fruit of forgetfulness; Iliad and Odyssey**.

Nephesh and ***Neshamah*** see **Kabbalah**; *Nafs* and *Ruh*; **Old Testament and the soul; Soul; Soul, tripartite**.

Nero. Nero Claudius Caesar Drusus Germanicus (54–68 CE). This infamous Roman emperor is not to be confused with either of his two predecessors, Tiberius Claudius Nero Caesar (14–37 CE) or Tiberius Claudius Drusus Nero Germanicus (41–54 CE). The biographer and moralist Plutarch (46–119?CE) mentions that Nero Claudius was reborn as a frog for all of his sins.

See also **Paul of Tarsus; Plutarch; *Redivivus*; Romans, Ancient; Simon Magus**.

Netherton Method. This is a method advocated in the book *Past Lives Therapy* (1978) by Morris Netherton and Nancy Schiffrin. It uses word or phrase association to recall past lives. Here specific recurring or out-of-place words or phrases of the patient, especially those that seem to be accompanied by a strong emotional or body language response, are used to open up the subconscious by having the patient concentrate on and/or repeat those phrases. In many cases this will lead to a recall of some past life trauma. For Netherton this concentration automatically puts the patient into a mild self-induced trance state, but one of which the patient is always in control. This, in turn, has the advantage of the individual who is recalling a past life doing so directly without an intermediate person such as a hypnotist. Clearly, in the Netherton Method the boundary between the conscious and subconscious mind is far more permeable than it is thought to be where hypnotic regression is used. Morris Netherton founded the Association for the Alignment of Past Life Experience in California.

See also **Affect bridge; Blocked regression; Hypnotic age regression; Leading question; Past life readings; Reverie recall; Spontaneous recall.**

Neverdies. This group, also known as the Church of the Living Gospel or Church of the Everlasting Gospel, is of the Pentecostal tradition but includes the teaching of reincarnation. The exact date for its founding in West Virginia is not uncertain.

New Age Community Church. This is said to be a church for the Age of Aquarius (the New Age). The Church teaches that the differences between the major religions are relatively unimportant in comparison to the nine pathways that can lead to God. These nine are social relationships; meditation or mental discipline; psychic revelation, which includes channeling; a belief in and understanding of karma and rebirth; the ecstasy of music and dance; magical and sacramental rituals; wisdom and understanding through intellectual knowledge; healthful physical practices of yoga and diet; and worshipful devotion and adoration. The Church teaches that God, rather then being a personal deity, is all there is. In other words, the universe can be thought of as God's physical body. Also, Christ is to be thought of as the Logos or Higher Self of mankind. The Church further teaches that human beings are currently trapped on the wheel of reincarnation because people continue to believe in good and evil and this creates emotional values based on that belief. When we cease to create such values karma can no longer hold us and we will ascend to the level of the divine.

New Age religions. This term encompasses a variety of religious movements and sects of the 20th century, all of which have an optimistic view of human nature and a sense that there is a higher spiritual reality which it is the destiny of mankind to eventually discover. The New Age Movement is in a number of ways a revitalized continuation of 19th century New England Transcendentalism, new thought, **spiritualism**, **Theosophy**, 19th–20th century astrology, and Eastern religions. Most New Age believers reject the Western orthodox view of an eternal hell which is why many of them prefer the doctrine of reincarnation or **transmigration** in place of the orthodox Christian resurrection of the dead. Some authors who write about New Age religions include **neo-pagan religions** into the New Age category; however, those more nature based religions object to this inclusion.

See also **Aquarian Gospel of Jesus Christ; Ascended masters; Astrology and rebirth; Channeling; Christianity, esoteric; Resurrection, bodily; Sutphen, Dick; UFOism.**

New Testament *see* **Antinomianism; Christian atonement theories; Corinthians, 1st and 2nd; Ephesians; Galatians; Gnosticism, Hebrew; James 3:6; Jesus; John, Gospel of; John the Baptist; Luke, Gospel of; Mark, Gospel of; Matthew, Gospel of; Paul of Tarsus; Peter, 1st & 2nd; Romans; Revelation of John; New Testament and reincarnation; New Testament sacrificial concept; Palingenesis.**

New Testament and reincarnation. Many reincarnationists have tried to find some evidence of reincarnation (**metempsychosis**) in the canonical New Testament; however, any such evidence, even of a hidden nature, is more wishful thinking than anything else. Without doubt, many of the "apocryphal" gospels and letters that were refused inclusion into the canon did include a belief in metempsychosis. This was especially the case for various gnostic Christian texts of the very late first century to the third century CE, but not earlier. The reason for this is that the earliest Christian community, as represented by the writers of the earliest synoptic gospels **Mark** and **Matthew**, and **Paul of Tarsus** believed that **Jesus**, as the Christ (Messiah), would return from heaven in their "own generation"; therefore, these authors had no real need for any long term afterlife theory such as reincarnation, and so no such theory should be expected in their works. It was only after it became obvious that the return (the *Parousia*) of Christ might be some time away that more specific theological concerns about the afterlife were needed. It was at this point that some early gnostic Christian groups accepted a belief in metempsychosis.

It must be noted that it took three centuries for the church to decide which writings to accept as orthodox and which to reject. Moreover, this decision was made in various church council debates which are among the most well documented activities of their time. If the question of metempsychosis, either for or against, were a part of any of these early council debates the documentation on that issue would certainly have been preserved. Usually what modern day reincarnationists claim were council debates on reincarnation where really debates on the **soul's existence prior to embodiment,** which was ultimately declared heretical. However, even if prior existence had been accepted, this would not have automatically meant prior existence for more than one life. Without exception all pro-metempsychosis texts were rejected as too unorthodox for inclusion in the canon at the **Church Council of Laodicea** in 364 CE; a decision that was confirmed at the synod of Carthage in 397.

Despite the orthodox success in excluding metempsychosis from the canon many modern attempts have been made to still read it into the New Testament. This, of course, can only be done if the targeted passages, as **proof text,** are taken completely out of context. A number of modern "esoteric" Christians have done just this. Of course, the ability in the first place to make the claim that the New Testament subtly teaches reincarnation is made easier by the fact that the New Testament is very inconsistent in its views of both a general afterlife and, more specifically, the resurrection of the dead.

One of the first modern attempts to use this inconsistently in support of reincarnation in the New Testament was made by **Helena Blavatsky.** The claim on her part that Jesus taught reincarnation was clearly not only an attempt to undermine any Christian opposition to her **Theosophy,** but to try to prove that Theosophy was more of a truly universal religion than was orthodox Christianity.

Among the most common phrases or verses in the New Testament that have been used to support Christian reincarnation are those found in **Corinthians, 1st and 2nd, Ephesians, Galatians**, the four Gospels, **James 3:6,** and **Peter, 1st and 2nd**.

Whenever any claim is made that the New Testament secretly teaches reincarnation it should be clearly understood that although that text was originally written in Greek, it represents Jewish, not Greek, thinking when it comes to life and death. The Jews only conceived of the human personality as something contained in a physical body, not as a disincarnated soul. The latter notion was purely a Greek contribution to Western religious thought. It is true that by the Middle Ages Christian theology, especially as it applied to the cult of deceased saints, adopted more of that Greek view; however, that adoption was not until well after the Bible had been officially closed to new additions.

See also **Angels and reincarnation; Annihilationism, Biblical view; Aquarian Gospel of Jesus Christ; Arguments supportive of rebirth; Carpocrates; Christian atonement theories; Christian view of the afterlife; Christianity and reincarnation; Christianity, esoteric; Church Council of 553; Church Universal and Triumphant; Course in Miracles; Elijah; Essenes; False claims of support for reincarnation; Genesis;** *Gilgul;* **Gnostic Order of Christ; Gnosticism; Heaven's Gate; Jesus; Job; John, Gospel of; Helmont, Franciscus Mercurius van; I Am Movement; Justin Martyr; Karma and forgiveness; Karma and free will; Karma versus grace; Kingsford, Anna Bonus; Limbo; Lucifer; Luke, Gospel of; Melchizedek; New Testament sacrificial concept; Old Testament and the afterlife; Origin; Original sin, Christianity, and reincarnation; Paulicians; Predestination;** *Psychopannychism;* **Purgatory; Resurrection, bodily; Resurrection of Jesus; Romans; Sciomancy; Soul; Theodicy; Work of Mercy; Xenoglossy; Yogananda, Paramahansa; Zoroastrianism.**

New Testament sacrificial concept. One of the main Christian arguments against reincarnation is that it would weaken or even make unnecessary the suffering, dying, and resurrection of **Jesus** as atonement for humanity's sins. In particular, it would make the "sacrificial blood" of Jesus largely irrelevant. According to the New Testament, however, it was only through the expiating-shed blood of Christ that salvation (heavenly immortality) is at all possible. Among the biblical passages to this effect are **Romans** 3:25, 5:9; 1st **Corinthians** 5:7; 1st **John** 1:7, 5:6; **Hebrews** 9:12–14, 22–28; 10:5–10, 19, 29, 12:24, 13:20–21; **Ephesians** 1:7, 2:13–14; Colossians 1:20, 1st **Peter** 1:2, 19.

This need for blood as a general outward cleansing of sin, however, was not considered sufficient by the New Testament, since there was also a theophagic need to complete the salvific process. Theophagy refers to the belief and practice of eating what is believed to be the flesh and/or blood of a divine or sacred being, as in that the Eucharist. Here bread and wine are said to be transformed into the real flesh and blood of Christ, which must then be consumed so that at the final resurrection of the dead those who have partaken of the immortal essence of God the Son alone will inherit immortal life. Among the biblical passages supporting this belief are **Mark** 14:22–24; **Matthew** 26:26–29; **Luke** 22:17–19; John 6:47, 51–51, 52–58; and 1st Corinthians 10:16.

When some people try to find in the New Testament evidence for a secret or even deliberately hidden reincarnational theme they generally ignore all the sacrificial and theophagic language presented there. This is because such language points directly to the absolute seriousness of having only one life in which to attain salvation.

See also **Christian atonement theories; John, Gospel of; Melchizedek; Old Testament and the soul; Original sin, Christianity, and reincarnation; Peter, 1st and 2nd; Rebirth and moral perfection; Resurrection, bodily; Steiner, Rudolf.**

New Thought *see* **Spiritualism; Unity Christianity.**

Nightmare of eastern philosophy. More than anything else, this is a derogatory term employed by some Christians who consider that the belief in reincarnation seduces people away from the orthodox Christian truth. The term is also used by those modern secularists who believe that the doctrine of reincarnation encourages escape from the world, rather than trying to improve it through social engagement. Finally, it is used as a synonym for **blaming the victim** factor.

See also **Caste system; Noble lie; Old Brahmin moonshine; Rebirth and cyclical time.**

Nine doors. In **Vajrayana Buddhism** it is believed that the rebirth consciousness of the deceased can pass out of the body through one of nine openings (doors). Which door the consciousness will pass through depends on the fate awaiting the deceased in the next existence. If the **hell** realm awaits, the rebirth consciousness will pass out of the body through the anus; if it is the animal realm then that consciousness will leave through the sexual organs; if it is the **hungry ghost** realm then route is through the mouth; if it is back into the human realm then the exit is through the nose; if the *asura* realm is the destination then it is the ears; if the consciousness has earned the desire god (*deva*) realm (the lowest heaven) then the navel is the chosen way; if the form god realm (intermediate heaven) then it is through the eyes; if the formless god realm (highest heaven) then the exit is somewhere through the top of the head; and finally, if the **Pure-Land** realm of **Amitabha Buddha** is the destination then the consciousness passes through the aperture of Brahma at the crown of the head (highest of the *chakras*).

See also *Bardo;* **Third eye.**

Nirjara (Without birth). In **Jainism** this term means there are no more rebirths because all karma has been annihilated and, therefore, the person is forever liberated.

See also ***Moksha;* Rebirth and suicide; *Samsara.***

Nirvana and ***Parinirvana.*** These terms mean respectively "the blowing out" and the "supreme blowing out," in other words, the release from any further rebirth. Nirvana is a state of being (consciousness) in which one enters into and remains in during this life. The person achieving it has the realization that he or she will never again be reborn. *Parinirvana* is attained upon death, and is the nonreoccurrence of rebirth itself. These two states are the highest spiritual goal of Buddhism. The Pali equivalents of these two terms are *nibbana* and *parinibbana.*

See also ***Kaivalya; Moksha.***

Nirvikalpa Samadhi. In *Kundalini* (Serpent power) *Yoga* this is the seventh and highest concentrative state (S: *Samadhi*). Once attained, it is believed that the attainer can usually only remain embodied for 21 days, after which physical death occurs and the **soul** is forever free of further rebirths. In the case of some great saints continued embodiment is made possible by their ability to bring their concentration down to the sixth or, at most, the fifth *chakra* level.

See also ***Chakras;*** Yoga.

Noble lie. This is a belief that serves a psychologically or morally constructive purpose; hence is "noble," while at the same time, it is a belief that on close scrutiny is show to be logically incompatible either with the greater or more logical parts of some other belief. Buddhism, in acknowledging rebirth, yet teaching the non-existence of a soul (*anatman*), is a logical contradiction. The belief in rebirth therefore qualifies as a noble lie to the degree that it serves to encourage morality.

In a less benevolent sense the noble lie is also called a convenient fiction. For many people who are appalled at the way that the doctrines of rebirth and karma are used to support the horrendous inequities of the Indian **caste system** regards those doctrines as convenient fictions on the behalf of the Brahman caste.

See also **Annihilationism, Buddhist view; Blaming the victim vs. illusion of innocence; Course in Miracles; Karma and God; Karma and justice; Karma and rebirth; Monism; Rebirth and maturity; Rebirth, compensation and life fulfillment; Rebirth in Buddhism.**

No-rebirth wish. According to **Edgar Cayce** as long as a person wishes not to be reborn that person can be assured that he or she "will be" reborn. To exemplify this Lynn Elwell Sparrow, in her *Reincarnation: Claiming Your Past, Creating Your Future* (1988), offers the following story: Two disciples of a master are in the forest. When the master appears, one disciple asks the master how many more lives must he (the disciple) must live before reaching liberating enlightenment. The master says only three more lives. The disciples obviously discouraged at this prospect, returns to his meditation. Soon the second disciple comes dancing by and asks the same question of the master. The master says a thousand more lives. The disciple's response to this answer is glee, and becoming instantly enlightened, continues dancing through the forest.

Norton, Rosaleen (1917–1979). Sometimes described as Australia's best known witch, this occult artist believed that in one of her past lives she had been a rural English poltergeist.

No-soul (self) see **Anatman**.

Notovitch, Nicholas (1858–?). This Russian aristocrat, Cossack officer, war correspondent, journalist, and spy claimed that in visiting Ladakh (East Kashmir) in 1887 he broke his leg and had to be taken to a lamasery named Himis, where he discovered some ancient Tibetan verses that described the life of **Jesus** (Isa) during his stay in that region as a youth. Supposedly, having had the verses translated, Notovitch published them as *The Unknown Life of Jesus Christ* (French edition 1894, English edition 1895). Later visitors to the same lamasery reported that the monks had no knowledge of such verses in their collection of ancient texts.

Notovitch's story of his visit to Himis seems to be taken from *Isis Unveiled* by **Helena Blavatsky** where in the original the traveler with the broken leg was taken to a monastery on Mount Athos where he discovered the long lost text of Celsus' *True Word* in the monastic library.

Despite the debunking of Notovitch's claim, "The Young Jesus in India Theory" has enabled any number of later individuals and groups to claim that Jesus was instructed in and later taught the concept of reincarnation. According to Elizabeth Clare Prophet of the **Church Universal and Triumphant**, Notovitch, a year after his Indian discovery, was visiting Rome where he was told by an "unnamed cardinal" that the Vatican Library had a number of documents about "Jesus in India" brought back by Catholic missionaries.

See also **Ahmadiyya; Alexandria, Egypt;** *Aquarian Gospel of Jesus Christ*; **Origin**.

Nous see **Emanationism;** *Nafs and Ruh*; **Numenius of Apamea; Soul, tripartite;** *Thumos*.

Number of rebirths see **Finite or infinite number of rebirths**.

Numbers. After Genesis this is the second book of the Old Testament to specifically mention the underworld as **Sheol** (Numbers 16:30, 33). On the surface this certainly has nothing to offer in support of reincarnation; nonetheless, some Kabbalists find such support in the middle part of Numbers 16:22. But to do so they must ignore the first and last parts of the passage, which leaves the middle open to almost any interpretation. The whole passage reads, "But they prostrated themselves and said, '*O God, God of the spirits of all mankind*, if one man sins will you be angry with the whole community?'" The italicized words are the ones focused on by the Kabbalists.

See also **Angels and reincarnation; Kabbalah; Forty; Old Testament and the afterlife; Serpent**.

Numenius of Apamea (late 2nd century CE). This Syrian born Greek philosopher was the main force in the transition from Platonic idealism to the Neoplatonic synthesis of Pythagorean, Hellenistic, Persian (Zoroastrian), Indian, gnostic, and Jewish thought. Numenius is especially famous for his characterization of **Plato** as "an Atticizing (of Athenian) Moses." Also it is believed that Numenius had an influence on the thought of **Origin**.

The soteriological view of Numenius was not only based on a **body-soul dualism**, but on the idea that beings possess a two-fold soul, a rational (*nous* or *noos*) and an irrational one. It is the first of these that rightfully seeks to escape from its round of evil bodily **transmigration**. There are a number of surviving fragments of the writings of Numenius, one of which is *Peri Aphtharsias Psyches* (*On the Indestructibility of the Soul*).

See also **Gnosticism; Planetary descent and ascent of the soul; Priesthood, lack of an organized; Pythagoras; Zoroastrianism**.

Numerology and rebirth. Numerology (more correctly, arithmancy) is the use of numbers to interpret an inner or hidden meaning of a word or phrase. It is loosely based upon the Pythagorean concept that all things can be expressed in numerical terms because they are ultimately reducible to numbers. In particular, numerologists believe that every name has a significant number value as well as a psychic vibration that relates to it and which, in turn, is related to a specific personality type. For some numerologists who also accept reincarnation there is the belief that the name that prospective parents have chosen for their child will influence a reincarnating soul as to whether or not to be born to those parents.

See also **I, William the Conqueror; Kabbalah**.

Nupe. This is one of the tribal peoples of Nigeria who have a belief in a form of reincarnation. They believe that everyone has two souls, of which one goes to the ancestors at death while the other reincarnates.

See also **Africa; Souls, multiple.**

Nusayris/Nursaris. This is a religious community found in northern Syria, southeast Turkey and Lebanon. While they claim to be Shi'a Moslems, the main Shi'a community rejects this claim. The name of this group comes from that of its founder, Abu Shu'ayb Muhammad ibn Nusayr (died 880 CE). The Nusayris are actually regarded as a subsect of Alawis/Alevis, which is to say those that show adoration to the memory of Ali (Muhammad's martyred cousin and son-in-law) to the point of deification (*Ali Ilahis*, Arabic: Deifiers of Ali). The Nusayris, in fact, believe that Ali created Mohammad.

A major difference between the Nusayris and other Alevis, not to mention orthodox Muslims, is the unusual belief that women, unlike men, are generally soulless. This means that male souls alone reincarnate (Arabic: ***tanasukh***), and should a woman have a soul it is because the soul of a sinful man has reincarnated into a woman in order to experience the purgatory of a woman's soulless body. This, of course, creates the problem that the "deified Ali" is dependent for his status on having been the husband of the Prophet's daughter, Fatima. This seemingly contradictory fact is dealt with by having Fatima claim that she was a man, manifesting himself as a woman only to give birth to Ali's sons and imams, Hasan and Husayn. The Alevis also believe that all souls begin as stars and after seven reincarnations will return to being such bodies of light.

See also **Ahmadiyya; Babism and Bahaiism; Cult of Angels; Islam; Druzes; Finite or infinite number of rebirths; Yazidis.**

Oahspe: A Kosmon Bible in the Words of Jehovih [sic] ***and his Angel Ambassadors.*** This book was produced by John Ballou Newbrough (1828–1891) through **automatic (type)-writing** and was published in 1882 by Oahspe Publishing Association in New York. The name *Oahspe* is said to mean sky, earth, and spirit.

Newbrough, who was deeply interested in the **spiritualism** and **lost continents** movements of the late 19th century, claims that the book was actually written by an angel (*ashar*) channeled through him. Among the teachings in the book is that the doctrine of reincarnation is not only false, but has been taught to mankind by lower order malicious angels called *drujas*. These spiritual entities, which were actually created by the false **Jesus** of standard Christianity, seek to possess both the homes and bodies of human beings in attempts to corrupt them.

See also ***Aquarian Gospel of Jesus Christ;*** Channeling; ***Urantia Book.***

Oasis Fellowship. Founded by George and Alice White after being contacted by several spiritual entities via channeling, this Florence, Arizona based Fellowship advertises itself as following the teachings of **Jesus** and accepts psychic communication and a belief in reincarnation.

Ob Ugarins. These Siberian tribal people believe that men have five souls and women have four. The first of each is the shadow-soul, which is in people, animals, and even inanimate objects. At death this soul either follows the body to the grave o, abandoning the body, it can become a ghost-like entity. The second soul can leave the body during sleep, but with the exception of some shamans, it must be embodied during waking hours. The third soul takes on an independent form outside of the body but may enter the body during sleep. If this soul should die, then the person would die. The fourth soul is the reincarnating entity which re-embodies as an infant in the same clan as the deceased. The fifth soul, exclusive to men, is less well explained. It too is sometimes called a reincarnating soul, but at other times it is called "strength."

See also **Souls, multiple.**

Objective immortality. This is a term used by the philosopher Alfred North Whitehead (1861–1947) for the belief that each person is for all eternity a memory in the mind of God. This is because every thought, word, action, and experience an individual has is recorded in the divine memory. Obviously, objective immortality is in contrast to subjective immortality which is where each **soul** retains its individuality and autonomy. Objective immortality might be thought of as a more personal or dynamic version of the ***akashic*** record and as such is a possible source for what might be mistaken for past life memories.

See also **Griffin, David Ray; Immortality; Individuality and rebirth.**

Obsession. This is the term used by Harold Marrow Sherman, in his *You Live After Death* (1949), to account for past life recalls. He uses this term actually to attribute such recall not to one's own **soul**, but to **possession** by a foreign former living entity.

See also **Attached entity; Bjorkhem, John.**

Occult, the *see* **Esotericism versus Occultism; Grey occultists.**

Occult hierarchy *see* **Angels and reincarnation; Ascended masters.**

Oceania. This is a large cultural area in the Pacific that includes Melanesia, Micronesia, and Polynesia. A belief in reincarnation has been found in some parts of Melanesia, including Papua New Guinea, as for example among the **Orokaiva;** the Trobriand Islanders; and the Malkula of Vanuatu (formerly the New Hebrides). The belief in Micronesia is not well documented, and such a belief seems to have been unknown in Polynesia.

See also **Australian Aborigines; Christian missionary influence and reincarnation; Orokaiva**.

Ogdoad. In ancient Greek this term means any set of eight but, more specifically, it refers to eight high deities that resided in the realm of fixed stars (**Milky Way**). Since this realm was the original home of all souls, and the realm from which they descended or fell to earth for their original embodiment, it is presumed that the eight rulers had some influence over the descent process and possibly renascent of souls.

See also **Planetary descent and ascent of the soul; Plato.**

Ojas. In Hindu Tantric yoga this is the spiritual energy or psychic power that is within semen and which is needed to escape from the round of birth and death. Through yogi practice the disciple causes his semen to rise up through the ***chakra*** system to his crown (*sahasrara*), where it is stored in the brain as *ojas shakti* (divine power). The rising of *ojas* is achieved by meditation, especially on the ***atman***; by worship of the gods; by yogic breath practices (*pranayama*); and above all by avoiding any release of semen (celibacy: *brahmacharya*). Some Tantric texts imply that transforming sexual energy into *ojas* can also be done by woman via the ova and menstrual cycle.

Old Brahmin moonshine. This is a sarcastic 19th century British metaphor of the Brahmin claim to their high caste status as due to former good karma and, by extension, to the whole doctrine of reincarnation.

See also **Nightmare of eastern philosophy**.

Old Norse. In certain Eddic or Old Norse sagas there is mention of rebirth of certain heroic persons. In particular, in the two related sagas, *Heligakvitha Hjorvarthssonar* and the *Helgakvida Hundingsbana,* the hero Helgi and the heroine Svava undergo rebirth (*endrborin*). Svara was first reborn as the Valkyrie Sigrun and later as the Valkyrie Kara; while Helgi Hundingsbana (Helgi Sigmundson) is reborn as Helgi Haddingjaskati. Throughout these rebirths the two remain lovers until in one of those lives Kara, who has taken the form of a swan, is mistakenly hurt by Helgi's sword. After this Kara can no longer protect Helgi from him being killed by the enemy.

See also **Lapps (Saami).**

Old souls. For most of those who believe in universal reincarnation all souls are equally old, but not equally wise. In this regard an old soul is one that has not only been reincarnating for centuries or millennium, but one which during those incarnation, has gained great wisdom. For those who believe that only a minority of people have had past lives, the term old souls refers just to that minority.

See also **Deaths, violent and premature; Kabbalah; Population increase issue**.

Old Testament and the afterlife. There are a "minority" of Old Testament passages that might suggest the doctrine of reincarnation. However, considering the "majority" of Old Testament verses, in which the fate of the dead is at best a rather dismal place, called in Hebrew *Sheol,* any authentic reincarnational interpretation of such passages becomes highly improbable. *Sheol* was thought of as an underworld destination that was neither a place of punishment nor of reward for all the dead, whether virtuous or sinful. It was a dark cavernous region where the dead continued a cold, dry, lethargic and ghostly existence, mere shadows of their former selves. *Sheol* was, in fact, very similar to the early Greek **Hades**. For all practical purposes, death was equated with near annihilation, as in **Genesis** 3:19; **Psalm** 39:12–13, Psalm 49, and **Ecclesiastes** 9:5–6, and 10. This meant that immortality was essentially through one's biological descendents, as implied in Psalms 22:29.

Only in some of the later Old Testament books does the post-mortem view begin to change. The earliest possible "indirect" mention of resurrection is at Isaiah 26:19, and Ezekiel 37:12–13; and, possibly Hosea 13:14. These citations may suggest redemption from *Sheol*, which under the names *Abbadon* (Hebrew: Destruction) or *Gehenna,* is considered to be a place of punishment; however, these indirect passages do not specify either a rewarding afterlife in some sort of other-worldly heaven or a future heaven on earth. A possibly more heavenly affirming post-mortem future is implied in Malachi 3:16–4:3 and 2 Maccabees 7:9b–14; but the earliest biblical text to emphasize an indisputable positive future resurrectional state for the dead comes from the still later in **Daniel** 12:1–2, but even here the exact conditions after the resurrection are left undeveloped.

See also **Angels and reincarnation; Annihilationism, Biblical view; Bible and rebirth; Deuteronomy 5:2–3; Elijah; Essenes; Exodus; Ezekiel; Hell; Job; Judaism and the afterlife; Kabbalah; Karma, racial; Numbers; Old Testament and the soul; Proof text; Proverbs; Psalms;**

Resurrection, bodily; Sciomancy; Shadow or shade; Soul; Yogananda, Paramahansa.

Old Testament and the soul. Any attempts to read into the Old Testament ideas of reincarnation are complicated by the earliest concept of the soul as the life force that was equated with blood, as at Leviticus 17:10–14; and **Deuteronomy** 12:23. It was only much later that a concept of a **soul** independent of the blood developed in ancient Judaism.

See also **Hell; Old Testament and the afterlife.**

Olfactory psychic experience. This is a *déjà vu*-like experience in which one is suddenly overwhelmed by a smell that is actually not present, but presumably has been triggered by some significant past life recall. For example, a person who was burned to death in a former life might suddenly experience the scent of burning flesh during either a spontaneous or hypnotically induced recall moment. Rabbi Yonassan Gershom, in his *Beyond the Ashes*, mentions just such an olfactory psychic experience related to those who in their past life were thought to have been burned alive in synagogues by the Nazi.

See also **Jewish Holocaust.**

Omega. According to the entity Alexander, as channeled through Ramon Stevens in *Earthly Cycles* (1994), this is the second post-mortem level into which the disembodied **soul** must pass before attaining bodily rebirth. The other levels are ***theta*** and the **astral plane**.

See also **Embodiment, moment of; Ouija Board; Welcomers.**

On a Clear Day You Can See Forever. This was a 1960's hit Broadway musical by Alan J. Lerner with a hypnotic age regression to a past life as its theme.

Only Fair Religion. This group was founded by a Saint Kenny and a group of his followers. Neither the identity of Saint Kenny, nor any of his group, is disclosed in the group's literature. The Religion teaches that through reincarnation the soul progress through lower life forms to higher ones. When a being evolves to a point of gaining a sense of self-awareness, it simultaneously acquires an immortal soul. This soul moves through a series of reincarnations which are necessary for its development and which will eventually allow it to become a planetary ruling spirit. The name "The Only Fair Religion" is said to represent its teachings that there is eventual salvation for all.

Ontological leap or ontological discontinuity. This is a theological concept that attempts to assign a **soul** exclusively to the human species and yet acknowledges that the human body evolved from a lower, soulless pre-human form. The ontological leap (radical change in the nature of being or existence) is said to have occurred when God suddenly, and at only one critical point in human evolution, injected souls into the still evolving human species. This is one reason why the ontological leap theory of the soul can also be called the soul injection theory.

The ontological leap concept, even when superficially examined, offers a number of logical and moral problems. If God decided that he was going to implant or inject souls in "generation y" then, while that generation must be regarded as fully human, the parents of that generation ("generation x") must be have remained sub-human in status. This would make the two generations ontologically discontinuous, even though for all practical purposes there was no anatomical or biochemical difference between these two generations. This discontinuity means that this first ensouled generation is eternally denied the right to share the joys of heaven with their beloved parents, while all later generations of ensouled persons have such a privilege.

It might make more sense to propose a very gradual evolution of the soul, but the theologians clearly understand that such parallel physical and spiritual evolution has at its own set of three problematic ontological questions. For example, at what point in a gradual process was humanity morally responsible for its actions and entitled to a favorable or unfavorable afterlife; would there be souls in heaven or hell that were more primitive than other souls; and would this ontological inequality be an eternal status?

Gradual soul evolution that parallels bodily evolution also has a problem with the **population increase issue**, unless combined with generationism or traducianism.

The ontological leap problem also applies to reincarnation if one denies progressive reincarnation. If the earliest human souls did not evolve from animal souls, but at one point entered pre-historic sub-human bodies by the process of **infusionism**, the parent generation of those newly ensouled remained sub-human.

See also **Animals, domesticated; Creationism, soul; Generationism and Traducianism; Rebirth and the scientific theory of biological evolution; Soul Darwinism; Soul, origin of the.**

Open Court. This is the name of an American magazine published from 1887 to 1936 which, under its first editor, Paul Carus (1852–1919), sought to introduce Asian religious ideas to the American public. Several of its issues dealt with the more orthodox Asian concepts of rebirth and karma, as opposed to the more speculatively westernized views on these concepts offered by Theosophists or **Rosicrucians**.

See also **Maha Bodhi, The; Theosophy**.

Oracles see **Lethe; Lhamoi Latso Oracle; Orphism**.

Ordo Templi Orientis (Order of the Oriental Templars) see **Crowley, Aleister; Rosicrucians; Scientology; Spare, Austin Osman; Steiner, Rudolf; Templars**.

Origin or **Origenes Adamanthus** (185–254 CE). Origin, as the head of the catechetical school in Alexandria, was the most influential and seminal theologian of the early Greek Church. Origin's name is often used by Western reincarnation advocates as proof that the early Christian Church also had reincarnation advocates. There is little doubt that Origin favored both universal salvation (*apocatastasis*) and the Platonic view of the **soul's existence prior to embodiment**, but there is no proof that he favored a previously "embodied" existence of the soul concept.

Origin had taught that rational beings, after being created, neglected to worship God and so to various degrees, fell from His grace. Those souls that fell least became angels, while those that fell most became devils. Human souls experienced an intermediate fall and for these God created the material world to embody those souls for purposes of discipline-ship. Origin further speculated that to remind mankind that this material world was not its true home God periodically ordained such natural catastrophes (acts of God) as earthquakes and plagues. Since **metempsychosis** depends upon the pre-existence of souls it is easy to see how a shallow reading of Origin's views could be interpreted to suggest a belief in pre-embodiment. Moreover, while some of his early writings can be more easily interpreted as supporting such a belief, his later writings such as his *Commentary on Matthew* cannot be so interpreted. In fact, that Origin rejected a belief in the multiple lives is evidenced by his attack on the idea that **Elijah** had been reborn as **John the Baptist**.

Also, any idea that Origin was a believer in multiple embodiments is further disproved by his well documented rejection of the Platonic belief that human souls could be reborn as animals and vice versa, as found in his *Contra Celsum* (*Against Celsus*). This work is Origin's response to the anti-Christian *Logos Alethes* (*True Word*) by Celsus and it reminds the reader that the human soul, having been made in the image of God, could not possibly have that image obliterated by being reborn into the body of an irrational animal.

Origin's *Peri Anastaseos* (*On the Resurrection*), a treatise in support of the Christian doctrine of the resurrection of the dead, is a further indication of his opposition to metempsychosis. Origin even wrote a commentary on the Gospel of John with the express purpose of refuting Gnostic followers of **Valentinus**.

Both Origin's pre-existent and universalist views, especially his belief that eventually even the devils would be reconciled to God, were attacked early on by **Theophilus** (late 4th — early 5th century CE), the patriarch of Alexandria. It was not, however, until the mid sixth century that both of these views were finally declared heretical. This occurred at the synod convened by the eastern Roman emperor Justinian I in 543 where nine anathemas against Origin's work were proposed, and was finalized by the **Church Council of 553**. What is important to note is that there is, in this well documented declaration, no mention whatsoever of metempsychosis, the presence of which would be expected, if Origin did indeed advocate it.

See also **Christian fathers critical of reincarnation; Christianity and reincarnation; Christianity, esoteric; John, Gospel of; New Testament and reincarnation; Plato; Pre-existiani; Resurrection, bodily**.

Original or ancestral sin and reincarnation. It is tenet of a number of reincarnational belief systems that souls are trapped or imprisoned in the body because of some sin committed eons ago by previously "non-incarnated" souls. Some Christian reincarnationists, while rejecting the orthodox biblical view of how such sin arose, nonetheless, wish to keep the general concept of a pre-natal sin factor in mankind, and see past lives as a preferred explanation for it.

See also **Arguments supportive of rebirth; Fall of Souls; Original sin, Christianity, and reincarnation; Original sin versus karma; Morganwg, Iolo; Orphism; Steiner, Rudolf**.

Original sin, Christianity, and reincarnation. The concept of sin as defined in the New Testament goes far beyond that of the Old Testament; in the latter there was still considerable room for a self-made righteous man or woman to exist. This is declared to be impossible in standard Pauline Christianity, as in **Romans** 3:10–18; 5:12–19, where the sin of **Adam** is inherited by all his descendents in the form of the universal inevitability of death. This sin-death dyad was only overcome by the crucifixion and resurrection of Christ, whose obedience to the Father was the antithesis of Adam's disobedience. With this Pauline view in mind it should be clear why standard Christianity can find no place for any person purifying him or herself through multiple lives. In fact, from the Pauline view any attempt by a person to be virtuous through self effort is the further sin of pride and that person is twice damned.

Even if Christianity should be more amenable to the doctrine of reincarnation, it would not matter how many lives a person had; that person would still need to depend entirely on God freely choosing to forgive that person both Adam's sin and that person's personal sins. In other words, a person can only be redeemed by surrendering to the free grace (gift) of God; a grace that actually is not free since it was in theory paid for through the willing sacrificial crucifixion of God himself as Christ. In short, reincarnation would accomplish nothing for the Christian.

See also **Christian atonement theories; Creationism, soul; Exodus; Fall of Souls; Generationism and Traducianism; Karma and forgiveness; Karma versus grace; New Testament sacrificial concept; Original sin versus karma; Steiner, Rudolf; Theodicy.**

Original sin versus karma. Belief in reincarnation is often said to free people from the oppressive belief in the concept of Original Sin, the sin that infected all mankind due to the disobedience towards God by Adam and Eve. It is true that the biblical concept of Original Sin can be oppressive; however, it is questionable whether the concept of karma is any less oppressive. When it comes to Original Sin there are two factors that ameliorate its oppression. First, the guilt connected to this sin is assigned to humanity collectively; second, this collective guilt is assigned to a very far past. In most cases these two factors weaken any sense of personal responsibility and hence of any personal guilt for that long ago sin. This leaves only one's present life sins about which to feel guilty. The doctrine of karma-*vipaka*, on the other hand, burdens one not only with one's present life sins, but all of one's past life sins. It is therefore debatable whether or not the concept of karma is less or more oppressive than the concept of Original Sin.

See also **Arguments supportive of rebirth; Blaming the victim vs. illusion of innocence; Original sin, Christianity, and reincarnation; Rebirth, East and West.**

Orokaiva. These are a people of the Northern District of Papua New Guinea. At least before Christian missionary activity, they had a belief in reincarnation. In particular there was the belief that the spirit of a male child may be derived from either an agnatic (male) or a uterine (female) ancestor through reincarnation. This seems to have been a clear political utility as that dual allegiance pattern forms the basis of Orokaiva political alliances.

See also **Christian missionary influence and reincarnation; Oceania.**

Orpheus. Orpheus was a legendary mystical Greek musician. According to one story Orpheus is said to have died by being ripped apart during an orgiastic festival by the Maenads, the mad female worshippers of Dionysus. After this disembodiment the head of Orpheus, having been tossed into the sea, floated to the island of Lesbos where an oracle of Orpheus was established. On the other hand, according to the Myth of Er in Plato's *Republic* Orpheus was reincarnated as a swan to live an innocent and graceful existence as reward for his virtues.

Orphism. Orphism was one of the Greek mystery religions established at least by the 6th century BCE. Orphic doctrines were based on a particular mythic story about the god Dionysus Zagreus that explained both the immortality and **metempsychosis** of the **soul** (*psyche*). In this myth Dionysus is the son of Zeus, king of the gods and Persephone, queen of the underworld. Due to the jealousy of Zeus's wife Hera, the infant Dionysus is murdered by the evil Titans and all of his flesh, except his heart (soul-center), is consumed by them. The enraged Zeus destroyed the Titans with his thunderbolts and from the ashes of the Titans Zeus creates mankind, whose body is of the titan element and whose his soul is of the divine element (Zagreus).

Following the metaphysical implications of this myth the Orphics (*Orphikoi*) believed that since the souls of mankind were of a divine substance they were immortal unlike the body. Indeed, life in the body was thought to be a penance and only through suffering and the conquest of bodily passions could the divine element be disassociated and purified from its impure titanic prison (*phroura*). This could not be done in one lifetime so the soul had to go through the cycle of becoming (**kyklos genesion**) or metempsychosis, until it was pure enough to liberate itself. Part of this purification was to be achieved through a ritual enactment of the death and consumption of Zagreus, followed by a life of asceticism (*ascesis*). This asceticism included **celibacy**, the avoidance of wine, and **vegetarianism**.

There were apparently for two reasons for this vegetarian *ascesis*. First, since one could never be sure that an animal killed for food might have harbored a former human soul, killing it would amount to murder. Second, it allowed the human practitioner to arise above the level of a meat-eating beast.

Also, as might be expected from the name Orpheus, the sect apparently believed in the spiritually healing power of music.

Much of our information about the Orphic religion has come from texts inscribed on gold leaves (laminae) found in tombs assumed to be those of Orphic initiates. These texts appear to be advice to the souls of the deceased that would enable them to authenticate their divine (Dionysian) origins and, therefore, escape further **transmigrations**. Some of these leaves show that by the second century BCE at least one branch of Orphism had been influenced by the platonic shift of the dwelling place of the dead from the earth, or under the earth, to the celestial realm. Not only do the golden leaves place **Hades** and the Lake of **Mnemosyne** (Memory) on the moon; but they give instructions on avoiding drinking from the waters of **Lethe** and drinking of those of Mnemosyne instead, after which the soul will be able to travel on the right-handed path to the starry heavens.

While Orphism had significant influence over a number of later religious movements it never became as popular in Greece as some other mystery religions did. There were probably two main reasons for its minor popularity. First, the ascetic ideal of Orphism and its view of the body (Greek: *soma*) as an imprisoning tomb (*sema*) could not be in greater contrast to the more common Greek view of the human body, especially the well-proportioned athletic body, as the epitome of a beauty nearing divinity. Second, there was no strongly organized priesthood in Greece to support the spread of Orphism.

Despite the limited appeal of Orphism it still managed to influence the philosophies of **Empedocles** and **Plato**; and most of all it was through the later modified **Platonism**, called **Neoplatonism**, that the Orphic doctrine of metempsychosis was adopted by various gnostic sects, as well as still later heterodox Islamic sects, and possibly even Kabbalic Judaism.

See also **Beans; Body is the hell of the soul; Body-soul dualism; Cave; Double torches; Drink or fruit of forgetfulness; Druzes; Eggs; Egypt; Fall of Souls; Gnosticism; Greek afterlife, the ancient; Greeks and reincarnation; Hermes; Homer's Iliad and Odyssey; Kabbalah; Lethe;** *Ogdoad*; **Phaedo; Priesthood, lack of an organized; Right-hand path and left-hand path; Sufism; Symbola**.

Osho Movement. This is a Hindu-Buddhist movement founded by Rajneesh Chandra Mohan (1931–1990), also known as Bhagwan Shree Rajneesh. After beginning his guru career in India in 1966 he relocated with his disciples to the United States in 1981. There he established his headquarters in Oregon, where he sought to create a utopian community or Buddha-field. Much of his teaching focused on a modernized and modified Tantric concept of the sacred nature of sexuality.

As regards his views on reincarnation, Rajneesh claimed that the reason most people could not remember their past lives was because they were meat eaters. Meat, he said, blocked the necessary channel through which such lives could be remembered.

Rajneesh's Western following began to abandon him after he was arrested in 1985 for tax evasion, embezzlement, wire-tapping, and immigration offenses and he was deported back to India.

See also **Vegetarianism**.

Osiris *see* **Book of the Dead; Egypt; Khepra; Pyramidology; Rebirth, analogies from nature; Unarius Academy of Science**.

Ouija Board. Also called a witch-board, this is a flat board with the alphabet, the numbers 0 to 9, and the words yes and no printed on its surface. A second small, pointed, easily movable board, or *planchette*, is used as a pointer to spell out answers to questions asked of the board. Depending on one's view the answers come from either the spirit world or subconscious minds of the board's users. While the Ouija board has often been used as just a parlor game activity, a few individuals have been highly traumatized by its use.

According to the teachings in *Earthly Cycles* (1994) by the entity Alexander as channeled through Ramon Stevens, messages coming through the board that involve foul language, predictions of impeding calamity, and threatening demands are usually from very immature spirits. Despite the bad name often given the board, some have claimed that it can be used to discover one's past lives.

See also **Automatic writing; Michael (2); Omega; Sciomancy**.

Ouroboros (Greek: Tail-biter). This is the name for a circular symbol that depicts a **serpent** or dragon swallowing its own tail. In one form or another it has been employed in a widely diverse number of cultures. The interpretations given it are equally diverse. In Hinduism and Buddhism, however, it symbolizes the round or cycle of *samsara*. The end (the tail) of life merges into a new beginning (the mouth) or rebirth.

See also **Circle of Necessity; Swastika**.

Ouspensky, Pyotr D. (1878–1947). In his book *A New Model of the Universe* (1971), this former student of **Georgi Ivanovitch Gurdieff** provides a very unique and complex concept of reincarnation, though it can be difficult to understand and even more difficult to summarize. Ouspensky seems to say is that very few people have a correct understanding of time. That, in fact, everything is eternal and reincarnation is nothing more than part of an eternal reoccurrence. This means that souls reincarnate into "the past," not into the future; and so the normal concept of reincarnation is a complete distortion of the truth. Ouspensky believes that the plurality of existences implied in reincarnation is due to people "simultaneously" living more than one life.

Regarding karma, Ouspensky says that since any karmic debt was made in the past, it can only be unmade (resolved) by going back into the past to relive that life. He also says that some souls that have lived more evolved lives can escape reincarnation. This, however, does not annihilate the past lives they lived, and so some other souls will have to reincarnate into those lives. On the other hand, some people who have lived meaningless lives of hardship may simply experience the annihilation of their souls; but again, this also does not annihilate their past lives, and so some other souls may reincarnate into those lives in the hope of doing a better job at living them than was done by the former souls.

See also **Annihilationism; Collin, Robert; Grant, Joan Marshall; Parallel lives; Plurality of existences; Rebirth, simultaneous.**

Out-of-the-body experiences and **near-death-experiences** (OBE/NDEs). The first of these phenomena is a state in which a person feels that his consciousness has separated from his body and from a distance can view that body as though it was no longer a part of the self. In psychic terms this seemingly disembodied consciousness is usually referred to as the **astral body**.

Out-of-the-Body Experiences (OBEs), also labeled *ecsomatic* experiences, are often used as evidence of life after death. The argument for this is that if consciousness can leave the body while alive and then return to it then it ought to be possible for consciousness to leave one body at death and survive on its own to some degree and for some period of time. Although such survival does not prove reincarnation, OBEs have been used as support for such re-embodiment on the basis that if the soul can leave and then re-enter its own body, it should be able to do so with another body. This use of OBEs to prove post-mortem survival is immediately flawed by equating what can occur with a still living body with what can occur with a dead one.

In most of the popular Western literature describing OBEs, it is claimed that there is a **silver chord** that runs from the back of the head of the physical body to the astral body and that physical death is associated with the breaking of this cord. This chord concept alone should make it clear that a consciousness that can leave and return to a living body can not be equated with a consciousness that leaves a dead body. In other words, assuming that such a cord and astral body exist then all that could possibly be suggested is that while consciousness may temporarily distance itself from the physical body it must remain attached to that body for both to continue to exist.

There is no doubt that out-of-the-body experiences happen; however, their psychic rather than physiological nature has been challenged in a number of ways. First, most OBEs occur under circumstances when there is a decreased or insufficient amount of oxygen to the brain (cerebral *hypoxia*), such as under anesthesia or temporary heart failure. This easily leads to hallucinatory experiences. Similar results have been reported with high levels of carbon dioxide (cerebral *hypercarbia*).

Second, an out-of-the-body experience can result from a medically induced procedure such as electrical simulation to the right *angular gyrus* near the back of the brain. This simulation can cause people to experience themselves floating and looking down at their normal body just as in a non-medically induced OBE. It should also be noted that the same electrical stimulation to the left side of the *angular gyrus* will cause people to have the sensation of a shadowy person lurking behind them.

Third, there is a related laboratory procedure in which a person is filmed with video cameras from the back while they wear goggles that capture the view of the cameras. This give the person a stereoscopic view of their back and the person experiences himself as if he were physically embodying a space six to seven feet behind were he really is.

Fourth, OBEs can occur under the influence of drugs such as marijuana.

The logical conclusion is that OBEs can not prove an afterlife unless it can be proven that consciousness "actually" can leave the body, even if only temporarily.

Some challengers of the psychic origin of OBEs add to their "disproof" the fact that people of different cultures and religions describe their OBE, as well as NDE, experiences differently, thus suggesting that such experiences are subjective (inside the mind), not objective (outside of the body). This challenge is not as valid as the preceding ones because the supporters of psychic OBEs can point out that such cultural relativity of experience is to be expected, at least as surface phenomena; but that beneath that surface OBEs are a trans-cultural experience.

When OBEs occur during life-threatening conditions they are often referred to as Near-Death-Experiences (NDEs). In a majority of these NDEs, at least in the Western world, the subject claims to see a great white light or tunnel of light. Along with this light "beings of light" are often perceived, which seem to come as guides to the subject. The guide is sometimes a loved one who previously died or culturally specific religious figures. In the latter case, if the subject considers him/herself or a Christian the figure will usually be an angel, a saint, or even Jesus; if Jewish it might be an angel or Elijah; if Hindu it could be one of the gods; and if the subject is a confirmed atheist the light alone may be all that is perceived. To some this religiously and culturally relative factor proves that the vision is completely within the mind of the perceiver and nothing more.

It should be mentioned that while a majority of NDEs are described as being very positive and comforting upon the return to normal consciousness, a minority are felt to have been negative. In some cases the subject reports that he/she felt attacked by malevolent forces or as being pulled into hell.

The latest scientific research has shown that there is a common ground between near-death experiences and the brain's sleep-wake control system. For most of those who have reported near-death experiences they have also reported having a condition called REM intrusion at times in their lives. In this condition, the boundaries between sleep and wakefulness are blurred. The most extreme of such cases are those of narcolepsy (brief attacks of deep sleep), which are fairly rare. In the far more common mild forms of a REM intrusion condition the person feels a short term inability to move during waking hours. During a crisis this experience can convince the person that that he or she has died and only come back to life once the condition and crisis is over.

For an interesting analysis of near-death experiences see the article by Emily Williams Cook, Bruce Greyson, and **Ian Stevenson**, "Do Any Near-Death Experiences Provide Evidence for the Survival of Human Personality after Death?" (1998) Also informative is the chapter "Near-death experiences: ancient, medieval and modern" in Bremmer's *The Rise and Fall of the Afterlife* (2002).

See also **Altered states of consciousness; Alzheimer's Disease; Arguments supportive of rebirth; Astral plane; Body-brain (mind) dependency; Borderline state; Death.**

Over-soul, personal. This is believed to be the consciousness that collects and integrates all the experiences of an individual person's past, present and, according to some, future-lives. The personal over-soul is a greater identity than that of the presently perceived self. There are, therefore, as many personal over-souls as there are people presently living. It is believed that when a person "remembers a past life" they are reading from their personal over-soul. This over-soul can also be considered a personal *akashic* record.

Over-soul, universal *see* **Anima; Brahman; Group soul.**

Ovid or **Publius Ovidius Naso** (43 BCE– 17 CE?). Among the works of this Roman poet is the *Metamorphoses*. In this he offers various tales in which he utilizes the metempsychosis concept of **Pythagoras.**

Oxytocin *see* **Body-brain (mind) dependency; Memories, reasons for loss of past life.**

Palingenesis. This term is derived from two Greek words, *palin-* (again) and *-genesis* (birth) and has been translated variously as rebirth, new birth, regeneration, recreation, or renewal. The word was originally used in an alchemical sense for the ability to regenerate life from ashes. In other words, it attempted to prove that sentience survived physical destruction. Only later did it become one of the synonyms for rebirth, reincarnation, **metempsychosis**, or **transmigration**; however, it is almost never used in this way in modern rebirth literature. Nonetheless, the fact is that it is found in the New Testament at **Matthew** 19:28 and Titus 3:5 has encouraged some reincarnationists to claim that reincarnation is meant by the term, at least, in Matthew's, "I tell you [the disciples] this: in the world the is to be (*paligenesia*), when the Son of Man [Jesus] is seated on his throne in heavenly splendor, you, my followers, will have thrones of your own, where you will sit as judges of the twelve tribes of Israel." *Paligenesia* here is usually translated as either the "world to be" or "in the regeneration" and clearly refers to the rebirth of the world as the Kingdom of Heaven, not to an individual's rebirth.

In Titus the wording is, "But when the kindness and generosity of God our savior dawned upon the world, then, not for any good deeds of our own, but because he was merciful, he saved us through the water of rebirth (*paligenesia*) and the *anakinoseoz* (renewing) power of the Holy Spirit." The only way to make *paligenesia* mean reincarnation in either of these passages is to read them out of their proper context.

Panchen Lama (Tibetan: *bla-ma*). The Panchen Lama is regarded as a *tulku*, or incarnation of **Amitabha Buddha** (Tibetan: O Pame) and as such he the second most important religious figure in traditional Tibetan society after the **Dalai Lama**. The Panchen Lama's residence and court is situated in Shigatse, not far from Lhasa. The term Panchen Lama is actually an abbreviation of *Pan-*

dita-chen-po which is a combination of Sanskrit and Tibetan for Great Scholar.

See also **Incarnation versus reincarnation**.

Pantheism and panentheism. The first of these terms means "all God" and it is the belief that the universe in its entirety is God, and God is identical to the universe. The second term means "all in God" and is the belief that while the whole universe is God, God is greater than the universe. Panentheism is a compromise between pantheism and transcendental theism which makes the universe and God two entirely separate states of being. In pantheism and panentheism both the body and souls of all beings are made-up of, or are a part of, God. The transcendental theism of orthodox Christianity, Judaism, and Islam regard both pantheism and, to a lesser degree panentheism, as heretical, especially in that it they allow for no true independence of the human soul, much less an independent post-mortem existence. In other words, the human soul becomes an *atman*-like phenomenon with all the logical problems that this phenomenon has with regards to an afterlife.

See also **Brahman; Monism**.

Pantomnesia. Greek for universal (*panto-*) memory (*-mnesia*) see *Déjà Vu*.

Papa-purusha (Man of sin). (1) In traditional **Hinduism** this is the personification of all evil in human form. (2) In **Theosophy** it also means a **soul** that has been reborn after a stay in the lowest and worst of hells (*avichi*).

Paradise see *Devachan*; Empire of Jade; Heaven; Interim period; *Mandara*; Pure-Land or Blissful Land Buddhism; Summerland; *Swarga* or *Svarga*; *Vaikuntha*.

Parallel lives. This refers to the concept that we all live in more than one dimension simultaneously and, therefore, are living more than one life at the same time. Some people believe that such parallel existences may be the real explanation for the experience of what seem to be past and even future lives.

According to Alex Vilenkin in an article in *Natural History* magazine (2006) a recent cosmological theory called "eternal inflation" proposes that there ought to be an infinite number of parallel earths which have undergone, are undergoing, and will undergo all the histories we have and will experience. The only problem with this for reading past or future lives is that there seems to be no way for these parallel worlds to communicate with one another.

See also **Grant, Joan Marshall; Ouspensky, Pyotr D; Plurality of existences; Rebirth, simultaneous**.

Paramacca Maroons. These people are the descendents of Negro slaves who escaped from their Dutch owners into the jungles of Surinam. Despite being mostly Christian today they believe that almost everyone is a reincarnation of an ancestor and, most often, is of the same matrilineage and sex of the ancestor. Early in childhood the reincarnated ancestor (*nenseki*) is determined by divination, or personality or physical characteristics, or dreams. Reincarnation as *nenseki* is reward for "not" having been a witch in the previous incarnation. The bodies of those persons who were found to be witches in this life are taken at death to a remote place in the forest and abandoned without any proper burial rituals and without their name ever again mentioned. This ensures the permanent annihilation of that person.

See also **Rebirth, consanguineous**.

Paramnesia see *Déjà Vu*.

Parapsychology. This is the study of the proposed abilities of the mind beyond those abilities that are assumed to be its normal limits. Among these abilities would be clairvoyance, telepathy, precognition, and post-mortem survival, including reincarnation.

Parapsychologists can be divided into those who are only concerned with the abilities of living minds and those who are also concerned with possible non-embodied minds.

See also **Rhine, J. B.**

Parents in the next life. Most Western reincarnationists believe that the soul has some freedom in deciding who its next life parents will be. Eastern religions assume that karma itself will determine all future parentage. This difference of views reflects the West's greater insistence on personal freedom versus the East's greater acceptance of impersonal karma. An example of this greater freedom is the belief that premature death, especially of infants and young children, is often a voluntary event. In some of these cases it is due to the souls of the children deciding that they had made a mistake in being reborn either at that time and/or to those parents. In other cases, the children's souls had some **karma as unfinished business** to complete, but this only required a minimal embodiment to complete it. Also, it is believed that children that experience involuntary death not only try to reincarnate as soon as possible, but do so in such haste that they are often very unselective about their future parents. This can create a situation in which the child literally does not seem to belong to those parents.

See also **Australian Aborigines; Congenital retardation; Deaths, violent and premature;**

Dreams, announcing; Jewish Holocaust; Rebirth, East and West.

Parmenides. This 5th century BCE Greek philosopher was said to have been a student of Ameinias, who was a student of **Pythagoras** and as such was also a teacher of **metempsychosis**.

Parousia (Greek: Presence). In a Christian context it means the second coming of Christ.

See also **Millennialism; New Testament and reincarnation; Peter, 1st and 2nd; Resurrection of Jesus**.

Pascal's wager. Blaise Pascal (1623–1662), a French philosopher, in trying to justify the belief in God and an afterlife devised a set of four gambling propositions for that purpose. These are: (1) If we believe in God and an afterlife and it is true, we win; (2) If we believe in God and an afterlife and it is not true, we neither win nor lose; (3) If we disbelieve in God and an afterlife and it is true, we lose; (4) If we disbelieve in God and an afterlife and it is not true, we neither win nor lose. Since three out of the four propositions are either beneficial or neutral to the believer, the rules of chance tell us it is safer to believe than to disbelieve.

This same wager argument can be made for a belief in karma and rebirth by substituting that belief for a belief in God.

See also **Arguments pro and con on an afterlife in general; Arguments supportive of rebirth**.

Pasricha, Satwant K. Dr. Pasricha is a protégé of **Ian Stevenson** and, since 1973, has investigated about four hundred cases involving children who claim to remember previous lives. Dr. Pasricha has tried to respond to one of the most common arguments of skeptics regarding reincarnation. This is that most children who claim to remember their previous lives come from cultures or communities whose people believe in reincarnation. The skeptics rationalize these claims as being a kind of fantasy arising from the hereditary belief of their culture. In response to this Dr. Pasricha has found a few cases occurring among Sunni Moslems who, guided by their religious teachings, do not believe in reincarnation. A full analysis of Dr. Pasricha's four hundred child recall cases revealed twenty six Moslem subjects who remembered having been Moslems in the previous life (nineteen cases) and Hindus who remembered having been Moslems (seven cases). There were seven Moslems cases from where no change in religion was reported. Most of the remaining cases involve members in the religious communities of Hindus, Sikhs, and Jains, who do believe in reincarnation, as well as some Shiite Moslems who also endorse the idea of reincarnation.

See also **Children remembering past lives; Rebirth and cultural conditioning**.

Passing-memories adoption (PMA). PMA has been suggested as one of several possible psychic alternatives to past life memories due to rebirth. It has been proposed that some newly created or generated souls, while descending or passing into the material existence from their place of origin, often pick up (are imprinted by) the memories of souls that are ascending or passing back to their place of origin. The new or imprinted souls unintentionally adopt those passed on memories as their own. In particular, this imprinting idea has been favored by some Sufi traditions.

See also **Rebirth, alternative explanations to; Sufism**.

Past life fakery. The best way to fake a past life is to invent one that is well over a century old and, therefore, very difficult to verify, and equally difficult to disprove.

See also **Fraud; Honest lying; Past life memory recall; Rampa, Lobsang Tuesday**.

Past life journal. A number of past life counselors advise people who want to explore the possibility of past life recall to keep a journal for this purpose. Possible inclusions in this journal could be records of reoccurring night time dreams; reoccurring daydreams; insights gained during past life recall meditation practices; *déjà vu* experiences; and long held habits, desires, and fears (phobias) that do not seem to be related to anything in the present-life.

See also **Philias** and **phobias**.

Past life memory categories. When we think of memory we often first associate it with semantic memory, which is memory of general knowledge, such as the definition of words, facts, etc. Unless some strong emotion is connected with such memory it is thought that it would not carry over to another life. The parapsychologist James G. Matlock, however, has suggested an alternative view. He divides past life memories into four categories. The first is verbal, or informational, the ability to member names, dates, and events. This is usually very personal and emotionally laden, and hence it is believed to carry over from one life to another. The second memory category is imaged memory which is where a living person is able to identify (remember) people and places associated with a prior living person. This is also very personal and would be carried over. The first and second categories are sometimes grouped together as episodic memory. The third of Matlock's categories is behavioral, where there is a great similarity between the deceased and a living person in mannerism, habits, likes and dislikes, especially **philias** and **phobias**, skills, and so would have been carried over from the past. The fourth memory is physical and involves such traits as birthmarks, scars, or deformities of one person that are the same or very similar to those of a second person who died previously to the first person's birth. According to Matlock, in many cases only one or two of these four categories is present in the presumed reincarnated person; rarely, if ever, are all four fully present.

While any theory of a past life recall must take these different kinds of memory into account, at the same time, it must not be forgotten that all memories are actually modified by what is acceptable to our current personality. This means that we are loaded with false memories. With this the case, the question might be asked, how can anyone be sure that a set of so-called past life memories is accurate?

See also **Alzheimer's Disease; Karma and justice; Memories, ancestral or genetic; Memories, reasons for loss of past life; Memory, summation; Rebirth, qualifications for.**

Past life memory recall *see* **Rebirth, criteria for proof of.**

Past life psychic reader. A past life psychic reader must be carefully distinguished from a **past life therapist**. A past life psychic reader is someone who claims that, through some psychic ability, he or she can read a client's past life. Such a reader does not require any kind of state licensing, which a genuine past life therapist is required to have. According to Lynn E. Sparrow, in her *Reincarnation: Claiming Your Past, Creating Your Future* (1988), when seeking out a past life psychic reader the prospective client should be aware of a number of facts. First, although some psychics might have more consistently correct information than others there is almost certainly no such person as a totally accurate psychic. Second, all psychics have psychic on-days and psychic off-days. Third, some psychics and clients match well together and some do not. Fourth, even the best of psychic readings are apt to mix incorrect information with correct information. Fifth, no matter how pleasant or unpleasant the information from a past life reading may be, none of it should be uncritically accepted if it does not intuitively seem accurate and/or offer accurate or beneficial insight into one's current life.

See also **Past life readings; Past life therapist, finding a.**

Past life readings. These are readings done by a **past life psychic reader.** The most common ways this is done is either by the psychic in a non-trance state using a deck of regular cards or **tarot** cards or by the psychic conducting the reading through some form of **scrying**, more often than not in a trance state. Perhaps even more controversial is past life reading via **channeling**. In this case there is, at least in theory, a doubly indirect source through which the reading occurs. First, there is the channeled entity and second, there is the channeler.

Since in past life readings the individual whose life is being read is passively receiving information from a totally outside source, such readings are generally thought of as being of less value to the individual than past life information more actively acquired through past life regression. However, even such regression, in that it depends on a hypnotist, is to a degree second handed and the only truly first hand source for discovering a past life is through **spontaneous recall.**

See also **Netherton Method; Trance states.**

Past life recall. There are a number of theories as to what might account for what might be a genuine ability to recall memories of a past life. These include the ***akashic* record**, soul imprinting (**passing-memories adoption**), **possession, retrocognition**; and reincarnation.

See also **Clairaudience; Clairvoyance.**

Past life recall meditation. There are believed to be a number of meditation practices that can stimulate past life recall. Most of these involve using the image-forming abilities of the right brain to access the subconscious where past life memories are thought to be stored. It is thought that the best meditations involve the elements of visualization, concentration, and creative imagination. For example, focusing on one's astrological chart or the *chakras*, engaging in **scrying** exercises, or using **tarot** cards can be a part of such meditation. Certain mineral or gem stones and fragrances are also regarded by some as assisting in recall.

See also **Astrology and rebirth; Fluorite; I, William the Conqueror; Patanjali; Pyramidology.**

Past life regression and suggestibility. In a study conducted at the University of Kentucky by Robert Baker and reported in the *American Journal of Clinical Hypnosis* (1982), some sixty undergraduate students were divided into three groups of twenty students per group to undergo hypnotic age-regression. Beforehand, suggestions highly supportive of **past life therapy** were given to Group A. More neutral or non-committal statements about past lives were given to Group B. Skeptical and derogatory statements about past lives were given to Group C. The results showed that Group A recalled the most past lives while Group C recalled the least.

See also **Christos** (anointing) **technique; Hypnotic age regression.**

Past life therapist. This is a person with some psychological training who has also been licensed for psychological counseling by the state in which he or she is working. A past life therapist must be carefully distinguished from a **past life psychic reader** in that the latter does not require any kind of licensing from the state and thus a client has little recourse for claims of malpractice or fraud.

Past life therapist, finding a. Karl Schlotterbeck, in his *Living Your Past Lives* (1987), recommends that one uses the following guide lines in finding a past life therapist. Ask the following questions. What is the therapist's background and training? Does he belong to a certified association or organization? What percentage of his therapy has dealt with past lives? Is past life therapy his exclusive practice? Is it the only practice in which he is trained and has he been trained in more than one past life therapy technique? Is he also trained to provide general counseling? How long are his individual sessions? Does he encourage or discourage recoding the sessions for future playback if desired?

See also **Atlantic Guild for Past Life Awareness; Past life psychic reader.**

Past life therapy. This is the exploration of one or more past life scenarios, usually through hypnosis, for possible relevance to present life physical and/or psychological issues. Past life therapy began in Europe as early as 1862, but it did not become a more wide spread and legitimate form of therapy until the 1960s. Past life therapy seems to have no better and no worse chance of helping a client than do most other forms of therapy. The reasons for this are the same as for any successful treatment. The therapist and patient share the same worldview. The patient develops confidence in the therapist. Along with the past life examination the therapist also usually uses a number of standardized medical and behavioral change strategies. The patient expects to get well from the treatment.

Those therapists who recognize the therapeutic value of past life therapy, yet do not believe in past lives have suggested that the so-called past life acting as a personal myth can be therapeutically effective. In fact, it has been theorized that those under hypnosis intuitively choose to create a past life scenario that will be therapeutic.

One interesting aspect of past life hypnotherapy is that very often the therapy works faster than in some other forms of therapy. This may partly be due to the use of a past lives as very safe and therapeutically useful **screen memories**. This also makes past life therapy a fairly short-term therapy.

A major criticism of past life therapy is that it can easily allow both the patient and therapist to overlook the real cause of the patient's problem in this life. This might permit the patient from actually dealing with his problem on the basis that he can not change the past.

A major source for past life therapists is the **Association for Past Life Research and Therapy**, was founded in 1980.

See also **Atlantic Guild for Past Life Awareness; Hypnosis; Kelsey, Denys; Multiple personalities; Netherton Method; Past life regression and suggestibility; Placebo effect; Spiritism; Sutphen, Richard.**

Past lives. This refers to the idea that the souls of human beings, and perhaps animals, have lived in one or more bodies in the past. It is the same as rebirth, reincarnation, **metempsychosis**, and **transmigration**.

See also **Animals and rebirth, non–Western view; Animals and rebirth, Western view; Karma and justice.**

Patala. This is the collective term for the seven Hindu underworlds, inhabited by various kinds of supernatural beings. Although identified as in the underworld, *Patala* has nothing to do with **hell**. On the contrary, each division of *Patala* is, for the most part, a place of wonder and delight. Some sources state that though many souls passing through *Patala* may undergo some trials, it is a place of beneficial refreshment before their next rebirth.

Patanjali. This 4th century BCE Indian philosopher, who codified yoga, instructed how past lives can be recalled through meditation.

See also **Past life recall meditation.**

Patarines or **Patarenes**. This is the name for a dualist Christian sect that believed in metempsychosis and which had spread through the Balkans and Italy in the 12th and 13th century CE before being exterminated by the Catholic Inquisition. They were closely associated with the **Bogomils** and the **Cathars**. Their name for awhile came to signify for the Catholic authorities all heretics.

See also **Dualism; Paulicians.**

Pathological retrocognition. This is where an individual becomes so obsessed with his or her past life memories that these memories interfere with the person's present-life functioning.

Patton, George S. (1885–1945). This American general, a firm reincarnationist, believed that during his many past lives he had been a soldier in various wars. In keeping with the **repetition compulsion**, he believed that he had been an ancient Greek soldier fighting against the Persians, a member of the army of Alexander the Great, the Carthaginian general Hannibal, a soldier in the Hundred Year War and an officer in the army of **Napoleon Bonaparte**. He wrote a poem, "Through a Glass Darkly," detailing his belief in reincarnation. The poem's title comes from 1st **Corinthians** 13:12 where the glass refers to a mirror.

See also **Buddhist Poem; Hindu Poem; Masefield, John; Poetry on reincarnation.**

Paul of Tarsus (?10–67 CE?). Paul was the author of at least seven of the New Testament Letters and was the first known person to write anything about **Jesus** of Nazareth. In that there is no known precedence for his views about Jesus as the Christ (Messiah), about the resurrection of Jesus, or about Jesus as a sacrificial victim for mankind's sins, it has been argued that one or more of these ideas originated with Paul himself and that Paul, more than anyone else, was the real founder of Christianity. Whatever else can be said about Paul, his teaching on the exclusivity of the resurrection was certainly the major factor in preventing a serious consideration of reincarnation in later orthodox Christianity.

See also **Anabios; Annihilationism, Biblical view; Augustine, Saint Aurelius; Bogomils; Cayce, Edgar; Christian view of the afterlife; Corinthians, 1st and 2nd; Ephesians; Galatians; Gnosticism; Karma and free will; Karma versus grace; Mark, Gospel of; New Testament; New Testament and reincarnation; New Testament sacrificial concept; Old Testament and the soul; Original sin, Christianity, and reincarnation; Paulicians; Peter, 1st and 2nd; Resurrection, bodily; Resurrection of Jesus; Resurrection or reincarnation; Romans; Soul; Valentinus.**

Paulicians. This was a 7th to 9th century Christian gnostic sect found in Armenia and Thrace (Bulgaria) which believed in reincarnation. This sect probably had a number of its views in common with other dualist gnostic sects as well as with **Manichaeism**. The first of these views was that there were two Gods, one was the evil creator of the material world (the *demiurge*) and the other was the good ruler of the world of pure spirit. Since the evil one had trapped human souls into material bodies it was the Paulicians' religious goal to instruct mankind in how to liberate those souls from the world of matter. In keeping with their antimaterial or **body-soul dualism** teaching the Paulicians denied the physical incarnation of **Jesus**, even his birth from a human womb. In direct opposition to orthodox Christianity the Paulicians considered the Old Testament to be the revelation of the evil one. With such exceptions of the letters of **Paul of Tarsus** and the Gospel of **Luke** even other parts of the New Testament were unacceptable to them.

The Paulician teachings were ultimately suppressed by the orthodox Byzantine emperors, but apparently not before the Thracian Paulicians gave rise to the dualist **Bogomils**.

See also **Cathars; Doceticism; Dualism; Fall of Souls; Gnosticism; Gospel of; Patarines; Plato.**

Perception and reality. While there presumably is an objective reality or reality independent of our observation of it, it has also been scientifically documented that our perception of reality is very much influenced by the theories we create in our examination of that reality. In other words, what we observe is not reality itself, but reality as altered by what we need and want it to be. Nothing could reflect this more than the various conflicting views of the afterlife in general and the conflicting views on reincarnation in particular.

See also **Science and pseudo-science.**

Persephone. At least three myths were woven around this Greek goddess. In the first she is the daughter of the goddess Demeter and Zeus, and the reluctant wife of her uncle **Pluto**. As such Persephone lived half of the year above ground with her mother and half the year under the earth in **Hades** with her husband. It was said that her time spent above ground accounted for the growing season of spring and summer, while her time below ground accounted for the dying seasons of autumn and winter. The second myth makes Persephone the mother of Dionysus Zagreus by Zeus, and so she is of importance in **Orphism**. A third myth makes her the daughter of Zeus and Styx, the nymph of the Underworld. In reincarnation symbolism Persephone's dual existence represents the cycle of life and the **interim periods** between lives.

Persia (Iran) *see* **Assassins; Babism and Bahaiism; Gnosticism; Hashimiyya; Islam; Kanthaeans; Khurramiyya; Manichaeism; Mithraism; Yarsanism; Yazidis (Yezidis); Zoroastrianism.**

Personalists. These were a large group of early Indian Buddhists who rejected the extreme *anatman* (no soul) doctrine of other Buddhists. The Personalists pointed out that without at least a temporary soul-like factor (S: *pudgala*) rebirth was put into doubt. This Personalist view avoided most of the problems, both metaphysical and moral, with which the *Anatmanists* had to struggle. The Personalists, however, died out in India, along with all other forms of Buddhism by the 13th century.

Personality versus individuality. Although the term personality can be difficult to precisely define one general definition is "a unique pattern of individual behavior that remains consistent over time and in a variety of circumstances."

When it comes to the issue of personality and reincarnation the criticism has been that even if we have past lives, not remembering them is the equivalent of the death of our personality and so of the death of self. In response to this criticism many reincarnationists have proposed that the personality that we have in any one life is not our true or essential self, but a mask or outfit we put over our true self which is the "individual." It is believed that this distinction is all the more justified considering the etymological origin of the words personality and individual. The first comes from Latin "persona" meaning a mask an actor wears on stage and changes with each new role. The second comes from Latin "individus" meaning indivisible which implies something unchanging.

This view of personality versus individuality is actually a Western version of the Hindu distinction between the ever changing mortal sheaths (*kosha*) around the soul and the immortal soul or *atman*.

See also **Individuality and rebirth**.

Petavatthu (P). This is a minor book in the **Theravada Buddhist** canon which describes the fate of a certain group of the virtue-less deceased that do not immediately go on to a physically embodied human or animal rebirth. The word *peta* in general means ghost, but in the Buddhist context it means **hungry ghost**. The *Petavatthu* consists of fifty-one stories detailing the miserable state that these ghosts must suffer due to their unwholesome karma.

See also *Pretas*; Theravada Buddhism; *Vimanavatthu*.

Peter, 1st and 2nd. The first of these two texts in the New Testament gives encouragement to readers of the time, who were experiencing persecution. They are reminded that as followers of Christ they are the heir to the glorious promise if they merely keep faith in the resurrection of Jesus and look forward to the *Parousia* (Second Coming). In particular, the faithful are to know that a new life (rebirth) into salvation is available through **baptism** (1st Peter 1:23, 2:2).

Despite the obviousness of the main theme in this text there have been attempts to read support for reincarnation into 1st Peter 1:23, which reads, "You have been **born again**, not of mortal parentage but of immortal, through the living and enduring word of God." This passage, however, means born again in the same non-reincarnational way as that at **John** 3:3–4 and in no way implies reincarnation.

Second Peter is quite different from its predecessor in that its main theme is to warn against false, ungodly teachers, and damnable heretics (2nd Peter 2:1) upon whom the future judgment of God will fall as prophesied in the Old Testament. However, as in 1st Peter there is also one passage in here that pro-reincarnationists have focused upon. It is 2nd Peter 3:8 which reads, "...with the Lord one day is like a thousand years and a thousand years like one day." This is really a quote from Psalm 90:3, "For in thy sight a thousand years are as yesterday." Considerable effort has been made to claim that both the Psalm and Peter verses mean that there is a thousand year cycle between embodiments. Rather than having anything to do with reincarnation 2nd Peter, when read in its full context, is an attempt to explain the delay of the return of Christ (*Parousia*) and the general resurrection of the dead as is made very clear at 2nd Peter 3:4, 9, etc.

See also **Annihilationism, Biblical view; Christian view of the afterlife; Christianity and reincarnation; Christianity, esoteric; Harrowing of Hell; Hell; John, Gospel of; Karma in the Bible? Limbo; Lucifer; Millennialism; New Testament and reincarnation; New Testament sacrificial concept; Psalms; Purgatory; Rebirth and moral perfection; Resurrection, bodily; Resurrection of Jesus;** *Theosis*.

Phaedo. The subject of this text, by **Plato**, is Socrates, who has been condemned to death. Socrates is explaining to his distressed students on the needlessness for fear of death because of the immortality of the soul, which includes a belief in a succession of lives. Among the arguments given in support of such a belief is the cyclical aspect in nature and that all learning is really remembering (*anamnesis*) from past lives. There is a strong **body-soul dualism** stated here in which the true goal in life is to have the soul once and for all escape from the prison (*phroura*) that is the body. Such escape is only possible for the more or less ascetic philosopher. All others will return to earthly existence in some new corporeal form. The individual who has lived at least a civil and socially virtuous life will come back as a human being or one of the social insects (bees, wasps, or ants). The gluttonous individual will return in the body of an ass or similar beast. The individual who has committed acts of injustice, tyranny, and other forms of violence will assume the form of a wolf or bird of prey.

See also **Orphism; Rebirth, analogies from nature**.

Phantasmata. In occult circles this is a thought-form created by the human mind which can become independent enough to be able to communicate with its creators. It has been suggested that some channeled beings, including ones that support the concept of reincarnation are *phantasmata*.

See also **Channeling**.

Pherecydes of Syros (c. 550 BCE). Some ancient Greek sources claim that Pherecydes was the first philosopher to teach the immortality of the soul. A much later Byzantine source credits him with being the first Greek to teach **metempsychosis**. For this reason at least, he is also said to have been the teacher of **Pythagoras**; however, most of the earliest sources regard Pythagoras, not Pherecydes, as the first to teach the doctrine of metempsychosis. Pherecydes is sometimes called Terecides.

See also **Greeks and reincarnation;** *Kyklos Genesion*.

Philias and **phobias**. These are two forms of behavioral memory that are said to carry over from one life to another. For example, a deep seated fear of the ocean or even swimming pools that has no discernable cause in your present life is thought to mean that you or someone close to you may have drowned in a former life. On the other hand, an enormous fascination with the sea may suggest that in the past you were a sailor, a fisherman, etc.

See also **Bleed-over; Past life memory categories**.

Philippians *see* "Every knee should bend ... every tongue confess."

Philo Judaeus or **Philo of Alexandria** (20 BCE–54 CE). This Neoplatonic Jewish philosopher recorded in his work, *De Somniis*, " The air is full of souls: those who are nearest to Earth descending to be tied to mortal bodies return to other bodies, desiring to live in them." In his *De Gigantes* he wrote, "The company of disembodied souls is distributed in various orders. The law of some is to enter mortal bodies and after certain prescribed periods to be again free. But those possessed of a diviner structure are absolved from all local bonds of Earth. Some souls choose confinement in mortal bodies because they are corporeally inclined.... Yet those who are wise, like Moses, are also living abroad from home because they chose this expatriation from heaven in order to acquire knowledge and so came to dwell in earthly nature. While here they urge men to return to their original source." It is debatable whether Philo is here speaking about **metempsychosis**, resurrection, or even **possession**.

See also **Kabbalah, Old Testament and the afterlife**.

Phobias as screen memory *see* **Philias and phobias; Screen Memory**.

Phoenix. In Western mythology this is a great magical bird which, rather than laying eggs to continue the species, builds a nest that engulfs the mature phoenix in flames and from the ashes in the nest a new phoenix is reborn.

The word phoenix is the Greek form of the Egyptian Bennu. In **Egypt** the bird, represented as a heron, was a symbol of Ra, the sun god of Heliopolis (Biblical On, Egyptian Iunu) which died each evening and was reborn each dawn. Because of this rebirth process the phoenix eventually became a symbol of **metempsychosis** as well as of resurrection.

It is to be noted that the phoenix in Eastern Asian mythology is totally independent of the Western version and does not incinerate itself for rebirth or any other reason.

See also **Phoenix card set**.

Phoenix card set. This cartomancy (divination by cards) deck was designed by Susan Sheppard specifically for past life readings. Along with the card deck Sheppard has written *Phoenix Cards: Reading and Interpreting Past life Influences with the Phoenix Deck* (1990). This deck is a kind of modified **tarot** deck, only exclusively to be used to help people discover their past lives. Some other similar decks have been produced for the purpose, but most are of less quality than Shappard's.

Phoenix Rising. This is a non-profit referral service for certified hypnotherapists that practice past life regression therapy as well as a group forum for these therapists.

See also **Associations and organizations**.

Phowa or *Phoba*. This is a Buddhist Tantric practice which seeks to transfer the consciousness of a dying person to a more favorable realm of existence such as a **Pure-Land** rather than merely being reborn into the ordinary cycle of rebirth and re-death. It is believed that a sign of a successful transfer is the presence of a minute hole at the crown aperture of the deceased's skull.

See also **Pure-Land** or **Blissful Land Buddhism; Vajrayana Buddhism**.

Phren see **Soul, tripartite**.

Phylos the Tibetan. In 1883 the teenager Frederick Spencer Oliver (1866–1899), while living near **Mount Shasta**, California, began to experience a series of **automatic writing** episodes. These were said to originate from a being named Phylos who described himself as a Lemurian spirit who had lived several previous lives on the **lost continent** of Atlantis. Oliver claimed that this channeled spirit took him to one or more secret temples within the mountain to meet members of a mystic brotherhood. Oliver's writings seem to be the origin of the now widespread belief in the mystical and occult nature of Mount Shasta. Among Oliver's works that have been republished are *An Earth Dweller's Return* (1940), *A Dweller on Two Planets* (1974), and *Growth of a Soul* (1975).

See also **Channeling; I Am Movement**.

Physical plane. This is the plane of existence in which the every-day body functions, as opposed to the **astral plane**, **etheric plane**, and **mental plane**.

See also **Planes of existence, names of**.

Pilgrimages. It is a widespread belief in South and East Asia that going on pilgrimages to certain holy sites can significantly reduce bad karma, if not eliminate it entirely. In Buddhism, there are four great pilgrimages places. These are associated with the birth, enlightenment, teaching and death of the historical Buddha. These are respectively: Lumbini, Bod-Gaya, Sarnath and Kushinagara. It is believed by many Buddhists that anyone who dies while on pilgrimage to one of these places will be guaranteed a superior rebirth. In **Hinduism** it is the **Ganges River** that is the holiest of pilgrim sites and the one most closely related to improved rebirth.

Pindar (518/22–446/38). This Greek poet was considered the greatest choral lyricist of ancient Greece. Some of his odes incorporate not only elements from the standard Olympian religion but also from the mystery cult and the Orphic-Pythagorean tradition. In the latter case, this includes a familiarity with the concept of **metempsychosis**. Whether or not Pindar believed in it personally can not be determined from the odes.

See also **Orphism; Pythagoras**.

Pineal and pituitary gland. Both of these glands are thought to be related to psychic powers. The first of these is pea-sized and located just under the major mass of the brain. Its main function is to produce and secrete the hormone melatonin, which seemingly is involved in biological rhythms and reproductive behavior in animals and humans. The second gland is located just under the front mid section of the major mass of the brain and secretes hormones governing the metabolism and growth of the body.

Depending upon which authority one chooses, either the pineal or the pituitary gland, and even the thalamus in conjunction with the pineal, is associated with the **third eye**. Among the abilities of this psychic eye are reading one's own past lives and possibly those of others. It might be noted that it is in the pineal gland that the French philosopher **Rene Descartes** (1596–1650) imagined the **soul** to reside.

See also *Chakras*.

Pistis Sophia (Greek: *Faith Wisdom*). The surviving version of this Gnostic text is a 3rd century translation from the original Greek into Coptic (old Egyptian) and contains two works. The first purports to be a record of the teachings of **Jesus** given to his disciples, including Mary Magdalene, over an eleven-year period following his resurrection and initial glorification or investiture. It ends in the twelfth year with a second, even more glorious divine investiture. In conversations with his elite disciples Jesus gives a Gnostic interpretation of some of the Old Testament **Psalms**, Five Odes of Solomon, and even esoteric interpretations of some of his own otherwise public sayings.

The second work is preoccupied with the issue of the fall into sin and the redemption from this fall. The text teaches that those who will ultimately be saved are the ones who completely renounce the world and follow a strict ethic of compassion and love. The text teaches a general faith in both the **soul's existence prior to embodiment** and its **metempsychosis**. As a gnostic text two atypical elements of the *Pistis Sophia* are that nowhere in it is Jesus referred to as the Christ and there is no sign of antagonism towards Judaism.

See also **Gnosticism; Hermetic philosophy;** *Nag Hammadi Texts*.

Placebo effect. This is where a patient experiences a cure simply because he is convinced that the therapist, contrary to reality, has applied a curative procedure to the ailment. Some psychologists suggest that this is, in fact, all that **past life therapy** involves.

Planes of existence, names of. Different New Age and Theosophical Schools have some common names for the planes of existence and some that are unique to individual schools. Among the common names are **astral plane, etheric plane, physical plane,** and **mental plane**. Other names are angelic plane, archangelic plane, and celestial plane.

See also **Soul and spirit levels, Theosophical; Stelle Group; Theosophy**.

Planet of death *see* **Eighth sphere**.

Planetary descent and ascent of the soul. Beginning at least as early as **Plato** many classical philosophers and religious teachers believed that during the original descent or **fall of souls** from the **Ogdoad** (sphere of fixed stars) to the earth each **soul** passed through the seven spheres of the celestial bodies taking on the negative spiritual characteristic of each of those spheres. When the soul was finally ready for release from the cycle of **metempsychosis** its ascent had to retrace its descent and, in doing so, had to shed whatever negative characteristics it previously acquired. If it did not do so it could not complete its journey back to the kingdom of pure light (**Milky Way**). This theory that began with the Pythagoreans attained its most elaborate form as it first passed on by the Greek Stoic philosopher Posiedonius or Posidonius (about 135–51 BCE), who was considered the most learned man of his time, and then by the Neo-Pythagorean philosopher **Numenius of Apamea** (2nd Century CE).

There were at least three differing versions of this descent/ascent concept. The first descent/ascent version is associated with Poseidonius (1st century BCE). In this version the moon gives the soul tears, Jupiter (Zeus) gives laughter, Mars (Ares) gives anger, Venus (Aphrodite) gives birth, Saturn (Kronos) gives speech, Sol (Helios) gives sleep, and Mercury (Hermes) gives desire.

The second version was named the Egyptian, which is a puzzling name since the first reference to this particular descent/ascent concept seems to come from a commentary on *Book IV of the Aeneid* of Publius Vergilius Maro, or **Virgil,** by the commentator Servius Marius Honoratus (4th–5th century CE). In the Servius version each planetary sphere is associated with one of the seven major vices. The list is as follows: avarice from **Saturn**; desire for dominance and gluttony from Jupiter; violent passions or anger from Mars; pride from the sun; lust from Venus; envy from Mercury; and sluggishness from the **moon**. Some classical authors differ as to which vice to assign to which planet, for example, sluggishness is often assigned to Saturn instead of the Moon. It should be noted that each of these vices, which latter Christianity will call the Seven Deadly Sins, are all psychological characteristics as is befitting of a soul.

The third, or Orphic descent/ascent, version comes from a commentary by the Neoplatonic pagan Greco-Roman philosopher Theodosius Macrobius (395–423 CE) on a work called *Scipio's Dream* (*Somnium Scipionis*), which is found in the sixth book of the *Republic* (*De Republica*) by **Marcus Tullius Cicero** (106–43 BCE). This dream story is modeled on the Myth of Er by **Plato** in his *Republic*, but Macrobius has combined it with a planetary psychological system that goes back at least as far as the Tyrian born anti–Christian Neoplatonist **Porphyry Malchus** (234–305 CE). For Macrobius the acquired influences from the planets are quite positive. Saturn offers the power of contemplative reason and theorizing or right judgment; Jupiter offers the power of putting things into practice or proper exercise of the will; Mars offers the power of forceful expression or impulsiveness; the sun offers the power of opinion, sensing, and imagination; Venus offers the power of desire and love; Mercury offers the power of interpreting feelings; and the moon offers the power of mastering the physical body and its environment. It is from this schema that some Neoplatonists justified the art of astrology.

It must be remembered that this astrological schema was developed when it was still thought that the earth was at the center of the universe and when the only planets that could be seen with the naked eye were those noted here. The Egyptian and Orphic planetary order follow that of the Greco-Roman astronomer Claudius Ptolemaeus (2nd century CE), and was based upon what were considered to be both their distance from the Earth and the speed at which they moved through heaven. In these regards Saturn was both the farthest from the Earth and the slowest in movement, whereas the Moon was the closest and the fastest. The Pre-Ptolemaic order accepted by Plato and Poseidonius was only slightly different.

Despite its close association with both paganism and **Gnosticism** this astrological concept was influential in early and medieval Christian mystical systems. Here the descent and ascent of the soul, with any implication of metempsychosis, was dropped and in place of the pagan gods several sets of angelic rulers (*archons*) were assigned to each of the seven Ptolemaic celestial bodies or spheres. In some cases these rulers were looked upon as benevolent, or at least neutral, but in other cases they were thought to be malevolent. In fact, it even came to be theorized that seven demons driven out of the woman in **Luke** 8:1–3 were somehow related to those seven *archons*.

See also **Angels and reincarnation; Astrology and rebirth; Celestial gates; Chakras; Heracleides of Ponticus; Planets, other; Pluto, the planet; Poimandres; Pyramidology;** *Sephiroth***; Zodiac.**

Planets, other. Before the scientific understanding that none of the other planets within our solar system could have ever evolved intelligent life forms, some age-regression subjects would claim to have had a past life on one or more of these planets. Since then many individuals have taken **current knowledge discrepancy** into consideration, and as a result, any claim to have had a past life on another planet "within our solar system" has more or less ended. Instead, present day claimants to lives or other contacts with other planets have chosen planets well beyond the current scientific community's ability to challenge such a claim.

Oddly enough, a few members of UFO religions and channelers continue to claim contact with intelligent beings from planets Mars, Venus, Jupiter, and Saturn; but now, rather than claiming that it is the physical planets that is meant, it is said that it is the higher spiritual plane of such planets that are meant. The problem with this is that it opens the entire age-regression process to denigration from the public.

See also **Aetherius Society**; **Ascended masters**; **Astrology and rebirth**; **Celestial gates**; **Channeling**; **I Am Movement**; **Rampa, Lobsang Tuesday**; **Lost continents and reincarnation**; **Moon**; **Muller, Catherine Elise**; **Pluto, the planet**; **Ramtha**; **Rebirth and science**; **Scientology**; **Supernatural-in-the-gap process**; **UFOism**; **Wilcock, David**.

Plants. In **Theravada Buddhism** plants are not considered sentient beings so they do not have any karmic factor that would lead to rebirth. Later **Mahayana Buddhism** considers even the grasses and trees as needing to attain liberation. In **Jainism** plants also have to participate in the round of *samsara*.

Plato (428–348 BCE). This ancient Greek philosopher, and possibly the first Western theologian, certainly believed in the immortal soul, but he was not consistent in his views as to the afterlife. Four of his dialogues, the *Gorgias*, the **Phaedo**, the *Republic* (*Politeia*), and the *Phaedrus* give different mythical versions of the soul's fate. In the *Gorgias* three judges, Rhadamanthus, Aeacus, and Minos, probably borrowed from **Orphism**, examine every **soul** and send the good ones, especially philosophers, on to the Isles of the Blessed and the evil ones to **Tartarus**. In some of Plato's writing he also gives the name of Triptolemus as a fourth judge.

In the *Phaedo* four possible destinies await the soul. Here the judgment occurs at the Acherusian Lake. The incurably evil souls go to Tartarus forever. The curably evil also go to Tartarus, but only for a short time, provided that they are pardoned by those they have harmed. After this they will be reborn into the world of the living as an ass or a still lower beast. The ordinary good souls will be reborn into a life somewhat improved from their last one. The souls of philosophers, presumably including Plato's soul, will be liberated from all future rebirths. Also in the *Phaedo* Plato's argument for the soul's immortality is based on his belief that the soul had no parts and, therefore, could not break apart as physical things did when they died. Later Plato contradicted himself by teaching that the soul had three parts — appetite, passion (spirit), and reason (*logos*).

In his *Symposium* Plato tells of a myth that human beings originally had one of three double forms, male-female, male-male, and female-female, which the gods then split into separate halves. All souls since then have undergone **metempsychosis** in an effort to find their original other half or **soul mate** for no soul will be liberated from continued embodiment until it finds its other half.

In the *Phaedrus*, where metempsychosis is also acknowledged, Plato follows the lead of **Herodotus** (5th century) in suggesting that there is an **interim period** of a thousand years between re-embodiments and only up to three lives, for a three thousand year maximum.

In the tenth book of the *Republic* the soul's fate is described through the *Myth of Er*. This tells of a noble soldier named Er, the Son of Armenius, who, having been killed in battle, immediately travels to **Hades** where he is given visions concerning the fate of the dead. The good souls, traveling to the right and in an upwards direction are rewarded in heaven for a thousand years, while the evil souls, traveling to the left and in a downwards direction are punished in the deeper parts of Hades for an equally long time. After a millennium the truly evil souls are cast into Tartarus, the deepest part of Hades, forever. The redeemable souls are allowed to travel upwards, while good souls descend on a rainbow-like pillar of light, both ending up at the knees of the goddess Ananke (Necessity). Here the souls see the daughters of Ananke, the three Fates (Moirai) Lachesis, Klotho, and Attropos (past or spinner of the thread of life, present or disposer of lots in life, and future or cutter of the thread of life). It is through the gift of Lachesis that the souls choose their future mortal life on earth.

Er is next shown how some chose their next lives. Those who had spent a thousand years being punished were likely to be very careful and choose wisely, while those who had enjoyed a thousand years in heaven often chose foolishly. In a few cases, those who had suffered grievously in their past human life and wished to have nothing to do with human beings in their next life chose to be animals. For example, Agamemnon, king of Mycenae, decided to be an eagle; Ajax, the Trojan warrior, chose to be a lion; and Thamyras, the musician, opted to be a nightingale. After making their decisions the souls drink from the River of Forgetfulness (**Lethe**). This water dissolves all memories of the souls' past lives, and only then are they prepared to be reborn into new bodies.

The Myth of Er ends with Er being told that it is not really time for him to die. Instead, he is sent back into the land of the living where, after seeming to be dead for twelve days, he awakens to find his companions preparing to cremate his body. Arising from his funeral pyre he tells his companions about his vision.

It is to be carefully noted that in the Myth of Er version of rebirth the souls have been fully rewarded or fully punished prior to being reborn. This means that there is no particular moral reason why some people are reborn into good lives and some into bad lives. In other words, there is no doctrine of karma in its "primary function" as there is in Eastern Asia. This lack of a full karmic concept was a major weakness in the Greek metempsychosis schema. Mention of metempsychosis is also found in Plato's *Laws* (*Nomoi*) and *Memo.*

Regardless of the versions of rebirth that Plato offers us, it is certain that he was influenced by **Pythagoras** (6th century) and the Orphic religion. However, to complicate the issue of Plato and his after-life views, in his *Timaeus,* he abandons his earlier belief in an inherently immortal soul for one dependent on the good grace of the divine. Also, in this he regards only the "intelligence" (*nous*) of the soul as potentially immortal. From the perspective of the metaphysics of the soul, the *Timaeus* is one of Plato's greatest works. It is here that the metaphysic of the creation of the world, the gods, the human body, and the soul as found. It is also here that Plato makes absolutely clear that he acknowledges the existence of a supreme creator being (God); moreover, that it is this God that first formed the world soul (***anima mundi***) out of three constituents, those of sameness (*tauton*), otherness (*thateron*), and being or essence and not *creatio ex nihilo* (creation out of nothingness). In fact, this creator (***demiurge***) merely formed the material parts of the universe out of a chaotic state of pre-existent matter. It was, therefore, the inherent chaotic nature of this matter that accounted for evil in the world. Once the world soul was created it was placed in the circles of the planets or stars surrounding the earth. It was from this world soul that the rational and immortal aspects of human souls were created with their own *tauton, thateron,* and being constituents. The number of individual souls that were created was the equal of the number of stars, for it was into celestial bodies that the souls were first placed. The God also created the lesser deities (traditional Greek gods and demi-gods), to which He gave the task of fashioning the human body and the lower aspects of the human soul. The individual souls, after experiencing celestial existence and gaining knowledge of cosmic reality and the laws of destiny, were incarnated into material bodies to learn how to master physical passions and to live virtuously. For those that succeeded in this they left behind all materiality and returned to their home star. For those that did not learn such mastery and virtue they were reborn time after time as women or worst, as beasts, until they were somehow able to reverse their condition.

During the European Middle Ages the writings of Plato were often out of favor, partly because he advocated a belief in **metempsychosis** or **transmigration**, which was regarded by the church as a heresy. It was only during the **Renaissance** that both Plato and the concept of metempsychosis once again became a subject of renewed interest.

See also ***Anamnesis***; **Aquinas, Thomas**; **Archytas of Tarentum**; **Aristotle**; **Body is the hell of the soul**; **Body-soul dualism**; **Bogomils**; **Cathars**; **Drink or fruit of forgetfulness**; **Essenes**; **Gender issue of the soul**; **Greek afterlife, the ancient**; **Greeks and reincarnation**; **Lost continents and reincarnation**; **Moon**; **Neoplatonism**; **Ogdoad**; **Paulicians**; **Pherecydes of Syros**; **Planetary descent and ascent of the soul**; **Platonism**; **Plotinus**; **Pluto, The God**; **Priesthood, lack of an organized**; **Soul, tripartite**; **Theophilus**; **Virgil**.

Pleiades. This is the great cluster of stars in the constellation Taurus, especially the **seven** largest stars. The name of this cluster comes from the Greek *plein* meaning to sail, because the rising and setting of these stars opened and close the season for safe navigation on the Aegean Sea. Their rising and setting then made them a symbol for **metempsychosis**.

See also **Forty**; **Pyramidology**; **Satya**.

Plotinus (205–270 CE). This Egyptian born Neoplatonic philosopher and mystic followed the Platonic teachings that viewed mankind as having an inborn intuition about the One (God), with which all men ultimately longed to be united. This required a degree of both intellectual and spiritual contemplation that could only bear fruit over a number of life times.

Plotinus, unlike most of the earlier supporters of **metempsychosis**, came very close to affirming a karma-like law of reward or punishment. Those individuals who have spent lives of stupor will find themselves in the bodies of vegetables, while those who have excessively gratified the senses will be reborn as licentious beasts, while only those who have displayed virtuous lives will once again come into human form.

Plotinus apparently taught that through all successive lives it is never the **soul** that suffers, but the outward shadow since it is this aspect of the self that acts out the plots in the world. One of the students of Plotinus was **Porphyry Malchus**.

See also **Empedocles**; **Pherecydes of Syros**; **Plato**; **Priesthood, lack of an organized**.

Pluralism. This is a metaphysical view that physical and spiritual reality is composed of more than one or two basic kinds of entities. Pluralism is in contrast to **monism** and **dualism**. In general, pluralism with its multitude of fundamentally separate souls is more compatible with the concept of reincarnation than is monism.

Plurality of existences. This term can refer to the standard reincarnation belief that the **soul** has a whole series of existences or that a soul can have two or more existences simultaneously. In this second case it is the same as **parallel lives**.

See also **Rebirth, simultaneous**.

Plutarch or **Ploutarchos** (about 46–119 CE). This Greek writer mentions **metempsychosis** in his *On the Delays of the Divine Vengeance*. In this work the **soul** of the music loving, but criminally insane, Emperor **Nero** Claudius Caesar Drusus Germanicus (54–68 CE) was said to have been reborn into the body of a frog so he could sing (croak) all he wanted.

Pluto, the planet. In modern astrology Pluto has sometimes been suggested as the main governing body for reincarnation. The validity of this has been challenged by the question, "What was considered the governing planet for reincarnation before the discovery of Pluto in 1930?" One answer is that it would have been **Saturn**, since that planet for millennia has been associated with death. A major source of the pro–Pluto reincarnation view is *Pluto: The Evolutionary Journey of the Soul* by Jeff Green (1986).

On the other hand, in mundane astrology Pluto is the governing planet of organized labor groups or labor unions. The logic of this is said to be that the organized labor movement was only founded a few decades prior to the discovery of the planet.

A more chronologically secure association is with the fact that Pluto, as the god of death, was discovered only 10 years before the discovery of the element named after it, plutonium, which coincidentally or not turned out to be a major ingredient in nuclear bombs. Also, the start of World War II, which ended with the atomic bomb, might be attributed to the astrological influence of the discovery of Pluto. Considering this Pluto-nuclear link, it may be less of a surprising that there is even an association of Pluto with **Jesus** according to **Zhendao**. Jesus, who is just one of many gods, is said to have helped settle on Pluto the survivors of the nuclear war that created this solar system.

Another factor associated with this planet according to many astrologers is that of the subconscious, the treasure house of the psyche. This is considered to be supported by the fact that it was around the discovery time of Pluto that depth psychology became fashionable. Since the astrologer Fritz Brunhubner gave his opinion on the matter in 1934 Pluto has also been assign governance over the **pineal gland** and its **third eye** psychic properties. Again the question ought to be asked, "What, if anything, was considered governing this gland before the discovery of Pluto?"

As of August 2006 Pluto lost its status as a full planet and was reclassified as a dwarf planet. We will have to wait to see how astrologers deal with this plutonian downgrading and its supposed governance of reincarnation.

See also **Astrology and rebirth; Moon; Planetary descent and ascent of the soul; Planets, other**.

Pneumatikoi (Greek: Spirituals) This term referred to the people with the highest level of spiritual understanding in some forms of **Gnosticism** and as such could soon escape from *kyklos genesion* (cycle of birth and death). The opposite of these were considered *sarikoi, choikoi* or *hylikoi* which meant corporeal or material and so more or less earth bound. In between were the *psychikoi*, or those with some degree of spiritual understanding, but not enough to escape from birth and death.

See also **Seth; Trichotomy**.

Poetry on reincarnation. For a very extensive sampling of poetry on reincarnation see Eva Martin's *Reincarnation: The Ring of Return* (1963). R. F. Goudey's *Reincarnation: A Universal Truth* (1928) has a fourteen-page chapter on reincarnation poetry; and Walker in his *Reincarnation: A Study of Forgotten Truth* (1965) has a fifty-page chapter of poetry on reincarnation by Western authors and a smaller chapter by Eastern authors.

See also **Masefield, John; Patton, George S.**

Poimandres or **Pymander** (Latin and Greek: Shepherd of men). This book, produced about 200 CE, is the first text in the *Corpus Hermeticum* or Hermetic writings, which is why the entire corpus is sometimes given this name. The full name of the text is *The Divine Pymander of Hermes Mercurius Trimegistus*. In this text the god Hermes is describing his vision of Poimandres and the doctrines he learns from that vision.

All that is left of the original text is seventeen fragmentary writings brought together as one work, divided into separate chapters. The second chapter or book, called *Poimandres* or *The Vision,* is possibly the most famous of all Hermetic Fragments which is why the whole text is often given this name. The *vision* has at times been erroneously called *The Genesis of Enoch* but that mistake is rare today. The main character in the story is Poimandres who appears as a Great Dragon, which, in turn, is said to be the Mind of the Universe, the Creative Intelligence, and the Absolute Emperor of all.

Among the things the text describes is the **soul's existence prior to embodiment** in the **Eighth sphere** (**Milky Way**) from where all souls fell down, passing through the seven planetary rings to earth and from where, after purifying themselves, they must once again pass through in reverse order to return once and for all to the supreme, all good God.

Much of the language of the text is ambiguous on the matter as to whether **metempsychosis**, in the common sense, is supported because it also mentions evil souls being destroyed or there being a **second death** in which there is no salvation. On the other hand, the text mentions that many souls will have to wait until the Great Day when the wheel of the universe will stop, the souls shall be freed from their bodily sheaths, ascend to the seed-ground of the stars (Milky Way), and there await a new beginning.

See also **Hermetic Order of the Golden Dawn; Hermetic philosophy; Planetary descent and ascent of the soul**.

Polar star *see* **Zodiac**.

Polarities. This term describes two life times in which one assumes opposite roles. For example, in one life a person may be a wife then in another a husband. Parent-Child, victimizer-victim, employer-employee are also examples of such polarities.

See also **Karma, family**.

Population increase issue. A major and long-standing challenge to the concept of reincarnation is that human population has steadily increased over the last thirty plus thousand years. This being the case, there would have to be either an as yet not emptied reservoir of souls to draw from or new souls periodically coming into being.

This population issue is more of a Western concern than an Eastern one because the Eastern view is that the animal world or souls from other planets or other spheres of existence (heaven, hell) form the reservoir for rebirth and/or **transmigration** here on earth.

Western advocates of reincarnation, more often than not, reject the first of these reservoir possibilities, while some may accept the second and/or third possibility.

The first, or reservoir, solution tends to go along with the belief that there are only a finite number of souls and as soon as the reservoir has been emptied the human population increase will come to an end. This solution, as logical as it may be, leads to the question, "Until there are enough bodies for all souls to enter the cycle of birth and death do souls rotate in embodiments or not. For example, if soul "x" has been through the rebirth cycle forty times and is still not ready to leave the cycle permanently, is there a procedure that says it can or must leave the cycle and return to the reservoir temporarily to giving another soul, "y," that has never yet entered the rebirth cycle a chance to do so? Or must soul "x" continue to reincarnate until it is ready to leave the cycle permanently?

The other solution to the population increase issue is that as the population increases new souls come into existence. This solution would generally require an ever-creative force such as God to create souls anew and is very acceptable to theists.

Either of these solutions to the population increase issue would mean that as far as embodiments are concerned some souls have reincarnated many times, hence are old souls' and some souls have more recently started the embodiment processes, hence are new souls. This could even be used to explain why some people remember a past life and others do not.

Rudolf Steiner, the founder of Anthroposophy, had his own solution to the population increase issue. He believed in a fixed number of souls, which is to say that all the souls that would be came into existence at the same time. The population of humanity is dependent on the number of souls that want or need to be reborn at any time. Besides the fact that there is a large pool of souls that are still in need of experiencing embodiment, and who are doing whatever they can to encourage a high human birthrate, there is an increased number of former embodied souls wanting to be reborn. The reason for this is that in the past the more primitive conditions under which many souls had to live meant that they were not as eager to immediately return to embodiment. This has become less and less true as humanity has progressed materially, so there has been a gradual population increase over the past few millennia.

The population increase issue is a particularly sensitive question for Buddhism, since Buddhism teaches that it is very difficult to attain the privilege of a human birth.

See also ***Akashic* Record; Animals and rebirth, non–Western view; Animals and rebirth, Western view; *Bhavachakra*; Fall of Souls; Cleopatra Syndrome; Interim period; Fixed number or variable number of souls; Kabbalah; Karma and rebirth; Ontological leap or ontological discontinuity; Planets, other; Population increase issue and a theistic solution; Privilege of a human birth; Rebirth and science; Soul Darwinism; Soul-fission; Soul, origin of the; Tertullian**.

Population increase issue and the theistic solution. If, due to Western objections to cross-species **transmigration**, the possibility of animals being reborn into human bodies is not an acceptable answer to the increasing population problem nor is there any enthusiasm for a huge reservoir of souls, then the easiest solution would seem be to accept a creator God as the source of soul increase. In this solution God originally created all souls as immature entities, and He continues to create new, but immature, souls. This He does for an increasing population both to supply souls for any bodies not able to receive an old soul, or even for a stable population to replace souls that spiritually grow out of the cycle of rebirth. The majority of the population, however, in both cases continues to have a previously existing soul.

This theistic solution could also accommodate karma; but first it needs to be asked, "What if some first time ensouled persons were born into a suffering environment, would this not amount to the suffering of an innocent person since the suffering was not related to any past karma?" The easiest answer to this would be that God might only put those first time ensouled persons in an appropriately just environment in which to begin there karmic journey.

Of course, this theistic solution depends upon God really existing; yet, as noted in **arguments pro and con on an afterlife in general** (7 and 8) it is very weak logic to try to argue for the truth or reality of one thing (an afterlife) on the basis of the truth or reality of another thing (God) which itself is unproven.

See also **Brahma and rebirth in Buddhism; Fixed number or variable number of souls; Kabbalah; Karma and God.**

Porphyry Malchus (234–305 CE). Among the writings of this ancient Greco-Roman Neoplatonist philosopher and supporter of **metempsychosis** were *On Abstinence from Animal Food*, a treatise on **vegetarianism**; *Life of Pythagoras*; and *Against the Christians*. Porphyry was the student of **Plotinus**, and **Iamblichus** was one of the students of Porphyry.

See also **Celestial gates; Julian, Flavius Claudius; Karma and free will; Neoplatonism; Planetary descent and ascent of the soul.**

Possession. In its broadest meaning possession is the act of a spiritual entity taking command of a physical body. In this broader sense reincarnation is a form or subset of possession. On the other hand, in its narrower and more common meaning possession is where a spiritual entity (soul) of a deceased person or other supernatural entity invades a body that "already has its own soul"; therefore, in this narrower sense possession must clearly be distinguished from reincarnation.

In what is assumed to be possession, the person being invaded is usually aware that an alien personality is trying to take over him or her and most often there is also a violent aspect of this invasion. If the invasion is successful the invading personality may so overwhelm the person invaded that the invaded person's own personality will seem to be radically replaced by the alien one. Possession of this kind, using the terminology of the American occultist Paschal B. Randolph (1825–1875), is *atrilism*.

According to the researcher **H. N. Banerjee** some of the signs of this kind of possession are that the top register of the normal voice of the possessed person is displaced; the invading entity usually reveals a vulgar attitude, fundamentally opposed to accepted ethical and religious norms; the possessed victim usually becomes irritable, if not violent; and the possession itself lasts for only brief periods, which are marked by an alarmingly sudden entering and exiting of the possessing entity.

It is to be noted that the preceding description of possession emphasizes the involuntary nature of the possession; however, there is also a voluntary or "invitational" possession, one form of which goes under the name of **channeling**, while another form would be deity possession. In the latter case, examples of this would range from possession of shamans by divining spirits, various gods in **Afro-American religions**, and possession by the Holy Spirit in Pentecostal Christian churches. In some reported cases of possession, especially in Brazil, it is thought that the possessing entity had some past karmic connection with the possessed person. In Randolph's terminology the more voluntary possession is called "blending," in that the alien entity does not interrupt the host's self-awareness or mental activities.

From a Western monotheistic position the greatest weakness in the theory of reincarnation is that it is impossible to separate that theory from possession. Past life practitioners, however, consistently point out that in the experiencing of a genuine past life the current personality, while remembering that it has lived before, continues to be aware that the past personality is not identical to the current personality.

While many reincarnationists entirely reject the concept of possession as an out-dated belief, other reincarnationists do accept that some past life memories are due to being possessed by an alien disincarnated spirit, rather than due to genuine memories of one's own past life. Also, it must be remembered that many conservative Western religious authorities consider most cases of non-fraudulent past life recall to be the result of possession by malicious supernatural entities. As proof of the reality of such possession they tend to cite such New Testament passages as **Matthew** 8:28–32, **Luke** 4:33–36, **Acts** 16:16–18, and 19:11–16. In fact, some Christian fundamentalists go as far as stating that the entire concept of past lives is due to the working of demons who are trying to sabotage Christian resurrection teachings. Obviously, this implies that these Christians believe that all of South and East Asia has been thoroughly deceived by and perhaps lost to demonic forces.

Possession, however, need not be thought of as

totally separate from reincarnation. For example, if a possessing entity were to take possession of an infant's body well before the infant had a chance to develop any independent personality of its own, for all practical purposes this could be considered the equivalent of reincarnation. In fact, leaving aside the hostile Christian attitude of reincarnation as possession, it might be suggested that with or without universal reincarnation this possession-reincarnation might be very characteristic of souls of those who died prematurely or with major unfinished business.

The concept of incarnated lamas offers another possible blurring of possession and reincarnation. For example, among most Tibetans it is believed that the **Dalai Lama** is an "incarnation" of the **Avalokiteshvara**, the *Bodhisattva* of compassion. When one Dalai Lama dies his divine spiritual essence (the ***bodhisattva***) takes possession of a new body. The question then becomes does the selected fetus or new born infant lack its own human or non-divine soul and only the divinity enters it, or does it have its own human soul which either merges with the divinity or is completely and permanently suppressed by the divinity? If suppression is the case, what happens to that soul after the death of the body it shares with the divinity? Does it continue in rebirth association with the divinity or does it go its own way. If it goes its own way is it karmicaly responsible for the actions of the divinity or free of such responsibility? Clearly, in this case the possession versus rebirth issue is very complex.

It should be further noted that even **Ian Stevenson**, in his *Twenty Cases Suggestive of Reincarnation* (1996), acknowledges that there is a continuous progression between mere possession and authentic reincarnation. In this continuum Stevenson lists partial temporary possession, complete temporary possession, complete permanent possession beginning years after birth, complete permanent possession occurring a day to several weeks after birth, complete permanent possession after conception, complete permanent possession at conception. Stevenson regards the last two forms of possession as constituting true reincarnation. In other words, he says that if a possessing personality is associated with a body either at conception or sometime during embryonic development it is reincarnation, while any later association is true alien possession. Since some authorities allow for the reincarnating entities to embody themselves at the moment of birth or very soon after that Stevenson's view of authentic rebirth might have to include the last three rather than just the last two categories of possession.

One question that is rarely asked in studying children's recall ability is whether or not they, as just starting to develop their own wills, are more prone to possession than are adults, and that as the children mature is the possessing entity that is being mistaken for a past life scenario forced to gradually abandon its host? Another question is whether or not individuals in cultures that strongly believe in reincarnation are more susceptible to possession than are individuals in cultures that do not believe in reincarnation?

Modern psychology offers several explanations for what it considers so-called malevolent possession. Among these are mental illnesses, epilepsy, or conscious or unconscious deception. In the last case psychologists and anthropologists point out that the conviction or pretence that an alien entity has taken control of a person has given that person (victim) the freedom to act in ways that would normally be denied by society. Hence subconscious desires and fantasies can be acted upon without the so-called possessed person having to take personal responsibility for the actions.

See also **Africa; Attached entity; Automatic writing; Children remembering past lives; Elijah; Etheric body; Guenon, Rene; John the Baptist; Kabbalah; Karma and rebirth; Karma as unfinished business; Multiple personalities; Rebirth, alternative explanations to; Walk-ins; Xenoglossy.**

Prabhavananda, Swami (1893–1976). This disciple of **Vivekananda** continued to work for the spread of his master's teachings via the **Vedanta Society**. It was under Prabhavananda that the society attracted the support of such men as Aldous Huxley and Christopher Isherwood. Members are not required to believe in either reincarnation nor karma; nonetheless, they are included in the teachings of the Society.

See also *Atman*; **Monism; Yogananda, Paramahansa.**

Prakriti (Mature, matter, physicality). In the **Samkhya Yoga School** this term is contrasted with ***purusha*,** meaning (essential) person or, in other words, the soul. In Advaita Vedanta *prakriti* is synonymous with the illusory characteristic of **maya** versus the exclusive reality of the *atman* (soul). In both of these religious systems attachment to *prakriti*, either through sensuality or ignorance keeps one trapped in the round of rebirth and re-death. In Tantric **Hinduism**, *prakriti* is equated with the divine magical creative power called *Shakti* and is viewed in a more positive manner than in the other two schools.

See also **Monism**.

Prana (Breath) *see* **Aetherius Society; Etheric body; Kosha; Soul and spirit levels, Theosophical.**

Prarthana. This Sanskrit term means a formal wish for rebirth.

Pratitya-samutpada/Paticha-samuppada (Dependent Causality). Buddhism teaches that a close examination or analysis of one's psychophysical development can demonstrate the complete non-necessity for any supernatural or metaphysical concept such as God or **Brahman** as a determining factor in one's development. Instead, Buddhism says that the entire psychophysical development of a person can be understood as a process of natural causality in which one stage of development is dependent upon an earlier stage of development.

While the *sutras* (holy texts) supply a number of different examples of the dependent origination schema the most developed one is that which has **twelve** factors or twelve or links (*nidanas*). This chain begins with ignorance (S: *avidya*); which causes or conditions volitional activity (***samskara***); which causes or conditions consciousness (*vijnana*); which causes or conditions the psychophysical organism of name and form (*nama-rupa*); which causes or conditions the six senses (*sad-ayatana*); which causes or conditions contact (*sparsha*); which causes or conditions sensation (*vedana*); which causes or conditions craving (*trishna*); which causes or conditions clinging (*upadana*); which causes or conditions becoming (***bhava***; which causes or conditions birth (*jati*) which causes or conditions old age and death (*jara-marana*) and hence dissatisfaction in life.

At some point in its development this twelve link schema came to be used to explain the rebirth process without having to postulate a permanent soul. Yet, for a variety of reasons, some scholars believe that this twelve factor chain is a later development of an earlier and simpler causal or conditional scheme that had nothing to do with rebirth. Instead, they believe that it was originally an explanation of the process by which the mind comes to cling to, or grasp after the self, others, and things which Buddhism teaches is the root of our ***duhkha***.

Besides dependent causality *pratitya-samutpada* has been variously translated into English as dependent origination, conditioned genesis, conditioned co-production, causal genesis, and sometimes simply as causation.

See also *Anatman*; **Psychophysical aggregates; Rebirth in Buddhism.**

Prayers for the dead. In many religious traditions intercessional prayers are a standard practice. Such prayers have even been accepted in some of those traditions where the future of the deceased is determined by the impersonal power of karma rather than a personal interceding deity. In **Theravada Buddhism** and **Mahayana Buddhism**, giving donations to monks in the name of the deceased is believed to aid in a better rebirth for both the deceased and the donor. Also, in Mahayana Buddhism prayers to the various ***bodhisattva***s on behalf of the dead can achieve the same result. Some New Age channeled entities have also supported the idea of such prayers as providing reincarnational benefits for the deceased.

See also **Ancestor worship.**

Precession of the equinox and rebirth *see* **Steiner, Rudolf.**

Pre-conception or post-conception, pre-birth or post-birth rebirth *see* **Embodiment, moment of; Hovering of the soul.**

Predestination. In general, this is the teaching that the fate of the soul has been determined well in advance of physical death or even prior to birth. In a Christian sense it means that due to the absolute sinfulness of "fallen mankind" no one by there own effort can do sufficient good works to make themselves worthy of salvation as far as God is concerned. Therefore, it is only by the arbitrary choice of God that some have been predestined to benefit from the saving power of Christ's sacrifice (single predestination); and others, as reprobates, have been predestined not to be saved (double predestination). This is also called "salvation of the elect or chosen of God."

There are a number of passages in the **Old Testament** that tell of God's foreknowledge which implies predestination. As for the New Testament, the predestination sources include **Matthew** 20:23 and 24:31; 25:35; **John** 10:29; **Romans** 8:28, and 9:10–24; **Ephesians** 1:4–5, and 9; 2nd Timothy 1:9; Titus 1:1–2; Jude 1:4; and in the most extreme version of such predestination the exact number of the saved souls is given as 144,000 according to the **Revelation of John** 7:4–8.

In light of these Christian predestination passages, there should be no reason to believe that early Christianity had any belief in **metempsychosis.**

See also *Apocatastasis*; **Fall of Souls; Karma and free will; Karma versus grace; Limbo; New Testament and reincarnation; Purgatory; Resurrection of Jesus.**

Pre-existence of the soul *see* **Soul's existence prior to embodiment**

Pre-existiani. This is the word used in ancient Roman sources for a believer in the **soul's existence prior to embodiment.**

See also **Clement of Alexandria; Origin.**

Presley, Elvis. Considering the near religious iconic status Presley achieved after, if not before, his death it should be no surprise that sooner or later he should be identified as a candidate for reincarnation. According to an article by Michael Logan in *Spirit Guide* (2004) the Hollywood psychic Kenny Kingston believes that Presley has to have been reborn in December of 2007 and is to become a holistic healer who is "almost Christ-like."

See also **Wilcock, David**.

Pretaloka. In **Hinduism** this is the place where the deceased reside for a year while waiting for the *shraddha* (supplementary funeral rites) to be completed. From here the deceased will move on to their next rebirths. This place is not to be confused with the ***Pritiloka***.

Priesthood, lack of an organized. Considering the familiarity with the concept of **metempsychosis** found in the classical Greco-Roman period it has often been questioned why this concept never became the dominant ideology in the West. Among the reasons that have been suggested is that while both the Greeks and Romans had priests there never developed an organized pro-reincarnationist priesthood to push forward a reincarnationist agenda, as was the case with the Brahmins in India.

In contrast to this pagan Greco-Roman lack of priestly organization, the Christian clergy in the later Roman Empire developed a strong, well-disciplined, hierarchical priestly organization that aggressively propagated its resurrectional belief. This Christian organizational superiority must partly be attributed to the sense of religious urgency that was created by a belief that only one lifetime meant only one chance for salvation. Furthermore, it was the disciplined organizational ability of the Christian clerical authorities which attracted the rapidly disintegrating late Roman State as a possible organizational tool to stop its disintegration and maybe even reverse it. Thus, with the official adoption of Christianity as the Roman state religion the teaching of multiple lives through metempsychosis was repressed in favor of a belief in a single life and the eventual resurrection of the dead.

See also **Ethicalized or karmic rebirth; Karma in the ancient and modern west; Neoplatonism; Plato; Platonism; Pythagoras; Resurrection, bodily**.

Priscillian (died 385 CE). This Christian bishop of Avila, Spain was known to support extreme views on the need for clerical **celibacy** and even on the ungodliness of lay marriage. These views brought him under suspicion of being a gnostic or Manichaean heretic, and hence a believer in **metempsychosis**. His church enemies had him tried, not as a heretic, but as a practitioner of magic, and by order of the Western Roman emperor Magnus Maximus he was executed. The majority of churchmen, however, condemned the emperor's actions. The execution of Priscillian was the first execution on grounds related to heresy in Christian history. While there is still some debate as to Priscillian's orthodoxy, at present the majority opinion seems to regard him as having been innocent.

See also **Astrology and rebirth; Manichaeism**.

Pritiloka. In Sanskrit this means the world (*loka*) of the ancestors (*priti*) and it is considered a restful place in **Hinduism** were virtuous souls temporarily dwell, but once their accumulated merit has been exhausted they must return to earthly rebirth to continue their goal of ultimate liberation from rebirth and re-death. The *pritiloka* is not to be confused with the *pretaloka*, which is the realm of the deceased in general and in some cases can be translated as realm of the **hungry ghosts**.

See also ***Linga Sharia*; Moon; Reincarnation, origins of; *Surya-marga***.

Privilege of a human birth. In Buddhism it is believed that only in the human state can a being have a chance to gain liberation from the round of birth and death (***samsara***). This is because the beings in the other realms of existence (***bhavachakra***) are too ignorant, too involved in their suffering, or too intoxicated with their temporary state of bliss for them to seek liberation (**nirvana**). Only in the human realm are the pleasures and pains of existence balanced sufficiently for there to be the freedom to choose whether to stay or leave such existence. Because of this privileged situation, Buddhism also teaches that it is very difficult to be born into human existence. This may seem to be contradicted by the huge number of people in the world at present, but Buddhism would answer that compared to the number of beings in the other realms of existence the human realm is under-populated. Nonetheless, modern Buddhism is faced with the **population increase issue**.

Proclus (411–485 CE). This Neoplatonist teacher believed that he was a reincarnation of an ancient Pythagorean and so studied all the religions and philosophies available to him. However, he apparently argued against the human soul being reborn as an animal.

See also **Plato; Pythagoras; Transmigration, regressive**.

Procrastination, charge of. A major criticism of reincarnation by Christianity is that it leaves the believer of multiple lives ample opportunity to postpone any real effort at the moral purification necessary for spiritual salvation, whereas the Christian belief in a single life time makes such effort imperative. This charge might have some validity for the Western believer who tends to think of rebirth in very positive, if not adventuresome, terms; but for the south or central Asian believer the unadventuresome monotony implied in repeated births and deaths is no more or less a motivation for attaining spiritual perfection than is the Christian view.

See also **Rebirth, East and West**.

Progression therapy. This is the process whereby one experiences aspects of a future reincarnation under hypnosis. It is the opposite of past life or regression therapy.

See also **Future-lives; Over-soul, personal; Time and the simultaneous past, present, and future**.

Promise of the cycle. This phrase expresses a **Wicca** belief that the cycle of rebirth is a phenomenon more of progression to better conditions than of digression to lesser conditions.

Proof for and against reincarnation argument. The sheer number of cases of reported past life recall, which includes those both well investigated and those taken on face value, might normally lead to an easy belief in past lives; however, the overwhelming disagreement about who or what reincarnates, and how, when, why, and where reincarnation takes place makes for major complications in any easy acceptance or an otherwise wide spread reincarnational belief. When all the disagreements about the **interim period**, including whether there is even such a period, the justification for any acceptance is still further undermined. Finally, when all the possible alternative explanations, both psychic and non-psychic, are taken into consideration the reason for believing in reincarnation seems to shift too significantly to that of faith alone, which is beyond logical argument. In the name of such faith some rebirth advocates have simply taken the position that absence of proof for reincarnation is not proof against reincarnation. This argument, of course, has been used for centuries to challenge a disbelief in God, and just as it is a very weak and dubious theistic argument it is equally weak as a reincarnation argument.

According to Woolger, in his *Other Lives, Other Selves* (1988), a further difficulty in proving reincarnation through hypnotic recall is that it doesn't matter whether the hypnotized subject believes in reincarnation or not. The unconscious mind will almost always produce a past life story when invited in the right way. This is the case even if the conscious mind is highly skeptical; in short, the unconscious is a true believer.

Yet another problem with trying to prove reincarnation is that to do so one would first need to eliminate as inapplicable all of the other possible non-psychic and psychic alternative explanations for past life recall such as the *akashic* **record; leading questions; possession; retrocognition;** telepathy with the living; and telepathy with the dead, etc.

See also **Rebirth, alternative explanations to; Rebirth and the preponderance of evidence**.

Proof of rebirth, criteria *see* **Rebirth, criteria for proof of**.

Proof of rebirth (Western Buddhist) *see* **Rebirth, proof of (Western Buddhist)**.

Proof text. This is a scriptural passage offered as proof for a theological doctrine or principle, which in most cases is taken out of the larger context in which the passage is found and once taken out of its proper context it can be used to prove any number of views contrary to the original in context view. There are two kinds of proof texting, the passive and the active. Passive proof texting is the deliberate searching of the scriptures to find something that seems to match a later condition. Active proof texting is the deliberate molding of a later condition to match an earlier scriptural one. Proof texting is heavily used by many Western reincarnationists to prove that various passages in the Bible imply reincarnation.

See also **Augustine, Saint Aurelius; Book of the Dead; Jesus; Jung, Carl; New Testament and reincarnation; Old Testament and the afterlife; Resurrection of Jesus**.

Protology. This is the study of metaphysical views dealing with the birth or pre-birth of the world, the soul, etc. The biblical myth of the Garden of Eden would be an example of this, especially since it is said to record the birth of sin and death due to the fall of mankind. Protology is the opposite of eschatology. One of the advantages to the concept of reincarnation, especially in its Eastern forms, is that the origin of the world and the soul can be pushed far enough back in time that the origin becomes almost irrelevant. The nature of biblical mythology requires that it must find a much more recent origin, which obviously has lead to the debate between biblical creationism and Darwinian evolutionism.

Proverbs. At least the following two out of the many proverbs in the **Old Testament** have been cited as suggesting a doctrine of reincarnation. Proverbs 17:5 reads, "A man who sneers at the poor insults his Maker, and he who gloats over another's ruin will answer for it." That this might imply a doctrine of post-mortem punishment is reasonable, but the suggestion that this post-mortem is of a reincarnational type is clearly reading into the passage what is not there.

The second passage is Proverbs 8:22–31. It reads, "The Lord created me the beginning of his works, before all else that he made, long ago. Alone, I was fashioned in times long past, at the beginning, long before earth itself." Despite some attempts to claim that this passage is referring to the **soul's existence prior to embodiment**, and in particular of the soul of King Solomon, the passage, without the slightest doubt, describes in anthropomorphic form the pre-existence of Divine Wisdom (Hebrew: *Chokmah* or *Hohhma*), not any ordinary soul. In fact, the proverb continues on for eight more verses, making its subject very clear.

See also **Karma in the Bible?**

Proximity burial. This refers to the belief that the closer the deceased is buried to his or her kinfolk the greater is the chance of the deceased being reborn into the same family (consanguineous rebirth). The **Igbo of Nigeria** are especially known for this belief.

See also **Africa; Akan; Rebirth, consanguineous; Yoruba.**

Proximity reincarnation *see* **Rebirth, proximity.**

Psalms. In general the theme of these **Old Testament** poems is to praise and give thanks to God, and/or to lament a personal situation; nonetheless, a number of Psalms have been cited as implying a doctrine of reincarnation. The first of these is Psalms 81:4–5 which is sometimes cited as a **proof text** that the Old Testament taught that King David was the reincarnation of both the Joseph of Genesis and of **Moses**. The passage reads, "This is the law for Israel, an ordinance of the God of Jacob, laid as a solemn charge on Joseph when he came out of **Egypt.**"

In trying to fathom such an identity we first need to remember that traditional biblical legend says that all the Psalms were written by King David under divine inspiration. The next thing we need to remember is in **Exodus** 13:19 when Moses left Egypt he took the bones (presumably the mummified body) of Joseph with him. In other words, the claim is being made that Moses was taking his former body with him out of Egypt. This act, from a reincarnationist view, was thought to be very symbolic in that the soul of the man, who brought the Israelites into Egypt now, in a different body, delivered the Israelites out of Egypt.

A second Psalm removed from its context and given a reincarnationist reading is Psalm 90. Indeed, this psalm is used twice for this purpose. Psalm 90:1 reads, "Lord, thou hast been our refuge from generation to generation." This in its proper context refers to biological generations, not a series of embodiments of the same soul. Then two verses below this is 90:3 which reads, "...for in thy sight a thousand years are as yesterday." This has been used to claim that there is a thousand year **interim period** between rebirths. Psalm 102: 26–27 uses the metaphor of the **body as a mere garment of the soul** that is cast of at death to be replaced with a new garment. Reincarnationists claim that this garment is a new body. The passage reads, "They shall pass away, but thou endurest: like clothes they shall all grow old; thou shalt cast them off like a cloak, and they shall vanish; but thou art the same and thy years shall have no end; ..." The reason this passage otherwise fails to have such a meaning is that the verse just before it makes it perfectly clear that what is being referred to are the earth and heaven and in no way should be interpreted as involving a human body.

Some supporters of "Jesus is David reborn" have used **Acts** 2:25–36, which in turn is quoting Psalm 16:9–10 which reads, "... my body too rests unafraid; for thou wilt not abandon me to Sheol nor suffer they faithful servant to see the pit." There is no question that this passage is referring to a "resurrection," not a reincarnation.

A Psalm much ignored by reincarnationists, and for obvious reasons, is 78:39, which is actually one of the annihilationist passages in the Old Testament.

See also ***Akashic (Akashik*) Record; Annihilationism; Aquinas, Thomas; Corinthians, 1st and 2nd; Harrowing of Hell; Karma in the Bible? Melchizedek; Millennialism; Old Testament and the afterlife; Peter, 1st and 2nd; *Pistis Sophia*; Resurrection of Jesus.**

Pseudepigrapha. These are writings that do not come from the author to whom they are attributed. Many ancient and not so ancient works dealing with reincarnation are pseudepigrapha.

Psychic archaeology. This is the belief that one can uncover facts about lost civilizations through psychic means. Many who write about ancient past lives claim that they can offer information about the cultures of those ancient times that can not be discovered through ordinary archaeological means.

See also **Cummins, Geraldine.**

Psychic cord *see* **Silver Cord.**

Psychic powers. Historically, in the reincarnationist community there is some debate about how much talk of psychic powers should or should not be publicly associated with the advocacy of reincarnation. Since the two subjects do not necessarily overlap the more conservative approach is to separate them on the basis that psychic powers are far more open to scientific criticism then reincarnation. In the present, however, the majority of pro-reincarnation writers have favored a more liberal willingness to associating psychic powers with reincarnation.

See also **Abhijna; Cayce, Edgar; Esotericism versus Occultism; Lost continents and reincarnation.**

Psychic psychodrama. This is a technique in psychotherapy in which, through spontaneous impersonations of the patient's problems, the patient is provided an opportunity to act out the conflicts which are at the core of his mental problem. It has been proposed that hypnotic age-regression to past lives is a form of psychodrama. It is possible that some elements of the subconscious take on the role of a fictitious personality in order to gain insight into the otherwise hidden aspects of that person's real personality.

Psychic recycling. This is a term used in some **Wicca** groups as a synonym for reincarnation.

Psychical Research Foundation. This Foundation was established in 1960 to support research on survival after death. The bulletin of the Foundation is *Theta* (1). The name of the bulletin comes from the Greek letter name of the first letter of the word *Thanatos* (Greek: Death).

See also **Associations and organizations.**

Psychics supportive of rebirth *see* **Cayce, Edgar; Cooke Grace; Eady, Dorothy; Grace-Loehr; Grant, Joan Marshall; Kingsford, Anna Bonus; Leek, Sybil; Montgomery, Ruth; Rosemary case; Steiner, Rudolf.**

Psychoanalysis *see* **Free-association; Id, ego, and superego; Electra/Oedipus Complex and rebirth; Jung, Carl; Unconscious, the.**

Psychography *see* **Automatic writing.**

Psychokinesis *see* **Maternal impressions or maternal psychokinesis.**

Psychology, abnormal. According to Master Djwal Khul, one of the **ascended masters,** many of the maladjustments of people in the present world are due to the fact that souls are not spending sufficient adjustment time in the **interim period** and thus are being reborn far too soon after death. The reason for this premature rebirth is that the material world's overpopulation has resulted in a like overpopulation of the post-mortem realm.

See also **Arcane School; Church Universal and Triumphant; Population increase issue; Rudolf Steiner**

Psychomancy *see* **Sciomancy.**

Psychometry. This is the purported psychic ability to perceive the history of objects by having someone (the psychometer) touching or handling the object. It has been theorized that this psychometrizing of an object is what actually happens in some rare cases that are otherwise assumed to be personal memories of a past life.

See also **Rebirth, alternative explanations to.**

Psychopannychism. This Greek derived term comes from the words soul (*psyche*), all (*pan*), and nightly (*nychios*); and refers to the soul, upon corporeal death, entering into a kind of sleep or hibernation until a future awakening at their resurrection.

Psychopannychism has been accepted at times by various Christian traditions, in contrast to the idea that the soul entered heaven or hell immediately after death. The Catholic Church, however, at the **Church Council of Lyons** (1274) and **Council of Florence** (1439), declared *psychopannychism* a heresy, partly because it conflicted with the cult of the saints in heaven. This declaration was reaffirmed at the Fifth Lateran Council in 1513.

The fact that some Old and New Testament passages could be interpreted to support *psychopannychism* was countered by the church's view that all such passages were simply metaphorical. While John Calvin and his Presbyterian followers also were opposed to *psychopannychism* Martin Luther and a number of other Protestant reformers were more favorable to it.

Among the biblical passages that speak of death as sleep are **Daniel** 12:2; **Matthew** 27:52; **John** 11:11–14; **Acts** 13:36; and I Thessalonians 4:14. Also, while John 5:25–30 does not mention sleep, it does say that all who are dead and in the grave "shall hear the voice of the Son of God, and all who hear shall come to life." These will be judged and rise to [eternal] life or rise to hear their doom. It has been this biblical support for *psychopannychism* that is used as a reason to reject the concept of reincarnation.

See also **Annihilationism, Biblical view; Christian view of the afterlife; Judgment of the Dead; Resurrection, bodily; Resurrection of Jesus.**

Psychophore (Mind-carrying). This term was coined by **Ian Stevenson** to describe the factor that carries memory from one life to another. It replaces the common term "soul."

See also *Diathanatic; Psychoplasm;* **Scientology.**

Psychophysical aggregates *see* **Skandha/Khandha.**

Psychoplasm. A term found in Paul von Ward's *The Soul Genome* (2008) to refer to the nonmaterial template that carries the cognitive, behavioral, and even physical pattern from one life to another.

See also *Psychophore.*

Psychopomps. (Greek: Soul conductor). This term refers to a conductor of souls to the afterworld. While throughout the world the most common psychopomp is the dog, in ancient Europe and parts of Asia the horse and/or cock (rooster) also served this function.

See also **Greek afterlife, the ancient; Hermes; Rescue circles.**

Psychosomatic illnesses. It is believed that a variety of psychosomatic illnesses that seem to have no present life explanation can be attributable to a past life. During hypnotic age regression procedures sometimes a past life explanation is offered for the illness. It has even been proposed that certain forms of mental illness, such as schizophrenia, are the result of a soul that has not fully embodied itself, so it exists in two separate worlds which accounts for its so-called split personality.

See also **Arguments supportive of rebirth; Cryptomnesia; Irrational fears; Karmic diseases; Multiple personalities; Screen memories**

Psychostasis. (Greek: Weighing of the soul). A number of cultures, past and present, have depicted the judgment of the soul after death as being weighed upon a scale against some symbol for truth.

See also **Egypt; Hell, the Chinese.**

Punar-janman/puna-bhava (Again birth or re-becoming) *see Bhava*; **Rebirth factor; Rebirth, simultaneous; Reincarnation, origins of.**

Puranas (Stories of Old). These Hindu works are mostly in verse and deal with the creation, history, and destruction of the universe, the genealogies of the gods and patriarchs, the reign of the 14 Manus (supernatural men), and the history of the solar and lunar dynasties. The *puranas* can be dated from the 2nd century CE and onwards. There are 18 major works *(mahapuranas)* and an equal number of minor or auxiliary ones *(upapuranas)*. One of the major stories is the *Garuda Purana* which deals with funeral rites, the recreation of new bodies for the *preta*, the judgment of deeds and misdeeds, and the various stages between death and rebirth. This particular *Purana* also presents the unique theory that the consciousness of the father at the time of impregnation will, through his semen, affect the nature of his offspring.

See also **Hinduism; Karma, parental.**

Pure-Land or Blissful Land Buddhism. (*Jingtu/Ching-t'u*, Japanese: *Jodo*). This Mahayana Buddhist afterlife realm is also called happiness or blissful land (S: *Sukhavati*) or even *Buddhaksetra* (Buddha Field). While each celestial **Buddha** has a paradise or Pure-Land that has been created by his astronomically great merit, most of these have not become of any cult significance. It is only the Western *Sukhavati* of **Amitabha Buddha**, which overshadowed all the others, to become of cultic significance.

A Pure-Land is to be clearly distinguished from a heavenly state. The latter is one of the *bhavachakra* realms into which one can be reborn as a god (*deva*) entirely due to one's own merit. Thus heaven is exclusively dependent on the law of karma. One is reborn into a Pure-Land, especially Amitabha's, due less to one's own merit than to faith in the saving grace of this Buddha; hence birth into the Pure-Land is not karmicaly dependent.

In Amitabha's Pure-Land all souls are said to be reborn as male, in order for there to be no distractions from the task of final liberation. So while female devotees can enter the Pure-Land, either on their way there or immediately upon reaching the Pure-Land their rebirth factor must change genders. In particular, it is to facilitate the change from a this-world female body and rebirth factor to a male one that women pray to **Bhaishajyaraja-guru.**

Among many Pure-Land believers a process of **conscious dying** is encouraged whereby the dying person tries to visualize Amitabha greeting him or her at the entrance to the Pure-Land.

See also *Bodhisattva*; **Chinese religion and reincarnation; Gender issue of the soul;** *Jataka Tales*; **Karma versus grace; Merit, transfer of; Nine doors;** *Phowa*.

Pure Mind Foundation. According to the website of this organization it was formed under the direct supervision of the In-Perpetuum reincarnate Mahan Agass, whose purpose is to explain Universal Nature's veritable pathway to Pure Mind, a spiritual practice that empowers perpetual reincarnation; hence a self-creation process leading to eternal life.

The Foundation's mission is to support all spiritual meditative practices, in particular the Path that leads to Pure Mind as detailed for the first time in the book *Beyond Forever: Unlocking the Door to Eternal Life*. (Manhattan, Kansas: Wheelbarrow Publishing, 1998).

The website further states that "reincarnation is not automatic and must be attained, vigorously maintained, and its movement controlled by living virtuously the Pure Mind Wheel."

Purgatory (Latin: Purgatorium). This is usually thought of as a temporary place of punishment for those who have not been bad enough to deserve eternal **hell**, but not good enough to go to heaven right after death.

Purgatory is not specifically mentioned in the Bible; nonetheless, 1st **Peter** 3:19; 4:6 and 1st Peter 4:6 have in some cases been interpreted to refers to purgatory rather than hell and/or limbo. Also, **John** 14:2 and **Matthew** 12:32 have been used at times to suggest the possibility of purgatory. These and other even less specific biblical passages allowed the concept of purgatory to be an officially accepted doctrine in the Roman Catholic Church since the 13th century **Church Council of Lyon** (1274) **and the Council of Florence** (1439). This was again confirmed in 1562–63, the last two years of the Council of Trent. This original acceptance of purgatory may have been part of the response to the threat of the so-called heretical reincarnation teachings of the **Cathars**.

The Roman Catholic Church specifically defines purgatory as the state in which the souls of those who have sinned after baptism and having repented die in grace (God's forgiveness) but before making satisfaction for their sins through worthy acts of penance. Such souls are then purged by a limited after death punishment or purification. From this definition it is clear that, at least, Catholic purgatory is not some half-way state between heaven and hell for general mild sinners. Nonetheless, a concept of purgatory has appealed to some Christian reincarnationists.

Geddes MacGregor in chapter ten, "Reincarnation as Purgatory," of his *Reincarnation and Christianity* (1978) tries his best to imply that Christian purgatorial teachings are proto-reincarnational, but his argument is unconvincing. Instead, what seems clear is that both Christian concepts of purgatory and hell work against any early or late Christian acceptance of reincarnation.

It might further be noted that while Judaism does not have a formal purgatory, the Jewish hell acts as one to the degree that Judaism does no accept that anyone is sent to hell for all eternity, no matter how bad they have been. This is because as bad as a person may be there is always some tiny good that they have done to someone, so this will in time free them from hell, at least according to Rabbi Gershom in his *Beyond the Ashes* (1992).

Most standard Protestants denominations either do not accept purgatory or leave it to be an open question.

See also **Eighth sphere; John, Gospel of; Kabbalah; Karma versus grace;** *Naraka*; **Predestination.**

Purusha. This Sanskrit term originally referred to a mythical cosmic man who sacrificed himself to bring about creation. It later took on the meaning of the essential element (soul) of every being, especially in **Samkhya Yoga**.

See also *Jiva; Prakriti.*

Purvanivasanusmrti/pubbenivasanussati (S/P). This term means "remembering of former births." It is said to be a one of the psychic or supernatural attainments of a *bodhisattva* upon realizing Buddhahood. Thus the Buddha, Gautama, is said to have gained this ability at the time of his enlightenment.

For those who regard the spontaneous past life recall of young children as good evidence of rebirth it must be wondered why such spiritually underdeveloped minds have a power otherwise mainly credited to fully awakened beings. To add to this question, why would the children be so prone to lose such memories and even memories of having had any past life recall as they become older? Do fully enlightened beings return a child-like mind?

See also *Abhijna*; **Memories, reasons for loss of past life; Rebirth in Buddhism;** *Samma Sambuddha.*

Pyramidology. This is the belief in the spiritual or psychic power inherent in pyramid shapes, especially those with the shape of the great Egyptian pyramids of Giza.

According to some **New Age religions** what have traditionally been called the air shafts in the Kings Chamber of the Great Pyramid of Cheops (Khufu) represent two possible destinies for the deceased. The shaft that is inclined to the celestial pole to the north represents liberation into the eternal stars of the circumpolar region. The shaft that is inclined south to the constellation Orion, which is associated with the mummified god of the dead Osiris, represents reincarnation into the constantly being born (ascent) and dying (descent) of the **zodiac**.

Sitting in a pyramidal shape or even having a small pyramidal shape over or on the head is believed by some New Agers to enhance past life recall.

See also **Agasha Temple of Wisdom; Egypt; Cayce, Edgar; Fluorite; Past life recall meditation; Pleiades; Planetary descent and ascent of the soul; Ramtha; Sirius; Solar Temple, Order of.**

Pythagoras (570–500 BCE). The first known mention of **metempsychosis** in Western literature is linked to this ancient Greek religious philosopher. In a satiric poem by the later Greek philosopher Xenophanes (about 560–478) it is stated that one day Pythagoras, while walking past a dog being beaten told the beater to stop hitting the dog because he [Pythagoras] recognized the voice of an old friend in the cries of the dog. Regardless of how true this statement is, it is almost certain that Pythagoras was the first Greek teacher to systematically teach that souls go through a series of lives. According to Pythagoras the soul seeks liberation from the body and this requires the soul to first gain a deep knowledge of philosophy. This knowledge probably included an understanding of the mystical nature of numbers, especially as such numbers were related to music, an essential part of Pythagoras's teachings seem to have been based on the concept of the "Music of the Spheres." It is believed that Pythagoras taught that the heavenly bodies (stars and planets) move in accordance with one another in such a manner that they produce celestial music. This music could only be heard by the soul, which upon liberation from metempsychosis, ascended into the heavens. In fact, it was probably the ability of the soul to eternally be enraptured by this music that was the supreme spiritual goal in the early Pythagorean religion. Much of this may explain the Pythagorean preference for the worship of Apollo, the god of music, and his daughters, the Muses.

A second Pythagorean liberating requirement was a vow to live a communal life in which all goods were shared. It is known that a number of such communal Pythagorean communities, some with considerable political clout, were established in **Magna Graecia** (Southern Italy), especially in the cities of Kroton (Croton), Metapontion (Metapontum), and Tarentum (Taranto) from the 6th–4th century BCE.

A third requirement for the liberation of the soul from the body was a vegetarian diet, perhaps in a fashion similar to that of the later **Empedocles of Acragas**.

According to **Diogenes Laertius**, Pythagoras believed that he had been given by the god **Hermes** the gift of seeing his own past lives as well as those of others. This ability to remember a previous life (*mathesis*) was for Pythagoras a primary function of life. He believed that he could identify as some of his past lives Aethalides, son of Hermes; the Trojan Euphorbus, son of Panthus; Hermotimus, a prophet of the Ionian city of Lazomenae; a humble fisherman; and the philosopher of Samos.

Present day **Theosophy**, believes that the **ascended master** Kuthumi of the **Great White Brotherhood** was a re-embodiment of Pythagoras.

See also *Anamnesis*; **Archytas of Tarentum; Bruno, Giordano; Greeks and reincarnation; Herodotus; Homer's Iliad and Odyssey; Marlowe, Christopher; Orphism; Pherecydes of Syros; Plato; Porphyry Malchus; Priesthood, lack of an organized; Y.**

Qabbalah *see* **Kabbalah**.

Qiyamah (Arabic: Judgment Day) *see* **Islam; Judgment of the Dead**.

Qlippoth/kelipoth (Hebrew: shells or husks). In the **Kabbalah** this term has a general meaning of evil or demonic entities. In the writings of the great Kabbalic teacher **Isaac Luria** (1534–1572) the *Qlippoth* are given a Neoplatonic meaning and used in the Lurianic creation. In this story during the creation of the universe by God the vessels (*Qlippoth*) carrying seven of the ten **sephiroth** which emanated out from God were too weak to contain their contents and shattered. The shards of these vessels were animated by the particles of divine life light still attached to them. Those shards became physical bodies and the particles of light became souls trapped in the shards of the *Qlippoth*. Those soul particles of light yearn to be free and to return to their divine source. These particles must undergo **transmigration** (*gilgul*) until they can be restored or redeemed (*tiqqum* or *tikkum*). This restoration is achieved by intense mystical concentration on God, following the Law (*Torah*), and through unceasingly struggling against evil. It is this Lurianic restoration process that has greatly influenced Hasidism and its interpretation of the Kabbalah. It is obvious that the fall of divine light into non-divine matter was borrowed from the very similar teachings of a number of sects of Neoplatonic **Gnosticism**.

See also **Fall of the Soul; Samael**.

Questions of King Milinda *see* **Milinda Panha**.

Quetzalcoatl *see* **Kulkulcan**.

Quimby Center. Founder by Dr. Neva Dell Hunter (d. 1978) in 1966 in Alamogordo, New Mexico, the purpose of the Center is to promote the concept of the fatherhood of God and the brotherhood of mankind. Also, like its namesake, Phineas P. Quimby, the founder of New Thought, the Center teaches that mankind, as a direct expression of God, can gain self-mastery by applying the Center's metaphysical teachings to human illness. The Center also accepts a belief in reincarnation, life on other planets, and that present upheavals are a preparation for entering into the Aquarian Age.

Quran *see* **Doceticism, Islam; Kiramu-l-Katin**.

Ra (1). This was a channeled entity through **David Wilcock**.

Ra (2). This entity was channeled through Carla Ruecket from 1981–1984. It described itself as a "Social Memory" or a group of completely integrated souls (**group soul**). The teachings of this entity became the basis of the book by Don Elkins, *The Law of the One*. (Louisville, KY: L/L Research, 1981).

See also **Channeling; Egypt; Equinox; Franklin,**

Benjamin (2); Hilarion; Lazaris; Mafu; Homosexuality; Ramtha; Ryerson, Kevin; Satya; Seth; Torah (2).

Race and rebirth *see* **Caste system; Himmler, Heinrich; Karma, racial; Lost continents and reincarnation; Metagenetics; Rastafarians; Rebirth, ethnic.**

Racial karma *see* **Karma, racial.**

Racial memories *see* **Ancestral Memories; Archetypes; Collective Unconscious.**

Rain. In some late **Vedic Religion** literature it was taught that deceased souls returned to the earth from the moon for rebirth through rain, as a kind of lunar semen.

Rajneesh *see* **Osho Movement.**

Ram Dass, Baba (1931–present [2009]). Born Richard Alpert, this former Harvard University professor, after abandoning some experimentation with psychedelic drugs in the early 1960's, journeyed to India where he adopted various Hindu beliefs, which included reincarnation. His book *Remember, Be Here Now* (1972) furthered a popularization of the concept of reincarnation.

See also **Body-brain (mind) dependency; Out-of-the-body experiences and near-death-experiences (NDEs).**

Rampa, Tuesday Lobsang (1910–1981). This is the pseudonym of the author of the immensely popular book *The Third Eye: Autobiography of a Tibetan Lama* (1956). In this book the author claimed that he was a Tibetan lama who as a novice monk had undergone a mysterious secret surgery in Tibet to open the psychic or **third eye** which enhanced his already natural psychic powers. Upon investigation it was discovered that the writer, far from being a lama, much less Tibetan, was an Irish ex-plumber named Cyril Henry Hoskins who also had recently presented himself under the name of Dr. Kuan-Suo. As a result of this revelation Mr. Hoskins changed his claim from being a lama in this life to having been one in his most recent past life. According to him, in 1949 the original personality called Hoskins voluntarily left his physical body so that it could be taken over (possessed) by the disembodied personality of Rampa, whose physical body was likely to soon die.

Despite the exposure, Hoskins went on to author nineteen more books about his life as a lama; auras; the law of karma; the lost years of **Jesus**; future wars; and extraterrestrials. Most of these books were not outside of what psychic power aficionados could accept as possible. However, his later claims that he had journeyed to the hollow center of the earth and that he had traveled on an alien spaceship to Venus were more than even his most ardent readers could accept.

See also **Planets, other; Possession; UFOism.**

Ramtha, the Enlightened One. According to J. Z. Knight this channeled entity is a high spiritual being that first appeared to Knight in 1977 in a ten foot bodily form as a result of her experiments with pyramid power (**pyramidology**). By the next year Ramtha was channeling through Knight while she was entranced. Ramtha claims to be a 35,000 year old being that lived on the **lost continent** of Lemuria. His people, the Lemurians, originally arrived on earth from a world beyond the North Star. At the early age of 14 Ramtha led an army against the oppressing forces of the lost continent of Atlantis which regarded the Lemurians as soulless. His defeat of this enemy made him a great warlord. Eventually he evolved into an androgynous god-like being of light. As in a number of **New Age religions,** the teachings of Ramtha include both the idea of reincarnation and of **soul mates.**

See also **Aetherius Society; Channeling; Egypt; Equinox; Fall of Souls; Franklin, Benjamin (2); Mafu; Michael (2); Lazaris; Planets, other; Ra (1); Ra (2); Ryerson, Kevin; Seth; Torah (2); Wilcock, David.**

Ransom Report *see* **Ian Stevenson.**

Rastafarians. This is the name adopted by the followers of an Afro-Caribbean religion founded in Jamaica in the first half of the 20th century. Rastafarian beliefs arose out of a prophecy by "the return to **Africa** advocate" Marcus Garvey (1887–1940). The prophecy was that salvation would come to the Black people of the Americas from Africa with the crowning of an African king. The coronation of the Ethiopian prince Ras Tafari as the emperor Haile Selassie in 1930 convinced some Jamaicans that this was the fulfillment of Garvey's prophecy. The basis of this conviction was that the Ethiopian emperors held the titles of the "King of Kings" and the "Lion of Judah" because of a connection to the legendary son of the biblical King Solomon and the Queen of Sheba. The Rastafarians were further convinced that the emperor himself was, in fact, the (re)-incarnation of **Jesus,** and, hence, of God.

Also, the Rastafarian movement came to believe that the black Africans were the original Israelites and, according to Rastafarian theology, the souls of the original Israelites have always been reborn as black people.

See also **Afro-American religions; Karma, racial; Metagenetics; Rebirth, ethnic.**

Rawandiyah. This was the name of an obscure Middle Eastern (Iraqian) religious group who held pre–Islamic beliefs which included reincarnation. They were suppressed by the Caliph al-Mansur in 757–758.

See also **Hashimiyya; Kanthaeans; Khurramiyya; Yarsanism.**

Rawat, Kirti S. (dates not known). A retired professor from the University of Rajasthan, Rawat is the director of the International Center for Survival and Reincarnation Research and the author of *Raghunath Remembered: A Case Suggestive of Reincarnation* (1985).

Reap what you sow *see* **Karma; Karma in the Bible?**

Rebirth or **rebecoming.** Rebirth is the most general and most inclusive term for what is also called reincarnation, **transmigration**, **metempsychosis**, and **palingenesis.**

Although lengthy, one standard definition for rebirth is "the process in which some core aspect of a person or animal which, upon bodily death, manifests itself as the core in a new body, the existence of which has not overlapped in time with the former body." The last part of this definition is required to distinguish rebirth from **possession**. Also, usually included in the definition of rebirth is a requirement that the core aspect, having manifested itself in the new body, ceases to exist beyond the new body; however, this supplementary part of the definition can not be considered an absolute requirement because some peoples in **Africa**, and in Tibet, while believing in rebirth in accordance with the first part of the definition also believe in the possibility of simultaneous multiple rebirth.

To further clarify the meaning of rebirth, including its near synonyms metempsychosis, palingenesis, reincarnation, and transmigration, the following three conditions are normally expected to be present. First, rebirth only refers to the continued existence of some factor (i.e. a **soul** or its equivalent) of a living being which, after physical death, is re-embodied in an infant prior to or very shortly after its leaving the maternal womb. Second, the body of this infant must not have received a previous re-embodied factor. If a previous re-embodied factor is already present in the infant the new factor would be considered an **attached entity**, which would qualify as possession rather than rebirth. Third, in the case of a human being, the continuing factor must be regarded as an essential aspect of the infant's being, one without which the infant would not have a chance at becoming a complete functioning rational, and eventually socially, responsible being. The second and third conditions are needed because some proponents of rebirth have broadened the concept of rebirth to include a recently disembodied soul entering and reanimating the body of an infant or adult who has just died and whose soul has left that body. This situation is closer to possession or to a **walk-in**. Also, the second condition, while allowing for only one soul per person, does not excluded the possibility that a soul may be a complex phenomena, the parts of which may have diverse origins. In such a case, those parts would be in a necessarily complementary relationship. Finally, the third condition is needed to differentiate an individual human soul from the rebirth of a collective soul of an animal.

See also **Animals and rebirth, non–Western view; Animals and rebirth, Western view; Parallel lives; Plurality of existences; Rebirth factor; Rebirth in Buddhism; Rebirth, simultaneous.**

Rebirth, alternative explanations to. In trying to explain various claims to memories of past lives without invoking the concept of a **soul** passing from one body to another, a number of alternate explanations have been proposed. These alternative explanations fall into two groups, the non-psychic and the psychic (extrasensory). In the first group are found **cryptomnesia;** *déjà vu*; (lucid) **dreams; fraud; honest lying; memories, ancestral or genetic; Multiple personalities;** personal myth in **past life therapy; psychic psycho-drama; rebirth and cultural conditioning;** role-playing **fantasy;** and **screen memories.** In the second group there are *akashic* record reading; **attached entities** and/ or **possession; channeling; clairaudience; clairvoyance; a group soul; passing-memories adoption; psychometry; retrocognition; telepathy with the living;** and **telepathy with the dead.** All of the items in the first group have the characteristic of being an ability of a living or embodied consciousness, not of a disembodied one. The second group of alternative explanations requires a considerable amount of psychic ability. The fact is, however, that most subjects that sincerely believe that they have remembered their past lives, in general, demonstrate no more psychic abilities than those who have no such memories.

Rebirth proponents argue that no single item above, by itself, can account for what they believe are multiple lives. They further argue that any thorough alternative explanation would require most, if not all, of the above alternatives. Rebirth proponents then point out that simple rebirth is a better explanation than the complex mixing of those alternatives because a simply explained rebirth process would not violate the **law of parsimony** which says that the simplest, or least complex, explanation for any phenomenon is the best explanation for it.

See also **Bleed-through of lives; Extrasensory perception; Fantasy versus past life regression; Memories, ancestral or genetic; Possession; Rebirth and cultural conditioning; Time and the simultaneous past, present, and future.**

Rebirth, analogies from nature. Analogies from nature mean that the various cycles of birth and death existing in nature support the concept of rebirth. Among these cyclical processes are those of the **moon**, the seasons, the metamorphosing **butterfly**, **deciduous trees**, seeds, **serpents**, **stags**, and even the comings and goings of migratory birds. The "analogies from nature" argument is very popular in the **Neo-pagan** and **Wicca** communities, but it seems to have more to do with poetic metaphors than any possible proof of the rebirth of a **soul**.

See **Arguments supportive of rebirth; Gods, cyclically dying and rising; Old Testament and the afterlife; Phaedo; Reincarnation, origins of; Similes and rebirth.**

Rebirth and abortion. The whole Western religious argument against the abortion of a fetus primarily rests on the issue of when a **soul** becomes implanted into the fetus. By the time of Aurelius **Augustine**, Bishop of Hippo (354–430), it was commonly thought that the soul was added to the fetus by God forty days after conception. In more modern Christian views the soul is thought to be inserted into the embryo much sooner, which is why many church groups are opposed to abortion. Since Western monotheists believe that an ensouled being has only one life in which to attain salvation, it is completely logical for believers to display strong opposition to abortion.

In those religions that accept rebirth of some kind, no such single life restriction on salvation is necessary. This is the main reason that such religions have been far more accepting of abortion than has Western religion. This does not morally justify abortion, especially if it is assumed that the rebirthing entity or factor is present upon or shortly after embryonic conception, but it does permit both the non-reincarnationists and the reincarnationists to better understand the other's religious perspective.

See also **Deaths, violent and premature; Embodiment, moment of; Embryo and Fetus; Human embryo stem cell uses and rebirth; Reincarnation and artificial insemination; Reincarnation and Suicide; Resurrection and the aborted fetus.**

Rebirth and artificial insemination. The modern technology of artificial insemination in a medical laboratory creates certain obvious problems for any kind of rebirth concept. Since there is presumably no sexual copulation, then what would attract a rebirth entity to enter a womb, at least at this stage? Several possibilities have been suggested. First, all souls come directly from God and, as omnipresent, He is even in fertility laboratories. Second, there are now very sophisticated rebirth entities that check out fertility clinics. Third, only embryos produced in the normal sexual manner receive a re-embodied entity. Fourth, embodiment of a soul occurs sometime after conception and the woman leaving the clinic.

Although no one has yet cloned a human being, it is only a matter of time before this happens, and while any of the above possibilities could be true, there is now the added question of whether or not the **soul** of the body being cloned is also cloned?

See also **Child as its own reborn father or mother; Electra/Oedipus Complex.**

Rebirth and cultural conditioning. The fact that the great majority of cases of spontaneous past life memories have occurred in cultures where the belief in rebirth is widespread have lead to the suspicion that such past life claims are more due to cultural conditioning than to anything else.

One response to this suspicion is that the souls of some individuals from cultures that thoroughly accept rebirth are more likely to retain their memories of a former life than individuals from cultures that do not accept rebirth. This failure to remember past lives may be especially the case in cultures that regard rebirth as dogmatically unacceptable.

See also **Children remembering past lives; Druzes; Uttar Pradesh.**

Rebirth and cyclical time. One thing that distinguishes all south and east Asian religions from the Judeo-Christian-Islamic tradition is their respective understanding of time. Buddhism, **Hinduism**, and **Jainism** all believe in the cyclical, or ever repeating, nature of the birth and death of the universe. Even **Daoism** and Confucianism, in their own way, see the universe as a never beginning and never ending interplay of Yin and Yang forces.

Western religious traditions, on the other hand, teach a linear concept of time in which the universe had a unique historical beginning with its creation by God and will have an equally unique historical end with the coming of the Messiah and the Kingdom of Heaven. The difference in these two understandings of time has an important implication for a belief in rebirth, as well as for the issue of social justice.

First, cyclical traditions can integrate the concept of rebirth more easily than can linear traditions. This is one reason that orthodox Western traditions are more favorable to a single future resurrection of the dead.

Second, the concept of rebirth tends to better match cultures where the connection to the past, as in justifying the present by the past, is more important than the present or future. This is the case for the Indian caste system and the Chinese emphasis on the ancestors as the best model. Western culture, under the influence of Judeo-Christian messianic thought, values the future more than the past or present.

The difference in these two understandings of time has important social implications. In traditions of cyclical time human society is thought to go through cycles of good and bad periods no matter what mankind does or does not do. The result of this is that these traditions, see only a minimum reason to expend time and effort on improving the world materially, socially, or scientifically because since ultimately none of this will help humanity escape the brutal round of birth and death. In other words, if the nature of the universe is such that all human efforts will eventually be defeated by a future bad period, why expend time and effort futilely? Instead, the goal of cyclical time religions has been to escape from the whole miserable cycle as quickly as possible. This has naturally led to the general Western charge of "rebirth pessimism."

A Western pro-reincarnationist effort to challenge this charge of pessimism was first popularized in the late 19th century by the development of **Theosophy** and its related schools. It was the view of these schools that a more modern view of rebirth and karma, one that was free of Asian pessimism, could support human progress. This Westernized version of rebirth was characterized by a rejection of human to animal rebirth and replacement of an emphasis on punishment with an emphasis on purification and reform. This was clearly an attempt to merge Eastern personal cyclical time with Western social lineal time. Whether this merger is logically satisfactory is open to question. If everyone's karma is his own, than all anyone can be held responsible for is his or her own progress. As long as a person works to keep his karma moving towards perfection he is doing his part.

Perhaps the greatest problem with the Western "rebirth as a process of spiritual progress" is that without a memory of past successes and failures the individual must keep restarting his growth from the very beginning as a memory-less infant.

See also **Finite or infinite number of rebirths; Fixed number or infinite number of souls; Hell; Individuality and rebirth; Karma and justice; Karma in the ancient and modern west; Nightmare of eastern philosophy; Rebirth, East and West; Resurrection, bodily; Theosophical Society.**

Rebirth and famous supporters. The fact that many famous people have believed in rebirth is often used as an argument in favor of it. For example, among the philosophers that have believed in rebirth are such luminaries as **Pythagoras, Plato,** and **Voltaire**. As for scientists, there are Sir Oliver Lodge (English physicist and President of the British Association for the Advancement of Science), Alfred Russell Wallace (co-discoverer of the theory of evolution), Thomas Edison, and Sir Humphrey Davy (renowned English chemist). Added to these names could be many well-known artists such as **W. B. Yeats**, and actors such as **Shirley MacLaine**.

There are several reasons for questioning this association as a valid argument for rebirth. First, there are far more philosophers and scientists who have rejected the belief. In the case of the philosophers and scientists just mentioned who support rebirth, there is no evidence in their writings that they ever carefully examined the pros and cons of the subject. It seems that for personal reasons they accepted it at face value. In all fairness, it is probable that many of the philosophers and scientists that have rejected the view have done so equally for personal reasons and at face value. This, by itself, would simply neutralize any dependence on philosophers and scientists for or against the belief.

On the other hand, there are such researchers as **Elizabeth Kubler-Ross, Satwant K. Pasricha, Ian Stevenson,** and **Helen Wambach** who have tried to prove rebirth, but so far their data has been open to considerable criticism by a number of other researchers who have closely examined that data.

It is one thing to accept the personal opinions of famous names of important secular persons, and another to accept the personal opinions of those that are regarded as having reached what might be the highest state of consciousness. The opinion of these enlightened individuals should count for far more than that of any unenlightened persons. Individuals such as Mahavira of **Jainism**, the disciples of the **Buddha** of Buddhism, and Shankara of Vedantism fall into this group. But their opinions are countered by the views of what most in the West regard as sources of divine truth. These include the prophets of the **Old Testament**, the disciples of **Jesus**, many Christian mystics, Mohammed, and various Islamic mystics, all of whom have supported a single life concept.

See also **Aristotle; Arguments supportive of rebirth; Logic and pseudo-logic and rebirth; Widespread and multi-cultural belief argument.**

Rebirth and general morality. One of the arguments for rebirth is that the rebirth concept encourages general morality and does it better than a belief in a future resurrection. The first factor that seems to be constantly overlooked in all moral arguments for a post-mortem existence is that truly evil people do not appear to be in the least bothered by threats of being deprived of heaven and/or condemned to hell; second, there is no substantial proof that the majority of unbelievers in an afterlife lead any less moral lives than do believers.

In response reincarnationist advocates have claimed that while the issue of general morality may not be any better served by a belief in rebirth than in a belief in resurrection, holding to rebirth is a superior way to overcomes social class, racial, national, and religious prejudice by teaching that any one person may be reborn into any social class, race, nation, and religion. In one rebirth view it is even stated that hatred towards another group works as a magnet to draw one into being reborn into that group. As reasonable as this sounds, if India with its **caste system** is any example of a less prejudiced society, this argument is not so easily sustained.

See also **Arguments supportive of rebirth; Karma in the ancient and modern west; Rebirth and moral perfection; Rebirth and religious tolerance; Resurrection, bodily.**

Rebirth and logical symmetry. In the context of rebirth the argument for logical symmetry states that what has a beginning should have an end what was created should experience eventual destruction. If the human **soul** is thought to have an endless life it ought to have never been created, but to have always existed. The Western concept that every soul is newly born out of nothing but becomes immortal after its birth has no logical symmetry to it. To give it symmetry one would have to assume that what was born out of nothing should go back into nothing upon death. For something to be truly immortal it should be without a beginning. In Western religion such without a beginning and without an end is accepted as a logical statement about God, but not about human souls, which are considered a product of divine creation "in time." In rebirth, on the other hand, the pre-embodiment of souls and the post-embodiment of souls balance each other creating a logical symmetry; therefore, rebirth is said to be logically symmetrical while other post-mortem views, such as resurrection, are logically asymmetrical.

Based on the idea that symmetry is somehow superior to asymmetry, pro-reincarnationists have argued that a theory of a beginningless and endless series of lives is superior to a theory of a single life. A challenge to this symmetrical argument has been that while symmetrical rebirth may be mathematically more logical than asymmetrical resurrection, nonetheless, it merely demonstrates that one improvable immortality theory may be better than another improvable immortality theory.

The argument for rebirth from logical symmetry has more validity in **Hinduism** than in Buddhism. In Hinduism this symmetry takes the form of the soul arising out of God and returning into God. In this sense, Hinduism offers a beginningless and an endless existence of souls. In Buddhism, however, without knowing the origin of the **rebirth factor**, it is impossible to judge whether or not it is symmetrical or asymmetrical. Moreover, while in Buddhism the rebirth factor may be given a vaguely indeterminate long rebirthing past that, on a practical level more or less amounts to an eternity, it then teaches that in the distant future the rebirth factor will cease to be reborn due to its entrance into **nirvana**, which technically destroys any symmetry once and for all.

See also **Arguments supportive of rebirth; Immortality; Karma and the moral structure of the universe.**

Rebirth and maturity. One argument made in support of rebirth is that many people who do not believe in rebirth and karma blame their misfortunes on outside factors, and as a result there is a great deal of childish self-pity in the world. Belief in rebirth and karma holds people fully responsible for their misfortune and so encourages greater maturity and less self-pity.

See also **Arguments supportive of rebirth; Blaming the victim vs. illusion of innocence; Dehiscent or Seed-pod Principle; Noble lie.**

Rebirth and moral perfection. Many religions teach that the goal of humanity is to attain to moral perfection. For advocates of rebirth this can not be done in one lifetime and so they argue that a heavenly existence in a religion that allows for only one life would be full of imperfect entities, which is a very contradictory heaven. Of course, Christianity is, in one sense, one of those "perfectionist" religions in so far as it accepts the words ascribed to Jesus "to be perfect as the heavenly Father" (**Matthew** 5:48; 19:21) or even more so as in the *theosis* implied in 2nd **Peter** 1:4b, "Through this might [divine power of Christ] and splendor he has given us his promise, great beyond all price, and through them you may escape the corruption with which lust has infected the world, and come to share in the very being of God."

It is clear from Peter and similar citations that Christianity teaches that any perfection a person could attain has been has already been achieved through Christ's atoning sacrifice and/or has been made possible by the three elements of faith, baptism, and the Eucharist. This teaching is either forgotten or ignored by Christian reincarnationists who use the argument that multiple lives alone give sufficient time for moral perfection.

Also, opponents of rebirth point out that the problem for all reincarnationists is that it is difficult to justify how a series of lives could lead to moral perfection in the absence of some sort of memory of a past life. The perfecting of anything requires a building up from what came before, but without a memory of what came before there is nothing upon which to build.

A variation on the moral perfection argument is that all souls must gain a sufficiently great enough variety of experiences to eventually leave the cycle of birth and death, but such variety is almost impossible for the average person to experience in one life-time. This, however, is also open to the absence of memory criticism.

See also **Altruism and rebirth; Arguments supportive of rebirth; Karma and justice; Karma in the ancient and modern west; Karma versus grace; New Testament sacrificial concept; Peter, 1st and 2nd; Rebirth and general morality; School of Life.**

Rebirth and original sin *see* **Original sin versus karma.**

Rebirth and religious tolerance. One of the best arguments for a belief in multiple lives versus in a single life followed by an eventual resurrection is that the former is associated with far more "religious" tolerance than the latter. While there have been violent power struggles between the followers of such religions as **Hinduism** and Buddhism over the centuries these have rarely been justified on the basis of saving any souls. In other words, there have been few crusades or jihadist like activities, and no official inquisitional murdering of heretics by reincarnationists. Such killing has always been religiously justified on the basis that there is only one life and one chance to be saved from eternal damnation and any methods necessary to insure that a majority of souls are saved have been sanctified by God. The religious history of Christianity and **Islam** is infamous for the amount of blood that has been spilled in the name of saving souls. In contrast to this, if it is believed that if there is an indefinite number of opportunities to be saved, there can be far less justification, much less divine sanction, to force a person to believe the "true religion" or be killed so that the unbeliever does not contaminate others.

The belief in rebirth and karma, especially without a belief in God, has actually been one of the main reasons that Buddhist and Jain monks and nuns have historically been so reluctant to even defend themselves against aggression by the followers of theistic Islam. The absence of any belief in a supreme deity has meant that there is no God who could override or neutralize the detrimental karmic consequences of intentionally killing others; therefore, one can not escape from the karmic consequence of intentional violence in a future rebirth, even if it is in self-defense.

See also **Belgi Dorje; Karma and God.**

Rebirth and science. One major criticism made about many people who believe strongly in rebirth is that they have no interest in, and sometimes even no toleration of, modern scientific knowledge. Examples of this may be the refusal to even acknowledge the **body-brain (mind) dependency** evidence or **population problem issue**, the tendency to adopt the **supernatural-in-the-gap process**, the continued attachment to **lost continents**, and various aspects of the **inconsistent views of rebirth**.

Since a great many people who have no belief in rebirth also subscribe to a number of those un-scientific views there is no way of telling if reincarnationists are any more or less anti-science.

See also **Arguments pro and con on an afterlife in general (9); Arguments supportive of rebirth; Rebirth and the scientific theory of biological evolution.**

Rebirth and suicide. Monotheistic religions that teach that there is only a single life in which to gain salvation are generally opposed to suicide on the basis that since it was God alone who gave a person his or her **soul**, it should be God alone who determines when to surrender up that soul in death. In contrast, religions that advocate a belief in rebirth are in considerable disagreement with one another on the issue of the right to take one's own life. Those that are opposed to it generally say that it is a self-defeating act, since whatever the person left undone in one life will only have to be resolved in the next life, possibly under more unpleasant conditions than exist presently. On the other hand, many reincarnationists have no objection to the taking of one's own life under such circumstances as an extremely debilitating illness that may not only have destroyed all of one's own quality of life, but has become such a burden on one's loved ones that it is destroying their quality of life.

When it comes to religiously sanctified suicide, it is above all the Jains that come to mind. In **Jainism** it is both a permitted and an honored act for great holy men and women to commit ritual suicide by slow self-starvation (*sallekhana*). This very painful ascetic ritual is said to burn off the last vestiges of karma of the saint, which upon death will free him or her from further rebirth.

The Mahayana Buddhist canon also contain stories of religiously sanctified suicide; in particular it is sanctioned by the *Lotus Sutra*.

See also **Annihilationism, Buddhist view; Cathars or Cathari; Ganges; Heaven's Gate; Rebirth and abortion; Return and serve argument for reincarnation; Solar Temple, Order of**.

Rebirth and the preponderance of evidence. Like the belief in an afterlife or even in the existence of God, the belief in rebirth is a metaphysical issue and as such cannot be scientifically disproved or proven. The most any challenger to any such metaphysical issue can offer is whether or not the "preponderance of evidence" against such an issue is greater than the preponderance of evidence for the issue. The preponderance of evidence would seem to be against all forms of afterlife theories, in which case the belief in an afterlife must be based exclusively upon an "act of faith."

See also **Arguments pro and con on an afterlife in general; Proof for and against reincarnation argument**.

Rebirth and the scientific theory of biological evolution. Rebirth is said to both support and to be supported by the scientific theory of biological evolution. The teaching that there is a parallel spiritual evolution is said to reflect this. There are three problems with this claim. First, very few scientists add teleology to the evolutionary process. This means that science assigns no forethought to nature such that it is purposely striving to develop higher and higher life forms. Parallel to evolution in nature is devolution. This is where a formerly more complex organism has become less complex as a way of surviving. Formerly free living organisms, which have become internal parasites, are just one example of this.

Second, physical evolution has been generated by the law of the survival of the fittest. If there is a parallel spiritual level of biological evolution it should also follow a spiritual tooth and claw survival of the fittest law. Most reincarnationists would find such a law of spirituality as unacceptable.

Third, any evolutionary system of the **soul** that parallels bodily evolution has to deal with the problems related to the **ontological leap** issue.

The belief in spiritually parallel evolution is far more the product of Western rebirth beliefs than it is of Eastern beliefs. This is because of the **rebirth and cyclical time** factor.

See also **Arguments pro and con on an afterlife in general (9); Arguments supportive of rebirth; Karma in the ancient and modern west; Rebirth and cyclical time; Rebirth and science; Resurrection, bodily; Soul Darwinism; Teleological presumption**.

Rebirth and unilinear descent. In folk societies there appears to be a strong statistical relationship between a belief in rebirth and a line of descent that gives greater value to either the maternal or paternal kin. Such a relationship is far less common in bilateral descent society, which is where both the maternal and paternal kin are given equal value.

If the concept of karma is added to the belief in rebirth the unilateral descent factor is over-ridden by moral considerations and so tends to weaken any kinship element in rebirth.

See also **Ancestor worship; Karma and justice; Proximity burial; Rebirth, consanguineous; Rebirth, obligatory; Rebirth, proximity; Reincarnation, origins of**.

Rebirth, artificial *see* **Artificial rebirth**.

Rebirth as tedium *see* ***Duhkha*; Rebirth, East and West; Rebirth, compensation and life fulfillment**.

Rebirth as the natural order of all living things. One of the arguments made in support of rebirth is that physical birth exists to replace that which has physically died; therefore, the rebirth of a **soul** in a new body is merely the spiritual side of this natural physical order. The problem with this view of soul re-embodiment is that for a spiritual component to truly parallel the bodily process there should be the death of the spiritual body after it has insured, through spiritual "reproduction," its replacement. The closest to this reproduction would be traducianism; but even here reincarnation is a separate issue.

See also **Arguments supportive of rebirth; Generationism and Traducianism; Rebirth and science; Rebirth and the scientific theory of biological evolution;**

Rebirth, compensation and life fulfillment. For many people the prospect of rebirth allows them to believe that they will be rewarded or compensated in some fashion for any of the sacrifice of selfish desires they have made in order to live a responsible life. It can also allow them to believe that selfish people will be deprived or punished for having lived irresponsibly. This is also true of the Western concept of the resurrection of the dead and of heaven. So, rebirth does not have a stronger argument here than does final resurrection. On the other hand, this hope for compensation ignores the very realistic Eastern religious view of rebirth as tedium more than anything else.

See also **Arguments supportive of rebirth; *Duhkha*; Rebirth and moral perfection; Rebirth, compensation and life fulfillment; Rebirth, East and West; Resurrection, bodily**.

Rebirth, consanguineous. Consanguineous rebirth would occur when a person is reborn into the same family or kinship group as in a previous life. Investigators of rebirth consider claims for rebirths back into the same family to offer the weakest evidence for rebirth since the amount of information about the life of the former family member is likely to be readily available through natural means to the supposedly reborn child.

See also **Akan; Cannibalistic reincarnation; Karma, family; Leland, Charles Godfrey; Paramacca Maroons; Rebirth and unilinear descent.**

Rebirth, control of. This is the concept that the **soul** can determine to a large degree the kind of body into which it will be reborn.

Rebirth, criteria for proof of. Most modern advocates of reincarnation acknowledge that many claims to a past life are more purposefully fraudulent than authentic. For this reason there have been attempts to develop some criteria for sincere claims to reincarnation. One such attempt at a set of criteria has been developed by the past life therapist Raymond A. Moody in his book *Coming Back: A Psychiatrist Explores Past life Journeys* (1991). He has suggested twelve traits that are present in sincere claims of having remembered a past life. He states that it is not necessary to manifest all twelve, but a significant number of these should be present. These are: (1) a past life experience usually involves visual images; less often they are just thoughts; (2) a genuine past life regression seems to have a life of its own; (3) the images have an uncanny feeling of familiarity; (4) the subject having the experience identifies with one of the characters in the scene; (5) past life emotions may be experienced during regression; (6) past life events may be viewed in two distinct perspectives; (7) the experience often mirrors present life issues in the experiencer; (8) regression may be followed by genuine improvement in the mental state; (9) regression may affect present medical conditions; (10) regression develops according to meanings, not a historical timeline; (11) past life regression becomes easier with repetition; and (12) most past lives are mundane, not famous, infamous, or heroic.

The reincarnation researcher **Ian Stevenson** (1918–2007) has offered the following characteristic that he feels would prove a case of reincarnation: (1) the subject should be able to have considerably detailed recall; (2) a written report of the past life memories should be made before trying to verifying them; (3) the verification should be accurate; (4) besides just memories the individual should manifest some behavioral habits identical to the previously living individual; (5) some physical evidence, such as a birthmark, should relate the two lives; and (6) the reincarnated individual should demonstrate linguistic compatibility with the previous life.

Another researcher, Jonathan Venn (1986), has offered the following as an ideal set of criteria for cases of hypnotic recall: (1) the hypnotist would collect considerable data from multiple hypnotic sessions; (2) the data must pertain to a time and place for which historical documentation is available for individual lives; (3) the hypnotic sessions must be auditorily and/or visually recorded; (4) to prevent any contamination of the original data all hypnotic sessions would be recorded before an attempt to historically document the data; and (5) both positive and negative documentation would be offered in judging the likelihood of an authentic past life.

Since a human being is so complex, the question has been asked, mainly by Westerners, "How much of that complexity would need to carry over from one life to another?" Even without a body a human personality would still consist of memories, disposition, habits, talents, likes and dislikes. Some reincarnation advocates would add karmic merits and demerits. Ideally, the person in the so-called next life should lack as few of these as possible to consider that person to be the same as the one in the so-called former life. However, both critics and supporters of reincarnation have been willing to settle for far less. Most Western critics will reluctantly settle for memory alone as the absolute minimum for proof that reincarnation is a valid concept. This contrasts greatly with Hindus, Buddhists, and Jains who require only karmic merits and demerits to be reborn and since there is no way to measure such karma, or prove that it even exists, critics must regard the Indian view as extremely questionable.

The main problem with trying to prove reincarnation is that one has to deal with a catch-22 situation. If the life of a now deceased person is too well documented, then any claims by a currently living person to have been that deceased person in a past life is suspect as either **cryptomnesia, honest lying, role-playing fantasy**, or even outright **fraud**, on the grounds that the currently living person could have knowingly or unknowingly acquired any knowledge of the deceased through completely normal channels. On the other hand, if the life of a now deceased person is not documented well enough to check facts supposedly recalled by the currently living person then there is not sufficient evidence for reincarnation, so once again the recaller can be suspect of honest lying, role-playing fantasy, or fraud.

See also **Fantasy versus past life regression; Jewish Holocaust; Language inconsistency;**

Leading question; Memory alone critique; Past life fakery.

Rebirth, cross-species. This refers to the ability of animals to reincarnate as human beings and vice versa. It is synonymous with progressive and regressive transmigration.

See also **Africa; Animals and rebirth, Western view; Basilides; Christianity and reincarnation; Metempsychosis; Rebirth, non-backsliding; Transmigration, progressive; Transmigration, regressive; Yazidis (Yezidis).**

Rebirth, East and West. A major difference between Eastern and Western believers in rebirth is that the Westerners almost always perceive rebirth as a mainly positive prospect. A good example of this optimism is in the number of **past life therapy** resources available, where the clearly stated purpose of discovering past lives is to ensure a more psychologically healthy or satisfying present life. Such a positive view ignores the more pessimistic Eastern implications of reincarnation.

Because of the usual translation of *duhkha* as suffering, the common Western perception is that Indian religions consider life to be essentially suffering. However, Indian religions, whether **Hinduism**, Buddhism, or **Jainism**, have been just as aware of life's pleasures as have people of other religions. Indian rebirth traditions teach that life's dissatisfaction is not derived so much from pain as it is from the sheer boredom or the perceived meaninglessness of multiple life times.

Western advocates of rebirth tend to focus on the positive concept that rebirth means that in the end no one will ever be cheated of opportunities to gain what they believe was their due. Rebirth implies that if one did not gain what one wanted in this life, one had a second, a third, a fourth, or more chance to do so. On the hand, what if in this life one failed to get all one wanted for good karmic reasons, is it not possible that one will be equally, if not even more, frustrated in any succeeding life or lives? In other words, if life has not been kind to one in the present existence, can anyone be sure that future rebirths will be any kinder? Can anyone, after one or two more of these unhappy lives, simply say, "No More"? The reincarnation-karmic system is emphatic in saying "No."

The Eastern view goes still farther in that it asks what if this life was a very happy one; can anyone expect that enjoyment will be repeatable in those lives that follow? Even if the answer were yes, it needs to remember that rebirth implies that a person has to go through thousands, hundreds of thousands, even millions of lives. With numbers like these how much variation of happiness can there be? Sooner or later we must repeat over and over again all of our successes and joys, and as we go from births, through aging, to deaths. Can this be thought of as anything more than a pessimistic weariness and tedium? So even without having to repeat any undesirable physical and mental conditions rebirth becomes a repeated form of tedium, which is *duhkha*.

The Indo-Buddhist view of suffering is ultimately circular. The ordinary stresses and strains of life are objectively forms of dissatisfaction and they may or may not make life seem meaningless or worthless. But the moment the metaphysics of rebirth are added to this condition the "may not" disappears. Life is suffering because rebirth makes it a vicious circle. With this in mind it can be understood why rebirth in the Eastern view is never an end in itself, but a means to the end of being liberated from future rebirths. In the more naively optimistic West the more satisfactory view of life allows the believer in multiple lives to perceive rebirth as an end in and of itself.

A final difference between the East and West is that in those cultures in which the belief in rebirth has a long tradition, that belief is significantly integrated into most, if not all, other aspects of that culture. Thus the belief, both positively and negatively, affects the economic, social, political, and artistic aspects of the culture. This is not the case in the West. Here most religious concepts are compartmentalized and thus have much less effect on the material culture.

See also **Animals and rebirth, non–Western view; Animals and rebirth, Western view; Caste system; Finite or infinite number of rebirths; Fixed number or variable number of souls; Hell; Individuality and rebirth; Karma and justice; Karma, developmental; Karma in the ancient and modern west; Karma, retributive; Karma versus grace; Mental plane; Neo-pagan religions; Original sin versus karma; Procrastination, charge of; Rebirth and cyclical time; Rebirth in the modern West; Rebirth in Zen; Rebirth, qualifications for; Rebirth or rebecoming; Theodicy; Transmigration.**

Rebirth eschatology. Eschatology is the study of metaphysical views dealing with death, the afterlife, judgment, heaven, hell, and even the end of time. The term rebirth eschatology refers to any eschatology that emphasizes rebirth or reincarnation, but without the doctrine of karma; therefore, rebirth eschatology is in contrast to the more complex **karmic eschatology**. Rebirth eschatologies have been far more common throughout human history than have karmic ones.

Eschatology is not to be confused with thanatology (study of death), which is the study of bodily death. Eschatology is closely related to soteriology (study of salvation).

The opposite of eschatology is **Protology**.

See also **Judgment of the Dead; Karma in the ancient and modern west; Millennialism; Ontology.**

Rebirth, ethnic. This is the belief that a particular racial group will always have the same set of souls born into it. If this occurs for some karmic reason than it is usually called ethnic or racial karma.

See also ***Dor deah*; Druzes; Jewish Holocaust; Karma; Karma, racial; Metagenetics; Proximity burial; Rebirth Proximity; Rastafarians.**

Rebirth, expectational. This refers to the occurrence of reincarnation only for individuals who are expected to reincarnate and/or reincarnation in cultures were it is expected to occur. In other words, souls are more likely to reincarnate in India than in the United States.

See also **Rebirth, obligatory; Rebirth, selective.**

Rebirth factor. This term is used as a substitute for the word soul when in a full Buddhist context. It serves as a reminder that Buddhism rejects the substantiality implied in the term soul.

See also ***Anatman; Karma* with minimal rebirth; *Manas*; Rebirth; Rebirth in Buddhism.**

Rebirth, general. This is the belief that the overwhelming majority of souls are assumed to reincarnate. It is the opposite of selective or special rebirth in which only a selective minority of souls undergo rebirth.

See also **Rebirth, selective.**

Rebirth, group. This is the processes whereby the same sets of souls are reborn more or less simultaneously due to karmic ties which necessitate a continued interaction with each other. According to **Helen Wambach** 87 percent of her regressed clients reported knowing people in a past life that they also know in the present-life.

See also ***Dor deah*; Guirdham, Arthur; Kabbalah; Karma, family; Soul groups.**

Rebirth in Buddhism. Standard Buddhism teaches that if a person has not been liberated by enlightenment then upon death that person will be reborn into one of the six ***bhavachakra*** realms which are those of human beings, animals, **hungry ghosts**, denizens of hell, anti-gods (*asura*), and denizens of heaven (*devachan*).

On the surface, the issue of rebirth in Buddhism can at times seem rather simple and uncontroversial, but as soon as the issue is explored more deeply it becomes complex and controversial. There are two reasons for this. The first reason centers on the problem of having to reconcile the Buddhist doctrine of rebirth with the Buddhist doctrine of ***anatman*** which is that there is no-self/-soul (*atman*) that passes from one life to another. Indeed, it is this no-soul teaching that explains the Buddhist reluctance to use the term reincarnation, since this term implies some concrete entity (a soul) that passes from one body to another. In place of reincarnation Buddhists prefer to use the more generalized term rebirth or re-becoming (***bhava***) as less likely to imply any transmigrating soul-like entity.

As might be expected, throughout the history of Buddhism the subject of a soulless rebirth has been most controversial issue for Buddhism. If there is no-soul, what, if anything, can go on to another life? If something does go on, is this not the same, or equivalent, of a soul? If it is not a soul, then what is it?

Because of the denial of a soul, yet with its affirmation of rebirth, orthodox Buddhism has often had to resort to saying that while no person passes from one life to another the karma of each person does pass from life to life. This then requires a carrier of karma of some kind to pass from death to birth or, more specifically, to conception.

In some scriptures (S/P: *sutras/suttas*) the Buddha is quoted as saying that for a human conception to take place the following factors are required: a mother who is in her fertile period, a father, sexual congress, and the presence of a ***gandharva***. The last factor is nowhere further explained in the *sutras*, but in the commentaries *gandharva* has been interpreted as a rebirth (linking) consciousness (*patisandhi vinnana*).

When the term *gandharva* is not being used, still other sutric terms are used for the so-called rebirth link or karmic carrier in the early Buddhist canon. Among these links are the *samskara/sankara* (volitional activities, also translated as past karma), ***chitta/citta*** (mind), and *vijnana/vinnana* (consciousness). A non-sutric or commentarial candidate for the karmic carrier is *bhavanga*, which is defined as subliminal consciousness; and still another term is *samtana/santana*, which means a continuity of consciousness. In other words, no "consistent" technical term, nor phenomenon, is found anywhere in the early Buddhist canon to unquestionably account for the rebirth process.

What is most paradoxical in all of these terms is that they openly state that it is "consciousness" in some form that carries the karma and yet there are passages in the same canon that categorically state that consciousness (*vinnana*), or at least personal consciousness, does not pass on from life to life but disintegrates like the rest of the **psychophysical aggregates** (*skandha/khandha*).

The second reason for the complexity and controversy regarding rebirth in Buddhism is that in the early Buddhist canon there are numerous conflicting statements about an after-life in general. Below are some major examples of these conflicts taken from the Pali canon. The *suttas* say that the Buddha told his fellow monks that to ask whether you live or die in the past or do not live or die in the past or will or will not live or die in the future are unwise questions that interfere with realizing **nirvana/nibbana**. [Tripitaka, Suttapitaka (T, S) MLS I, 10–11; DN III, 130; AN II, 90; SN III, 88] Furthermore, the suttas say that a truly Enlightened One (Buddha) makes no lamentation over the past, nor yearns not after the future. [(T, S) SN I, 8] These *sutta* words, at the very least, would support a reluctance to indulge in the metaphysics of rebirth.

On the other hand, other *suttas* say that the Buddha taught how to meditate to ensure a good future birth and avoid a bad one. [(T, S) MLS III, 139] Elsewhere, the heavens and hells are defined as being the six senses. What is sensed as ugly is hell and as beautiful is heaven. [(T, S) SN IV, 81] This may or may not be related to another saying attributed to the Buddha, namely that a person's present physical beauty or ugliness depends on their past life disposition.

In still another *sutta* it is implied that a belief or non-belief in an after-life is optional. The Buddha is quoted as saying that what is important is to live the Brahma faring (celibate) life; that this is all that is necessary to realize *nibbana* (nirvana). The *sutta* reads, "If there be no world beyond, no fruit (***vipaka***) and ripening of deeds done, well or ill, yet in this very life I hold myself free from enmity and oppression, without sorrow and well, this is an *Aryan* (noble) discipline's bliss of Brahma (comfort)." [(T, S) AN I, 175] In other parts of the *suttas* rebirth is again affirmed by applying it to the four **Buddhist stages of liberation**. Lastly, the Buddha, himself, is said to have claimed to remember numerous past lives (***purvanivasanusmrti***). In fact, the wording in the *suttas* reads, "In that life, at that time I was (then a name follows)."

The various conflicting statements about rebirth attributed to the Buddha lead to the following questions. If he did not believe in a cyclical passing from one life to the next, why did he talk of rebirth? If he believed in something, whether called a soul (self) or not, yet still soul-like, why did he talk of no-soul/-self? If it is not a soul or self, why did he not say what it is? If something went on then why say it was not necessary to believe it? Why say that consciousness (*vijnana*) does not go on and then allow for the possibility that it does? Why did he say it was unwise to talk or even think about past or future lives, and yet say that there was an afterlife heaven and hell? Is it possible that only a Buddha can understand this mystery, which being so profound can not even be communicated to the unenlightened? If this last is the case then why, in another part of the canon, in the *Kalama Sutta*, are we advised not to believe something just because tradition or even the Buddha says it is true? Yet from the canonical view point the only proof or reason for believing in rebirth is that according to the canon the Buddha says that it is true. In fact, the only reason the canon can give to justify the doctrine of rebirth and post-mortem karma is to say that the Buddha experienced the validity of these through the supernatural powers (***abhijna***) he gained at the moment of his enlightenment.

Ultimately we can not be sure that the Buddha taught or did not teach the doctrine of rebirth. We can only be sure that the authors of the canon had various views on what he said or did not say on the subject. But for such various views to exist in the first place suggests that the Buddha did not teach his disciples a single very well defined view about rebirth, and/or that realizing the obvious conflict between doctrines of no-soul/-self and rebirth the compilers of the early canon had little choice but to vacillate on the subject of rebirth. In either case, if the earliest Buddhist movement emphasized enlightenment in this very life then there would be far less need to be concerned with rebirth since it is entirely future life oriented. If this is true then a limited interest in rebirth could have been remembered sufficiently enough by at least some of the Buddha's successors to be preserved in the earliest *suttas*. An argument can thus be made for the idea that the contradictions in the canon represent a later time when the extremely spartan nature of the Buddha's teachings needed to be greatly elaborated and metaphysicalized to become part of a popular religion. In other words, there are clearly enough inklings in the earliest canon to suggest that what the Buddha did say about rebirth was different from what later dogmatic Buddhism claimed he said.

It is important to note that any lack of consistency with regards to rebirth does not necessarily suggest a lack of concern with regards to karma. On the contrary, the concern for karma on the part of the Buddha and the earliest Buddhist community is reinforced by many canonical statements that uphold the absolute efficacy of karmic actions (*kiriya*) for spiritual training. Indeed, according to the *suttas*, those ascetics who had practiced under one or more teachers other than the Buddha and who then wished to join the Buddhist order were allowed to do so without a probationary period if they were believers in karma (*kiriyavada*).

This concern about karma, however, seems to have had less to do with an ontological view, which included post-mortem existence (rebirth), than it had to do with a moral view. In other words, the Buddha's interest in rebirth may have been no more than what was absolutely necessary to avoid being misunderstood as a materialist-annihilationist (an *ucchedavadin*) or as one who claimed that karmic producing behavior was not necessary for liberation (an *akiriyavadin*). If a disbelief in a post-mortem existence did not undermine a person's commitment to living a moral life then such disbelief may have been perfectly acceptable. If disbelief did undermine morality it was not acceptable. Indeed, this possibility has led some scholars to suggest that the Buddha may even have looked upon the concept of rebirth as an expedient means or **noble lie**.

Despite all the canonical inconsistencies on the subject of rebirth, from the earliest Buddhist beginnings in India, the belief in rebirth was accepted by lay Buddhists and most clerics without much questioning. The reason for this was that the rebirth doctrine was never a mere religious belief in India, but a social belief. This is to say that the entire sociopolitical structure (*caste system*) of India depended on it. Whatever else an average Indian might have questioned in his or her culture the conviction of the truth of rebirth was rarely one of these. Thus, any explanation that Buddhism would have given to account for rebirth would probably have been accepted by the masses. Furthermore, in spite of the official doctrine of rebirth without a real soul, all but a very few academically oriented Buddhists ignored the no-soul aspect and thought of rebirth in terms of a very real soul. Even the academic attempt to replace the soul with the concept of a rebirth consciousness has some of the aspects of trying to reinstate the soul indirectly or through a back door.

In modern times some Buddhists have suggested that western science may offer a solution to the problem of rebirth without a permanent soul in the form of the catalytic process. A catalyst is a substance or element which, while necessary to produce a chemical reaction, does not become a part of the final product. Thus the *gandharva* could, rather than being a substitute soul, be a karmic transferring catalytic agent that once the transference took place and the embryo was conceived, the *gandharva* itself then ceased to exist. Of course, this still leaves the problem of how to have such catalytic activity passing from one body (the dead) to another (the one being conceived) without some sort of physical contact. The obvious solution would be some psychic phenomena, a disembodied something which, with the exception of Tibetan Buddhists, most Buddhists prefer not to concern themselves with.

Regardless of the process by which rebirth is said to occur, it must always be remembered that a primary purpose for the belief in rebirth is to say that a person's existence is not just due to the sexual desire and action of that person's parents, but that each person is at least partly responsible for his or her own coming into being. What this means is that Buddhism, or for that matter **Hinduism** and **Jainism**, is opposed to any person thinking, "I did not ask to be born, I am an innocent victim of my parents' desires."

See also *Alayavijnana*; Annihilationism, Buddhist view; Arguments supportive of rebirth; Buddha; Buddhism, folk; Buddhist stages of liberation; Interim period; Karma and justice; Karma and rebirth; Karma in the ancient and modern west; Karma, origins of; Karma with minimal rebirth; *Milinda Panha*; Personalists; *Pratitya-samutpada*; Psychophysical aggregates; *Punar-janman*; Rebirth and cultural conditioning; Rebirth in Zen; Rebirth in the West; Rebirth, qualifications for; Reincarnation, origins of; *Skandha*.

Rebirth in the modern West. According to a 2000 Harris Poll 27 percent of the general population in the United States believes in reincarnation. Furthermore, among those in the population that are 20–30 years old this percentage rises to 40 percent, while among those over 65 years old it drops to only 14 percent. Similar percentages have been found in Europe.

A number of reasons have been suggested for this growing acceptance for rebirth. One major reason is that many Westerners have lost the belief in the concept of a future miraculous bodily resurrection. However, rather than abandon all hope for a life after death they have adopted the far less miraculous seeming belief in rebirth. Another major reason is that many people can not harmonize the idea of a just and loving God with the resurrection related idea of an eternal **hell**. A third reason is the still very strong idea of the spiritual superiority of the East.

See also **Arguments supportive of rebirth;** *Ex Oriente Lux*; **Rebirth, East and West; Resurrection, bodily.**

Rebirth in Zen Buddhism *see* **Zen Buddhism, rebirth in.**

Rebirth, instantaneous. This refers to any rebirth that occurs immediately after a death with absolutely no **interim period** between death and rebirth. Technically, **Theravada Buddhism**, in denying any interim period supports instantaneous rebirth. What complicates the Theravada position is that all rebirths are not necessarily corporeal. In fact, only two out of the six sentient states of being of the ***bhavachakra*** (Wheel of Becoming) are corporeal, namely the human and animal realms. The other four realms (the heaven (*devaloka*), ***asuras*** (anti-gods), ***hungry ghosts***, and denizens in **hell**) are for all practical purposes serve as a kind of non-corporeal interim period realm.

See also **Child as its own reborn father or mother; Corporeal versus non-corporeal afterlife; Druzes.**

Rebirth, intra-cultural versus inter-cultural *see* **Rebirth, proximity.**

Rebirth, lateral *see* also **Transmigration, lateral.**

Rebirth, minimal *see* **Karma with minimal rebirth.**

Rebirth, minority *see* **Rebirth, selective.**

Rebirth, moment of *see* **Embodiment, moment of.**

Rebirth, natural concept of. This is the concept of reincarnation without any particular moral principle involved such as karma. It must be noted that outside of the Indian cultural sphere of influence most concepts of reincarnation have been of this natural type.

See also **Karma and faith; Reincarnation, origins of.**

Rebirth, non-backsliding. This is the concept that while a higher animal soul might evolve into a human soul and attain human rebirth, once human it can never revert to an animal soul or be reborn in an animal body. This is accepted by some who otherwise oppose the concept of regressive transmigration. This can also be called single-direction rebirth.

In Buddhism it is taught that once a person sincerely takes and never renounces the three refuges (the Buddha, the Dharma, and the Sangha) and five Buddhist lay moral precepts he or she can never again fall into a less than human birth.

See also ***Bhavachakra***; **Rebirth, cross-species; Transmigration, lateral; Transmigration, regressive.**

Rebirth, obligatory. In certain cultures the deceased are obliged to reincarnate within the same clan or family to which they formerly belonged (consanguineous rebirth).

See also **Rebirth, consanguineous; Reincarnation, Expectational.**

Rebirth, partial. This is the idea that the soul is not a single entity, but a compound one. Thus only part of a soul may be reborn while the other part or parts exist in some other state.

See **Africa; American Indians; Chinese Religion and Reincarnation; Egypt; Soul fragmentation.**

Rebirth pessimism *see* **Nightmare of eastern philosophy; Rebirth and cyclical time.**

Rebirth, proof of (Western Buddhist). The growing Western interest in rebirth has lead to a very un-traditional attempt to "scientifically" prove rebirth. This has even encouraged many Eastern researchers to join in this effort. Finding such proof is difficult enough if one accepts the idea of a **soul**, but to try to find proof of, much less make logical sense of, a soulless rebirth, as Buddhism expects, is truly taking on a heroic challenge.

To begin with, the investigators have obliviously trapped themselves in at least three major and inter-related contradictions. The first of these comes from a number of attempts to explain so-called past life memories as proof of a continuity of identity from one life to another. But what these Buddhists, Western or Eastern, seem to over look is that if such a memory could be scientifically proven to be genuine this would be detrimental to the Buddhist doctrine of no-soul (self) or ***anatman***. An authenticated continuity of memory from a past life to a present one is in itself a sufficient definition of a soul. This would then give more support to the Hindu-like concept of a soul (***kosha-atman***) reincarnating from one body to another than it would to a Buddhist denial of such a reincarnating soul. Of course, the truth is that most Buddhists have always favored the concept of a soul despite the standard denial of it.

See also **Karma in the ancient and modern west; Rebirth, East and West; Rebirth in Buddhism; Rebirth, qualifications for; Resurrection or reincarnation.**

Rebirth, proximity. This occurs when the **soul** seeks rebirth within a relatively small geographic area. For example, in some American Indian cases it is expected that people will be reborn into some future generations of their own or closely related families (consanguineous rebirth). Among the Balla of Zimbabwe this recycling of ancestral souls is even more specific. Here the first born son is considered a rebirth of his deceased grandfather, while all later sons are reincarnations of deceased grand uncles. Daughters, in turn, are believed to be reincarnations of paternal great aunts (grandfather's sisters).

In the cases reported from south Asia and Lebanon by **Ian Stevenson** the presumed rebirth, while usually happening outside of the same family, most often happens in another local community that is rarely more than one hundred miles away, which is still within the same cultural boundaries. Also, the time between death and rebirth in these separate community rebirths ranged from only a few weeks to up to nine years. Thus, there is rarely ever any claim to have been some person who lived far away and long ago.

Rebirth, distant in place and in time, is more characteristic of Western claims. Although most Westerners usually claim former births as Westerners, many do not. The greater mobility of modern Western people could account for this willingness to at least accept geographically distant reincarnation while the greater awareness by educated Westerners of past cultures might make for a greater acceptance of rebirth relating to those historically distant cultures.

Some rebirth skeptics consider proximity or intra-cultural rebirth as part of the proof that rebirth is simply a cultural supporting fantasy. They say that this is because the place and time of rebirths tends to follow the expectation of a culture. While it can not be denied that part of this is true at the same time such proximity rebirth is very logical. Presumably, most souls would not be any more adventuresome than most living people are. They would naturally be drawn back to a location and to people that were familiar to them.

Whatever the proposed reasons for proximity rebirth they certainly can add to the problems for strong supporters of rebirth. Rebirth of a person too close to a presumed former home makes it much easier for the claimant to have consciously or subconsciously heard and seen clues regarding a recently deceased person. These then could be used by the claimant to create a past life scenario. For this reason there might be far less suspicion if a person from Lebanon was able to describe a past life as an Inuit hunter.

Considering the unlikelihood of children, especially of very young ones, having any opportunity to acquire any real information about foreign cultures, especially ones long past, it would give considerable support to the rebirth theory if a five-year-old Zulu claimed to have recently lived as a modern Japanese or even more astonishingly as a sixteenth-century Aztec.

It must be noted that proximity rebirth is more often than not found in societies that lack ethicalized or karmic rebirth.

See also **Africa; Ancestor worship; Fantasy versus past life regression; Incremental change of identity; Karma, racial; Proximity burial; Rebirth, consanguineous; Rebirth and unilinear descent.**

Rebirth, qualifications for *see* **Arguments supportive of rebirth; Children remembering past lives; Karma with minimal rebirth; Memory, Episodic; Memories, ancestral or genetic; Memories, reasons for loss of past life; Mental plane; Past life memory categories; Rebirth, criteria for proof of.**

Rebirth, restricted. From a human perspective any rebirth that is not assumed to eventually lead to a human one must be considered restricted. For example, a number of tribal people believe that upon death a human soul will be reborn into an animal body of some kind, but what happens to the soul after that is unspecified. This is not to be confused with selective reincarnation.

See also **American Indians; Aztecs; Dayaks; Finite or infinite number of rebirths; Rebirth, selective.**

Rebirth, selective. This is the belief that only a selective minority of souls undergo rebirth. One example of selective rebirth would be that only souls under certain conditions, such as experiencing a violent or otherwise pre-mature death or because of having committed certain extremely vile sins, are reborn while all other souls upon death go to heaven or hell. A second example would be that only an elite few souls are reborn while all others face annihilation.

Selective rebirth is sometimes called special rebirth. Under either name it is in contrast to general rebirth in which the overwhelming majority of souls are assumed to be reborn. The earlier **Kabbalah** literature, in particular, viewed rebirth as selective in the first sense, while some sects of **Gnosticism** viewed rebirth in the second sense. Selective rebirth is not to be confused with restricted rebirth.

See also **Andaman Islanders; Deaths, violent and premature; Finite or infinite number of rebirths; Rebirth, general; Rebirth, restricted.**

Rebirth, simultaneous. This is a belief found in Tibet and a few other places such as among the Inuit and Northwest Pacific Coastal American Indians. According to this belief it is possible for a soul to be reborn into two or more entities at the same time. Another version of this simultaneous rebirth does not require that any double rebirth be at the same time; for example, a single soul may be shared by one person living from 1940 – 2015 and a second person living from 1955 – 2030.

See also **Africa; Grant, Joan Marshall; Parallel lives; Plurality of existences; Rebirth, partial; Rebirth or rebecoming; Souls, multiple; Swarm of bees theory; Zhendao.**

Rebirth, two logical views of. There are two possible logical beliefs about rebirth. The first is that there is an immortal soul, or its equivalent, which goes from birth to birth until it attains salvation, which ends the rebirth process. The second is that the immortal soul is reborn eternally with no ending of rebirth. This view is found in many tribal societies where there is no concept of wishing to escape from rebirth since that would mean the end of the ancestors and eventually of their descendents.

Rebirth versus possession *see* **Rebirth.**

Rebirth versus resurrection *see* **Resurrection or reincarnation.**

Rebirths, number of *see* **Finite or infinite number of rebirths.**

Redivivus. This is the Latin word for living again; but it can cover concepts as diverse as revival, resurrection, and reincarnation.

Re-embodiment *see* **Incarnation versus reincarnation.**

Reincarnation. The earliest recorded use of this term in English to signify a renewal or rebirth of an individual life was in 1858. It is composed of re- (again) -in- (into) -carna- (flesh) -tion (noun suffix). In other words, it means re-infleshment and refers to the surviving soul or some other spiritually significant aspect of a deceased being assuming a (new) "un-souled body" and, hence, having another life. It is important to emphasize the idea of un-souled, because any soul that was said to enter a body that already had a soul of its own would be called **possession**.

Some modern authorities restricted the term reincarnation to inter-human (non-animal) rebirth and, therefore, do not consider it synonymous with **transmigration** or **metempsychosis** which are often reserved for cross species multiple embodiments. This is particularly true among Western reincarnationists who believe that the purpose of reincarnation is to help the soul evolve to a higher state of being. In this case, an animal rebirth would be regarded as devolution of the soul, not evolution.

In this encyclopedia the term reincarnation is mainly used in reference to the issue of exclusively human multiple embodiments.

See also **Animals and rebirth, non–Western view; Animals and rebirth, Western view; Animals, domesticated; Evolutionary transmigration of souls; Ontological leap or ontological discontinuity; Rebirth, cross-species; Rebirth; Rebirth, non-backsliding; Rebirth and the scientific theory of biological evolution.**

Reincarnation (Periodical). This is the title of a monthly periodical, edited by Weller Van Hook and C. Shuddemagen, which was published as the official organ for the Karma and Reincarnation Legion (Chicago) from 1914 to 1931. For a time Van Hook was the General Secretary of the American Section of the Theosophical Society. According to a statement by Annie Besant in the first issue of *Reincarnation* the purpose of the Legion, as founded by Van Hook, was to spread the doctrine of karma and reincarnation among the masses of the American people.

Reincarnation and divine grace *see* **Bhagavad Gita; Bhakti Yoga; Grace; Karma; Karma versus grace; Pure-Land or Blissful Land Buddhism.**

Reincarnation bibliographies. There are at least two significant, separately published, reincarnation bibliographies, both of which were published in 1996. The first is *Reincarnation: A Bibliography* by Joel Bjorling. It lists 1,612 items in ten categories: Eastern Religions and Reincarnation, Reincarnation in Comparative Religions and Philosophy; Reincarnation in Occult Traditions; Reincarnation in Christianity, Judaism, and Islam; Cases Suggesting Reincarnation; Past Life Therapy; Astrology and Reincarnation; Popular Works on Reincarnation; reincarnation in World Literature; and Reference Works. It includes an Author Index.

The second bibliography is *Reincarnation: A Selected Annotated Bibliography* by Lynn Kear. It lists 562 works by author; but unlike Bjorling's book, it annotates each entry. It also lists some 17 organizations in an appendix. Both are indispensable resources for anyone interested in the subject of reincarnation and karma.

While not a separately published bibliography, the book *Karma and Rebirth in Classical Indian Traditions*, edited by Wendy Doniger O'Flaherty (1980) has an excellent scholarly bibliography on rebirth and karma.

Reincarnation, ethnic *see* **Karma, racial.**

Reincarnation International Magazine. This periodical was published by Roy Stemman in London from 1994 to at least 1999 before its name was changed to *Life and Soul Magazine*. The current status of the periodical is not known.

Reincarnation, origins of. In the book *Birth of the Gods: The Origin of Primitive Beliefs* by Guy E. Swanson (1960), the author uses a sociological theory to explain the origin of reincarnation beliefs among pre-industrialized or folk societies. He does this by statistically correlating the belief in reincarnation among folk religions with a particular social structure. He notes that reincarnation has been statistically shown to correlate to such settlement patterns as stable physically or socially isolated neighborhoods, nomadic bands, and extended family compounds. In fact, even the Indian **caste system**, which on the surface may not seem to support this correlation, when carefully examined does appear to fit this pattern. This is to say that in traditional caste society there is little social, or even travel, mobility; each village is divided into caste-like or sub-caste like neighborhoods; marriage between these is forbidden; therefore, there is a need to intensify social bonding within tiny endogamous groups. This need can be met by the belief that one's ancestors are born into later generations *ad infinitum.*

Peter Fab, in his *Man's Rise to Civilization* (1969), using Swanson's theory comes to the same conclusion. However, a problem with Swanson's sociological theory, especially as stated by Fab, is that Swanson makes the rather peculiar statement that, "Reincarnation is considerably different from the mere belief in spirits that the Eskimo and the Shoshone have." This statement, as least as it applies to the Eskimo (Inuit), is in complete conflict with the studies found in *Amerindian Rebirth: Reincarnation Belief among North American Indians and Inuit* (1994), edited by Antonia Mills and Richard Slobodin. Also, the belief in reincarnation among a culture such as that of the early European Druids would also seem to weaken Swanson's theory.

Competing with this sociological theory about the origin of reincarnation is speculation that connects reincarnation to the need for a totemic life force to be recycled from one generation to another, as among **Australian Aborigines**. Still another theory, specific to South Asia, is that the reincarnation concept is related to rice cultivation. Rice is planted twice, first as a seed and then as a seedling that is replanted. Rice is also harvested more than once a year. This multiple life cycle may have made it a natural symbol for multiple lives.

Some East Indian scholars prefer to find an autonomous Indian origin for that sub-continent's belief system. These scholars note that in middle to late Vedic thought there appears the concept that there were two paths to heaven. One of these was the path of the gods (S: *deva-yana*) and the other was the path of the fathers (S: *pitr-yana*). The first was attained through religious austerities of the Brahmins and lead to a permanent dwelling in the heavenly world of Brahma. The second was attained through ordinary sacrificial means, but lead to a temporary lunar existence. Eventually, these *pitr-yana* would require a re-death (S: *punarmrtyu*) or return (S: *punaravrtti*) through the rain which would be absorbed into plant life that would become food for animals and men. Entering into semen the souls would be reconceived in a womb. Even without the idea of two separate paths to heaven, it has been thought that the phases of the **moon**, in which it seems to be continuously dying only to be continuously reborn, might have suggested to the pre-scientific mind in India, and possibly outside it, the idea of reincarnation.

See also **Ancestor worship; Jainism; Karma, origins of;** *Pritiloka;* **Rebirth and unilinear descent; Rebirth, Buddhist; Rebirth in the West; Reincarnation, origins of;** *Upanishads;* **Vedic Religion.**

Reincarnation Report. This was a monthly magazine published for Reincarnation, Inc. by Valley of the Sun Publishing Company, Malibu, California, from 1982 until 1987.

See also **Sutphen, Richard (Dick).**

Renaissance. The European Renaissance (14th to 17th century) was a time in which classical Greek and, to a lesser degree, classical Roman culture was once again glorified by both the secular and religious authorities. Some reincarnationists believe that, in line with **national character reappearances**, this was due to a large number of souls from the classical period being reborn into that later era.

See also **Aristotle; Bruno, Giordano; Lost Continent(s); Platonism; Theosophy.**

Re-occurring patterns of behavior. Some reincarnationist believe that certain behavior patterns to which people are more or less addicted and which have arisen from no seemingly rational cause in the present life can be explained as behavior patterns developed in a past life and which continue to exist as unfinished business.

See also **Arguments supportive of rebirth; Dreams; Repetition compulsion.**

Repeater children (Ogbanje). This refers among the Igbo of Nigeria to two or more successive infant deaths occurring in the same family. It is believed that for some unknown reason the same soul is purposely seeking rebirth in that family, only to decide to die. To end this unpleasant situation the body of the last deceased child is mutilated as a message to the soul that it either stop trying to reincarnate into that particular family or to successfully be reborn into and grow to adulthood in that family.

See also **Africa.**

Repentance *see* **Karma as absolute or relative; Restitution negates retribution.**

Repetition compulsion. This refers to a subconscious drive to repeat the same life patterns over several life times.

See also **Karmic boomerang effect; Patton, George S; Re-occurring patterns of behavior.**

Republic (*Politeia*) *see* **Plato.**

Researchers of rebirth. Among major researchers of rebirth are **Banerjee, H. N.; Bowman, Carol; Chari, Dr. C.T.K.; Ivanova, Barbara; Kubler-Ross, Elizabeth; Rhine, Joseph Banks; Stevenson, Ian;** and **Wambach, Helen.**

Rescue circles. These are said to be mature souls who meet with those who have died suddenly and who are very confused about their new state.

See also **Deaths, violent and premature;** *Psychopomps*.

Residue karma *see* ***Jivanmukti***; **Karma,** *Prarabdha*.

Restitution negates retribution. In general most teachings that include a belief in karma acknowledge that restitution can counter the bad karma one might have otherwise earned from a certain unskillful action. From a Buddhist perspective such restitution should be a part of genuine repentance for the negation to be as complete as possible.

See also **Karma as absolute or relative.**

Resurrection and the aborted fetus. One long standing issue for those who defend or criticizes the Christian theory of the resurrection is whether or not an aborted fetus would partake of the final resurrection. Of course, this issue is bond up with at what stage in the conception and gestation period God is thought to infuse a soul into the fetus. If such infusion is early on and the mother spontaneously aborts what happens to the soul of that fetus? If it resurrected, would it do so in the partially developed form in which it died or would God miraculously bring it to its full normal development?

Reincarnationists see the aborted fetus issue as one of the weaknesses of the resurrection concept, and point out that the concept of reincarnation can deal with the issue in a less questioning fashion.

See also **Rebirth and abortion.**

Resurrection, bodily. This is the belief that in a messianic future God will, in some highly disputed manner, reunite the souls of all the deceased with either new bodies or their former bodies. Such bodily resurrection is held as orthodox in Judaism, Christianity, and Islam; however, many reincarnationists find major logical problems with the resurrection concept. While each of the three traditions has a different understanding of resurrection, from a reincarnationist perspective, these differences are slight enough that the Christian version should suffice for listing the problems reincarnationists find in it.

Since the New Testament is ambiguous on the exact manner in which the souls of the deceased will attain resurrectional re-embodiment the exact manner has been a widely discussed and debated subject from early Christian times to the present. **Paul of Tarsus** implies at 1st **Corinthians** 15:42–45 that the resurrected body is a new imperishable spiritual one, not an old flesh and blood physically perishable one. At 2nd Corinthians 5:3–4 Paul refers to the heavenly (new) body put over the old (the one in which we groan) rather than finding ourselves first stripped naked of the old one and then put in the new body. On the other hand, in the Latin form of the Athanasian Creed (5–6th century CE) it is stated that all men shall rise again with "their" bodies (*resurgere habent cum corporibus suis*). This was reaffirmed more specifically, as a rising in "their very own present bodies" (*omnes cum suis propriis resurgent corpoibus, quae nunc gestant*) by the Roman Catholic Lateran Council (1215) and **Church Council of Lyon** (1274), both of which were deliberately convened to counter the metempsychosis belief of the heretical **Cathars**.

The "very own present bodies" view, in contrast to Paul's view, was regarded as being supported by the New Testament claim that the tomb, in which the corpse of the crucified Jesus had been laid, was empty. This meant that the resurrected Christ must have had the same body as the one that died. Furthermore, in **Luke** 21:18, it is stated, "But not a hair of your head shall be lost." This Lucian statement obviously did not take into consideration that all the molecules in all the bodies that have died and been buried or cremated eventually get recycled innumerable times into other bodies, be these plants, animals, or other human bodies; therefore, it would be impossible to resurrect all human bodies with their original molecules. That the author of the gospel of Luke did not take into account this recycling fact is certainly due to the assumption of the author that the messianic era, and hence the general resurrection, was only a short time away. By the Middle Ages such naiveté could no longer be accepted. By that time, holding on to the idea that the resurrected body must be the exactly same one that died led to the following scholastically interesting questions. "If one person kills another person and eats the flesh of that person, part of the body of the eaten person will be part of the body of the eater. When the resurrection comes, how can all of the flesh of both persons be equally resurrected in their same flesh?" "Also, if not a hair is lost, does all the hair lost in a life time, as well as finger nail clippings, decayed teeth, etc. once more become part of the resurrected body?"

Despite such questions as these the Church continued to hold to the identical body belief. One of the main reasons for this was popular piety which was based around the veneration of the bodily relics of saints. It was thought that the soul of the saint in heaven would pay no attention to the venerator of its bodily relic if that relic was not going to be part of the saint's future body. Support for this veneration of saints, in fact, must have been a major reason for the church's rejection of ***psychopannychism***, for if the saints were asleep in their graves they could hardly be of assistance to anyone. However, this also led to a set of questions. If *psychopannychism* is rejected and souls, both saintly and more ordinary, go directly to heaven or **hell** after death why would there even be a need for a future bodily resurrection? Do those previously embodied in heaven and hell exist in these realms in a still incomplete state which only a bodily resurrection can complete?

In accordance with modern science, for bodily resurrection to occur God would have to keep a record of every person's genetic code as well as a record of all of their memories, which brings up a further question. Would God first repair any genetic defects with which a person had been born, and/or would He mercifully eliminate all traumatic memories with which people suffered before their deaths? Christian reincarnationists point out that if everyone, except Jesus, passes through many lives before the final resurrection then only the body everyone earned karmicaly at that finality would be of any concern.

See also **Arguments supportive of rebirth; Body-brain (mind) dependency; Body-soul dualism; Christian view of the afterlife; Christianity and reincarnation; Christianity, esoteric; Creationism, soul; Essenes; Egypt; Gnosticism; Kabbalah; Millennialism; New Testament and reincarnation; Old Testament and the afterlife; Purgatory; Rebirth in the West; Resurrection, bodily; Resurrection of Jesus; Rebirth and cyclical time; Sacred Bone; Zoroastrianism.**

Resurrection cultural and technological age discrepancy issue. This refers to the presumed situation that re-embodied souls of very different cultural and technological periods would all be found living side by side at a future resurrection. Reincarnationists noting this have asked the following questions. Could a 1st century re-embodied soul be expected to understand the technologically advanced 21st century re-embodied soul, or could the 21st century re-embodied soul understand the distant future re-embodied soul? Even if there are no televisions and spaceships in the kingdom of heaven on earth, will not the 1st century re-embodied soul have to learn about these technologies if they are to be equal, and not inferior, to the most technologically sophisticated re-embodied souls? It must be remembered that the early Christian movement did not know that there were still stone age tribes existing in the world and so this problem would not have occurred to them; moreover, those Christians originally expected the resurrection of the dead and subsequent arrival of the kingdom of God to occur within no more than one or two generations from the death of **Jesus**.

Since bodily resurrection implies having vocal cords and a tongue it might be assumed that the once-again living would be using those for communicating with one another. So besides technological differences, might it logically be thought that there would be enormous language problems, unless in the kingdom of heaven all languages would be miraculously "un-babel-ed"? Also, for the linguistically curious, which language would that everyone speak? Would it be Old Testament Hebrew, the Aramaic spoken by Jesus, the Greek of the New Testament, or some specifically revealed language of angels? Perhaps, although having physical vocal abilities, the once again living would also be able to communicate telepathically.

As proponents of reincarnation point out, having multiple lives avoids this cultural and technological age discrepancy issues because all souls are periodically recycled into more modern cultural and technological conditions and the language issue in this multicultural world does not require a single intercultural language.

See also **Arguments supportive of rebirth; Resurrection, bodily; Resurrection individual age discrepancy issue.**

Resurrection individual age discrepancy issue. Another question asked by reincarnationists about resurrection is based on this discrepancy. According to Christianity all souls that have either been baptized and or have accepted Christ over the past two thousand years, and will accept Christ in the future will share in the kingdom of heaven on earth. This ought to mean that many of the residents in the kingdom will be the souls of new born babies and young children who have prematurely died. If they are give new immortal bodies as Christianity teaches will they have to remain their death age for eternity? Immortality implies not only never dying, but never growing or aging, since growing and aging is the process of cellular birth and death. Obviously, reincarnation avoids this issue by giving every soul the opportunity to completely mature prior to any freedom from the reincarnational round.

See also **Age factor and rebirth; Arguments supportive of rebirth; Resurrection cultural and technological age discrepancy issue.**

Resurrection of Jesus. Most of the Christian opposition to the doctrine of rebirth has been based on its core belief in the doctrine of the resurrection of the dead. This focus on resurrection is, in turn, based on the conviction that **Jesus** arose from the grave after his death on the cross. This is most clearly stated in 1st **Corinthians** 15:14–15, "If there was no resurrection, the Christ was not raised; and if Christ was not raised, then our gospel is null and void, and so is your faith; and we turn out to be lying witnesses for God." There is, however, a logical problem with basing a general belief in resurrection upon that of Jesus. In the case of Jesus we are not talking about someone who resurrected after being long dead as with the general resurrection theory. The gospels say that Jesus was in the tomb for no more than a day and a half or 36 to 40 hours. This number comes from the gospel statement that the dead Jesus had to be removed from the cross and at least temporarily entombed before the beginning of the Sabbath at sundown on Friday and that the tomb was supposedly empty by early Sunday morning.

It is because of this time factor that many Christian reincarnationists believe that the issue of the resurrection of Jesus should to be dealt with separately from that of any general resurrection concept. On the other hand, from an orthodox Christian point of view any separation of the specific and general resurrections would weaken the Christian whole belief in both resurrections.

See also **Ahmadiyya; Arguments supportive of rebirth; Christianity and reincarnation; Daniel, Book of; Irenaeus; Islam; Judgment of the Dead; Luke, Gospel of; Mark, Gospel of; Matthew, Gospel of; Millennialism; Moon; Old Testament and the afterlife;** *Psychopannychism***; Rebirth, analogies from nature; Resurrection, bodily; Resurrection versus Resuscitation.**

Resurrection of Jesus as circular thinking. One of the responses to Christian challenges to reincarnation is for reincarnationists, at least non–Christian ones, to point out the circular nature of resurrectional thinking. It goes as follows. (Supporter) "The resurrection of Jesus is true because the New Testament says it is." (Questioner) "But why believe the New Testament?" (Supporter) "It should be believed because it was written (dictated) by God." (Questioner) "How do you know it was written by God?" (Supporter) "We know it because the church says so." (Questioner) "How do you know the church is right?" (Supporter) "We know it is right because the church is the body of Christ." (Questioner) "How do you know the church is the body of Christ?" (Supporter) "We know it because the New Testament says so."

In logic this is obviously the process of "both circular reasoning and begging the question"; and this is why standard Christianity declares that the resurrection of Jesus and future resurrection of all Christians must be accepted on the basis of blind faith.

See also **Logic and pseudo-logic and rebirth.**

Resurrection of the dead *see* **Resurrection, bodily.**

Resurrection or reincarnation. Both these concepts have conceptual advantages and disadvantages. An advantage to reincarnation is that it does not depend on a belief in an indeterminate future miraculous and apocalyptic event. Instead, it is put forth as a simple universal and natural law of cause and effect. The disadvantage to reincarnation is that as such a natural law it ought to be clearly discernable or provable, which currently it is not.

The advantage to resurrection is that, being a future miraculous event, it can never be the subject of scientific inquiry and possible disproof, unlike reincarnation. The disadvantage to resurrection is that it must be believed in on the basis of blind faith and when some of the logical problems concerning it are examined faith must include a complete suspension of critical thinking.

While the two post-mortem concepts of resurrection or reincarnation may seem in opposition to one another, some Christian supporters of rebirth believe that it is possible to harmonize them. In this harmonized version people will remain in the cycle of rebirth only until a future point when some divine intervention will bring the cycle to an end through a general resurrection.

See also **Arguments supportive of rebirth; Christianity and reincarnation; Christian view of the afterlife; Creationism, soul; Infusionism; Judgment of the Dead; Karma as natural law; Millennialism; New Testament and reincarnation; Old Testament and the Afterlife; Rebirth and religious tolerance; Resurrection, bodily; Resurrection cultural and technological age discrepancy issue; Resurrection individual age discrepancy issue; Sikhism.**

Retroactive inhibition *see* **Children remembering past lives.**

Retrocognition. This is a supposed psychic ability that is said to allow one to perceive past events as though the perceiver was a present observer. While there have been a number of reports of such retrocognition that clearly have nothing to do with experiencing a past life, some reincarnation critics believe that some past life recalls may actually be retrocognition experiences. These critics argue that cognition of the past does not automatically imply that the experiencer lived that life in the past.

Committed reincarnationists argued that retrocognition alone is an inadequate explanation for past life memories in that such retrocognition can often focus both on present and past lives, some of which may overlap in time; but reincarnation memories focus in on only the past, and if on more than one life, they are generally non-over-lapping. Retrocognition shares with the *akashic* record theory the problem of frozen or unedited memories.

See also **Chronoportation; Katsugoro case; Possession; Psychometry; Rebirth, alternative** explanations to; Telepathy; Time and the simultaneous past, present, and future.

Retrofitting. Retrofitting occurs when either spontaneously, or through hypnosis, a person makes a highly generalized statement about a presumed past life element that can be easily manipulated to fit later more specifically acquired information. For example, a person might state that in his most recent past life he died near water. If it is later found that a previously living individual that is thought to have reincarnated into that presently living person died even remotely near a stream, lake, ocean, swimming pool, or even water tower, that more specific data can be fitted to match the original over generalized statement. This seems to give legitimacy to the original statement that it may not deserve.

Return and serve argument for reincarnation. According to this argument reincarnation is just a natural extension of the desire for people to have an opportunity to return and serve one's country, one's religious community, or all humanity. This argument was especially used by the Japanese government in World War II. The Japanese soldiers were encouraged to believe that dying in the war service of the emperor would guarantee them the right to be reborn seven more times to serve future emperors. This argument was particularly directed at those *kamikaze* soldiers that were making suicide attacks against the enemy. This was epitomized by the white headband (*hachimaki*) they wore which had the words "*Shichisho Hokoku* (*Serve the Nation for Seven Lives*)" written on it. The most modern representation of this same dedication was seen in the life of the prize winning Japanese author Yukio Mishima. Not only did many of his stories include reincarnationist themes, but at the time of his nationalism motivated suicide he wore the *Shichisho Hokoku hachimaki*. The reason for the choice of seven lives may be due to the fact that there are seven gods of luck in the **Shinto** pantheon or that because, in accordance with the **Buddhist stages of liberation**, anyone who attained to the first or stream enterer (S: *shrotapanna*) stage of enlightenment was guaranteed that full liberation would be attain within a maximum of seven lifetimes. Since the Japanese Buddhist clerical hierarchy had not only indorsed the war effort, but had declared it a sacred duty of the soldiers to defeat the enemy, from the point of view of the common soldier that soldier was on the first sage of liberation.

It might be thought that the obvious militaristic nature of this argument should disqualify it as a reincarnation argument; however, this would be an inappropriately hasty reaction. This return and serve argument is, in fact, a simple modification of the standard Mahayana Buddhist **bodhisattva** vow to sacrifice **nirvana** and loyally return to **samsara** *bodhisattva*-like in the service of the suffering Japanese nation.

Before judging the Japanese as having perverted high spiritual values, it should also be noted that according to the Hindu **Bhagavad Gita**, a warrior has a spiritual right to kill, as long as he does so impersonally as part of his duty. In fact, the *Gita* teaches that if a warrior is absolutely faithful in following his duty it will free him from further reincarnation. This is the basis of the karma yoga of the Indian warrior in the **caste system**.

Finally, we need to remember that this "die for duty" is not confined to religions that believe in reincarnation, they are the exact equivalent of the Christianity and Islam "die for duty" Crusades and *Jihads*.

See also **Arguments supportive of rebirth; Rebirth and suicide; Karma yoga**.

Revelation of John (also, Apocalypse of John). Not only in order of books is this the last book in the New Testament, but it was the last book of that collection to be accepted as canonical. Its late acceptance was largely due to its profound and even nearly incomprehensible strangeness, visions, allegories, and symbols.

To say the least, with a text as open to interpretation as is this one, is it is to be expected that reincarnation might be read into it. In fact, there are two main passages in this book that reincarnationists favor. The first is Revelation 3:12 which reads, "He who is victorious — I will make a pillar in the temple of my God, and he shall never leave it." Some translations replace "leave it" with "go no more out of it" and use of this replacement wording has suggested to some reincarnationists that it means that only when a person is completely victorious over sin, which will take more than one life-time, will the soul no longer go out of the body into another body but will be allotted an eternal place in paradise.

The second favorite reincarnationist passage in the book is Revelation 20:12–15 which reads, "I could see the dead, great and small, standing before the throne; and books were opened. Then another book was opened, the roll of the living. From what were written in these books the dead were judged upon the record of their deeds. The sea gave up its dead, and Death and Hades gave up the dead in their keeping; they were judged, each man on the record of his deeds. Then Death and Hades were flung into the lake of fire. This lake of fire is the second death and into it were flung any whose names were not to be found in the roll of the living." It takes some imagination to read reincarnation into these passages, but this has been done by focusing on the concept of books of names and as representing multiple lives.

See also *Akashic (Akashik)* Record; Crowley, Edward Aleister; Genesis; Heaven's Gate; Karma in the Bible?; Kingsford, Anna Bonus; Millennialism; Predestination; *Redivivus*.

Reverie recall. This is a method used to recall a past life. Here the subject does not enter a trance or hypnotic state, but is encouraged by the monitor to first relax and then to describe any scene that comes into the subject's conscious mind. At first a great deal of both relevant and irrelevant information will present itself which must be sorted out by the monitor. This is done by cross-checking which information more consistently keeps arising and by evaluating what information seems directly related to the subject's problem and seems to offer a solution. While this is a relatively simple method, it is also a rather long drawn out one.

See also Artificial (past life) recall; *Déjà vu*; Hypnotic age regression; Past life recall; Netherton Method; Spontaneous recall.

Reynaud, Jean *see* **Spiritism**.

Rhine, Joseph Banks (1895–1980). Rhine was the former head of the Institute for **Parapsychology** at Duke University in Durham, North Carolina. According to Rhine **hypnotic age regression** cannot prove reincarnation until it can be proven that there is a psychic factor capable of existing separate from the body, even if only for a very short time.

Richardson, Alan (1951–). Richardson is author of *Dancers to the Gods* (1985). This book includes transcripts of reincarnational memoirs of Charles R. F. Seymour (1880–1943) and Christine Hartley (1897–1985), who were two members of the Fraternity of the Inner Light of **Dion Fortune**.

Richter, Johann Paul Friedrich, also called Jean Paul (1763–1825). This German novelist and humorist was very favorable to the idea of reincarnation, although he rejected regressive transmigration and was critical of some of the Kabbalic ideas connected to the concept.

See also **Transmigration, regressive**.

Right-hand path and left-hand path. Among some Pythagorean groups the right-hand path was the one of remembrance of former lives due to not partaking of the Drink of Forgetfulness. This then became the path of liberation from metempsychosis or the road to paradise (Elysium Fields). The second, or sinister, path was that of forgetfulness due to partaking of the drink. Naturally, this meant that the soul would once again have to enter into embodiment.

See also **Drink or fruit of forgetfulness**; **Greek afterlife, the ancient**; **Orphism**; **Plato**; **Pythagoras**; **Tantrism**.

Ring pass not. This is said to be a circle within which all are confined (trapped) who still are deluded by a sense of separateness from the whole. In other words, it means a barrier to release from reincarnation.

Ringu jukai or ***Rinju shukke***. Both of these terms translate as "deathbed tonsure" and refer to a former Japanese Buddhist practice of having one's head shaved and taking monastic vows on one's deathbed to gain the merit and better rebirth due to dying as a monk or nun.

Roberts, Jane *see* **Seth**.

Romans. As in his earlier **Galatians**, the apostle **Paul of Tarsus**, in this New Testament letter, repeats the theme that humanity is so deeply contaminated by and trapped in sin that not even a scrupulous keeping of the moral Law (*Torah*) of the Old Testament or doing good works "in the hope of salvation" can save one. Because of this inability of mankind to save himself God has sent Jesus, His son, to pay the necessary price for mankind's salvation by His sacrifice on the accursed cross and His subsequent resurrection. Having paid the price for mankind's sins (ransomed him from sin) the believer who identified with and was baptized in Jesus' death was himself dead to sin and so (re-)born into eternal life in the kingdom of God, which Paul expected to arrive very soon. Also in Romans, as in 1st **Corinthians**, Jesus is again called the second **Adam**, based on the idea that as Adam brought sin and death into the world, the second Adam was sent into the world to overcome sin and death.

Any attempt to read the idea of reincarnation into this letter requires a great deal of creative thinking. Nonetheless, attempts at this have still been made as with Romans 9:10–13 and Romans 14:8–9. The first of these passages describe how in **Genesis** God favored Jacob over his brother Esau even before they were born. The concept of "before they were born" is interpreted by some reincarnationists to mean that the **soul's existence prior to embodiment**, and from this that the two brothers had past lives. When this passage is read in the context of the thought of Paul it becomes clear that it is referring to Paul's belief that God as the creator does not need to explain his preferences and that **predestination** is perfectly within keeping of God's plan for this world. Romans 14:8–9 reads, "If we live, we live for the Lord, and if we die, we die for the Lord. Whether therefore we live or die, we belong to the Lord. This is why Christ died and came to life again, to establish his lordship over the dead and the living." Some reincarnationists have claimed that "Lord of the dead" refers to the **interim period** and "Lord of the living" refers to the embodied life.

See also **Angels and reincarnation; Annihilationism;** *Apocatastasis*; **Christianity and reincarnation; Christian atonement theories; Ephesians; "every knee should bend ... every tongue confess"; Gnosticism; John, Gospel of; Karma in the Bible?; New Testament and reincarnation; Peter, 1st and 2nd; Predestination.**

Romans, Ancient. The Romans essentially borrowed their view of the afterlife, including that of **metempsychosis**, from the Greeks. While most Roman citizens did not pay much attention to the belief, a number of emperors apparently found it appealing. For example, the emperor Commodus (161–192 CE) imagined himself to be either a "reborn" or an "incarnation" of Hercules. With this in mind he would dress as such and with club or bow and arrows enter the circus arena to slay animals. Also, at least two emperors, Caracalla (188–217 CE) and Flavius Claudius Julian (reign 361–363 CE), believed themselves to be Alexander the Great reborn.

See also *Anamnesis*; **Dweller on the Threshold; Egypt; Ennius, Quintus; Greek afterlife, the ancient; Julian, Flavius Claudius; Incarnation versus reincarnation;** *Lethe*; **Lucretius; Mithraism; Pluto, The God; Porphyry Malchus; Pre-existiani; Priesthood, lack of an organized;** *Redivivus*; **Virgil.**

Rosemary case. In 1931 a British spiritualist medium named Rosemary, the pseudonym for Ivy Carter Beaumont, began to speak what was thought to be authentic ancient Egyptian. Rosemary, through a control (disincarnated spirit) named Nona, supposedly learned that she had formerly lived as an Egyptian temple dancer during the reign of the 18th dynasty pharaoh Amenhotep III (1406–1370). This case was published under the title *Ancient Egypt Speaks: A Miracle of Tongues*, (London: Rider & Co., 1937), by A.J.H. Hulme and F. H. Wood. The case began to lose credibility when Hulme, who claimed to be a qualified Egyptologist, was found to have no such qualifications. Moreover, the so called transcribed ancient Egyptian was found to be a mixture of middle and late Egyptian which are about as different as Latin is from Italian. Further inconsistencies such as the reported presence of camels in Egypt centuries before their introduction further discredited the case.

See also **Current knowledge discrepancy; Language inconsistency; Xenoglossy.**

Rosicrucians. This is the name for several groups that have claimed to teach an esoteric religious philosophy. The name literally means rose cross or rosy cross. The earliest known mention of this name is from a German source of the early 17th century. Although Rosicrucianism claimed to be a revival of Near Eastern (Arabian, Syrian, Egyptian, or Moroccan) gnosis (occult knowledge) it seems to have been more closely related to the **Kabbalah** and European Renaissance alchemy. This version of Rosicrucianism actually had a not too disguised anti–Catholic and pro–Lutheran Protestant agenda and was very short-lived. Despite some of its Kabbalic elements, however, it did not include any belief in reincarnation.

There was a brief, but not too successful, revival of Rosicrucianism and pseudo-Rosicrucianism in the 18th century which early 20th century Rosicrucianism has used to try to bridge the gap between itself and the original movement.

Today, there are a number of competing Rosicrucian groups in the United States that claim an unbroken descent, not only from the 17th century, but from much farther back in time. Only some of these, however, include reincarnation and karma in their teachings and of these four are noteworthy. The oldest is the Fraternitas Rosae Crucis, which was founded in 1858 by an African-American, Paschal Beverly Randolph (d. 1875). The "inner teachings" of the FRC included a system of occult sexuality called Eulistic, a word derived from the Eleusian mysteries. Randolph's teachings had a major influence on the sex magic of the **Ordo Templi Orientes** of **Aleister Crowley**. Unfortunately, in contrast to Randolph's teaching Crowley tried to channel those teachings into black magic. Acting as an outer order of the FRC is the Church of Illumination which is open to the public unlike the inner order with its Aeth Priesthood. The FRC headquarters is in Quakertown, Pennsylvania.

The second is the Ancient and Mystical Order Rosae Crucis (AMORC), founded in 1904 by Harvey Spencer Lewis (1883–1939) under the name of the Rosicrucian Research Society or the New York Institute for Psychic Research. This group seems to have been derived from the German occult Order of the Temple of the Orient (Ordo Templi Orientis). The AMORC took its present name in 1915 or 1916. Like a number of other modern Rosicrucians groups the AMORC have continued to believe that their teachings have a Near Eastern link, only they trace this link all the way back to ancient Egypt. For example, the AMORC claims to have been originally founded in 1489 BCE by order of the Egyptian Pharaoh Thutmose III. From him the order was passed on through other members of what became known as the **Great White Brotherhood**. Among the later members of this brotherhood were the Pharaoh Akhenaton, King Solomon, **Pythagoras, Plato, Plotinus, Ammonius Saccas, Jesus**, and the followers of Hermes Trismegistus. The AMORC headquarters has been located in San Jose, California since 1927.

The third Rosicrucian group is the Societas Rosicruciana in America which was founded in 1907 by Sylvester C. Gould and George Winslow Plummer. The S.R.I.A. was created to offer non–Masons access to a Masonic Rosicrucian order. Its teaching include a belief in a single infinite intelligence and the need for the spiritual evolution of each soul through reincarnation.

The fourth major contemporary Rosicrucian group to include reincarnation in its teachings is the Rosicrucian Fellowship founded in 1909 by Max Heindel, also known as Max Grashof (1865–1919). This group grew out of the **Theosophy** of **Helena Blavatsky** and the anthroposophy of **Rudolf Steiner**. According to Heindel, the Fellowship was founded under the guidance of highly spiritual beings, which along with their 17th century master Christian Rosenkreuz (German, Christian Rose-Cross), were hierophants of the lesser mysteries and were called the Elder Brothers of the Rosicrucian Order. The Fellowship regards itself as a form of esoteric Christianity. Since 1910 its headquarters have been in Oceanside, California.

See also *Ankh*; **Ascended masters; Cayce, Edgar; Christianity, esoteric; Esotericism versus Occult; Egypt; Hermetic Order of the Golden Dawn; Hermetic philosophy; Lost continents and reincarnation;** *Open Court*; **Saint Germain; Mount Shasta.**

Rosicrucian's cycle *see* **Interim period.**

Roy, Raja Ram Mohan (1772–1833). This Hindu reformer and founder of the Brahma Sabha in 1828, later renamed the Brahmo Samaj, advocated a pure Unitarianism, without images, priests (Brahmans), or sacrifices. Roy also rejected the **caste system** and the belief in reincarnation that sustained the caste system.

Ruah or *Ruach* (Hebrew: Spirit) *see* **Kabbalah;** *Nafs* **and** *Ruh*; **Old Testament and the soul; Original sin, Christianity, and reincarnation; Spirit.**

Ruh (Arabic: Spirit) See *Nafs* **and** *Ruh*.

Russia, reincarnation in. While various individuals in pre-soviet Russian may have believed in reincarnation, with the exception of **Helena Blavatsky**, none of them seemed to have made any great attempt at developing any kind of successful organization to further the belief. For the most part, a belief in rebirth was mainly associated with the non–Christian and non–Islamic native peoples of the country. Of these the most well known have been the various Altaic Buddhists the majority of which belong to the Gelupa school of **Vajrayana Buddhism**. This form of Buddhism is practiced by the Mongol-speaking Buryats of South-central Siberia, east of Lake Baikal; by the Turkic-speaking Tuvinians of Siberia adjacent to Northwest Mongolia; and by the Mongol-speaking Kalmyks (Kalmucks) of the area on European Russia on the west side of the lower course of the Volga River, along the northwest shore of the Caspian Sea.

See also **Artificial rebirth; Dalai Lama; Gurdjieff, Georgi Ivanovitch; Heschel of Opatov, Abraham Joshua. Notovitch, Nicholas.**

Ryerson, Kevin (1953–). This channeler has been the medium through which a number of former embodied souls are said to have made contact with the present. Among these are a former oriental story-teller named Japu, who has a particular interest in reincarnation; John, a member of the **Essenes**; Tom McPherson, from Elizabethan Ireland; Obadiah, and a Haitian.

According to Walter Semkiw, in his *Return of the Revolutionaries* (2003) and *Born Again: Reincarnation Cases Involving International Celebrities ...* (2006), Ryerson's most currently main entity is Ahtun Re. Ahtun Re is said to be of Egyptian or Nubian origin, who has evolved through a series of human lives, the last of which was as a high priest of the Pharaoh Akhenaton (1379–1362 BCE). Ahtun Re identifies the past lives of various well known modern individuals for Semkiw.

See also **Channeling; Egypt; Equinox; Facial architectural consistency; Franklin, Benjamin (2); Hilarion; Kevin; Lazaris; Mafu; Michael (2); Ra; Ramtha; Satya; Seth; Torah (2).**

Saint Germain (1691/6?–1785?). This is the mysterious alchemist and occultist who, among other pseudonyms, called himself Le Comte de Saint Germain. Thought by some of his contemporaries to be either a Freemason or Rosicrucian he was probably neither. Saint Germain in his later life claimed that he was Prince Rakoczy, the son and heir of the last independent ruling prince of Transylvania. Also claiming to have discovered the elixir of life (immortality), Saint Germain ingratiated himself in various European courts, but never one from which he did not eventually have to flee. Saint Germain died in Schleswig some time between 1780 and 1785, but under what circumstances it is not known. Although condemned by many in his time as a charlatan, he has become one of the **ascended masters** or **dhyani chohans** in **Theosophy** and some of its offshoots.

Guy Warren Ballard, founder of the **I Am Movement**, claimed that Saint Germain had previous lives as the prophet Samuel and Francis Bacon. The modern writer Chelsea Quinn Yarbro transformed Saint-Germain into a heroic **vampire**, first in the novel *Hotel Transylvania,* (New York: St. Martin Press, 1978), and then in a series of following novels. This is the same Yarbro who has documented the teachings of the channeled entity **Michael**.

See also **Church Universal and Triumphant; Dweller on the Threshold; Michael (2); Rosicrucians; Mount Shasta**.

Saintly versus diabolical persons argument. This argument in favor of an afterlife is that if, instead of an after-life, there is only extinction then one minute after the deaths of people like Gandhi and Albert Schweitzer they will have the identical moral status as people like **Adolf Hitler** and Joseph Stalin. There will be nothing to tell us which of these to emulate and which to shun. History will immortalize both the monstrously evil and the saintly good, giving each of them an equal value. The naiveté of this argument should be obvious in that it mistakenly ties human moral reasoning to the survival issue. With or without an after life, it is obvious that saintly figures will be judged as better than diabolical ones in all but the most diabolical societies.

See also **Arguments supportive of rebirth**.

Sallustius (Greek, Saloustios) the Neoplatonist (4th century CE). This philosopher was a student of **Iamblichus** and a member of the Pergamum School. Sometime between 363 and 394 Sallustius wrote a compendium of the (pagan) doctrines of the Pergamum School called *On the Gods and the World (Universe)*. This most likely was written, not only in defense of the classical paganism that was being attacked by the newly empowered Christian movement, but in posthumous support of the attempt by the Roman emperor **Julian the Apostate** (331–363) to reinstate paganism as the official religion of the empire. The work has a chapter that promotes a concept of **transmigration**.

According to Sallustius a rational soul that transmigrates into a human body becomes the soul of that body. On the other hand, a rational soul that becomes associated with a non-rational creature only accompanies that creature from outside the body much as a guardian spirit does for a rational being. In the view of *On the Gods and the World* there are a limited number of souls which are born into miserable conditions in this world or in **Hades** if in the past they have failed to live virtuous lives. At the same time virtuous persons are purified of bodily existence and are united with the gods and share with them the governing of the world.

See also **Greek afterlife, the ancient; Hermetic philosophy; Neoplatonism; Priesthood, lack of an organized**.

Samkhya or ***Sankhya* Yoga**. This is an ancient school of Indian philosophy that teaches that liberation of the soul (*purusha*) can only be attained through karmicaly purifying ascetic practices (yoga) and the uncompromised realization of the fundamental distinction (*viveka*) between *purusha* and *prakriti* (the material body).

See also **Dualism**.

Samma Sambuddha (P). 1. The standard Buddhist meaning of this term is Supreme Wisdom Buddha. 2. In **Theosophy** this term is sometimes interpreted to mean the miraculous ability to remember one's own past lives (***Purvanivasanusmrti***), something every Buddha is believed to be able to do.

Samsara (S. Journeying). In Buddhism this refers to the world of dissatisfaction (***duhkha***) and impermanence (S: *anitya*) through which we travel. Nothing is thought to manifest this more than the repeated cycles of rebirth and re-death, which are brought about through craving, hatred, and ignorance. *Samsara* is the opposite of **nirvana and *parinirvana***.

See also ***Bhavachakra; Bodhisattva; Kyklos Genesion; Shunya;* Three Roots (*Mulas*) of *Samsara***.

Samskara/sankara (volitional activities). These are impressions left from past actions, so the term has also been translated as past karma.

See also ***Pratitya-samutpada*; Psychophysical aggregates; Rebirth in Buddhism; *Skandha*; *Vasanas***.

Samuel, First Book of *see* **Old Testament and the afterlife; Old Testament and the soul; Sciomancy**.

Samvara. In Jainism this term refers to preventing karma from adhering to the *jiva* (soul), which if successful will lead to liberation from birth and death.

See also ***Moksha; Nirjara***.

Sanskrit language. This is the old Indian classical language that was used to for both Hindu religious texts and various secular works. It was not used to record Buddhist teachings until the rise of **Mahayana Buddhism**. A sister language of Sanskrit is the Pali language of the Theravada Buddhist canon.

Many Western esoteric sources that deal with reincarnation prefer to retain Sanskrit, or in rare cases, the Pali, vocabulary rather than translating a word into a Western language; for example, *akashic* record, *linga-sharia*, *samskara*

Santeria (Santerismo). This is a Cuban **Afro-American religion** that was developed during the days of slavery by the Lucumi (people of **Yoruba** ancestry). In Santeria one of the most important deities (Orishas) is Orunla (Orula or Orunmila). This is the deity of divination (*awo*). For this reason he is also called *Ifa* (oracle). As *Ifa* he is considered the spiritual father of those priests (*santeros*, saints) that will become high priests (*babalaos*, (*baba*, father of—*l'awo*, mystery). When it comes time for a soul (*ori*) to choose its earthly destiny (*iwa*), Orunla is present as a witness. If the soul in its first incarnation does not fulfill that destiny Orunla will require it to reincarnate until it does so. During the slavery period, when it was necessary to disguise slave deities as Catholic saints (*ocha*), Orunla was identified with Saint Francis of Assisi. In the late 19th century Santeria was greatly influenced by, and absorbed elements of, the Spiritism of **Allen Kardec**. Many Santerians refer to their religion as the *Regla de Ocha* or Religion of the Saints.

See also **Africa; Kardecismo; Possession; Umbanda.**

Satan *see* **Lucifer (1).**

Sathya Sai Baba. Born Sathya Narayana Raju in 1926, Baba left home at the age of 13 or 14 declaring that he was the reincarnation of a Shiridi Sai Baba from the village of Shiridi, who was a Moslem saint who died in 1918. According to the present Sai Baba he will voluntarily disembody at the age of 96, and will, eight years later, reincarnate in his third and last Sai Baba embodiment under the name of Prema Sai Baba in a village in Kerala (Southern India). Some of Sai Baba's disciples regard him as a reincarnation of **Jesus.**

Saturn, the planet. Saturn is the Latin name for the Greek Kronos, which early on was identified with *Chronos* (Greek: time) and as such, in traditional Western astrology, it came to be considered the Great Malefic, with Mars (Ares) being the lesser malefic. This malefic nature is thought to be especially strong when Saturn is found in the eighth astrological house which governs death. It is also to be noted that in Hindu astrology Saturn (Hindi: *Shani*) likewise has a connection to destructive situations.

One of the original reasons for the maleficent reputation of Saturn was originally due to the fact that, with its 29.5 year revolution, it was for the ancients the slowest moving visible planet; therefore, it represented old age, finality, and endings. In fact, its slowness made it the prototype for our Father Time.

The astrologer Robert Powell (1947–), in his *Hermetic Astrology: Towards a New Wisdom of the Stars*, (Kinsau, Germany: Hermetika, 1987) believes that Saturn is a major factor in the rebirth process. Powell takes exception with the majority of astrologers in that he considers only the sidereal zodiac and the heliocentric chart, as opposed to the older and more traditional imaginary zodiac and the geocentric chart, to be useful in gaining insight into reincarnation from the astrological view.

Another well known astrologer, Jeanne Avery, has published *Astrology and Your Past Lives: Reincarnations through Saturn's Placement in Your Chart*. (New York: Simon and Schuster, 1987).

See also **Angels and reincarnation; Astrology and rebirth; Dweller on the Threshold; Lords of Karma; Mann, Tad; Moon; Planetary descent and ascent of the soul; Pluto, the planet.**

Satya. According to the channeler Barbara Marciniak, this is an entity from the **Pleiades** cluster of stars in the constellation of Taurus that has been channeled through her since 1988. The entity supports the concept of reincarnation, karma, and past life exploration. Whether by design or coincidence the word "Satya" is also **Sanskrit** for Truth.

See also **Channeling; Equinox; Franklin, Benjamin (2); Hilarion; Lazaris; Mafu; Ra (1); Ra (2); Ramtha; Ryeron, Kevin; Satya; Seth; Torah (2).**

Schiller, Friedrich von (1759–1805). This German poet and dramatist, in his early writings, seemed to strongly favor the idea of reincarnation, but this interest waned in his later works.

School of Life. There is a very old adage that says, "Life is a school in which through suffering and joy we must learn as much as we can before we die." Most people simply accept this adage as it is without asking, "Why we are supposed to learn as much as possible?" The orthodox Christian answer might be because God appreciates such learning and/or it improves our chances of going to **heaven** and/or it makes us more educated denizens of heaven. The reincarnationist, on the other hand, will point out that the overwhelming majority of people do not take the opportunity to learn much in this or any one life and so heaven must either be very underpopulated or very full of unschooled inhabitants. It is only by proposing a series of lives (rebirths) that most people could learn most of what they should learn. In this sense the School of Life argument for rebirth is basically the same as the **rebirth and**

moral perfection argument and as such is open to the same weakness or counter argument as that position.

Schopenhauer, Arthur (1788–1860). This German philosopher was highly influenced by Buddhism. He interpreted the Buddhist concept of soulless (***anatman***) rebirth (***bhava***) as the rebirth of each person's impersonal "will to live." Schopenhauer was the first to collect and publish references to the doctrine of rebirth from early to contemporary times. In these he pointed out that the doctrine of **metempsychosis** was far older and more widespread than most of his contemporaries believed.

See also *Ex Oriente Lux*; Karma with minimal rebirth.

Science and pseudo-science *see* Logic and pseudo-logic and rebirth.

Science of Mind. A part of the New Thought movement, Science of Mind, also known as Religious Science, was founded by Ernest Shurtleff Holmes (1887–1960). Although reincarnation is not an official doctrine of this church, the church is open to the concept.

Scientology. This New Age Organization was founded by Lafayette Ronald Hubbard (1911–1986). In his book *Dianetics: The Modern Science of Mental Health* (1950) Hubbard claimed to have discovered a new and more advanced way to cure emotional and psychosomatic illnesses. Moving from the simple mental therapy of *Dianetics*, Scientology was officially initiated as a religion in 1954, which is a blending of psychoanalysis, Western **Gnosticism**, and Eastern religion. One reason for the name Scientology seems to be due to the group's use of the presumed techno-scientific e-meter (electropsychometer), a kind of lie detector device that monitors the psychogalvanic reflex or galvanic skin response, an indicator of stress.

Scientology's religious dimension was especially represented in Hubbard's *Have You Lived Before This Life? A Scientific Study: A Study of Death and Evidence of Past Lives* (1958); and *Mission into Time* (1973). The first of these is purported to be a collection of forty-one cases of past lives obtained from auditing with the e-meter. Among these past lives are ones that are said to have occurred as an animal and on other planets. In the introduction to *Have You Lived Before* Hubbard states that Scientology and *Dianetics* techniques differ greatly from hypnotism. He says that in hypnotism the aim is to put the client to sleep and make him as irresponsible as possible for his answers. In contrast, in Scientology and *Dianetics*, the person is made more and more alert, more and more responsible and truthful. Hubbard further states that past lives are not the same as the theory which has been called "reincarnation in Hinduism." Having made the last statement the book's explanation of past lives is more or less the "same" as in Hinduism. Finally, many of the cases in *Have You Lived Before* read more like poorly researched history and/or poorly written science fiction. For example, case 8 states that the person lived 3,225 years ago as a member of the Roman army. This date was 700 years before the founding of Rome. Case 10 states the person lived 55 quiatillion (18 zeros) years ago as a manta ray. The earth is only four billion (9 zeros) years old. Case 13 has a past life as a person living on Mars nearly 5 hundred million years ago. Hubbard's *Mission into Time* is even less reliable.

The understanding of reincarnation in Scientology is based on the concept of the "*Theta*" and the "*Thetan*." These terms comes from the name of the Greek letter *theta*, which was said to represent thought. To this Hubbard added a "-n" suffix to make it appear more like a proper English noun. The -n is also said to represent the power of the *theta* to the "nth" or unlimited degree. According to Scientology the *theta* is the mathematical symbol for static thought or the static thought itself. The term is used to refer to creative energy specific to life, as well as to the thought and spirit embodied in the individual. The *theta* entity is called a *thetan* and this refers to the single unit of beingness that is each person. The *thetan* is that which has awareness of its own awareness. It is the innermost, hence real, personality beneath body and mind.

According to Hubbard *thetans* are immortal celestial beings, which billions of years ago created matter, energy, space and time. In an experiment with trying to experience life in material bodies they inadvertently became trapped. This caused them to forget most of their celestial origins. The *thetans* must now undergo constant reincarnation until they can once again be come free of materiality. This freedom can only be achieved first through clearing all of the traumatic impressions (*engrams*) on the subconscious (reactive) mind. If this is not done these *engrams* will pass on into the person's next reincarnation and cause one unnecessary suffering. Once the *engrams* have been cleared, a series of carefully guarded consciousness training will be required to produce an operant *thetan*. This is a *thetan* that is, not only fully conscious both of its origin and of God; but is a master of matter, energy, space, and time (a MEST). It is just such a clear, operant, and "mest *thetan*" that **Jesus** was according to Hubbard. During the reincarnation process the *thetan* is said to take over a new body a few days or weeks before the birth of that host-to-be's body.

Between the years 1945 and 1946 Hubbard was,

to some degree, involved with the California branch of the occult sexual order Ordo Templi Orientis with Jack Parson, a disciple of **Aleister Crowley**; thus, it is not unexpected that some of Crowley's thought has been passed on via Scientology.

See also **Affect bridge; Blocked regression; Crowley, Aleister; Eckankar; Fall of the Souls; Netherton Method; Planets, other;** *Psychophore*; **Zhendao.**

Sciomancy. This is the proper term for the communication with the souls (shades) of the dead for the purpose of divination, as can be seen from its root *scio* (from the Greek: *skia*), meaning a **shadow** or **shade**, as in the sense of a soul in **Hades**. Unfortunately the term **necromancy** is more commonly, but incorrectly, used for such divination. The Greek root "necro" refers to a corpse, not the soul. Necromancy, therefore, should strictly be used to refer to any attempt to use a dead body for divinational purposes. A synonym of sciomancy is psychomancy (soul-divination) and a person who invokes the spirits of the dead is sometimes called a psychogogues. Perhaps one reason that necromancy is substituted for sciomany is that sciomancy can also mean divination by observing shadows. Sciomancy is also at times confused with theurgy, which properly used is the art of persuading or compelling a god or beneficent supernatural power to do or not do some activity.

Many modern conservative religious groups regard past life inquiry as sciomancy and along with **Spiritualism** and **channeling** consider them to be witchcraft and/or demonomancy. These groups readily point towards those verses in the Old Testament that condemn such witchcraft (Hebrew: *kishuph*) activities. Among these are Exodus 22:18; Leviticus 19:31; 20:6, 27; Deuteronomy 18:12; 2 Kings 21:6; 23:24; 2 Chronicles 33:6; Isaiah 8:19–20; 19:3; 47:9–14; Jeremiah 27:9; and Malachi 3:5. 1 Samuel 28:6–20; while 1 Chronicles 10:13 even condemns the practice of sciomancy as an action worthy of execution.

In defensive of such condemned activities, a number of their more sophisticated practitioners argue that most of those passages were really opposing the worship of the dead or ancestors, not only by the neighboring tribes around ancient Israel, but also among the early Israelites. The spiritualist, channeler, and past life recallers further argue that the biblical condemnations were part of the attempt by Judean authorizes to center all religious activities on the Temple of Solomon in Jerusalem and the Yahwehist tradition, and regarded spiritualist activities as threatening competition.

See also **Astral plane; Old Testament and the afterlife; Possession.**

Score, John (1914–1979). Score was one of the lesser known figures in the modern witchcraft revival. As early as 1948 Score's desire for a more spiritual dimension to his life caused him to seek to purify his body by turning to **vegetarianism**. Becoming aware of the newly arising neo–Pagan and Wicca movements in the 1960s, Score was drawn to them by recognizing that they had great similarities to the solar worship that he felt he had practiced in **Egypt** in a distant past life. In fact, Score believed that he could remember past lives as far back as one on the lost continent of Atlantis.

In 1968 Score became the editor of the newsletter *The Wiccan*, published by the Pagan Federation, and through this newsletter he was able to establish the Pagan Front, a British organization for the support and defense of Neo-Paganism. This organization changed its name to the Pagan Federation in 1981, and its publication became the *Pagan Dawn*.

See also **Lost continents and reincarnation; Neo-pagan religions; Wicca.**

Screen memories. These are false memories produced by the unconscious mind to protect the conscious mind from remembering some event that is otherwise too traumatic for the person to deal with consciously. For example, seemingly unaccounted for phobias (irrational fears) can lead to screen memories. Under hypnosis many subjects have been asked to go back to the time in this life when they first experienced the cause of a particular phobia. In many of those cases the individuals seems unable to locate that time. The hypnotist may then ask them to go back to former lives and locate the cause of the phobia. This very often results in a past life scenario that explains the origin of the phobia. The same process has often worked in locating the origin of psychosomatic illnesses. Skeptics of such past life origins suggest that finding the source of a trauma in a past life is simply psychologically less threatening than finding it in the present life.

See also **Affect bridge; Blocked regression; Memory, suppressed; Past life therapy.**

Scrying or **Skrying.** This is the concentrated gazing at any highly polished monochromatic surface. It is believed by some that concentrated gazing at any such surface may aid the mind in a vision of a past life. There are a great variety of surfaces at which to gaze: most commonly a glass or crystal sphere (crystal(l)omancy); but also a bowel of liquid (hydromancy) such as water; oil (leconomancy), treacle (molasses), black ink, red wine, fresh blood, or narcotic power in magnetized water;

a small polished pendulum; a mirror (catoptromancy or enoptromancy); a lamp or candle flame (lampadomancy) or a fire (pyromancy, fire of Azrael). Each of these serve as a speculum, a shiny, reflective surface used to focus all of one's gaze in such a manner as to enter into some degree of a trance state.

Strictly speaking scrying differs from crystal gazing (crystal(l)omancy) in that the scryer is using a crystal surface in an attempt either to contact spirits or to have an inner vision of the future. A crystal gazer, on the other hand, is looking for a vision or sign of the future within the crystal itself.

One modern replacement for a crystal ball is a galvanic mirror. This is a magnetized disc made by joining together concave copper and convex zinc parts. It differs from a normal scrying mirror, which is basically a piece of clear glass with its back side painted black.

See also **Lhamoi Latso; Moody, Raymond A. Jr; Phoenix Cards; Tarot; Sciomancy; Trance states.**

Séance *see* **Astral plane; Blavatsky, Helena Petrova; Sciomancy**

Seasons. In temperate climates the perpetual cycle of spring birth, summer youth, autumn aging, and winter death were certainly one of the analogies in nature that suggests the concept of rebirth.

See also **Rebirth, analogies from nature.**

Second death. This term has two religious meaning. The first is found in various ancient and modern folk religions, while the second is found in modern **Theosophy** and related systems.

A number of folk religions, while acknowledging an afterlife, believe that some or all souls only experience a temporary afterlife. This belief in a temporary afterlife can take two general forms. The first involves the memories of the living. For example, in several ancestral worshipping religions the deceased survive only as long as there are living family members who periodically remember the deceased through some ritual procedure. Since each generation of ancestors will eventually be replaced by newer ancestral generations in the memory of their descendents, memory of the older ones will fade into a secondary and permanent death. Many tribal people in Africa hold this view of a second death.

In the second form of folk religion second death it is believed that an after-life is dependent on the behavior of the soul. An example of this is the belief that every soul is required to undergo judgment in an afterlife. Those that are judged good continue on indefinitely in some happy state. Those that are judged bad are either immediately extinguished or first punished in some very unhappy state and then face extinction. The people of ancient Egypt and, in some cases, the ancient Greeks are associated with this view. Even some Christian groups, over the centuries, have felt that this second death concept is more in keeping with a God of mercy than is the idea of an eternal hell, although, in the **Revelation of John** the term second death is found in the context of the wicked being cast into a lake which burns with fire and brimstone.

The Theosophical view of the second death refers to one of two situations. The first is the death of the **astral body** upon the soul entering the **mental plane** of existence, a necessary phase before an eventual rebirth. The second is the annihilation of the soul in the **eighth sphere.**

See also **Annihilationism, Biblical view; Annihilationism, Buddhist view; Astral plane; Buddha's necklace; Chinese Religion and Reincarnation; Etheric revenant.**

Seelenwanderung. This is the standard dictionary German phrase for **transmigration** or **metempsychosis** of souls. It literally translates as the wandering of many souls. Another word that has been used is *Wiedermenschwerdung*, but this appears to be more of a recently made up word, using various German roots. It literally means "people becoming people again." It does not appear in standard dictionaries.

Self-Realization Fellowship *see* **Yogananda, Paramahansa.**

Sensation body. This is an alternative name for the **etheric body.** It is called this because it is thought that the physical body only has sensation in union with this sensation body.

Sephiroth (Hebrew: numerations). These are the ten emanations of God that form the Kabbalic "Tree of Life." These ten descend in the order of (1) *Kether* (Crown); (2) *Chokmah* (Wisdom), (3) *Binah* (Understanding); (4) *Chesed* (Mercy); (5) *Geburah* (Severity); (6) *Tipareth* (Beauty); (7) *Netzach* (Victory) (8) *Hod* (Glory); (9) *Yesod* (Foundation); and (10) *Malkuth* (Kingdom). According to the medieval Kabbalic teacher **Isaac Luria** it was due to a fault in the original emanations of the *Sephiroth* that souls became trapped in matter and thus must go through **transmigration** (*gilgul*) until they can escape.

See also **Angels and reincarnation; Astrology and rebirth; Blavatsky, Helena; Kabbalah; Milky Way; Moon; Planetary descent and ascent of the soul;** *Qlippoth.*

Septenary nature of man *see* **Soul and spirit levels, Theosophical.**

Serial lives. This is term for a set of linear multiple lives; in other words, for rebirths, reincarnations, **transmigrations**, etc.

Serpent or **snakes.** Although modern supporters of rebirth no longer use the serpent analogy, ancient people certainly did. The habit of serpents sloughing off their skin only to reveal a new one beneath it was thought suggestive of rebirth.

See also **Ouroboros; Rebirth, analogies from nature.**

Seth. In 1963 Jane Roberts (1929–1984) and her husband Robert Butts began experimenting with a **Ouija board** which brought through an entity that at first called itself Frank Withers, but preferred to be known as Seth. It was not long before the Ouija board was replaced with clairaudience and **automatic writing** while Roberts was in a trance. Seth described itself as a bisexual fragment of a larger entity. This description ultimately applied to Roberts and everyone else. According to Seth he had experienced many lives on Earth, including one on the **lost continent** of Atlantis, but eventually evolved into an energy personality essence that is no longer dependent on physical reality. At the same time Seth suggested a time schema very similar to that of **Joan Marshall Grant** where our so-called Past, Present, and Future lives all exist simultaneously.

The 1963 date of Seth's appearance actually made Roberts the earliest of the modern channelers; moreover, while Roberts continued to channel Seth until her death in 1984, she later also channeled other entities, including a Seth Two, who was part of the same collective entity as Seth One. Among the works on reincarnation from Seth, via Roberts is *The Seth Material* (1970); *Seth Speaks: The Eternal Validity of the Soul* (1972); and *Dreams, Evolution, and Value Fulfillment* (1986). These and other extensive recorded writings of Seth encouraged the establishment of Seth Centers which perform past life regressions.

It needs to be noted that Robert's Seth is quite distinct from three other occult Seths. The first is the Egyptian name for the murderous brother of the god Osiris; hence the representation of all that was thought to be evil. This Seth is sometimes spelled as Set. The second Seth, modeled on the Egyptian Seth, is the deity of The Temple of Seth, which is a modern Satanic group founded in 1975 by Michael Aquino. The third Seth is the name of the third and youngest son of the biblical **Adam**. Since according to Genesis, Noah was descended from Seth all post-flood humanity was descended from this Seth. This ancestry encouraged several traditions of **Gnosticism**, called Sethian gnostics, to surround this biblical Seth with an esoteric significance as a *pneumatikoi*.

See also **Attached entity; Channeling; Egypt; Equinox; Franklin, Benjamin (2); Hilarion; Karma, developmental; Lazaris; Mafu; Parallel lives; Plurality of existences; Ramtha; Ryerson, Kevin; Satya; Time and the simultaneous past, present, and future; Torah (2); Trance states; Wilcock, David.**

Seven. This number is regarded in both the West and East as of particular esoteric significance. This universality is probably due to the original (pre-telescope) seven visibly moving celestial bodies, the seven **Pleiades** stars, and/or the Big Bear or Big Dipper. In the Old Testament, for example, seven is mentioned seventy-seven times, beginning with the seven days of creation. It is a number also frequent in the New Testament, where in the **Revelation of John** it occurs forty times. With such esoteric popularity it is no surprise that the number seven has significance in various reincarnational systems.

See also *Aquarian Gospel of Jesus Christ*; *Archons*; **Ascended masters; Astrology and rebirth; Blavatsky, Helena Petrova; Buddhist stages of liberation Buddhist stages of liberation;** *Chakras*; **Colton, Ann Ree; Critical time periods; Cult of Angels and reincarnation; Finite or infinite number of rebirths; Genesis; Heaven; Hell, the Chinese; Interim period; Kabbalah; Lords of Karma; Lucifer; Matthew 18:21–22; Mental plane; Mithraism;** *Nirvikalpa Samadhi*; **Planetary descent and ascent of the soul; Poimandres; Rebirth in Buddhism; Return and serve argument for reincarnation;** *Sephiroth*; **Seven rungs of the heavenly ladder; Seven Veils, Dance of; Soul and spirit levels, Theosophical; Yarsanism.**

Seven rungs of the heavenly ladder. In various esoteric systems a ladder with seven rungs symbolizes the seven steps or actions needed to attain liberation from birth and death. This symbolism was especially important in **Mithraism**. This was originally based on the seven moving celestial bodies.

See also **Genesis; Planetary descent and ascent of the soul; Seven; Seven Veils, Dance of the.**

Seven times seven *see* **Bardo; Matthew, Gospel of.**

Seven Veils, Dance of the. The famous Dance of the Seven Veils by Salome before King Herod is believed in some esoteric traditions to actually represent the soul divesting itself of seven layers of materiality in order to ascend to paradise. While the dance is mentioned in **Mark** 6:22 and **Matthew** 14:6, there is no mention of any removal of clothing. This was the invention of Oscar Wilde in his play *Salome*, which was then made into an opera by Richard Strauss.

Wilde's concept of the removing seven veils may have come from the Sumerian myth of Inanna and Dumuzi. The goddess of love and fertility, Inanna (later Ishtar), lost her mortal lover Dumuzi (Tammuz) to death and to retrieve him she has to descend into the land of the dead which has seven gates. At each gate she had to remove a piece of clothing until she is finally naked, as were all the inhabitants of the underworld. This left the world without fertility and that returned only when the goddess, with her lover, returned to the surface. This descent and ascent was really represented the dying of life in autumn and winter, followed by its rebirth in the spring and summer, so as a source for a reincarnationist interpretation this myth is weak. A stronger reincarnationist interpretation would use the **planetary descent and ascent of the soul**.

See also **Seven rungs of the heavenly ladder**

Seventeenth century renewed interest in rebirth. With the rise of the Cambridge Platonists in the sixteenth century there gradually developed an interest in the subject of **metempsychosis**. This interest is witnessed by the number of books published in the late seventeenth century in English on the subject of metempsychosis, pro and con. This, of course, demonstrates that the suppression of unorthodox religious ideas found in the 16th and earlier centuries had significantly diminished, at least in Protestant England.

A search for books from the 15th–17th centuries on the subject of reincarnation in Early English Books Online (EEBO), an electronic data base, resulted in only three finds which interestingly are all inter-related. The first has a not uncommon extended title of that period which is *Two hundred queries moderately propounded concerning the doctrine of the revolution of humane souls and its conformity to the truths of Christianity* (*De Revolutione Animarum*, for short) by the Kabbalist Franciscus Mercurius van Helmont (1614–1699). This 88-page book was printed in London in 1684. (A related book by this author, not in EEBO, was *Seder Olam; or the Order, Series or Succession of All the Ages, Periods, and Times of the Whole World is theologically, philosophically and Chronologically Explicated and Stated also the Hypothesus of the Pre-existency and Revolution of the Human Souls* ... [Holland 1693], which was translated from the Latin and published in London in 1694).

The second EEBO listing is *Truth and innocency defended against calumny and defamation in a late report spread abroad concerning the revolution of humane souls: with a further clearing of the truth by a plain explication of my sence, &c* by George Keith (1639?–1716). This 20-page book, printed in Philadelphia in 1692, was written to counter a charge made by an unspecified person that George Keith was in fact the real author of the Helmont book. In this book the author not only denies the charge, but reaffirms his orthodox Christian belief against the revolution of humane souls (reincarnation) and for the resurrection.

The third book has the even more elaborate title of *The harmless opinion of the revolution of humane souls as a probable hypothesis, and very serviceable to clear many doubts, and answer many objections of atheists against the divine providence, and the Holy Scriptures. Modestly defended in a reply to a late treatise, signed by J.H. printed at Oxford, and called by him, An answer to some queries, proposed by W.C. or a refutation of Helmont's pernicious error, &c* by an anonymous author. This 48-page book was printed in 1694 in London and tries to defend the views of the Helmont book and challenges the criticism of Keith.

Other 17th-century publications in England dealing with reincarnation included *Philosophical Poems: A Platonick Song of the Soul, treating of the Life of the Soul, her Immortality, the Sleep of the Soul, the Unitie of the Souls, and Memorie after Death* by Henry More (1647); *Works* by John Goodwin (1652), which defended **soul's existence prior to embodiment;** *Lux Orientalis: or an Inquiry into the opinions of the Eastern sages concerning the Prae-existence of Souls. Being a key to unlock the Grand Mysteries of Providence in Relation to man's sin and misery* by Joseph Glanvil (1662), the chaplain to King Charles II; *A Free and Impartial Censure of the Platonic Philosophie, with an account of the Origenian Hypothesis, concerning the Pre-existence of Souls* by (Bishop) Samuel Parker (1666); *No Pre-existence, or a brief Dissertation against the Hypothesis of Human Souls living in a state antecedaneous to this* by Edward Warren (1667); *An Essay on Transmigration, in Defense of Pythagoras* by Whitelock Bulstode (1692); and *The Visions of the Soul before it comes into the Body* by John Dunton (1692). Outside of England there was at least *De metempsycosi dissertation* by Heinrich Wolfgang Schilling, Lipsiae [Lipzig] (1679); *De animarum transmigratione* by Heinrich Henrici (1699); and *The Book on the Rashith ha Gigalim (revolutions of the soul or scheme of reincarnation)* by the Christian Kabbalist Baron Knorr von Rosenroth (1636–1689), place of publication unknown.

See also **Internet and reincarnation;** *Metempsychosis, or the Transmigration of Souls, Systematically Considered...*

Seventh heaven see **Heaven; Planetary descent and ascent of the soul.**

Sewer lifetime *see* **Solity**.

Sexual activity and rebirth *see* **Creationism, soul; Electra/Oedipus Complex and rebirth; Kabbalah;** *Pratitya-samutpada***; Rebirth and artificial insemination; Rebirth in Buddhism**.

Shadow or **shade**. These two terms have been used to refer to the deceased as continuing to exist not only in English but in other languages. For example, the Roman term *umbra* meant, not only the shadow created by blocking light, but the part of the tripartite soul that remained near the body after death. In ancient **Egypt** the shadow (*khaibi* or *haidit*) had a more positive connotation. It was believed a person could not exist without this in this life or the next.

See also **Archetypes; Astral plane; Greek afterlife, the ancient; New Testament and reincarnation; Old Testament and the afterlife; Scientology; Sciomancy; Shinto; Soul; Soul, tripartite**.

Shadow body. This term, though widely used in both esoteric and occult circles, may signify not only the dark (demonic) side of a person, but also the **etheric body**, the **astral body**, or the **Dweller on the Threshold**. The shadow body may also be called the double. It is believed by some occultists that such a shadow body may linger about the deceased physical body due to its attachment to the material world.

See also **Shadow** or **shade**.

Shakespeare, William (1564–1616). There is no doubt that Shakespeare was familiar with the concept of **transmigration**. If nothing else, this is shown by its brief mention in his play, *Twelfth Night* (1601/02). In this play the dour, puritanical Malvolio lampoons the Pythagorean idea that a human soul can happily be reborn as a bird. Whether Shakespeare had a more positive and more personal belief in transmigration is an arguable issue. A number of readers of the bard's sonnets believe that they, rather than his plays, at least hint at a favorable view of it. The sonnet most commonly thought of as pro-transmigrational is *Sonnet LIX*. The first four lines of this fourteen lined poem read, "If there be nothing new, but that which is /Hath been before, how are our brains beguiled, /Which, belaboring for invention, bear amiss /The second burden of a former child."

Shamanism *see* **Bon-pa [po] religion; Channeling; Dalai Lama; Greeks and reincarnation; Koryaks; Kwakiutl; Neo-pagan religions; Possession; Shinto**.

Shanti Devi case. This is one of the most widely cited cases for proof of reincarnation. Devi was born in India in 1926 and her memories of a past life were said to begin when she was three years old. She claimed to remember the village she used to live in, which was about 80 miles away; to remember her former husband; caste; previous family; house; and even the fact that she had buried some money under her former house. Upon Shanti Devi's visit to her presumed former village she is said to have been correct on many of these recollections. Unfortunately, no scientifically controlled investigation of this case was attempted until after the village visit, which for all practical purposes makes it useless as evidence for reincarnation.

See also **Children remembering past lives; Katsugoro case; Possession**.

Shared or duplicate recall memories *see* **Soul-fission**.

Shasta, Mount *see* **Mount Shasta**.

Sheep. In the Welsh tale of Peredur, in the *Mabinogion*, there are two flocks of sheep, one white, the other black, which were separated by a river. Every time a white sheep crossed to the black sheep side it turned black, while the opposite happened to a black sheep crossing to the white side. One esoteric interpretation of this is that the river is said to represent the boundary between life and death. The white sheep crossing it represents the soul descending from heaven (death) to earth to be reborn, while the black sheep crossing it represents the soul at death ascending to heaven.

See also **East-West, Traveling**.

Sheol (Hebrew: abyss, cave) *see* **Elijah; Genesis; Hades; Harrowing of Hell; Hell; Numbers; Old Testament and the afterlife; Shinto/Shintoism; Unarius Academy of Science**.

Shinto/Shintoism (Japanese: Way of the spirits or gods). This is the native shamanic religion of Japan. Like many folk religions it did not originally have a very promising attitude towards an afterlife. In fact, the Shinto view was very similar to that of the ancient Greek **Hades** and the Hebrew *Sheol* in that the underworld was a place of gloomy shades. It was not until Buddhism was introduced into the country that a more positive vision of an afterlife was offered the Japanese. One of the reasons for Buddhism's great success in Japan was because of it promise of rebirth into heavens and **Pure Lands**. Of course, Buddhism also brought to Japan its first taste of **purgatory** (Japanese: *Jigoku*). Since the introduction of Buddhism most Japanese have tended to practice both religions side by side. As in many folk religions there is no clearly defined doctrinal or dogmatic view about the **soul** (*tama* or *mitama*) in Shinto.

See also **Animism; Emma-o; Greek afterlife, the ancient;** *Hotoke*; **Old Testament and the afterlife; Shadow or shade;** *Tama*.

Shiva. In **Hinduism** this is one of the three personal manifestations of the universal soul or self (**Brahman**). When envisioned as just one of the three high gods he is simply called the Destroyer, as opposed to Brahma the Creator and **Vishnu** the Sustainer. But when worshipped as a completely separate entity, particularly in the form of a dancing figure (*Nataraja*: Lord of the Dance), Shiva dances the universe into being, sustains it by his rhythm, and eventually dances it into annihilation. As the god of generation his symbol is the *lingam*. As Shiva the great meditating ascetic he also represents the great effort to liberate oneself from the round of reincarnation.

Shotoku Taishi (574–622). The efforts of this imperial Japanese prince and de facto ruler of Japan in the spread of Buddhism were great enough for him to have been thought to be, not only the **Buddha** Shakya-muni (Gautama) reborn, but also to be the one who will be reborn on earth in the future as the Buddha to come, Maitreya Buddha.

Sikhism. This is a religious sect founded in the Punjab (northwestern India) by Guru Nanak (1469– 1539) that originally sought to bridge the gap between Muslims and Hindus. Animosity between these two very different religions turned out to be far too deeply seated to be bridged. This resulted in Nanak's followers becoming a separate and autonomous sect from both **Islam** and **Hinduism**. While the sect adopted an undiluted monotheism from Islam, it adopted its belief in karma and reincarnation (*awagaun*) from Hinduism. The Sikhs, however, added to the Hindu view the Islamic idea of a last judgment, only with the Hindu-like belief that all souls, upon ceasing to reincarnate, would be absorbed back into God.

See also **Eckankar; Kabirpanthi; Resurrection or reincarnation.**

Silent watchers. In Theosophy these are supremely enlightened spirits who are more or less omniscient and who have taken upon themselves the role of assisting mankind in its evolution. As omniscient they are superior to the **ascended masters**.

See also **Dweller on the Threshold.**

Similes and rebirth. A number of similes have been employed to argue for rebirth. Among these are the alternating of wakefulness and sleep, day and night, summer and winter, and the fact that all the cells in our body are said to undergo replacement at least every **seven** years. The use of such similes may be very poetic, and on the surface seem very apt, but a deeper look at them makes for a very weak argument for rebirth. The mental and physical activity of an individual may be greatly reduced in sleep compared to wakefulness, but the body while asleep does not disintegrate as it does at death, nor does the planet earth as a whole change radically (die) during its daily rotation or yearly revolution. Also, at no time in the process of cell replacement does the body as a whole cease to function.

See also **Rebirth, analogies from nature.**

Simon Magus (Simon the Magician or Sorcerer). This semi-legendary 1st century CE individual seems to have been a Gnostic teacher of some kind. As was not an uncommon among Gnostics, he believed that the female personification of Divine Wisdom (Greek: *Sophia*), the first emanation from God had, through some cosmic tragedy fallen from heaven to earth and been trapped in a series of earthly female embodiments, among which was Helen of Troy. The salvation of mankind from **metempsychosis** was impossible until she could be liberated. Legend has it that Simon found Sophia in her latest embodiment as a prostitute in a brothel in the Phoenician city of Tyre.

See also **Fall of Souls; Gnosticism; Valentinus.**

Single-direction rebirth *see* **Rebirth, non-backsliding; Transmigration.**

Sinnett, Alfred Percy (1840–1921). Sinnett is the author of *The Occult World* (1881), *Esoteric Buddhism* (1883), *Growth of the Soul: A Sequel to Esoteric Buddhism* (1896), and the article "*Obscure Problems of Karma and Rebirth*" (1902). Each of these works was written as a result of Sinnett's meeting **Helena Blavatsky** (1879) and being converted to her **Theosophy**. The material for *Esoteric Buddhism* was purportedly given to him by two members of the **ascended masters (***dhyani chohans***)**, *Mahatma* (El) Morya and, especially, Master Koot Hoomi (Kuthumi). The letters that formed the bases of *Esoteric Buddhism* were later independently published as *The Mahatma Letters to A.P. Sinnett* (1924). Sinnett and his wife were also associated with the **Hermetic Order of the Golden Dawn**, the pioneering ceremonial magic society.

See also **Esoteric Buddhism; Soul and spirit levels, Theosophical.**

Sirius (dog star). This star in the constellation Canis Major is the brightest (true) star in the northern sky. It has been important in a number of ancient and not so ancient religious systems. Its worship by some pagan Arab tribes is even mentioned in the Quran (53:49). It has figured in several more modern occult systems in conjunction with the concept of reincarnation. Old Christian lore names it as the home of **Lucifer**.

See also **Crowley, Edward Aleister; Solar Temple, Order of**.

Six sentient states of being *see **Bhavachakra**.*

Skandha/Khandha (S/P). This term is the collective designation for the five causally conditioned factors or aggregates of which a living being is composed, according to Buddhism. These five are body (*rupa*), feelings or sensations (*vedana*), perception (*samjna/sanna*), *vijnana/vinnana* (consciousness), and (*samskara*). The exact meaning of the term *samskara* is debatable since it has a variety of definitions, one of which is subconscious habit patterns that result from past experiences or simply karmic formations. A possible modern definition might be genetic dispositions. This five component analytical schema was an attempt to explain the development and functioning of the body and mind complex without having to resort to a belief in a permanent soul that acts as the vitalizing agent of a mere material body, in other words "a ghost in the machine." In other words, it is because no one of these can be considered to be at the heart of selfhood that Buddhism theoretically teaches that there is no permanent self (*anatman*). Various Buddhist texts, however, have suggested that it is either *samskara* or *vijnana* that is involved with the rebirth process. This has led some critics to accuse Buddhism of teaching the existence of at least a temporary self or soul despite Buddhist disclaimers not to do so.

While this Buddhist schema is far more naturalistic than the older soul as animating agent concept, it should not be assumed that it is a more scientific analysis of the body-mind complex. The *skandha* concept arose to support a particular sectarian view, not to develop a scientific explanation.

See also *Anatman*; **Death**; *Pratitya-samutpada*; **Rebirth; Rebirth in Buddhism; Soul**.

Social status in past lives. Critics of reincarnation have sometimes claimed that most persons who purport to remember past lives remember lives as upper status individuals despite the fact that most of humanity has lived as low status individuals. The psychologist **Helen Wambach** is one of the few that have tried to address this issue.

See also **Cayce, Edgar; Egypt; Important person criticism**.

Society for Psychical Research. This is the leading organization in Great Britain for the study of paranormal phenomena, including claims of various kinds of post-mortem survival. The Society was established in 1882.

See also **American Society for Psychical Research; Associations and organizations**.

Society for Spiritual Regression. This organization was founded by Dr. Michael Newton, the author of *Journey of Souls* (2003) and *Destiny of Souls* (2003). According to the Society's website the Society provides information and referral services to people interested in achieving an experiential understanding of their nature as an eternal spiritual being through the process of Life-Between-Lives Spiritual Regression. This method offers individuals a means to access soul memories through a trance-induced "superconscious" state of awareness.

See also **Associations and organizations**.

Solar Temple, Order of (French: Ordre du Temple Solaire). This order was founded in the 1980's by Luc Jouret (1947–1994) and Joseph Di Mambro (1924–1994). As leaders of the order they taught a mixture of AMORC Rosicrucianism, Egyptian mortuary occultism, **Pyramidology**, Knights Templar mythology, and a belief in **ascended masters** of the **Great White Brotherhood** who were thought to dwell in Agartha, a secret subterranean center. Both men believed strongly in reincarnation, in fact, Jouret considered himself a reincarnation of Saint Bernard of Clairvaux (1090–1153), who was a major influence in the establishment of the medieval military monastic order of the Poor Knights of Christ and of the Temple of Solomon, in short, the **Templars**. Di Mambro believed that he was the reincarnation of an Egyptian pharaoh, of one of the apostles of Christ, and of an **ascended master** named Manatanus. The members of the Solar Temple order were mainly French speakers from Switzerland, France, and Quebec.

The order received world wide attention in October of 1994 when authorities discovered that a mass murder-suicide of five temple members in Quebec and forty-eight members in Switzerland had occurred. This was to be followed the next year with sixteen more deaths in France, in which some of the victims and been drugged, shot, and had their bodies burned. Finally, in1997, there were five more suicides found, who appear to have burned themselves to death. As best as can be determined the motivation for these seventy-four deaths was the order's belief that the world was very soon to experience an apocalyptic transition from the Age of Pisces to the Age of Aquarius and that this would be preceded by the earth being engulfed in fire. The only way to escape this catastrophe was to be specially trained and prepared in some esoteric fashion for a de-corporealization by the soul which would then be able to transit safely to the star **Sirius** A.

The reason for the burning of the victim's bodies seems to have been based on the idea that some of the de-corporealized souls might have lost courage after beginning their astral journey and tried to re-corporealize in their former bodies. This would not be possible if the souls knew that their bodies had been destroyed.

See also **Agasha Temple of Wisdom; Crowley, Edward Aleister; Egypt; Heaven's Gate; Koresh, David; Planets, other; Rosicrucians.**

Solity. This term is said to refer to an individual soul that, after several dozen lives, integrates all the positive aspects of its past personalities into a single super-personality (solity). This super-personality itself does not as a whole re-embody; instead it regenerates a series of new individual personalities that will, one by one, re-embody. In the process of winnowing the positive from the negative aspects of the past lives, the negative aspects must be properly disposed of. This may be done by voluntarily draining the negativity into a "sewer lifetime" which is a life characterized by moral, emotional, and/or physical ill health. Since it is an end process in creating the solity, presumably this life, unlike most other ill characterized lives, would not involve the acquisition of new negative karma.

Solomon, King *see* **Jesus; Phoenix;** *Pistis Sophia***; Proverb 8:22–31; Rastafarians; Rosicrucians; Star of David** or **Sign of Solomon; Wisdom of Solomon 8:19–20.**

Solomon, Temple of *see* **Sciomancy; Solar Temple, Order of; Templars.**

Somatic rebirth. This is a supposedly more scientific name for reincarnation. Presumably it could be turned into the verb re-ensomatization.

See also **Existential seriality; Hetero-recognition.**

Soteriology. (From the Greek soter: savior). This is the study of religious salvation. For example, the various methods by which the soul is liberated from the round of rebirth and re-death (*samsara*) would be considered soterial or soteriological in nature. Soteriology is closely related to eschatology.

See also **Karmic eschatology; Ontology; Protology; Rebirth eschatology.**

Soul. This term is commonly understood as being one or more metaphysical elements of selfhood that is/are non-material or non-physical in nature and is able to continue to exist after the death and/or destruction of the body.

Jerome Elbert, in his *Are Souls Real?* (2000), suggests that we could classify souls into four types — the life soul, the ego soul, the free soul, and the surviving soul. The first of these has been thought to be what all living things (plants to people) have and which distinguish them from non-living matter. When an organism loses this soul it dies. This type of soul could also be called a life-force and has been accepted by much of mankind over the millennia. The second soul type would be what carries the mental, emotional, and other aspects of an ego and as such is traditionally associated with human being alone. The third would be the soul or entity that can freely leave the human body during sleep or unconsciousness and has been traditionally associated with dreams and out-of-the-body experiences. The fourth type would be that which survives the death of the body for a longer or shorter time and occupies an afterlife world or re-embodies itself.

It is rare to find belief systems that keep these soul types clearly delineated and it is far more common to find a belief in souls that are mixed or have overlapping aspects of these. In fact, Elbert mentioned the "comprehensive immortal soul" as one that would be a unification of all four types.

The very fact that any definition of a soul can have at least as many aspects as Elbert offers demonstrates the problem of finding a single or universal definition of soul. A good example of this problem can be found with the ancient Egyptian understanding of soul in that, unlike most modern western definitions of the soul, the Egyptian one did not exclude the physical body. The whole point to the great expenditure on mummification of the dead body demonstrates this. The Egyptians believed that if the dead body was not in some manner preserved from destruction the various non-material aspects of selfhood, the "ba," the "ka," the spiritual aspect of the physical heart, the name (*ren*), and the shadow would be unable to retain any personal identity; therefore, they would either altogether cease to exist or, at best, would cease to have any meaningful existence.

When dealing with the modern day issue of the soul, a very careful distinction must be made between the Western (Judeo-Christian-Islamic) concept of it and the various Indian concepts of it, whether Hindu, Jain, or Buddhist. This is especially so when dealing with the issue of the retention of personal memories and personality traits which are of crucial significance to the Western mind, but not necessarily to the Indian mind.

The Western view of the soul generally envisions it as a permanent or eternally abiding carrier of an intensely personal identity (memories), which as a moral agent is itself the object of salvation. In the Hindu view, the soul is a never changing impersonal entity (*atman*) that is surrounded by a set of sheaths that contain the various changeable elements of individuality or personality.

When Buddhism, at least in theory, denies the whole concept of an eternal soul it is even denying the *atman* as a permanence entity. Buddhism in denying any eternal self factor says that the only thing that one could possibly identify with as a self is a subtle constantly changing compound. This position is based on the two Buddhist concepts of impermanence (S: *anitya*) of all conditioned things and the psychophysical aggregate (**Skandha**) nature of sentient bodies.

In both Western religion and non–Buddhist Indian religions a major characteristic assigned to the soul after immortality is that of autonomy. However, the early Buddhist canon points out that one should not associate anything called self with real autonomy. A person can not successfully command himself not to become sick, not to age, and not to die. In all of these the person is powerless or subject to forces other than a self. To believe otherwise is to be deluded, which leads to a life of painful frustration or *duhkha*. This lack of autonomy of soul (self) should not be confused with any kind of fatalistic **determinism** because Buddhism has always upheld the freedom and ability of each person to liberate his or her practical or conventional self.

From a Buddhist perspective to try to identify with any other impermanent autonomous-less worldly phenomenon as a self, or a self with anything that seems at least semi-permanent and semi-autonomous, only results in a false sense of security which guarantees the person still further frustration, anxiety and grief. This is the case, whether that semi-permanence is some concrete presently reality or some imaginary factor associated with eternalism such as God. This is why the Buddhist scriptures (S: *sutras*; P: *suttas*) say that any grasping after a theory of soul (self), hence egotism, is as defeating to the realization of **nirvana** (the real deathless) as is grasping after sensual pleasure.

While some Western critics have seen the idea of no-soul/-self (***anatman***) as a threat to morality, Buddhism has also pointed out that to believe in a permanent self is the basis of our efforts to benefit ourselves at the expense of others. To let go of this belief can lead to living a selfless and morally upright life.

Despite all the Buddhist belief in no-soul/-self it must be understood that Buddhism is not saying that there is no practical I or self that functions in the every day world. This temporary self is easily acknowledged by Buddhism, but only as a mortal and world dependent self versus any so-called eternal and autonomous self.

Clearly the standard Buddhist teaching of no-soul (self) seems in diametric opposition to the soul (self) beliefs of such Indian religions as **Hinduism** and **Jainism**, but this may be more the case on the surface than below it. The Jains have always held to the idea of individual souls that, upon final liberation from the material body lose all individual personality characteristics and ascend into a cosmic realm where they remain eternally in a state of extreme blissfulness.

In the Hindu **Upanishads** there is teaching about an eternal soul (self) or *atman* that is really a part of a universal soul (self) or **Brahman** or God. The goal in this Hindu view is to realize Brahman as impersonal beingness, consciousness and bliss. Having achieved such realization the soul upon death is liberated by being dissolved into the beingness of Brahman.

At a first glance nothing could be more different from one another than the Buddhist no (personal) soul (self), the Jain's very real, but absolutely isolated soul (self), and the Upanishadic universal, but impersonal soul (self). However, from a psychological perspective they may amount to more or less the same thing. All three deny the personal uniqueness and importance of the individual; each sees the illusion of individuality as the real source of suffering; and all three agree that once individuality is abolished enlightenment and liberation is guaranteed once and for all. Thus, both the Buddhist denial of soul (self) and the non–Buddhist affirmation of impersonal soul (self) might be seen as just two sectarian or dogmatic explanations of a single pan–Indian attitude.

The most obvious problem with the Buddhist rejection of a soul is that this ought to leave nothing that could be reborn into a new body. Yet standard Buddhism insists that such rebirth occurs. Because of this dilemma, as well as the religious requirement that East Asian people venerate the souls of their ancestors, folk Buddhism has more or less acknowledged the reality of a soul in all but name.

If all of the preceding were not enough to demonstrate that the common Western view of the soul, as requiring personal identity, is not merely a culturally relative view, then the issue of the multiplicity versus singularity of the soul should be a sufficient demonstration of such relativity. In many cultures the Western idea of a single unified soul is readily replaced with a dual or even multiple-soul. The Chinese, Eskimos, and most African peoples envision a concept of a duality of souls, while the earlier example of the ancient Egyptian "ba and ka," etc. is a multiple soul concept. This would appear to lead back to a minimal definition for the soul, namely, that it is the element of selfhood that is not annihilated with the death of the body. This, however, would still be misleading in that the various biblical understandings of the soul conflict even with such a minimal definition.

The earliest biblical concepts of the soul mention

it under the Hebrew term **nephesh** (Arabic: *Nafs*) which, while the body was alive, was the *nephesh hayyim* (breath of life) and when the body was dead it was the *nephesh met* (dead breath). But the *nephesh* as an animating force could also apply to God, Himself. However, when confined to mankind this *nephesh* was only distinguishable from the body by the fact that it could have some vague ghostly existence after the death of the body.

What is most important to understand is that the *nephesh* was never thought of as an inner essential self because the early Jews never conceived of a real self as something not in the physical body. In fact, in some cases the soul was regarded as synonymous with the person's blood, as in Deuteronomy 12:23. This, obviously, has little to do with what modern people envision as a soul.

The ancient Jews also referred to something called the **Ruah or Ruach** (Arabic: *ruh*) which is generally translated as **spirit**. Etymologically it implies air in motion, hence the wind or the breath. At times the terms *nephesh* and *ruah* are used interchangeably, but more often *ruah* was more closely associated with God than with man. In other words, *ruah*, rather than being the mere animating ability of the *nephesh*, could be understood as the creative power of God. Even when applied to a person *ruah* suggested a greater than normal, divinely supplied, energy or strength on the part of the person. This is most obvious when in the Old Testament it is written that the Spirit of God (*Ruah Elohim*) inspires men with great courage, wisdom, artistic genius, and prophecy.

When the Old Testament was translated into Greek its translators always equated *nephesh* with the Greek *psyche*, but rarely equated *ruah* with *psyche*. Most of the time *ruah* was translated as the Greek *pneuma* (spirit), which also had a connotation of wind and breath.

The definition as to what is and what is not the human soul, biblically, is further complicated by the fact that the person in the earliest parts of the Old Testament is dichotomic which is to say that of a two-fold body and soul. Only in the later parts of the Old Testament does the trichotomy of body, soul, and spirit making a significant appearance. In contrast, through the trichotomic influence of **Paul of Tarsus,** Christianity in general adopted a trichotomic view of man.

It is true that in the New Testament the *psyche* (soul) and *pneuma* (spirit) of the living person are often accepted as equivalent to one another, especially in the Gospels. However, in the writings of Paul, the *psyche* is never equated with the *pneuma*. This is because the *psyche* has had no natural or inherent capacity to survive death ever since the "Sin of **Adam**" deprived it of its original inherent right to immortality. In other words, the *psyche* is automatically bound to the body (*soma*) or flesh (*sarx*), but the *pneuma* is not; therefore, when something specifically concerning the human will or desire is implied *psyche* is the term that is exclusively used, as in Jude 19, where the term "*psychikos*" has been variously translated as "natural man" or "unspiritual."

The New Testament further makes it clear that when the spirit (*pneuma*) is withdrawn, the soul sleeps in a kind of suspended state until the messianic resurrection and final judgment of the dead. Some Christian theologians try to settle the soul to spirit relationship by proposing a distinction between a human spirit (*pneuma tou anthropou*) and the Spirit of God or Holy Spirit (*Pneuma Hagion*). Finally, it should be noted that despite what Christian orthodoxy demands, the "popular" Christian view of the human being is dichotomic, with the terms soul and spirit being synonymous. This is not due to a preference for an Old Testament view over a New Testament one, but a long held preference for the simpler classical Greek view of the person as a mortal body and an inherently immortal soul.

See also ***Amrita***; Arguments pro and con on an afterlife in general; Body-soul dualism; Chinese Religion and Reincarnation; Creationism, soul; Gender issue of the soul; Generationism and Traducianism; Greek afterlife, the ancient; Egypt; Individuality and rebirth; Infusionism; Kabbalah; Karma and justice; ***Linga Sharia***; Memories, ancestral or genetic; Memories, reasons for loss of past life; Memory, Episodic; Mental plane; Mind; ***Nafs* and *Ruh***; New Testament and reincarnation; Nusayris (Nursaris); Old Testament and the afterlife; Old Testament and the soul; Original sin, Christianity, and reincarnation; Pineal and pituitary gland; ***Pneumatikoi***; Population increase issue; Rebirth factor; Rebirth, qualifications for; Rebirth, simultaneous; Scientology; Soul, Fixed and Free; Soul and spirit levels, Theosophical; Soul, origin of the; Soul, tripartite; Soul's existence prior to embodiment; Trichotomy.

Soul and spirit levels, Theosophical. The Theosophical movement as started by **Helena P. Blavatsky** and others, as well as several of its offshoots, such as those of **Rudolf Steiner** and **Alice Bailey**, envisioned a seven level (septenary) esoteric body-soul-spirit system which is more complex than in most other metaphysical systems. Each of these individuals used slightly different terms for the various levels, which has lead to a fair amount of confusion between their respective systems.

The earliest of these septenary listings appears

to come from *Fragments of Occult Truth* by A. O. Hume in the *Theosophist*, Oct. 1881. Here they were listed from the lowest to the highest levels as physical body (*rupa*); vital principle or *jiv-atma*; **astral body** or ***linga sharia***; astral shape or ***kama rupa*** (body of desire); animal, physical intelligence, or consciousness of ego; higher or spiritual intelligence, or spiritual ego; spirit or the absolute. This listing was soon modified in the book *Esoteric Buddhism* by A. P. Sinnett, who gave the following order: *rupa* (physical body), *prana-jiva* (vitality), ***linga-sharia*** (astral body), *kama-rupa* (animal soul), ***manas*** (human soul), *buddhi* (spiritual soul), and *atma* (spirit). Various later theosophical listings included seven out of the following eight terms. These were the physical (body) *sthula sharira*; the **etheric body** or *prana*; astral body or *linga sharira*; mental body (*manas*); intuitional or *buddhi*; spiritual, nirvanic or *atmic*; monadic or *anupadaka*; and the divine or *adi*. Still another, though rarer, septenary version considered the fourth place *kama-rupa* as will- form, but placed the animal soul in fifth place with the translation of *linga deha* (body) . The sixth place had spiritual soul, which was translated as both ***atman*** and *mayavi-rupa* (illusory body); and in seventh place was spirit or *maha-atma*.

Taking into consideration the most common version, little needs to be said about the physical body (*rupa* or *sthula sharira*), but the others do needs some further explanation. The etheric body (*prana* or *prana-jiva*) is considered to be the basic animating factor for the physical body, which would be inanimate matter without it. Death then is the separation of the etheric body from the physical body. The astral body is sometimes called the dream body since it is thought to be able to partially divorce itself from the sleeping physical body and etheric parts and travel during that time, leaving us with our **dreams**. The astral body is also called the desire body, since it the seat of the emotional life. Shortly after physical death the etheric body dissolves which leaves the astral body free to reflect on the past life of the deceased person.

The *manas* is said to have a dual nature or a lower level and a higher level. It is the lower *manas*, which, while not directly partaking of embodiment, is able to transmit higher truth to the embodied levels. The term *buddhi* is from Sanskrit *budh* meaning "enlighten," as the word implies this is level of enlightened consciousness. The *atmic* is derived from *atma*, a shortened form of *atman* and is the self as one with the universal divine spirit, hence the deified self. The term *anupadaka* means "parent-less or self-existing" and *adi* means "the first or primordial."

In theosophical and related systems there seems to be agreement mostly on the lower two level names, and disagreement on all the names for the positions above those two. For example, the *linga sharira*, as noted above, is the equivalent of the astral body in some texts, yet other texts equate it with the much higher **causal body**. Also, the term *kama rupa* (desire body) which in some texts is the same as the astral body, in other texts is given the position just above the astral body and when this happens the *manas* is forced into the position allocated to the intuitional body. Likewise, the term *buddhi* may be used for the second to the highest rather than the as the fourth level; hence, it would be the equivalent of the spiritual body (spiritual soul); while the *atmic* may be used at the highest level in the sense of the divine as *atma*, rather than as a synonym for the spiritual level. There, at least, seems some agreement among most of these systems that the terms soul and spirit are not synonymous. The soul refers only to the lower level self, while spirit refers to the higher level self.

The terms etheric, astral, mental, and causal are also used by other New Age teachers less connected to **Theosophy**, such as John-Roger Hinkins, who in breaking away from the ***Eckankar*** movement, established his own Movement of Spiritual Inner Awareness Church.

See also **Astral travel; Buddhism, esoteric; Consciousness and Mind; *Devachan*; Id, ego, and superego; Kabbalah; Monad; Soul**.

Soul and rebirth in Ch'an and Zen Buddhism *see* **Rebirth in Zen**.

Soul cohorts. These are two or more souls who have lived and interacted with one another in one life and wish to continue that interaction into the next life by being reborn under circumstances that will maximize the chances for that continued interaction.

See also **Soul family**.

Soul, collective. It is believed by the most Western reincarnationists that only beings that have full self-awareness have individual souls and that each animal species, or maybe each genus of a non-self-aware animal, and possibly even plants, have a single collective soul. Presumably our pre-hominid ancestors also had only a collective soul, but upon our species evolving self-awareness that collective soul broke into individual souls. It should be noted that this would make it impossible for animals to be reborn as humans or humans as animals. This would also make it impossible to use the animal kingdom to solve the **population increase issue**.

This evolutionary view would also suggest that there was only one point in time that individual self-aware souls evolved out of the collective. This being the case, there should be only a very limited number of souls available for reincarnation. It would seem that the only way then to account for an increased population of souls would be through **soul-fission** or creation of new souls by God.

The term collective soul should not be confused with the term **group soul**, since in the collective there have never been any formerly discernable separate entities that make up that soul as is the case with a group soul.

See also **Creationism, soul; Ontological leap or ontological discontinuity.**

Soul creationism *see* **Creationism, soul**.

Soul Darwinism. This is the concept that there has been a gradual evolution of the human soul that parallels the evolution of the human body. Soul Darwinism has a distinct problem when it comes to the theory of reincarnation in that it ties the soul so tightly to a limited number of our ancestral bodies. Because of this tie there is no explanation for where the new fully evolved souls of the ever increasing human population come from. In other words, there is no surplus of souls in a spirit world to reincarnate.

See also **Generationism and Traducianism; Ontological leap or ontological discontinuity; Population increase issue; Rebirth and the scientific theory of biological evolution; Soul, collective; Soul, origin of the**.

Soul, external. This is the belief that the soul of a person, rather than residing within that person's own physical body, resides in a separate body external to the person. This external body can be an animal, more often than not, a wild one versus a domesticated one; a plant, especially a tree; or even an inanimate object, such as a weapon, tool, roof of the house, or an amulet. The person who has identified the residing body of his soul tries to be very careful about the safety of that body since it is believed that if it is harmed or destroyed, the same will happen to the person. James Frazer, in his *The Golden Bough* (1963) has a detailed chapter on this external soul concept. There is no information on whether or not an external soul can be subject to reincarnation.

See also **Ob Ugrians**.

Soul family. This refers to a group of companions with whom a person has shared past lives and, therefore, among which karmic ties have developed.

See also **Karma, family; Rebirth, consanguineous; Rebirth, group; Soul cohorts; Soul-siblings**.

Soul-fission. This is the idea that souls could actually split or duplicate themselves asexually like an amoeba. It is one of the proposed solutions to the **population increase issue**.

This solution, however, leads to several questions. (1) Do all souls divide or do only some souls divide? (2) Do souls automatically fission or do they do so only under specific circumstances and what would those circumstances be? (3) If only some souls divide, what determines which souls divide and do not divide? (4) Do souls divide during the **interim period** or in the embodied period?

This soul-fission concept could actually justify two or more persons claiming to have been the same person in a past life. In other words, it could account for the number of people claiming to have been Cleopatra or Louis XIV. In this regard, soul-fission would be similar to the **swarm of bees theory**. Soul-fission is not to be confused with **soul fragmentation**.

See also **Cleopatra syndrome; Embodiment, moment of; Generationism and Traducianism; Home, Daniel Douglas; Soul, collective; Soul, origin of the; Soul twins**.

Soul fragmentation. This is the idea that the soul can divide into two or more parts when reincarnating although at some point each of these parts will seek to reunite. In the mean time it is thought possible that one living person may meet another person unaware that they share the fragments of the same soul. One aspect of this theory is that when two or more of those formerly separately embodied souls reunite the person could have the recall-memory of two or more individuals that lived at the same time. Soul fragmentation is not to be confused with **soul-fission** in that in the latter case there is no reunification of the divisions.

See also **Hypnosis; Rebirth, simultaneous; Soul mates; Swarm of bees theory**

Soul, free *see* **American Indians; Australian Aborigines; Soul**.

Soul fusion *see* **Embryonic fusion**.

Soul groups. This term is not to be confused with the term **group soul**. Soul groups are said to be families of souls that may have up to thousands of individual members which in various manners support each other through the reincarnation process. It is further thought by some that these families are divided into smaller groups called tribes, which continually reincarnate around the same time and place. An even smaller and more intimate soul group would be smaller families with karmic ties.

See also ***Celestine Prophecy*; Karma, family; Rebirth, group.**

Soul imprinting *see* **Passing-Memories Adoption**.

Soul injection theory *see* **Ontological leap or ontological discontinuity**.

Soul intrusion. This is said to be the rather rare process whereby part of one person's soul, intentionally or unintentionally, intrudes into another person's soul. The cause of such an intrusion is thought to be due to some trauma experienced by one or both of the souls. It has been suggested that such an intrusion can last over several lifetimes causing much distress to both souls.

See also **Death trauma**.

Soul mates. This term has been used in a narrow sense to signify a relationship of only two souls that either are closely related to one another and/or in some manner interact with one another over many life times. The term also has a broader meaning of more than two souls in a relationship over many lives. The narrower sense of the term can be traced back at least as far as the romantic Greek myth mentioned in the *Symposium* of **Plato** that told the story of the division of all the primordial souls into pairs, which ever since have sought to find and reunite with one another. One of the lesser **arguments supportive of rebirth** is that the phenomenon of "love at first sight" is the immediate recognition between soul mates on their first meeting in new lives.

It should be emphasized that the romantic, even optimistic, nature of the Platonic story is far more a Western creation, than an Eastern one. In **Hinduism**, Buddhism, and **Jainism** rebirth is primarily a punitive condition caused by worldly desires, therefore, to wish that you and your mate be reborn to meet again is to wish that you and your mate suffer again. According to the rules of karma this well might happen, but not to the joy of either party. Also, there is nothing to prevent karma from bringing one into a "hatred at first sight" relationship. In short, karma is not given to romanticism.

Since in Christianity the **soul's existence prior to embodiment** is denied, there is no orthodox basis for a soul mates concept and certainly not in such a romantic form as the so-called "marriage made in heaven." However, the pagan Greek soul mate concept has a loose analogy in the Judeo-Christianity tradition by way of the biblical myth in Genesis 2:23, where God creates Eve out of Adams flesh (rib) after which Adam says, "Now this, at last —/bone from my bones,/flesh from my flesh?—/this shall be called woman [Hebrew: *ishshah*],/for from man [Hebrew: *ish*] was this taken." This is followed by the narrator's statement, "That is why a man leaves his father and mother and is united to his wife, and the two become one flesh." Using this biblical justification it can be seen how easy it was for the pagan Greek soul mate attitude to enter Christianity and even more so in Kabbalic Judaism where successful or unsuccessful marriages depend on finding one's soul mate.

According to the **Grace-Loehr Life Readings** true soul mates are, *Symposium*-like, the two halves of an originally undivided soul; however, while many people look for their soul mates, the two halves "purposely" do not come together very often because to do so makes their togetherness so satisfying that they lose the desire for further growth and development. To prevent this one mate remains un-embodied while the other is embodied.

Soul mates, in a broader sense, do not necessarily require that there be only two souls, or that the souls be those of lovers or to even be amicable. It can include three or more family members, friends, business partners, teachers and students, even enemies. It is also thought that such soul mates may not be present in every rebirth, but only in those where they are able to further fulfill their common destiny.

A number of past life memories have implied that a process of role reversal is often a significant aspect of soul mate relationships. This is where a present-life husband might have been a past life father, brother, or son. It is also, where the gender roles of husband and wife, mother and son, etc. may have been reversed.

The author Gloria Chadwick, in her *Reincarnation and Your Past Life Memories* (1988), divides soul mates into three categories — companion soul mates, twin soul mates, and twin flame soul mates. The first refers to persons that one has spent only a brief time with in a past life and who help one to accomplish a goal or to fulfill a specific purpose in this life because the soul mate did the same for them in a past life. Beyond this the bond between one and the other is not very strong. With a twin soul mate the bond is much stronger. These are persons with whom one has shared various lives of close friendship or family relationships. The strongest bond is between a person and his or her twin flame soul mate who is a soul mate in the truest way possible for, according to Chadwick, each person has only one such soul mate. This is the person who one falls deeply in love with at first sight and he or she reciprocates; however, a person does not meet a flame twin in every life. Even though both do not share all lifetimes together, together or separately both mates are working towards spiritually evolving in similar ways.

See also ***Anamnesis*; Cycle mates; Gender issue of the soul; Homosexuality and transsexuality; Karmic romances; Plato; Ramtha; Rebirth, East and West; Rebirth, group; Soul fragmentation; Soul groups; Soul twins**.

Soul-personality. Among some **Rosicrucians** man is considered to be composed of a mortal body; a reincarnating soul-personality; and an immortal, perfect, and non-reincarnating soul. The soul-personality suggests something like the Hindu reincarnating part of the soul, while the non-reincarnating part would be the equivalent of the *atman*.

Soul, psychology of. A psychological investigation of why people believe in a soul, or for that matter believe in spirits, gods, or God, goes back to at least to the early 19th century, but that investigation depended as much on philosophy as it did on science. This was even true of the early 20th century depth psychology of Freud and Jung. It has only been from the mid 20th century that sufficient understanding of the human mind has been achieved that this investigation came to be based upon more verifiable scientific data.

According to some psychologists one source of a soul belief is the "Agent Detection Factor," which is the tendency to assume the presence of an agent behind otherwise agent-less motions. It would seem that this factor was originally one of the survival mechanisms that we inherited from our prehistoric ancestors. If a caveman was out hunting and his peripheral vision detected motion it was ultimately safer to assume that it was related to an agent, such as a predatory animal, than to something as harmless as a bush bending in the breeze. If it was a bush he lost nothing; if it was a predator, he had a chance to defend himself. This agent detection factor means that the human brain is primed to presume the working of an agent (spirit, deity, etc) behind any number of events or occurrences in the world to which logic would not necessarily assign agency.

A second source of soul belief is due to our "causal reasoning." The human brain has the capacity and tendency to impose a chronological and cause-effect narrative on even the most obviously random events. We are very reluctant to accept apparently meaningless reasons for things that strongly affect our lives. In other words, we automatically ask "Why something happened?" and if we can not find an easy answer, we may very well, if only semi-consciously, invent a meaningful reason, even though it may not be complimentary to our self-image; for example, "It happened because of our breaking a taboo."

A third source of soul belief is a social intuition concept called the "Theory of Mind," also, known as "Folk-psychology." This is essentially our ability to assume the existence of minds other than our own, or more specifically, it is the ability to imagine oneself in another person's head. This may seem such a totally inherent ability as not to even need a specially labeled theory to remind us of it; but it is not as inherent as it at first seems. Severely autistic individuals are more or less incapable of imagining being in another's mental world, which is why they have such difficulties in managing any social relationships.

The ability to imagine oneself as if in another living person also allows one to imagine himself as existing outside of his own body, that is to say as a bodiless entity (soul or spirit). An extension of this folk-psychology makes it nearly impossible for a person to think about not being able to think; or in other words, impossible to conceptualize oneself as not existing.

Finally, it would seem that if to the elements of agent detection factor, causal reasoning, and theory of mind, we add the ability to vividly dream of the deceased, we have more than enough sources to not merely allow for, but to encourage, a belief in the post-mortem existence of the individual in some manner.

See also **Dreams; Dreams, lucid.**

Soul-siblings. These are two or more souls which were biological siblings in their past lives and still feel a bond even though they are not biologically related in their present life.

Soul, Stoic. In classical Greek Stoicism the soul was often regarded as a particle of God (*apospasma tou theu*). This view was later adopted by several forms of ancient **Gnosticism** and modern **Theosophy.**

Soul travel *see* **Astral travel; Essenes; Greek afterlife, the ancient; Hades; Plato**

Soul, tripartite. A number of cultures have viewed the soul as less of a unity and more of a composite. A belief in a composite soul of three parts was especially common in the Greco-Roman and later the Christian world.

Plato, in his *Phaedrus*, seems to have been one of the earliest recorded advocates of this tripartite concept. According to Plato's there is the lowest soul or appetitive soul (*epithumia*) that resides in the stomach or navel region and/or groin; the intermediary, passionate, or spirited soul (*thumos*) that is located in the heart; and the rational soul (*nous* or *to logistikon*) that dwells in the head. This scheme gave rise to the myth that the human body was specifically created by the divine with a narrow neck in order to isolate the rational soul from too much contamination from the other two souls. Also, it was only the rational soul that would undergo **metempsychosis.**

A somewhat later triad schema suggested by Plato is found in his *Republic*. In this there is a single soul that has three elements to it. The first of these is the appetitive element and this is responsible for the numerous demanding and yet conflicting desires of a person. The second is the judgmental element and this is responsible for rational thought. The third is the spiritual element and it is responsible for control of the appetite element and the longing for spiritual autonomy. Plato regarded these three aspects of the soul as being reflected in society at large. The general populace represented the appetite element, the statesman represented the judgmental element, and the army-police (in the ideal state) represented the spiritual element.

Modern democratic society might look strangely upon Plato's equating the higher spiritual aspect of the soul with the either military forces or police, but one's to remember two things about Plato. First, he was no lover of democratic rule, since he related it to the appetitive part of the soul; his political ideal was of an aristocracy (Greek: government of the best) of philosophers lead by a philosopher-king. Second, in Plato's ideal state the army-police would act as a benevolent source for order. However, Plato was an enemy of any kind of tyranny.

Plato is not the only source for a tripartite vision of the soul. **Aristotle**, in his *De anima*, divides the soul into the vegetable (*anima herba*), animal or sensitive (*anima bruta*), and human or rational levels (*anima humana*). The first is concerned with nutrition and growth, the second with sense experience and movement, and the third with rational thought. There seems to be some question as to whether Aristotle believed in the immortality of the soul, but if he did it was only of the rational part, the *nous*. This tripartite soul view of Aristotle is in keeping with the spirit of Plato's earlier soul view.

The Romans had an alternative tripartite soul. For them there was the *manes* that at death went either to the Elysium Fields or to **Tartarus**, the *anima* (spirit) that returned to the gods, and the *umbra* (shadow) that stayed near the deceased body.

A much later version of the tripartite soul is found in the **Kabbalah**. Here the lowest, vegetative, or life soul is the *nephesh*; the vital or speaking soul is the *ruah* (spirit); and the highest part of the soul, the rational soul, is called the *neshamah*. This third and highest soul level is sometimes described as the angelic or even divine aspect of the soul. There is a disagreement among Kabbalist writers as to whether all three parts of the soul undergo **gilgul** (**transmigration**) or only the first two levels. Later Kabbalists added two more levels to the soul making it a pentad. This, however, remained less popular than the three-fold soul.

The tripartite soul is not to be confused with the **trichotomy** of later Christianity, which views, not just the soul, but the whole person as a three-fold of body, soul, and spirit.

See also **Aquinas, Thomas; Augustine, Saint Aurelius; Old Testament and the afterlife; Old Testament and the soul; Zhen Dao.**

Soul twins. This term can refer to three different phenomena. First, in some metaphysical systems souls are thought, not only to be bisexual, but to have the capacity for temporary reincarnation in two separate bodies, each of a different sex. Second, this is where two souls are said to come into individualized existence, usually by being drawn out from the same part of the universal soul, at the same time. This creates a very strong bound between the two, although not as strong as **soul mates**, which are two parts of the same original soul-body. Soul twins, more so than soul mates, are thought by some to have no restrictions on their being contemporarily embodied. Third, there is considerable debate about the nature of the souls in identical twins, triplets, etc. as they develop in the womb. One view is that an embryo acquires a soul at the moment of conception, in which case two or more fetuses arising from the same embryo would have to either all share a single soul, or the original soul would have to undergo **soul-fission**, the division of an original single soul into two or more identical souls, one for each fetus.

In an alternate view, it is assumed that the fetus does not acquire its soul until some later intrauterine stage when such fission is no longer possible and the two or more fetuses are clearly individualized. A major current view is that such fission would cease to be possible somewhere between the end of the second and third week of gestation. An even simpler possibility would be that the soul does not taken on bodily form until the moment of birth or very shortly afterwards (postpartum). In these cases there would really be no reason to even speak of twin souls.

According to **Edgar Cayce**, Adam and Eve, and Jesus and Mary his mother were soul twins in the above first sense.

See also **Cycle mates; Embryonic fusion; Gender issue of the soul; Twins, identical.**

Soul, virgin. This term can imply either a soul never before embodied and/or a soul that has been so freed from material impressions as to be as pure as it was before its first embodiment.

Souls, complementary. This refers to souls that are so similar in temperament and personality as to be near copies of one another. Such souls are thought to travel through lives together, especially as twins or triplets.

Soul's existence prior to embodiment This is the belief that souls exists prior to any conception of an embryo; that souls existed prior to the physical evolution of mankind; or even that souls existed before the start of life on earth. Obviously, all versions of rebirth imply pre-existence in some manner, but all versions of pre-existence do not automatically imply rebirth. For example, the gospel of John clearly attributes pre-existence to Jesus (**John** 1:1–2, 8:58, and 17:24), but in none of these passages is **metempsychosis** suggested.

See also **Aetherius Society; Church Council of 553; Creationism, soul; Infusionism; Gender issue of the soul; Generationism and Traducianism; Kabbalah; Mormonism; Nemesius; Origin** or **Origenes Adamanthus; Pre-existiani; Scientology; Soul, origin of the; Unarius Academy of Science.**

Souls, fixed and free. The fixed soul is one that is regarded as essential for the maintenance of all normal physical processes of the body in which it dwells. The free soul is one that can leave and return to the body without a major disruption of the life processes. In many cultures it is believed that everyone has both kinds of souls with the free one being able to go and come during sleep or in shamanic trance.

See also **American Indians; Australian Aborigines; Dreams; Soul.**

Souls, multiple. In many cultures the soul is not considered to be a simple unified entity. Rather it may be composed of two or more independent parts. This concept was especially widespread among North American Indians, except in the Southwest area; and is also found among the **Ob Ugarins**.

See also **Chinese Religion and Reincarnation; Egypt; Nupe; Rebirth, simultaneous; Soul fragmentation; Souls; Swarm of bees theory; Zhen Dao.**

Soul, origin of the. Speculation on the origin of souls is of far less concern for Eastern religions than for Western ones. In **Hinduism**, Buddhism, and **Jainism** the origin of souls is pushed so far back into time that their origin is a mute point; moreover, these three traditions accept that animal souls can transmigrate into human bodies just as human souls can transmigrate into animal bodies. This further frees those traditions from speculating on the origins of souls.

Among many Westerner reincarnationists the issue of origins is not so easily avoided. Most Western advocates of reincarnation accept that souls may have pre-existed either since the beginning of the universe or at least prior to the evolution of the human body from that of the ape. This has given rise to the question, "What bodies, if any, did souls inhabit before the human bodies came into existence?" This question is especially problematic for those Western believers who reject the possibility of human souls ever inhabiting an animal form. One of the easier ways to answer this question is to inject some form of intelligent design (creator God) into the issue.

See also **Animals, domesticated; Animism; Creationism, soul; Fall of Souls; Generationism and Traducianism; Infusionism; Kabbalah; Karma and the moral structure of the universe; Ontological leap or ontological discontinuity; Population increase issue; Rebirth and the scientific theory of biological evolution; Soul, collective; Soul Darwinism; Soul's existence prior to embodiment; Soul-fission.**

Sowing and reaping *see* **Karma in the Bible?**

Spare, Austin Osman (1888–1956). Spare was a trance artist and occultist who claimed that his former lives as animals and humans, while deeply imbedded in his unconscious mind, were accessible through the trance state. Through his belief in reincarnation Spare came to the conclusion that humanity had the mystical purpose of an atavistic resurgence (tracing previous lives to their primal roots). This was to be done through the use of occult symbols (*sigils*) and a state of trance in which the person entered what he called "the Death Posture." That posture required a person to practice gazing at his or her reflection in a tall mirror until the image blurred and the person was unsure of the identity of the gazer. The eyes were then closed and light visualized. This, when done daily, could lead to a full and detailed knowledge of one's past lives.

Spare was influenced by **Aleister Crowley** and both the Astrum Argentinum and Ordo Templi Orientis in creating his own set of sigils. Spare also claimed possession by the artist William Blake, whose art he emulated.

See also **Trance states**.

Specific age spontaneous recall *see* **Spontaneous recall.**

Spirit. There are several possible definitions for this word. 1) This is a non-physical part of an embodied human being that many believe survives physical death, and may or may not be equated with the term **soul**. 2) This is a non-physical conscience entity that has never been embodied in human form such as in an angel and a demon (**daimones**). 3) In Christianity this is the part or aspect of God that connects Him to human beings, as in the Holy Spirit (*Hagia Pneuma*, or *Spiritus Sanctus*).

See also **Soul and spirit levels, Theosophical.**

Spiritism. In its broadest sense this term simply means a belief in spirits. In a far narrower sense it refers to a movement beginning in mid–19th century France in which there was the belief that it was possible for the living to communicate with the souls (spirits) of the deceased while the latter were in between embodiments (reincarnations). The ground work for the founding of French Spiritism was in place by the 1830s. By then an influx of religious ideas from Hinduism and Buddhism, a rise in socialism, a matching anti-clericalism, and a perception of a growing tension between Christianity and science made a significant portion of the French literati open to the concept of reincarnation. While there were other influential popularizers of this concept at this time it was one Jean Reynaud who cleverly reminded his listeners that reincarnation was part of the religion of the ancient **Druids** of pre–Romanized Gaul (France) and as such was part of the true spirit of that country. To say the least, Reynaud did everything he could to down-play some of the more primitive elements of ancient Druidism, such as polytheism and human sacrifice, so as to raise the level of cultural sophistication of the Druids to that of the ancient Greeks and to make it the moral equal of Christianity. For Reynaud one of the most important aspects of multiple lives was that it gave the individual the opportunity to progress spiritually in a parallel fashion to what society should be doing to create a socialist system of equality for all.

With the new rage for spirit communications arriving from the United States in the 1850s the second element of Spiritism was present and in the hands of Hippoltyte Leon Denizard Riail (1804–1869), better known by his pseudonym Allan Kardec, Spiritism was officially born. Riail took his pseudonym from what he claimed was his name in a previous life as a Druid in ancient Breton.

In developing Reynaud's views into Spiritism Kardec taught that many human psychological illnesses were not only the result of conditions in the present life, but leftovers from past lives. For this reason mediumship was useful in diagnosing these illnesses. In this sense Kardec is one of the fathers of **past life therapy**. In fact, it was this emphasis on past lives that more than anything else distinguished French spiritism from the majority of English and American Spiritualists who tended to reject reincarnation. This rejection was strong enough to encourage the famous Scottish medium **Daniel Douglas Home** (1833–1886) to claim that the post-mortem spirit of Kardec eventually denounced the belief in reincarnation.

Spiritism went through a rapid rise in popularity in France in the 1860s and 1870s, only to experience an equally rapidly loss of popularity in the 1880s and 1890s. Spiritism regained some of that influence in the 20th century, but less so in France than in Brazil, Cuba, and the Philippines under the name Kardecism.

Kardec's most famous written work is his *Le Livre des Esprits* (1856), published in English as the *Spirits Book* (1875). This was followed by the *Book of Mediums: A Guide for Mediums and Invocators* (1864), *The Gospel According to Spiritism* (1864), *Heaven and Hell: the Divine Justice Vindicated in the Plurality of Existences* (1865), *Genesis: The Miracles and Predictions According to Spiritism* (1867), *Experimental Spiritism and Spiritist Philosophy* (1881), and *The Four Gospels* (1881).

See also **Afro-American Religion; Kardecismo; Possession; Santeria; Scientology; Spiritism and the Catholic Church; Spiritualism; Umbanda.**

Spiritism and the Catholic Church. In response to increasingly unorthodox Christian practices in the second half of the 19th century the Catholic Church, in 1856 under Pius IX, condemned "Magnetism," the original term for hypnosis. In 1864 Rome condemned all attempts to communicate with the dead (Spiritism and Spiritualism); and in 1898 Leo XIII threatened to excommunicate anyone who acted as a medium or participated in such condemned activities. In particular, the church felt especially threatened by the spiritist view that through reincarnation no souls could ever be condemned to eternal punishment, since reincarnation obviously undermined the Church's interest in saving people from endless hell. For the most part the Church's attitude was that such spiritist views were the workings of the devil.

Spiritualism. In its original sense spiritism meant any belief that all reality is in essence spiritual rather than material. In this sense such diverse religious systems as Hindu Vedanta and Christian Science are forms of spiritualism. In the more recent sense spiritualism refers to the belief that spirits (souls) of the dead can communicate with the living, especially through a medium. In this sense spiritualism is a quasi-religious movement that had part of its roots in the teachings of **Swedenborg**, in mesmerism (hypnosis), and in a white American's romanticizing of American Indian religion.

The formal beginning of spiritualism was in Rochester, New York, in 1848 when the fifteen- and-nine-year-old Fox sisters first claimed that they were able to receive messages from the spirits of the dead. This claim started a movement that rapidly spread all over the United States and Europe. By the turn of the century the movement was in decline, but went through a brief revival after the First World War.

With such exceptions as the **Spiritism** of Allan Kardec, the spiritualism of the 19th century largely sought to accommodate itself to the standard

Christian view of a future resurrection rather than any kind of reincarnation. In fact, the National Spiritual Association of Churches (NSAC) in 1930 explicitly rejected the concept of reincarnation. Among the most famous of such spiritualists to endorse such rejection were **Andrew Jackson Davis**; **J.J. Morse**; and **Carl A. Wickland**. The (NSAC) opposition to the doctrine of reincarnation did not go completely unchallenged. In fact, it led to the founding of the reincarnation accepting **Independent Spiritualist Association of the United States of America** in 1924.

Many of the late 20th century spiritualist teachers, however, became more accepting of Eastern religious ideas, including reincarnation and karma. This is particularly true of the much modified form of spiritualism of the very late 20th century better know as Channeling.

See also **Aquarian Foundation; Blavatsky, Helena;** *Oahspe*; **Sciomancy; Summerland.**

Split brain. In some patients when the brain is surgically split in order to stop certain kinds of seizures the result is two separate mental states. Each half has independent memories, perceptions, and desires co-existing in the same person. This has led to the following question. If there is a soul that holds consciousness then why does the person's consciousness not remain unified, since presumably surgery can not split a soul? It may also be asked, if two consciousnesses then exist, which one would reincarnate as the person?

Spontaneous recall. This is recall of what are believed to be memories of a past life without the aid of hypnosis or other indirect or non-spontaneous methods. This is said to occur more often in children than in adults. It is also considered more reliable in children than adults since there is much less likelihood of such recall being contaminated by **cryptomnesia, fraud, honest lying, multiple personalities,** or **screen memories.**

On the other hand, there seems to be something that might be called specific age spontaneous recall. In this, a person suddenly begins to recall a past life only at an age in the present life that corresponds to the age in a past life at which something that was especially traumatic occurred. An example of such "anniversary recall" would be for a person at the age of thirty-five suddenly to recall a former life in which the person in that former life was killed at the age of thirty-five. It is believed that in the case of such anniversary recall the subconscious is encouraging us to remember, but only those memories which would be helpful to the present life.

See also **Artificial rebirth; Artificial (past life) recall; Bowman, Carol; Children remembering past lives;** *Déjà vu*; **Hypnotic age regression; Netherton Method; Reverie recall; Stevenson, Ian.**

Stags. Among the **Druids** the autumnal shedding and spring re-growth of the antlers of stages was one of the analogies from nature that suggested rebirth of souls.

See also **Rebirth, analogies from nature.**

Stake a claim. This is the concept that a soul, even before it is ready to become embodied, will choose its future body and do so in some way will ensure that another soul does not move in on its claim.

See also **Embodiment, moment of.**

Star of David or **Sign of Solomon.** This is the six pointed star which is composed of two overlapping triangles. From a reincarnationist point of view the two triangles represent the descent (rebirth) and ascent (death) of the soul.

Stearn, Jess. A prolific writer on life after death and reincarnation, Stearn's writings display a particular interest in the work of **Edgar Cayce**. Among these works are *Edgar Cayce: the Sleeping Prophet* (1967), *A Prophet in His Own Country: The Story of Young Edgar Cayce* (1974), and *Intimates Through Time: The Life of Edgar Cayce and His Companions Through the Ages* (1989). Among Stearn's other works are *The Search for the Girl with the Blue Eyes* (1968), *The Search for A Soul: Taylor Caldwell's Psychic Lives* (1973), *A Matter of Immortality: Dramatic Evidence of Survival* (1976), and *Soul Mates* (1984).

See also **MacIver, Joanne.**

Steiger, Brad. This author has written at least eight books on reincarnation either alone or with a co-author. These include *The Enigma of Reincarnation* (1967), *Other Lives* (1969), *You will Live Again* (1978), and *Discover Your Past Lives* (1987).

Steiner, Rudolf (1861–1925). In 1904 **Annie Besant** made the German born Steiner the head of "The Esoteric Society" for Germany and Austria, which was originally created in 1888 by **Helena P. Blavatsky,** independent of the Theosophical Society. In that same year Steiner also began to build his own esoteric society which had a more Egypto-Hermetic-Masonic Rosicrucian flavor than the more theosophically oriented Esoteric Society. In fact, what caused Steiner to break with **Theosophy** in 1907 was the latter's increasing drift into Eastern mysticism, which finally culminated in the proclaiming of Krishnamurti, as not only the reincarnation of the Hindu god Krishna and Christ but as the coming world Messiah. For Steiner there was no need for a new messiah because **Jesus** of Nazareth was the messiah to end all messiahs. In this regard Steiner rejected the Theosophical view that Jesus was just one of many great world teachers. Steiner believed that the spilled etherized blood of the Christ essence that took possession of Jesus and the resurrection of the etheric body of Christ Jesus had been slowly working to spiritually transform this world for the past 2000 years. The subordination of Eastern religions to esoteric Christianity can be seen in Steiner's belief that in the Gospel of **Luke** the angel that heralded the birth of Christ to the shepherds was the Buddha.

By 1914 Steiner's own esoteric society gave way to his new school which he called Anthroposophy (Wisdom of Man). In the mean time, Steiner was also involved with the occult group Mysteria Mystica Maeterna, an autonomous national section of the Ordo Templi Orientis, founded in 1896, and he also was involved with the closely related Order of the Illuminati.

Steiner claimed to be able to access the ***akashic records*** from which he learned about his own past lives and the true history of humanity. According to these records, human kind originally lived free of a material plane of existence, but in time fell into it and was trapped in what is the round of birth and death and it is freedom from this entrapment that the soul now seeks. To accomplish this freedom the soul must pass and evolve through the various zodiacal periods or processional years. Every 2,160 solar years, the time it takes for the sun to enter a new sign of the zodiac, is one processional year. From one of these years to the next the evolution of the earth is believed to be radically different. In this way each soul is reborn under a different astrological sign for at least every twelve lives or 25,920 years, after which the zodiacal cycle repeats itself.

It is also part of the human evolutionary process that a person must be reborn at least once in each sign, with the standard number being two times, once as a man and once as a woman. In fact, according to Anthroposophy, with some exceptions, there is a law of reincarnation that requires each soul to alternate in gender with each new life. Anthroposophy also advocates the evolution of latent spiritual awareness in order to contact a higher world composed of pure thought. It is through non-backsliding reincarnation that much of this evolution is advanced.

Steiner also believed that there were two sets of superior spiritual beings, the first worked to assist mankind in its evolutionary process, while the second were opposed to such progress. Since Jesus the Christ is considered to be one of these great supportive beings, Anthroposophy considers itself an Esoteric Christian Theosophy with a blending of Rosicrucianism, but at the same time a system of thought that puts man, not God, at the center.

Steiner seems to have further believed that the year 1899 was the dawn of a new age of light in which people would, in the not-too-distant future, begin to remember their past lives. In the meanwhile, in a series of lectures given in 1924, but not published until 1955–1966 as *Karmic Relationships: Esoteric Studies*, Steiner claimed that Charles Darwin was in a former life the 8th century Arab commander and conqueror of Spain, Gebel al Tarik; that the Caliph al Mamun (790–823) was reincarnated as the astronomer and mathematician Perre-Simon Laplace (1749–1827); and that the Abbasid Caliph Haroun al Raschid (764–809) reincarnated as Francis Bacon (1561–1626). In terms of his own rebirth Steiner is said to have believed that he was the reincarnation of the Medieval Christian theologian **Thomas Aquinas**.

Steiner offered a rather interesting idea about the purpose for mummification in **Egypt**. He said that the whole purpose of such elaborate preservation of the body was to prevent a new descent of the soul into a material body, which allowed the soul to remain indefinitely in the spirit world.

Steiner wrote some fifty books on reincarnation, the majority of which have been published by Anthroposophic Press. The headquarters of the Anthroposophical Society is in Switzerland.

See also **Ascended masters; Astrology and rebirth; Besant, Annie; Crowley, Aleister; Elijah; Fall of Souls; Finite or infinite number of rebirths; Kingsford, Anna Bonus; Lost continents and reincarnation; Moltke, Helmuth Graf von; Mummy, The; Population increase issue; Rebirth, non-backsliding**.

Stelle Group. This Illinois based group was founded in 1963 by Richard Kieninger (b. 1927), a former member of the **Lemurian Fellowship**. The same year the group was formed, *The Ultimate Frontier* (1963), written by Kieninger under a pen-name, Eklal Kueshana, was released. This book is said to be autobiographical and forms the basics of the Stelle teachings. In the book Kieninger claims that on his 12th birthday he was contacted by a Dr. White, the first of several mysterious persons. Kieninger was informed about his past lives, including ones as the biblical King David and Pharaoh Akhenaton, and that his mission was to found a new nation. Later that year Kieninger was given a secret name and told about the 12 Brotherhoods (five greater and seven lesser). Included in the teachings Kieninger received was knowledge of the angels and archangels such as Jehovah, **Lucifer**, and **Melchizedek**-Christ who created and ruled over the earth; the **akashic record**; the various planes of existence (physical, etheric, astral, mental, angelic, archangelic, and celestial); extraterrestrial beings;

the **lost continents** (Atlantis and Mu-Lemuria); **pyramidology**; the "Young **Jesus** in India Theory" and that all the traditional churches in the world were to be consider at best **Grey occultists** and at the worst priestly Black Mentalists, both in the service of the anti–Christ. In 1945, Dr. White further informed Kieninger as to the ideal community site which he and his students should establish. This became Stelle City, Illinois.

In *The Ultimate Frontier* it is predicted that at the end of the twentieth century a massive natural catastrophe leading to a rearrangement of the land masses would be triggered by the alignment of the planets in this solar system (May 5, 2000), but even the year before this there would be, in the form of an atomic war, the Battle of Armageddon as prophesized in Revelation, and less than a tenth of the world's population would survive into 2001.

Despite being the founder of the Stelle Group Kieninger was eventually forced out of its leadership due to charges of financial irregularities and sexual misconduct. In response Kieninger formed a new organization called Adelphi which he claimed was established to carry out "The Great Plan of the Brotherhood."

Stevenson, Ian (1918–2007). A psychiatrist with the University of Virginia, Stevenson was the most well known modern investigator of rebirth claims. Stevenson's interest in reincarnation may have initially stemmed from his mother's interest in **Theosophy**, which has been used to suggest that Stevenson's investigations were not as objective as they should have been. A major critic of Stevenson's research is Champe Ransom, a former assistant of Ian Stevenson. Ransom, as quoted in *Reincarnation: A Critical Examination* (1996) by **Paul Edwards**, faults Stevenson in a number of ways. First, there was Stevenson's tendency to ask **leading questions**; second, the question periods were too short for a thorough investigation; third, there was too much time having elapsed between the occurrences of past life recall and the investigation of them; fourth, the imaginative capacities of the children were not being well explored; fifth, there was a tendency on Stevenson's part to unintentionally "fill in" an investigated story to make it more complete; sixth, there was too much reliance on potentially biased witnesses; and seventh, there was the fact that in 90 percent of the researched cases the families of the recalling children had met with the families of the deceased before Stevenson's research began.

In actuality, Stevenson tended to avoid any out and out statement that his research proved reincarnation. Instead, he said that his research was highly suggestive of reincarnation. Perhaps to lessen any suggestion that his work had a religious bias Stevenson implied that his cases of likely reincarnation had shown no relationship to karma.

Stevenson published more than a dozen works on reincarnation. Among his most well know are *Twenty Cases Suggestive of Reincarnation* (1966), *Unlearned Languages: New Studies in Xenoglossy* (1984), *Children Who Remember Previous Lives* (1987), *Where Reincarnation and Biology Intersect* (1997), and *European Cases of the Reincarnation Type* (2003).

See also **Extrasensory perception; Grant, Joan; International cases; Karma; Male births, greater proportion of; Pasricha, Satwant K.; Possession; Proof of Rebirth, Criteria;** *Psychophore*; **Rebirth and cultural conditioning; Rebirth, proximity; Uttar Pradesh.**

Stygian sexuality (Sexuality beyond the River Styx [River of Death], the most well known of the five mythological rivers of the ancient Greek underworld). This is a metaphor for the sexuality that is said to be evidenced between disembodied souls or spirits. Another term for such post-mortem sexuality is second state sexuality, as identified in *Journeys Out of the Body* (1973) by Robert A. Monroe. Stygian sexuality is not to be confused with necrophilia, which is a living person having sex with a corpse, or with spectrophilia, which is a living person having sex with the spirit of a deceased person or other spiritual entity. Presumably, stygian sexuality means that two entities in the **interim period** could have a sexual relationship which implies that the soul possesses gender between death and birth.

See also **Boullan, Joseph-Antoine; Gender issue of the soul**.

Subconscious, mystifying of. Many proponents of reincarnation claim that past life memories survive death by being stored in the subconscious, which of course means that the subconscious mind must survive death while the conscious mind does not. There is, however, no scientifically logical reason for assuming that the subconscious can in any way exist independently from the conscious mind, much less independently from the whole body-brain complex. Even if this were possible, reincarnationists seem to ignore the fact that the term subconscious is far more often associated with the primitive aspects of the brain (i.e. the reptilian and the mammalian), rather than the higher human levels of the conscious mind. For the advocates of a survival of the subconscious to avoid the **body-brain (mind) dependency** of the subconscious they have to mystify that mind level and then metaphysicalize it into a substitute soul. It would be far less open to criticism to just attribute any survival of memories to a completely metaphysical, hence religious, factor such as a soul, than to try to seem more psychological, hence scientific, in arguing for such survival.

Subtle body. This is the collective name for all the proposed psychic bodies surrounding the physical body.

See also **Astral body; Causal body; Etheric body;** *Linga Sharia;* **Soul and spirit levels, Theosophical.**

Sufism. Although some orthodox Islamic authorities consider Sufism in general as unorthodox, other Islamic authorities accept the more conservative Sufi Schools as orthodox. One of the main characteristic that separate these two versions of Sufism is that the more orthodox reject reincarnation (***tanasukh***) while the less orthodox accept the Neo-Platonist belief in *tanasukh.*

See also **Ahmadiyya; Druzes; Indonesia; Islam; Neo-Platonism; Passing-Memories Adoption.**

Suggestion and past life regression *see* **Past life regression and suggestibility.**

Suicide *see* **Rebirth and suicide.**

Summerland. Among advocates of spiritualism this is the name for heaven, which was believed to be either within the **Milky Way** or just beyond it. It is believed that here all the spirits sooner or later will reside for an indefinite period. Among Neo-Pagans Summerland is where souls temporarily dwell in between embodiments. In other words, for them it is only an **interim period** place of rest.

See also **Astral plane;** *Devachan;* **Diakka.**

Supernatural-in-the-gap process. This process occurs when a non-scientific explanation such as God, karma, etc. is inserted in a present-day gap in scientific knowledge.

See also **Current knowledge discrepancy; Lost continents and reincarnation; Planets, other; Rebirth and science.**

Suras (Arabic: Writings) *see* **Doceticism; Islam; Islam; Judgment of the Dead.**

Surya-marga. In Hinduism this means path of the sun and is the name for the spiritual road taken by those souls that are liberated forever from rebirth as opposed to the **moon** path which leads to a rebirth.

See also *Pritiloka.*

Sutphen, Richard ("Dick," 1937–). Sutphen is the founder of the new age organization called the Valley of the Sun. He has been a strong opponent of fundamentalist Christianity and advocates the unity of all religions as well as belief in reincarnation and karma. He supports such practices as meditation, the use of the pendulum, and automatic writing. Sutphen was the founder of Reincarnationists, Inc., in 1982, which, until its demise in 1987, published *Reincarnation Report*. In 1983 Sutphen married Tara Sutphen who, through automatic writing, began channeling a spirit named Abenda.

Sutphen has authored and co-authored a number of books on reincarnation. One of these is *Past Life Therapy in Action*, co-authored with Lawrence Leigh (1983). Also, Tara Sutphen, with the help of Abenda, wrote the book *Blame It on Your Past Lives: Personal Problems and Supernatural Solutions* (1992).

See also **Channeling; Walk-ins.**

Sutratman (Thread of the *atman*). In **Hinduism** this is the part of the self that goes from one life to another like beads on a thread.

See also *Kosha; Linga Sharia.*

Swarga or *Svarga*. Meaning Good Kingdom, this is the general name for heaven in **Hinduism**, and more specifically the name for the heaven of the storm and warrior god Indra. Dwelling here are the lesser gods and beatified mortals, but even for the souls that have earned time in this heaven those souls will eventually be drawn back into the rebirth cycle.

See also *Vaikuntha.*

Swarm of bees theory. This is the theory that the soul is actually a collective of particles like a swarm of bees. At death the collective (swarm) breaks up and the numerous particles go their separate ways in search of rebirth into a new body with which it will share other particles that formerly belonged to different collectives. It is this changing collective nature of souls that is said to account for a number of people remembering the same former life. In other words, most of the people who claim to have memories of being Marie Antoinettes, Alexander the Great, or **Napoleon Bonaparte** do have such memories because the various particles that comprised such person's soul reincarnated separately in numerous people. Thomas Edison is credited with suggesting this theory.

See also **Cleopatra Syndrome, Home, Daniel Douglas; Population increase issue; Rebirth, simultaneous; Soul-fission; Soul fragmentation; Souls, multiple.**

Swastika or **Svastika.** Meaning "well-being" or "good fortune," this image is also called the fylfot cross and is one of the most widely used symbols in the world. It is found on most continents and its appearance extends back beyond recorded history. It appears, more than anything else, to be a symbol of the movement of the sun, and hence of fire and light. As a symbol of enlightenment legend has it that it was engraved on the souls of the Buddha's feet at birth. It is also often found on the exposed chest of images of the Buddha and is used in East Asia on maps to designate the location of Buddhist temples.

In **Jainism** the swastika is a symbol that represents the movement of the soul in the round or cycle of existence. The four arms of this symbol represent for the Jains the four possibilities of rebirth: the realms of humanity, animals, hell, and heaven. The Nazi's corrupt employment of the symbol ultimately derives from its use in ancient Germanic paganism.

See also *Bhavachakra*; **Christianity, esoteric; Ouroboros; Possession; Spiritualism.**

Swedenborg, Emanuel (1688–1772). This famous Swedish mystic in 1743 began to have visions of **heaven, hell, Jesus,** Satan and God that differed in major ways from orthodox Christianity. In none of these, however, was there any place for the belief in reincarnation. In fact, Swedenborg was of the opinion that what might be thought of as a reincarnating entity was actually an **attached entity.** Some reincarnationists in an attempted to discredit Swedenborg, have pointed out that in some of his visions he saw and described the inhabitants of the other planets in our solar system.

Symbola (Greek: passwords). In **Orphism** these were words, phrases, or sentences that were written on gold leaves and buried with the dead and which were believed to assist the soul to enter paradise, thus escaping rebirth.

Symposium *see* **Gender issue of the soul; Plato; Soul mates.**

Synchronicity. This is a more scientific term for particularly meaningful occurrences without any apparent cause, or in common English, amazing coincidences. An example of such synchronicity would be when two **soul mates** were not only born about the same time, but met each other at what seems like just the most appropriate time.

See also **I, William the Conqueror; Kennedy, John F.**

Synesius of Cyrene (370–415?). This Christian bishop of Ptolemais, Libya was also a Neoplatonic philosopher. Before answering the call to be a bishop, Synesius freely published philosophical views which were not fully in accord with standard Christian teachings. In particular, he cited differences of opinion regarding the relationship of the soul to the body and the resurrection. Among his written works was the *Aegyptus sive de providential* (*Egypt or On providence*) in which he appears to have affirmed a belief in **metempsychosis.**

See also **Christian fathers critical of reincarnation; Neoplatonism.**

T'ai-Yueh-Ta-Ti (WG). In the Chinese heaven things run like a civil service and T'ai-Yueh-Ta-Ti (Great Emperor of the Eastern Peak) is one of its bureaucrats; in fact, he is the chancellor and second-in-command among the heavenly figures. T'ai-Yueh-Ta-Ti looks after the affairs of both men and animals, and besides determining births, deaths, marriages, and the number of children to be had, he registers good and evil deeds and their appropriate retributions during and after death. In other words, he is associated with fate (fortune, destiny), and karma. He is also called Tung-Yueh-Ta-Ti and T'ai-Yo Ta-Ti.

Talbot, Michael. The author of *Your Past Lives: A Reincarnation Handbook* (1987), Talbot describes step-by-step exercises and techniques to explore a person's past lives.

Tanasukh (Arabic: to copy, in the sense of from life to life). This term has three different meanings. First it can mean the **evolutionary transmigration of souls** (mineral to plant to animal to human to transhuman). Second, it can refer to ordinary reincarnation from one human life to another human life. Neither of these is acknowledged in orthodox **Islam** and the second is even regarded as a clear heresy. Nonetheless, some Shiite sects believe in one or both of these, as do many Muslims in India and **Indonesia**. The third meaning of *tanasukh* is the Shiite belief that the soul of the supreme religious leader, the Imam, reincarnate several times in a kind of ***tulka*** fashion. Among the Isma'ilis Shiites it was believed that souls could not be reborn until released by their Imam (secret or hidden spiritual leader).

Tanasukh is never to be confused with *hulul* which means descent or incarnation of the divine into human form, and is considered the heresy of heresies in orthodox Islam; and the minority of Shiites who believe in it are considered *ghulat* (extremists).

See also **Dabistan; Druzes; Neoplatonism; Nusayris (Nursaris); Sufism; Yarsanism; Yazidis (Yezidis).**

Tantrism. This esoteric teaching is found in both a Hindu and a Buddhist form. The teaching regards itself as the quick way to liberation from rebirth through the power of sacred or magical rituals. This is in contrast to the non-esoteric Hindu and Buddhist paths which often require a long series of rebirths dedicated to the purifying or extinguishing of the passions through ascetic practices.

The justification for Buddhist Tantric teachings is based on the Age of Dharma Decline Theory.

Early Buddhism had taught that the true Dharma would eventually fall on hard times and enlightenment would become more and more difficult for the average practitioner, until no one would be capable of realizing release through the original ascetic path taught by Shakyamuni (the Buddha). It was for this reason that the esoteric path was finally revealed after having been kept in secret reserve up until the time of decline.

Since Tantric Buddhism had several centuries of development it naturally went through a number of phases before its present state. Chinese Tantrism (Chen-yen) and Japanese Tantrism (Shingon) represents mainly the earlier phases of Tantrism, while the Central Asian or Tibetan-Mongol, Tantrism (**Vajrayana**) represents the later phases; nonetheless, all forms teach what they consider an accelerated esoteric path to liberation from the cycle of rebirth and re-death.

See also **Antinomianism; Bardo; Buddhism, esoteric; Vajrayana Buddhism; Vegetarianism; Vijnanavada (Consciousness only) School.**

Tanya (Aramaic: It was taught). This is the more common name for the *Likkutei Amarim* (*Collection of Statements*) published in 1797. In this work by the Hasidic master Sh'neur Zalman of Laydi *gilgul* (reincarnation) is offered as an explanation for conversions to Judaism. According to the text, those converts are really Jewish souls trapped in non-Jewish bodies who have found their way back to Judaism. According to the *Tanya* and based on the account in Exodus that there were six hundred thousand "souls" present at Mount Sinai that is the number of root Jewish souls, which since then have split, spread out, and reunited in the millions of Jewish bodies over the generations.

See also **Kabbalah**.

Taoism *see* **Daoism**.

Tarot cards. The Tarot deck is divided into Fifty-six Minor Arcana or suit cards, and twenty-two Major Arcana or tarot proper cards. The former is roughly the same as a modern deck of playing cards except for its four extra cards royal cards (Pages). It has been suggested that there is a connection between the Tarot and the "**Kabbalah**"; however, this is entirely due to the belief that the twenty-two letters of the Hebrew alphabet appear to be related to the highly symbolic twenty-two Major Arcana cards.

Some tarot cartomancers (diviners by cards) are said to be able to read a person's past life or lives through the cards. For example, the Major Arcana card "Justice" is thought to focus on a person's karma, while the Wheel of Fortune card is recommended for **Past life recall meditation**. On the other hand, some taroists regard the Temperance card as dealing with reincarnation, especially in its symbolism of pouring one liquid (life/soul) from one vessel (body) into another vessel. Even the colors of the vessels, one either red (earth) or silver (moon) and the other purple-violet (heaven) or yellow (sun) are said to represent this back and forth movement of the soul. This association of the Temperance card with rebirth has also been encouraged by the fact that the classical Greek word for such a pouring act is metagiosmos which is then associated with **metempsychosis**.

All the relationships between the tarot and past life are, in the sense of the psychology of **Carl Jung**, said to be due to the images in the Major Arcana representing **Archetypes** stored in the **Collective Unconscious**.

Among the works on the tarot and reincarnation and karma are the *Karmic Tarot: A New System for Finding Your Lifetime's Purpose* (1988) by W. C. Lammey; *Past Life and Karma Tarot* (2004) by Edain McCoy; and the *Tarot of Reincarnation* (2007) by Massimiliano Filadoro.

See also **Hermetic Order of the Golden Dawn; Past life readings; Phoenix Cards; Scrying.**

Tartarus. For the ancient Greeks this was the deepest and worst part of hells (the **Hades** beneath Hades) and it was reserved mainly as a place to confine and punish various Titans, gods, and those human souls which were so evil that instead of rebirth were condemned to endless punishment.

See also **Essenes; Greek afterlife, the ancient; Hades; Peter, 1st and 2nd; Plato; Soul, tripartite; Virgil**.

TAU. According to **Alice Bailey** in her *A Treatise of White Magic*, TAU is the power sound which symbolizes reincarnation.

Taylor, Thomas (1758–1835). This great English Platonist openly rejected Christianity as "bastardized and barbarous" and publicly admitted to a personal worship of the old classical Greco-Roman deities, as well as to a belief in reincarnation. He is regarded as one of the founders of the non–Druid wing of the Neo-pagan revival.

See also **Neo-pagan religions**.

Techiyat Hameitim. This is the Hebrew phrase for revival or resurrection of the dead and not to be confused with *gilgul* (reincarnation).

See also **Resurrection, bodily**.

Teleological presumption. This presumption is that either nature itself or some intelligence behind nature (e.g. God) has as its ultimate creative goal the creation of rational beings. Once this presumption has been considered valid it is easy to further presume that inherent to this rational beingness is a continuation of that beingness after death.

The first part of this dual presumption is the basis of intelligent design theory which seeks to challenge the Darwinian evolutionism or Natural Selection which denies any teleological aspect to nature and her evolution. The second part of this teleology presumption can be used to support either the concept of resurrection or reincarnation.

Telepathy (telegnosis) with the living. This is said to be the ability of one living person to read the thoughts produced by another living person. It is one of the psychic abilities that are sometimes suggested as accounting for what otherwise might be thought of as an indication of past life recall. H. N. Banerjee argues that most subjects who have experienced past lives generally demonstrate no more telepathic abilities than an otherwise ordinary person; thus, he believes a telepathic explanation for the reincarnation phenomenon is largely invalid.

Telepathy is also a problematic explanation in the case of the children who seem to remember a past life. To create the sometimes elaborate set of memories of the past life those children would have to telepathically "chose" from the memories of a several adults, and then do so very selectively so as not to recall the wrong lives.

See also *Déjà Vu*; **Psychometry; Rebirth, alternative explanations to; Telepathy with the dead.**

Telepathy with the dead. This has been suggested as one of the possible sources for so-called past life recall. One problem with such a telepathic explanation, especially with regards to children, is that those who are thought to demonstrate mediumship abilities show those abilities almost in every case while in some form of altered state of consciousness (trance); but all the children studied recalled the past in a normal state of consciousness.

See also **Rebirth, alternative explanations to; Telepathy (telegnosis) with the living.**

Templars. This is the abbreviated name of a medieval Catholic monastic military order whose full name was the Poor Knights of Christ and of the Temple of Solomon. The order was established by some French knights around 1119/1120 in Jerusalem after the city's conquest during the First Crusade. Thanks to large charitable donations offered to the order over the years the order became extremely wealthy. The Templar's wealth and secrecy came under criticism and enabled the king of France, who coveted their wealth, to charge the order with heresy, sodomy, and blasphemy and to persuade the Pope to abolish the order in 1312.

In modern times the various mysteries surrounding the Templars have given rise to diverse claims of the order being the ancestor of Free Masonry and the **Rosicrucians**, and to having a belief in reincarnation. However, during the various trials for heresy that the Templars underwent there was never any accusation of a belief in **metempsychosis**; so it is highly unlikely that the order held to such a belief.

See also **Ordor Templi Orientis; Solar Temple, Order of.**

Ten Dam, Hans. This author's book, *Exploring Reincarnation: The Classical Guide to the Evidence for Past Life Experiences* (2003), has a very extensive bibliography on the subject of reincarnation. It covers some Dutch, German, French, Italian, Spanish, and Portuguese language sources, as well as English.

Termas see Bardo.

Tertullian (155/160–220? CE). This Church Father's full Latin name was Quintus Septimius Florens Tertullianus. He is thought to have been the first Christian theologian to question the logic of **metempsychosis**. In his *De Anima* (*Treatise on the Soul*) he applies both the **age factor and rebirth** and **population problem issue** arguments against metempsychosis. With regards to the later argument Tertullian was especially critical of **transmigration** of animal souls into human bodies.

See also **Animals and rebirth, Western view; Christian fathers critical of reincarnation; Christianity and reincarnation; New Testament and reincarnation; Transmigration, progressive.**

Theodicy. This Greek derived term means "divine justice." It refers to the attempt to explain why there is evil in the world if ultimately the world was created and is ruled by a loving, or at least just, deity. In the Western religious claim that God is all good the presence of evil has always been a major problem. This is especially true when it comes to the suffering of presumably innocent people whether at the hands of other people or natural catastrophes. In the Old Testament this seeming contradiction is most fully explored, but not resolved, in **Job**. Christianity makes a questionable attempt at explaining the problem of evil by placing all the blame on humanity through the doctrine of **Original Sin** and countering the problem of the innocent suffering by the **deferred payment plan** (for the Soul).

In religions that acknowledge rebirth and karma **blaming the victim** leaves no need to account for injustice in anyway that includes God. In other words, theodicy is not a problem in Buddhism, **Hinduism, Jainism**, and **Sikhism**.

See also **Arguments supportive of rebirth; Job 1:20–21; Kabbalah; Karma and justice; Weber, Max.**

Theophilus (?–412 CE). This Christian patriarch of Alexandria, Egypt was violently intolerant of all non–Christian beliefs. He is most infamous for two of his actions. First, it was he, with permission the Roman emperor Theodosius I (379–395), who destroyed the pagan temples of the gods Mithra, Dionysus, and Sarapis. This included the burning to the ground of the Sarapeum library in 391 with its irreplaceable collection of classical Greco-Roman literature.

Second, Theophilus was one of the earliest Christian theologians to attack the views of **Origin**, who supported the Platonic, hence pagan, idea of the **soul's existence prior to embodiment**. These two actions almost certainly began the as yet unofficial Christian condemnation of **metempsychosis**.

See also **Christian fathers critical of reincarnation; Christianity and reincarnation; New Testament and reincarnation; Platonism;** *Pre-existiani*.

Theory of Mind *see* **Mind, Theory of.**

Theosis. This is a synonym for deification. It is the call to man to become God-like. One of the arguments for reincarnation is that this is the ultimate goal of humanity and the only way for any individual to achieve this is to have many life-times to perfect one's soul to this end.

The most unambiguously supportive statement of *theosis* in the New Testament, or anywhere else in the Bible, is 2nd **Peter** 1:3–4 which reads, "His divine power has bestowed on us everything that makes for life and true religion, enabling us to know the One who called us by his own splendor and might. Through this might and splendor he has given us his promise, great beyond all price, and through them you may escape the corruption with which lust infested the world, and come to share in the very being of God." 2nd Peter goes on in verses 5–7 to state the standards for such sharing "...in the very being of God" would require. These are to have faith [in the promise], virtue, knowledge [of the divine], temperance, patience, godliness, brotherly love, and divine love. It is argued by some Christian reincarnationists that for the average believer to meet such heroic standards would require more than one life and that requirement "indirectly" proves that 2nd Peter is subtly acknowledging reincarnation.

See also **Rebirth and moral perfection; Resurrection or reincarnation.**

Theosophy. This school of thought derives its name from the Greek *Theo-sophia*, meaning Divine-wisdom. In the most general sense of this term Theosophy is the belief that truly authentic knowledge of God comes, not through reason or the senses, but through a direct mystical insight or experience. Along with this mystical aspect, most forms of Theosophy also favor esotericism, occultism, and pantheism, or some other form of monism. In this sense the teachings of **Pythagoras, Plato**, various Gnostic and Neoplatonists teachers, and even a number of Medieval and Renaissance Christian, Jewish, and Islamic mystic could be considered Theosophists.

In the narrower sense of the term Theosophy is the esoteric system of teachings founded by **Helena Blavatsky**, Colonel Henry Steel Olcott, and **William Q. Judge** in 1875. This system, as represented by Blavatsky's book *Isis Unveiled* (1877), revolved around Egyptian Gnostic and **Rosicrucian** works with some influence from **Hinduism**. Soon, however, a more Hindu-Buddhist influence came to dominate Theosophy as represented in Blavatsky's *The Secret Doctrine* (1888). While it is questionable whether the first book dealt with reincarnation and karma, the second one clearly did, and this lead to a major revival of interest in the concept of reincarnation.

The impact of Theosophy, however, went well beyond that of groups that officially identify as theosophical. It led to a resurrection, at least in name, to several Rosicrucian groups, and to the development of the Anthroposophy of **Rudolf Steiner**; the **I Am Movement**, and the **Liberal Catholic Church, Province of the United States**, etc. Each of these accepted the concept of reincarnation.

See also *Akashic* **Record; Apollonius of Tyana; Aquarian Foundation; Arcane School; Ascended masters; Astral plane; Besant, Annie; Chnoumis (Chnouphis); Church Universal and Triumphant;** *Devachan*; **Dhyani Chohans; Ego; Egypt; Eighth sphere; Esotericism versus Occult; Etheric body; Gnosticism; Higgins, Godfrey; Kabbalah; Khepra; Kingsford, Anna Bonus; Limbo;** *Linga Sharia*; **Lords of Karma; Lost continents and reincarnation; Lost soul; Lucifer;** *Manas*; **Mental plane; Moon; New Age; New Testament and reincarnation;** *Open Court*; **Planes of existence, names of; Rebirth and cyclical time; Rosicrucians; Saint Germain;** *Samma Sambuddha*; **Second death; Silent watchers; Sinnett, Alfred Percy; Steiner, Rudolf; Stevenson; Ian; Yeats, William Butler; Zoroastrianism.**

Therapeutic value of past life therapy *see* **Past life therapy.**

Theravada Buddhism. This is the Buddhism of the south Asian countries of Sri Lanka, Myanmar

(Burma), Thailand, Laos, and Cambodia. This form of Buddhism has retained many more of the earliest Buddhist traits than has the **Mahayana Buddhism** of East Asia or the **Vajrayana Buddhism** of central Asia. Among these earlier traits is a rejection of an **interim period**.

See also **Buddhism; Merit, transfer of; Monism**.

Theta (1). This is the bulletin published by the Psychical Research Foundation.

See also **Associations and organizations; International Association for Regression Research and Therapy; Thanatology**.

Theta (2). According to the entity Alexander, as channeled through Ramon Stevens and reported in *Earthly Cycles* (1994), theta is the third postmortem level into which the disembodied soul must pass before attaining bodily rebirth. The other levels are **Omega** and **Astral plane**.

Theta (3) *see* **Scientology**.

Theta waves. These are the brain waves associated with the twilight state, Dreams, and creative thinking. It is claimed that spontaneous psi (psychic phenomenon) has been associated with these waves and that there may be some relationship between them and past life recall.

See also **Hypnotic age regression**.

Third and fourth generation, punishment to *see* **Exodus**.

Third eye. This is believed to be a spot in the middle of the forehead just above the normal eye level that is a focal point for psychic powers. In Sanskrit it is called the *dyoya-drsti* and in Indian thought it is sometimes linked with both the sixth **chakra**, called *ajna*, and the pineal gland, which is found just below the front mid section of the brain. Practitioners of Kundalini Yoga claim that if one can raise the *kundalini* (psychic) energy to this level all past karma can be destroyed. Also, some advocates of rebirth believe that if the soul is able to leave the body upon death through this *chakra* it need never again be reborn.

Since the pineal gland is sometimes associated with this occult eye it is sometimes called the pineal or parietal eye. Other names for it are the Eye of *Dangma* (Purified Soul), the Eye of **Shiva**, and the Eye of the Buddha. Buddhists often equate this third eye with the *urna*, which is a small circle of hair that is said to grow at this chakra spot on all Buddhas. The early western authority on the *chakra* system, Arthur Avalon (Sir John George Woodruff), called this psychic spot the *Juanachakrasha*.

See also **Nine doors; Rampa, Lobsang Tuesday; Pineal and pituitary gland**.

Thirty-three years *see* **Interim period**.

Thoth, Book of. This legendary book is named after Thoth, the ancient Egyptian ibis-headed god of writing, mathematics, and of knowledge, especially of the esoteric kind. *The Book of Thoth* actually refers to at least three different works.

The first is a legendary book (scroll) containing powerful spells and knowledge, said to have been buried in a princely tomb in the City of the Dead. The reader, even though he was dead and in the world of ghosts, could come back to the earth in the form he once had. On the other hand, anyone unauthorized who read the book was punished by the gods.

The second *Book of Thoth* is the *Eine Einweihung im Alten Agypten nach dem Buch Throth* (*An initiation in ancient Egypt according to the Thoth Book*, 1922) by Woldemar von Uxkull. Among the themes encountered in Uxkull's work are the theory that Egyptians had their origin in Atlantis, an extensive **pyramidology** mysticism, and reincarnation.

Since the late 18th century, beginning with some French occultists, the **Tarot**, especially the major arcana, has also been called the *Book of Thoth*. In fact, the tarot deck and the book that goes with it by **Aleister Crowley** (1944) is specifically called the *Book of Thoth*, but this work has more to do with the Kabbalah than with reincarnation.

See also **Cayce, Edgar; Egypt; Hermetic philosophy; Lost continents and reincarnation**.

Three lives only *see* **Kabbalah; Plato**.

Three refuges and five Buddhist lay precepts. It is believed in Buddhism that once a person takes the three refugees and five precepts that s/he can never again fall into a less than human birth. The refuges are in the Buddha (teacher), the Dharma (Buddhist teaching), and the Sangha (Buddhist order of monks and nuns as teachers). The minimum precepts that a lay person takes are to avoid harming other life forms (**ahimsa**), to avoid harmful speech, to avoid taking what is not rightfully yours to take, to avoid sexual misconduct, and to avoid becoming intoxicated.

See also ***Bhavachakra*; Rebirth, Non-backsliding**.

Three roots of *Samsara* *see* ***Mulas***.

Threefold (law of) return. This is a Neo-Pagan or **Wicca** version of karma. According to this law any evil a practitioner does to another will be returned to the doer in a triple degree. The first will be for intent, the second for execution, and the third for outcome. Presumably the same applies to good intent, execution, and outcome.

See also **Neo-pagan religions**.

Thumos or thymos see **Soul, tripartite**.

Tibet see **Animals and rebirth, Western view;** *Aquarian Gospel of Jesus Christ*; **Ascended masters;** *Bardo*; **Belgi Dorje; Blavatsky, Helena Petrova; Bon-pa [po] religion; Dalai Lama; Dehiscent or Seed-pod Principle;** *Lhamoi Latso Oracle*; **Panchen Lama; Rebirth and maturity; Rebirth, simultaneous; Swastika;** *Tulku*; **Vajrayana Buddhism**.

Timaeus (*Timaios*). This dialog by **Plato** is spoken by *Timaeus* a Pythagorean philosopher, who gives an exposition on the origin and nature of the universe. In the beginning God created the universe from the two substances of ideas and material elements. From these he formed the heavens, the earth, the world soul, and the lesser gods. It is the latter that create animal and human bodies in accordance with certain geometric formulae. The three kinds of souls that inhabit man and the fate of these souls after death are also described. The preliminary myth of Atlantis is also given here, but this will be continued in a following work, *Critias*. *Timaeus* is by far the most cryptic and mystical of all Plato's dialogs.

See also **Gender issue of the soul; Pythagoras**.

Time and consciousness. A consciousness of time is what may distinguish human beings from other animals. In fact, all religions could be thought of arising from such consciousness. It is our ability to look back to our youth and compare it to our present, and to compare these to our imagined future which means consciousness of our death. Some higher animals seem to have a rudimentary awareness of death of another, but not of their own inevitable death. Human consciousness of time and the presumed lack of it in animals have been offered as one argument for rebirth being exclusively a human possibility.

See also **Animals and rebirth, non–Western view; Animals and rebirth, Western view; Animals, domesticated; Transmigration**.

Time and the simultaneous past, present, and future. This is the idea that the past, present, and future do not exist in a linear fashion, but exist simultaneously. This is thought by some to be the reason that the mind can experience lives of people long dead, or even lives of people normally thought of as not having lived yet. In other words it is said to account for **Retrocognition** and Precognition.

See also **Future-lives; Grant, Joan Marshall; Lazaris; Parallel lives; Plurality of existences; Rebirth and cyclical time; Seth**.

Time, cyclical see **Rebirth and cyclical time**.

Time-recall challenge. On many occasions during supposed past life recall the subject, either on his or her own or in response to the regressor, will give the year(s) in which the past life occurred. In those cases where the modern western calendar was not in use at that time in theory the subject sought not to be able to report the year in modern terms. For example, if the past life was as an ancient Egyptian, Greek, Chinese, etc. the Christian use of BC/AD would be meaningless. The fact that the subject supplies the date in BC/AD terms is used as proof that the subject's subconscious is merely creating a fantasy. The response to this criticism has been that no matter how much the subject may be recalling a past life he/she still has an underlining awareness of the present life and in fact is filtering the past-life through the current one which allows the subject to use present information in the recall of the past life.

Timothy, 1st and 2nd see **Annihilationism, Biblical view; Apocatastasis; Hell; Karma versus grace; Predestination; Universalism**.

Titiksha. This Sanskrit term means a cheerful and patient acceptance one's karma.

Ti-ts'ang (WG). This is the translation of the Sanskrit **Kshitigarbha** see *Bodhisattva*.

Titus see **Elect or chosen of God; Karma versus grace; Palingenesis; Predestination**.

Tomb to womb. This is a metaphor, like **coffin to cradle** or **death to breath**.

See also **Cave; Crypt**.

Torah (1). This is the collective name for the first five books of the Old Testament.

See also **Kabbalah**.

Torah (2). This is a channeled entity described as an inter-dimensional consciousness by the Los Angeles channeler Shawn Randall. According to Randall, Torah has ceased to reincarnate and has not adopted any of the characteristics or personality traits of his former lives.

See also **Channeling; Equinox; Franklin, Benjamin (2); Grace-Loehr life readings; Hilarion; Lazaris; Mafu; Michael (2); Ra (1); Ra (2); Ramtha; Ryerson, Kevin; Satya; Seth**.

Trance states. The entering into a trance state is not as rare as many people assume. In fact, most people probably enter some degree of a trance state on a near daily basis. Being totally absorbed in music, watching a movie, or reading a book to the point where you have become unaware of everything else are forms of a trance state. Driving on the freeway and suddenly realizing that you have been on a kind of auto-pilot is a type of trance state. Also, as many people intuitively know, intense prayer and meditation are very obvious trance states. One can also enter into a trance state that is sometimes called a walking vision. This is when one has a sudden or spontaneous visionary experience of being in a different time and/or place which may be interpreted as a past life vision. In a trance state the usual rational and linear consciousness is suspended and replaced by a non-rational and non-linear consciousness. Note that non-rational does not mean irrational.

The ability of ordinary people in ordinary circumstances to enter into some type of trance state should make the hypnotic trance state that a past life therapist puts one into seem far less mysterious. This should also make it clear why more than 90 percent of the population can be hypnotized. It does seem, however, that children and young adults are better hypnotic subjects than are middle aged and older persons.

See also **Automatic writing; Channeling; Full participation; Hypnotism.**

Transcorporation. This is a very rarely used synonym for reincarnation.

Transmigration. The earliest recorded use of this term in English to signify a renewal of an individual life was in 1559. In its broadest sense this term is an alternative name for **rebirth** or **rebecoming, reincarnation, metempsychosis** and **palingenesis.** In its narrowest sense it is used by those who believe that human souls can be reborn (transmigrate) into animals and vice versa. Reincarnation is generally the term preferred by those who reject such cross-special movement.

See also **Animals and rebirth, Western view; Animals, Domestic; Aristotle; Rebirth, cross-species; Rebirth, non-backsliding; Ontological leap or ontological discontinuity; Origin** or **Origenes Adamanthus; Rebirth in the West.**

Transmigration, alternating lives. This is the belief that each time a human being dies his or her soul must automatically be reborn in a non-human body such as an animal just prior to being once again reborn into a human body.

See also **Kwakiutl.**

Transmigration, lateral. This term means that a human soul can only be reborn into a human body. It is also called circular rebirth because one is recycled back into another human body. Lateral or circular rebirth is in contrast to either regressive or progressive transmigration.

See also **Rebirth, non-backsliding; Transmigration, progressive; Transmigration, regressive.**

Transmigration of Souls. This is the name of a critically hailed choral and orchestral work by the California composer John Adams in commemoration of those who lost their lives in the terrorist attack on New York City on September 11, 2001.

Transmigration, progressive. This term means that an animal soul can be reborn into a human body.

See also **Animals and rebirth, Western view; More, Henry; Rebirth, non-backsliding; Rebirth in the West; Transmigration, lateral; Transmigration, regressive.**

Transmigration, regressive. This term means that a human soul can be reborn into a non-human body.

See also **Animals and rebirth, Western view; More, Henry; Transmigration, lateral; Transmigration, progressive; Rebirth, non-backsliding; Rebirth in the West.**

Traveler's Tale. This is a long narrative poem by Clifford Bax and published in 1921. It tells the story of the soul of an enlightened spiritual teacher which had previously reincarnated as a Stone Age person, a Babylonian, a Greek scribe, a Roman soldier, a medieval bishop, and a more recent English vicar. In each of these lives the soul learns some important lesson on its way to it enlightenment.

Trichotomy. This refers to the biblical view in which the human being is thought to be not just a dichotomy of the body and the soul, but a threefold being of body (*sarx*), soul (psyche), and spirit (*pneuma*). While a dichotomy seem to be justified by some New Testament passages, a trichotomy is more commonly implied. The trichotomy is not to be confused with the tripartite soul.

See also *Pneumatikoi*; **Soul, tripartite.**

Tri dhatu or *tri loka* (Three realms). In Buddhist cosmology these are the realms one can be reborn into. They comprise the ***kama dhatu*** and two higher meditative realms of form (*rupa dhatu*) and formlessness (*arupa-dhatu*). The latter two are only open to very spiritually advanced individuals.

See also **Buddhist stages of liberation**

Trinity, soul as *see* **Augustine, Saint Aurelius.**

Tripart soul *see* **Soul, tripartite.**

Trobriand Islanders. These Melanesian people have the most well documented belief in reincarnation in all of Oceania.

Tulku (Tibetan: sprul-sku). This term, meaning "manifest body," is used in Tibet, Bhutan and Mongolia for high-ranking monks in **Vajrayana Buddhism** who are considered to be incarnated ***bodhisattvas*** or celestial Buddhas. The term *tulku* must be distinguished from the term rebirth. The latter refers to the soul, or its equivalence, of an ordinary human or animal taking on a new body after the death of its previous body. The spiritual component of a *tulku* has technically never been that of an ordinary or mundane being. Instead, it is a celestial or divine essence or factor that has taken on successive material forms (a human body) in order to guide humanity to liberation; in short, an ***avatar***. It is this status as divine that has for the past seven centuries gives *tulkus* a supernatural authorization to rule Tibet and neighboring areas. The earliest historical designation of a person as a *tulku* appears to have been the second Karmapa Lama (Tibetan: bKa'gdams-pa bla-ma) Karma Pakshi (1206–1283), of the Kagyu-pa (Tibetan: bKa'brgyud-pa) School. It may or may not be a coincidence that this it was at this time that the Buddhist clerical hierarchy was assuming full temporal power in Tibet and even today the candidates for such *tulku*-ship are not chosen exclusively by spiritual evidence, but also by the current political needs of the monasteries and of society at large.

The **Dalai Lama**, who is considered the incarnation of the transcendental manifestation of compassion, the *bodhisattva* Avalokiteshvara, and the **Panchen Lama** who is considered the incarnation of the transcendental manifestation of the celestial Buddha **Amitabha** are the most well known examples of *tulkus*.

See also **Arguments supportive of rebirth; Avalokiteshvara; Incarnation versus reincarnation; Jesus; Lama;** *Lhamoi Latso* **Oracle; Possession; Rebirth and maturity.**

Twelve. This number is a nearly universal symbol for time, hence of birth and death as well. This is probably due to there being just over twelve lunar months (12.368) in a solar year. In cultures with more sophisticated astronomical interests this has often been reinforced by the fact that the orbit of Jupiter is nearly twelve years (11.86). It is possible that the twelve links (*nidanas*) of the ***pratitya-samutpada*** wheel has its origin in such celestial cycles.

See also **Zodiac.**

Twin Souls *see* **Soul twins.**

Twins, conjoined (Siamese) *see* **Embryonic fusion.**

Twins, identical. These are twins that have an identical genetic inheritance since they developed from the same fertilized egg; hence monzygotic, as opposed to fraternal twins (dizygotic). If these twins were raised in the same household it would be assumed that they should have identical personalities. This is not always the case. Even with conjoined (Siamese) twins there are personality differences. This has led advocates of rebirth to suggest that a non-biological or independent extra-genetic factor or factors must be present to account for the differences. Theoretically, this factor ought not to be that of two newly God-created souls because those souls would have no prior personality differentiations that would explain the differences in the twins; therefore, reincarnationists argue that the factor must be two unrelated souls that had prior lives and identities.

One counter argument to this may be found in the form of L1 retrotransposons which make up 20 percent of the human genome. These are pieces of DNA that have the ability to make copies of themselves and then to insert these onto new spots in the genome. It is thought that the activity of some of these virus-like genes jumping from one place to another in the brain may help explain why the brains even of identical twins are different.

To complicate the whole twin issue there is the very rare form of semi-identical twins which is where a single egg is fertilized by two different sperm.

See also **Arguments supportive of rebirth; Embryonic fusion; Soul twins.**

Tzror ha-Chayyim (Hebrew: bonds of Life) or **Otzar** (Treasury [of souls]). In kabbalic literature this is the resting place of righteous souls before they reincarnate into new bodies. As the treasury of souls it is said to be beneath God's Throne of Glory.

See also ***Enoch, Third Book of*; *Guf ha-Briyot*; Kabbalah.**

Ubar see **Kabbalah.**

UFOism or **Ufology.** Although UFO is the acronym for Unidentified Flying Objects, when applied to any of the **New Age religions** it can mean any of those that believe that the Earth has been visited by or been put into contact with intelligent extra-terrestrials "with or without" an interplanetary vehicle. UFO groups generally can be divided into those that regard the space travelers as hostile aliens, and those that regard them as friendly, even benevolent aliens. The first group is often labeled apocalyptic UFOism in that it is often believed that the aliens are intent on either destroying or enslaving mankind. Among the second group of UFOers are those who claim that the space visitors have come to teach us a higher wisdom. In a number of cases this wisdom includes reincarnation and other theosophical-like teachings. Only rarely is it claimed that these benevolent interplanetary teachers make contact in their own bodily form. Instead, they are said to usually contact earthlings either through **channeling** or by having purposefully incarnated into human form, especially as **walk-ins**. These incarnated teachers presumably have retained the full memory of their previous lives on their home planet. It might be noted that claims of past lives as aliens is not uncommon among those who claim that they were temporarily abducted by UFO entities.

The modern UFO movement had it beginning on June 24, 1947, when Kenneth Arnold, a civilian pilot, reported seeing a chain-like formation of nine shiny objects flying at some 1600 miles per hour in the sky over the Cascade Mountains in western Washington. It was his description of them as "flying erratic, like a saucer if you skip it across the water" that led to the term flying saucer. While the present UFO groups are obviously all post–1947 development, some of their roots are in earlier non–UFO groups. Those earlier groups that embraced communication with angels and those that believed in ascended masters were in many ways precursors to the UFOers.

See also **Aetherius Society; Aquarian Foundation;** *Fiat Lux***; Heaven's Gate; Rampa, Lobsang Tuesday; Lost continents and reincarnation; Planets, other; Unarius Academy of Science.**

Umbanda. This is a popular Brazilian mediumship religion that began around 1900 and is a blending of native Indian (Tupi), African (Yoruba), European (Catholic), and Eastern religious elements. In particular this includes belief in both reincarnation and karma, which it adopted from **Kardecismo**. Umbanda sacred literature includes the *Secrete Doctrine of Umbanda*, the *Tight Fundamentals of Umbanda*, and the *Revelation of the Hexagramatic Cross*. The last of these contains details on how to receive spiritual protection, how to help others, and how to properly serve the Masters of Karma.

There are 3 branches of Umbanda: the Gege-Nago (the most African), the Angola-Congo (the more mixed), and the Caboclo (the most syncretic).

See also **Afro-American religions; Astral plane (2); Kubitschek, Juscelino.**

Umbra see **Shadow.**

Unarius Academy of Science. This is one of the **New Age religions** that combine a belief in reincarnation, karma, **lost continents**, and non-apocalyptic **UFOism**. Unarius was founded in 1954 by Ernest (d. 1971) and Ruth (d.1993) Norman, when the first announcement of it appeared in Ernest Norman's book *Voice of Venus* (1954).

The Unarius name is an acronym derived from the title Universal Articulate Inter-dimensional Understanding of Science. The Academy is said to have begun from both the ability of the Normans to channel messages from extraterrestrials and to extensively read into their own past lives. According to the Unarius Academy, Ernest Norman's higher self was the archangel Raphael (Hebrew: God heals), while Ruth Norman's higher self was the archangel Uriel (Hebrew: Fire of God). This later archangel, at least according to the twentieth chapter of the Christian apocryphal, *The Book of Enoch*, is the leader of the heavenly host and guardian of *Sheol*, the underworld. Ruth Norman, however, also considered the Uriel name to be an acronym for Universal Radiant Infinite Eternal Light.

The Normans claimed that they could remembered their past lives as far back as those of extraterrestrials from the 700 light-years distant planet Lemuria who, along with other Lemurians, arrived on the Earth some 156,000 years ago. These interplanetary beings established the Earth's first civilization on the now lost continent which they obviously named after their home planet. These Lemurian lives of the Normans were said to have been followed by lives on the pre-deluge Atlantis and then, some 14,000 years ago, as the Egyptian god-king Osiris and goddess-queen Isis; these were followed by a life as **Jesus** of Nazareth and Mary of Bethany, who was betrothed to Jesus.

After the death of her husband, Ruth Norman wrote her past life autobiography *Visitations: A saga of Gods and Men* (1985). In this she described some of her further past lives as the female Pharaoh Hapshepsut, Socrates, Charlemagne, the Toltec (Mexican) god-king Quetzalcoatl (**Kulkulcan**), Elizabeth the I of England, Peter the Great of Russia, the Mogul Indian emperor Akbar, the empress Maria Theresa of Austria, the Inca emperor Atahualpa, etc. Among Ruth Norman's writings on reincarnation are *Principles and Practices of Past Life Therapy* (1984); *The Proof of the Truth of Past Life Therapy* (1988); and *The Last Inca, Atahualpa: An Eyewitness Account of The Conquest of Peru in 1535* (1993).

See also **Aetherius Society; Angels and reincarnation; Heaven's Gate; Old Testament and the afterlife; Planets, other; Ramtha; Silent watchers; UFOism.**

Unconscious, the. This is the region of the mind that is presumed to produce mental processes that are neither autonomic nor conscious. In depth psychologies such as psychoanalysis it is regarded as the repository of repressed impulses and memories. The psychotherapeutic approach of such psychologies is to bring these repressions to the surface conscious mind. It is theorized by many believers in reincarnation that the memories of past lives reside in this unconscious and that psychotherapy can sometimes lead to past life recall.

See also **Id, Ego, Superego**.

Underworld *see* Greek Afterlife, Ancient; Hell; Hell, the Chinese; Old Testament and the afterlife; Purgatory; Shinto.

Unity School of Christianity. Unity Christianity is a version of "New Thought." This is the name of a loosely structured movement that began in the United States in the latter part of the 19th century. It was mainly centered on the belief that a benevolent God of pure spirit had never meant for humanity to suffer illness or disease; therefore, most forms of illness were due to a false belief in the material reality of illness and lack of faith in God's benevolence. While most New Thought teachers and practitioners considered themselves to be authentically Christian, as might be expected, they did not emphasize sin, eternal damnation, or a future physical resurrection. In fact, a number of New Thought groups, for example Christian Science, regarded death as being just as illusory as disease. With the exception of Unity Christianity none of the other New Thought groups adopt a belief in reincarnation and karma.

Unity Christianity was founded in 1889 by Charles Fillmore (1854–1948) and his wife Myrtle Fillmore (1845–1931). The Filmores were students of Emma Curtis Hopkins, who was an associate of Mary Baker Eddy, the founder of Christian Science. Like Eddy's group, Unity emphasizes spiritual healing through prayer. However, Unity also accepted lateral reincarnation as a way to perfect oneself in order to eventually leave the physical body behind and to assume a purely spiritual one, like that of the resurrected Christ. While accepting karma Unity has never regarded it as an immutable law, but considers it to be under the will of God.

See also **Christianity, esoteric; Karma versus grace; Liberal Catholic Church; Reincarnation, Lateral; Science of Mind**.

Universal Church of the Master. Established in 1908, this is one of the larger Spiritualist religious groups. It teachings are primarily based on the ***Aquarian Gospel of Jesus the Christ***. Besides acknowledging the ability to communicate with the dead, it also accepts a belief in reincarnation.

Universalism. This is the doctrine that all souls will eventually be redeemed (*apocatastasis*) from **hell** or some other less desirable state, such as **limbo**. Most believers in rebirth, especially in the West, subscribe to some form of universalism.

Christian Universalists have often cited **Romans** 11: 25–32; 14: 9–12 and especially 1st Timothy 2:4 in support of their rejection of eternal punishment. Some Christian Universalists believe that such universal salvation is achieved through a pre-messianic series of reincarnations.

See also **Annihilationism, Biblical view; Origin; Predestination**.

Upanishads. This is the ancient Hindu sacred literature that conceives of God in a very monistic or pantheistic manner. It is the earliest known Indian literature to acknowledge the doctrine of rebirth. While certain passages in the pre–Upanishad literature called the *Brahmanas* may hint at the idea of rebirth, the earliest text to clearly mention rebirth is probably in the third and fourth chapter of the *Brhadaranyaka Upanishad*, which was probably composed shortly before the 6th century BCE. The only other early *Upanishads* to mention rebirth are the *Chandogya Upanishad* and the *Kausitaki Upanishad*. Even in these the concept of rebirth is regarded as a secret teaching known only to some non–**Brahman** (non-priestly) teachers. This suggests that the concept of rebirth originated from a source outside of the **Vedic Religion**, most likely among the pre–Aryan (pre–Vedic) population.

See also ***Bhagavad Gita***; **Caste system; Hinduism; Jainism; Karma, origins of; Yeats, William Butler**.

Urantia Book. The anonymous author of this 1955 **new age religion** book claims that it is a record of the teachings of certain high spiritual (angelic) beings channeled through the author while asleep, but recorded by a University of Chicago psychiatrist, Dr William Samuel Sadler (1875–1969). Included in the titles and names of these beings are Chief of Archangels, Chief of Seraphim, Bright Evening Star (**Lucifer**), and **Melchizedek**. The book has a detailed cosmology and an alternative account of the life and teachings of **Jesus**. Perhaps the most interesting teaching found in the Urantia Book is the idea that Urantian believers can invite some of these high spiritual beings, as "Thought Adjusters," to take possession of the believers. In this way the angelic adjusters can communicate with, and teach, the believer's higher selves to let go of fear and uncertainty and in their place to experience of the presence of God. The name of this book comes from the name these beings use for the planet Earth. Unlike a number of New Age writings the Urantia Book, (Urantia Foundation, Chicago, 1955), states that the belief in reincarnation is an absurd and barbaric left over concept from **ancestor worship**.

See also **Angels and reincarnation;** *Aquarian Gospel of Jesus Christ*; **Ascended masters; Auto-**

matic writing; Channeling; Christianity, esoteric; *Oahspe*; Possession.

Uttar Pradesh. It is in this north central India state that the belief in reincarnation seems to be more strongly adhered to than in other parts of India. This is also the part of India in which **Ian Stevenson** has found most of his Indian cases of presumed reincarnation.

Vaikuntha (land of no hindrance). This is the name for the personal paradise of the Hindu Saguna **Brahman** god Vishnu and is attained through ***bhakti*** (devotional) yoga. It *Vaikuntha* is not the ultimate spiritual goal in Vaishnavism, but is a place for the soul of the devotee to rest in between lives. After a longer or shorter stay in this blissful realm the soul is once again reborn into a worldly body to continue its ultimate goal of merging back into an impersonal Brahman, in short *moksha*.

See also **Hinduism; Incarnation versus reincarnation; Karma versus grace;** *Swarga* or *Svarga*.

Vajrayana Buddhism. (Sanskrit: Diamond Vehicle) This is the Tantric form of Buddhism that is dominant in Tibet, Bhutan, Mongolia, parts of Russia, and formerly in Manchuria. It is best known through its association with the ***Bardo*, Dalai Lama, Panchen Lama,** and other ***Tulku*** manifestations.

See also **Amitabha Buddha; Avalokiteshvara;** ***Bodhisattva*; Buddhism, esoteric; Dehiscent or Seed-pod Principle;** ***Gandharva/Gandhabba*; Interim period; Mahayana Buddhism; Merit, transfer of; Nine doors;** ***Phowa*; Rebirth and maturity; Russia, reincarnation in; Tantrism; Theravada Buddhism.**

Valentinus (ca. 136–ca. 165 CE). This Egyptian born teacher was one of the more important figures in Christian **Gnosticism.** His teachings were a fusion between the Christianity of **Paul of Tarsus** and the Gnosticism of **Basilides.** Like the latter he believed that the material world had been created by an inferior deity (*demiurge*) and not the father of Christ. Christ was seen as the offspring of Sophia (the Divine Wisdom) which was a secondary emanation from a primary emanation of the Father (near unknowable supreme God). It was this Christ who was sent to help liberate souls trapped by the *demiurge* in their reincarnational round. *Adversus omnes Haereses* (*Against the Heresies*) by **Irenaeus** was particularly directed against the teachings of Valentinus.

See also **Origin** or **Origenes Adamanthus;** ***Pneumatikoi*; Simon Magus.**

Vampires. In several versions of the Dracula story the beloved wife of the count, thinking he has been killed in battle, commits suicide. When the count returns home he finds that his beloved is not only dead, but as a suicide victim has been refused burial in consecrated ground. It is his cursing of God for this injustice that turns him into a member of the undead. Centuries pass and the count discovers that his wife's soul has finally reincarnated into the body of an English woman with whom he becomes determined to reunite. In another particularly imaginative association of reincarnation and vampires, the horror writer J.N. Williamson, in his book *Death-Coach* (1981), managed to bring together **Pythagoras,** a Greek-American community in Indiana, and vampires.

See also **Astral plane; Attached entity; Bogomils; Chinese Religion and Reincarnation; Crowley, Edward Aleister; Diakka; Etheric body; Etheric revenant; Immortality; Saint Germain.**

Vasanas. In Buddhism these are the inner tendencies or impressions latent in each person that are inherited from a past life and that act as karmic seeds in the present and future lives.

See also *Samskara*.

Vedanta *see* **Monism; Yogananda, Paramahansa; Vedanta Society; Vivekananda, Swami.**

Vedanta Society. Swami Vivekananda (1863–1902), the first Hindu teacher to attract an American following, arrived in the United States in 1893. He organized the Vedanta Society in 1896. Under Vivekananda's disciple, Swami Prabhavananda (1893–1976), the society attracted the support of such men as Aldous Huxley and Christopher Isherwood. Both reincarnation and karma are included in the teachings of the Society.

See also *Atman*; **Yogananda, Paramahansa.**

Vedic Religion. This is the name given by scholars to the religion of the Aryan people in northern India before that religion gradually evolved into **Hinduism.** The name Vedic comes from the sacred texts known as the "Veda," which is Sanskrit for wisdom. The Vedic religion is the religion that both Buddhism and **Jainism** rose to challenge. It was only in the last Vedic phase that the concept of rebirth and karma were found. This suggests that the concepts of reincarnation entered into late Vedic writings from some non–Vedic source.

See also *Bhagavad-Gita*; **Rain;** *Upanishads*.

Vegetarianism. Many believers in **transmigration** feel that since a human soul might reincarnate into an animal's body eating meat might be paramount to cannibalism. Also, it is believed by some teachers that eating meat, or in some cases any animal product, is a major impediment to remembering one's past lives. Among the religions that believe in rebirth **Jainism** is the one most thoroughly committed to vegetarianism. **Hinduism** and Buddhism encourage vegetarianism, but they generally do not require it. There are, however, a small number of Mahayana Buddhist texts that have a very negative view of meat eating. One example of such a text is the renowned *Lankavatara Sutra*. This text claims that eating meat will result in being reborn as an ill-smelling, contemptuous, and insane member of the untouchable caste; as if that was not bad enough, from there the person will be reborn as a *dakini* (ogress) or even as a cat.

In contrast to advocating vegetarianism, Left-handed **Tantrism** regards meat (S: *mamsa*) and fish (*matsya*) eating as part of the esoteric way to spiritual liberation or freedom from birth and death, specifically because eating meat and fish are two of the five forbidden practices (*pancamakara*) in non–Tantric (exoteric) circles. The other three forbidden or antinomian practices are the use of intoxicants (*mada*), aphrodisiacs (*mudra*), and ritual sexual intercourse (*maithuna*).

On the other hand, the founder of the **Osho Movement** taught that the inability of most people to remember their past lives was due to the fact that meat eating blocked the necessary channel through which such lives could be remembered. This seems to agree with the view of **Helena Blavatsky** that meat possessed a kind of magnetism that anesthetized the psychic power in its eaters.

India-originating religions were not the only ones to associate meat-eating with rebirth. The ancient Greek Pythagoreans and followers of **Orphism** also regarded some degree of vegetarianism as essential for liberation from the wheel of rebirth (*kyklos genesion*). Also, according to a folk Chinese belief, being a vegetarian and teaching your children to be the same will help a person to avoid suffering in the third Court of Hell.

See also **Aetherius Society**; *Ahimsa*; **Antinomianism; Beans; Empedocles;** *Fiat Lux*; **Hell, the Chinese; Kingsford, Anna Bonus; Porphyry; Pythagoras.**

Venus, the planet *see* **Aetherius Society; I Am Movement; Lucifer; Planets, other; Rampa, Tuesday Lobsang; Unarius Academy of Science.**

Vijnana (S. Consciousness) *see Pratitya-samutpada*; **Psychophysical aggregates; Rebirth in Buddhism; Soul.**

Vijnanavada (S: Consciousness) **School of Buddhism.** This is one of the two main philosophical schools of **Mahayana Buddhism**; the other being the Madhyamika School. The name of the school comes from the fact that it teaches that the mind or consciousness (*vijnana*) can never be sure how real the outer world is. The only thing it can be certain of is that there is a consciousness which is called "I." This is much like the view of the seventeenth century French philosopher **Descartes**, as well as the Western system called Subjective Idealism.

Vijnanavada divides consciousness into eight levels. The first five levels correspond to the five senses of sight, hearing, smell, taste, and touch. The sixth (*manovijnana*) and seventh (***manas***) levels are respectively the lower and higher forms of intellectual consciousness. The *manovijnana* is the thinking consciousness that coordinates the previous five consciousnesses. The *manas* in unenlightened persons is "defiled" by delusion of self consciousness. The eighth, or ***alayavijnana***, is not consciousness in any ordinary sense as are the other seven. Rather it is the non-reflected or non-self-aware consciousness that underlines the others. The name *alaya* means womb or storehouse and refers to where the seeds (*bija*) of good and bad karma reside or are stored. It is only when consciousness manifests itself as the *manas* that the person begins to have the basis for a sense of self or ego develop. Of course, this happens as a result of the karmic seeds in the *alayavijnana*. These seeds sprout into all the delusions that we call the world and the self.

Other names applied to this philosophical school are *Chittamatra* (Intention-only), *Vijnaptimatrata* (consciousness-matrix-only), *Dharma-Laksana* (Dharma-characters), and *Yogachara* (Yoga way). The last name is given to this school because it teaches that only through the right meditation practice (yoga) can one realize this "conscious-only" condition and thus gain awakening (Buddhahood) which meant the end of rebirth. One of the main reasons for the development of this school was to try to answer the Buddhist dilemma of how there could be rebirth without a soul (***anatman***).

See also ***Alayavijnana***; **Annihilationism, Buddhist view; Zen.**

Vilna Gaon (Elijah ben Solomon Kramer, 1720–1797). This Lithuanian Kabbalist wrote a commentary on the biblical book of Jonah that envisions it as an allegory for reincarnation.

See also **Kabbalah.**

Vimanavatthu. In the canon of **Theravada Buddhism** this is a minor book which describes the fate of a certain group of the virtuous deceased that instead of being immediately reborn into a new human body, are born into the blissful state of the gods (*devas*). The *Vimanavatthu* tells eighty-three stories detailing with how the wholesome (*kusala*) karma of those individuals brought them to their celestial births.

See also ***Bhavachakra***; ***Petavatthu***; ***Pretas.***

Vintras, Eugene (1807–1875). In 1839 Frenchman claimed that he had been visited by Saint Joseph for the purpose of announcing the "Reign of Love" in order to prevent the end of the world. This Reign of Love turned out to be more a reign of sexual libertinism than anything else. Despite a five year imprisonment for collecting money under false pretenses, Vintras continued to attract followers up until his death, by which time he had become convinced that he was the reincarnation of the prophet **Elijah** and of John the Baptist. Vintras was apparently sufficiently notorious to merit condemnation by the equally disreputable occultist Eliphas Levi.

See also **New Testament and reincarnation**.

Violent and premature deaths *see* **Deaths, violent and premature**.

Vipaka (S/P: ripening, maturing). This refers to the consequence (fruit: *phala*) of karma. Technically karma is only the cause and *vipaka* is the effect of an action. In this sense a person sows karma but reaps *vipaka*.

See also **Karma and forgiveness**.

Virgil (70–19 BCE). This ancient Roman writer, whose full name was Publius Vergilius Maro, was the author the *Aeneid*. In book six of this epic poem the author combines Orphic and Pythagorean ideas in his views of the afterlife. In the Aeneid the Trojan hero Aeneas, in visiting the underworld, sees how the wicked are punished in *Tartarus* and the good are rewarded in the Elysium Fields. Aeneas also sees those souls that, after drinking from the river **Lethe**, will eventually be reincarnated as illustrious Romans.

See also **Greek afterlife, the ancient; Greeks and reincarnation; Orphism; Pythagoras**.

Virgin conception. It has been believed in many folk societies that the man's semen is not necessary for conception. At most the male is thought to serve only to open up the womb so that a reincarnating spirit can enter and produce a fetus.

See also **Australian Aborigines**.

Virgo (Hebrew: *Elul*). In the Kabbalic thought of Isaac Luria this is the astrological period in which non-premeditated murder victims reincarnate for the purpose of continuing to fulfill their cosmic obligations to repair the split between God and the soul (Hebrew: *tikun*).

See also **Kabbalah**.

Vishnu *see* **Avatar; Babbitt, Elwood; Brahman; Incarnation versus reincarnation; Karma versus grace; Lenz, Frederick; Shiva; Vaikuntha**.

Vivekananda, Swami (1863–1902). This Indian holy man, in visits to Europe and America, sought to give the West a new image of **Hinduism**. Rather than it being a primitive polytheism he tried to show that it was the truth behind all religions in that it taught the unity of humanity through universal human divinity. Vivekananda attended the 1893 Parliament of Religions in Chicago which lead to his acquiring a group of western disciples. It was from his teachings that the **Vedanta Society** was founded in 1896 in New York City. Vivekananda's vision was carried on in the West by his disciples, in particular by **Swami Prabhavananda**. While the Vedanta Society does not require any belief in reincarnation, as an offshoot of Hinduism it does not discourage the belief.

See also **Self-Realization Fellowship; Yogananda, Paramahansa**.

Voltaire, Francois-Marie Arouetde (1694–1778). This French philosopher was said to have stated that the doctrine of **metempsychosis** is neither absurd nor useless, and that it is no more surprising to be born twice than it was to be born once. Whether this statement meant that Voltaire actually believed in reincarnation or was merely pointing out its logical possibility has long been under debate.

Wagner, Richard. According to the diaries of Wagner's wife, Cosima Wagner, the musician began to write a prose sketch for an opera on a Buddhist-reincarnation theme called *Die Sieger* (*The Victor*) but never completed it. It must be noted that this does not necessarily mean that Wagner was either a true believer in reincarnation, much less a Buddhist, any more than his Christian or German pagan themed operas imply that he was a committed Christian or pagan.

Walk-in. This term refers to an alien soul or being that is believed to take over the body of a person who is about to die. The alien is said to be able to rejuvenate the body for its own use. According to **Ruth Montgomery**, in her *Strangers Among Us* (1979), there are hundred of thousands of such walk-ins living on Earth; and while the majority of these walk-ins are enlightened entities from Earth, according to her *Alien Among Us* (1983), a few of them are thought to be extraterrestrials. Montgomery believed that most of these walk-ins are benevolent entities trying to teach humanity higher spiritual truths. Interestingly, Montgomery considers **Richard Sutphen** as having become a walk-in. Montgomery's *Threshold to Tomorrow* (1982) also deals with this subject.

See also **Attached entity; Possession; Rebirth or rebecoming; UFOism**.

Wallace, Henry A. (1818–1965). This vice-president of the United States from 1941–45 was a

Freemason, Theosophist, and between 1925 and 1930 a member of the **Liberal Catholic Church**. He believed in reincarnation and karma, and that he had been an Indian brave, possibly Iroquois, in a past life. Wallace was instrumental in having the Masonic mystic eye-pyramid placed on the left side of the one-dollar bill.

Wambach, Helen (1925–1986). This American psychologist specialized in group hypnotic regression and claimed that some ninety percent of the participants believed that they had some degree of past life recall. Wambach stated that the ten percent of her subjects that did not have past life memories could be divided into two groups. The first were those persons who wanted so desperately to have past life experiences that they could not relax enough to have those experiences. The second were those that were very doubtful about reincarnation and would not let themselves relax sufficiently to experience past lives; indeed, they had concluded before-hand that no such experience would occur.

Wambach was of the opinion that among the best evidence for reincarnation was the fact that in her sample of over a thousand subjects about 50.6 percent claimed to have been males and for 49.4 percent to have been females in their last past life. Wambach noted that this was just what would be expected in genuine population statistics. Besides gender, Wambach analyzed the social status of her subject's past lives; and using a sample of 1,100 subjects, she said that only 10 percent claimed upper class status, 60–70 percent acknowledged lower class status, and the remaining 20–30 percent would have been of the middle class. This would more or less match historical reality. Wambach also reported that in a study of twenty-five subjects under **hypnosis** who were regressed back to 1400 and up to 1945 CE that between those dates the average number of lives for each subject was five.

A major criticism of Wambach's work has been that she began her study with a very favorable view of reincarnation which automatically prejudiced her result. Wambach's research is documented in her books *Reliving Past Lives: Evidence under Hypnosis* (1978) and *Life before Life* (1979).

See also **Deaths, violent and premature; Rebirth, group; Researchers; Social Status of Past Lives**.

Wandering soul. This refers to the soul of a deceased person that usually has been so disoriented by the loss of its body at death that it moves from place to place until it can somehow orient itself to its disembodied condition.

Watchers *see* **Dweller on the Threshold; Silent watchers**.

Weber, Max (1864–1920). This German sociologist of religion was probably the first European scholar to examine the doctrine of karma from a socio-economic view point. He wrote that the doctrine of karma ideologically transformed the Indian world into a strictly rational, ethically-determined cosmos, the result of which was the most consistent **theodicy** ever produced. However, the karma doctrine also made revolutionary ideas or progressivism inconceivable in the Indian world as manifested in the conservative rigidity of the **caste system**.

Welcomers. According to the entity Alexander, as channeled through Ramon Stevens in *Earthly Cycles* (1994), welcomers are a family of souls that have evolved beyond the **astral plane** yet meet recently disembodied souls and help them in their post-mortem transition. These welcomers surround each soul, even the most monstrous ones, with deep compassionate wisdom and unconditional love.

See also **Embodiment, moment of; Omega; Theta (2)**.

Wheatley, Dennis Yates (1897–1977). This enormously popular British novelist of the macabre was a firm believer in reincarnation. In his later years he was the editor of the *Library of the Occult* which comprised more than 40 volumes.

Wheel of Life *see* ***Bhavachakra; Kyklos Genesion.***

White Brothers and Blue Sisters *see* **Great White Brotherhood**.

White Eagle. This was the name for the Amerindian spirit guide (channeled entry) of **Grace Cooke**. He was said to have guided Cooke in discovering several of her past lives. The more recent channeler, Jill Cook [note similarity of last names], has claimed to be in contact with this same spirit guide.

White Lodge. Founded in 1941 by Lady Elizabeth Carey, a representative of the British **White Eagle Lodge**, the teachings of the White Lodge were said to come from a member of the **Great White Brotherhood** named Azrael and channeled through Carey. Azrael's messages focused on the approaching Age of Aquarius, the healing power of prayer and a belief in reincarnation and karma. The White Lodge was eventually absorbed into the **Church Universal and Triumphant**.

See also **Cooke, Grace**.

Wicca. This is the modern name for the Neo-Pagan religious movement of benevolent (white) witchcraft. According to its practitioners "Wicca" is said to be derived from the Anglo-Saxon word for "wisdom," although others have traced it back to a Germanic root meaning "to twist" or "to bend."

Although some Wiccans claim their practice to be an uninterrupted continuation of pre–Christian European paganism, it really developed as a result of the publication of *The Witch Cult in Western Europe* (1921) and *God of the Witches* (1931) by Margaret Murray and *Witchcraft Today* (1954) by Gerald Gardner. The view of Wicca as a modern revival was vehemently challenged in 1968 by the New York feminist organization WITCH (Women's International Conspiracy from Hell) which wrote a manifesto declaring that witchcraft was, indeed, the pre–Christian religion of Europe.

Wicca emphasizes worship of the earth as the mother goddess and sometimes of a subordinate horned male deity companion. Many Wicca practitioners believe in reincarnation, which is sometimes referred to as "psychic recycling." The Wiccan belief is based on a rejection of the Christian doctrine of the resurrection of the dead as well as the tendency to find analogies for rebirth in nature.

See also **Crowley, Aleister; Druids; Fortune, Dion; Hell; Leland, Charles Godfrey; Neopagan religions; New Age religions; Rebirth, analogies from nature; Resurrection, bodily; Roberts, Jane; Sciomancy; Score, John.**

Wickland, Carl August (1861–1945). Wickland was the founder of the Psychopathetic Institute of Chicago and the National Psychological Institute (NPI). Through the mediumship of his wife, over a period of thirty years, Wickland was supposedly able to cure patients of obsessing **attached entities**. He stated that those who died believing in reincarnation carry that belief into the next world where, imagining that they would be reincarnated, they instead lost opportunities to spiritually progress. In fact, Wickland claimed that the spirit of **Helena Blavatsky** recanted her belief in reincarnation. Wickland was the author of *Thirty Years among the Dead* (1924).

See also **Davis, Andrew Jackson; Home, Daniel Douglas; Morse, J.J.; Spiritualism.**

Widespread and multi-cultural belief argument. This argument in favor of rebirth is based on the fact that many totally unrelated cultures around the world, both primitive and advanced, have accepted rebirth as a truism. The same counter argument made about **rebirth and famous supporters** can be made here also. While many cultures do accept rebirth, the majority of known cultures have not accepted it.

See also **Arguments supportive of rebirth; Channeling; Rebirth and cyclical time; Reincarnation, origins of.**

Wieland, Christopher Martin (1733–1813). This German writer, beginning with his first important work *Die Natur der Dinge* (The Nature of Things, 1751), had a major positive impact on a growing interest in reincarnation among many of his country's intellectuals.

Wilcock, David. According to the book *The Reincarnation of Edgar Cayce* (2004), Wilcock, who was born in 1973, is the reincarnation of Cayce who died in 1945. Part of the proof for this claim is said to come from a complex, or group soul, entity by the name of **Ra (1)** who is channeled through Wilcock. Ra states that "it" evolved millions of years ago on Venus and that presently it is the oversoul for earth. Ra has told Wilcock that Cayce's prophecy that California, New York, and Tokyo would in inundated and disappear into the ocean in 1998 was false because the entity Halahiah that revealed this false information to Cayce was, in reality, a negative source and should not have been trusted.

See also **Cayce, Edgar; Channeling; Lazaris; Michael (2); Planets, other; Presley, Elvis; Ramtha; Ryerson, Kevin; Seth.**

Willing suspension of disbelief. This phrase was offered by the writer Henry James as a the mental process by which people believed in something of which there is no possible concrete or objective proof, such as the existence of God, the soul, or an afterlife.

Wilson, Ian. In his book, *Mind Out of Time: Reincarnation, Hypnotic Regression, Stigmata, Multiple Personality, and Other Little-Understood Powers of the Mind* (1982), originally published under the name All in the Mind (1981), Wilson offers a major critique of reincarnation. Wilson also wrote *The After Death Experience* 1987.

See also **Edwards, Paul.**

Winnebago. According to a study by the anthropologist Paul Radin (1983) the Winnebago believe that reincarnation is confined only to prominent tribal members and members of the Medicine Dance secret society.

Wisdom of Solomon 8:19–20. This is one of the biblical passages that Christian reincarnationists use to claim that this apocrypha supports reincarnation. The passage reads, "As a child I was born to excellence, and a noble soul fell to my lot: or rather, I myself was noble, and I entered into an unblemished body:.." This passage certainly suggests the **souls existence prior to embodiment**; however, a pre-existing soul entering a body does not automatically imply that this happens more than once.

See also **Solomon, King.**

Witchcraft and reincarnation *see* **Wicca**.

Witness position. This is said to be a post-mortem state of consciousness from where the deceased entity can review his or her most recent life, but from a safely detached state of mind, almost as if it were the life of another person.

Women. In a number of societies the concept of rebirth is used to marginalize women, especially by making them believe that their present gender is due to poor karma, and that if they obey the male authorities they will be rewarded by being reborn as men. One version of this marginalization is the dogma that it is only as a male that one could ever manifest as a Buddha. The most extreme case of marginalization of women is found in the **Nusayris** doctrine that only men have souls and thus only they can reincarnate.

See also **Aztecs; Bhaishajyaraja-guru; Caste system; Gender issue of the soul; Jataka Tales; Kabbalah; Kingsford, Anna Bonus; Nusayris (Nursaris); Pure-Land or Blissful Land Buddhism**.

Work of Mercy. This was an occult cult begun in France by Eugene Vintras, a factory worker, who claimed to be the reincarnation of John the Baptist and to have been visited by both the archangel Michael and the Virgin Mary. Before his death in 1875 Vintras passed the leadership on to **Joseph-Antoine Boullian**, who himself claimed to be the reincarnation of the Baptist, as well as of the prophet **Elijah**.

See also **New Testament and reincarnation; Old Testament and the afterlife**.

World Catalyst Church. Founded in 1967 in Butte, Montana, the Church teaches that there is an inner internal light that is beyond the self in wisdom, power and scope, and that it is the church's responsibility to lead its members from their present ignorant state into that eternal light. Each person is regarded as bound by natural law and by his/her oneness with others. No one will enter into eternal perfection until all are able to do so. This will require each person to be reincarnated in various dimensions to learn the lessons of those dimensions.

World Wide Web *see* **Internet and reincarnation; Seventeenth century renewed interest in rebirth**.

Wraith *see* **Astral body**.

Xenoglossy. This Greek derived term is from xeno- for foreign and -glossa for tongue; it is sometimes replaced with *xenolalia* (foreign-language). The term was coined by the French physiologist Dr. Charles Richet and refers to speaking, reading, or understanding of a real language which, presumably, one has never learned. Usually xenoglossy occurs while in some degree of an altered state of consciousness.

There are actually two types of xenoglossy, the recitative and the responsive. In the first, which is the most common type, the speaker uses words and phrases of which he does not understand the meaning. It is thought that this form of xenoglossy is, more likely than not, to be related to **cryptomnesia**.

Responsive xenoglossy, which is much rarer, is where the speaker does understand the meaning of what he is saying. It is in this form that xenoglossy is thought by some to be related to memories of a past life.

Some of the more conservative Christian churches views xenoglossy as related to demonic **possession**. Xenoglossy is not to be confused with **glossolalia**.

See also **Arguments supportive of rebirth; Language inconsistency; New Testament and reincarnation; Possession; Rosemary case; Xenography**.

Xenography. This ability to writing in a presumed unlearned language is believed by some to suggest recall from a past life.

See **Automatic writing; Xenoglossy**.

Xenophanes *see* **Pythagoras**.

Xenophrenia. This is an altered state of consciousness such as during a past life hypnotic trance.

Y symbol. This symbol was used by the Pythagoreans to signify the two possible destinations with which the soul was eventually faced. The left path represented reincarnation, while the right path represented the Elysium Fields.

See also **Greek afterlife, the ancient; Pythagoras**.

Yama. In the Vedas this is the name for the mythological first human being to experience bodily death, which gave him the right to become the king of the after-life world. This world at first was thought to be located in the heavens, but soon was believed to be in an underworld. Originally a light-hearted ruler of ancestral souls in a morally indifferent world, Yama in post–Vedic literature became a severe judge of the dead ruling over a hellish place of punishment (***naraka***). Iconographically Yama is depicted as green in color with red eyes, wearing red garments. He carries a noose, and a mace which is often decorated with a skull; he rides a black water buffalo.

According to Hindu mythology when a person is about to die, Yama sends to that person his Bird of Doom (crow and/or pigeon). Once the person is dead the messenger of Yama, Yamduta, will guide the soul of the deceased to the underworld which involves passing by two ferocious four-eyed dogs of Yama, the Sarameyas, which guard Yama's palace, Kalichi, in the city of the dead, Yamapura. Once in Yamapura, the dead meet **Chintra-Gupta**, the Registrar of the Dead, who reads out the *Agrasandhani*, the register of all the deceased's deeds. This is followed by the judgment of Yama who will send some souls to hell, others to heaven (*swarga*) and still others to immediate earthly rebirth.

The journey to the underworld is said to take 4 hours and 40 minutes, so the body of the deceased must not be cremated before this time.

In the *Tibetan Book of the Dead* Yama, having been borrowed from Hinduism, carries a mirror that reflects all the good and evil actions of a person's most recent embodiment.

See also **Emma-o; Hell, the Chinese; Vedic Religion; Yen-Lo.**

Yanomamo. Among these Indians of Venezuela there is a belief that the souls of the deceased, after a rest and rejuvenation period on the **moon**, return to earth as rain that is absorbed by the penises of the men, who, through sexual intercourse, will then transfer them into the womb of their mates. The Yanomamo also believe one alternates gender each life. In fact, these people believe that if a child dies during or shortly after its birth the death was due to it having mistakenly entered a body with the identical gender of its last one.

See also **American Indians; Gender issue of the soul.**

Yarsanism. A religion which is concentrated in southern Kurdistan (Iran and Iraq), Yarsanism possesses an impressive body of religious cosmogony. It holds that the world was created when the Universal Spirit (Haq), who resided in Pre-Eternity in (or as) a pearl, manifested itself in a primary *avatar* as the Lord God (Khawandagar). This signaled the First of the Seven Epochs of universal life. The Lord God then proceeded to create the world. The Spirit further manifested itself in five secondary *avatars* to form the Holy Seven with the Spirit itself.

Yarsanism teaches that all souls start their evolutionary development by entering inanimate objects, eventually advancing into plants, then animals, and finally human beings. Once transmigrating into human form most souls begins a transmigratory journey which can last for 1,000 life-times. This is the equivalent in time to the 50,000 years that it is thought the universe will exist. At the end of this evolutionary journey a man or woman reaches salvation and becomes a holy perfect being which is then privileged to dwell in the high heavens and experience total union with the Universal Spirit.

While it is thought very rare, a person of exceptional quality and effort may in a single life-time reach the highest state. Morally inadequate persons, on the other hand, may regress to an animal form; but such a life is not then counted among the 1,000 lives. Also, not counted is the life-time of an infant that dies before reaching a minimum of 40 days. If after the 1,000 lives, or at the end of the universe's 50,000 years, whichever comes first, a soul has not yet reach the status of a holy person then that soul will be judged at the Final Judgment or Pardivari (the bridge crossing).

See also **Cult of Angels; Evolutionary transmigration of souls; Hashimiyya; Islam; Kanthaeans; Khurramiyya;** *Tanasukh.*

Yazidis or **Yezidis**. These are a non–Muslim Kurdish speaking people of northern Iraq who honor as their founder the 11th century Sufi saint Sheikh Adi b. Musafir. The Yazidis believe that Satan (Arabic: Shaitan), as a fallen angel, repented of his crime and was forgiven by God. Since the term Shaitan was his pre-repentant name it is forbidden for the Yazidis to use it. Instead, this figure is venerated under the title of the Peacock Angel (Aramaic: *Malak Taus*). In accordance with their belief in **transmigration**, if the dying person has led a good life he will be reborn as human being; and if he has lived a bad life he will be reborn as an animal. The Yazidis constitute less than 5 percent of the Kurdish population.

See also **Assassins; Babism and Bahaism; Cult of Angels; Druzes; Evolutionary transmigration of souls; Islam; Mesopotamia; Nusayris (Nursaris); Rebirth, cross-species; Sufism;** *Tanasukh.*

Yeats, William Butler (1865–1939). This Noble Prize–winning Irish poet had a major interest in Platonism, Neoplatonism, the prophetic works of William Blake and **Swedenborg** and in the esoteric and the occult in general. He founded the Irish Hermetic Society in 1885 and from 1887 to 1890 he was a member of the Irish Theosophical Society. This was followed by his joining the British Isis-Urania Lodge of Hermetic Order of the Golden Dawn and still later the Order of the Stella Matu-tina (Morning Star). In 1917 Yeats married Georgie Hyde-Lees, who very shortly afterwards began experimenting with automatic writing. The success of this experiment was manifested by making contact with entities Yeats referred to only as "the Communicators." These spirits communicated an entire esoteric system based on the twenty-eight phases of the **moon** and other astrological elements. In this lunar system the soul works its way through the phases of the moon both during this life and continuing on in between one life and another. The nature of this esoteric system was privately published in 1925 under the title of *A Vision,* which in 1937 was republished in a much revised form, which showed more influence from the Upanishads than in the earlier edition. Further esoteric ideas of both a mystical and magic nature are found in the volume of collected essays of Yeasts titled **Ideas of Good and Evil** (1903).

See also **Astrology and rebirth; Sinnett, Alfred Percy; Theosophy**

Yellow Springs (Huang Quan, WG). In Chinese mythology this is the name for the underground abyss where the souls of the dead reside while awaiting rebirth.

Yen-Lo. This is the Chinese pronunciation for the Sanskrit **Yama**, the lord of the underworld. In the Buddhist-influenced Chinese folk religion Yen-lo was the king of the first hell, but the Jade Emperor decided that he was too merciful towards evil souls and so demoted him to the fifth hell. One of the major significances to this fifth hell is that it is here that the Bank of Hell is located. This is where all the funeral money offered to the deceased by their surviving kin is deposited. With this money the deceased are able to bribe the corrupt officials of hell to let the souls pass quickly through hell and on to their next rebirth. This is the hell for those who either slandered the Buddha or do not believe in karma.

See also **Chinese Religion and Reincarnation; Chuan-lun wang; Emma-o; Hell, the Bank of; Hell, the Chinese.**

Yin and Yang forces *see* **Acupuncture; Chinese Religion and Reincarnation; Rebirth and cyclical time.**

Yoga. According to the "Yoga Sutras" (400CE) past lives can be recalled through yogic meditation.

See also *Bhagavad Gita*; *Bhakti Yoga*; Karma yoga; *Nirvikalpa Samadhi*; Samkhya Yoga.

Yogachara School of Buddhism *see Alayavijnana*; Karmic seeds; *Manas*; Vijnanavada School.

Yogananda, Paramahansa (1893–1952). Having arrived in America from India in 1920 to address the International Congress of Religious Liberals Yogananda remained in the country lecturing on and teaching a Westernized version of Vedantism to record crowds. In 1935 he and his followers established the Self-Realization Fellowship. While the Fellowship, in an effort to be compatible with liberal Christianity does not require any belief in reincarnation and karma, as an offshoot of **Hinduism** it does not discourage the belief. In fact, it appears that Yogananda even thought that some of the passages in the Bible implied reincarnation, such as **Genesis** 9:6.

See also **Atman; Old Testament and the afterlife; Vedanta Society; Vivekananda, Swami.**

Yoruba. This is a tribe of highly urbanized people of southwest Nigeria and neighboring areas. Unlike a number of other African people the Yoruba believe that a person's moral behavior affects his afterlife condition. In the case of a person who has not lived an upright life the creator god Olorun (Olodumare), to whom the dead must confess, can exile him to a place of punishment. If the person has lived an upright life Olorun can offer some degree of reincarnation.

See also **Africa; Afro-American religions; Akan; Igbo; Nupe; Santeria; Zulu.**

Yukaghir. This is one of the Siberian native people who, according to Waldemar Jochelson (1855–1937) in his *The Yukaghir and Yukarghirized Tungus* (1910), believed in reincarnation.

See also **Chukchi; Inuit; Koryaks, Lapps (Saami).**

Zen Buddhism, rebirth in. While most people know the school of Buddhism under the Japanese name Zen it is also called *Chan* (Chinese), *Son* (Korean), and *Thien* (Vietnamese). Zen developed in China under Daoist and Confucianist influences, and eventually spread to Korea, Japan, and Vietnam. The belief system in Zen ranges from folk Zen to philosophical Zen. In the first of these there is all of the standard Buddhist supernaturalism. It accepts the reality of celestial Buddhas and ***bodhisattva***s, gods, ghosts, witches, animals that transformed themselves into human beings, exorcism, protective amulets, prayers for healing, rain, for the defense of the country, and for a good rebirth. Folk Zen has the problem about rebirth that is found in Buddhism in general, namely how can there be rebirth without a soul?

Philosophical Zen places all of its emphasis on living in the "Here and Now" as a prelude to experiencing the "Eternal Now"; therefore, it makes a belief in rebirth and karma entirely optional.

See also **Chinese religion and reincarnation; Mahayana Buddhist rebirth texts; Rebirth in Buddhism.**

Zenith. This term is sometimes used as a synonym for escaping the cycle of birth and death. It is said that to pass from the vault of heaven (a temporary or mere **interim period** place of rest) to the zenith is to pass from life, or the finite, to the eternity or the infinite.

Zhendao/Chen Tao (Chinese: True-Way). The organization by this name has also advertised itself as God's Salvation Church. Its main teachings have been taken from Daoism, Pure Land Buddhism, apocalyptic Christianity, techno-science, and UFO-ism. Zhendao had its beginnings in the 1950s when a woman named Yu-Hsia Chen formed the Association for Research on Soul Light in Taiwan. The purpose of the Association is to better the health, spiritual powers, and karma of its members. Under the later leadership of Hon-Ming Chen prophetic and millennial elements have been added to the group's teachings.

The group's headquarters were relocated from Taiwan to the United States in 1995 due to the belief that after the annihilation of much of the Earth's population in 2043, God will relocate the North American continent onto Mars and transform it into the Kingdom of Heaven/the Pure Land. Just before the annihilation Jesus will arrive in a spaceship to take the members of Zhendao to a safe haven in the interior of the planet. Perhaps another reason for relocating to the United States is the Yu-Hsia Chen's belief that nine and a half million years ago Christ and eleven **bodhisattvas** created humanity in this country or, more specifically, in Texas.

Zhendao teaches that everyone has a tripartite soul. These are the main spiritual light, the physical soul, and the conscious soul. The first of these actually produces the other two upon embodiment. At death each of these souls goes its own way. The main spiritual light is the only one that, upon death, is reincarnated, while the other two will themselves become main spiritual lights if their karma is good, or they will become evil spirits (devils) in hell if their karma is bad. Somewhat like Scientology, Zhendao uses an electronic meter to test the worthiness of its members' souls.

See also **Planets, other; Pluto; Soul, tripartite**.

Zodiac. Since the stars in the zodiac descend below the horizon as the year moves on the zodiac came to be identified with death and rebirth by ancient peoples. This was in contrast to the polar star which remained visible all year round and represented non-rebirth or escape from rebirth. Also, since the polar star represented the northern direction that direction too was associated with such escape, and so the southern direction was given the opposite meaning of continuing rebirth.

See also **Astrology and rebirth; Celestial gates; Moon; Planetary descent and ascent of the soul; Pleiades; Pyramidology; Steiner, Rudolf**.

Zohar see **Adam; Frank, Jacob; Kabbalah**.

Zoroastrianism. This is a dualist Persian (Iranian) religion founded by the prophet Zoroaster some time between the tenth and sixth century BCE, which has survived as a minority religion in Iran and India. Zoroastrianism proposes the existence of two separate cosmic principles, one good called Mazda (God) and one evil called Ahriman. These two principles or beings are in a cosmic struggle in which humanity is also involved. It is the moral responsibility of human beings to ally with God and help defeat evil. Along with a belief in an angelic and demonic hierarchy, Zoroastrianism holds to a belief in a future Messiah, the Resurrection of the Dead, and a Last Judgment at the end of time. Zoroastrianism has no traditional belief in reincarnation; however, some modern Indian members of the faith, called the Parsees (Persians), have adopted the belief in reincarnation under theosophical influence. There is, for example, the esoteric Zoroastrian movement called Ilm-e-khshnoom (Persian: Knowledge of gratification), founded in 1907 by Behramshah Shroff (1858–1927) and established as the Zoroastrian Radih Society in 1919. According to Shroff his teachings are derived from his communication with a secret colony of masters in an Iranian cave who taught, among other teachings, the doctrine of reincarnation.

Nasarvanji Bilimoria, in his *Zoroastrianism in the Light of Theosophy* (1898), has a chapter titled *Transmigration in the Avesta* which states that there is an obscure reference in the *Vendidad*, the most orthodox text of the Zoroastrian canon, that the souls or consciousnesses of dogs, highly regarded animals in Zoroastrianism, upon death reincarnate into Udra (water-dogs) which are mythical beasts, possibly modeled on the seal. Beyond this there is no current evidence for any original belief in reincarnation in Zoroastrianism.

See also **Angels and reincarnation; Ascended masters; Dualism; Gnosticism; Islam; Manichaeism; New Testament and reincarnation; Old Testament and the afterlife; Resurrection, bodily**.

Zulu. These South African people believe that upon death the soul (*idhozi*) remains for a while near the corpse, but then leaves and travels to the Place of Beasts (Esilweni) where it takes on the partial form of an animal, due to the soul's partial animal nature. Eventually it drops this partial animal form and proceeds on to a place of rest where, in time, it dreams about a future life state and upon awakening it is reborn into a human body. The soul repeats this process until it develops sufficiently to become one with the Universal Spirit (Itongo).

See also **Africa**.

Sources Consulted

Acker, Jack. *Journey of a Skeptic: A Quest to Discover the Continuity of Life*. Atlanta: Literary Legends, 2002.

Agate, Joanne. "The Reincarnation Lecture." *Skeptical Briefs* 15, no. 4 (December 2005): 1.

Alcock, James E. "Channeling: Brief History and Contemporary Context." *Skeptical Inquirer* 13, no. 4 (Summer 1989): 380–384.

Alegretti, Wagner. *Retrocognitions; an Investigation into Memories of Past Lives and the Periods Between Lives*. Miami: International Academy of Consciousness, 2004.

Algeo, John. *Reincarnation Explored*. Wheaton, IL: Theosophical Publishing House, 1987.

Almeder, Robert. "A Critique of Arguments Offered against Reincarnation." *Journal of Scientific Exploration* 11, no. 4 (1997): 499–526.

Altizer, Thomas J. J. *Oriental Mysticism and Biblical Eschatology*. Philadelphia: The Westminster Press, 1961.

Anderson, Jerome A. *Reincarnation: A Study of the Human Soul*. San Francisco: Lotus, 1896.

Andrade, Hernani Guimarães. *A Case Suggestive of Reincarnation: Jacira and Ronaldo*. São Paulo: Instituto Brasilieriro de Pesquisas Psicobiofisicas, 1980.

_____. *Morte, Renascimento, Evolucão*. São Paulo: Editora Pensamento, 1983.

_____. *Reencarnacão no Brazil: oito casos que sugerem renascimento*. Matão, Est. de São Paulo: O Clarim, 1988.

Andrews, Ted. *Uncover Your Past Lives*. St. Paul, MN: Llewellyn, 2004.

Angus, S. *The Religious Quests of the Greco-Roman World: A Study in the Historical Background of Early Christianity*. New York: Scribner's, 1929.

Aquinas, Thomas. "The Resurrection of Man." In *Immortality*, edited by Paul Edwards. Amherst, NY: Prometheus Books, 1997.

Archiati, Pietro. *Reincarnation in Modern Life: Towards a New Christian Awareness*. London: Temple Lodge, 1997.

Arifuku, Kogaku. "The Immortality of the Soul and the Problem of Life and Death in the Zen-Buddhist Thought of Dogen." In *Progress, Apocalypse, and Completion of History and Life After Death of the Human Person in the World Religions*, edited by Peter Koslowski, 22–39. Dordrecht: Kluwer Academic Publishers, 2002.

Arthur, Joyce. "Fetal Pain: A Red Herring in the Abortion Debate." *Free Inquiry* 25, no. 5 (Aug.–Sept. 2005): 44–47.

Arvey, Michael. *Reincarnation: Opposing View Points*. San Diego: Greenhaven Press, 1989.

_____. *A Soul's Journey. Empowering the Present through Past Life Regression*. Austin: Boru Books, 1996.

Ashley, Leonard R. N. *The Complete Book of Devils and Demons*. Fort Lee, NJ: Barricade Books, 1996.

Atkinson, William Walker. *Reincarnation and the Law of Karma*. Chicago: Yogi Publication Society, 1936.

Auerbach, Loyd. *Reincarnation, Channeling and Possession: A Parapsychologist's Handbook*. New York: Warner Books, 1993.

Auken, John Van. *Reincarnation: Your Secret Life*. New York: Ballantine Books, 1991.

Avery, Jeanne. *Astrology and Your Past Lives: Reincarnations through Saturn's Placement in Your Chart*. New York: Simon and Schuster, 1987.

_____. *A Soul's Journey: Empowering the Present through Past Life Regression*. Austin: Boru Books, 1996.

Babb, Lawrence A. "Destiny and Responsibility: Karma in Popular Hinduism." In *Karma: An Anthropological Inquiry*, edited by Charles F. Keyes and E. Valentine Daniel, 163–181. Berkeley: University of California Press, 1983.

Bach, Richard S. *The Bridge Across Forever*. New York: William Morrow, 1984.

_____. *Jonathan Livingston Seagull*. New York: Macmillan, 1970.

Bache, Christopher M. *Lifecycles: Reincarnation and the Web of Life*. New York: Paragon House, 1990.

Bailey, Alice A. *A Treatise of White Magic*. New York: Lucis, 1952.

_____. *Treatise on the Seven Rays: Esoteric Astrology*. New York: Lucis, 1951.

Baker, Robert A. "The Effects of Suggestion on Past Lives Regression." *American Journal of Clinical Hypnosis* 25, no. 1 (July 1982): 71–76.

Baker, Robert A., and Joe Nickell. *Missing Pieces: How to Investigate Ghosts, UFOs, Psychics, and Other Mysteries*. Buffalo, NY: Prometheus Books, 1992.

Balche, Robert W., and David Taylor. "Heaven's Gate: Implications for the Study of Commitment to New Religions." In *Encyclopedic Sourcebook of UFO Religions*, edited by James R. Lewis, 211–237. Amherst, NY: Prometheus Books, 2003.

Ballard, Guy Warren. *The Magic Presence*. Chicago: Saint Germain Press, 1935.

_____. *Unveiled Mysteries*. Chicago: Saint Germain Press, 1934.

Banerjee, H. N. *Americans Who Have Been Reincarnated*. New York: Macmillan, 1980.

_____. *Lives Unlimited: Reincarnation East and West*. Garden City, N.Y: Doubleday, 1974.

_____. *The Once and Future Life: An Astonishing Twenty-five-year Study on Reincarnation.* New York: Dell, 1979.

Barash, David. "When Are Souls Handed Out?" *Los Angeles Times,* July 18, 2005, B11.

Beckwith, C. A. "Soul and Spirit, Biblical Conception of." *The New Schaff-Herzog Encyclopedia of Religious Knowledge,* edited by Samuel Macauley Jackson. vol. 11, 12–14. New York: Funk and Wagnalls, 1911.

Belanger, Michelle. *Walking the Twilight Path: A Gothic Book of the Dead.* Woodbury, MN: Llewellyn, 2008.

Benard, Elisabeth. "The Tibetan Tantric View of Death and Afterlife." In *Death and Afterlife: Perspectives of World Religions,* edited by Hiroshi Obayashi, 169–180. New York: Greenwood Press, 1992.

Bengtson, David R. *Past Lives of Famous People; Journeys of the Soul.* Woodside, CA: Bluestar Communications, 1997.

Bensley, D. Alan. "Can Minds Leave Bodies?" *Skeptical Inquirer* 27, no. 4 (Jul/Aug. 2003): 34–39.

Berg, Philip S. (Rabbi). *Wheels of a Soul; Reincarnation, Your Life, Today and Tomorrow.* Revised edition. New York: Kabbalah Learning Centre, 1991.

Berger, Arthur S. "Order Out of Chaos in Survival Research." *Skeptical Inquirer* 14, no. 4 (Summer 1990): 390–396.

Berger, Arthur, and Joyce Berger. "Appendix B, Annotated Bibliography of Works in English." In *Reincarnation: Fact or Fable.* Wellingborough, Northamptonshire: The Aquarian Press, 1991.

Berling, Judith A. "Death and Afterlife in Chinese Religions." In *Death and Afterlife: Perspectives of World Religion,* edited by Hiroshi Obayashi, 181–192. New York: Greenwood Press, 1992.

Berman, Michael. *Soul Loss and the Shamanic Story.* Newcastle: Cambridge Scholars Publishing, 2008.

Bernstein, Morey. *The Search for Bridey Murphy.* Garden City, NY: Doubleday, 1956.

Besant, Annie. *The Ancient Wisdom: An Outline of Theosophical Teachings.* Adyar, Madras: Theosophical Publishing House, 1897.

_____. *Death and After?* London: Theosophical Publishing Society, 1914. (Theosophical Manuals. No. 3).

_____. *Karma,* 8th edition. Wheaton, Illinois: Theosophical Publishing House, 1971.

_____. *The Necessity for Re-Incarnation.* London: Theosophical Publishing Society, 1904.

_____. *Reincarnation.* London: Theosophical Publishing Society, 1892. (Theosophical Manuals. No. 2).

_____. *A Study in Karma.* 2nd edition, Adyar, Madras: Theosophical Publishing House, 1917.

Besant, Annie, and C.W. Leadbeater. *The Lives of Alcyone,* co-authored with Adyar. Madras: Theosophical Publishing House, 1924.

Besterman, Theodore. "The Belief in Rebirth of the Druses and Other Syrian Sects." *Folk-Lore: A Quarterly Review of Myth, Tradition, Institution, and Custom,* vol. 39, no. 2 (June 30, 1928): 133–148.

Bevir, Mark. "The West Turns Eastward: Madame Blavatsky and the Transformation of the Occult Tradition." *Journal of the American Academy of Religion* 62, no. 3 (Fall 1994): 747–767.

Biddle, Kenneth. "Ghost Photographs: Orbs or Dust?" *Skeptical Briefs* 18, no. 3 (September 2008).

Bilimoria, Nasarvanji F. *Zoroastrianism in the Light of Theosophy.* Bombay: Theosophical Society, Blavatsky Lodge, 1898.

Bjorling, Joel. *Reincarnation: A Bibliography.* New York: Garland Press, 1996.

Blackmore, Susan. "Beyond the Self: The Escape from Reincarnation in Buddhism and Psychology." In *Reincarnation: Fact or Fable,* edited by Arthur and Joyce Berger, 117–129. London: The Aquarian Press, 1991.

_____. "What Can the Paranormal Teach Us About Consciousness?" *Skeptical Inquirer* 25, no. 2 (Mar/Apr. 2001) 22–27.

Blakeslee, Sandra. "Out-of-Body Experience? Your Brain Is to Blame." *New York Times,* October 3, 2006, D1.

_____. "This Is Your Brain Under Hypnosis." *The New York Times,* November 22, 2005, D1.

Blavatsky, Helena Petrovna. *An Abridgement of the Secret Doctrine.* London: Theosophical Publishing House, 1966.

_____. *Isis Unveiled: A Master Key to the Mysteries of Ancient and Modern Science and Theology.* Pasadena, CA: Theosophical University Press, 1972.

_____. *The Secret Doctrine: The Synthesis of Science, Religion and Philosophy.* London: Theosophical Publishing House, 1950.

_____. *The Theosophical Glossary.* Los Angeles: The Theosophy Company, 1990.

Bodde, Derk. "The Chinese View of Immortality: Its Expression by Chu Hsi and Its Relationship to Buddhist Thought." *The Review of Religion* 6, no. 4 (May 1942), 369–383.

Bokenkamp, Stephen R. *Ancestors and Anxiety: Daoism and the Birth of Rebirth in China.* Berkeley: University of California Press, 2007.

Bolduc, Henry Leo. *The Journey Within: Past Life Regression and Channeling.* Independence, VA: Adventures into Time, 1988.

Bower, Bruce. "Night of the Crusher: The Waking Nightmare of Sleep Paralysis Propels People into a Spirit World." *Science News* 168, no. 2 (July 9, 2005): 27–29.

Brady, Michael J. *Infinite Horizons: A Psychic Experience.* Virginia Beach: Norfork Unilaw Library, 1982.

Brandon, S.G.F. *The Judgment of the Dead: The Idea of Life After Death in the Major Religions.* New York: Scribner's, 1967.

Bregman, Lucy. "Three Psycho-mythologies of Death: Becker, Hillman, and Lifton." *Journal of the American Academy of Religion* 52, no. 3 (Sept. 1984): 461–479.

Bremmer, Jan N. *The Rise and Fall of the Afterlife: The 1995 Read-Tuckwell Lectures at The University of Bristol.* London: Routledge, 2002.

Brennan, J.H. *The Reincarnation Workbook: A Complete Course in Recalling Past Lives.* Wellingborough, Northamptonshire: The Aquarian Press, 1989.

Brody, Jane E. "When a Brain Forgets Where Memory Is." *The New York Times,* April 17, 2007.

Brox, Norbert. "The Early Christian Debate on the Migration of Souls." In *Reincarnation or Resurrection?,* edited by Hermann Haring and Johann-Baptist Metz, 75–80. London: SCM Press, 1993. (Concilium 1993/5).

Bruno, Giordano. *Spaccio de la bestia trionfante* [*Expulsion of the Triumphant Beast*], edited by Hilary Gatti. Aldershot Hants, England: Ashgate, 2002.

Bruns, J. Edgar. *The Christian Buddhism of St. John: New Insights into the Fourth Gospel.* New York: Paulist Press, 1971.

Buddhadsa (Bhikkhu). *Paticcasamuppada: Dependent*

Origination. Bangkok: The Foundation of Sublime Life, 1986.
Bunson, Matthew. *The Vampire Encyclopedia.* New York: Crown, 1993.
Burman, Edward. *The Assassins: Holy Killers of Islam.* Northampton, Wellingborough: Aquarian Press, 1987.
Bynum, Caroline Walker. "Material Continuity, Personal Survival, and the Resurrection of the Body: A Scholastic Discussion in its Medieval and Modern Context." *History of Religions* 30, no.1 (August 1990): 51–85.
Callahan, Tim. "A New Mythology: Ancient Astronauts, Lost Civilizations, and New Age Paradigm." *Skeptic* 13, no. 4 (2008): 32–41.
Canizares, Raul. *Walking with the Night: The Afro-Cuban World of Santeria.* Rochester, VT: Destiny Books, 1993.
Cannon, Alexander. *The Power of Karma in Relation to Destiny.* London: Rider, 1936.
_____. *The Power Within.* New York: E.P. Dutton, 1953.
Caramutto (Ven Bhikkhu). "What Is Reborn — and Why?" *The Middle Way: Journal of The Buddhist Society* 48, no. 2 (August 1973): 71–74.
Carey, Benedict. "A Neuroscientific Look at Speaking in Tongues." *Los Angeles Times,* November 7, 2006, D5.
Carrier, Richard C. "The Burial of Jesus in Light of Jewish Law." In *The Empty Tomb: Jesus Beyond the Grave,* edited by Robert M. Price and Jeffery Jay Lowder, 369–392. Amherst, NY: Prometheus Books, 2005.
_____. "The Plausibility of Theft." In *The Empty Tomb: Jesus Beyond the Grave,* edited by Robert M. Price and Jeffery Jay Lowder, 349–368. Amherst, NY: Prometheus Books, 2005.
_____. "The Spiritual Body of Christ and the Legend of the Empty Tomb." In *The Empty Tomb: Jesus Beyond the Grave,* edited by Robert M. Price and Jeffery Jay Lowder, 105–231. Amherst, NY: Prometheus Books, 2005.
Carroll, Robert Todd. *The Skeptic's Dictionary: A Collection of Strange Beliefs, Amusing Deceptions, and Dangerous Delusions.* Hoboken. NJ: John Wiley, 2000.
Cassiel. *Encyclopedia of Black Magic.* New York: Mallard Press, 1990.
Cavendish, Richard, editor. *Encyclopedia of the Unexplained: Magic, Occultism and Parapsychology.* London: Arkana, 1989.
Cayce, Edgar Evans. *Edgar Cayce on Atlantis.* New York: Warner Books, 1968.
Cerminara, Gina. *Many Lives, Many Loves.* Marina Del Rey, CA: DeVorss, 1963.
_____. *Many Mansions: The Edgar Cayce Story on Reincarnation.* New York: Penguin, 1967.
_____. *The World Within.* New York: William Sloane Associates, 1957.
Cerve, W. S., and James Ward. *Lemuria: The Lost Continent of the Pacific.* San Jose, CA: Rosicrucian Press, AMORC College, 1931.
Chadwick, Gloria. *Reincarnation and Your Past Life Memories.* New York: Gramercy Books, 1988.
Champhausen, Rufus C. *The Encyclopedia of Sacred Sexuality: From Aphrodisiacs and Ecstasy to Yoni Worship and Zap-lam Yoga.* Rochester VT: Inner Traditions, 1999.
Chapple, Christopher. *Karma and Creativity.* Albany: State University of New York Press, 1986.
Chari, C.T.K. "Paramnesia and Reincarnation." *Proceedings of the Society of Psychical Research* 53 (December, 1962): 264–286.
_____. "Paranormal Cognition, Survival and Reincarnation." *Journal of the American Society of Psychical Research* 56 (October 1962): 158–183.
_____. "Regression 'Beyond Birth.'" *Tomorrow* 6 (1956): 87–96.
_____. "Reincarnation Research: Method and Interpretation." In *Signet Handbook of Parapsychology,* edited by Martin Ebon, 313–324. New York: New American Library, 1978.
Chevalier, Jean, and Alain Gheerbrant. *A Dictionary of Symbols.* Translated by John Buchanan-Brown. London: Penguin Books, 1996.
Chidester, David. *Patterns of Transcendence: Religion, Death, and Dying.* Belmont, CA: Wadsworth, 1990.
Chinchore, Mangala R. *Anatta/Anatma: An Analysis of the Buddhist Anti-Substantialist Crusade.* Delhi: Sri Satguru, 1955.
Chittick, William C. *Sufism: A Short Introduction.* Oxford: Oneworld, 2000.
Christie-Murray, David. *Reincarnation: Ancient Beliefs and Modern Evidence.* Bridgeport, Dorset: Prism Press, 1981.
Churchward, James. *Children of Mu.* Washburn, NY: Ives, 1931.
_____.*Cosmic Forces of Mu.* Washburn, NY: Ives, 1934.
_____. *The Lost Continent of Mu: The Motherland of Man.* New York: W.E. Rudge, 1926.
_____. *The Sacred Symbols of Mu.* Washburn, NY: Ives, 1933.
Clarke, Peter B. *Black Paradise: The Rastafarian Movement.* Wellingborough, Northamptonshire: Aquarian Press, 1986.
Clifton, Chas S. *Encyclopedia of Heresies and Heretics.* Santa Barbara, CA: ABC-CLIO, 1992.
Clow, Barbara Hand. *Eye of the Centaur: A Visionary Guide into Past Lives.* St. Paul, MN: Llewellyn, 1987.
Cohen, Daniel. *The Encyclopedia of the Strange.* New York: Avon, 1985.
Collin, Robert. *The Theory of Celestial Influence.* London: Vincent Stuart, 1954.
_____. *The Theory of Eternal Life.* London: Vincent Stuart, 1956.
Collins, Steven. *Selfless Persons: Imagery and Thought in Theravada Buddhism.* Cambridge: Cambridge University Press, 1982.
Collis, J. S. "Reincarnation and Karma." *The Aryan Path* 9, no. 6 (June 1938): 288–290.
Colton, Ann Ree. *Draughts of Remembrance: Memories of Past Lives, The Seven-Year Etheric Cycles of the Soul.* Glendale, CA: Ann Ree Colton Foundation of Nescience, 1959.
Cook, Emily Williams, Bruce Greyson, and Ian Stevenson. "Do Any Near-Death Experiences Provide Evidence for the Survival of Human Personality after Death? Relevant Features and Illustrative Case Reports." *Journal of Scientific Exploration* 12, no.3 (1998): 377–406.
Cook, Ryan J. "News Media and the Religious Use of UFOs: The Case of Chen-Tao, The True Way." In *Encyclopedic Sourcebook of UFO Religions,* edited by James R. Lewis, 301–320. Amherst, NY: Prometheus Books, 2003.
Cooper, Irving S. *Reincarnation: The Hope of the World,* 7th edition. Wheaton, IL: The Theosophical Press, 1964.
Corelli, Marie. *Ardath: The Story of a Dead Self.* London: Richard Bentley, 1889.

_____. *The Life Everlasting, A Romance of Reality*. New York: Grosset and Dunlap, 1911.
_____. *A Romance of Two Worlds*. London: Richard Bentley, 1886.
_____. *Ziska: The Problem of a Wicked Soul*. New York: Stone and Kimball, 1897.
Cowie, Susan D., and Tom Johnson. *The Mummy in Fact, Fiction and Film*. Jefferson, NC: McFarland, 2002.
Cranston, Sylvia, and Carey Williams. *Reincarnation: A New Horizon in Science, Religion, and Society*. New York: Julian Press, 1984.
Creel, Austin B. "Contemporary Philosophical Treatments of Karma and Rebirth." In *Karma & Rebirth: Post Classical Developments,* edited by Ronald W. Neufeldt, 1–14. Albany: State University of New York Press, 1986.
Cross, F. L., and E. A. Livingstone, editors. *The Oxford Dictionary of the Christian Church*. Oxford: Oxford University Press, 1997.
Crowley, Aleister. *Magick in Theory and Practice*. Paris: Privately Published, 1929.
Cuevas, Bryan J. "Intermediate States." In *Encyclopedia of Buddhism*, edited by Robert E. Bushwell, vol. one, 377–380. New York: Thomson Gale, 2004.
Cummins, Geraldine Dorothy. *Beyond Human Personality*. London: Ivor Nicholson & Watson, 1935.
_____. *Mind in Life and Death*. London: Aquarian Press, 1956.
_____. *Road to Immortality*. London: The Psychic Book Club, 1947, originally 1932.
_____. *The Scripts of Cleophas*. London: Rider, 1928.
_____. *Swan on a Black Sea: A Study of Automatic Writing*. London: Routledge & K. Paul, 1965.
_____. *They Survive*. London: Rider, 1946.
D. Ph. "Reincarnation in the English Novel." *The Aryan Path* 9, no. 6 (June 1938): 281–284.
Damian-Knight, Guy. *Karma and Destiny in the I Ching*. New York: Routledge & Kegan Paul, 1987.
Danelek, Allen J. *Mystery of Reincarnation: The Evidence & Analysis of Rebirth,* St. Paul, MN: Llewellyn, 2005.
Davidson, Gustav. *A Dictionary of Angels, Including the Fallen Angels*. New York: Macmillan, 1967.
Davis, Stephen T. *Risen Indeed: Making Sense of the Resurrection*. Grand Rapids, MI: William B. Eerdmans, 1993.
Dawn, Rose. *The Miracle Power*. San Antonio, TX: Mayan Press, 1959.
Day, Harvey. *Occult Illustrated Dictionary*. New York: Oxford University Press, 1976.
Deardorff, James W. *Jesus in India: A Reexamination of Jesus' Asian Traditions In the Light of Evidence Supporting Reincarnation*. Lanham, MD: International Scholastic Publications, 1994.
Dee, James H. "The Silver Bullet Question That Kills the Immortal Soul." *Free Inquiry* 24, no.3 (April/May 2004): 47–49.
Dennis, Geoffery W. *The Encyclopedia of Jewish Myth, Magic and Mysticism*. Woodbury, MN: Llewellyn, 2007.
De Silva, Lynn A. *The Problem of the Self in Buddhism and Christianity*. London: Macmillan, 1979.
_____. *Reincarnation in Buddhist and Christian Thought*. Colombo: The Study Centre for Religion and Society, 1968.
Dethlefsen, Thorwald. *The Challenge of Fate*, London: Coveture, 1979.

_____. *Voices from Other Lives: Reincarnation as a Source of Healing*. New York: M. Evans, 1977.
Deutsch, Eliot. *Advaita Vedanta: A Philosophical Reconstruction*. Honolulu: The University of Hawaii Press, 1969.
Dhammananda, K. Sri. *Do You Believe in Rebirth?* Kuala Lumpur: The Buddhist Missionary Society, Jalan Berhala, 1981. (Buddhist Missionary Society Series no. 2, Rev. edition).
Dharmasiri, Gunapala. *A Buddhist Critique of the Christian Concept of God*. Colombo: Lake House Investments, 1974.
Donnelly, Ignatius. *Atlantis, or the Antediluvian World*. New York: Harper, 1882.
Dowling, Levi H. *Aquarian Gospel of Jesus Christ*. London: C. F. Cazenone, 1908.
Drange, Theodore M. "Why Resurrect Jesus?" In *The Empty Tomb: Jesus Beyond the Grave*, edited by Robert M. Price and Jeffery Jay Lowder, 55–67. Amherst, NY: Prometheus Books, 2005.
Drury, Nevill. *Dictionary of Mysticism and the Occult*. San Francisco: Harper and Row, 1985.
_____. *The Dictionary of the Esoteric*. London: Watkins, 2002.
_____. *The History of Magic in the Modern Age: The Quest for Personal Transformation*. New York: Carroll & Graf, 2000.
_____. *Reincarnation, Exploring the Concept of Reincarnation in Religion, Philosophy and Traditional Cultures*. New York: Barnes and Noble, 2002.
Ducasse, Curt John. *A Critical Examination of the Belief in a Life After Death*. Springfield, IL: Charles C. Thomas, 1961.
_____. *Is a Life After Death Possible?* Berkeley: University of California Press, 1948.
_____. *Nature, Mind, and Death,* Chicago: Open Court, 1951.
_____. "Survival as Transmigration." In *Immortality,* edited by Paul Edwards. Amherst, NY: Prometheus Books, 1997.
Duenwald, Mary. "The Biology of Sex Ratios." *Discover* 26, no. 6 (June 2005): 20–21.
Dunwich, Gerina. *The Concise Lexicon of the Occult*. New York: Carol Publishing Group, 1990.
Eady, Dorothy. *The Search for Om Sety: A Story of Eternal Love,* Garden City, NY: Doubleday, 1987.
Eady, Dorothy, and Hanny El Zeini. *Abydos: The Holy City of Ancient Egypt*. Los Angeles: L L, 1981.
Eason, Cassandra. *Discover Your Past Lives*. London: Foulshan, 1996.
Eberhard, Wolfram. *A Dictionary of Chinese Symbols: Hidden Symbols in Chinese Life and Thought*. Trans. G. L. Campbell. London: Routledge & Kegan Paul, 1986.
Ebon, Martin. *Reincarnation in the Twentieth Century*. New York: New American Library, 1970.
Edelmann, Jonathan, and William Bernet. "Setting Criteria for Ideal Reincarnation Research." *Journal of Consciousness Studies* 14, no.12 (2007): 92–101.
Edwards, Paul. "The Dependence of Consciousness on the Brain." In *Immortality,* edited by Paul Edwards. Amherst, NY: Prometheus Books, 1997.
_____. "Karma. Tribulations." In *Immortality,* edited by Paul Edwards. Amherst, NY: Prometheus Books, 1997.
_____. *Reincarnation: A Critical Examination,* Amherst, NY: Prometheus Books, 1996.

Efthimiou, Costas J., and Sohang Gandhi. "Cinema Fiction vs. Physics Reality: Ghosts, Vampires, and Zombies." *Skeptical Inquirer* July/Aug. vol. 31, no. 4 (2007): 27–34.

eHRAFWorld Cultures. New Haven, CT: Human Relations Area Files, http://www.ehrafworldcultures.Yale.edu.

Elbert, Jerome W. *Are Souls Real?* Amherst, NY: Prometheus Books, 2000.

Elkin, A.P. *The Australian Aborigines*. Garden City, NY: Anchor Books, 1964.

Elkins, Don, Carla R. Ruecket, and Jim McCarthy. *The Law of the One*. Louisville, KY: L/L Research, 1981.

Ellwood, Robert S. "UFO Religious Movements." In *America's Alternative Religions*, edited by Timothy Miller, 393–399. Albany: State University of New York Press, 1995.

Ellwood, Robert S., editor. *Eastern Spirituality in America: Selected Writings*. New York: Paulist Press, 1987.

Evans, Arthur. *The God of Ecstasy: Sex-Roles and the Madness of Dionysus*. New York: St. Martin's Press, 1988.

Evans-Wentz, W.Y. *The Tibetan Book of the Dead or the After-Death Experiences on the Bardo Plane, According to Lama Kazi Dawa-Samdup's English Rendering*. 3rd edition. New York: Oxford University Press, 1960.

Fab, Peter. *Man's Rise to Civilization*. New York: Avon, 1969.

Fales, Evan. "Taming the Tehom: The Sign of Jonah in Matthew." In *The Empty Tomb: Jesus Beyond the Grave*, edited by Robert M. Price and Jeffery Jay Lowder, 307–348. Amherst, NY: Prometheus Books, 2005.

Ferm, Vergilius. "Soul." In *Encyclopedia of Religion*, edited by Vergilius Ferm, 728–729. Paterson, NJ: Littlefield, Adams, 1964.

Fernandez Olmos, Margarite, and Lizabeth Paravisini-Gebert. *Creole Religions of the Caribbean: An Introduction from Voudou and Santeria to Obeah and Esiritismo*. New York: Oxford University Press, 2003.

Feuerstein, Georg. "Tantrism and Neotantrism." *The Journal of Divine Ecstasy* 1, no. 4 (1992): 4–10.

Filadoro, Massimiliano. *Tarot of Reincarnation*. Torino: Lo Sacarabeo, 2007.

Finkelstein, Adrian. *Your Past Lives and the Healing Process: A Psychiatrist Looks at Reincarnation and Spiritual Healing*. Malibu, CA: 50 Gates, 1997.

Firenze, Paul. "Spirit Photography: How Early Spiritualists Tried to Save Religion by Using Science." *Skeptic* 11, no. 2 (2004): 70–78.

Fisher, Joe. *The Case for Reincarnation*. Toronto: Bantam Books, Inc., 1985.

Flew, Anthony. "Transmigration and Reincarnation." In *Reincarnation: Fact or Fable*, edited by Arthur and Joyce Berger, 101–116. London: The Aquarian Press, 1991.

Flournoy, Theodore, and Helen Smith. *From India to the Planet Mars: A Study of a Case of Somnambulism with Glossolalia*. New Hyde Park, NY: University Books, 1963.

Foer, Joshua. "The Psychology of Déjà vu." *Discover* 26, no. 9 (Sept. 2005): 18–19.

Forrest, Peter. "Reincarnation Without Survival of Memory or Character." *Philosophy East and West*, 28, no.1 (January 1978): 91–97.

Forster, Allan. *Success through Discovering Your Past Lives*. New York: Body Well Press, 1994.

Fortune, Dion. *Psychic Self-Defense*. London: Rider, 1930.

Franklin, J. Jeffrey. *The Lotus and the Lion: Buddhism and the British Empire*. Ithaca: Cornell University Press, 2008.

Frazer, James George. *The Golden Bough*. New York: Macmillan, 1963.

Frazier, Kendrick. "How to Study Reincarnation: Guidelines for Research." *Skeptical Inquirer* (May/June 2008): 13.

Free, Wynn, and David Wilcock, *The Reincarnation of Edgar Cayce: Interdimensional Communication and Global Transformation*. Berkeley, CA: Frog, 2004.

Freeman, James Dillet. *The Case for Reincarnation*. Unity Village, MO: Unity Books, 1986.

Freidel, David. "Betraying the Maya." *Archaeology* 60, no. 2 (March/April 2007): 36–41.

Freke, Timothy & Peter Gandy. *Jesus and the Lost Goddess: The Secret Teachings of the Original Christians*. New York: Harmony Books, 2001.

Gardner, Gerald. *Witchcraft Today*. London: Rider, 1954.

Gardner, Martin. *Fads and Fallacies: In the Name of Science*. New York: Dover, 1957.

Gaynor, Frank. *Dictionary of Mysticism*. New York: Philosophical Library, 1953.

Glaskin, G. M. *A Door to Eternity: Proving the Christos Experience*. London: Wildwood House Limited, 1979.

———. *Windows of the Mind: Discovering Your Past and Future Lives through Massage and Mental Exercise*. New York: Delacorte Press, 1974.

———. *Worlds Within*. 2nd edition. London: Arrow Books Limited, 1978.

Geisler, Norman L., and J. Yutaka Amano. *The Reincarnation Sensation*. Wheaton, IL: Tyndale House, 1986.

Gellatly, Angus, and Oscar Zarate. *Introducing the Mind and Brain*. Cambridge: Icon, 1999.

Gellene, Danise. "Out-of-Body Feeling Created in Labs." *Los Angeles Times*, August 24, 2007, A24.

George, Marie I. "Aquinas on Reincarnation." *The Thomist* 60, no.1 (January 1996): 33–52.

Gershom, Yonassan. *Beyond the Ashes; Cases of Reincarnation from the Holocaust*. Virginia Beach, VA: A.R.E. Press, 1992.

Givens, Terryl L. *When Souls Had Wings: Pre-Mortal Existence in Western Thought*. New York: Oxford University Press, 2010.

Glasse, Cyril. *The Concise Encyclopedia of Islam*. San Francisco: Harper & Row, 1989.

Glausiusz, Josie. "When the Brain Loses the Body." *Discover* (Dec. 2007): 23.

Godwin, Joscelyn. "The Case Against Reincarnation." *Gnosis: A Journal of the Western Inner Traditions* no. 42 (winter 1997): 28–32.

Goldberg, Bruce. *Past Lives Future Lives*. New York: Ballantine Books, 1982.

Goodacre, Mark, and Nicholas Perrin, editors. *Questioning Q: A Multidimensional Critique*. Downers Grove, IL: InterVarsity Press, 2004.

Goudey, R. F. *Reincarnation: A Universal Truth*. Los Angeles: The Aloha Press, 1928.

Gragnani, Carlos. "Another Life or a Life of Another?" *The Middle Way: Journal of the Buddhist Society* 50, no. 1 (May 1975): 29–36.

———. *Birth, Life, and Death of the Ego*. Kandy, Sri Lanka: Buddhist Publication Society, 1975. (The Wheel Publication no. 215).

Graham, David. *The Practical Side of Reincarnation*. Englewood Cliffs, NJ: Prentice-Hall, 1976.

Grant, Frederick C., editor. *Hellenistic Religions: The Age of Syncretism.* New York: Liberal Arts Press, 1953.

Grant, Marcel. *The Religion of the Chinese People.* Trans. Maurice Freedman. New York: Harper & Row, 1975.

Greasley, Peter. "Management of Positive and Negative Responses in a Spiritualist Medium Consultation." *Skeptical Inquirer* 24, no. 5 (Sept/Oct. 2000): 45–49.

Green, Jeff. *Pluto: The Evolutionary Journey of the Soul.* St. Paul, MN: Llewellyn, 1986.

Green, Miranda J. *Dictionary of Celtic Myth and Legend.* London: Thames and Hudson, 1992.

———. *The World of the Druids.* London: Thames and Hudson, 1997.

Greene, Liz. "The Ancient Shape of Fate." In *Karma: Rhythmic Return to Harmony.* 3rd edition, edited by V. Hanson, R. Stewart, and S. Nicholson, 150–168. Wheaton, IL: Theosophical Publishing House, 1990.

———. *Saturn: A New Look at an Old Devil.* New York: Samuel Weiser, 1976.

Greer, John Michael. *The New Encyclopedia of the Occult.* St. Paul, MN: Llewellyn, 2003.

Grettings, Fred. *Encyclopedia of the Occult: A Guide to Every Aspect of Occult Lore, Belief, and Practice.* London: Rider, 1986.

Grof, Stanislav, and Christiana. *Beyond Death: The Gates of Consciousness.* London: Thames and Hudson: 1980.

Gruber, Elmar R. & Holger Kersten. *The Original Jesus: The Buddhist Sources of Christianity.* Shaftesbury, Dorset: Element, 1995.

Guenon, Rene. *Introduction to the Study of the Hindu Doctrines.* London: Lazac, 1945.

Guiley, Rosemary E. *The Encyclopedia of Angels.* 2nd edition. New York: Checkmark Books, 2004.

———. *Harper's Encyclopedia of Mystical and Paranormal Experience.* San Francisco: Harper, 1991.

Guirdham, Arthur. *Cathars and Reincarnation.* London: Neville Spearman, 1970.

———. "Clinical Evidence of Reincarnation." *The Middle Way: Journal of the Buddhist Society* 48, no. 2 (August 1973): 75–78.

———. *A Foot in Both Worlds.* Jersey: Neville Spearman, 1973.

———. *The Lake and the Castle.* Jersey: Neville Spearman, 1976.

———. *We Are One Another.* Jersey: Neville Spearman, 1974.

Gunaratana, V. F. *Rebirth Explained.* Kandy, Sri Lanka. Buddhist Publication Society, 1980. (The Wheel Publication no. 167/168/169).

Gunter-Jones, Roger. "Release from Rebirth." *The Middle Way: Journal of the Buddhist Society* 43, no. 4 (February 1969): 161–164.

Haggard, H. Rider. *Ayesha: The Return of She. In the Classic Adventures: Ayesha: The Return of She: An African Romance.* Poole, England: New Orchard Editions, 1986. (Oxford World's Classics).

———. *She.* Oxford: Oxford University Press, 1998.

———. *She and Allen.* New York: Ballantine Books, 1978.

Halbfass, Wilhelm. "Karma, Apurva, and 'Natural' Causes: Observations on the Growth and Limits of the Theory of Samsara." In *Karma and Rebirth in Classical Indian Traditions,* edited by Wendy Doniger O'Flaherty, 268–302. Berkeley: University of California Press. 1980.

Halevi, Z'ev ben Shimon. *Kabbalah and Exodus.* Boulder: Shambala, 1980.

Hall, Calvin S., and Lindzey, Gardner. *Theories of Personality.* New York: John Wiley, 1970.

Hall, Harriet. "Seek and Ye Shall Find: A Review of *The God Code: The Secret of Our Past, the Promise of Our Future* by Gregg Braden." *Skeptic* 11, no. 4 (2005): 85–86.

Hall, Judy. *Deja Who? A New Look at Past Lives.* Tallahassee, FL: Findhorn Press, 1998.

Hall, Manly Palmer. *Astrology and Reincarnation.* 2nd edition. Los Angeles: The Philosophical Research Society, 1980.

———. *Death to Rebirth: Five Essays.* Los Angeles: The Philosophical Research Society, 1979.

———. *Past Lives and Present Problems: How to Prepare for a Fortunate Rebirth.* Los Angeles: The Philosophical Research Society, 1977.

———. *Reincarnation: The Cycle of Necessity.* Los Angeles: The Philosophical Research Society, 1956.

———. *Research on Reincarnation.* Los Angeles: The Philosophical Research Society, 1964.

———. *The Secret Teachings of All Ages.* New York: Jeremy P. Tarcher/Penguin, 2003.

Hamilton, Malcolm. *Sociology and the World's Religions.* New York: St. Martin's Press, 1998.

Hammerman, David, and Lisa Lenard. *The Complete Idiot's Guide to Reincarnation.* Indianapolis, IN: Alpha Books, 2000.

Hanayama, Shoyu. *An Introduction to the Buddhist Canon: 139 Buddhist Scriptures.* Tokyo: The Buddhist Promoting Foundation, 1995.

Hanson, Virginia. "The Other Face of Karma." In *Karma: Rhythmic Return to Harmony.* 3rd edited by Virginia Hanson, Shirley Nicholson, and Rosemarie Stewart, 242–254. Wheaton, IL: Theosophical Publishing House, 1990.

Hart, George. *A Dictionary of Egyptian Gods and Goddesses.* London: Routledge, 1986.

Harvey, Peter. *The Selfless Mind: Personality, Consciousness, and Nirvana in Early Buddhism.* Richmond, Surrey: Curzon Press, 1995.

Harvey, Van A. *A Handbook of Theological Terms.* New York: Macmillan, 1964.

Hastings, Arthur. *With the Tongues of Men and Angels. A Study of Channeling.* Fort Worth, TX: Holt, Rinehart and Winston, 1991.

Hathaway, Michael R. *The Complete Idiot's Guide to Past Life Regression.* Indianapolis, IN: Alpha, 2003.

Hathaway, Nancy. *The Friendly Guide to Mythology.* New York: Viking, 2001.

Head, Joseph, and S. L. Cranston, editors. *Reincarnation: An East-West Anthology.* Wheaton, IL: The Theosophical Publishing House, 1961.

———. *Reincarnation in World Thought.* New York: Julian Press, 1967.

———. *Reincarnation: The Phoenix Fire Mystery.* New York: Julian Press, 1977.

Hearn, Lafcadio. *Gleanings in the Buddha-Field: Studies of Hand and Soul in the Far East.* Boston: Houghton Mifflin, 1897.

Heijke, Jan. "Belief in Reincarnation in Africa." In *Reincarnation or Resurrection,* edited by Hermann Haring and Johann-Baptist Metz, 46–53. London: SCM Press, 1993. (Concilium 1993/5).

Heine, Steven, and Charles S. Prebish. *Buddhism in the Modern World, Adaptations of an Ancient Tradition.* Oxford: Oxford University Press, 2003.

Henig, Robin Marantz. "Darwin's God." *New York Times Magazine,* March 4, 2007: 35–43, 58, 62, 77–78, 85.

Herder, Johan Gottfriend. "Dialogues on Metempsychosis." In *Prose Writers of Germany,* translated by Frederic H. Hedge. New York: C.S. Francis, 1856.

Hick, John H. *Death & Eternal Life,* San Francisco: Harper & Row, 1976.

Higgins, Godfrey. *Anacalypsis: An Attempt to Draw Aside the Veil of the Saitic Isis: Or, an Inquiry into the Origin of Languages, Nations, and Religions.* Vol. 2. London: Longman, Rees, Orme, Brown, Green, and Longmen, 1836.

_____. *The Celtic Druids.* London: R. Hunter, 1827.

Highwater, Jamake. *Myth and Sexuality.* New York: Penguin, 1991.

Hodgson, Joan. *Reincarnation through the Zodiac.* Vancouver, WA: CRCS Publications, 1978.

Hodson, Geoffrey. *Reincarnation, Fact or Fantasy? An Explanation and Exposition of the Doctrine of Rebirth.* Adyar, Madras: The Theosophical Publishing House, 1965.

Hoffman, Edward. "The Kabbalah and the Afterlife." *Gnosis: A Journal of the Western Inner Traditions* no. 42 (winter 1997): 60–65.

Hoffman, Frank J. *Rationality and Mind in Buddhism.* Varanasi: Motilal Banarsidass, 1987.

Horowitz, Mitch. *Occult America: The Secret History of How Mysticism Shaped Our Nation.* New York: Bantam Books, 2009.

Hornung, Erik. *The Secret Lore of Egypt: Its Impact on the West.* Trans. David Lorton. Ithaca, NY: Cornell University Press, 2001.

House, H. Wayne. *Charts of World Religions.* Grand Rapids, MI: Zondervan, 2005.

_____. "Resurrection, Reincarnation, and Humanness." *Bibliotheca Sacra* 148, No. 590 (April 1991): 132.

Howe, Quincy, Jr. *Reincarnation for the Christian.* Wheaton, IL: The Theosophical Publishing House, 1974.

Howell, Olive Stevenson. *Heredity and Reincarnation.* London: The Theosophical Publishing House Limited, 1926.

Hubbard, Lafayette Ronald. *Dianetics: The Modern Science of Mental Health.* Wichita, Kansas: Wichita Publishing Company, 1951.

_____. *Have You Lived Before This Life? A Scientific Study: A Study of Death and Evidence of Past Lives.* Los Angeles: Church of Scientology of California, 1989.

_____. *Mission into Time.* Los Angeles: Bridge Publishing, 1973.

Hubbell, C. Lee. "Immortality, Reincarnation, and God." *American Rationalist* 40, no. 5 (1996): 71.

Huffman, Robert W., and Irene Specht. *Many Wonderful Things.* Los Angeles: DeVorss, 1957.

Hughes, Thomas. Patrick. *A Dictionary of Islam: Being a Cyclopaedia of the Doctrines, Rites, Ceremonies and Customs, Together with the Technical and Theological Terms of Muhammadan Religion.* Lahore: Premier Book House, 1995.

Hull, Richard. "It's a BA-by!" *Free Inquiry* 27, no. 1 (December/January 2007): 27–31.

Hulme, A.J.H., and F. H. Wood. *Ancient Egypt Speaks: A Miracle of Tongues.* London: Rider, 1937.

Hulusi, Ahmed. "Will You Return to This World Again?" *Religious Misunderstandings.* http://www.ahmedbaki.com/english/books/din33.htm (Accessed 9/24/2003).

Humphreys, Christmas. "Karma and Rebirth." *The Middle Way: Journal of the Buddhist Society* 53, no.3 (Autumn 1978): 131–133.

Hyman, Ray. "How Not to Test Mediums: Critiquing the Afterlife Experiments." *Skeptical Inquirer* 27, no. 1 (Jan/Feb. 2003): 20–30.

_____. "Hyman's Reply to Schwartz's 'How Not to Review Mediumship Research.'" *Skeptical Inquirer* 27, no. 3 (May/June 2003): 61–64.

Irwin, Lee. *Coming Down from Above: Prophecy, Resistance, and Renewal in Native American Religions.* Norman: University of Oklahoma Press, 2008.

Isaason, Ben. *Dictionary of the Jewish Religion,* edited by David Gross. New York: Bantam Books, 1979.

J.S. "The Sufis and Reincarnation." *The Aryan Path* V, no. 3 (March 1934): 194–197.

Jack, Alex. *The New Age Dictionary.* Brookline, MA: Kanthaka Press, 1976.

Jaini, Padmanabh S. "Karma and the Problem of Rebirth in Jainism." In *Karma and Rebirth in Classical Indian Traditions,* edited by Wendy Doniger O'Flaherty, 217–240. Berkeley: University of California Press, 1980.

Jast, L. Stanley. *Reincarnation and Karma; a Spiritual Philosophy Applied to the World of Today.* New York: Bernard Ackerman, 1944.

Jayatilleke, K. N. *Survival and Karma in Buddhist Perspective.* Kandy, Sri Lanka: Buddhist Publication Society, 1980 (The Wheel Publication No. 141/142/143).

Jipa, Thupten, and Gyurme Dorje. "Glossary of Key Tibetan, Buddhist and Sanskrit Terms." In *A Handbook of Tibetan Culture,* edited by Graham Coleman, 275–420. Boston: Shambala, 1994.

Jocelyn, Beredene. *Citizens of the Cosmos: Life's Unfolding from Conception through Death to Rebirth.* New York: Continuum, 1981.

Johnson, Paul. "Imaginary Mahatmas: Who Were Madame Blavatsky's Masters?" *Gnosis: A Journal of the Western Inner Traditions* no. 28 (summer 1993): 24–30.

Johnson, Paul K. "Afterlife Visions of a Sleeping Prophet." *Gnosis: A Journal of the Western Inner Traditions* no. 42 (winter 1997): 34–40.

Johnson, Raynor. "Preexistence, Reincarnation and Karma." In *Immortality,* edited by Paul Edwards. Amherst, NY: Prometheus Books, 1997.

Johnson, Sarah. *Historical Fiction: A Guide to the Genre.* Westport, CT: Libraries Unlimited, 2005.

Jones, Gladys V. *The Flowering Tree: A Mystical Interpretation of Reincarnation.* New York: William Sloane Associates, 1965.

Jordan, Michael. *Encyclopedia of Gods.* New York: Facts on File, Inc., 1993.

_____. *Witches: An Encyclopedia of Paganism and Magic.* London: Kyle Cathie Limited, 1996.

Judge, William Q. *The Ocean of Theosophy.* Pasadena, CA: Theosophical University Press, 1964.

Kampman, Reima, and Reijo Hirvenoja. "Dynamic Relation of the Secondary Personality Induced by Hypnosis to the Present Personality." In *Hypnosis at Its Bicentennial: Selected Papers,* edited by Fred H. Frankel, 183–188. New York: Plenum Press, 1978.

Kapleau, Philip. *The Wheel of Life and Death: A Practical and Spiritual Guide.* New York: Doubleday, 1989.

Kardec, Allan. *Experimental Spiritism. Book on Mediums.* Trans. Emma A. Wood. Boston: Colby and Rich, 1874.

_____. *Genesis: The Miracles and the Predictions According to Spiritism.* Translated by the spirit-guides of W.J. Colville. Boston: Colby and Rich, 1883.

_____. *The Gospel According to Spiritism.* London: Headquarters, 1987.

_____. *Heaven and Hell.* London: Trübner, 1878.

_____. *The Spirits Book.* New York: Cosimo Classics, 1966.

Karr, Andy, Norman Fischer, Robin Korman, and Alahn Amaro. "Forum: How Does Karma Work?" *Buddha dharma,* 5 no. 3 (Spring 2007): 48–57, 64–67.

Kaspary, Joachim. *The Science of Re-incarnation or the Eternity of the Soul.* London: Humanitarian Publishing Society, 1916.

Katz, Nathan. *Buddhist Images of Human Perfection.* Delhi: Motilal Banarsidass, 1982.

Kaufman, Whitley R.P. "Karma, Rebirth, and the Problem of Evil." *Philosophy East and West.* 53, no. 1 (January 2005): 15–32.

Kear, Lynn. *Reincarnation: A Selected Annotated Bibliography.* Westport, CT: Greenwood Press, 1996.

_____. *We're Here: An Investigation into Gay Reincarnation.* Atlanta, GA: Brookhaven, 1999.

Keck, Leander E. "Death and Afterlife in the New Testament." In *Death and Afterlife: Perspectives of World Religions,* edited by Hiroshi Obayashi, 83–96. New York: Greenwood Press, 1992.

Kelly, Sean, and Rosemary Rogers. *Who in Hell: A Guide to the Whole Damned Bunch.* New York: Random House, 1996.

Kemp, Daren. *New Age Guide: Alternative Spiritualities from Aquarian Conspiracy to New Age.* Edinburgh: Edinburgh University Press, 2004.

Keyes, Charles F. "Merit-Transference in the Kammic Theory of Popular Theravada Buddhism." In *Karma: An Anthropological Inquiry,* edited by Charles F. Keyes and E. Valentine Daniel, 261–286. Berkeley: University of California Press, 1983.

Khantipalo (Bhikkhu). *The Wheel of Birth and Death.* Kandy, Sri Lanka: Buddhist Publication Society, 1970. (The Wheel Publication no.147/148/149).

Kingsford, Anna Bonus. *Clothed with the Sun: Being the Illuminations of Anna (Bonus) Kingsford.* London: George Redway, 1889.

_____. *The Perfect Way, or the Finding of Christ.* London: Watkins, 1882.

Kipling, Rudyard. "The Finest Story in the World." In *The Phantom Rickshaw and Other Ghost Stories.* New York: R.F. Fenno, 1899.

Kirby, Peter. "The Case Against the Empty Tomb." In *The Empty Tomb: Jesus Beyond the Grave,* edited by Robert M. Price and Jeffery Jay Lowder, 233–260. Amherst, NY: Prometheus Books, 2005.

Klimo, Jon. *Channeling: Investigation on Receiving Information from Paranormal Sources.* Los Angeles/New York: Jeremy P. Tarcher, 1987.

Kline, Milton V. "Multiple Personality: Psychodynamic Issues and Clinical Illustrations." In *Hypnosis at Its Bicentennial: Selected Papers,* edited by Fred H. Frankel, 189–196. New York: Plenum Press, 1978.

_____, editor. *A Scientific Report on "The Search for Bridey Murphy."* New York: The Julian Press, 1956.

Klostermair, Klaus K. "Contemporary Concepts of Karma and Rebirth Among North Indian Vaisnavas." In *Karma & Rebirth: Post Classical Developments,* edited by Ronald W. Neufeldt, 83–108. Albany: State University of New York Press, 1986.

Knappert, Jan. *Pacific Mythology: An Encyclopedia of Myth and Legend.* London: The Aquarian Press, 1992.

Konik, Alan. *Buddhism and Transgression: The Appropriation of Buddhism in the Contemporary West.* Leiden: Brill, 2009.

Krippner, Stanley. "The Role of 'Past life' Recall in Brazilian Spiritistic Treatment for Multiple Personality Disorders." In *Reincarnation: Fact or Fable,* edited by Arthur and Joyce Berger, 169–185. London: The Aquarian Press, 1991.

Krishan, Yuvraj. *The Doctrine of Karma: Its Origin and Development in Brahmanical, Buddhist and Jaina Traditions.* Delhi: Motilal Banarsidass Publishers Private, 1997.

Kubler-Ross, Elizabeth. *Death Is of Vital Importance: On Life, Death and Life After Death.* Barrytown, NY: Station Hill Press, 1995.

_____. *On Death and Dying.* New York: Macmillan, 1969.

_____. *On Life After Death.* Berkeley, CA: Celestial Arts, 1991.

Kueshana, Exlal. *The Ultimate Frontier.* Chicago: The Stelle Group, 1963.

Kurth-Voigh, Lieselotte E. *Continued Existence, Reincarnation, and the Power of Sympathy in Classical Weimar.* Rochester, NY: Camden House, 1999.

Lai, Whalen. "The Chan-ch'a Ching: Religion and Magic in Medieval China." In *Chinese Buddhist Apocrypha,* edited by Robert E. Bushwell, 175–206. Honolulu: University of Hawaii Press, 1990.

Lamb, Geoffrey. *Magic, Witchcraft, and the Occult.* New York: David and Charles, 1983.

Lammey, W. C. *Karmic Tarot: A New System for Finding Your Lifetime's Purpose.* San Bernadino, CA: Borgo Press, 1988.

Lane, Barbara. *16 Clues to Your Past Lives! A Guide to Discovering Who You Were.* Virginia Beach, VA: A.R.E. Press, 1999.

Langley, Noel. *Edgar Cayce on Reincarnation.* New York: Warner Books, 1967.

Larson, Gerald James. "Karma as a 'Sociology of Knowledge' or 'Social Psychology' of Process/Praxis." In *Karma and Rebirth in Classical Indian Traditions,* edited by Wendy Doniger O'Flaherty, 320–316. Berkeley: University of California Press, 1980.

Laszlo, Ervin. *Science and the Akashic Field.* Rochester, VT: Inner Traditions, 2004.

Lauritsen, Poul. *Reincarnation and Freedom, with an Appendix on Astrology.* Gylling, Denmark: Narayana Press, 1987.

Layton, Felix. "Karma in Motion." In *Karma: Rhythmic Return to Harmony.* 3rd edition, edited by V. Hanson, R. Stewart, and S. Nicholson, 3–9. Wheaton, IL: Theosophical Publishing House, 1990.

Leadbeater, C. W. *The Chakras: a Monograph.* Wheaton, IL: Theosophical Publishing House, 1994.

_____. *A Textbook of Theosophy.* Adyar, Madras: Theosophical Publishing House, 1912.

Lear, Martha Weinman. "Why Do We Forget Things?" *Parade, the Sunday Newspaper Magazine* (January 6, 2008): 10–11.

Leek, Sybil. *Reincarnation: The Second Chance.* New York: Stein and Day, 1974.

Legge, Francis. *Forerunners and Rivals of Christianity: From 330 B.C. to 330 A.D.* New Hyde Park, NY: University Books, 1964.

Leland, Charles Godfrey. *Aradia, The Gospel of the Witches.* London: D. Nutt, 1899.
_____. *Etruscan Roman Remains in Popular Tradition.* London: T.F. Unwin. 1892.
Lenz, Frederick. *The Last Incarnation.* Malibu, CA: Lakshmi, 1983.
_____. *Lifetimes: True Accounts of Reincarnation.* Indianapolis: Bobbs-Merrill, 1979.
Lester, David. *Is There Life After Death? An Examination of the Empirical Evidence.* Jefferson, NC: McFarland, 2005.
Lewis, H. Spencer. *The Mystical Life of Jesus.* San Jose, CA: Rosicrucian Press (AMORC College), 1926.
Lewis, James R. *The Astrology Encyclopedia.* Detroit, MI: Visible Ink Press, 1994.
_____. *The Death and Afterlife Book: The Encyclopedia of Death, Near Death, and Life After Death.* Detroit, MI: Visible Ink Press, 2001.
_____. "Eckankar." In *New Religions: A Guide. New Religious Movements, Sects and Alternative Spiritualities*, edited by Christopher Partridge. New York: Oxford University Press, 2004.
_____, editor. *The Encyclopedia of Cults, Sects, and New Religions.* 2nd edition. Amherst, NY: Prometheus Books, 2002.
Lewis, James R., and Evelyn Dorothy Oliver. *Angels A to Z.* Detroit, MI: Visible Ink Press, 1996.
Lichter, David, and Lawrence Epstein. "Irony in Tibetan Notions of the Good Life." In *Karma: An Anthropological Inquiry*, edited by Charles F. Keyes and E. Valentine Daniel, 223–260. Berkeley: University of California Press, 1983.
Lindsay, Ronald A. "Stem Cell Research: An Approach to Bioethics Based on Scientific Naturalism." *Free Inquiry* 27, no. 1 (December/January 2007): 23–26.
Livingston, Marjorie. "Reincarnation: A Historical and Critical Review." *The Aryan Path* 9, no. 6 (June 1938): 295–299.
Logan, Michael. "King of Kings." *Spirit Guide: Your Door to the Spiritual and the Supernatural. Soap Opera Digest* (Fall/Winter 2004): 60–62.
Loning, Karl. "Reincarnation or Resurrection? Resurrection and Biblical Apocalyptic." In *Reincarnation or Resurrection?*, edited by Hermann Haring and Johann-Baptist Metz, 67–74. London: SCM Press, 1993. (Concilium 1993/5).
Lopez, Donald S., Jr. "Lobsang Rampa: The Mystery of the Three-Eyed Lama." *Tricycle: The Buddhist Review* 8, no. 2 (winter 1998): 36–41.
Lowder, Jeffery Jay. " Historical Evidence and the Empty Tomb Story: A Reply to William Lane Craig." In *The Empty Tomb: Jesus Beyond the Grave*, edited by Robert M. Price and Jeffery Jay Lowder, 261–306. Amherst, NY: Prometheus Books, 2005.
Lucretius. "The Mind and the Spirit Will Die." In *Immortality*, edited by Paul Edwards. Amherst, NY: Prometheus Books, 1997.
_____. *On the Nature of the Universe.* Trans. R.E. Latham. New York: Penguin Books, 1951.
Luntz, Charles E. *The Challenge of Reincarnation.* St. Louis, MO: Charles E. Luntz, 1957.
Lurker, Manfred. *An Illustrated Dictionary of the Gods and Symbols of Ancient Egypt.* London: Thames and Hudson, 1980.
Lynn, Steven Jay, Elizabeth F. Loftus, Scott O. Lilienfeld, and Timothy Lock. "Memory Recovery Techniques in Psychotherapy: Problems and Pitfalls." *Skeptical Inquirer* 27, no. 4 (Jul/Aug 2003): 40–46.
MacGregor, Geddes. *Immortality and Human Destiny.* New York: Paragon House, 1985.
_____. *Reincarnation in Christianity: A New Vision of the Role of Rebirth in Christian Thought.* Wheaton, IL: The Theosophical Publishing House, 1978.
Mack, Burton L. *The Lost Gospel: The Book of Q and Christian Origins.* San Francisco: Harper, 1993.
MacTaggart, John Ellis. *Human Immortality and Pre-existence.* New York: Longmans, Green, 1915.
_____, and C.D. Broad. *The Nature of Existence.* 2 vol. Cambridge: Cambridge University Press, 1921 and 1927.
Madelung, Wilferd. *Religious Trends in Early Islamic Iran.* Columbia Lectures on Iranian Studies, no. 4. Albany: Bibliotheca Persica, 1988.
Madison, Arnold. *Mummies in Fact and Fiction.* New York: Franklin Watts, 1980.
Mann, A. T. *The Divine Plot: Astrology, Reincarnation, Cosmology and History.* London: Allen & Unwin, 1986.
_____. *The Elements of Reincarnation.* Shaftesbury, Dorset: Elemental Books, 1995.
Marrs, Texe. *Texe Marrs Book of New Age Cults and Religions.* Austin, TX: Living Truth, 1990.
Martin, Eva, editor. *Reincarnation: The Ring of Return.* New Hyde Park: University Books, 1963.
Mascaro, Juan. *The Bhagavad Gita.* Baltimore: Penguin Books, 1962.
Matlock, James G., and Antonia Mills. "Appendix: A Trait Index to North American Indian and Inuit Reincarnation." In *Amerindian Rebirth: Reincarnation Belief Among North American Indians and Inuit*, edited by Antonia Mills and Richard Slobodin, 299–326. Toronto: University of Toronto Press, 1994.
Matsunaga, Daigan, and Alicia Matsunaga. *The Buddhist Concept of Hell.* New York: Philosophical Library, 1972.
Matthews, John, editor. *The World Atlas of Divination: The Systems, Where They Originate, How They Work.* Boston: Bulfinch Press, 1992.
Mauze, Marie. "The Concept of the Person and Reincarnation Among the Kwakiutl Indians." In *Amerindian Rebirth: Reincarnation Belief Among North American Indians and Inuit*, edited by Antonia Mills and Richard Slobodin, 177–191. Toronto: University of Toronto Press, 1994.
Mbiti, John S. *African Religions and Philosophy.* 2nd revised and enlarged edition. London: Heinemann, 1990.
McClelland, Bruce A. *Slayers and Their Vampires: A Cultural History of Killing the Dead.* Ann Arbor: The University of Michigan Press, 2006.
McConkie, Bruce R. *Mormon Doctrine.* 2nd edition. Salt Lake City, UT: Bookcraft, 1979.
McCoy, Edain. *Past Life & Karmic Tarot.* St. Paul, MN: Llewellyn, 2004.
McDermont, James Paul. *Development in the Early Buddhist Concept of Kamma/Karma.* New Delhi: Munshiram Manoharlal, 1984.
_____. "Karma and Rebirth in Early Buddhism." In *Karma and Rebirth in Classical Indian Traditions*, edited by Wendy Doniger O'Flaherty, 165–192. Berkeley: University of California Press, 1980.
McGraw, John J. *Brain & Belief: An Exploration of the Human Soul.* Del Mar, CA: Aegis Press, 2004.
McNamara, Patrick, editor. *Where God and Science Meet:*

How Brain and Evolution Studies Alter Our Understanding of Religion. Vol. 1. Westport, CT: Praeger, 2006.

Melling, Leonard. *The Logical Aspects and Processes of Reincarnation.* Manchester: Torh, 1954.

Melton, J. Gordon. "Edgar Cayce and Reincarnation: Past Life Readings as Religious Symbology." In *Encyclopedic Sourcebook of New Age Religions*, edited by James R. Lewis, 82–95. Amherst, NY: Prometheus Books, 2004.

_____. *The Vampire Book: The Encyclopedia of the Undead.* Detroit, MI: Visible Ink Press, 1999.

Melville, Herman. *Moby-Dick.* New York: Pearson Longman, 2007.

Mendenhall, George E. "From Witchcraft to Justice: Death and Afterlife in the Old Testament." In *Death and Afterlife: Perspectives of World Religions*, edited by Hiroshi Obayashi, 67–81. New York: Greenwood Press, 1992.

Mendoza, Ramon G. "Metempsychosis and Monism in Bruno's Nova Filosofia." In *Giordano Bruno: Philosopher of the Renaissance*, edited by Hilary Gatti. Aldershot, Hants: Ashgate, 2002.

Mestel, Rosie. "Jumping Genes Aid Brain Diversity." *Los Angeles Times,* June 18, 2005, A21.

Metz, Johannes Baptist. "Time Without a Finale: The Background to the Debate on Resurrection or Reincarnation." In *Reincarnation or Resurrection*, edited by Hermann Haring and Johann-Baptist Metz, 124–131. London: SCM Press, 1993. (Concilium 1993/5).

Metzger, William. "Choosing: Karma & Dharma in the 21st Century." In *Karma: Rhythmic Return to Harmony*, edited by V. Hanson, R. Stewart, and S. Nicholson, 181–191. 3rd edition. Wheaton, IL: Theosophical Publishing House, 1990.

Miller, Sukie. *After Death: Mapping the Journey.* New York: Simon & Schuster, 1997.

Mills, Antonia. "Reincarnation Belief Among Indian and Inui." In *Amerindian Rebirth: Reincarnation Belief Among North American Indians and Inuit*, edited by Antonia Mills and Richard Slobodin, 15–37. Toronto: University of Toronto Press, 1994.

Mirza, Nadarbeg. *Reincarnation in Islam.* Adyar, Madras: Theosophical Publishing House, 1927.

Monaghan, Patricia. *The Book of Goddesses and Heroines.* New York: E. P. Dutton, 1981.

Monastersky, Richard. "Religion on the Brain: The Hard Science of Neurobiology Is Taking a Closer Look at the Ethereal World of the Spirit." *The Chronicle of Higher Education* (May 26, 2006): A15–19.

Monroe, Robert A. *Journeys Out of the Body.* Garden City, NY: Anchor Press, 1973.

Montgomery, Ruth. *Alien Among Us.* New York: Coward, McCann, Geoghegan, 1985.

_____. *Companions Along the Way.* New York: Popular Library, 1974.

_____. *Here and Hereafter.* Greenwich, CT: Fawcett, 1968.

_____. *Strangers Among Us.* New York: Coward, McCann, Geoghegan, 1979.

_____. *Threshold to Tomorrow.* New York: G.P. Putnam's, 1982.

Moody, Raymond A., Jr. *Life After Life.* Harrisburg, PA: Stackpole Books, 1976.

_____, and Paul Perry. *Coming Back: A Psychiatrist Explores Past Life Journeys.* New York: Bantam Books, 1991.

Mooier, Christine. *Buddhism and Taoism: Face to Face Scripture, Ritual, and Iconographic Exchange in Medieval China.* Honolulu: University of Hawaii Press, 2008.

Moore, Marcia, and Howard Sunny Alltounian. *Journey into the Bright World.* Rockport, MA: Para Research, 1978.

Moore, Marcia, and Mark Douglas. *Reincarnation: Key to Immortality.* York Cliffs, ME: Arcane, 1968.

Morema, Christopher M. *Beyond the Threshold: Afterlife Beliefs and Experiences in World Religions.* Lanham, MD: Rowan & Littlefield, 2008.

Morey, Robert A. *Reincarnation and Christianity: Has the Traditional Viewpoint of the Church Been Right?* Minneapolis, MN: Bethany Fellowship, 1980.

Morgan, Richard. "Planet Xena Rocks The Solar System." *Discover,* 27, no. 1 (January 2005): 58.

Motoyama, Hiroshi. *Karma and Reincarnation.* New York: Avon Books, 1992.

Mundis, Hester. *101 Ways to Avoid Reincarnation or Getting It Right the First Time.* New York: Workman, 1989.

Murnane, William J. "Taking It with You: The Problem of Death and Afterlife in Ancient Egypt." In *Death and Afterlife: Perspectives of World Religions*, edited by Hiroshi Obayashi, 35–48. New York: Greenwood Press, 1992.

Murphy, Joseph M. *Santeria: An African Religion in America.* Boston: Beacon Press, 1988.

Murray, Margaret. *God of the Witches.* Oxford: Oxford University Press, 1931.

_____. *The Witch Cult in Western Europe.* Oxford: Oxford University Press, 1921.

Murry, J. Middleton. "The Reasonableness and Practicality of Reincarnation." *The Aryan Path* 9, no. 6 (June 1938): 271–276.

Narain, Raj. "Reason and Reincarnation." *The Aryan Path* 9, no. 6 (June 1938): 277–280.

Na-Rangsi, Sunthorn. *The Buddhist Concept of Karma and Rebirth.* Bangkok: Mahamakut Rajavidyalaya Press, 1976.

Nataf, Andre. *The Wordsworth Dictionary of the Occult.* Ware, Hertfordshire: Wordsworth Reference, 1994.

Netherton, Morris, and Nancy Schiffrin. *Past Lives Therapy.* New York: William Morrow, 1978.

New English Bible with the Apocrypha. New York: Cambridge University Press, 1971.

Newton, Michael. *Destiny of Souls; New Case Studies of Life Between Lives.* St. Paul, MN: Llewellyn, 2003.

_____. *Journey of Souls; Case Studies of Life Between Lives.* St. Paul, MN: Llewellyn, 2003.

Nicholson, R.A. *The Idea of Personality in Sufism.* Lahore: Sh. Muhammad Ashraf, Kashmiri Bazar, 1964.

Norman, Ernest. *Voice of Venus.* El Cajon, CA: Unarius Academy of Science, 1954.

Norman, Ruth. *The Proof of the Truth of Past Life Therapy.* El Cajon, CA: Unarius, 1988.

_____. *Visitations: A Saga of Gods and Men.* El Cajon, CA: Unarius Educational Foundation, 1985.

Norman, Ruth, and Charles Spaegel. *The Last Inca, Atahualpa: An Eyewitness Account of the Conquest of Peru in 1535.* El Cajon, CA: Unarius Educational Foundation, 1993.

_____. *Principles and Practices of Past Life Therapy.* El Cajon, CA: Unarius Educational Foundation, 1984.

North, Helen F. "Death and Afterlife in Greek Tragedy and Plato." In *Death and Afterlife: Perspectives of World*

Religions, edited by Hiroshi Obayashi, 49–66. New York: Greenwood Press, 1992.

Obayashi, Hiroshi. "Death and Eternal Life in Christianity." In *Death and Afterlife: Perspectives of World Religions*, edited by Hiroshi Obayashi, 109–124. New York: Greenwood Press, 1992.

Obeyesekere, Gananath. *Imagining Karma: Ethical Transformation in Amerindian, Buddhist, and Greek Rebirth*. Berkeley: University of California Press, 2002.

———. "The Rebirth Eschatology and Its Transformations: A Contribution to the Sociology of Early Buddhism." In *Karma and Rebirth in Classical Indian Traditions*, edited by Wendy Doniger O'Flaherty, 137–164. Berkeley: University of California Press, 1980.

O'Flaherty, Wendy Doniger. "Introduction." In *Karma and Rebirth in Classical Indian Traditions*, edited by Wendy Doniger O'Flaherty, ix–xxv. Berkeley: University of California Press, 1980.

———. "Karma and Rebirth in the Vedas and Puranas." In *Karma and Rebirth in Classical Indian Traditions*, edited by Wendy Doniger O'Flaherty, 3–37. Berkeley: University of California Press, 1980.

Oliver, Frederick Spencer. *A Dweller on Two Planets*. San Francisco: Harper & Row, 1974.

———. *An Earth Dweller's Return*, Milwaukee, WI: Lemurian Press, 1940.

———. *Growth of a Soul*. Monterey, CA: Angel Press, 1975.

Olmos, Margarite Fernandez, and Lizabeth Paravisini-Gebert. *Creole Religions of the Caribbean: An Introduction from Vodou and Santeria to Obeah and Espiritismo*. New York: New York University Press, 2003.

Olsen, Roger E. "Rudolf Steiner, Esoteric Christianity, and the New Age Movement." In *Encyclopedic Sourcebook of New Age Religions*, edited by James R. Lewis, 50–62. Amherst, NY: Prometheus Books, 2004.

Oneywuenyi, Innocent C. "A Philosophical Reappraisal of African Belief in Reincarnation." *International Philosophical Quarterly*, 22, no. 3 (September 1982): 157–168.

Osborn, Arthur W. *The Meaning of Personal Existence: in Light of Paranormal Phenomena, The Doctrine of Reincarnation and Mystical States of Consciousness*. Wheaton, IL: The Theosophical Publishing House, 1966.

Ouspensky, P.D. *A New Model of the Universe: Principles of the Psychological Method in Its Application to Problems of Science, Religion, and Art*. New York: Random House, 1971.

Palmer, Marti, and Joanne O'Brien. *The Book of Reincarnation and the Afterlife*. London: Judy Piatkus, 1996.

Parrinder, Geoffrey. *The Indestructible Soul: The Nature of Man and Life After Death in Indian Thought*. New York: George Allen & Unwin, 1973.

Parsons, Keith. "Peter Kreeft and Ronald Tacelli on the Hallucination Theory." In *The Empty Tomb: Jesus Beyond the Grave*, edited by Robert M. Price and Jeffery Jay Lowder. Amherst, NY: Prometheus Books, 2005.

Pasfield, W.R. "The Archetype of Rebirth." *The Middle Way: Journal of the Buddhist Society* 43, no. 1 (May 1968): 32–33.

Patil, Pareimal G. *Against a Hindu God: Buddhist Philosophy of Religion in India*. New York: Columbia University Press, 2009.

Paul, Annie Murphy. "The First Ache: When Does the Experience of Pain Begin?" *New York Times Magazine*, Feb. 10, 2008, 45–49.

Paul, Gregory S. "The Great Scandal: Christianity's Role in the Rise of the Nazis." *Free Inquiry* 23, no. 4 (October/November 2003): 20–29.

Paulson, Genevieve Lewis, and Stephen J. Paulson. *Reincarnation: Remembering Past Lives*. St. Paul, MN: Llewellyn, 1998.

Pedersen, Clarence R. "The Source of Becauses." In *Karma: Rhythmic Return to Harmony*, edited by V. Hanson, R. Stewart, & S. Nicholson, 51–60. Wheaton, IL: Theosophical Publishing House, 1990.

Penn, Gregory E. *Reincarnation: The Same Old, Brand New You!* Newport Beach: Harbour House, 1981.

Perkins, James S. *Experiencing Reincarnation*. Wheaton, IL: The Theosophical Publishing House, 1977.

Peters, Ted. "UFOs, Heaven's Gate, and the Theology of Suicide." In *Encyclopedic Sourcebook of UFO Religions*, edited by James R. Lewis, 259–260. Amherst, NY: Prometheus Books, 2003.

Phillips, Stephen. *Yoga, Karma, and Rebirth: A Brief History and Philosophy*. New York: Columbia University Press, 2009.

Pickthall, Mohammed Marmaduke. *The Meaning of the Glorious Koran*. New York: The New American Library, n.d.

Pieris, Aloysius. "Reincarnation in Buddhism: A Christian Appraisal." In *Reincarnation or Resurrection?*, edited by Hermann Haring and Johann-Baptist Metz, 16–22. London: SCM Press, 1993. (Concilium 1993/5).

Pike, Sarah M. *New Age and Neo-pagan Religions in America*. New York: Columbia University Press, 2004.

Pilkington, J. Maya, and the Diagram Group. *Who Were You?* New York: Ballantine Books, 1988.

Plato. "Release of the Soul from the Chains of the Body." In *Immortality*, edited by Paul Edwards. Amherst, NY: Prometheus Books, 1997.

Pope, Douglas. "I Have Been Here Before." *The Aryan Path* 9, no. 6 (June 1938): 288–290.

Potter, Karl H. "The Karma Theory and Its Interpretation in Some Indian Philosophical Systems." In *Karma and Rebirth in Classical Indian Traditions*, edited by Wendy Doniger O'Flaherty, 241–267. Berkeley: University of California Press, 1980.

Powell, Robert. *Hermetic Astrology: Towards a New Wisdom of the Stars*. Kinsau, Germany: Hermetika, 1987.

Prabhupada, A.C. Bhaktivedanta Swami. *Coming Back: The Science of Reincarnation*. Los Angeles: Bhaktivedanta Book Trust, 1982.

Price, Robert M. "Apocryphal Apparitions: 1 Corinthians 15:3–11 as a Post-Pauline Interpolation." In *The Empty Tomb: Jesus Beyond the Grave*, edited by Robert M. Price and Jeffery Jay Lowder, 69–104. Amherst, NY: Prometheus Books, 2005.

———. "By the Time He Stinketh: The Attempts of William Lane Craig to Exhume Jesus." In *The Empty Tomb: Jesus Beyond the Grave*, edited by Robert M. Price and Jeffery Jay Lowder, 411–431. Amherst, NY: Prometheus Books, 2005.

Pugh, Judy F. "Astrology and Fate: The Hindu and Muslim Experiences." In *Karma: An Anthropological Inquiry*, edited by Charles F. Keyes and E. Valentine Daniel, 131–146. Berkeley: University of California Press, 1983.

Punnadhammo (Bhikkhu). "The Soul of Buddhism: Mind, Karma, Rebirth and the Buddhist Middle Path Philosophy." *Right view Quarterly* (Summer 2007): 6–13.

Querido, Rene M. *Questions and Answers on Reincarnation and Karma.* Sprint Valley, NY: St. George, 1977.

Quincy, Howe, Jr. *Reincarnation for the Christian.* Wheaton, IL: The Theosophical Publishing House, 1974.

Quinn, Noreen. *She Can Read Your Past Lives.* Los Angeles, CA: Religious Research Press, 1975.

Quintman, Andrew. "Karma Pa." In *Encyclopedia of Buddhism*, edited by Robert E. Bushwell, Jr. New York: Macmillan Reference USA, 2004.

Quran. Elmhurst, NY: Tahrike Tarsile Quran, 2005.

Quran. Trans. Ali Unal. Somerset, NJ: The Light, 2007.

Qur'an: Arabic Text with Corresponding English Meanings. Riyadh: Saheeh International Abulqasim Publishing House, 1997.

Quran: The Guidance for Mankind. Houston, TX: The Institute of Islamic Knowledge, 1997.

Rabinovitch, Shelly, and James Lewis. *The Encyclopedia of Modern Witchcraft and Neo-Paganism.* New York: Kensington, 2002.

Radford, Benjamin. "Measuring Near-Death Experience." *Skeptical Inquirer* 31, no. 3 (May/June 2007): 31.

———. "Soul Scales." *Skeptical Inquirer* 31, no. 1 (January/February 2007): 28.

Radin, Paul. "The Reincarnations of Thunder Cloud, a Winnebago Indian." In *Amerindian Rebirth: Reincarnation Belief Among North American Indians and Inuit*, edited by Antonia Mills and Richard Slobodin, 55–66. Toronto: University of Toronto Press, 1994.

Raman, N. S. S. "Reincarnation and Personal Immortality: The Circle and the End of History in Hinduism." In *Progress, Apocalypse, and Completion of History and Life After Death of the Human Person in the World Religions*, edited by Peter Koslowski, 8–21. Dordrecht: Kluwer Academic Publishers, 2002.

Ram Dass, Baba. *Remember, Be Here Now.* San Cristobal, NM: Lama Foundation, 1972.

Rampa, Tuesday Lobsang. *The Third Eye: Autobiography of a Tibetan Lama.* London: Secker & Warberg, 1956.

Randi, James. *An Encyclopedia of Claims, Frauds, and Hoaxes of the Occult and the Supernatural.* New York: St. Martin's Griffin, 1995.

———. *Flim-Flam: Psychics, ESP, Unicorns and Other Delusions.* Buffalo, NY: Prometheus Books, 1982.

Raphael, Katrina. *Crystal Enlightenment: The Transforming Properties of Crystals and Healing Stones*, vol. I. New York: Aurora Press, 1985.

Ravenscroft, Trevor. *The Spear of Destiny: The Occult Power Behind the Spear Which Pierced the Side of Christ.* New York: G. P. Putnam's Sons, 1973.

Rawat, Kirti S. "Raghunath Remembered: A Case Suggestive of Reincarnation." *Venture Inward,* 1 (Nov./Dec. 1985): 11–12.

Rawlinson, Andrew. *The Book of Enlightened Masters: Western Teachers in Eastern Traditions.* Chicago: Open Court, 1997.

Redfield, James. *Celestine Prophesy.* New York: Warner Books, 1993.

Reed, Graham. "The Psychology of Channeling." *Skeptical Inquirer* 13, no. 4 (Summer 1989): 385–390.

Reese, William L. *Dictionary of Philosophy of Religion.* Atlantic Highlands, NJ: Humanities Press, 1980.

Reichenbach, Bruce R. *The Law of Karma: A Philosophical Study.* Honolulu: University of Hawaii Press, 1990.

Reisner, Andrew D. "A Psychological Case Study of 'Demon' and 'Alien' Visitation." *Skeptical Inquirer* 25, no. 2 (Mar/Apr. 2001): 46–50.

Renard, John. *101 Questions and Answers on Islam.* New York: Gramercy Books, 1998.

Richardson, Alan. *Dancers to the Gods.* Wellingborough, Northamptonshire: Aquarian, 1985.

Rinbochay, Lati, and Jeffrey Hopkins. *Death, Intermediate State and Rebirth in Tibetan Buddhism.* Ithaca, NY: Snow Lion Publications, 1979.

Roach, Mary. *Spook: Science Tackles the Afterlife.* New York: W. W. Norton, 2005.

Roberts, Jane. *Dreams, Evolution, and Value Fulfillment.* New York: Prentice-Hall, 1986.

———. *The Seth Material.* Englewood, NJ: Prentice-Hall, 1970.

———. *Seth Speaks: The Eternal Validity of the Soul.* Englewood, NJ: Prentice-Hall, 1972.

Rogo, Scott. *The Search for Yesterday: A Critical Examination of the Evidence for Reincarnation.* Englewood Cliffs. NJ: Prentice-Hall, 1985.

Rohmann, Chris. *A World of Ideas: A Dictionary of Important Theories, Concepts, Beliefs, and Thinkers.* New York: Random House, 1999.

Rose, Nanci Hoetzlein. "The Nechung State Oracle in Dharamsala." *Shaman's Drum: A Journal of Experiential Shamanism.* Number 40 (Winter 1996): 50–55.

Rosenberg, Roy A. *The Concise Guide to Judaism: History, Practice, Faith.* New York: Penguin, 1990.

Ross, Anne. *Pagan Celtic Britain.* London: Cardinal, 1974.

Rossum, Rogier Van. "Reincarnation in Connection with Spiritism and Umbanda." In *Reincarnation or Resurrection?*, edited by Hermann Haring and Johann-Baptist Metz, 81–87. London: SCM Press, 1993. (Concilium 1993/5).

Rothstein, Mikael. "The Idea of the Past, the Reality of the Present, and the Construction of the Future: Millenarianism in the Aetherius Society." In *Encyclopedic Sourcebook of UFO Religions*, edited by James R. Lewis, 143–156. Amherst, NY: Prometheus Books, 2003.

Ruether, Rosemary Radford. *Goddesses and the Divine Feminine: A Western History.* Berkeley: University of California Press, 2005.

Sachs, John R. "Resurrection or Reincarnation? The Christian Doctrine of Purgatory." In *Reincarnation or Resurrection?*, edited by Hermann Haring and Johann-Baptist Metz, 81–87. London: SCM Press, 1993. (Concilium 1993/5).

Sadakata, Akira. *Buddhist Cosmology: Philosophy and Origins.* Tokyo: Kosei, 1997.

Saliba, John A. "The Earth Is a Dangerous Place: The World View of the Aetherius Society." In *Encyclopedic Sourcebook of UFO Religions*, edited by James R. Lewis, 123–142. Amherst, NY: Prometheus Books, 2003.

———. "UFOs and Religion: A Case Study of Unarius Academy of Science." In *Encyclopedic Sourcebook of UFO Religions*, edited by James R. Lewis, 191–208. Amherst, NY: Prometheus Books, 2003.

Sanford, John A. *Soul Journey; a Jungian Analyst Looks at Reincarnation.* New York: Crossroad, 1991.

Schlinger, Henry D. "Consciousness Is Nothing but a Word." *Skeptic* 13, no. 4 (2008): 58–63.

———. "How the Human Got Its Mind: Debunking the Last Great Myth in Psychology." *Skeptic* 11, no. 4 (2005): 48–53.

Schlotterbeck, Karl. *Living Your Past Lives: The Psychology of Past Life Regression.* New York: Ballantine Books, 1987.

Schoegl, Irmgard. "Death and Rebirth." *The Middle Way: Journal of the Buddhist Society* 57, No. 1 (May 1982): 15.

Scholem, Gershom. *Kabbalah*. New York: New American Library, 1974.

_____. *On the Mystical Shape of the Godhead: Basic Concepts in the Kabbalah*. New York: Schocken Books, 1991.

Schroeder, John. *Cults: From Bacchus to Heaven's Gate*. London: Carlton, 1999.

Schueler, Gerald & Betty. *The Truth About Enochian Magick*. St. Paul, MN: Llewellyn, 1993.

Schulman, Martin. *Karmic Astrology: Retrogrades and Reincarnation*. New York: Samuel Weiser, 1977.

Schwartz, Gary E. "How Not to Review Mediumship Research." *Skeptical Inquirer* 27, no. 3 (May/June 2003): 58–61.

Scott, Miriam Van. *Encyclopedia of Heaven*. New York: St. Martin Press, 1998.

_____. *Encyclopedia of Hell*. New York: St. Martin Press, 1999.

Scriber, Scott, and Gregory Wheler. "Cosmic Intelligence and Their Terrestrial Channel: A Field Report on the Aetherius Society." In *Encyclopedic Sourcebook of UFO Religions*, edited by James R. Lewis, 157–171. Amherst, NY: Prometheus Books, 2003.

Semkiw, Walter. *Born Again: Reincarnation Cases Involving International Celebrities, India's Political Legends and Film Stars*. New Delhi: Ritana Books, 2006.

_____. *Return of the Revolutionaries: The Case for Reincarnation and Soul Groups Reunited*. Charlottesville, VA: Hampton Roads, 2003.

Service, Elman R. *Profiles in Ethnology*. New York: Harper and Row, 1958.

Sharp, Lynn L. *Secular Spirituality: Reincarnation and Spiritism in Nineteenth-Century France*. Lanham, MD: Rowan & Littlefield, 2006.

Shelley, Violet M. *Reincarnation Unnecessary*. Virginia Beach, VA: A.R.E. Press, 1979.

Sheppard, Susan. *Phoenix Cards: Reading and Interpreting Past Life Influences with the Phoenix Deck*. Rochester, VT: Destiny Books, 1990.

Sherman, Harold. *You Live After Death*. Greenwich, CT: Fawcett, 1972.

Shermer, Michael. *Why People Believe Weird Things; Pseudoscience, Superstition, and Other Confusions of Our Time*. New York: W.H. Freeman, 1997.

Shroder, Tom. *Old Souls: The Scientific Evidence for Past Lives*. New York: Simon and Schuster, 1999.

Sinnett, A. P. *Esoteric Buddhism*. 5th edition. Minneapolis, MN: Wizard Bookshelf, 1973.

_____. *Growth of the Soul: A Sequel to Esoteric Buddhism*. London: Theosophical Publishing House, 1918.

_____. *The Mahatma Letters to A.P. Sinnet*. Adyar, Madras, India: Theosophical Publishing House, 1972.

_____. "Obscure Problems of Karma and Rebirth." London: Theosophical Pub. Society no. 36 (1902).

_____. *The Occult World*. London: Theosophical Publishing Society, 1921.

Sircar, Mahendranath. "The Process of Reincarnation in Hindu Philosophy and Psychology." *The Aryan Path*. 9, no. 6 (June 1938): 267–270.

Siwek, Paul. *The Enigma of the Hereafter: Theories of Reincarnation of Souls*. New York: Philosophical Library, 1952.

Slobodin, Richard. "Kutchin Concepts of Reincarnation." In *Amerindian Rebirth: Reincarnation Belief Among North American Indians and Inuit*, edited by Antonia Mills and Richard Slobodin, 136–155. Toronto: University of Toronto Press, 1994.

Smith, F. LaGard. *Out on a Broken Limb*. Eugene, OR: Harvest House, 1986.

Smith, Idleman, and Yvonne Yazbeck Haddad. *The Islamic Understanding of Death and Resurrection*. Albany, NY: State University of New York Press, 1981.

Smith, Margaret. "The Doctrine of Re-incarnation in Islamic Literature." *The Aryan Path* 4, no. 1 (January 1933): 33–39.

_____. "The Doctrine of Re-incarnation in Persian Thought." *The Aryan Path*. 14, no. 1 (January 1943): 10–15.

Smith, Roy C., editor. *Incarnation and Reincarnation*. Grand Island, FL: Religious Research Press, 1975.

Snellgrove, David L., and Hugh Richardson. *A Cultural History of Tibet*. Boulder: Prajna Press, 1980.

Sparrow, Lynn Elwell. *Edgar Cayce and the Born Again Christian*. Virginia Beach, VA: The Association for Research and Enlightenment, 1985.

_____. *Reincarnation, Claiming Your Past, Creating Your Future*. San Francisco: Harper & Row, 1988.

Spence, Lewis. *An Encyclopedia of Occultism*. Mineola, NY: Dover, 2003.

Spencer, W. Baldwin. "Reincarnation and Spirit Children Among the Aboriginals of Australia." *Reincarnation* 5, no. 9 (May-June 1920): 259–262.

Spong, John Sheby. *Resurrection: Myth or Reality?* San Francisco: Harper, 1994.

Stanislav, Grof. *Ancient Wisdom and Modern Science*. Albany: State University of New York Press, 1984.

Stanislav, Grof, Hugh Lynn Cayce, and Raynor C. Johnson. *The Dimensions of Dying and Rebirth: Lectures from the 1976 Easter Conference at the Association for Research and Enlightenment, Inc*. Virginia Beach, VA: A.R.E. Press, 1977.

Stanislav, Grof, and Joan Halifax. *The Human Encounter with Death*. New York: Dutton, 1977.

Starr, Aloa. *Prisoners of Earth: Psychic Possession and Its Release*. Los Angeles: Aura Books, 1987.

Starr, James. "Does 2 Peter 1:4 Speak of Deification?" In *Partakers of the Divine Nature: The History and Development of Deification in the Christian Tradition*, edited by Michael J. Christense and Jeffery A. Wittung, 81–92. Madison, NJ: Farleigh Dickinson University Press, 2007.

Stcherbatsky, Theo. *The Soul Theory of the Buddhists*. Delhi: Bharatiya Vidya Prakashan, 1976.

Stearn, Jess. *Edgar Cayce: The Sleeping Prophet*. Garden City, NY: Doubleday, 1967.

_____. *Intimates Through Time: The Life of Edgar Cayce and His Companions Through the Ages*. New York: Harper & Row, 1989.

_____. *A Matter of Immortality: Dramatic Evidence of Survival*. New York: New American Library, 1976.

_____. *A Prophet in His Own Country: The Story of Young Edgar Cayce*. New York: William Morrow, 1974.

_____. *The Search for a Soul: Taylor Caldwell's Psychic Lives*. Garden City, NY: Doubleday, 1973.

_____. *The Search for the Girl with the Blue Eyes*. Garden City, NY: Doubleday, 1968.

_____. *Soul Mates*. New York: Bantam Books, 1984.

Stecher, Carl. "Faith, Facts, and the Resurrection of Jesus: A Review of the Resurrection of the Son of God by N. T. Wright." *Skeptic* 11, no. 4 (2005): 73–78.

Steiger, Brad. *Discover Your Past Lives.* West Chester, PA: Whitford Press, 1987.
———. *The Enigma of Reincarnation.* New York: Ace Books, 1967.
———. *You Will Live Again.* New York: Dell, 1978.
Steiger, Brad, and Loring G. Williams. *Other Lives.* New York: Hawthorn Books, 1969.
Steiner, Rudolf. *Karmic Relationships: Esoteric Studies.* 8 vols. London: Steiner Press, 1955–66.
Steinerbooks Dictionary of the Psychic, Mystic, Occult. Blauvelt, NY: Rudolf Steiner, 1973.
Stemman, Roy. *One Soul, Many Lives: First-hand Stories of Reincarnation and the Striking Evidence of Past Lives.* Berkeley, CA: Ulysses Press, 2005.
Stevens, Ramón. *Earthly Cycles: Reincarnation, Karma and Consciousness.* Ojai, CA: Pepperwood Press, 1994.
Stevenson, Ian. "Cultural Patterns in Cases Suggestive of Reincarnation Among the Tlingit Indians of Southeastern Alaska." In *Amerindian Rebirth: Reincarnation Belief Among North American Indians and Inuit,* edited by Antonia Mills and Richard Slobodin, 242–262. Toronto: University of Toronto Press, 1994.
———. *European Cases of the Reincarnation Type.* Jefferson, NC: McFarland, 2003.
———. *Twenty Cases Suggestive of Reincarnation.* New York: American Society for Psychical Research, 1966. (Proceedings of the American Society for Psychical Research, 26).
———. *Unlearned Languages: New Study in Xenoglossy.* Charlottesville: University Press of Virginia, 1984.
———. *Where Reincarnation and Biology Intersect.* Westport, CT: Praeger, 1997.
Storey, John Andrew. "The Doctrine of Reincarnation." *The Middle Way: Journal of the Buddhist Society* 44, no. 2 (August 1969): 70–71.
Sullivan, Lawrence E. *Icanchu's Drum: An Orientation to Meaning in South American Religions.* New York: Macmillan, 1988.
Sumedho (Ven. Bhikkhu). "Kamma and Rebirth." *The Middle Way: Journal of the Buddhist Society* 57, no. 1 (May 1982): 17–19.
Sutphen, Dick, and Lawrence Leigh Taylor. *Past Life Therapy in Action.* Malibu, CA: Valley of the Sun, 1983.
Sutphen, Dick, and Trenna. *The Master of Life Manuel.* Scottsdale, AZ: Valley of the Sun, 1980.
Sutphen, Tara. *Blame It on Your Past Lives: Personal Problems and Supernatural Solutions.* Malibu, CA: Valley of the Sun, 1992.
Swanson, Guy E. *The Birth of the Gods: The Origin of Primitive Beliefs.* Ann Arbor, MI: University of Michigan Press, 1960.
Synder, John. *Reincarnation vs. Resurrection.* Chicago, IL: Moody Press, 1984.
Talbot, Michael. *Your Past Lives: A Reincarnation Handbook.* New York: Fawcett Crest, 1987.
Tanabe, George J., Jr. "The Orthodox Heresy of Buddhist Funerals." In *Death and the Afterlife in Japanese Buddhism,* edited by Jacqueline I. Stone and Mariko Namba Walter, 325–348. Honolulu: University of Hawaii, 2008.
Taylor, John H. *Death and the Afterlife in Ancient Egypt.* Chicago: University of Chicago Press, 2001.
Ten Dam, Hans. *Exploring Reincarnation: The Classical Guide to the Evidence for Past Life Experiences.* London: Rider, 2003.
Tertullian. "The Refutation of the Pythagorean Doctrine of Transmigration." In *Immortality,* edited by Paul Edwards. Amherst, NY: Prometheus Books, 1997.
Thapar, Romila. *A History of India.* Vol. I. Harmondsworth, Middlesex, England: Penguin Books, 1966.
Thera, Piyadassi. *Dependent Origination: Paticca Samuppada.* Kandy, Sri Lanka: Buddhist Publication Society, 1981. (The Wheel Publication No. 5 a/b).
Thomason, Sarah Grey. "Entities in the Linguistic Minefield." *Skeptical Inquirer* 13, no. 4 (Summer 1989): 391–396.
Thornton, Penny. *The Forces of Destiny: Reincarnation, Karma, and Astrology.* London: The Aquarian Press, 1990.
Tierney, John. "Are Scientists Playing God? It Depends on Your Religion." *New York Times.* Nov. 20, 2007, D1.
Tipitaka. Suttapitaka, Anguttaranikaya (AN). The Book of the Gradual Sayings (Anguttara-Nikaya) or More Numbered Suttas. Translated by F.L Woodward, vols. 1, 2, 5; and E. M. Hare, vols. 3 and 4. London: Pali Text Society, 1965, 1972, 1973, 1979.
Tipitaka. Suttapitaka. Dighanikaya (DN). Dialogues of the Buddha. Translated by T.W. Rhys Davids. Parts I–III. London: Pali Text Society, 1977.
Tipitaka. Suttapitaka. Majjhimanikaya (MLS). The Collection of the Middle Length Sayings (Majjhima-Nikaya). Translated by I.B. Horner. Vols. 1–3. London: Pali Text Society, 1976, 1975, 1977.
Tipitaka. Suttapitaka. Sanyuttanikaya (SN). The Book of the Kindred Sayings (Sanyutta-Nikaya) or Grouped Suttas. Translated by C.A.F. Rhys Davids, vol. 1; and F.L. Woodward, vols. 2–4. London: Pali Text Society, 1971, 1972, 1972, 1975.
Todeschi, Kevin J. *Edgar Cayce on the Reincarnation of Biblical Characters.* Virginia Beach, VA: A.R.E. Press, 1999.
Toolan, David S. "Reincarnation and Modern Gnosis." In *Reincarnation or Resurrection?,* edited by Hermann Haring and Johann-Baptist Metz, 81–87. London: SCM Press, 1993. (Concilium 1993/5).
Tucker, Ruth A. *Another Gospel: Alternative Religions and the New Age.* Grand Rapids, MI: Zondervan Pub. House, 1989.
Tull, Herman W. *The Vedic Origins of Karma: Cosmos as Man in Ancient Indian Myth and Ritual.* Albany: State University of New York Press, 1989.
Tumminia, Diana. "Appendix 2: The Unarius Society." In *Encyclopedic Sourcebook of UFO Religions,* edited by James R. Lewis, 429–459. Amherst, NY: Prometheus Books, 2003.
Turner, Edith. "Behind Inupiaq Reincarnation: Cosmological Cycling." In *Amerindian Rebirth: Reincarnation Belief Among North American Indians and Inuit,* edited by Antonia Mills and Richard Slobodin, 67–81. Toronto: University of Toronto Press, 1994.
Valantasis, Richard. *Gnosticism and Other Vanished Christianities.* New York: Doubleday, 2006.
Valea, Ernest. "Reincarnation, Its Meaning and Consequences. A) Reincarnation in Eastern Religion, Meaning and Consequences." *Many Paths to One Goal.* http://www.comparativereligion.com/reincarnation.html (accessed 8/3/2003).
———. "Reincarnation, Its Meaning and Consequences. B) Past life recall as proof for Reincarnation" *Many Paths to One Goal.* http://www.comparativereligion.com/reincarnation1.html (accessed 8/3/2003).

_____. "Reincarnation, Its Meaning and Consequences." C) Reincarnation and cosmic justice." *Many Paths to One Goal.* http://www.comparativereligion.com/reincarnation 2.html (accessed 8/3/2003).

_____. "Reincarnation, Its Meaning and Consequences. D) Reincarnation and Christianity. *Many Paths to One Goal.* http://www.comparativereligion.com/reincarnation 3.html (accessed 8/3/2003).

Van Scott, Miriam. *Encyclopedia of Heaven.* New York: St. Martin Press, 1998.

Van Zeyst, Henri. *Dependent Origination.* Colombo, Sri Lanka: Metro Printers, 1979.

Venn, Jonathan. "Hypnosis and Reincarnation: A Critique and Case Study." *Skeptical Inquirer* 12, no. 4 (Summer 1988): 386–391.

_____. "Hypnosis and Reincarnation Hypothesis: A Critical Review and Intensive Case Study." *The Journal of the American Society for Psychical Research* 80, no. 4 (Oct. 1986): 409–425.

Vilenkin, Alex. "Beyond the Big Bang." *Natural History* 115, no. 6 (July/August 2006): 42–47.

Von Gernet, Alexander. "Saving the Souls: Reincarnation Beliefs of the Seventeenth-Century Huron." In *Amerindian Rebirth: Reincarnation Belief Among North American Indians and Inuit,* edited by Antonia Mills and Richard Slobodin, 38–54. Toronto: University of Toronto Press, 1994.

Von Ward, Paul. *The Soul Genome: Science and Reincarnation.* Tucson, AZ: Fenestra Books, 2008.

Wadley, Susan S. "Vrats: Transformers of Destiny." In *Karma: An Anthropological Inquiry,* edited by Charles F. Keyes and E. Valentine Daniel, 147–162. Berkeley: University of California Press, 1983.

Waite, Arthur Edward. *The Book of Black Magic and of Pack.* London: George Redway, 1898.

Walker, Benjamin. *The Hindu World: An Encyclopedia Survey of Hinduism.* 2 vols. New York: Frederick A. Praeger, 1968.

_____. *Masks of the Soul: The Facts Behind Reincarnation.* Wellingborough, Northamptonshire: The Aquarian Press, 1981.

Walker, E.D. *Reincarnation: A Study of Forgotten Truth.* New Hyde Park, NY: University Books, 1965.

Walters, Derek. *Chinese Mythology: An Encyclopedia of Myth and Legend.* London: Aquarian Press, 1992.

Wambach, Helen. *Life Before Life.* New York: Bantam Books, 1979.

_____. *Reliving Past Lives; the Evidence Under Hypnosis.* New York: Barnes & Noble Books, 1978.

Wapnick, Kenneth. *Absence from Felicity: The Story of Helen Schucman and Her Scribing of a Course in Miracles.* Roscoe, NY: Foundation for "A Course in Miracles," 1991.

Warren, Christopher, Kevin Logan & Arvin Gibson. "Reincarnation: The Great Delusion." *New Covenant Church of God: Reincarnation.* http://www.nccg.org/25 Art-Reincarnation.html (accessed 12/1/2003).

Wayman, Alex. *Untying the Knots in Buddhism: Selected Essays.* Delhi: Motilal Banarsidass, 1997.

Weber, Max. *The Religion of India: The Sociology of Hinduism and Buddhism.* New Delhi: Munshiram Manharlal, 2000.

Wedeck, H.E., and Wade Baskin. *Dictionary of Pagan Religions.* New York: Philosophical Library, 1971.

Wedeck, Harry. *Dictionary of the Occult.* New York: Philosophical Library, 1956.

Werner, Karel. *A Popular Dictionary of Hinduism.* Richmond, Surry: Curzon, 1994.

Wessinger, Catherine. "Hinduism Arrives in America: The Vedanta Movement and the Self-realization Fellowship." In *America's Alternative Religions,* edited by Timothy Miller, 173–190. Albany: State University of New York Press, 1995.

Westen, Robin. *Channelers: A New Age Directory.* New York: The Putnam Publishing Group, 1988.

Westwood, Jennifer. "Soul Birds." In *Macmillan Encyclopedia of Death and Dying,* edited by Robert Kastenbaum, vol.2, 773–775. New York: Macmillan Reference, 2003.

Whitton, Joel L., and Joe Fisher. *Life Between Life.* New York: Warner Books, 1986.

Wickland, Carl August. *Thirty Years Among the Dead.* San Bernardino, CA: Borgo Press, 1924.

Wilkinson, Tracy, and Louis Sahagun. "Vatican Panel Condemns Limbo to Eternal Dustbin: An Advisory Study, Approved by the Pope, Concludes that Unbaptized Babies May Go to Heaven After All." *Los Angeles Times,* April 21, 2007, 3A.

William, Kevin. "Testimonials of those who have seen Jesus." *Christian NDEs and Reincarnation.* http://www.near-death.com/origen.html (accessed 9/29/2003).

Williams, C.A.S. *Outline of Chinese Symbolism and Art Motives: An Alphabetical Compendium of Antique Legends and Beliefs, as Reflected in Manners and Customs of the Chinese.* 3rd Revised Edition. New York: Dover, 1976.

Williams, George M. "Swami Vivekananda's Conception of Karma and Rebirth." In *Karma & Rebirth: Post Classical Developments,* edited by Ronald W. Neufeldt, 41–60. Albany: State University of New York Press, 1986.

Williamson, J.N. *Death-Coach.* New York: Zebra Books, 1981.

Willson, Martin. *Rebirth and the Western Buddhist.* London: Wisdom Publication, 1987.

Wilson, Cyril H. "Re-birth — Fact or Fiction?" *The Middle Way: Journal of the Buddhist Society* 48, no. 2 (August 1973): 66–70.

Wilson, Ian. *The After Death Experience.* New York: William Morrow, 1987.

_____. *All in the Mind.* London: Gollancz, 1981.

_____. *Jesus: The Evidence.* San Francisco: Harper & Row, 1984.

Wiseman, Richard, and Ciaran O'Keefee. "A Critique of Schwartz et al.'s After-death Communication Studies." *Skeptical Inquirer* 25, no. 6 (Nov/Dec. 2001): 26–30.

Woerlee, G. M. "Darkness, Tunnels, and Light." *Skeptical Inquirer* 28, no. 3 (May/Jun 2004): 28–32.

Woodward, Mary Ann. *Edgar Cayce's Story of Karma.* New York: Berkley Books, 1972.

Woolger, Roger J. *Other Lives, Other Selves: A Jungian Psychologist Discovers Past Lives.* New York: Bantam Books, 1988.

World Almanac of the Strange. New York: New American Library, 1977.

Wright, Tom. *The Original Jesus: The Life and Vision of a Revolutionary.* Grand Rapids, MI: William B. Eerdmans, 1996.

Yarbro, Chelsea Quinn. *Message from Michael.* New York: Playboy Paperbacks, 1979.

Yeats, William Butler. *Ideas of Good and Evil*. London: A. H. Bullen, 1903.

Yewdale, Merton S. "The Path of Souls." *The Aryan Path* 9, no. 6 (June 1938): 263–266.

Young, Robert & Loy, and Lucia Capacchione. *Reincarnation Handbook*. Santa Monica, CA: Reincarnation Research and Education Foundation, 1980.

Zhu, Rui. "Myth and Philosophy: Form a Problem in Phaedo." *Journal of the American Academy of Religion* 73, no. 2 (June 2005): 453–473.

Zolar. *Zolar's Book of Reincarnation: How to Discover Your Past Lives*. New York: Simon & Schuster, 1996.

INDEX

References in ***bold italics*** indicate main encyclopedic entries.

Abelard, Peter 61
Abenda 263
abhavya ***9***
abhijna ***9***, 227
abhimsa 12
abhinna ***9***
abortion 86, ***129***
Abraham of Posquieres, Isaac ben ***9***
Absence from Felicity (Wapnick) 68
Abydos: The Holy City of Ancient Egypt (Eady and El Zeini) 80
accidentalism ***9***, 172
Acts of the Apostles 9, 54; 2:39 ***9***, 100, 105, 207, 213
acupuncture ***9***
Adam ***9–10***, 54, 61, 68, 91, 99, 105, 133, 189, 190, 327, 245, 252, 255, 257
Adelphi 262
adhi-bhautika duhkha ***10***
adhi-daivika duhkha ***10***
adhyatmika duhkha 10
adrishta ***10***
Advaita Vedanta: A Philosophical Reconstruction (Deutsch) 79, 127, 175, 208
Adversus nationes (Arnobius the Elder) 29
Adversus omnes Haereses (Irenaeus) 122, 274
Aegypyus sive de providential 264
Aeneas of Gaza ***10***
Aeneid (Virgil) 202, 276
Aetherius Society ***10***
affect bridge 10–11
A-field ***11***
Africa ***11***, 13, 20, 39, 42, 50, 55, 117, 217, 232, 244, 251, 272, 281, 282
Afro-American religions ***11***, 207, 241, 272
The After Death Experience (Wilson) 278
afterlife 24, 62, 68
Against the Christians (Porphyry) 207
Agartha 249
Agasha Temple of Wisdom ***11–12***
Agass, Mahan 214
age factor and rebirth ***12***, 266
agra-sandhani ***12***, 61
ahankara ***12***, 82

Ahasi, Shayky Ahmad 37
ahimsa ***12***, 268
ahmadiyya ***12***
Ahnenerbe 111
Ahriman ***12***
Ahtun Re 57, 239
AIDS 95
Airaudi, Oberto 72
Ajivikas ***13***, 17
Akan (tribal group) 11, ***13***
akashic record 11, ***13–14***, 22, 29, 31, 47, 54, 67, 94, 101, 160, 186, 193, 196, 21, 218, 235, 261
Akhenaton 83, 89, 154, 239, 261
Alayavininana ***14***, 140, 151, 275
Alcott, Bronson 15
Alcott, Louisa May 15–16
Alegretti, Wagner 12; *Retrocognitions* 86, 12
Aleut (tribal group) 15
Alevism 70
Alexandria, Egypt ***14***, 181
Ali, Mirza Husayn 37
Aliens Among Us (Montgomery) 276
Almeder, Robert: *A Critic of Arguments Offered Against Reincarnation* 174
Alpert, Richard 217
Alpha and Omega Lodge 94
Alpha Bootes 24
Al-Shahrastani 136, 152
altered states of consciousness (ASC) ***14***
altruism and rebirth ***14***
Alzheimer's disease and reincarnation
amata ***16***
Ambedkar, Bhim Rao 15
Ambrose of Milan 15
American Indians and reincarnation ***15***, 20, 114, 229, 230, 258, 259, 280
American Society for Psychical Research ***15***, 31, 131
American Temple 113
American Transcendentalists ***15–16***, 91
Americans Who Have Been Reincarnated (Banerjee) 38
Amerindian Rebirth: Reincarnation Belief among North American Indians and Inuit (Mills) 232

Amitabha Buddha ***16***, 50, 61, 76, 118, 161, 184, 193, 214, 271
Ammonius Saccas ***16***, 181, 239
Ammut (Ammit or Amemait) 83
amrita ***16***, 118
anabios ***16***
Anacalypsis: An Attempt to Draw Aside the Veil of the Saitic Isis: or, an Inquiry Into the Origins of Languages, Nations, and Religions (Higgins) 111
anamnesis ***16***, 199
anastasis ***16***
anatman 12, 13, ***16–18***, 21, 28, 31, 38, 46, 48, 51, 106, 119, 150, 151, 173, 184, 198, 226, 242, 249, 251, 275
anatta ***16–18***
ancestor worship ***19***, 107, 108
Ancient and Mystical Order Rosae Crucis (AMORC) 20, 238, 249
Ancient Egypt Speaks: A Miracle of Tongues (Hulme and Wood) 238
The Ancient Science of Soul Travel 81
Andaman Islanders (tribal group) ***19***
Andrade, Hernani Guimarãre ***19***; *A Case Suggestion of Reincarnation: Jacira and Ronaldo, Morte, Renascimento, Evolução, Reencarnacão no Brasil* 19
angelic planes 201
angels and reincarnation ***19***, 32, 33, 56, 153, 258, 261, 280
anima ***19***, 23, 162, 257
anima mundi 31, 48, 49, 204
animals and rebirth: non–Western view ***19–20***; Western view ***20***
animals, domesticated 20
animus 23
ankh ***20–21***
Ann Ree Colton Foundation of Nescience 66
annihilationism: Biblical view ***21***; Buddhist view ***21***, 172
anniversary recall phenomenon ***21***
Anselm (Saint) 61
antara-bhava 18
anthroposophy 206, 239, 261
anthropotathism ***21–22***
antimimon pneuma ***22***
antinomianism ***22***

299

Apadana 36
apocatastasis 22, 189, 273
Apocryphon of John 180
Apollonius of Tyana 22
Applewhite, Marshall Herff 107
Aquarian Foundation 22
Aquarian Gospel of Jesus Christ (Dowling) 13, 22–23, 55, 126, 273
Aquarius, Age of 33, 77, 182, 249, 277
Aquinas, Thomas 23, 2, 33, 261; *De Anima Commentarium* 23; *Aristotelis Librum* 23; *Scriptum Super Sententiis* 23; *Summa Contra Gentiles* 23; *Super Evangelium S. Matthaei* 23
Aradia, the Gospel of the Witches (Leland) 157
Arcane School 37
archetypes 23, 131, 265
archons 24, 202
Archy and Mehitabel 24
Archytas of Tarentum 24
Arcturus 24
Ardath (Corelli) 68
Are Souls Real? (Elbert, Jerome) 250
Argenteum Astrum 70
arguments: pro and con on an afterlife in general 24, 207; specifically against rebirth 25; supportive of rebirth 25–28, 114, 180, 255; that challenge rebirth on a logical basis 28
arhat/arahat 9, 28, 52, 125, 143
Aries 33
Aristophanes 97
Aristotelis Librum (Aquinas) 23
Aristotle 28–29, 109, 181, 257; *De Anima* 257; *Metaphysics* 28; *Physics* 28
Arnobius the Elder 29; *Adversus nationes* 29
Arnold, Edwin Lester 151
Arnold, Kenneth 272
artificial rebirth 29
Asahara, Shoko 35
ascended masters 29–30, 56, 65, 76, 100, 102, 116, 126, 158, 166, 213, 216, 240, 248, 249
asceticism 30, 172
Ashoka (Indian king) 30
Ashtar 22
Asia 30
asmi-mana 30
Assassins 30
Association for Past Life Research and Therapies 31, 197
Association for Research and Enlightenment 93
Association for the Alignment of Past Life Experience 31
Association for the Study of Karma 31
associations and organizations 31
Astara 31
Astraea 31
astral body 31, 32, 38, 54, 76, 90, 121, 136, 154, 159, 192, 244, 247, 253

astral light 31
astral plane 13, 31–32, 80, 90, 170, 188, 201, 268, 277
astral soul 32
Astrological Reincarnation Time Scale (ARTS) 165
astrology and rebirth 32–34, 64
Astrology and Your Past Lives: Reincarnations through Saturn's Placement in Your Chart (Avery) 241
asuras 32, 34, 40, 100, 136, 166, 184, 226, 229
Atlantic Guild for Past Life Awareness 31, 34
Atlantis 49, 54, 71, 94, 101, 111, 161, 200, 217, 243, 245, 262, 268, 269
atman 12, 28, 34–35, 50, 51, 96, 98, 104, 106, 119, 127, 154, 169, 171, 173, 178, 187, 194, 199, 208, 226, 250, 251, 253, 256, 263
atonement 61–62
atrilism 207
attached entity 35, 140, 178, 218, 26, 278
Augustine, St. Aurelius Augustinus 15, 35, 61, 64, 219; *De Civitate Dei* 35
Aum Shinrikyo 35
Aum Temple of Universal Truth 35–36
Aumism of Mandarom 36
Aurum Solis 80
Australian aborigines 36, 147, 232
automatic speech 36
automatic writing 22, 36, 68, 175, 186, 200, 245, 263
Ava-Ciripa (tribal group) 15
Avadana 36
Avalokiteshvara 36, 72, 159, 208, 271
Avalon, Arthur: *Juana-chakrash* 268
avatar 10, 12, 36–37, 40, 70, 72, 118, 271, 280
Avery, Jeanne: *Astrology and Your Past Lives: Reincarnations through Saturn's Placement in Your Chart* 241
avichi 37, 194
awagaun 37, 248
Awareness Research Foundation 31, 37
Awareness Technique 37
Ayesha, the Return of She (Haggard) 105
Aztec Mummy vs. the Robot (movie) 179
Aztecs 37, 52, 168

Babb, Lawrence A.: *Destiny and Responsibility: Karma in Popular Hinduism* 111
Babbitt, Elwood 37
Babism 37
Bach, Richard S. 130; *Jonathan Livingston Seagull* 130
Bahaism 37
Bahaullah 37
Bahir 9

Bailey, Alice A. 37–38, 171; *A Treatise of White Magic* 265; *Treatise on the Seven Rays: Esoteric Astrology* 161
Baker, Robert 196
Ballard, Edna 115
Ballard, Guy Warren 115, 116, 240; *The Magic Presence* 116; *Unveiled Mysteries* 116, 177
Banerjee, H.N. 38, 91, 123, 207, 232, 266; *Americans Who Have Been Reincarnated* 38; *Lives Unlimited: Reincarnations East and West* 38; *The Once and Future Life: An Astonishing Twenty-Five-Year Study on Reincarnation* 38, 123
baptism and reincarnation 38, 199
Bardesanes 33
bardo 38, 69, 94, 120, 274
Bardo Thodol 38
Basil (Basilus) of Caesarea 39, 103
Basil the Great 39
Basilides 39, 274
Bax, Clifford: *Traveler's Tale* 270
beans 39
Beaver (tribal group) 15
behavioral memory 39
Belgi Dorje 39
Beng (tribal group) 11
Bengston, David 13: *Past Lives of Famous People: Journeys of the Soul* 13
Benin (tribal group) 11, 39–40
Berg, Philip S.: *Wheels of a Soul* 127, 134
Bernard of Clairvaux 249
Bernstein, Morey 49; *A Scientific Report on "The Search for Bridey Murphy"* 49; *The Search for Bridey Murphy* (book) 49
Beruchim, Abraham 40
Besant, Annie 32, 40, 90, 156, 171, 231, 260
Bey, Hamid 67
Beyond Forever: Unlocking the Door to Eternal Life (Pure Mind Foundation) 214
Beyond Human Personality (Cummins) 71
Beyond the Ashes: Cases of Reincarnation from the Holocaust (Gershom) 127
Bhagavad-Gita 12, 40, 122, 126, 150, 236
Bhaishajyaraja-gurn 40, 50, 161, 214
bhakti yoga 40, 149, 274
bhava 40, 209, 226, 242
bhavachakra 32, 40, 210, 214, 226, 229
bhavanga 40
Bi-Amir, al Hakim 78
Bible and rebirth 41
Biblical deluge and reincarnation 41
bija 41
Bilimoria, Nasarvanji: "Transmigration in the Avesta" in *Zoroastrianism in the Light of Theosophy* 282

Bimstein, Louis 29
birds, soul *41–42*
birth trauma *42*
birthmarks 27, *42*, 143, 167, 196
Bjorkhem, John 42
Bjorling, Joel: *Reincarnation: A Bibliography* 231
black hole 42
Black Mentalists 103
Blake, William 258
Blame It on Your Past Lives: Personal Problems and Supernatural Solutions (Sutphen) 263
blaming the victim vs. illusion of innocence 19, *42*, 53, 63, 67, 74, 126,142, 143, 150, 159, 171, 180, 184, 266
Blavatsky, Helena Petrovna 13, 29, 31, 32, 37, 40, *43–44*, 76, 90, 91, 111, 130, 146, 153, 156, 161, 164, 171, 183, 186, 239, 248, 260, 267, 275, 278; *Isis Unveiled* 43, 11, 186; *The Secret Doctrine* 43, 161
bleed-over 44
bleed-through of lives 44
blocked regression 44
Blood from the Mummy's Tomb (movie) 179
Blue Cliff Record 163
bodhisattva 36, 37, 39, 43, *44–45*, 48, 50, 60, 72, 74, 107, 125, 149, 154, 159, 161, 164, 171, 208, 209, 215, 236,271, 281, 282
body as a mere garment of the soul 23, *45*, 68, 212
body-brain (mind) dependency 12, *45*, 57, 169, 222, 262
body is the hell of the soul 46
body-soul dualism 17, *46*, 53, 79, 185, 198, 199
Bogomils *46–47*, 53, 79, 90, 197, 198
Bonaparte, Napoleon 165, *180*, 198, 263
Bon-pa [po] religion *47*
The Book of Black Magic and of Packs (Waite) 89
Book of Life 47
The Book of Mediums: A Guide for Mediums and Invocators (Kardec) 259
Book of Serenity 164
Book of the Dead (Egyptian) 47
Book of the Dead (Tibetan) 38–39, 69, 280
Book of the Law (Crowley) 70
Book of the Law (Elkins) 113
Book of Thoth 268
Book of Thoth (Crowley) 268
Book of Thoth (Uxkull) 268
The Book on the Rashith ha Gigalim (Revolution of the Soul or Scheme of Reincarnation (Rosenroth) 246
borderline state *47*
"born again" *47–48*, 128, 199
Born Again: Reincarnation Cases Involving International Celebrities (Semkiw) 92, 239
Bostwick, Lewis S. 65
Boulder Fellowship Foundation *48*

Boullan, Joseph-Antoine *48*, 279
Bourdin, Gilbert 36
Bowman, Carol *48*, 232
Brahma and rebirth in Buddhism *48*
brahmacarya (celibacy) 49, 124
Brahman 17, 35, 40, *48–49*, 51, 118, 119, 126, 127, 139, 154, 165, 168, 175, 209, 248, 251, 273, 274
Brahmanas 48, 273
Branch Davidians 153
Bremmer, Jan N.: *The Rise and Fall of the Afterlife* 103, 193
Brennan, J.H.: *The Reincarnation Workbook* 101
Bridey Murphy case 48, *49*, 70
bridges 49, 108
Brighton, Earl W. 112
Brotherhood of Light 163
Brotherhood of the White Temple *49*
Bruno, Giordano *49*; *Spaccio de la bestia trionfante* 49
Brunton, Paul *50*; *Hermit in the Himalayas* 50
Buchan, Sir John *50*; *Pilgrim's Way* 50
Buddha 9, 10, 16, 18, 30, 36, 40, 44, 48, *50*, 61, 65, 76, 98, 106, 107, 113, 124, 126, 140, 143, 149, 156, 161, 164, 171, 178, 184, 191, 193, 201, 214, 215, 220, 226, 227, 229, 240, 248, 261, 264, 265, 268, 271, 275, 279, 281, 282
Buddha's necklace *50*
Buddhism 9, 12, 13,16–18, 19, 30, 32, 34, 40, 48, 49, *50–51*, 75, 79,82, 89, 93, 94, 96, 98, 100, 106, 107, 108, 109, 110, 113, 114, 117, 118, 119, 120, 124, 125, 126, 136, 137, 138, 139, 140, 141, 142, 143, 149, 150, 151, 152, 154, 156, 157, 158, 159, 161, 163, 164, 165, 166, 171, 172, 173, 175, 177, 178, 180, 184, 191, 193, 198, 199, 200, 201, 203, 208, 209, 210, 214, 215, 216, 219, 220, 221, 222, 223, 225, 226–228, 229, 236, 237, 239, 240, 242, 248, 249, 250, 251, 255, 258, 259, 261, 264, 265, 266, 267, 268, 270, 271, 274, 275, 279, 281, 282; esoteric *51*; folk *51*, 98, 251; see also Mahayana Buddhism, Theravada Buddhism, Vajrayana Buddhism, *Vijnanavada* School of Buddhism, *Yogachara* School of Buddhism
Buddhist stages of liberation *51–52*, 227, 236
Bulstode, Whitelock: *An Essay on Transmigration, in Defense of Pythagoras* 246
Bulwer-Lytton, Sir Edward: *Zanoni: A Rosicrucian Tale* 80
Burke, George 100
Butler, Hiram 88
butterfly *51*, 219

cabales or caballi *51*
Cancer (the Crab) 33, *52*, 55

Candia Debate 52
Candomble 11, 136
cannibalistic reincarnation *52*
Cannon, Alexander *52*, 96, 102; *The Power of Karma in Relation to Destiny* 52; *The Power Within* 52
Cao Dai *52*
Capricorn (the Goat horn) 33, *53*, 55
Caracalla 238
Cardiac, Jean-Louis 58
Carey, Elizabeth 277
Caropocrates 22, *53*
Carus, Paul 188
A Case Suggestive of Reincarnation: Jacira and Ronaldo (Andrade) 19
caste system 42, *53*, 135, 137, 146, 165, 184, 220, 228, 231, 236, 239, 277
casual body *54*, 122, 253
Cathars and Reincarnation (Guirdham) 104
Cathars or Cathari 47, *53–54*, 64, 79, 90, 94, 104, 111, 120, 132, 197, 215, 233
Catholic Church 28, 35, 47, 53, 62, 63, 81, 95, 111, 120, 125, 131, 132, 152, 159, 173, 185, 197, 213, 215, 235, 238, 241, 259, 266, 272
Catimbo 11
cats *54*
cave *54*
Cayce, Edgar 10, 13, 24, 33, *54–55*, 109, 126, 16, 168, 169, 184, 257, 260, 278
celestial gates 33, *55–56*
celestial planes 29, 201
Celestine Prophecy (Redfield) *56*
celibacy (*brahmacharya*) 49, 60, 88, 93, 124, 165, 177, 187, 190, 210, 227
Celsus 185, 189
Celtic Druids (Higgins) 111
Cerminara, Gina: *Many Mansions* 129
Cervé, W.S.: *Lemuria: The Lost Continent of the Pacific* 177
Chadwick, Gloria: *Reincarnation and Your Past Life Memories* 255
chakras *56*, 65, 184, 187, 268
Chalice of Oblivion 78
The Challenge of Fate (Dethlefsen) 155
Chan-ch'a sha-0-yeh-pao ching 56
Chaney, Earlyne 31
Chaney, Robert 31
Channelers: A New Age Directory (Western) 57
channeling 36, *56*, 65, 74, 112, 186, 196, 207, 218, 24, 260, 271
Chari, Dr. C.T.K. *57*, 232; *Paramnesia and Reincarnation* 57; *Paranormal Cognition, Survival and Reincarnation* 57; *Regression Beyond Birth* 57; *Signet Handbook of Parapsychology* 57
Charlemagne 165, 180, 272
Charvakas *57*
child as its own reborn father or mother *57*

child prodigies or geniuses 26, **58**
children remembering past lives **58**
Children Who Remember Previous Lives (Stevenson) 262
child's epitaph **59**
chimera 86
Chinese religion and reincarnation **59–61**
Chintra-gupta **61**, 280
chirognomy 61
chirology 61
chiromancy **61**
chirosophy 61
chit **61**
chitta **61**, 165, 226
Chizuo, Matsumoto 35
chnoumis, chnouphis **61**
Christ 16, 22, 24, 30, 35, 45, 47, 48, 53, 55, 61, 62, 63, 70, 87, 90, 93, 100, 109, 112, 113, 118, 126, 130, 149, 153, 156, 157, 158, 168, 169, 173, 177, 180, 182, 183, 185, 198, 199, 201, 233, 234, 238, 249, 260, 261, 266, 273, 274, 282
Christ the Savior Brotherhood 113
Christian Scientists 63, 273
Christianity: atonement theories **61–62**; esoteric 35, **63–64**, 168; fathers critical of reincarnation **62**; lost chord of **64**; missionary influence and reincarnation **62**; and reincarnation **62–64**; view of the afterlife **62**
Christopher, Daniel 112
Christos technique **64**
Christward Ministry **64**
Chronicles 243
chronoportation **64**
Chuan-lun wang **64**
Chukchi (tribal group) **65**
Church Council: of 553 **64**, 189; of Laodicea **65**, 183; of Lyons **65**, 213, 215, 233
Church of the Divine Man **65**
Church of the People 105
Church of the White Eagle Lodge 67
Church Truth Universal-Aum 35
Church Universal and Triumphant **65**, 116, 185, 277
Cicero, Marcus Tullius 16, **65**, 102; *De Republica* 202
Circle of Necessity **65**
Citizens of the Cosmos (Jocelyn) 12, 13, 33, 55, 161, 176
clairaudience **65**, 218
clairvoyance **65**, 218
Clarion 22
Clement of Alexandria **65–66**
Cleopatra Syndrome **66**, 254, 263
Closs, Hannah: *High Are the Mountains* 104
Clothed with the Sun: Being the Illuminations of Anna (Bonus) Kingsford 153
The Cloud on the Sanctuary (Von Eckarshausen) 102
coffin to cradle **66**, 70, 73, 269
collective birth of extraordinary men and women **66**

collective soul 103
collective unconscious 23, **66**, 131, 265
Collin, Robert **66**; *The Theory of Celestial Influence* 66; *The Theory of Eternal Life* 66
Collin, Rodney **165**
Collins, Mortimer: *Transmigration* 151
Colton, Ann Ree **66**; *Draughts of Remembrance: Memories of Past Lives, The Seven-Year Etheric Cycle of the Soul* 66
come-as-you-were parties **67**
Coming Back: A Psychiatrist Explores Past Life Journeys (Moody) 175, 224
Committee for the Scientific Investigation of the Paranormal (CSIOP) **67**
Commodus 238
Community of the Inner Light 94
conditional immortality **67**
Confucianism 52, 60, 219, 281
congenital retardation **67**
conscious dying **67**, 214
consciousness continuity, sleep versus death **67**
Cook, Emily Williams: "Do Any Near-Death Experiences Provide Evidence for the Survival of Human Personality After Death" 193
Cooke, Grace **67**, 277; *The Illumined Ones* 67
Cooke, Maurice B. 111
Cooper, Irving: *Reincarnation: The Hope of the World* 121
Coptic Fellowship of America **67**
Cordovero, Moses 67
Corelli, Marie **67–68**, 105, 151; *Ardath* 68; *The Life Everlasting* 68; *A Romance of Two Worlds* 68; *Ziska* 68
Corinthians, 1st and 2nd 21, 22, 54, **68**, 100, 145, 148, 183, 198, 233, 234, 237
corporeal versus non-corporeal afterlife **68**
Corpus Hermeticum 110
cosmic picture gallery 13
Cosmoplanetary Messenger 36
Cott, Jonathan: *The Search for Om Sety: a Story of Eternal Love* 80
Council of Florence **65**, 213, 215
Council of Sirmium, Fourth 105
Course in Miracles **68**
A Course in Miracles (Schuchman) 68
creationism 98; soul **68–69**, 96
Critias (Plato) 269
A Critic of Arguments Offered Against Reincarnation (Almeder) 174
A Critical Examination of the Belief in Life after Death (Ducasse) 49
critical time periods **69**
Cromwell, Oliver 13
Crowley, Aleister 29, 57, **69–70**, 238, 243, 258, 268; *Book of the Law* 70; *Book of Thoth* 268; *Magick in Theory and Practice* 70
Crux Ansata **20–21**
crypt **70**
cryptesthesia **70**
cryptomenesia 29, 49, 59, **70**, 127, 218, 224, 260, 279
Cult of Angels 37, **70–71**, 280
Cummins, Geraldine Dorothy **71**; *Beyond Human Personality* 71; *Mind in Life and Death* 71; *Road to Immortality* 71; *The Scripts of Cleophas* 71; *Swan on a Black Sea: A Study of Automatic Writing, the Cummins-Willet Transcripts* 71; *They Survive* 71
cumulative argument **71**
current knowledge discrepancy **71**, 202
cycle mates **71**

Dabistan **71**
daimones **71**, 258
Dakelhnes (tribal group) 15
Dakini 274
Dalai Lama 36, **72**, 117, 118, 158, 193, 208, 274
Dali, Salvador **72**
Damanhur **72**
Dancer to the Gods (Richardson) 237
Danelek, Allen J.: *Mystery of reincarnation* 49
Daniel, Book of 13, **72**, 96, 114, 187, 213
Daoism 60, **72**, 108, 118, 159, 219
Dark Brotherhood **72**
Darwin, Charles 211, 254, 261, 266
David (King) 10, 54, 95, 133, 153, 169, 171, 212, 260, 261
Davis, Andrew Jackson **72–73**, 260; *The Diakka and their Earthly Victims* 76
Dawn, Rose: *The Miracle Power* 168
Dayaks (tribal group) **73**
De Anima (Tertullian) 266
De Anima Commentarium (Aquinas) 23
De Animarum Transmigratione (Henrici) 246
De Bello Galico (Julius Caesar) 78
De Civitate Dei (Augustine) 35
De Metempsycosi dissertation (Schilling) 246
De Republica (Cicero) 202
Dead Sea Scrolls 109, 168
death **73**
Death-Coach (Williamson) 274
Death Is of Vital Importance (Kubler-Ross) 154
death panorama **73**
death to breath 66, 70, **73**, 269
death, violent and premature **73**
deciduous trees **74**, 219
deferred payment plan for the soul **74**, 266
dehiscent or seed-pod principle 43, **74**
déjà vu 27, 59, **74**, 188, 195, 218

demiurge 22, 23, 39, 46, 53, **74,** 97, 198, 204, 274
demonomancy **74**
Dene-Tha (tribal group) 15
Deo non fortuna 94
depth psychology 82
De Rochas, Col. Albert **75**: *La Vies Successives* 75
Descartes, René 56, **75**, 173, 201, 275
Destiny and Responsibility: Karma in Popular Hinduism (Babb) 111
Destiny of Souls (Newton) 249
determinism 9, 13, 63, **75**, 172, 251
Dethlefsen, Thorwald: *The Challenge of Fate* 155; *Voices from Other Lives: Reincarnation as a Source of Healing* 155
Deuteronomy **75**, 132, 145, 188, 243, 252, 252
Deutsch, Eliot: *Advaita Vedanta: A Philosophical Reconstruction* 175
devachan **75–76**, 106, 136, 226
devaloka 9, 32, **76,** 120
devas 32, 33, 34, 40, 76, 100, 136, 160, 166, 184, 214, 275
dharma 30
Dharma Shastras **76**
dhyani chohans 29, 72, **76**, 111, 117, 126, 240, 248
diakka **76**
The Diakka and their Earthly Victims (Davis) **76**
"Dialogues on Metempsychosis" (Herder) 109
Diamond Cutter Sutra's Revilement **163**, 164
Dianetics: The Modern Science of Mental Health (Hubbard) 242
diathanatic **76**
dibbuk, dybbuk **76**, 135, 136
dichotomy **76**
Diogenes Laertius **76**, 216; *Lives and Opinions of Eminent Philosophers* 76
Dionysus **76–77**
Diordus Silculus 78
Discover Your Lives (Steiger) 260
disincarnation **77**
dissociation **77**
divided consciousness **77**
The Divine Plot (Mann) 34, 165
Divine Science of the Soul 81
doceticism **77,** 85
A Door to Eternity (Glaskin) 64
dor deah **77**
Doreal, M. 49
double torches **77**
Dowling, Levi H. 22–23; *Aquarian Gospel* of Jesus Christ 13, 22–23, 55
Draughts of Remembrance: Memories of Past Lives, The Seven-Year Etheric Cycle of the Soul (Colton) 66
dreams **77–78**, 253; announcing **78**; lucid **78**, 218
Dreams, Evolution, and Value Fulfillment (Roberts) 245
drink or fruit of forgetfulness **78**

drugs 30–31, 45, 103, 170, 176, 192
Druids **78,** 90, 176, 179, 259, 265
Druzes 30, 55, 71, **78–79**
dual or double souls 36
dualism 17, 46, 53, **79**, 89, 185, 198, 199, 204
Ducasse, Curt John **79**; *A Critical Examination of the Belief in Life after Death* 49, 79; *Is a Life After Death Possible?* 79; *Nature, Mind, and Death* 79
duhkha/dukkha 10, 17, 18, 30, 48, **79,** 107, 209, 224, 24, 251
Dunton, John: *The Visions of the Soul Before It Comes into the Body* 246
Dweller on the Threshold **80**, 247
A Dweller on Two Planets (Oliver) 177, 201
dying in peace 27, **80**
Dzogchen 39

Eady, Dorothy **80**; *Abydos: The Holy City of Ancient Egypt* 80
Earth-bound **80**, 124
An Earth Dweller's Return (Oliver) 201
Earthly Cycles (Stevens) 86, 191, 268, 277
East-West Traveling **80**
Ecclesiastes **80–81**, 82
Ecclesiasticus or the Wisdom of Jesus son of Sirach 80, **81**
Eckankar **81**, 253
Eckart, Dietrich 112
Eclesia Catholic Cristiana **81**
Eddy, Mary Baker 273
Edgar Cayce and the Born Again Christian (Sparrow) 55
Edgar Cayce: The Sleeping Prophet (Stearn) 260
Edison, Thomas 263
Edwards, Paul 31, 174, 262; *Reincarnation: A Critical Examination* 31, 262
eggs 81
ego 12, 32, 54, 68, 75, **80–81**, 117, 165, 170, 173, 251, 253, 275
Egypt 13, 23, 30, 69, 71, **82–84,** 89, 91, 94, 101, 102, 110, 151, 152, 179, 180, 200, 201, 202, 212, 244, 247, 249, 250, 251, 261, 264, 267, 268, 269
Eighth sphere **84**, 205, 244
Eike, Erika Bertschinger 93
Elbert, Jerome: *Are Souls Real?* 250
Elder Brothers of Mankind 29
Elder Brothers of the Rosicrucian Order 239
Elect or Chosen of God 84
Electra/Oedipus Complex and rebirth **84**, 96, 173
Elements of Reincarnation (Mann) 34, 165
Elijah 53, 129, 189, 193, 276, 279
Elisha 97
Elkins, Don: *Book of the Law* 113, 216
Elysium Fields 102, 237, 257, 276

El Zeini, Hanny: *Abydos: the Holy City of Ancient Egypt* 80
emanationism 68
embodiment, moment of **86**
embryonic fusion **86**
Emerson, Charles 15
Emerson, Ralph Waldo 15, 91
Emma-o **87,** 107
Empedocles or Acragas **87,** 163, 190, 216
Empire of Jade **87**
engrams **87**
The Enigma of Reincarnation (Steiger) 260
Ennius, Quintus **87**
Enoch, Books of **87**, 168, 272
ensomatosis **87**
Ephesians **87**, 91, 148, 183, 209
Equinox 57
The Equinox (periodical) 70
Erziechung des Menschengeschlechts (Lessing) 157
Esoteric Buddhism (Sinnett) 51, 136, 248
Esoteric Christianity 88
Esoteric Fraternity **88**
An Essay on Transmigration, in Defense of Pythagoras (Bulstode) 246
Essene Center **88**
Essenes **88–89**, 239
Essenes of Arkashea 89
The Eternal (movie) 179
The Eternal Return (Mann) 34, 165
eternalism **89**, 172
Etherian Religious Society of Universal Brotherhood **89–90**
etheric body 32, 54, 80, **90**, 121, 136, 159, 244, 253
etheric plane **90**, 201
etheric revenant **90**
Etruscan Roman Remains in Popular Tradition (Leland) 157
Eucharist 62
Europe and reincarnation **90**
European Case of the Reincarnation Type (Stevenson) 115, 262
"every knee should bend ... every tongue confess" 63, **90**
evolution 27
evolutionary transmigration of souls **91**, 264
ex oriente lux **91**
existential seriality **91**
Exodus 91, 99, 129, 133, 212, 243, 265
Experiencing Reincarnation (Perkins) 76
Experimental Spiritism and Spiritist Philosophy (Kardec) 259
Exploring Reincarnation: The Classical Guide to the Evidence for Past Life Experiences (Tan Dam) 266
extinctivist **91**
extrasensory perceptions 57, **91–92**
Ezekiel **145**, 187

Fab, Peter: *Man's Rise to Civilization* 232
facial architectural consistency **92**
facial blank **92**

faculty X **92**
fall of the souls **92,** 176, 201
false claims of support for reincarnation **92**
false-memory syndrome **92–93**
false messiahs 95, 131
Falun Gong **93**
fantasy prone personality **93,** 115, 218
fantasy versus past life regression **93,** 218
far memory **93**
Far Memory (Grant) 101
Fellowship of the Inner Life **93**
Filadoro, Massimiliano: *Tarot of Reincarnation* 265
Fillmore, Charles 273
Fillmore, Myrtle 273
The Finest Story in the World (Kipling) 153
finite or infinite number of rebirths **93**
Finland **94**
fixed number or variable number of souls **94**
Flavius Claudius Julian 117
Flournoy, Theodore 178; *From India to the Planet Mars: A Study of a Case of Somnabulism with Glossolalia* 178
fluorite **94**
A Foot in Both Worlds (Guirdham) 104
The Forces of Destiny (Thornton) 34
Fortune, Dion **94,** 237; *Psychic Self-Defense* 94
forty 91, **94,** 102, 206, 219, 245
forty-nine 38, 69, 96, 109, 120
Foundation for Reincarnation and Spiritual Research 31, **94**
Foundation for the Realization of Inner Divinity 163
The Four Gospels (Kardec) 259
Fox Koan 164
Frank, Jacob **95**
Frankel, Fred H. 179; *Hypnosis at Its Bicentennial: Selected Papers* 179
Franklin, Benjamin 57
Fraternity of Light **95**
Fraternity of the Inner Light 237
fraud **95,** 218, 224, 260
Frazer, James George 155; *Golden Bough* 155
A Free and Impartial Censure of the Platonic Philosophie ... (Parker) 246
free association 95, 114
free soul 15, 36
Freud, Sigmund 37, 78, 82, 117, 173, 256
From India to the Planet Mars: A Study of a Case of Somnabulism with Glossolalia (Flournoy) 178
full participation **95–96**
future lives 74, 94

Ga (tribal group) 11
Gabriel **96,** 176
Galatians 21, 22, 48, 96, 145, 183, 237

Galya Raza **96**
gandharva/gandhabba **96–97,** 226, 228
Ganges river **97,** 201
Garbhavakranti-nirdesha-sutra 164
garden of waiting **96,** 102
Gardner, Gerald: *Book of Shadows* 70; *Witchcraft Today* 278
Garvey, Marcus 217
Gatti, Hilary: *Giordano Bruno* 50
Gehazi **97**
gehenna **97,** 134, 187, 187
Gemini 33
gender issue of the soul **97**
generationism and traducianism 68, **98,** 120
Genesis 9, 19, 91, **98–99,** 127, 135, 168, 187, 237, 245, 255, 281
Genesis: The Miracles and Predictions According to Spiritism (Kardec) 259
Genii of Nations, Knowledge and Religion 88
Gershom, Yonassan 127, 188, 215; *Beyond the Ashes: Cases of Reincarnation from the Holocaust* 127, 215
ghost 90
gilgul or *gilgulim* **99,** 110, 130, 132, 133, 134, 135, 216, 244, 25, 265
gilgul neshamot 99
Gilgulim, Sefer ha- (Vital) **99**
Giordano Bruno (Gatti) 50
Glanvil, Joseph: *Lux Orientalis: or an Inquiry into the Opinions of the Eastern Sages Concern the Pre-existence of Souls....* 246
Glaskin, G.M. 64; *A Door to Eternity* 64; *Windows of the Mind* 64; *Worlds Within* 64
Gleanings in Buddha Fields (Hearn) 152
glossolalia **99–100,** 178, 279
glottologues **100**
Gnostic Order of Christ **100,** 113
Gnostic Orthodox Church of Christ in America **100**
Gnosticism 22, 33–34, 46, 71, 74, 79, **100,** 110, 122, 165, 180, 202, 205, 23, 242, 245, 256, 274
Gnostics 23, 24, 33, 39, 46, 49, 53, 54, 63, 65, 77, 83, 85, 90, 91, 92, 96, 97, 106, 124, 126, 128, 136, 152, 166, 180, 181, 182, 185, 189, 190, 198, 201, 210, 230, 245, 248, 267, 274
God and rebirth in the West **100**
God of the Witches (Murray) 278
Gods, cyclically dying and rising **101**
Goethe, Johann Wolfgang von **101**
Golden Bough (Frazer) 155
Goodwin, John: *Works* 246
The Gospel According to Spiritism (Kardec) 259
Goudey, R.F.: *Reincarnation: A Universal Truth* 41, 93, 121, 205
Grace-Loerh Life Readings 13, 71, 93, 98, **101,** 159, 255
Grant, Joan Marshall **101–102,** 152, 245: *Far Memory* 101; *Many Lifetimes* 152; *Now and Then: Rein-*

carnation, Psychiatry, and Daily Life 152
Great Pyramid 109
Great White Brotherhood 10, 30, 35, 65, 70, 72, 76, 102, 113, 116, 216, 239, 249, 277
Great White Lodge 102
Greek afterlife, the ancient **102**
Greeks and reincarnation **102–103**
Green, Jeff: *Pluto: The Evolutionary Journey of the Soul* 205
Greene, Liz: *Saturn: A New Look at an Old Devil* 80
Gregory of Nazianus **103**
Gregory of Nyssa 39, 64, **103**
grey occultists **103,** 262
Greyson, Bruce: "Do Any Near-Death Experiences Provide Evidence for the Survival of Human Personality After Death" 193
Griffin, David Ray **103**
Grof, Stanislav **103**
group soul **103–104,** 114, 172, 216, 218, 254
Growth of a Soul (Oliver) 201
Growth of the Soul: A Sequel to Esoteric Buddhism (Sinnett) 248
Guardian of the Threshold 80
Guayaki (tribal group) 15
Guernon, Rene: *Introduction to the Study of the Hindu Doctrines* 104
Guf ha-Briyot **104**
guided imagery **104**
Guild of the Master Jesus 94
Guirdham, Arthur **104**: *Cathars and Reincarnation* 104; *A Foot in Both Worlds* 104; *The Lake and the Castle* 104; *We Are One Another* 104
Gurdjieff, Georgi Ivanovitch 31, 66, **104–105,** 191
Gwenved **105**

Hades 44, 101, 102, **105,** 117, 158, 175, 187, 190, 198, 203, 226, 240, 24, 265
Haggard, H. Rider 67, **105,** 151
Hall, Manley Palmer **105,** 172; *The Secret Teachings of All Ages: An Encyclopedic Outline of Masonic, Hermetic, Qabbalistic and Rosicrucian Symbolical Philosophy* 105, 172
Hapshepsut 83
The Harmless Opinion of the Revolution of Humane Souls as a Probable Hamsa 105
harrowing of hell **105,** 158
Hartley, Christine 237
Hashimiyya **106**
Hasidism 99, **106,** 110, 122, 127, 130, 147, 216, 265
Hauntings 104, **106**
Have You Lived Before This Life? A Scientific Study: A Study of Death and Evidence of Past Lives (Hubbard) 242
Hawkman **106**
Hearn, Lafcadio: *Gleanings in the Buddha Fields* 152

heaven 24, 25, 26, 27, 33, 35, 37, 38, 47, 52, 54, 59, 62–63, 65, 71, 76, 79, 80, 82, 84–85, 87, 88, 90, 99, 103, 106, 107, 158, 159, 162, 167, 173, 175, 178, 193, 206, 241, 263, 264, 280
Heaven and Hell: The Divine Justice Vindicated in the Plurality of Existences (Kardec) **259**
heaven, hell, and Buddhist no-soul (Self) **106**
heavens, Buddhist **106**
Heaven's Gate **107**
Hebrews, Book of 62, 109, 168, 183
hedonism **107**, 172
Heimarmene **107**
Heindel, Max 239
hell 24, 34, 37, 38, 60, 62, 106, **107–108**, 114, 120, 125, 130, 139, 144, 158, 159, 162, 166, 171, 178, 180, 184, 197, 206, 228, 229, 234, 264, 273, 280; Chinese **108**, 275; realm 32
Helmont, Franciscus Mercurius van **109**; *Seder Olam; or the Order, Series or Succession of All the Ages, Periods, and Times of the Whole World....* 246; *Two Hundred Queries....* 109, 246
Henrici, Heinrich: *De Animarum Transmigratione* 246
Heracleides of Ponticus **109**
Herder, Johann Gottfried von **109**; "Dialogues on Metempsychosis" 109
Hermes **109**, 216
Hermes-Thoth 31
Hermes Trismegistus 31, 110, 239
Hermetic Astrology: Towards a New Wisdom of the Stars (Powell) 241
Hermetic Brotherhood of Luxor 29, 44
Hermetic Order of the Golden Dawn 29, 69, 94, **110**, 135, 153, 248, 280
hermetic philosophy 31, 49, 54
Hermetic Society for World Service **110**
Hermit in the Himalayas (Brunton) 50
Herod (King) 85, 245
Herodotus **110**, 203; *The Histories* 110
heroic "I" **110**
Heschel of Opatov, Abraham Joshua **110**
Hesiod 105
hetero-retrocognition **110**
Hezyonat, Sefer ha- (Vital) **111**
hidden observer **111**
Higgins, Godfrey **111**; *Anacalypsis: An Attempt to Draw Aside the Veil of the Saitic Isis: or, an Inquiry Into the Origins of Languages, Nations, and Religions* 111; *Celtic Druids* 111
High Are the Mountains (Closs) 104
Hilarion 57, 72, 76, 111, 117
Himmler, Heinrich **111**
Hinduism 12, 19, 32, 34, 40, 48, 49, 61, 75, 76, 79, 93, 94, 98, 105, 106, 108, **111**, 118, 119, 120, 124, 127, 135, 137, 138, 143, 149, 157, 160, 168, 171, 175, 177, 180, 191, 194, 195, 201, 208, 210, 219, 220, 222, 224, 228, 248, 250, 251, 255, 258, 259, 263, 264, 266, 267, 274, 275, 276, 280, 281
Hinkins, John-Roger 177, 253
Hirvenoja, Reijo 179
Historical Fiction: A Guide to the Genre 151
The Histories (Herodotus) 110
Hitler, Adolf **112**
Hodgson, Joan: *Reincarnation through the Zodiac* 33
Hollywood and reincarnation **112**
Holmes, Ernest Shurtleff 242
holy lying 95
Holy Order of Ezekiel **112**
Holy Order of Mans 100, 112
Holy Spirit (*Pneuma Hagion* or *Spiritus Sanctus*) 100, 117, 193, 207, 252, 258
Home, Daniel Douglas **113**, 259
Homer 55, 87, 181
homosexuality and transsexuality 27, 84, **113**
honest lying 95, 113, 163, 218, 224, 260
Honoratus, Servius Marius 202
Hopkins, Emma Curtis 273
Hosea 145, 187
Hoskins, Cyril Henry 217
Hotel Transylvania (Yarbro) 240
Hotoke **113**
hovering of the soul **113**
Hubbard, Lafayette Ronald 70, **242**; *Dianetics: The Modern Science of Mental Health* 242; *Have You Lived Before This Life? A Scientific Study: A Study of Death and Evidence of Past Lives* 242; *Mission into Time* 242
Huffman, Robert W. 48: *Many Wonderful Things* 48
Hulme, A.J.H.: *Ancient Egypt Speaks: A Miracle of Tongues* 238
human embryo stem cell uses and rebirth **113–114**
Human Immortality and Pre-existence (MacTaggart) 163
human personality complexity **114**
hungry ghosts 32, 40, 60, **114**, 120, 136, 171, 184, 199, 210, 226, 229
Hunter, Neva Dell 216
hunting cultures and reincarnation 114
Hussein, Saddam **114**
Hutin, Serge **114**
Huxley, Aldous 274
Huxley, Thomas Henry **114**
Hyde-Lees, Georgie 280
hypermnesia **114**
hypnosis 29, 47, 49, 75, 77, 113, 114, 162, 179, 197, 242, 259, 277
hypnotic age regression 12, 49, 122, 237
hypoamnesia **114**, 115
Hypothesis....(W.C.) 246

I Am Movement 65, 115, 177, 240, 267
I, William the Conqueror: a meditation on an improbable past life **116–117**
Iamblichus of Chalcis **117**, 207, 240; *Peri Psyches* 117
ibbur 99, 117, 135
Ichantika 9, 117
id, ego and superego **117**, 173
Ideas of Good and Evil (Yeats) 281
idolatry of the brain **117**
Igbo of Nigeria 11, 33, 212
Illiad and *Odyssey* (Homer) **117**
Illuminati 102
The Illumined Ones (Cooke) 67
illusion of innocence **42**
immortality 67, **117–118**, 136
Immortality and Human Destiny: A Variety of Views (MacGregor) 162
important person criticism **118**
Inca Indians **118**
incarnation versus reincarnation **118**
incest and reincarnation **118**
inconsistent views and reincarnation **118–119**, 222
incremental change of identify **119**
Independent Spiritualist Association of the United States of America 31, 260
India 119
Indian Institute of Parapsychology 38
individuality and rebirth **119–120**
Indonesia 120, 264
infusionism 68, 97, 120, 188
The Inner I 31
Inquisition, Catholic 53, **120**
Inter-human reincarnation **120**
Interim period 11, 12, 43, 57, 65, 68, 69, 73, 75, 79, 94, 96, 109, **118**, 129, 144, 160, 161, 163, 164, 174, 176, 198, 203, 211, 212, 213, 229, 238, 254, 262, 263, 268, 281
Interlife **121**
Internal-external rule **121**
International Association for Regression Research and Therapy 31, **121**
International Board for Regression Therapy 31, **121**
International cases **122**
International Society for Krishna Consciousness **122**
Internet and reincarnation **121**
Interplanetary Parliament 10
Intimates Through Time: The Life of Edgar Cayce and His Companions through the Ages (Stearn) 260
Introduction to the Study of the Hindu Doctrines (Guenron) 104
Inuit (tribal group) 15, 73
Inupiaq (tribal group) 114
Irenaeus 64, **122**, 274; *Adversus omnes Haereses* 122, 274
irrational fears 27, **121**
Is a Life After Death Possible? (Ducasse) 79
Isaac, Jacob, the Seer of Lublin **122**
Isaac the Blind 9

Isaac the Pious 9
Isaiah, Book of 13, 116, 129, 166, 187, 243
Isherwood, Christopher 208, 272, 274
Isis Unveiled (Blavatsky) 43, 111, 185, 267
Islam 30, 47, 71, 79, 106, 120, *122*, 124, 131, 153, 164, 165, 177, 179, 181, 194, 195, 220, 232, 236, 248, 250, 264, 267
Isma'ilis 44, *124*, 264
Israel, Manasseh ben *124*; *The Soul of Life* 124
Ivanova, Barbara *124*, 232; *The Golden Chalice* 124

Jacira and Ronaldo (Andrade) 19
Jacob (Biblical) 10
Jainism 12, 13, 17, 19, 34, 46, 49, 75, 79, 93, 94, 98, 100, 105, 106, 108, 120, *124*, 127, 136, 138, 139, 141, 171, 184, 195, 203, 219, 220, 222, 224, 228, 250, 251, 255, 258, 264, 266, 274, 275
James, Henry 278
James, Letter of 21, *125*, 183
Janua Coeli, Janua Inferni *125*
Jataka Tales 36, 60, 125
Jehovah's Witnesses 63
Jeremiah, Book of 9, 145, 243
Jerome, Eusebius Hieronymus *125*
Jesus 10, 12, 14, 22, 23, 39, 54, 62, 65, 68, 76, 77, 88, 94, 96, 98, 100, 105, 107, 220, *126*, 128, 129, 130, 131, 145, 153, 156, 158, 161, 165, 166, 167, 169, 182, 183, 185, 186, 193, 198, 199, 201, 205, 212, 217, 233, 234, 235, 237, 239, 241, 242, 257, 258, 260, 261, 262, 264, 272, 273
Jewish Holocaust *126*
Jews, Ashkenazi and Sephardic *127*
jigoku 87, 154, 247
Jiva 13, 16, 124, *127*, 240, 253
Jivakosha 127
Jivamukta *127-128*
Jivaro (tribal group) 15
Jnana chakrasha 268
Job, Book of 81, *128*, 132, 145, 266
Jocelyn, Beredene: *Citizens of the Cosmos* 12, 13, 33, 55, 161, 176
Jochelson, Waldemar: *The Yukaghir and Yukarghirized Tungus* 281
John Chrysostom *128*
John, Gospel of 21, 47, 66, 85, 122, *128-130*, 156, 183, 189, 199, 209, 213, 215, 258
John the Baptist 48, 53, 129, 189, 276, 279
Johnson, Sarah: *Historical Fiction: A Guide to the Genre* 151
Jonah, Book of 275
Jonathan Livingston Seagull (Bach) 130
Josephus, Flavius 88
Jouret, Luc 249
Journal of Regression Therapy *121*
Journal of the American Society for Psychical Research 15

Journey into the Bright World (Moore) 176
Journey of Souls (Newton) 249
Journeys Out of the Body (Monroe) *262*
Judaism 9, 79, 89, 95, 97, 100, 122, 131, 132, 147, 158, 190, 194, 201, 215, 231, 233 250, 255, 267
Judaism and the afterlife 130, 131, 252
Judas Syndrome *130*
Jude 148
Judge, William Q. 64, 130, 267; *Ocean of Theosophy* 29
Judgment of the Dead *131*, 153, 177, 248, 282
Julian, Flavius Claudius or Julian, the Apostate *131*, 238, 240
Julius Caesar 78; *De Bello Galico* 78
Jung, Carl 23, 78, 82, 131, 157, 174, 265
Jupiter 10, 33, 202
Justin Martyr 64, *131-132*

Kabbalah 44, 76, 97, 100, 127, 130, *132-135*, 158, 162, 168, 190, 230, 238, 257, 265, 268, 271, 275, 276
Kabirpanthi *135*
kaivalya 136
Kalama Sutta 227
kamadhatu 32, 106, *136*, 270
kamaloka 32, 106, *136*, 176, 107, 176
kama-manas 165
kamarupa 31, 32, 76, *136*, 253, 270
Kampman, Reima 59, 179
Kant, Immanuel *136*
Kanthaeans 136
Kardec, Allan 52, 81, 113, 136, 241, 259: *The Book of Mediums: A Guide for Mediums and Invocators* 259; *Experimental Spiritism and Spiritist Philosophy* 259; *The Four Gospels* 259; *Genesis: The Miracles and Predictions According to Spiritism* 259; *The Gospel According to Spiritism* 259; *Heaven and Hell: The Divine Justice Vindicated in the Plurality of Existences* 259; *Le Livre des Esprits* 259
Kardecismo 11, *136*, 272
Karet *136*
Karma/*kamma* *136*, 190; as absolute or relative 141; in the ancient and modern west *144*; attitudinal *143*; in the Bible 96, *145-146*; bodily *143*; classification *143*; delayed *144*; developmental *144*; family *144*; and free will 75; geographic *144*; global *114*; and God *138*; group *144*; and justice *138*; justice, and infancy *146*; and logic *140*; marital *146*; and the moral structure of the universe *140*; national or state *146*; as natural law *142*, 149; organic or organismic *146*; origins of *146*; parental *147*; place or site *147*; Prarabdha *147*; racial *147-148*; and rebirth 84, *140*; redemptive *148*; relationship *148*; retributive *148*; symbolic *148*; as unfinished business *142-143*, 194; versus grace *148-149*; vocational *150*; with and without rebirth *150*; with minimal rebirth *150*; yoga 40, *150*
Karma and Rebirth in Classical Indian Traditions (O'Flaherty) 231
Karma and Reincarnation League 231
Karma in Motion (Layton) 161
karma-nemesis *146*
karma-*vipaka* as a long term moral tendency 149
karmic: astrology 33, *150*; bankbook *150*; boomerang effect 145, *150*; carrier 98, 159, 226; carry-over *151*; disease *151*; eschatology 106, 108, 144, *151*, 224; romances 74, 151; script *151*; seeds 41; ties 152
Karmic Astrology: Retrogrades and Reincarnation (Schulman) 33
Karmic Relationships: Esoteric Studies (Steiner) 261
Karmic Tarot: A New System for Finding Your Lifetime's Purpose (Lammay) 265
Katsugoro case *152*
Kear, Lynn: *Reincarnation: A Selected Annotated Bibliography* 231
Keith, George: *Truth and Innocency Defended Against Calumny and Defamation....* 246
Kelsey, Denys *152*: *Many Lifetimes* 152; *Now and Then: Reincarnation, Psychiatry and Daily Life* 152
Kennedy, John F. *152*
Kenny, Saint 188
Kerr, Katherine 151
Kevala 124
Khepra 83, *152*
Khnum 83
Khul, Djwal 213
Khurramiyya 71, 152
Kieninger, Richard 261; *The Ultimate Frontier* 261
King, Elizabeth Delvine 35
King, George 10
Kings, Book of 243
Kingsford, Anna Bonus *152-153*; *Clothed with the Sun: Being the Illuminations of Anna (Bonus) Kingsford* 153; *The Perfect Way, or the Finding of Christ* 153
Kipling, Rudyard *153*; *The Finest Story in the World* 153
Kiramu-l-katibin *153*
Kirkisani 130; *Sefer ha-Orot* 130
Klemp, Harold 81
Kline, Milton V. 179
Koot Hoomi 31
Koresh, David *153*
Koryaks (tribal group) 65
Kosha 34, *154*, 159, 199
Krishna 10, 12, 37, 40, 48, 122, 126, 150, 156, 160
Krishnamurti, Jiddu 40, 156, 260
Kshitigarbha Bodhisattva *154*, 159, 161, 269

Kubitschek, Juscelino *154*
Kubler-Ross, Elizabeth *154,* 220, 232; *Death Is of Vital Importance* 154; *On Death and Dying* 154; *On Life After Death* 154; *On Life, Death and Life After Death* 154
Kueshana, Eklal: *The Ultimate Frontier* 103
Kulkulcan *154,* 272
kundalini yoga 56, 268
Kwakiutl (tribal group) 15, *154*
kyklos genesion 107, *154,* 190, 205, 275

Lactantius, Lucius Caelius Firmianus *155*
Ladder *155*
The Lake and the Castle (Guirdham) 104
lama 155, 217
Lama Yoga 31
Lammay, W.C: *Karmic Tarot: A New System for Finding Your Lifetime's Purpose* 265
Language inconsistency *155*
Lankavatara Sutra 275
Lao Tzu 10
Lapps (Saami) *155*
Larkin, E.L. 177
The Last Inca, Atahualpa: An Eyewitness Account of the Conquest of Peru in 1535 272
The Last Incarnation (Lenz) 157
Last thought *155*
Last Word: Therapies, Inc. 31, *156*
Laszlo, Ervin 11; *Science and the Akashic Field* 11
Lateran Council 233
Lauritsen, Poul 34; *Reincarnation and Freedom* 34
law of parsimony 13, 218
Laws (Plato) 204
Layela 78, *156*
Layton, Felix: *Karma in Motion* 161
Lazaris 57, *156*
Leadbeater, C.W. 32, 40, 90, 156, 158, 171; *A Textbook of Theosophy* 32, 90, 156, 171
Leading questions *156,* 211, 262
Leek, Sybil 156; *Reincarnation: the Second Chance* 156
Leibniz, Gottfried Wilhelm von *156;* *Philosophische Schriften* 156
Leigh, Lawrence: *Past Life Therapy in Action* 263
Leland, Charles Godfrey *157; Aradia, the Gospel of the Witches* 157; *Etruscan Roman Remains in Popular Tradition* 157
Lemuria (Mu) 10, 49, 157, 161, 217, 261
Lemuria Fellowship *157,* 261
Lemuria: The Lost Continent of the Pacific (Cervé and Ward) 177
Lenape (tribal group) 15
Lenz, Frederick *157; The Last Incarnation* 157; *Lifetimes: True Accounts of Reincarnation* 157
Leo 33
Leo, Alan *157*

Leo XIII, Pope 259
Lerner, Alan J.: *On a Clear Day You Can See Forever* 188
Lessing, Gotthold Ephraim *157; Erziechung des Menschengeschlechts* 157
Lethe *158,* 175, 18, 190, 203
Levi, Eliphas Zahed 29, 80, 153
Levirate marriage *158*
Leviticus 91, 188, 243
Lewis, H. Spencer 238; *The Mystical Life of Jesus* 55
Lhamoi Latso Oracle 72, *158*
Liberal Catholic Church International 158
Liberal Catholic, Province of the U.S.A. 100, 156, *158,* 267, 276
liberation 51–52
Libra 33
Library of the Occult (Wheatley) 277
Life After Life (Moody) 175
Life Before Life (Wambach) 277
The Life Everlasting (Corelli) 68
Life of Apollonius of Tyana 22
Life of Pythagoras (Porphyry) 207
Life script problem *158*
Lifetimes: True Accounts of Reincarnation (Lenz) 157
limbo 25, 62, 90, 105, *158,* 273
Limited life or soul substance 159
linga sharia 31, 54, 119, 154, *159,* 253
lingam 248
Lingbao Scripture of the Most High Concerning Karmic Retribution 159
Lipika 12, 140, 160, 161
Lives and Opinions of Eminent Philosophers (Diogenes) 76
Lives Unlimited: Reincarnations East and West (Banerjee) 38
Living Your Past Lives: The Psychology of Past Life Regression (Schlotterbeck) 34, 197
Le Livre des Esprits (Kardec) 259
Loehr, Franklin 101
Loehr, Grace Wittenberger 101
Logan, Michael 210; *Spirit Guide* 209
Logic and pseudo-logic and rebirth *159–160*
Logic of physical cause and effect *160*
Lords of Karma 10, 140, *160–161*
lost continents 10, 49, 54, 71, 94, 101, 111, 151, 157, *161,* 175, 186, 200, 217, 222, 245, 262, 272
lost soul *160*
Lotus Ashram *160*
Lotus Sutra 151, 223
Louis XIV 113, 254
Lucian *160*
Lucifer *160,* 249, 261, 273
Lucifer (publication) 44
Lucretius, Carus Titus 162
Luke, Gospel of 21, 53, 62, 77, 84, 85, 96, 122, 145, *162,* 166, 167, 198, 202, 207, 233, 261
Luria, Isaac 67, 96, 99, 106, 127, 133, 136, 147, *162,* 177, 216, 244, 276

Lux Orientalis: or an Inquiry into the Opinions of the Eastern Sages Concern the Pre-existence of Souls.... (Glanvil) 246

Maccabees, Book of 187
MacGregor, Geddes *162,* 215; *Immortality and Human Destiny: A Variety of Views* 162; *Reincarnation and Christianity* 215
MacIver, Joanne *162–163*
MacIver, Ken 162
Maclaine, Shirley 112, *163,* 220
Macrobius, Theodosius 202
MacTaggart, John Ellis *163: Human Immortality and Pre-existence* 163; *The Nature of Existence* 163
Macumba 11, 136
Madhi 12, 131
Mafu 57, 84; *163*
Magdalene, Mary 201
The Magic Presence (Ballard) 116
Magick in Theory and Practice (Crowley) 70
Magna Graecia 103, *163,* 216
Magnetic attraction metaphor *163*
The Maha Bodhi 163
Maha-brahma 48
Mahayana Buddhism 16, 36, 45, 50, 79, 118, 120, 149, 154, 161, *163,* 171, 203, 209, 240, 268, 275
Mahayana Buddhist rebirth texts *163–164*
Maher Baba *164*
maiden embodiment or incarnation *164*
mala 50
Malachi, Book of 13, 85, 187, 243
Malaysia *164*
Male births, greater proportion of *164*
Malkula (tribal group) *164,* 187
Mambro, Joseph di 249
manas 32, 54, 61, 82, *165,* 173, 175, 253, 275
mandalas 80
Mandara *165*
Mani 165
Manichaeism 15, 35, 71, 79, 100, 122, 144, *165,* 171, 198
Mann, A. Tad. 34, *165,* 180; *The Divine Plot* 34, 165; *Elements of Reincarnation* 34, 165; *The Eternal Return* 34, 165
Man's Rise to Civilization (Fab) 232
Manson, Charles Willie *165*
Manu-Sanhita 165
Many Lifetimes (Kelsey and Grant) 152
Many Mansions (Cerminara) 129
Many Wonderful Things (Huffman & Specht) 48, 49
Mara 76, 107, *165–166*
Marciniak, Barbara 241
Mark, Gospel of 21, 53, 62, 68, 77, 84, 85, 99, 100, 122, *166,* 167, 183, 245
Mark-Age, Inc. *166*

Marlowe, Christopher *167*; *The Tragedy of Doctor Faustus* 167
Mars 10, 33, 109, 178, 202
Martin, Eva: *Reincarnation: The Ring of Return* 205
Masefield, John *167*
Masonry 105, 110, 177, 239, 260, 266, 277
Masters of the Great White Brotherhood of Cosmic Light 22
maternal impressions or maternal psychokinesis 42, *167*
Mathesis *167*
Matlock, James G. 195, 196
A Matter of Immortality: Dramatic Evidence of Survival (Stearn) 260
Matthew, Gospel of 21, 53, 62, 77, 84, 85, 90, 99, 122, 145, 158, 162, 166, *167–168*, 183, 193, 207, 209, 213, 215, 245
Maya *168*, 208
Mayan Indians 83, 154, *168*
Mayan Order *168*
Mayan Temple *168*
Mazda 12
McClelland, Bruce 47; *Slayers and Their Vampires* 47
McCoy, Edain: *Past Life and Karma Tarot* 265
meditation 18, 36, 48, 50, 60, 64, 76, 94, 107, 112, *168*, 174, 182, 185, 187, 195, 196, 197, 263, 265, 270, 275, 281
medium *168*
Melanesia 187, 190
Melchizedek 10, 54, 89, 100, 157, *168–169*, 261, 273
Melville, Herman *169*; *Moby Dick* 169
Memo (Plato) 16, 204
Memoires (Talleyrand-Périgord) 180
memory: ancestral or genetic *169*; contamination *170*; problem 13; reasons for loss of past life *169–170*; summation *170*; suppressed *170*
memory alone critique *170*
mental body 54
mental plane 32, *170–171*, 201, 244
mental retardation *171*
Mercury 33, 109, 202
Merit, transfer of 171
Mesopotamia 94, 99, 101, 136, 171
Messiah 12, 36, 40, 62, 84, 85, 88, 89, 95, 101, 104, 105, 126, 131, 133, 153, 156, 166, *171*, 182, 198, 219, 260, 282
metagenetics *171*
Metamorphoses (Ovid) 193
Metaphysics (Aristotle) 28
metempsychosis 10, 16, 18, 20, 24, 29, 34, 35, 39, 46, 50, 52, 53, 62, 64, 65, 66, 68, 102, 109, 110, 111, 117, 126, 129, 136, 114, 153, 155, 161, 162, 167, *171*, 172, 175, 177, 181, 182, 189, 190, 193, 195, 197, 200, 201, 203, 204, 205, 207, 209, 210, 215, 218, 237, 238, 242, 244, 248, 256, 257, 264, 265, 266, 276

Metempsychosis, or the Transmigration of Souls.... 172
metensomatosis 66, 171, *172*
Michael (1) 37; *172*, 279
Michael (2) 57, *172*, 240
Michael's Teachings (Yarbro) 172
Micronesia 187
Middle Way or Middle Path 9, 21, 50, 75, 89, *172*, 201
midnight *172*
Milinda Panha *172*
Milky Way 84, 109, *173*, 187, 205, 206, 263
Millennialism *173*
Mills, Antonia: *Amerindian Rebirth: Reincarnation Belief Among North American Indians and Inuit* 232
mind 14, 23, 34, 36, 45, 56, 57, 64, 70, 74, 75, 78, 109, 111, 114, 117, 130, 136, 140, 151, 154, 155, 165, 168, 172, *173–174*, 175, 182, 191, 192, 193, 194, 199, 205, 209, 211, 214, 215, 237, 242, 243, 249, 256, 258, 262, 269, 272–273, 275, 278
Mind in Life and Death (Cummins) 71
Mind Out of Time: Reincarnation, Hypnotic Regression, Stigmata, Multiple Personality, and Other Little-Understood Powers of the Mind (Wilson) 278
mind, theory of *174*, 256
minimal reincarnation hypothesis 174
The Miracle Power (Dawn) 168
Mirza, Nadarbeg K.: *Reincarnation in Islam* 123
Mission into Time (Hubbard) 242
Mithraism 55, 71, *174–175*, 245, 267
Mnemosyne *175*, 190
Moby Dick (Melville) 169
Mohan, Rajneesh Chandra 191
moksha 9, 127, 144, *175*, 274
Moltke, Helmuth Graf von *175*
monad *175*
monism 81, *175*, 204
Monroe, Robert A: *Journeys out of the Body 262*
Montgomery, Ruth Shick *175*, 276; *Aliens Among Us* 176; *Strangers Among Us* 276; *Threshold to Tomorrow* 276
Moody, Raymond A., Jr. *175*; *Coming Back: A Psychiatrist Explores Past Life Journeys* 175, 224; *Life After Life* 175
moon 33, 55, 84, 90, 96, 102, 121, *175–176*, 202, 219, 232, 263, 280
Moore, Marcia *176*; *Journey into the Bright World* 176; *Reincarnation: Key to Immortality* 176
More, Henry *176*; *The Immortality of the Soul* 176; *Philosophical Poems: A Platonick Song of the Soul, ...* 246
Morganwg, Iolo (Edward Williams) *176*

Mormonism 22, 63, *177*
Moroni 22
Morse, J.J. *177*, 260
*Morte, Renascimento, Evoluç*ão, *Reencarnacão no Brasil* (Andrade) 19
Moses, the Old Testament prophet 22, 75, 85, 91, 133, *177*, 185, 200, 212
Mother, mule, and son 177
Mount Shasta 115, *176*, 200
Movement of Spiritual Inner Awareness Church *177*, 253
Mozart, Wolfgang Amadeus 58
Mu 10, 49
Muhammad Ahmad *177*
Muhammad, Mirza Ali 37
mula 177–178
Muller, Catherine Elise (Smith, Helen) *178*
multiple personalities 57, 59, 92, 110, *178–179*, 218, 260
The Mummy 179
The Mummy Lives (movie) 179
The Mummy Returns (movie) 179
mumukshatwa 179
Murphy, Bridey 49
Murray, Margaret *278*; *God of the Witches* 278; *The Witch Cult in Western Europe* 278
Murro, Jonathan 66
Myers, F.W.H. 104, *179*
Mysteria Mystica Maeterna 261
Mysteria Mystica Maxima 70
Mystery of Reincarnation (Danelek) 49
The Mystical Life of Jesus (Lewis) 55
mystical states 14

Nada-Yolanda 166
nafs and *ruh 179*
Nag Hammadi Texts 100, 126, *180*
Nahmanides 132
Nanak, Guru 248
Nandi (tribal group) 11
naraka 108, 136, *180*, 279
natal defects 143, *180*
Nataraja (Lord of the Dance) 248
national character reappearances 27, *180*, 232
National Psychopathetic Institute 278
National Spiritual Association of Churches 260
nations, their rise and decline argument *180*
Die Natur der Dinge (Wieland) 278
Nature, Mind, and Death (Ducasse) 79
The Nature of Existence (MacTaggart) 163
Naylor, James *180*
Nazi 111, 126, 188, 264
Ndembu (tribal group) 11
necromancy *180–181*, 243, 262
Nemesius of Emesa *181*; *Peri Physeos Anthropou* 181
Neo-pagan religions 171, *181*, 182, 219, 243, 263, 265

Neoplatonism 16, 30, 74, 79, 100, 110, 122, 132, 144, 165, 175, *181*, 190, 263, 264, 267, 280
Nepenthean veil *181*
nephesh 134, 252, 257
Neptune 33
Nero, Claudius Drusus Germanicus *181*, 205
Nero, Tiberius Claudius 112, 181
neshamah 134, 257
Netherton, Morris: *Past Lives Therapy* 182
Netherton Method *182*
Nettles, Bonnie Lu 107
Neverdies *181-182*
New Age Community Church *182*
New Age religions 35, 45, 65, 81, 169, 181, 182, 215, 217, 271, 272, 273, *182*, 215, 217, 271, 272, 273
New Testament 9, 16, 21, 22-23, 41, 47, 53-54, 62, 64, 68, 76, 84, 96, 100, 105, 108, 125, 129, 138, 145, 161, 168, 182, 18, 19, 198, 209, 213, 233, 234, 235, 245, 252, 266, 270; and reincarnation *182-183*; sacrificial concept 61, 62, *183-184*
New Thought 88, 273
New York Institute for Psychic Research 238
Newbrough, John Ballou 186
Newhouse, Flower A. 64
Newton, Michael: *Destiny of Souls* 249; *Journey of Souls* 249
nidhi 39
Nightmare of eastern philosophy *184*
nine doors 56, *184*
Nirjara 184
nirman-rati 107
nirvana 16, 18, 44, 52, 76, 144, 159, 175, *184*, 210, 221, 227, 236, 240, 251
nirvikalpa samadhi 184
No Pre-existence, or a Brief Dissertation Against the Hypothesis of Human Souls Living in a State Antecedaneous to This (Warren) 246
no-rebirth wish *184-185*
noble lie 43, 139, 175, *184*, 228
Norman, Ernest 272; *Voices of Venus* 272
Norman, Ruth 272: *The Last Inca, Atahualpa: An Eyewitness Account of the Conquest of Peru in 1535* 272; *Principles and Practices of Past Life Therapy* 272; *The Proof of the Truth of Past Life Therapy* 272
Norton, Rosaleen *185*
Notovitch, Nicholas 65, *185*; *The Unknown Life of Jesus Christ* 185
nous 85, 256, 257
Now and Then: Reincarnation, Psychiatry, and Daily Life (Grant and Kelsey) 152
Numbers *185*
Numenius of Apamea *185*, 202; *Peri Aphtharsias Psyches* 185
Numerology and rebirth *185*

Nupe (tribal group) 11, *185-186*
Nusayr, Abu Shu'ayb Muhammad ibn 186
Nusayris 98, *186*, 279

Oahspe: A Kosmon Bible in the Words of Jehovih [sic] and His Angel Ambassadors 186
Oasis Fellowship *186*
Ob Ugarins *186*, 258
Obadiah 145
Obeah 11
Objective immortality *186*
Obscure Problems of Karma and Rebirth (Sinnett) 248
obsession 35, 42, *186*
Occult Hierarchy 102
The Occult World (Sinnett) 248
Ocean of Theosophy (Judge) 29
Oceania *186-187*, 190, 270
Octavian (Roman Emperor) 13
O'Donnell, Margaret O. 101
O'Flaherty, Wendy Doniger: *Karma and Rebirth in Classical Indian Traditions* 231
Ogdoad *187*, 201
ojas 187
Olcott, Henry Steel 130, 267
old Brahmin moonshine *187*
Old Norse *187*
old souls 135, 161
Old Testament 21, 22, 39, 41 53-55, 62, 71, 72, 75, 80, 81, 83, 96, 98, 105, 127, 130, 132, 145, 158, 185, 189, 199, 201, 209, 211, 212, 213, 220, 23, 237, 243, 245, 252, 266, 269; and the afterlife *187*; and the soul *188*, 252
Olfactory psychic experience *188*
Oliver, Frederick 177, 200; *A Dweller on Two Planets* 177, 201; *An Earth Dweller's Return* 201; *Growth of a Soul* 201
Oliver, Frederick Spencer 200
Omega *188*, 268
On a Clear Day You Can See Forever (Lerner) *188*
On Abstinence from Animal Food (Porphyry) 207
On Death and Dying (Kubler-Ross) 154
On Life After Death (Kubler-Ross) 154
On Life, Death and Life After Death (Kubler-Ross) 154
On the Delays of the Divine Vengeance (Plutarch) 205
The Once and Future Life: An Astonishing Twenty-five-year Study on Reincarnation (Banerjee) 38
oneriomancy 78
Only Fair Religion *188*
ontological leap or ontological discontinuity 20, *188*, 223
Open Court *188*
Order of Melchizedek of the Order of the Holy Cross 100
Order of the Illuminati 261
Order of the Temple of the Orient 238

Ordo Templi Orientis 70, *189*, 238, 243, 258, 261
Origin 16, 64, 125, 185, 189, 267
original or ancestral sin and reincarnation *189*
original sin, Christianity, and reincarnation 38, 43, 62, 69, 87, 98, 103, 148, 158, *189-190*, 266
original sin versus karma *190*
Orokaiva (tribal group) 187
Orpheus 190
Orphism 39, 46, 77, 83, 89, 100, 101, 103, 117, 129, 165, *190-191*, 198, 202, 203, 264, 275, 276
Osho Movement *191*, 275
Osiris 83, 84, 152
Other Lives (Steiger) 260
Other Lives, Other Selves (Woolger) 211
Ouija board 36, 172, *191*, 245
Ouroboros 191
Ouspensky, P.D. 66, *191-192*; A New Model of the Universe 191
out-of-the-body and near-death experiences 14, 27, 45, 154, *192*
Over-soul, personal 193
Ovid or Publius Ovidius Naso *193*; *Metamorphoses* 193
Ovimbundu (tribal group) 11

Padmasambhava 39
Pagan Dawn 243
Pagan Federation 243
Pagan Front 243
Pali canon 143, 227
Palingenesis 171, *193*, 218
Panchem Lama 16, *193*, 274
pantheism and panentheism *194*
pantomnesia 74, *194*
papa-purusha 194
parallel lives *194*, 204
Paramacca Maroon (tribal group) 15, *194*
Paramahansa Yogananda 99
Paramananda Saraswatti 163
paramnesia 74
Paramnesia and Reincarnation (Chari) 57
para-nirmita-vashavartin 107
Paranormal Cognition, Survival and Reincarnation (Chari) 57
parapsychology *194*
parents in the next life *194*
parinirvana 44, 175, *184*, 240
Parker, Samuel: *A Free and Impartial Censure of the Platonic Philosophie....* 246
Parmenides *195*
parousia 90, 173, 182, *195*, 199
partial reincarnation 11, 15
Pascal, Blaise 195
Pascal's wager 25, 27
Pasricha, Satwant K. *195*, 220
passing-memories adoption *195*, 196, 218
past life: fakery *195*; journal *195*; life therapy 55, 124, 152, 182, 196, *197*, 201, 224, 259; memory categories *195*; psychic reader *196*, 197; reading *196*; recall 65, 79,

114, **196**; recall meditation 94, **196**, 265; regression and suggestibility 77, 93, **196**; therapist **197**, 218
Past Life and Karma Tarot (McCoy) 265
Past Life Therapy in Action (Sutphen and Leigh) 263
past lives **197**
Past Lives of Famous People: Journeys of the Soul (Bengston) 13
Past Lives Therapy (Netherton and Schiffrin) 182
Patala **197**
Patanjali **197**
Patarines 79, 90, **197**
Path of the Western Tradition of the Priesthood 100
pathological retrocognition **197**
Patton, George S. **197–198**
Paul of Tarsus 16, 22, 35, 46, 54, 62, 68, 96, 138, 148, 182, **198**, 233, 237, 252, 274
Paulicians 47, 79, 90, 165, **198**
Pelagian heresy 148
perception and reality 198
The Perfect Way, or the Finding of Christ (Kingsford) 153
Peri Aphtharsias Psyches (Numenius of Apamea) 185
Peri Physeos Anthropou (Nemesius of Emesa) 181
Peri Psyches (Iamblichus of Chalcis) 117
Perkins, James S.: *Experiencing Reincarnation* 76, 112, 147
Persephone **198**
persona 23
personalists 18, **198**
personality after Death (Cook, Greyson and Stevenson) 193
personality versus individuality **198**
Petavatthu 199
Peter, 1st and 2nd 21, 47, 105, 129, 145, 158, 161, 183, **199**, 215, 267
Phaedo (Plato) 16, **199**, 203
Phaedrus (Plato) 203
phala 276
phantasmata **199**
Pherecydes of Syros **200**
philias and phobias 39, 195, **200**
Philippians 13, 63, 90
Philo Judaeus or Philo of Alexandria **200**; *De Gigantes* 200; *De Somniis* 200
Philosophical Poems: A Platonick Song of the Soul, ... (More) 246
Philosophical Research Society 105
Phoenix **200**
Phoenix card set **200**
Phoenix Cards: Reading and Interpreting Past Life Influences with the Phoenix Deck (Sheppard) 200
Phoenix Rising 31, **200**
phowa or *phoba* **200**
phroura 46
Phylos the Tibetan 57, **200**
physical handicaps 143
physical plane 31, 172, **201**
Physics (Aristotle) 28
pilgrimages **201**

Pilgrim's Way (Buchan) 50
Pindar **201**
pineal and pituitary gland **201**, 205
Pisces 3
Pistis Sophia 126, **201**
Pius IX, Pope 259
Pius XII, Pope 23
placebo effect **201**
planes of existence **201**, 261
planetary ascent and descent of the soul 13, 34, 175, **201–202**
planets, other **202–203**, 278
plants 203
Plato 16, 23, 74, 97, 102, 109, 120, 129, 181, 185, 199, 201, 202, **203–204**, 256, 257, 267, 269; *Critias* 269; *Laws* 204; *Memo* 16, 204; *Phaedo* 16, 199, 203; *Phaedrus* 203, 256; *Republic* 190, 203, 256; *Symposium* 203, 220, 239, 255; *Timaeus* 269
Platonism 35, 88, 144, 190, 265, 280
Pleiades 91, 94, **204**, 241, 245
Plotinus 16, 144, 181, **204**, 207, 239
pluralism 46, 175, **204**
plurality of existence 204
Plutarch or Ploutarchos **205**; *On the Delays of the Divine Vengeance* 205
Pluto 33, 105, 198, **205**
Pluto: The Evolutionary Journey of the Soul (Green) 205
Pneuma 252, 258, 270
Pneumatikoi **205**, 245
poetry on reincarnation **205**
Poimandres or Pymander **205–206**
polarities 206
Polynesia 187
population increase issue 13, 20, 63, 75, 94, 127, 188, **206**, 210, 222, 253, 254, 266; and the theistic solution **206–207**
Porphyry Malchus 55, 202, **207**; *Against the Christians* 207; *Life of Pythagoras* 207; *On Abstinence from Animal Food* 207
Posidonius 78, 202
possession 15, 25, 35, 56, 57, 58, 76, 85, 90, 99, 100, 104, 135, 174, 186, 196, 200, **207–208**, 211, 218, 279
Powell, Robert: *Hermetic Astrology: Towards a New Wisdom of the Stars* 241
The Power of Karma in Relation to Destiny (Cannon) 52
The Power Within (Cannon) 52
Prabhavananda, Swami **208**, 274, 276
prakriti **208**, 240
Pramanavarttika 164
Prarthana 209
pratitya-samutpada 139, **209**, 271
prayers for the dead **209**
Precious Records 109
Precognition 194, 269
predestination 22, 75, 87, **209**, 237
pre-existiani 66, **209**
Premananda, Swami 81

Presley, Elvis **209–210**
preta 114, 214
pretaloka **210**
priesthood, lack of an organized **210**
Principles and Practices of Past Life Therapy 272
Priscillian 33, **210**
priti 114
pritiloka **210**
privilege of a human birth **210**
Proclus **210**
procrastination, charge of **210–211**
progression therapy **211**
The Proof of the Truth of Past Life Therapy (Norman) 272
proof text 126, 183, **211**, 212
Prophet, Elizabeth Clare 65
Prophet, Mark 65
A Prophet in His Own Country: The Story of Young Edgar Cayce (Stearn) 260
protology **211**, 226
Proverbs 145, **211**
proximity burial **212**
Psalms 13, 105, 145, 168, 199, 201, **212**
Psalmtic (Pharaoh) 13
pseudepigrapha **212**
psyche 52, 173, 252
psychic archaeology **212**
psychic powers **212–213**
psychic psychodrama **213**, 218
psychic recycling **213**, 278
Psychic Self-Defense (Fortune) 94
Psychical Research Foundation 31, **213**
psychology, abnormal **213**
psychomanteum 175
psychomatic illness 27
psychometry 29, 65, **213**, 218
psychopannychism 46, 65, 131, **213**, 233
Psychopathetic Institute of Chicago 278
psychophore **213**
psycho-physical aggregates 79, 226
psychoplasm **214**
psychopomp 172, **214**
psychosomatic illnesses **214**
psychostasis 108, 213
Ptolemaeus, Claudius 202
Puranas **214**
Pure-Land 61, 76, 98, 107, 113, 149, 200, 214, 247, 282
Pure-Land or Blissful Land Buddhism 63, **214**
Pure Mind Foundation **214**: *Beyond Forever: Unlocking the Door to Eternal Life* 214
purgatory 32, 40, 62, 87, 108, 13, 136, 166, 176, 180, **214**, 247
purusha **215**, 240
purvanivasanusmrti/pubbenivasanussati 9, 170, **215**, 240
pyramidology 11, 49, **215**, 217, 249, 261, 268
Pythagoras 76, 87, 102, 103, 110, 117, 161, 162, 163, 167, 185, 193, 195, 200, 204, **215–216**, 220, 239, 247, 267, 274, 276

Qabbalistic and Rosicrucian Symbolical Philosophy (Hall) 105, 172
Qadiyani, Mirza Ghulam Ahmed 12
Qlippoth/kelipoth **216**
Quimby, Phineas P. 216
Quimby Center **216**
Quinn, Noreen 93
Quran 47, 77, 122–123, 153, 248

Ra 57, 84
Ra (1) **216**, 278
Ra (2) 113, 216
racism 43, 102
Radin, Paul 278
Raghunath Remembered: A Case Suggestive of Reincarnation (Rawat) 218
Raikov, Vladimir 29
rain **217**
Rajneesh, Bhagwan Shree 191
Ram Dass, Baba **217**; *Remember, Be Here Now* 217
Ramadam 79
Rampa, Tuesday Lobsang **217**; *The Third Eye: Autobiography of a Tibetan Lama* 217
Ramses I 83
Ramtha, the Enlightened One 57, 84, 217
Randall, Shawn 269
Randolph, Paschal Beverly 207
Ransom, Champe 262
ransom theory 61
Raphael 29, 85
Rastafarians 11, 148, 171, **217**
Ravenscroft, Trevor: *The Spear of Destiny: The Occult Power Behind the Spear Which Pierced the Side of Christ* 112
Rawandiyah **218**
Rawat, Kirti S. **218**; *Raghunath Remembered: A Case Suggestive of Reincarnation* 218
rebirth 48, 113–114, 163–164, 184–185; and abortion **219**; alternative explanations to **218**–**219**; analogies from nature 74, **219**; and artificial insemination **219**; compensation and life fulfillment **223**; consanguineous **224**; control of **224**; criteria for proof of **224**; cross species 19, 20, 39, 40, 206, **225**; cultural conditioning **219**; and cyclical time **219**; East and West **225**; and famous supporters **220**, 278; and general morality **220**–**221**; and logical symmetry **221**; and maturity **221**; as the natural order of all living things **223**; and the preponderance of evidence **223**; rebirth and moral perfection **221**–**222**, 241–242; rebirth and science **222**; and religious tolerance **222**; and the scientific theory of biological evolution **223**; and suicide **222**–**223**; and unilinear descent **223**
rebirth eschatology 144, 151, **225**–**226**; or becoming **218**; in

Buddhism **226**–**228**; ethnic **226**; expectational **226**; general **226**; group **226**; instantaneous **228**; in the modern West **228**; natural concept of **229**; non-backsliding **229**; obligatory **229**; partial **229**; proof of (Western Buddhist) **229**; proximity **229**; restricted **230**; selective **230**; two logical views of **230**
rebirth factor 38, 69, 76, 98, 120, 149, 220, **226**
Rebirth: Reincarnation Belief among North American Indians and Inuit (Mills and Slobodin) 232
recurring patterns of behavior 27
Redfield, James: *The Celestine Prophecy* 56
Redivivus **231**
Regla de Ocha 241
Regression Beyond Birth (Chari) 57
reincarnation 11, 15, 52, 62–64, 114, 1818–119, 120, 121, 174, 182–183, 189, 205, **231**, 234, 236, 239; bibliographies **231**; origins of **231**; the term **231**
Reincarnation (periodical) **231**
Reincarnation: A Bibliography (Bjorling) 231
Reincarnation: A Critical Examination (Edwards) 262
Reincarnation: A Selected Annotated Bibliography (Kear) 231
Reincarnation: A Study of Forgotten Truth (Walker) 205
Reincarnation: A Universal Truth (Goudey) 41, 93, 121, 205
Reincarnation and Freedom (Lauritsen) 34
Reincarnation and Your Past Life Memories (Chadwick) 255
Reincarnation: Claiming Your Past, Creating Your Future (Sparrow) 149, 184, 196
Reincarnation in Christianity: A New Vision of the Role of Rebirth in Christian Thought 162
Reincarnation in Islam (Mirza) 123
Reincarnation International Magazine **231**–**232**
Reincarnation: Key to Immortality (Moore) 176
Reincarnation of Edgar Cayce (Wilcock) 278
Reincarnation Report **232**, 263
Reincarnation: The Hope of the World (Cooper) 121
Reincarnation: The Second Chance (Leek) 156
Reincarnation through the Zodiac (Hodgson) 33
Reincarnation Unnecessary (Shelley) 24, 34
The Reincarnation Workbook (Brennan) 101
The Religion of Light and Sound 81
Religious Research Foundation of America 101
Reliving Past Lives: Evidence Under Hypnosis (Wambach) 277

Remember, Be Here Now (Ram Dass) 217
Renaissance 49, 66, 171, 172, 204, **232**
re-occurring patterns of behavior **232**
repeater children (Obanje) **232**
repetition compulsion 13, 151, 197, **232**
reptilian and mammalian brain 262
Republic (Plato) 190, 203
rescue circles **232**–**233**
researchers of rebirth **232**
restitution negates retribution **233**
restricted rebirth 15, 37, 42, **230**
resurrection: and the aborted fetus **233**; bodily **233**, 282; cultural and technological age discrepancy issue 26; individual age discrepancy issue **234**; of Jesus 62, 68, 126; of Jesus as circular thinking **234**; or reincarnation **234**
retardation 67
retroactive inhibition 58
retrocognition 13, 29, 58, 86, 110, 196, 197, 211, 218, **235**, 269, 269
Retrocognitions (Alegretti) 86, 112
retrofitting **236**
return and serve argument for reincarnation **236**
Return of the Revolutionaries (Semkiw) 92, 239
Revelation of John 13, 70, 90, 99, 107, 145, 153, 161, 173, 209, 244, 245, 262
Revelation of the Hexagramatic Cross 272
reverie recall **237**
Reynaud, Jean 259
Rhine, Joseph Banks 232
Rhinehart, the Rev. Keith Milton 22
Riail, Hippoltyte Leon Denizard 259
Richardson, Alan **237**; *Dancer to the Gods* 237
Richter, Charles 70, 279
Richter, Johann Paul Friedrich **237**
right-hand path and left-hand path **237**
Rig-pa ngo-sprod gcermthong ranggrol 39
ring pass not **237**
ringu jukai or *ringu shukke* **237**
The Rise and Fall of the Afterlife (Bremmer) 103, 193
Road to Immortality (Cummins) 71
Roberts, Jane: *Dreams, Evolution, and Value Fulfillment* 245; *The Seth Material* 245; *Seth Speaks: The Eternal Validity of the Soul* 245
role-playing fantasy 224
A Romance of Two Worlds (Corelli) 68
Romans (Ancient) 77, 83, 87, 90, 166, 174, 210, **236**, 256, 257, 276.
Romans, Letter to the 21, 22, 47, 62, 84, 88, 145, 148, 183, 189, 20, 273

Rosemary case **238**
Rosenkreuz, Christian 239
Rosenroth, Baron Knorr von: *The Book on the Rashith ha Gigalim (Revolution of the Soul or Scheme of Reincarnation* 246
Rosicrucian Fellowship 239
Rosicrucian Research Society 238
Rosicrucians 20–21, 29, 121, **238**, 249, 256, 260, 261, 266, 267
Roy, Raja Ram Mohan **239**
ruah or *ruach* 134, 252, 257
Rubin, Penny Torres 163
Ruecket, Carla 216
rupa-dhatu and *arupa-dhatu* 52, 270
Russia, reincarnation in **239**
Ryerson, Kevin **239**

Sadat, Mohammed Anwar 13
Saddharmas-metyupasthana-sutra 164
Sadler, William Samuel 273
Sagittarius 33
Saint Germain, Comte de 65, 76, 115
saintly versus diabolical persons argument **240**
sallekhana (suicide) 17, 124, 222
Sallustius the Neoplatonist 117, **240**; On the Gods and the World (Universe) 240
Salome (Wilde) 245–246
samkhya or *sankhya yoga* 46, 79, 208, 21, **240**
Samma Sambuddha **240**
samsara 34, 37, 44, 48, 51, 76, 86, 107, 136, 166, 172, 178, 191, 203, 210, 236, **240**, 250
samskara 209, **240**, 249
samvara **240**
Sananda 166
Sanema-Yanoama (tribal group) 15
Sanskrit language 13, 28, 34, 39, 40, 48, 50, 51, 54, 76, 87, 118, 124, 146, **240**, 241
Santeria (Santerismo) 11, **241**
Satan 53, 54, 70, 102, 161, 173, 245, 264, 280
Sathy Sai Baba **241**
Saturn (planet) 10, 13, 33, 55, 80, 161, 202, 205, 241
Saturn: A New Look at an Old Devil (Greene) 80
satya 57
Schiffrin, Nancy: *Past Lives Therapy* 182
Schiller, Friedrich von **241**
Schilling, Heinrich Wolfgang: *De Metempsycosi Dissertation* 246
Schlotterbeck, Karl 34; *Living your Past Lives: the Psychology of Past Life Regression* 34, 197
School of Life **241–242**
Schopenhauer, Arthur **242**
Schuchman, Helen 68; *A Course in Miracles* 68
Schulman, Martin 33: *Karmic Astrology: Retrogrades and Reincarnation* 33

Science and the Akashic Field (Laszlo) 11
Science of Man 113
Science of Mind **242**
Scientific Report on "The Search for Bridey Murphy" (Bernstein) 49
scientific theory of biological evolution 27
Scientology 65, 70, 81
sciomancy 57, 74, 180, 243
Score, John **243**
Scorpio 33
screen memories 11, 29, 127, 170, 179, 19, 218, 243, 260
The Scripts of Cleophas (Cummins) 71
Scriptum Super Sententiis (Aquinas) 23
scrying or skrying 175, 196, 243
The Search for a Soul: Taylor Caldwell's Psychic Lives (Stearn) 260
The Search for Bridey Murphy (Bernstein) 49
The search for Bridey Murphy (movie) 49
The Search for Om Sety: A Story of Eternal Love (Cott) 80
The Search for the Girl with the Blue Eyes (Stearn) 163, 260
seasons **244**
second death 32, 90, 206, 244
Secret Book of John 180
The Secret Doctrine (Blavatsky) 43, 161, 267
Secret or Inner Chiefs 29
Secret Doctrine of Umbanda 272
The Secret Teachings of All Ages: An Encyclopedic Outline of Masonic, Hermetic Seder Olam; or the Order, Series or Succession of All the Ages, Periods, and Times of the Whole World.... (Helmont) 246
seelenwanderung 244
Sefer ha-Gilgulim (Vital) **99**
Sefer ha-Hezyonat (Vital) 111
Sefer ha-Orot 130
Sefer-ha-Temunah 133
Self Revelation Church of Absolute Monism 81
Self-Realization Fellowship 281
sema 46
Semkiw, Walter: *Born Again: Reincarnations Cases Involving International Celebrities* 92, 239; *Return of the Revolutionaries* 92, 123, 239
sensation body **244**
sephiroth 216, **244**
serial lives **245**
serpents or snake 73, 191, 218, 245
Seth 57, 84, 245
The Seth Material (Roberts) 245
Seth Speaks: The Eternal Validity of the Soul (Roberts) 245
Seti I 83
seven **245**, 248
seven deadly sins 202
seven rungs of the heavenly ladder **245**
seven veils (dance) **245**

seventeenth century renewed interest in rebirth **246**
Seymour, Charles R.F. 237
shadow body **247**
shadow or shade 23, 32, 243, **247**, 257
Shakespeare, William **247**; *Sonnet LIX* 247; *Twelfth Night* 247
shamanism 15, 39, 47, 56, 72, 103, 153, 155, 181, 186, 207, 247, 258
Shango 11
Shanti Devi case **247**
Sharpe, Pauline 166
She (Haggard) 105
She and Allen (Haggard) 105
sheep **247**
Shelley, Violet M. 24: *Reincarnation Unnecessary* 24, 34
Sheol 84, 99, 101, 102, 105, 128, 185, 187, 212, 247, 272
Sheppard, Susan: *Phoenix Cards: Reading and Interpreting Past Life Influences with the Phoenix Deck* 200
Sherman, Harold Marrow: *You Live After Death* 186
Shinto/Shintoism 113, **247**
Shiva 35, 48, 159, **246**, 268
Sh' neur Zalman of Laydi 265; *Tanya (Likkutei Amarim)* 265
Shotoku Taishi **248**
Shuddemagen, C. 231
sidereal periods 33
Signet Handbook of Parapsychology 57
Sikhism 37, 81, 135, 138, 177, 195, **248**, 266
Silent watchers **248**
silver chord 31, 192
Similes **248**
Simmons, Ruth 49
Simon Magus **248**
Singh, Kirpal 81
Sinnett, Alfred Percy: *Esoteric Buddhism* 51, 136
Sirius (dog star) **248**, 249
skandha/khandha **249**
Skeptical Inquirer 67
Slayers and Their Vampires (McClelland) 47
Slobodin, Richard: *Amerindian Rebirth: Reincarnation Belief Among North American Indians and Inuit* 232
Smith, Helen (Muller, Catherine Elise) 178
Smith, Joseph 22, 177
Social status in past lives **249**
Societas Rosicruciana in Anglia 80
Society for Psychical Research 179, **249**
Society for Spiritual Regression 31, **249**
Society of Inner Light 94
Solar Temple, Order of **249**
solity 250
Solomon (King) 54, 201, 212, 239, 243
soma 46
somatic rebirth 250

Sonnet LIX (Shakespeare) 247
soteriology 226, **250**
soul 201–202, 250; cohorts **253**; collective **253**; Darwinism **254**; external **254**; family **254**; fission 86, **254**, 257; fragmentation **254**; groups 103, **254**; intrusion **255**; mates 9, 97, 203, 217, **255**, 257, 264; psychology of **256**; stoic **256**; tripartite **256**, 270; twins **257**; virgin **257**
The Soul Genome (Ward) 214
Soul Mates (Stearn) 260
The Soul of Life (Israel) 124
soul-personality **256**
soul-siblings **256**
souls: complementary **257**; existence prior to embodiment 10, 68, 87, 96, 103, 125–126, 176, 177, 183, 189, 201, 205, 209, 212, 237, 255, **258**, 267, 278; fixed and free **258**; multiple **258**; origin of **258**
Spaccio de la bestia trionfante (Bruno) 49
Spare, Austin Osman **258**
Sparrow, Ellen: *Edgar Cayce and the Born Again Christian* 55; *Reincarnation: Claiming Your Past, Creating Your Future* 149, 184, 196
The Spear of Destiny: The Occult Power Behind the Spear Which Pierced the Side of Christ (Ravenscroft) 112
spectrophilia 262
spirit 33, 76, 173, 252, **258**
Spiritism 113, 136, 241, **258–259**; and Catholic Church 259
Spiritualism 22, 31, 44, 74, 76, 152, 168, 173, 175, 182, 186, 243, **259**
Spiritualist Cristiana Church 81
split brain 260
spontaneous recall 29, 58, 196, 260
Sri Chinmoy 157
stags 219, **260**
stake a claim **260**
Stanford, John A. 131; *Soul Journey: A Jungian Analyst Looks at Reincarnation* 131
Star of David or Sign of Solomon **260**
Stearn, Jess 162–163, **260**; *The Search for the Girl with the Blue Eyes* 163; *Edgar Cayce: The Sleeping Prophet* 260*i* Intimates Through Time: The Life of Edgar Cayce and His Companions through the Ages 260; *A Matter of Immortality: Dramatic Evidence of Survival* 260
Steiger, Brad **260**; *Discover Your Lives* 260; *The Enigma of Reincarnation* 260; *Other Lives* 260; *You Will Live Again* 260
Steiner, Rudolf 85, 93, 120, 136, 161, 175, 206, 239, **260–261**, 267
Stella Matutina 94, 280
Stelle, Robert D. 157
Stelle Group 261–262
Stevens, Ramon: *Earthly Cycles* 86, 188, 191, 268, 277

Stevenson, Ian 58, 73, 92, 94, 115, 121, 144, 155, 164, 174, 193, 195, 208, 213, 220, 224, 232, **262**, 274: *Children Who Remember Previous Lives* 262; "Do Any Near-Death Experiences Provide Evidence for the Survival of Human Personality After Death" 193; *European Cases of the Reincarnation Type* 262; *Twenty Cases Suggestive of Reincarnation* 92, 262, 208; *Unlearned Languages: New Studies in Xenoglossy* 155, 262; *Where Reincarnation and Biology Intersect* 262
Strangers Among Us (Montgomery) 276
Street, Coleen 161
Street, Noel 161
stygian sexuality **262**
subconscious, mystifying of **262–263**
subtle body **263**
Sufiism 12, 71, 104, **263**
suicide 17, 97, 124, 222
Sumerian civilization 83
Summa Contra Gentiles (Aquinas) 23
Summerland 32, 76, **263**
Summit Lighthouse 65
Super Evangelium S. Matthaei (Aquinas) 23
supernatural-in-the-gap process 58, 222, **263**
Surya-marga **263**
Sutphen, Richard **263**; *Past Life Therapy in Action* 263; *Reincarnation Report* 263
Sutphen, Tara 263: *Blame It on Your Past Lives: Personal Problems and Supernatural Solutions* 263
Sutra of Entering the Womb 164
Sutra of Perfect Enlightenment 164
Sutra on Stability in Mindfulness of the True Dharma 164
Sutratman **263**
Swan on a Black Sea: A Study of Automatic Writing, the Cummins-Willet Transcripts (Cummins) 71
Swanson, Guy E.: *Birth of the Gods: The Origins of Primitive Beliefs* 231
Swarga or *Svarga* **263**, 180
swarm of bees theory 254, **263**
swastika or *svastika* **263**
Swedenborg, Emanuel 72, 259, **264**, 280
Swygard, William 37; *Awareness Technique* 37
symbola **264**
Symposium (Plato) 203, 255
synchronicity 117, 152, **264**
Synesius of Cyrene **264**; *Aegypyus sive de providential* 264

Ta'amei ha-Mizat 133
T'ai-Yueh-Ta-Ti 264
Talbot, Michael 131, **264**; *Your Past Lives: A Reincarnation Handbook* 131, 264

Talleyrand-Périgord, Charles Maurice de: *Memoires* 180
Tammuz 101
tanasukh 71, 79, 106, 122, 124, 136, 152, 185, 263, **264**
tankas 38
Tantrism 39, 47, 51, 56, 157, 187, 191, 200, 208, **264–265**, 274, 275
Tanya (Likkutei Amarim) 265
Taoism **72**
Tarkajvala 164
tarot 29, 110, 116, 196, **265**, 268
Tarot of Reincarnation (Massimiliano) 265
Tartarus 102, 105, 203, 257, **265**, 276
tau 265
Taurus 33
Taylor, Thomas **265**
Techiyat Hameitim 265
Techniques of Past Lives Recall 37
teleological presumption **265**
teleology 223
telepathy 29
telepathy (telegnosis) with the living 218, **266**
telepathy with the dead 218, **266**
Templars 249, **266**, 249
Ten Dam, Hans **266**: *Exploring Reincarnation: The Classical Guide to the Evidence for Past Life Experiences* 266
terma 38
tertons 39
Tertullian 12, 20, 53, 64, **266**: *De Anima* 266
A Textbook of Theosophy (Leadbeater) 32, 90, 171
thanatology 225
Thelema 69
theodicy 43, 132, **266**, 277
Theon, Max 29
Theophilus 64, 189, 267
The Theory of Celestial Influence (Collin) 61
The Theory of Eternal Life (Collin) 61
theory of mind **174**, 256
theosis 221, **266**
Theosophical Society 40, 110, 156, 157, 231, 260, 280
theosophy 13, 22, 31, 32, 51, 54, 61, 65, 75, 76, 80, 82, 84, 90, 11, 115, 136, 152, 159, 161, 165, 170, 174, 175, 176, 182, 183, 194, 216, 220, 239, 240, 244, 248, 253, 256, 260, 261, 262, **267**
Theravada Buddhism 46, 50, 117, 118, 120, 149, 163, 171, 173, 175, 199, 203, 209, 229, **267**, 275
Thessalonians 213
Theta (1) 213, **268**
theta (2) 188, **268**
theta (3) 242
theta waves 115, **268**
thetan 242
They Survive (Cummins) 71
third eye 56, 64, 205, 217, **268**
The Third Eye: Autobiography of a Tibetan Lama (Rampa) 217

Thirty Years Among the Dead (Wickland) 278
Thoreau, Henry David 15
Thornton, Penny: *The Forces of Destiny* 34
Thoth, Book of **268**
The Tragedy of Doctor Faustus 167
Three refuges and five Buddhist lay precepts **268**
Threefold (law of) return **268**
Threshold to Tomorrow (Montgomery) 276
Tibet 23, 30, 31, 36, 37, 38, 39, 43, 47, 50, 65, 67, 72, 74, 76, 111, 118, 126, 146, 158, 185, 193, 208, 217, 218, 228, 230, 265, 271, 274, 279
Tibetan Book of the Dead 38, 280
Tierney, John: "Are Scientists Playing God? It Depends on Your Religion" 113–114
Tighe, Virginia 49
Tight Fundamentals of Umbanda 272
Timaeus 78, **269**
Time and consciousness **269**
Time and the simultaneous past, present, and future **269**
Time-recall challenge **269**
Timothy, 1st and 2nd 21, 22, 88, 148, 209, 273
Tipitaka 52
Titus 84, 148, 193, 209
Tlingit (tribal group) 15
Toltec 83, 154, 168, 272
tomb to womb 54, 66, 70, 73, **269**
Torah (1) 22, 57, 96, 98, 132, 216, 237, **269**
Torah (2) **269**
traducianism 68, 96, 223
trance states 14, **269-270**
trance therapy 54
transcorporation 270
transmigration 11, 18, 20, 29, 37, 39, 52, 57, 78, 101, 102, 130, 133, 144, 171, 181, 185, 191, 204, 206, 218, 240, 244, 245, 247, 257, 266, **270**, 274, 280, 282; alternating lives **270**; lateral **270**; progressive **270**; regressive **270**
Transmigration (Collins) 151
"Transmigration in the Avesta " in *Zoroastrianism in the Light of Theosophy* (Bilimoria) 282
Transmigration of Souls (Adams) **270**
Traveler's Tale (Bax) **270**
A Treatise of White Magic (Bailey) 265
Treatise on the Seven Rays: Esoteric Astrology (Bailey) 161
trees 74
trichotomy 257, **270**
tri-dhatu or *tri-loka* 270
Trimurti 48
Trobriand Islanders (tribal group) 187
trzor ha-chayyim or *Otzar* 104
Tukano (tribal group) 15
tulkus 16, 72, 118, 126, 193, 264, **271**, 274

Tushita Heaven 107
Twelfth Night (Shakespeare) 247
twelve **271**
Twenty Cases Suggestive of Reincarnation (Stevenson) 92, 208, 262
twins, identical **271**
Twitchell, Paul 81
Two Hundred Queries (Helmont) 109
Tzevi, Shabbettai 95
Tzror ha-Chayyim **271**

UFOism or ufology 10, 30, 93, 107, 202, **271-272**
The Ultimate Frontier (Kieninger) 103, 261–262
Umbanda 11, 32, 136, **272**
Unarius Academy of Science **272**
the unconscious 66, **272-273**
Unity School of Christianity 273
Universal Church of the Master **273**
universalism 22, **273**
The Unknown Life of Jesus Christ (Notovitch) 185
Unlearned Languages: New Studies in Xenoglossy (Stevenson) 155, 262
Unveiled Mysteries (Ballard) 116
Upanishads 15, 17, 48, 98, 154, 251, **273**, 281
Urantia Book **273**
Uranus 33
Urhobo (tribal group) 11
Uttar Pradesh **274**
Uxkull, Woldemar von: *Eine Einweihung im Alten Agypten nach dem Buch Throth* 268

Vaikuntha **274**
Vajrayana Buddhism 16, 36, 38–39, 45, 50, 51, 56, 72, 74, 76, 96, 120, 171, 184, 239, 265, 268, 271, **274**
Valentinus 122, 189, **274**
vampire 32, 47, 60, 70, 90, 118, 240, **274**
van Hook, Weller 231
Vasanas **274**
Vedanta Society 208, **273**, 276
Vedic religion 51, 111, 124, 146, 147, 176, 273, **274**, 180
vegetarianism 93, 153, 165, 190, 207, 243, **274**
Vendidad 282
Venn, Jonathan 224
Venus 10, 30, 33, 109, 154, 16, 202, 217, 278
La Vies Successives (De Rochas) 75
vijnana 14, 61, 154, 165, 209, 226, 227, 249, 275
Vijnanavada School of Buddhism 14, 18, 41, 151, 165
Vilenkin, Alex 194
Vintras, Eugene **276**, 279
vipaka 36, 136, 140, 141, 142, 143, 146, 150, 151, 161, 164, 190, 227, **276**
Virgil **276**: *Aeneid* 202, 276
virgin conception **276**
Virgo 33, **276**

Vishnu 37, 48, 157, 118, 149, 157, 248, 274
A Vision (Yeats) 281
The Visions of the Soul before It Comes into the Body (Dunton) 246
Visitations: A Saga of Gods and Men (Norman) 272
Vital, Hayim: *Sefer ha-Gilgulim* **99**, 133; *Sefer ha-Hezyonat* 111
Vivekananda, Swami 208, 274, **276**
Voices from Other Lives: Reincarnation as a Source of Healing (Dethlefsen) 155
Voices of Venus (Norman) 272
Voltaire, François Marie Arouet de 220, **276**
Von Eckarshausen, Karl: *The Cloud on the Sanctuary* 102
Voodoo 11

Wagner, Richard **276**
Waite, Arthur Edward: *The Book of Black Magic and of Packs* 89
Walker, E.D.: *Reincarnation: A Study of Forgotten Truth* 205
walk-in 175, 218, 272, 276
Wallace, Alan B. 117
Wallace, Alfred Russell 220
Wallace, Henry A. **276-277**
Wambach, Helen 73, 121, 220, 226, 232, 24, **277**; *Life Before Life* 277; *Reliving Past Lives: Evidence Under Hypnosis* 277
wandering soul 277
Wapnick, Kenneth: *Absence from Felicity* 68
Ward, James D.: *Lemuria: The Lost Continent of the Pacific* 177
Ward, Paul von: *The Soul Genome* 214
Warren, Edward: *No Pre-existence, or a Brief Dissertation Against the Hypothesis of Human Souls Living in a State Antecedaneous to This* 246
Watcher on the Threshold 80
W.C.: *The Harmless Opinion of the Revolution of Humane Souls as a Probable Hypothesis....* 246
We Are One Another (Guirdham) 104
Weber, Max 277
Welcomers 277
Western, Robin: *Channelers: A New Age Directory* 57
Western Waripiri (tribal group) 36
Wheatley, Dennis Yates **277**; *Library of the Occult* 277
Wheel of Fate 34
Wheels of a Soul (Berg) 127, 134
Where Reincarnation and Biology Intersect (Stevenson) 262
White, Alice 186
White, George 186
White Brothers and Blue Sisters 102
White Eagle 67, **277**
White Lodge **277**

White Temple Church 49
Whitehead, Alfred North 103, 186
Whitman, Walt 16
Wicca 94, 219, **268**, 277
The Wiccan 243
Wickland, Carl August 44, 260, **278**; *Thirty Years Among the Dead* 278
widespread and multi-cultural belief argument **278**
wiedermenschwerdung 244
Wieland, Christopher Martin **278**; *Die Natur der Dinge* 278
Wilcock, David 55, **278**; *Reincarnation of Edgar Cayce* 278
Wilde, Oscar: *Salome* 245–246
Williams, Edward 176
Williamson, J.N.: *Death-Coach* 274
willing suspension of disbelief **278**
Wilson, Ian **278**; *The After Death Experience* 278; *Mind Out of Time: Reincarnation, Hypnotic Regression, Stigmata, Multiple Personality, and Other Little-Understood Powers of the Mind* 278
Windows of the Mind (Glaskin) 64
Winnebago **278**
Wisdom of Solomon 19–20 **278**
The Witch Cult in Western Europe (Murray) 278
Witchcraft Today (Gardner) 278

Witness position **279**
women **279**
Wood, F.H.: *Ancient Egypt Speaks: A Miracle of Tongues* 238
Woolger, Roger J.: *Other Lives, Other Selves* 211
Work of Mercy **279**
Works (Goodwin) 246
World Catalyst Church **279**
Worlds Within (Glaskin) 64

xenoglossy 100, **279**
xenography **279**
xenophrenia **279**

Y symbol **279**
Yama 61, 87, 107, **279–280**, 281
Yanomamo (tribal group) 15, **280**
Yarbro, Chelsea Quinn: *Hotel Transylvania* 240; *Michael's Teachings* 172, 240
Yarsanism **280**
Yazdanism 70
Yazidis (Yezidism) 70, 91, **280**
Yeats, William Butler 89, 220, **280–281**; *Ideas of Good and Evil* (Yeats) 281; *A Vision* 281
Yellow Spring 60, **281**
Yen-lo 108, **281**
Yin-Yang 59
Yoga **281**

Yoga Sutra **281**
Yogachara School of Buddhism 75
Yogananda, Paramahansa 99, **281**
Yoruba (tribal group) 11, 241, **281**
You Live After Death (Sherman) 186
You Will Live Again (Steiger) 260
Your Past Lives: A Reincarnation Handbook (Talbot) 131, **264**
Yukaghir (tribal group) **281**
The Yukaghir and Yukarghirized Tungus (Jochelson) 281

Zabchos zhikhro dgongs-pa rang-grol 39
Zanoni: A Rosicrucian Tale (Buler-Lytton) 80
Zen Buddhism, rebirth in **281**
Zenith **281**
Zeus 105, 175, 190, 198, 202
Zhendao/Chen Tao 205, **281–282**
Ziska (Corelli) 68
zodiac 24, 33, 34, 52, 53, 84, 215, 241, 261, 282
Zohar 10, 132, 133, 135, 156, 177
Zolar's Book of Reincarnation 34
Zoroastrianism 12, 54, 79, 122, 164, 165, 168, 185, **282**
Zoroastrianism in the Light of Theosophy (Bilimoria) 282
Zulu (tribal group) 11, **282**

www.ingramcontent.com/pod-product-compliance
Lightning Source LLC
Chambersburg PA
CBHW081539300426
44116CB00015B/2688